W9-BJJ-082

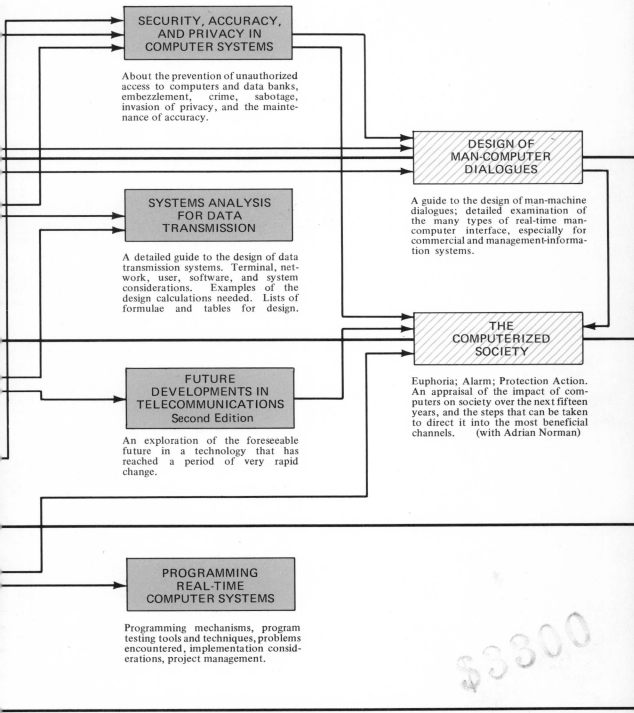

SECURITY, ACCURACY, AND PRIVACY IN COMPUTER SYSTEMS

About the prevention of unauthorized access to computers and data banks, embezzlement, crime, sabotage, invasion of privacy, and the maintenance of accuracy.

DESIGN OF MAN-COMPUTER DIALOGUES

A guide to the design of man-machine dialogues; detailed examination of the many types of real-time man-computer interface, especially for commercial and management-information systems.

SYSTEMS ANALYSIS FOR DATA TRANSMISSION

A detailed guide to the design of data transmission systems. Terminal, network, user, software, and system considerations. Examples of the design calculations needed. Lists of formulae and tables for design.

THE COMPUTERIZED SOCIETY

Euphoria; Alarm; Protection Action. An appraisal of the impact of computers on society over the next fifteen years, and the steps that can be taken to direct it into the most beneficial channels. (with Adrian Norman)

FUTURE DEVELOPMENTS IN TELECOMMUNICATIONS Second Edition

An exploration of the foreseeable future in a technology that has reached a period of very rapid change.

PROGRAMMING REAL-TIME COMPUTER SYSTEMS

Programming mechanisms, program testing tools and techniques, problems encountered, implementation considerations, project management.

COMPUTER DATA - BASE
ORGANIZATION

A *James Martin* BOOK

Prentice-Hall
Series in Automatic Computation

AHO, ed., *Currents in the Theory of Computing*

AHO and ULLMAN, *The Theory of Parsing, Translation, and Compiling,* Volume I: *Parsing;* Volume II: *Compiling*

ANDREE, *Computer Programming: Techniques, Analysis, and Mathematics*

ANSELONE, *Collectively Compact Operator Approximation Theory and Applications to Integral Equations*

AVRIEL, *Nonlinear Programming: Analysis and Methods*

BENNETT, JR., *Scientific and Engineering Problem-Solving with the Computer*

BLAAUW, *Digital System Implementation*

BLUMENTHAL, *Management Information Systems*

BRENT, *Algorithms for Minimization without Derivatives*

BRINCH HANSEN, *The Architecture of Concurrent Programs*

BRINCH HANSEN, *Operating System Principles*

BRZOZOWSKI and YOELI, *Digital Networks*

COFFMAN and DENNING, *Operating Systems Theory*

CRESS, et al., *FORTRAN IV with WATFOR and WATFIV*

DAHLQUIST, BJORCK, and ANDERSON, *Numerical Methods*

DANIEL, *The Approximate Minimization of Functionals*

DEO, *Graph Theory with Applications to Engineering and Computer Science*

DESMONDE, *Computers and Their Uses,* 2nd ed.

DIJKSTRA, *A Discipline of Programming*

DRUMMOND, *Evaluation and Measurement Techniques for Digital Computer Systems*

ECKHOUSE, *Minicomputer Systems: Organization and Programming (PDP-11)*

FIKE, *Computer Evaluation of Mathematical Functions*

FIKE, *PL/1 for Scientific Programmers*

FORSYTHE, MALCOLM, and MOLER, *Computer Methods for Mathematical Computations*

FORSYTHE and MOLER, *Computer Solution of Linear Algebraic Systems*

GEAR, *Numerical Initial Value Problems in Ordinary Differential Equations*

GILL, *Applied Algebra for the Computer Sciences*

GORDON, *System Simulation*

GRISWOLD, *String and List Processing in SNOBOL4: Techniques and Applications*

HANSEN, *A Table of Series and Products*

HARTMANIS and STEARNS, *Algebraic Structure Theory of Sequential Machines*

HILBURN and JULICH, *Microcomputers/Microprocessors: Hardware, Software, and Applications*

HUGHES AND MICHTOM, *A Structured Approach to Programming*

JACOBY, et al., *Iterative Methods for Nonlinear Optimization Problems*

JOHNSON, *System Structure in Data, Programs, and Computers*

KIVIAT, et al., *The SIMSCRIPT II Programming Language*

LAWSON and HANSON, *Solving Least Squares Problems*

LORIN, *Parallelism in Hardware and Software: Real and Apparent Concurrency*

LOUDEN and LEDIN, *Programming the IBM 1130,* 2nd ed.

MARTIN, *Communications Satellite Systems*

MARTIN, *Computer Data-Base Organization,* 2nd ed.

MARTIN, *Design of Man-Computer Dialogues*

MARTIN, *Design of Real-Time Computer Systems*

MARTIN, *Future Developments in Telecommunications,* 2nd ed.

MARTIN, *Principles of Data-Base Management*

MARTIN, *Programming Real-Time Computer Systems*

MARTIN, *Security, Accuracy, and Privacy in Computer Systems*

MARTIN, *Systems Analysis for Data Transmission*

MARTIN, *Telecommunications and the Computer,* 2nd ed.

MARTIN, *Teleprocessing Network Organization*

MARTIN and NORMAN, *The Computerized Society*

MCKEEMAN, et al., *A Compiler Generator*

MEYERS, *Time-Sharing Computation in the Social Sciences*

MINSKY, *Computation: Finite and Infinite Machines*

NIEVERGELT, et al., *Computer Approaches to Mathematical Problems*

PLANE and MCMILLAN, *Discrete Optimization: Integer Programming and Network Analysis for Management Decisions*

POLIVKA and PAKIN, *APL: The Language and Its Usage*

PRITSKER and KIVIAT, *Simulation with GASP II: A FORTRAN-based Simulation Language*

PYLYSHYN, ed., *Perspectives on the Computer Revolution*

RICH, *Internal Sorting Methods Illustrated with PL/1 Programs*

RUDD, *Assembly Language Programming and the IBM 360 and 370 Computers*

SACKMAN and CITRENBAUM, eds., *On-Line Planning: Towards Creative Problem-Solving*

SALTON, ed., *The SMART Retrieval System: Experiments in Automatic Document Processing*

SAMMET, *Programming Languages: History and Fundamentals*

SCHAEFER, *A Mathematical Theory of Global Program Optimization*

SCHULTZ, *Spline Analysis*

SCHWARZ, et al., *Numerical Analysis of Symmetric Matrices*

SHAH, *Engineering Simulation Using Small Scientific Computers*

SHAW, *The Logical Design of Operating Systems*

SHERMAN, *Techniques in Computer Programming*

SIMON and SIKLOSSY, eds., *Representation and Meaning: Experiments with Information Processing Systems*

STERBENZ, *Floating-Point Computation*

STOUTEMYER, *PL/1 Programming for Engineering and Science*

STRANG and FIX, *An Analysis of the Finite Element Method*

STROUD, *Approximate Calculation of Multiple Integrals*

TANENBAUM, *Structured Computer Organization*

TAVISS, ed., *The Computer Impact*

UHR, *Pattern Recognition, Learning, and Thought: Computer-Programmed Models of Higher Mental Processes*

VAN TASSEL, *Computer Security Management*

VARGA, *Matrix Iterative Analysis*

WAITE, *Implementing Software for Non-Numeric Application*

WILKINSON, *Rounding Errors in Algebraic Processes*

WIRTH, *Algorithms + Data Structures = Programs*

WIRTH, *Systematic Programming: An Introduction*

YEH, ed., *Applied Computation Theory: Analysis, Design, Modeling*

COMPUTER

DATA - BASE ORGANIZATION

Second Edition

JAMES MARTIN

IBM Systems Research Institute

PRENTICE-HALL, INC., Englewood Cliffs, New Jersey 07632

Library of Congress Cataloging in Publication Data

MARTIN, JAMES   (date)
    Computer data-base organization.

    (Prentice-Hall series in automatic computation)
    Includes bibliographical references and index.
    1. Data base management.   I. Title.
QA76.9.D3M36   1977   001.6'442   76-52450
ISBN   0-13-165423-3

Computer Data-Base Organization, 2nd edition
James Martin

© 1977, 1975 by Prentice-Hall, Inc.
Englewood Cliffs, N. J.

All rights reserved. No part of this book may be
reproduced in any form, by mimeograph or any other
means, without permission in writing from the publisher.

10   9

Printed in the United States of America.

PRENTICE-HALL INTERNATIONAL, INC., *London*
PRENTICE-HALL OF AUSTRALIA PTY. LIMITED, *Sydney*
PRENTICE-HALL OF CANADA, LTD., *Toronto*
PRENTICE-HALL OF INDIA PRIVATE LIMITED, *New Delhi*
PRENTICE-HALL OF JAPAN, INC., *Tokyo*
PRENTICE-HALL OF SOUTHEAST ASIA PTE. LTD., *Singapore*
WHITEHALL BOOKS LIMITED, *Wellington, New Zealand*

TO CHARITY

CONTENTS

PART **II**   PHYSICAL ORGANIZATION

PREFACE

INTENT   One of the most badly needed courses in universities and other establishments which teach computing is a course on the realities of data-base technology. The 1970's is the decade of the data base. Probably the biggest difference between the next generation of computers and the present will be massive on-line storage and its software. By the start of the 1980's, much of the computing in industry and government will relate to the data bases which have been painfully constructed piece by piece, and management effectiveness will relate to the quality of their organization's data sources and the versatility with which they can be used.

At the time of writing, data-base technology is widely misunderstood. Its role as the foundation stone of future data processing is often not appreciated. The techniques used in many organizations contain the seeds of immense future difficulties. Data independence is often thrown to the winds. Data organizations in use prevent the data being employed as it should be. And most educational establishments do not yet teach a data-base course. This book is being used at the IBM Systems Research Institute as the text for such a course.

ACKNOWLEDGEMENTS   The author wishes to thank many students who have reviewed the text critically. He is very grateful for the detailed comments from Mr. R. M. Gale, Dr. E. F. Codd, Mr. R. W. Holliday, Mr. C. P. Wang, Mrs. S. Snook, Mr. Andy Chiu and Mr. H. S. Meltzer. The author is especially grateful to his wife for her logical and physical assistance. Miss Cora Tangney, who helped with the manuscript, was immensely appreciated by the author and admired for her professional competence.

The author, having been sustained when writing late at night by consuming large quantities of cookies, feels that acknowledgements are also warranted to Pepperidge Farm and Cadbury.

James Martin

INDEX OF BASIC CONCEPTS

The basic concepts, principles, and terms that are explained in this book are listed here along with the page on which an introductory explanation or definition of them is given. There is a complete index at the end of the book.

PROLOGUE

1 INTRODUCTION

The development of corporate data bases will be one of the most important data-processing activities for many years to come. Data will be increasingly regarded as a vital corporate resource which must be organized so as to maximize their value. In addition to the data bases within an organization, a vast new demand is growing for data-base services, which will collect, organize, and sell data.

The files of data which computers can use are growing at a staggering rate. The growth rate in the size of computer storage is greater than the growth in size or power of any other component in the exploding data-processing industry. The more data the computers have access to, the greater is their potential power. In all walks of life and in all areas of industry, data banks will change the realms of what it is possible for man to do. In centuries hence, historians will look back to the coming of computer data banks and their associated facilities as a step which changed the nature of the evolution of society, perhaps eventually having a greater effect on the human condition than even the invention of the printing press.

Some of the most impressive corporate growth stories of the generation are largely attributable to the explosive growth in the need for information. Already, as we move to an increasingly information-oriented society, about 20% of the U.S. Gross National Product is devoted to the collection, processing, and dissemination of information and knowledge in all its various forms [1].

The vast majority of this information is not yet computerized. However, the cost of data-storage hardware is dropping more rapidly than other costs in data processing. It will become cheaper to store data on computer files than to store them on paper. Not only printed information will be stored. The computer industry is improving its capability to store line drawings, data in facsimile form, photographs, human speech, etc. In fact, any form of information other than the most intimate communications between humans can be transmitted and stored digitally.

The falling cost per bit is related to the fact that increasing quantities of data are being stored. Figure 1.1 shows how the capacities of on-line data files have grown (*on-line* means that the data can be read directly by the computer, usually in less than a second, without any human intervention such as loading a tape). The curve shows the maximum amount of storage found on the largest working commercial systems at any time. Note that the vertical scale is logarithmic, not linear, indicating that the growth is becoming faster at a very rapid rate.

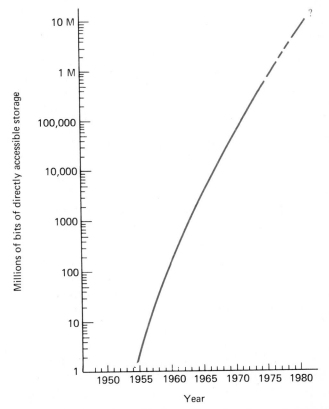

Figure 1.1 Capacity of on-line data files directly accessible by the computer. The curve represents maximum amount of storage likely to be found on large systems in each area. (Note that the vertical scale does not ascend in steps of equal magnitude. Each major division represents a tenfold increase.)

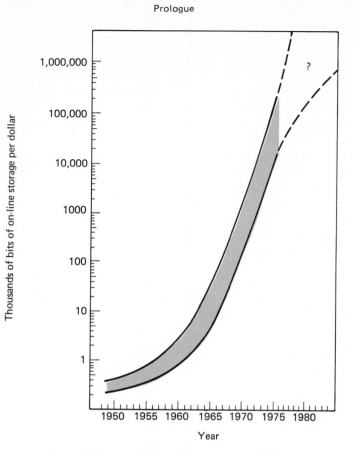

Figure 1.2 The drop in cost of on-line storage.

As the capacities go up, the costs per bit of the storage in Fig. 1.1 come down; this is shown in Fig. 1.2. The costs in Fig. 1.2 refer to the storage devices and media that are used, and this cost is divided by the number of bits on-line. If the costs were divided by the number of bits which could be loaded onto the storage devices from the tape or disk library, the costs would be a fraction of those in Fig. 1.2. The largest tape and disk libraries at any point in time have typically contained an order of magnitude more data than that shown on-line in Fig. 1.1.

The curves in Figs. 1.1 and 1.2 will continue their upward trend, possibly with the same exponential growth rate. New storage technologies that are appearing suggest that the exponential growth *could* continue for a decade or two if we can find suitable applications for it, and it is fascinating to reflect upon the implications of this for data-base design, software requirements, and the way data will be used in industry.

There are two main technology developments likely to become available in the near future. First, there are electromechanical devices that will hold much more data than disks but have much longer access time. Second, there are solid-state technologies that will give low access times but capacities smaller than disk. Disks themselves may be increased in capacity somewhat. For the longer-term future (7 years, say) there are a number of new technologies which are currently working in research labs which may replace disks and may provide very large fast devices. A steady stream of new storage devices is thus likely to reach the marketplace over the next 10 years, rapidly lowering the cost of storing data.

Given the available technologies, it is likely that on-line data bases will use two or three levels of storage: solid-state technology with microsecond access times, magnetic bubble memory with millisecond access times, electromagnetic storage with access times of a fraction of a second, and electromechanical storage with access times which may be several seconds. If two, three, or four levels of storage are used, physical storage organization will become more complex, probably with paging mechanisms to move data between the levels. Solid-state storage offers the possibility of parallel search operations and associative memory. Both of these demand data organization techniques different from those in today's software.

Both the quantity of data stored and the complexity of their organization are going up by leaps and bounds. The first trillion-bit (1,000,000,000,000 bits) on-line stores are now in use. In a few years' time, stores of this size may be common, and stores 10 times as large may be emerging.

To make use of the huge quantities of data that are being stored, two system facilities are needed in addition to the storage. These are *data transmission*—the ability to access the data base from remote locations where its information is needed, by means of telecommunications—and *man-computer dialogues*, which enable the users to make inquiries, browse in the files, modify the data stored, add new data, or solve problems which use the data. Both of these subjects are as complex in their own right as is the design of the data base itself. This book deals only with the organization of the data. The other two topics are dealt with in the author's related books.

In all three areas the designer is confronted with a complex array of alternatives. The more alternatives he can consider in a rational fashion, the more likely he is to produce an optimal design. Many of the poor designs of data-base systems (and there are many) result from a designer considering only certain of the alternatives. The majority of systems analysts have a limited range of knowledge and are sometimes enthusiastic about particular techniques which they understand well to the exclusion of others, some of which might be better.

A particularly important consideration in data-base design is to store the data so that they can be used for a wide variety of applications and so that the way they are used can be changed quickly and easily. On computer installations prior to the data-base era it has been remarkably difficult to change the way data are used. Different programmers view the data in different ways and constantly want to modify them as new needs arise. Modifications, however, can set off a chain reaction of changes to existing programs and hence can be exceedingly expensive to accomplish. Consequently, data processing has tended to become frozen into its old data structures.

To achieve the flexibility of data usage that is essential in most commercial situations, two aspects of data-base design are important. First, the data should be independent of the programs which use them, so that they can be added to or restructured without the programs being changed. Second, it should be possible to interrogate and search the data base without the lengthy operation of writing programs in conventional programming languages. Data-base query languages are used.

The job of designing a data base is becoming increasingly difficult, especially if it is to perform in an optimal fashion. The software is becoming increasingly elaborate, and its capabilities are often misunderstood, misused, or not used to advantage. There are many different ways in which data can be structured, and they have different advantages and disadvantages. Not the least of the complicating factors is that there are so many different types of data needing to be organized in different ways. Different data have different characteristics, which ought to affect the data organization, and different users have fundamentally different requirements. The needs are sufficiently diverse that, often, no one data organization can satisfy all of them—at least with today's hardware. *Hence, the designer steers a delicate course through compromises.*

Given the falling cost of data storage and the increasing capability to transmit data, it is clear that data banks will have a major part to play in the running of industry. It is a formidable task to identify all the data items that are needed for the running of a corporation and to work out where and how they can best be recorded and stored. Today there is much redundancy in the data that is used in organizations, and the same item of data is often defined slightly differently by different groups. It is often true that when computers are installed they reveal how vague was the earlier thinking or how imprecise the previous methods. Cleaning up the imprecision in the way data is defined and used must go hand in hand with the design and stage-by-stage integration of data bases. This is one of the major tasks in the development of data processing in the years ahead. Data dictionaries defining all the data items that are in use will be built up in corporations. The definitions will have to be agreed upon between one department and another. Many different ways of organizing the data items will be employed in the vast data stores.

Frequently, one sees systems today in which data-base design decisions were made in a shortsighted manner. Indeed, in many situations straightforward design calculations do not provide the answers because there are intricate trade-offs between one aspect of the design and another—trade-offs, for example, between storage utilization and time utilization, between response time and complexity of data structure, between design which facilitates unanticipated inquiries and design for well-defined operational requirements. The trade-offs which involve user psychology are subjective. They can be made confidently only by a systems analyst who is experienced, and probably also well read, in the art of designing man-computer dialogues.

There are many interlocking questions in the design of data-base systems and many types of technique that one can use in answer to the questions—so many, in fact, that one often sees valuable approaches being overlooked in the design and vital questions not being asked. It is the intention of this book to make the reader familiar with the many alternatives possible in data organization and with the trade-offs between them.

There will soon be new storage devices, new software techniques, and new types of data bases. The details will change, but most of the principles will remain. Therefore, the reader should concentrate on the principles. The systems analyst must be able to *adapt* the techniques illustrated to his own needs.

REFERENCES

1. *Markets for Data-Base Services,* Frost and Sullivan Inc., New York, July 1973.

2 BASIC TERMINOLOGY

The terminology used for describing files and data bases has varied substantially from one authority to another and even from one time to another in the same organization. It is necessary that a consistent terminology be used throughout this book, and it would help if the industry terminology became consistent. In this chapter we will describe the terminology we will use, which has been taken, where possible, from the most widely accepted sources. The knowledgeable reader may skip the chapter with a glance at the figures.

We will describe the wording used to describe the hardware first and then the data.

HARDWARE TERMINOLOGY

Figure 2.1 shows wording used to describe the file hardware.

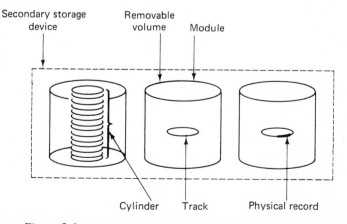

Figure 2.1 Wording which describes the file hardware.

Peripheral (or Secondary) Storage Device

Because the main memory of a computer is relatively small, most data are stored in storage devices connected to the computer by means of a channel. The latter are referred to as *peripheral* or *secondary* storage devices. They include tape and disk units, drums, and devices on which data are stored in demountable cells or cartridges.

Volumes

The demountable tapes, disk packs, and cartridges are referred to as *volumes.* The word volume also refers to a drum or other nondemountable storage medium. A volume is normally a single physical unit of any peripheral storage medium. It has been defined as "that portion of a single unit of storage medium which is accessible to a single read/write mechanism"; however, some devices exist in which a volume is accessible with two or more read/write mechanisms.

Module

A module of a peripheral storage device is that section of hardware which holds one volume, such as one spindle of disks.

Direct-Access Storage Device

A *direct-access* storage device (sometimes abbreviated to DASD) is one in which each physical record has a discrete location and a unique address. Disks and drums are direct-access devices; tape units are not. Records can be stored on a direct-access device in such a way that the location of any one record can be determined without extensive scanning of the recording medium. Records can be read or written directly, at random, rather than having to be read or written in a fixed serial sequence.

Track

A track on a direct-access device contains that data which can be read by a single reading head without changing its position. It may refer to the track on a drum or disk which rotates under a reading head.

Cylinder

An access mechanism may have many reading heads, each of which can read one track. A cylinder refers to that group of tracks which can be read without moving the access mechanism.

Cell

Cell is used as a generic word to mean either a track, cylinder, module, or other zone delimited by a natural hardware boundary such that the time required to access data increases by a step function when data extend beyond the cell boundaries. If the cells are such that data can be read from more than one cell at the same time, we will refer to them as *parallel* cells. This use of the word *cell* will appear in the names of techniques discussed later in the book, such as *cellular multilist*.

DATA TERMINOLOGY

Logical and Physical

Descriptions of data and of the relationships between data are of one of two forms: *logical* or *physical*. Physical data descriptions refer to the manner in which data are recorded physically on the hardware. Logical data descriptions refer to the manner in which data are presented to the application programmer or user of the data. The words *logical* and *physical* will be used to describe various aspects of data, *logical* referring to the way the programmer or user sees it, and *physical* referring to the way the data are recorded on the storage medium.

A physical record may contain several logical records in order to save storage space or access time. The structure of the data and the associations between the data may be different in the programmer's view of the data and in the physical organization of the data. We use the terms *logical relationship, logical structure,* and *logical data description* to describe the programmer's or user's view. *Physical relationship, physical structure,* and *physical data description* describe actual ways in which the data are stored. Figure 2.2 gives a simple example of difference between a logical and physical structure: physical records on a disk contain shorter logical records which are chained together. The programmer requires a file of logical records in the sequence of the chain. He does not necessarily know about the chain. The software presents his program with logical records in the required sequence. Other programs might be given records in a different sequence. There can be many other types of differences between the logical and physical organization.

The reasons the logical and physical views of the data are different will be discussed later in the book. It is a function of the software to convert from the programmer's logical statements and descriptions to the physical reality.

WORDS DESCRIBING DATA

There are many alternate words used for describing data. A widely accepted authority on data bases that is not associated with a specific computer manufacturer is CODASYL, and this book uses their wording where possible—in particular the wording of the CODASYL Data Base Task Group.

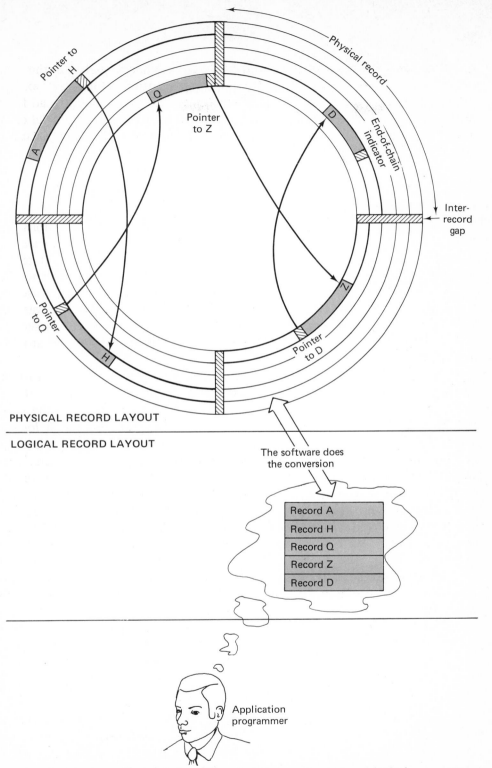

PHYSICAL RECORD LAYOUT

LOGICAL RECORD LAYOUT

Figure 2.2 An example of the difference between physical and logical data organization.

It is not always possible. Some concepts, such as the IBM concept of a "segment," do not have an exactly equivalent CODASYL word, and relational data bases need a vocabulary of their own, so some non-CODASYL vocabulary appears. The choice of the CODASYL wording is merely to achieve uniformity and hence clarity in the text; it does not necessarily imply preference for the Data Base Task Group (DBTG) languages or techniques.

Figure 2.3 shows the words used to describe the application programmer's view of the data.

Byte

A byte is the smallest individually addressable group of bits—conventionally eight bits.

Data Item

A data item is the smallest unit of named data. It may consist of any number of bits or bytes.

A data item is often referred to as a *field* or *data element.* In COBOL it is called an *elementary item.*

Data Aggregate

A data aggregate is a collection of data items within a record, which is given a name and referred to as a whole. For example, a data aggregate called DATE may be composed of the data items MONTH, DAY, and YEAR.

A data aggregate is called a *group* or *group item* in COBOL.

There can be two types of *data aggregates:* vectors and repeating groups. A *vector* is a one-dimensional, ordered collection of data items such

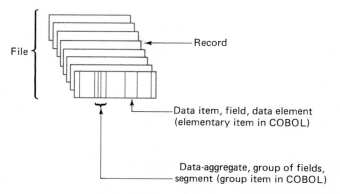

Record

Data item, field, data element
(elementary item in COBOL)

Data-aggregate, group of fields,
segment (group item in COBOL)

File

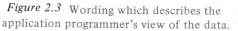

Figure 2.3 Wording which describes the
application programmer's view of the data.

as DATE above. A *repeating group* is a collection of data which occurs multiple times within a record occurrence, for example, deposits and withdrawals in a savings bank account record. A repeating group may consist of single data items, vector data aggregates, or other repeating groups.

Record

A record is a named collection of data items or data aggregates. When an application program reads data from the data base it may read one complete (logical) record. Often, however, *logical data-base record* refers to a data structure which incorporates multiple groups of data items (segments), not all of which need be read at one time. There is no upper limit to the number of possible occurrences of a particular record type (given sufficient hardware), whereas there is normally an upper limit to the number of repeating groups within a record.

Segment

It is the view of some authorities that there is no need to differentiate between a data aggregate and a record because each is a collection of data items. Each is referred to as a *segment* in terminology used by IBM and others. A segment contains one or more data items (usually more) and *is the basic quantum of data which passes to and from the application programs under control of the data-base management software.*

File

A file is the named collection of all occurrences of a given type of (logical) record. In a simple file every logical record has the same number of data items, as in Fig. 2.3. In a more complex file the records may have a varying number of data items because of the existence of repeating groups.

Data Base

A data base is a collection of the occurrences of multiple record types, containing the relationships between records, data aggregates, and data items. In the next chapter we will discuss the nature of a data base.

Data-Base System

In most systems the term *data base* does not refer to *all* the record types but to a specified collection of them. There can be several data bases in one system; however, the contents of the different data bases are assumed to be separate and disjoint. A term is needed for the collection of data bases, and *data-base system* is used.

Data bank sometimes refers to a collection of data bases. Other authorities interchange the meanings of *data base* and *data bank*, saying that a data base is a collection of data banks. The term *data bank* is often used in the literature in an imprecisely defined fashion. To avoid confusion, the term *data bank* will be generally avoided in this text.

**PHYSICAL
STORAGE**

The form in which the data are stored physically is often quite different from their logical form. The reasons for the differences will be clarified later in the book. Figure 2.4 shows the wording used to describe the physical storage of data.

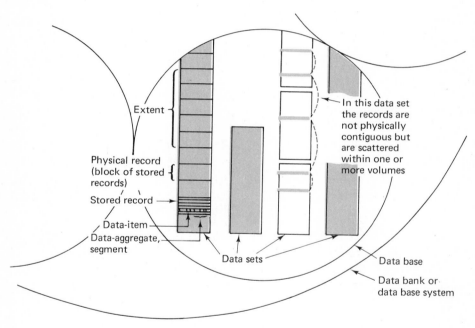

Figure 2.4 Wording which describes the stored data.

Physical Record

A physical record is that basic unit of data which is read or written by a single input/output command to the computer. It is those data which are recorded between gaps on tape or address markers on disk. One physical record often contains multiple logical records, or segments.

On most systems the length of a physical record is determined by the system programmer; on some devices it is of fixed length.

Block of Stored Records

The group of data which compose a physical record is referred to as a *block*.

Extent

An extent is a collection of physical records which are contiguous in secondary storage.

How many records are in an extent depends on the physical size of the volume and the user's request for space allocation. Associated records are not necessarily stored contiguously; this depends on the storage organization.

Data Set

A data set is a named collection of physical records. It includes data used for locating the records, such as indices. A data set may occupy one or more extents. It may be contained within one volume or spread over many volumes.

Bucket

Some addressing and indexing techniques provide as their output the address of a stored record. Others are less precise and provide the address of an area where a group of records is stored. We will refer to an area holding a group of records which are addressed jointly as a *bucket*. The bucket could be a physical record, a track, or a cell, but often it is a grouping determined by an addressing technique such as hashing and not necessarily related to the hardware. Some authorities use other words for this grouping, such as *pocket* or *slot*.

SUMMARY   Different data-base software systems employ different words to describe the data. Figure 2.5 shows equivalent words used in some of the most common software. This text uses the wording on the top line of Fig. 2.5 except when describing a specific software product.

A *data item* may be a quantity on an invoice. A *data aggregate* may be a line item on the invoice which is repeated multiple times and is hence a *repeating group*. The line item may be an individually addressable group of data in IBM (or other) software which refers to it as a *segment*. The *logical record* may be the entire invoice. The *physical record* may be as many logical records as can fit on one track. The *data set* may be the entire

The wording of CODASYL	Data item	Data aggregate	Record	Set	Data base
Wording commonly used for non-data-base systems	Field		Record	File, data set	
Wording commonly used in IBM	Data element	Segment	Record	File, data set	Data base (data bank)
COBOL	Elementary item	Group item	Record	File	
IMS (IBM's Information Management System)	Field	Segment		File	Data base
MARK IV (Informatics, Inc.)	Field	Segment		File	Master file
IDS (Honeywell's Integrated Data Store)	Data field	Group item	Record	File	File
TDMS (System Development Corporation's Time-shared Data Management System)	Element	Repeating group	Entry	File	Data base

Figure 2.5 Words used to describe data. (The words in the two right-hand columns are only approximately equivalent.)

collection of invoice records. The *data base* may include the invoice data set, the accounts receivable data set, and the customer data set. The *data-base system* may incorporate many such data bases.

VIRTUAL AND TRANSPARENT DATA
The word *virtual* referring to computer facilities or to data indicates that the item in question *appears to exist to the application programmer* when in fact it does not exist in that form. The programmer may, for example, write his program as though he has infinite main memory when in fact memory is limited but the computer overcomes the shortage by means of a paging mechanism which transfers blocks of data or program backward and forward between main memory and the peripheral storage devices. A programmer may similarly refer to virtual data which appear to exist but in fact do not, at least in that form; the computer generates them in some way, possibly using a more compact form of storage, every time the programmer refers to them.

An application or systems program may refer to data as though they were on a disk when in fact they are on a cartridge of a mass storage device;

a control program quickly moves them to a disk thus simulating a *virtual* disk unit.

Transparent Data and Facilities

Whereas something virtual appears to exist but does not, something *transparent* appears *not* to exist but in fact does. Many of the complex mechanisms used in data storage and data transmission can be hidden from the programmer so that he does not have to understand or even know about them. In this way his work can be made simpler and his programs easier to understand. In particular the complexities involved in transforming the logical files into the physical data storage and vice versa can be made transparent to the application program. When the program calls for the logical record of a given entity it may receive only those fields which concern it. There are other data elements needed for other applications in the stored record, but these are "transparent" to the program. It is only by using transparency that we can afford to build some of the complex data-base structures that we will discuss. Without it, application programming and maintenance would be too difficult.

Note: Class questions are at the end of the book.

BOOK STRUCTURE

Part I

A fast path through Part I of the book:

Note: This fast path omits one of the most important chapters, Chapter 15.

PART **I** LOGICAL ORGANIZATION

3 WHAT IS A DATA BASE?

A much-publicized but impracticable idea of a data base says that a corporation keeps all its processable items of data in a large reservoir in which a diversity of data users can go fishing. The storage in which all the data are kept may be in one location or multiple locations, the latter possibly interconnected by telecommunications. Programs for a variety of applications have access to the data.

Such a data base would be highly complex, and in general the dream has not been achieved in reality. It may remain a worthy *long*-term goal of the development of data processing. A complex data base, however, has to be built up stage by stage. In reality, today most data bases serve a limited set of applications. One computer is often referred to as having many data bases. Eventually the data bases for separate related functions may become combined where this integration can increase the efficiency or usefulness of the overall system.

A data base may be defined as a collection of interrelated data stored together without harmful or unnecessary redundancy to serve multiple applications; the data are stored so that they are independent of programs which use the data; a common and controlled approach is used in adding new data and in modifying and retrieving existing data within the data base. The data is structured so as to provide a foundation for future application development. One system is said to contain a collection of data bases if they are entirely separate in structure.

In simpler data organizations a collection of records is designed for one application. The intention of a data base is that the same collection of data should serve as many applications as possible. Hence, a data base is often conceived of as the repository of information needed for running certain functions in a corporation, factory, government department, or other organization. Such a data base would permit not only the retrieval of data but also the continuous modification of data needed for the control of operations. It may be possible to search the data base to obtain answers to queries or information for planning purposes. The collection of data may serve several departments, possibly cutting across what were political boundaries.

A data base may be designed for batch processing, real-time processing, or in-line processing (in which single transactions are processed to completion one at a time but without the tight time constraints of a real-time system). Many data bases serve a combination of these processing methods. On many data-base systems real-time terminals are employed at the same time as batch processing.

REDUNDANCY In most tape or disk libraries prior to the use of data-base techniques a massive amount of duplication exists in the data that are stored. Many data items are stored redundantly in volumes for different purposes and in different update versions of the same data. A data base should remove much of this redundancy. A data base has sometimes been defined as a *nonredundant* collection of data items, but in reality some measure of redundancy exists in many data bases in order to give improved access times or simpler addressing methods. Some records are duplicated to provide the capability to recover from accidental loss of data. There is a trade-off between nonredundancy and other desirable criteria, and so it would be better to use the phrase *controlled redundancy* or *minimal redundancy*, or say that a well-designed data base removes *harmful* redundancy.

Uncontrolled redundancy has several disadvantages. First, there is the extra cost of storing multiple copies. Second, and much more serious, multiple updating operations are necessary to update at least some of the redundant copies. Redundancy is therefore more expensive on files with a large volume of updating or, worse, in which new items are frequently being inserted or deleted. Third, because different copies of the data may be in different stages of updating, the system may give inconsistent information.

In a large data processing operation without a data base there are so many redundant data that it is virtually impossible to keep them all at the same level of update. Too often the users or general management notice the apparent inconsistencies that this causes and distrust the computerized information. Inability to keep redundant data in the same state of update is a common cause of the anti-computer stories that managers too often tell.

CONSTANT GROWTH One of the most important characteristics of most data bases is that they will constantly need to change and grow. Easy restructuring of the data base must be possible as new data types and new applications are added. The restructuring should be possible without having to rewrite the application programs and in general should cause as little upheaval as possible. The ease with which a data base can be changed will have a major effect on the rate at which data-processing applications can be developed in a corporation.

It is often easy for a systems analyst to imagine that the data structure he has designed for an application represents its ultimate content and usage. He leaves some spare characters in the records and thinks that these will accommodate any change that will occur. Consequently he ties his data to a physical organization which is efficient for that particular structure. Time and time again such systems analysts have been proved wrong. The requirements have changed in unforeseen ways. The data structures have had to be modified, and many application programs have consequently had to be rewritten and debugged. The larger an installation's base of application programs, the more expensive is this process.

The term *data independence* is often quoted as being one of the main attributes of a data base. It implies that the data and the application programs which use them are independent so that either may be changed without changing the other. In particular, the application programmer is insulated from the effects of changes made to the data, their organization, or the physical devices on which they are stored. In reality, just as the data are rarely completely nonredundant, so they are rarely completely *independent*. As we will see, there are several variations on the theme of data independence. How much the programmer has to know about the data in order to access them varies from one data base to another. Nevertheless, data independence is one of the main reasons for the use of data-base systems.

MULTIPLE   When a single set of data items serves a variety of
RELATIONSHIPS   applications, different application programs per-
                         ceive different relationships between the data items.
To a large extent, data-base organization is concerned with the representation of associations between data items and records. A data base used for many applications can have multiple interconnections between the data.

In such an environment the control of the accuracy, privacy, and security of the data is more difficult than when simple noninterconnected files are stored. Concern with security and recovery from failure is of major importance in data-base design.

On some systems, a reason for using data-base techniques is to permit users to employ the data in a way which cannot be precisely anticipated by the system designers. One of the much-heralded advantages of "Management Information Systems" is that managers or their staff may ask unanticipated questions of their computer system. Instead of being organized into application-oriented files which are always addressed in the same way, the data are organized so that they can be addressed in a variety of different ways and can be used to answer a diversity of queries. All the interesting facts about entities are stored together rather than merely those facts needed for one application. The "reservoir" concept of management information systems, or other information systems, is much easier to conceive than to implement. It is proving a very complex and lengthy operation to build up such data bases, and with current hardware it is expensive to search sufficiently quickly to give real-time answers to unanticipated queries. For the forseeable future many of the most valuable data bases will be those structured for specific sets of operations rather than those for unstructured fishing.

EVOLUTION OF
DATA-BASE CONCEPTS
The term *data base* became current in the late 1960s. Prior to that time, the data-processing world had talked about files of data and data sets. As often happens when a new term becomes fashionable, many users promoted their files by changing their title to data base without changing their nature to include *data independence, controlled redundancy, interconnectedness, security protection,* or, in many cases, *real-time accessibility.* As the employment of better data management software spread, these characteristics spread with it. For reasons that will emerge later in the book, no single software package yet gives all the characteristics that an ideal data base should have, and the systems analyst (as often when he designs systems) has to select a compromise among different qualities.

Figure 3.1 illustrates the evolution of data-storage methods. Prior to the third generation of computers (first installed in 1965) most files were handled as in stage 1 of Fig. 3.1. The software executed the input/output operations of the storage devices and little else. The coding written into the application programs took care of the data organization, and this was done in an elementary manner, usually with simple serial files on tape. There was no data independence. If a change was made to the data organization or to the storage units, the application programmer had to modify his programs accordingly, recompile them, and then test the modifications. To update a file, a new file was written. The old one was retained and referred to as the *father.* The previous generation—*grandfather*—was also kept, and often earlier ancestors. Most files were used for one application only. Often other applications used the same data, but they usually needed it in a different form, often with different fields, so different files were created. There was therefore a high level of redundancy, with many different files containing the same data elements.

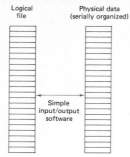

Logical file

Physical data (serially organized)

Simple input/output software

- Files organized in serial manner.
- Physical data structure essentially the same as logical file structure.
- Batch-processing with no real-time access.
- Several copies stored of the same file because previous generations of data are kept.
- Software handles only input/output operations.
- Application programmer designs the physical file layouts and embeds them in the application programs.
- If the data structure or storage device are changed, the application program must be rewritten, recompiled, and retested.
- Data is usually designed and optimized for one application.
- Hence the same data is rarely used across applications.
- High level of redundancy between data files.

STAGE 2: File Access Method (Predominant in the late 1960's)

Logical file

Serial data set

Logical file

Direct access data sets

Access method

Access method (with addressing mechanism)

- Serial access or random access is possible to records (not fields).
- Processing is batch, in-line, or real-time.
- Logical and physical file organization are distinguished but the relationship between them is fairly simple.
- Storage units can be changed without changing the application program.
- Data structures are usually serial, indexed sequential, or simple direct access.
- Multiple-key retrieval is generally not used.
- Data security measures may be used (but are rarely very secure).
- Data still tends to be designed and optimized primarily for one application.
- Much data redundancy still exists.
- If hierarchical files are used, the programmer usually has to construct the father-son relationships.
- The software provides "access" methods but not "data management"

Figure 3.1

STAGE 3: Early Data-Base Systems (Predominant in the early 1970's)

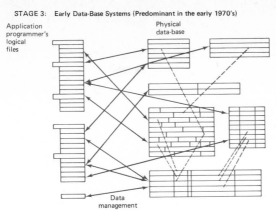

Application programmer's logical files

Physical data-base

Data management

- Multiple different logical files can be derived from the same physical data.
- The same data can be accessed in different ways by applications with different requirements.
- Software provides the means to lessen data redundancy.
- Data elements are shared between diverse applications.
- Absence of redundancy facilitates data integrity.
- The physical storage organization is independent of the application programs. It may be changed often in order to improve the data-base performance without application program modification.
- The data is addressable at the field or group level.
- Multiple-key retrieval can be used.
- Complex forms of data organization are used without complicating the application programs.

STAGE 4: Today's Requirement in Data-Base Systems

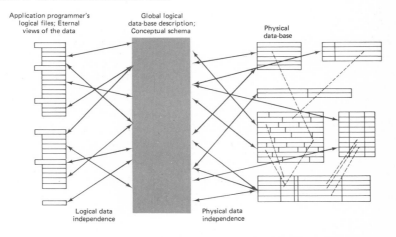

Application programmer's logical files; Eternal views of the data

Global logical data-base description; Conceptual schema

Physical data-base

Logical data independence

Physical data independence

- Software provides logical as well as physical data independence, allowing a global logical view of the data to exist independently of certain changes in the application programs' views of data or the physical data layouts. The data independence capabilities listed in Fig. 3.2 are provided.
- The data base may evolve without incurring high maintenance costs.
- Facilities are provided for a Data-Base Administrator to act as controller and custodian of the data, and ensure that its organization is the best for the users as a whole.
- Effective procedures are provided for controlling the privacy, security, and integrity of the data.
- Inverted files are used on some systems to permit rapid data base searching.
- Data bases are designed to provide answers to unanticipated forms of information request.
- Data migration is facilitated.
- The software provides a *data description language* for the Data-Base Administrator, a *command language* for the application programmer, and sometimes a *data interrogation language* for the user.

Some *random-access* files were used in the stage 1 era which permitted the user to access any record at random instead of scanning the entire file serially. The means of addressing them had to be built by the application programmer into his code. If the storage devices were changed, a major upheaval in the application program coding was necessary. In fact, the storage devices did change. New technology brought substantial reductions in the cost per bit of storage, and the sizes of the files often outgrew their earlier storage device.

The second stage in Fig. 3.1 recognized the changing nature of files and their storage devices. It attempted to insulate the application programmer from the effects of hardware changes. The software made it possible to change the physical data layout without changing the logical view of the data, provided that there was no change in record contents or in the fundamental structuring of the files.

The files used in this second era were, like the first, generally designed for one application or closely related applications. A set of files, for example, would be designed for the purchasing function in a corporation. A small group of systems analysts and programmers would design these files and include in them the set of data elements needed for the purchasing application. The files would be structured to serve that application as efficiently as possible. The accounts payable application needs much of the same information. A separate small group may design the files for accounts payable. It might be suggested to them that they use the purchasing files. However, they need a number of data items that are not in these files, and they want to permit inquiries to the files that would be difficult with files structured in the manner of the purchasing files. Consequently they produce their own files with separate computer runs. If the accounts payable and purchasing applications could have used the same files, both the total processing time and the total storage requirement would have been less.

WHEN DATA
STRUCTURE CHANGES

As commercial data processing evolved, it became clear that it was desirable to isolate the application programs not only from changes in file hardware and the effect of increasing file size but also from additions to the data that are stored, such as new fields and new relationships. If ideal data management software had been used, it would have been possible to develop the purchasing application and the accounts payable application separately and then, later, merge their files without having to rewrite the application programs. Data-base software—stage 3 of Fig. 3.1—attempts to accomplish this. It recognizes that a data base is something that is continually evolving and will be used for new applications. New types of records will be added and new data items will be included in existing records. The structure of the data base will be changed to improve its efficiency or to permit new types of inquiries. The users will change their needs and modify the types of inquiries they make of the data.

A data base in an organization is no more a *static* entity than are the contents of the organization's filing cabinets. The details of data stored, and the way it is stored, change continuously. If a computer system attempts to impose an unchangeable file structure on an organization, it is doomed to the types of pressure that will result in most of the programming effort being spent on modifying existing programs rather than developing new applications.

As multiple logical files can be derived from the same data, in stage 3, the same data may be *accessed* in different ways by applications with different requirements. This often leads to complex data structures. Good data-base software, however, protects the application programmer from the complexities of the data structure. Regardless of how the data are organized the application programmer should see the file as a relatively simple structure that is planned as he needs it for his application.

The data-base software must provide a means for mapping the application programmer's file structure (the left-hand side of the diagram in Fig. 3.1, stage 3) into the physical data structure that is actually stored (the right-hand side of the diagram) and vice versa.

The degree to which the application programmer is freed from having to know details of the physical data varies from one system to another. If you were going to the movies by means of a New York taxi, the degree of *data independence* possible would vary from one taxi driver to another. With some you could ask merely for "The Godfather," and the taxi driver would find the theater where that movie was playing. If the movie has been changed to another theater, you need not know or change your request—the taxi driver would find it. With a less helpful taxi driver you might have to know where the movie was playing and ask for "The Paris Theater." The driver would find the address of that theater. With another taxi driver you might have to find the address yourself and instruct the driver to go to "the Paris Theater on 58th Street at Fifth Avenue." Worse, with today's taxi drivers you might even have to navigate: "Turn left . . . drive five blocks . . . turn right," and so on.

Similarly, the application programmer may merely give the application name of the data item or record he wants. With different software he may have to give the identification of the data item and the name of the data set it is kept in. Worse, he may have to know how the data set is organized. He may have to know how to determine the machine address of the data. If there is no data independence, he will have to know the exact physical format of the record. Worst of all, he might have to "navigate."

The process of converting the application programmer's reference to a *logical record* and its data items into the machine's reference to a *physical record* and its data items is called *binding*. Binding is the association of a physical representation of data with the program that uses them.

LOGICAL AND PHYSICAL   When the early data-base systems had been in use
DATA INDEPENDENCE   for a short time it became apparent that a further
level of data independence was needed. The overall logical structure of the data became complex in many cases, and as the data base grew, the overall logical structure inevitably changed. It became important that it should be able to change without forcing a change in the many application programs which used it. In some systems, change in the overall logical structure of the data has become a way of life; it is constantly evolving. Because of this, two levels of data independence are needed called *logical* and *physical* data independence.

Logical data independence means that the overall logical structure of the data may be changed without changing the application programs. (The changes must not, of course, remove any of the data the application programs use.)

Physical data independence means that the physical layout and organization of the data may be changed without changing either the overall logical structure of the data or the application programs.

Stage 4 of Figure 3.1 illustrates the concept of logical and physical independence, and we will give detailed illustrations of it later in the book. The block in the center of the illustration represents the overall logical structure of the data. This view may be entirely different from the *physical* structure of the data and different from any individual application programmer's view of the data. The data-base software will, in effect, derive the application programmer's data from the overall logical structure and will then map the overall logical structure into the physical representation.

THE CONCEPTUAL   The central block in stage 4 of Fig. 3.1 is ex-
MODEL OF THE DATA   tremely important in modern data-base design.
This is the conceptual view of the data as a whole. From it the parochial views of programmers and end users are derived. It is sometimes referred to as a *model* of the data, or *conceptual model*; it is sometimes called a *schema* or *conceptual schema*. It should be designed to be as stable as possible. While the programmer's views of the data change and the

	No change in (other) application programs	No change in the global logical data description	No change in the physical storage organization
● A new application program is added, using existing types of data	X	X	X
● An application program uses a changed representation of existing data (e.g., floating-point instead of fixed-point)	X	X	X
● A new application program is added, using new types of data	X		
● New record occurrences are inserted, or old ones deleted	X	X	X
● The global logical data description is improved, or new relationships between data types are created	X		
● Two data bases are merged	X		
● The physical organization of data is improved; possibly different representations are used	X	X	
● The addressing methods are changed	X	X	
● The data is moved to a different type of volume	X	X	
● The software is changed	X	X	
● The hardware is changed	X	X	

Figure 3.2 The data independence capabilities desirable in advanced data-base systems.

physical storage and organization change, the conceptual model remains stable or grows to incorporate more data types. The conceptual model of the data should be a stable foundation on which much future data processing will be built. To make it stable it should be designed to represent the inherent properties of the data, as we discuss later.

If the conceptual model is badly designed, then it will have to be modified later as its usage evolves. This will necessitate the rewriting of programs which have employed the model. A major objective of data-base design is to avoid this burdensome rewriting of past programs as the system evolves.

The purpose of the structure shown in the stage 4 diagram is to permit the maximum freedom to change the data structures without having to rehash much of the earlier work on the data base. Figure 3.2 lists a number of changes that are common on a data-base system and indicates whether these can be accomplished without restructuring the physical storage organization, the global logical view of the data, or the application programs other than the one which initiated the change. The ticks in the columns of Fig. 3.2 represent an objective of contemporary data-base software design.

THREE TYPES OF ORGANIZATION In this book we are concerned with the organization of data. There are three aspects to the organization, corresponding to the three parts of Fig. 3.1, stage 4. We will refer to these as *external organization, global logical data organization*, and *physical storage organization.* These three types of organization are often entirely different.

External organization is concerned with the view of the data (such as that in Fig. 6.2) as perceived by the application programmer or end users. The programmer may, for example, view the files as a master record with subordinate detail records. He describes his view of the files in his application program.

Global logical data organization is the overall organization or conceptual model for the data base (such as that in Fig. 6.1) from which multiple external organizations may be derived. It is a logical view of the data, entirely independent of the physical storage organization. It will be described in a data description language which is part of the data-base management software.

Physical storage organization is concerned with the physical representation and layout and organization of the data on the storage units. It is concerned with the indices, pointers, chains, and other means of physically locating records and with the overflow areas and techniques used for inserting new records and deleting records. Part II of this book is concerned with physical storage organization.

The distinction between the three forms of organization will become clearer later in the book.

THE DATA-BASE ADMINISTRATOR To design and maintain the data base structures a new job title was introduced: *data-base administrator.*

The data-base administrator is the custodian of the corporation's data— or that part of it which his system relates to. He controls the overall structure of the data.

Note that being *custodian* of the data is quite separate from being its *owner*. A bank manager is the custodian of what is in his bank vault but not its owner. A department or an individual may *own* the data. The data administrator is responsible for safekeeping and controlling the data. The data may be *used* by any persons who are given authority to use it.

Note further that controlling the data does not mean that the data-base administrator knows the content of records. He knows that the PAYROLL record contains a SALARY data item, but he does not know the value recorded in this data item; indeed, he is specifically locked out of that data item so that he cannot read it. However, if the SALARY data item must be expanded from six digits to seven digits, only the data-base administrator can accomplish this change.

If an application programmer wants to create a new type of record or wants to modify an old record by including new data items or by expanding the size of a data item, he must apply to the data-base administrator for permission. The data-base administrator will make suitable arrangements to modify the data structures in whatever manner he thinks best for the system as a whole. An application programmer or a systems analyst working on one application is not permitted to change the overall data structures; only the data-base administrator or staff with a global viewpoint can be familiar with the overall economics of the data.

We will make many references to the data-base administrator as having the global view of how the data are organized. In reality the data-base administrator may be a department or group rather than one man. A complete understanding of the data base, its organization, its economics, its design criteria, and the requirements of its many users is too much for one man.

Note: Class questions are at the end of the book.

4 WHAT SHOULD BE THE OBJECTIVES OF A DATA-BASE ORGANIZATION?

There are many ways in which a data base can be organized. Which principles should guide us in selecting the organization techniques?

This question has been studied at great length by many bodies—by corporations which use computers, by government committees, and by confidential task forces in the computer manufacturers. The CODASYL Systems Committee has issued reports addressing the subject [1,2,3] (CODASYL—Conference on Data Systems Languages—is the organization that developed the language COBOL). SHARE and GUIDE (the influential organizations of IBM users) issued a classic report on the requirements for a data-base management system [4]. The ACM (Association for Computing Machinery) has studied the subject [6,7,9,10] and the American National Standards Institute (ANSI) X3 SPARC/DBMS Study Group has published an important report [11].

The ultimate objective of data-base systems is to make application development easier, cheaper, faster and more flexible. It is important not to lose sight of this overriding objective as we discuss the complex mechanics of data-base systems.

A data-base system should be a repository of the data needed for an organization's data processing. That data should be accurate, private, and protected from damage. It should be organized so that diverse applications with different data requirements can employ the data. Different application programmers and different end users will have different views of the data which must be derived from a common overall data structure. Their methods of accessing or searching the data will differ.

The ways in which end users want to utilize existing data will constantly change, and in some cases demands for new uses of the data will arise rapidly and urgently. The extent to which these demands can be satisfied determines the overall value of the data-base system.

The cost of change in data processing has become excessive. A seemingly trivial change in the data an application uses often starts a chain reaction of changes to other programs and results in many new programming bugs. Data-base software should permit the data for one application to be changed without causing the rewriting of other programs.

The overall logical structure of the data will serve diverse applications in the future. Because its uses cannot be fully foreseen it should be designed so as to represent the *true properties of the data.* In other words the groupings of data items and the associations between data items should represent the inherent structure of the data. In this way it will be as stable as possible, retaining its validity while the uses of the data change and the physical structures change. It should be a stable foundation on which future applications will be built.

Data bases of wide applicability will not be built overnight; they will grow a step at a time. Both the software and the logical structuring of the data should be designed to facilitate orderly data-base growth without disruption.

Where possible the end users should have their own access to the data which permits them to employ the data in spontaneous or creative ways without having to wait for application programs to be written. To do this they should have data-base interrogation and manipulation facilities which bypass the need for conventional programming, and are as easy to use as possible.

When a corporation achieves stable logical data-base structures and its computer users have powerful easy-to-use data-base interrogation and manipulation facilities and report and application generators, a higher level of automation will have been achieved which permits rapid, flexible development of data processing.

Some of the desirable characteristics of data-base systems should be as follows:

1. Ability to Represent the Inherent Structure
of the Data

In Chapter 15 we illustrate how to derive logical data structures which represent the associations inherent in the data—the true properties of the data. The data-base management system should be able to represent these structures and not force the data into structures which do not represent its inherent nature. A system which can only represent tree structures, for example, is inadequate.

2. Performance

Data-base applications designed for use by a terminal operator must give a response time appropriate for the man-terminal dialogue. In addition, the data-base system must be able to handle an appropriate throughput of transactions. On systems with a low traffic volume the throughput may place few constraints on the data-base design. On systems with a high traffic volume the throughput has a major effect on the choice of physical storage organizations.

On systems designed for batch processing only, response time is of no concern, and the physical organization method will be selected to give efficient batch operations.

The response time which is needed for a terminal system depends on the nature of the man-terminal dialogue. For certain categories of dialogue a response time of 2 seconds is needed (i.e., 2 seconds of elapsed time between the operator completing an input message at a terminal and the first character of the response appearing at that terminal). For single inquiries a much longer response time can often be tolerated. The requirements for different response time are discussed in detail in Chapter 18 of the author's book *Design of Man-Computer Dialogues.* Some of the physical storage organizations we will discuss make very fast response times possible, whereas others prevent fast responses.

3. Minimum Cost

To keep the cost down, techniques are selected which minimize the total storage requirements. Using those techniques the physical representation of data in storage may be quite unlike the representation which the application programmer uses. Software, or possibly hardware or micro-programming, does the conversion between the two. There is then a trade-off between the cost of the conversion algorithms and the storage savings.

The cost per bit of storage is dropping rapidly with improved technology, whereas the cost of programming is not. There is therefore an increasing need to keep the application programming simple, and *logical* data organizations should be designed with this objective.

4. Minimal Redundancy

Prior to the use of data-base techniques a very high level of redundant data has been growing in data-processing systems. Most tape libraries contain much redundant data. Even with data-base techniques, as increasing amounts of information are combined to form integrated data bases a great potential exists for the presence of redundant data. As we have noted, redundant data are expensive in that they take up more storage than is necessary, and require more than one updating operation. Because different copies of the data may be in different stages of updating, the system may give conflicting information.

An objective of the data-base organization should be to eliminate redundant data where it is economic to do so, and to control the inconsistencies that are caused by redundant data values.

5. Search Capability

The user of a data base may ask a wide variety of questions about the data that are stored. In the majority of today's commercial applications the types of queries are anticipated and the physical data organization is designed to handle them with suitable speed. There is an increasing requirement for systems to handle queries or produce reports that were *not* anticipated in detail. The user may enter spontaneous requests for information at a terminal. Unanticipated queries (and some anticipated queries) make it necessary to search parts of the data base. If a quick answer is needed at a terminal, the search will have to be fast. The capability to search a data base quickly and with different search criteria is highly dependent on the physical data organization. With many data organizations the search times are far too long for real-time responses at terminals. An objective of the data-base organization, then, may be to achieve fast and flexible search capability.

6. Integrity

When a data base contains data employed by many different users it is important that the data items *and* associations between data items not be destroyed. Hardware failures and various types of accidents will occur occasionally. The storage of data and its updating, and insertion procedures, must be such that the system can recover from these circumstances without harm to the data. An installation needs to be able to guarantee the integrity of the data it stores.

In addition to protecting data from systems problems, the integrity checks may also be designed to ensure that data *values* conform to certain specified rules. For example, they may be constrained to lie within certain ranges of values. Tests may be made by checking the relationship between several data values.

7. Privacy and Security

Data in data base systems must be kept secure and private. The information stored is sometimes of great value to a corporation. It must not be lost or stolen. The more vital the information in data bases becomes, the more important it is to protect it from hardware or software failures, from catastrophes, and from criminals, vandals, incompetents, and people who would misuse it [5].

Data security refers to *protection of data against accidental or intentional disclosure to unauthorized persons, or unauthorized modifications or destruction.*

Privacy refers to *the rights of individuals and organizations to determine for themselves when, how, and to what extent information about them is to be transmitted to others.*

Although the technology of privacy is closely related to that of security, privacy is an issue that goes far beyond the computer center. To a large extent it is a problem of society. To preserve the privacy of data about individuals, solutions are needed beyond the technical solutions. Future society, dependent upon a massive use of data banks, will need new legal and social controls if the degree of privacy of personal information that is cherished today is to be maintained.

Security is a highly complex subject because there are so many different aspects to it. A systems analyst responsible for the design of security needs to be familiar with all features of the system because the system can be attacked or security breached in highly diverse ways. Sometimes a great amount of effort is put into one aspect of security and other aspects are neglected.

The following seven requirements are essential for data-base security:

1. The data should be **protected** from fire, theft, or other forms of destruction.

2. The data should be **reconstructable** because, however good the precautions, accidents sometimes happen.

3. The data should be **auditable.** Failure to audit computer systems has permitted some of the world's largest crimes.

4. The system should be **tamperproof.** Ingenious programmers should not be able to bypass the controls.

5. No system today is completely tamperproof, but bypassing the controls can be made extremely difficult. Users of the data base must be positively **identified** before they can use it.

6. The system must be able to check that users' actions are **authorized**.

7. Users' actions should be **monitored** so that if they do something wrong they are likely to be found out.

8. The Interface with the Past

Organizations which have been using data processing for some time have a major investment in their existing programs, procedures, and data.

When an organization installs new data-base software it is important that it can work with the existing programs and procedures and that the existing data can be converted. This need for *compatibility* can be a major constraint in switching to a new data-base system. It is essential, however, that growth of data-base technology is not held back by too much attention to compatibility with the past. The biggest obstacle to software progress is overemphasizing the existing problems and *patching* them. Software producers can paint themselves into a corner with excessive patching of existing software.

9. The Interface with the Future

Most important is the interface with the future. In the future the data and its storage media will change in many ways. No commercial organization is static; change is a way of life. Change has been extremely costly to data-processing users. The *enormous cost of seemingly trivial changes* has held back application development seriously. This cost has resulted from the need to rewrite application programs, to convert data, and to deal with the many bugs that are introduced by the changes. Over the years the numbers of application programs grow in an organization until eventually the prospect of having to rewrite all of them is unthinkable. One of the most important objectives of data-base design is to plan the data base in such a way that changes can be made to it without having to modify the application programs.

To obtain this essential protection two characteristics are necessary in the data-base design, and both are complex to achieve. First, the application programs' view of the data must be severed from the physical representation of data, and the data management software must convert between one and the other. When changes are made to the physical organization of the data or to the hardware, these changes should be reflected in the data management software but should leave the application programs untouched. This severing is referred to as *physical data independence.*

Second, the application programs' view of data must be protected from changes in the global logical structure and changes in the data requirements of other application programs. The global logical data representation itself changes frequently in many organizations as new applications are added and old applications are modified. New fields must be added to logical records and new relationships created between existing data items. What was once a two-level hierarchy may become a three-level hierarchy, and so forth. It is important that these changes to the logical data organization can be made without having to rewrite application programs which are unaffected by them. To achieve this type of independence any single application program's view of the data needs to be severed from the overall logical data repre-

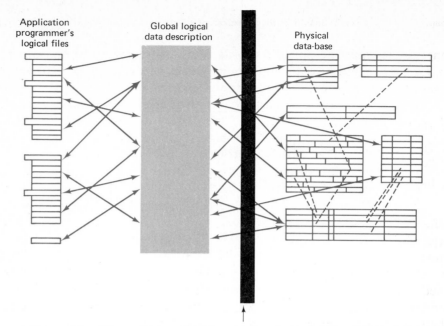

Figure 4.1 The software should sever the physical data organization from the logical data description as completely as possible, so that the physical data organization can be tuned or totally changed without necessitating any rewriting of the logical data description or application programs.

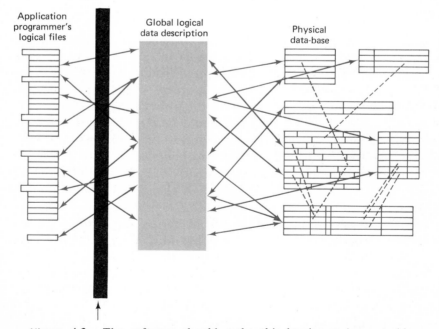

Figure 4.2 The software should make this barrier as inpenetrable as possible so that when on application program changes the data it uses, other application programs are not affected, and when the global logical data is restructured, the application programs need not be rewritten.

sentation. It must be possible to add new fields to a record without having to rewrite an existing application program which uses that record. This severing is referred to as *logical data independence.*

A data-base organization thus requires three separate views of the data:

1. The physical representation.
2. The overall data-base logical representation (referred to with the words "schema" or "conceptual model".
3. Individual application programs' or end users' representations.

It must be possible to change the first of these without changing the others. As indicated in Fig. 4.1, the severing of the physical data organization from the other two views should be as complete as possible. It must also be possible to change the global logical representation of the system's data without rewriting any application programming. When the data needs of one application program change, this change may necessitate modifications to the global logical data description but should not cause any changes to other application programs. As indicated in Fig. 4.2, the barrier between the application programs and the global logical data description should be as complete as possible.

In general the data independence shown in Fig. 3.2 should be provided. Some current systems provide some *physical data independence* and little or no *logical data independence.*

10. Tunability

Where on-line access to the data is needed, the users of the system are very much concerned with the time it takes the system to respond. With batch-processing systems there is concern with how large a throughput the system can handle or how long it takes to accomplish the work load. These factors are dependent on the time it takes to access the required data, and also dependent on the organization of the data and its positioning with the storage units. The difference between appropriate and inappropriate organizations can make a very large difference in response time and throughputs.

If the data storage is planned for a specific and well-understood set of operations, such as airline reservations, the organization can be selected and the data positioned in an optimal manner for those operations. The designer knows precisely what he is designing for. Often a designer is not so fortunate. In some cases he does not know exactly how the files will be used, how the data base will be interrogated, or how often. It is therefore necessary to adjust, or even to fundamentally change, the organization of the storage *after* the system has come into use and the usage pattern has become clear. With many data bases the usage continually changes as different persons become familiar with how the system can be used or as the application programs evolve. The adjustment of the storage organization to improve its performance is a continuing process.

Adjusting a data base to improve its performance is referred to as *tuning* the data base. The savings that have resulted from tuning have often, in practice, been great. Sometimes they have been so great as to make the difference between workable and unworkable applications. The data-base administrator or his group is responsible for the tuning and operation of the data base, and it is important that he should be free to make what changes he feels necessary without playing havoc with the application programs. Without appropriate software, tuning can incur unacceptably high costs in program maintenance and testing.

Effective tuning has two requirements. First, physical data independence is necessary. Second, it is desirable to automatically monitor the usage of the data base so that appropriate adjustments can be made. Future data-base systems may employ some measure of automatic tuning, for example, automatic data migration. Whether automatic or not, the system should be designed for ease of tuning.

11. Data Migration

Some data are referenced very frequently and others only occasionally. It is desirable to store the frequently referenced data in such a manner that they can be accessed quickly and conveniently. The rarely accessed data can be stored in a cheaper fashion. In an office the information which is used every day is in the secretaries' filing cabinets; information which is rarely if ever looked at may be in the basement, out of the way and inexpensively stored. The computer equivalent of the basement storage may be magnetic tape, and frequently accessed data may be on disk or drum, always readable in a fraction of a second. A complex data base may have multiple levels of ease of accessability.

Some stored data, like pop music, rapidly changes its popularity rating. In a stockbroker system, for example, there may be a high level of activity and inquiries for certain stocks which last month had little attention paid to them. On an airline there is high activity for the records of a flight and its passengers during the few days before it takes off. Ten months before it takes off there is little activity, although some bookings will be made. Two days after it takes off there is no activity, although the records must still be kept.

As the popularity of data changes it may be moved to forms of storage, or to positions in the data base, suited to its activity. Two days after an airline flight takes off, the records of the flight and its passengers are moved from the real-time disks to *archival* storage on tape. In some cases the data themselves are not moved, but references to them in the indices which are used for addressing them are changed so that they can be found more quickly. The process of adjusting the storage of data to suit its popularity rating is called *data migration*. In some systems it is done automatically. In others it is done by the system's programmers or the data administrator. In some it is regarded as part of the process of tuning the data base.

12. Simplicity

The means that are used to represent the overall logical view of data should be conceived in a simple and neat fashion. In many systems pointers are used in the logical representation to show relationships between data items. Glancing ahead, Figs. 6.8 and 9.13 show examples of logical pointers. A problem with logical pointers is that as more and more relationships are added between data items the overall collection of pointers becomes highly complex and it is difficult to represent the overall logical view of the data base with clarity. There are pointers to pointers to pointers. In some cases, as we will see, multiple pointer links in the user's representation of data can be highly misleading. There is no need for the complexity that exists in some logical data structures.

13. Powerful User Languages

It is possible that in the future the most important reason to have data-base systems will be that they permit end users to employ data *without* application programs necessarily having to be written. Powerful languages are coming into existence which permit untrained users to query, search, and update data in a data base; to manipulate the data; and to generate reports or documents which use it [11].

As computing power and storage drop rapidly in cost over the next 10 years, so it will become more difficult to program all the available machines with conventional application programming languages. The application backlog in most organizations is high today, and may become higher as computing becomes more economical. The economic attractiveness of end users *bypassing* the application programmers will grow. Appropriately designed data bases with powerful data-manipulation facilities will make this possible.

The collection of data in on-line data-base form will grow in corporations, and will become a highly valuable corporate resource if it can be put to use in a spontaneous and powerful manner. To maximize the usefulness of this resource the data must be structured in a clean, well-thought-out manner that is independent of the need of any *single* application.

Box 4.1 Objectives of Data-Base Organization

PRIMARY OBJECTIVES OF DATA-BASE ORGANIZATION

- **The Data Base is the Foundation Stone of Future Application Development**

    It should make application development easier, cheaper, faster, and more flexible.

- **The Data Can Have Multiple Uses**

    Different users who perceive the same data differently can employ them in different ways.

- **Intellectual Investmentment Is Protected**

    Existing programs and logical data structures (representing many man-years) will not have to be redone when changes are made to the data base.

- **Clarity**

    Users can easily know and understand what data are available to them.

- **Ease of Use**

    Users can gain access to data in a simple fashion. Complexity is hidden from the users by the data-base management system.

- **Flexible Usage**

    The data can be used or searched in flexible ways with different access paths.

- **Unanticipated Requests for Data Can Be Handled Quickly**

    Spontaneous requests for data can be handled without application programs having to be written (a time-consuming bottleneck), by means of high-level query or report generation languages.

- **Change Is Easy**

    The data base can grow and change without interferring with established ways of using the data.

- **Low Cost**

    Low cost of storing and using data, and minimization of the high cost of making changes.

- **Less Data Proliferation**

    New application needs may be met with existing data rather creating new files, thus avoiding the excessive data proliferation in today's tape libraries.

- **Performance**

    Data requests can be satisfied with speed suitable to the usage of the data.

- **Accuracy and Consistency**

    Accuracy controls will be used. The system will avoid having multiple versions of the same data item available to users in different stages of updating.

- **Privacy**

    Unauthorized access to the data will be prevented. The same data may be restricted in different ways from different uses.

- **Protection from Loss or Damage**

    Data will be protected from failures and catastrophes, and from criminals, vandals, incompetents, and persons who might falsely update them.

- **Availability**

    Data are quickly available to users at almost all times when they need them.

Box 4.1 *continued*

SECONDARY OBJECTIVES (to help achieve the primary objectives)

- **Physical Data Independence**

   Storage hardware and physical storage techniques can be changed without causing application program rewriting (Fig. 4.1).

- **Logical Data Independence**

   New data items can be added, or the overall logical structures expanded, without existing programs having to be rewritten (Fig. 4.2).

- **Controlled Redundancy**

   Data items will be stored only once except where there are technical or economic reasons for redundant storage.

- **Suitably Fast Access**

   Access mechanisms and addressing methods will be fast enough for the usage in question.

- **Suitably Fast Searching**

   The need for fast spontaneous searching of the data will grow as interactive systems usage spreads.

- **Data Standardization Within a Corporation**

   Interdepartmental agreement is needed on data formats and definitions. Standardization is needed between departments who would otherwise have created incompatible data.

- **Data Dictionary**

   A data dictionary, defining all data items used, is needed.

- **High-Level Programmer Interface**

   Application programmers should use simple, powerful data requests and be insulated from the complexities of file layout and addressing.

- **End User Language**

   A high-level query or report-generation language should permit some end users to bypass the application programming step.

- **Integrity Controls**

   Range checks and other controls should detect data inaccuracies where possible.

- **Fast Recovery from Failures**

   Automatic recovery without loss of transactions.

- **Tunability**

   The data base should be tunable, to improve performance without causing application program rewriting.

- **Design and Monitoring Aids**

   Aids which permit the designer or data administrator to predict and optimize performance.

- **Automatic Reorganization or Migration**

   Data migration or other automatic physical reorganization designed to improve performance.

- **Evolution to Distributed Data Base Operation**

   The system should be designed so that distributed processing and computer network operations can evolve.

SUMMARY OF
OBJECTIVES
Box 4.1 summarizes the objectives of data-base organization and, if these objectives are achieved, the advantages of the data-base approach over that of traditional computer files.

Note that the summary says nothing about "management information systems" and nothing about a data base handling "all the data needs of a corporation." Such phrases have confused rather than clarified the concept of data-base systems. In actuality most valuable data bases are used with a limited set of applications and contain only a portion of an organization's data. Data bases are an evolutionary step in an organization's data processing which will facilitate further application development and will help to ensure that computer data are put to the best uses.

In many systems the most important advantages of the data-base approach are physical and logical data independence (Figs. 4.1 and 4.2). Before using such techniques the application programs were constantly being modified to accommodate changes in the file organization or storage hardware, and the program *maintenance* costs became excessive. Only with the data independence given by good data-base techniques can an organization be free to allow its data base to change and evolve as the users' needs require.

REFERENCES

1. CODASYL Systems Committee, *Feature Analysis of Generalized Data Base Management Systems,* Technical Report, ACM (Association for Computing Machinery), New York, London, and Amsterdam, May 1971.

2. Data Base Task Group (DBTG) of CODASYL Programming Languages Committee, *Report,* ACM (Association for Computing Machinery), New York, London, and Amsterdam, April 1971.

3. National Bureau of Standards Handbook 113, CODASYL *Data Description Language Journal of Development,* U.S. Department of Commerce, National Bureau of Standards, Washington, D.C., 1974.

4. *Data Base Management System Requirements,* A report of the Joint GUIDE-SHARE Data Base Requirements Group, Nov. 1971. Available from GUIDE or SHAKE, New York.

5. Detailed discussion of data-base security in the author's *Security, Accuracy and Privacy in Computer Systems,* Prentice-Hall, Inc., Englewood Cliffs, N.J., 1973.

6. A.L. Dean, Jr., "Data Privacy and Integrity Requirements for Online Data Management Systems," *Proc. 1971 ACM SIGFIDET Workshop on Data Description, Access and Control.*

7. R. W. Engles, *An Analysis of the April 1971 Data Base Task Group Report* Presented to the Codasyl Programming Language Committee, May 1971. A precise statement of why IBM voted negatively to the CODASYL proposal. Also published in a revised form in *Proc. 1971 ACM SIGFIDET Workshop on Data Description, Access and Control.*

8. R. Canning, "The Debate on Data Base Management," *EDP Analyzer,* March 1972.

9. C. J. Date and P. Hopewell, "File Definition and Logical Data Independence," *Proc. ACM SIGFIDET Workshop on Data Description, Access and Control* (Nov. 1971), pp. 117-138.

10. C. J. Date and P. Hopewell, "Storage Structure and Physical Data Independence," *Proc. 1971 ACM SIGFIDET Workshop on Data Description, Access and Control.*

11. ANSI/SPARC Data Base Management System Study Group *Interim Report,* American National Standards Institute, Washington, D.C., 1975.

Note: The reader should answer the questions on page 665.

Thru pg. 59

5 ENTITIES AND ATTRIBUTES

Items about which we store information are referred to as *entities*. An entity may be a tangible object, such as an employee, a part, or a place. It may be nontangible, such as an event, a job title, a customer account, a profit center, or an abstract concept. An entity has various properties which we may wish to record, such as color, monetary value, or name. Often in data processing we are concerned with a collection of similar entities, such as employees, and wish to record information about the same properties of each of them. We will refer to such a collection of similar entities as an *entity set.*

The above wording describes the real world. The words used are those in the leftmost column of Fig. 5.1. The second column of Fig. 5.1 contains words we will use in describing information about the real world, without yet specifying how the information is kept. The information could be on paper documents in filing cabinets or in any other form. We commonly maintain a record about each entity, and records about similar entities are grouped into entity record sets. The records refer to attributes of the entities and contain values for these attributes. The attributes recorded about a house might include its address, number of rooms, land acreage, assessed valuation, the date it was built, and so forth.

THREE REALMS
As Mealy [1] and Engles [2] have pointed out, there are three realms which we may be talking about when we discuss information, and we tend, sometimes confusingly, to jump from realm to realm without warning. The first realm is the real world in which there are entities and in which the

48

Reality	Information *about real world*	Logical Data (as seen by the application programmer)	Stored Data (as seen by the Data Administrator)	Physical Storage
All the things in the enterprise with which the system is concerned.	The organized knowledge in the enterprise with which the system is concerned.		Data base system (containing multiple data bases) Data Bank	Library
			Date base Data bank	
Entity set	Entity record set	File	Data set	Volume
			Area Extent	Cell (track, cylinder, physical subdivision)
			Block of stored records Data base record	Physical record
Entity	Entity record	Logical record	Stored record Segment Tuple	
		Data-aggregate Group item Element group Group Segment		
Property of an entity	Attribute	Data-item Elementary item Field Data element		
	Attribute value	Data-item value Data value Field value Data element value Data item		

Figure 5.1   The vocabulary used to describe data. **The words in black will be used throughout this book;** the words in red are commonly used alternatives. (See Figs. 1.1 to 1.4.)

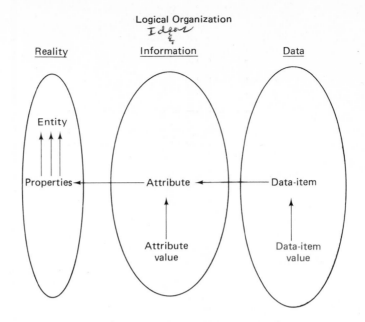

Figure 5.2   Three realms. The data-item value is what is actually stored; this must be associated with a particular attribute of a particular entity. (Redrawn from Engles [1].)

entities have certain properties. The second is the realm of ideas and information existing in the minds of men and programmers. Here we talk about attributes of entities and refer to the attributes symbolically, in English or programming. We assign values to the attributes. The third realm is that of data in which strings of characters or bits are used to encode items of information. Figure 5.2 illustrates these three realms.

The third realm can be further subdivided into the data perceived by the application programmer, the overall logical structure of data perceived by the data administrator, and the physical storage. Figure 5.1 summarizes the vocabulary relating to these different views of the data.

The collection of bits or characters representing a particular data-item value must be associated with the data item which has that value. The data item represents an attribute, and the attribute must be associated with the relevant entity. One attribute has a special significance in that it *identifies* the entity. A collection of bits or characters representing a single data-item value can exist independently of any information that is stored. It takes on meaning only when it is associated with the data items which assume that value. We could, for example, permanently store the data-item values BLUE, ORANGE, and PURPLE WITH GREEN STRIPES, and these values could be associated at a later time with specific data items.

Name of the attribute:	Employee-number	Name	Sex	Grade	Date	Department	Skill-code	Title	Salary
Form of representation:	N5	AV	B1	N2	N6	N3	N2	AV	N4
	53730	JONES BILL W	1	03	100335	044	73	ACCOUNTANT	2000
	28719	BLANAGAN JOE E	1	05	101019	172	43	PLUMBER	1800
	53550	LAWRENCE MARIGOLD	0	07	090932	044	02	CLERK	1100
	79632	ROCKEFELLER FRED	1	11	011132	090	11	CONSULTANT	5000
	15971	ROPLEY ED S	1	13	021242	172	43	PLUMBER	1700
	51883	SMITH TOM P W	1	03	091130	044	73	ACCOUNTANT	2000
	36453	RALNER WILLIAM C	1	08	110941	044	02	CLERK	1200
	41618	HORSERADISH FREDA	0	07	071235	172	07	ENGINEER	2500
	61903	HALL ALBERT JR	1	11	011030	172	21	ARCHITECT	3700
	72921	FAIR CAROLYN	0	03	020442	090	93	PROGRAMMER	2100

Value of the attribute:

Record or segment

Primary key

Secondary keys

Entity identifier

A set of values of one data-item type

Some attributes are themselves entity identifiers of another file.

Figure 5.3

51

FLAT
FILES

The most common way of associating a value with a data item and associating data items with the relevant attributes of the relevant entities is to store the data items together in a fixed sequence, as illustrated in Fig. 5.3.

Inside the box in Fig. 5.3 is a set of data items. The value of each data item is shown. Each row of data items relates to a particular entity. Each column contains a particular type of data item, relating to a particular type of attribute. At the top of the diagram, outside the box, the names of the attributes are written. The leftmost column in the box contains the data items which *identify* the entities. The attribute referred to as the entity identifier in this case is EMPLOYEE-NUMBER.

Below the name of the attribute in Fig. 5.3, the form of encoding used for representing the attribute value is shown. The attribute values must be stored using predetermined forms of encoding. Common types of representation are as follows:

Alphanumeric characters

Decimal, fixed-point numbers

Decimal, floating-point numbers

Binary, fixed-point numbers

Binary, floating-point numbers

Bit strings

The representation will indicate whether the data item is fixed-length or variable and if fixed, how large.

In Fig. 5.3 the representations have meanings such as the following:

N 6 = decimal, fixed-point, 6 digits

A V = alphanumeric, variable-length

B 1 = binary, 1 bit

The attribute names and value representations will not be recorded in the file, although they should be recorded elsewhere, for example, in a data dictionary which lists the names and types of all data items in the data base.

Note that some of the values of the attributes may themselves be the names or identifiers of entities in another file. DEPARTMENT in Fig. 5.3 is an attribute of the entity EMPLOYEE. Elsewhere there may be a DEPARTMENT file giving the attribute values of each department.

The group of data items forming a horizontal row in Fig. 5.3 may constitute an *entity record.* As we commented earlier, the stored record may differ from the record perceived by the application programmer; it may have more data items and perhaps in different sequence. The stored record may be substantially different from the *physical record*; the physical record may contain many stored records and may be compacted by techniques such as those discussed in Chapter 32.

The simple two-dimensional layout of data elements in Fig. 5.3 is sometimes referred to as a *flat* arrangement. Many files are *flat files,* and some classes of file organization are intended for flat files. As we will see in Chapter 6, programmers and systems analysts do not necessarily view their data as a collection of flat files but sometimes manipulate more complex arrangements of data elements.

Flat Files

TUPLES　　　　　　　　The grouping of data items shown in Fig. 5.3 represents a relationship between these data items. A related set of values is sometimes referred to as a *tuple* (pronounced to rhyme with "couple"). A tuple containing two values is called a *pair.* A tuple containing N values is called an *N-tuple.* The tuples shown in Fig. 5.3 are 9-tuples. A file consists of a set of tuples, each containing the same data-item types. It is thus a two-dimensional matrix of data items.

Data items are commonly handled in groups. Different software systems use different names for these groups. The term *record* is common. Some software designers use the term *segment*, and some use the term *tuple.* To avoid terminology problems we will sometimes refer to a record, segment, or tuple as a *group* of data items.

ENTITY　　　　　　　　It is necessary for the programmer or data admin-
IDENTIFIER　　　　　　istrator to be able to refer to a record or group
　　　　　　　　　　　　relating to a given entity, and it is necessary for the computer to be able to identify it and have a means of finding it in the storage unit. For this purpose one of the data items is usually designated an *entity identifier.* The entity identifier of an employee would be the EMPLOYEE-NUMBER (shown in Fig. 5.3). The entity identifier of an account record would be the ACCOUNT-NUMBER. The entity identifier must be unique; no other entity may have the same value of this particular data item.

Sometimes more than one data item is required in order to identify a record. For example, to identify a transaction made in an account the ACCOUNT-NUMBER and TRANSACTION-NUMBER may be necessary. To identify an airline flight record the FLIGHT-NUMBER and DATE are needed; FLIGHT-NUMBER alone is not enough because a flight with the same FLIGHT-NUMBER may take off every day.

PRIMARY   The entity identifier is referred to as the *key* of
KEY   the record or group. Strictly it is the *primary key*;
                     we will also refer to secondary keys, which do not
uniquely identify an entity. When more than one data item is used in the key
they will be shown joined by a + symbol: FLIGHT-NUMBER + DATE.
The combination is referred to as a *concatenated key.* Sometimes three,
four, or even five data items are needed to form the primary key. REVENUE
in the following group, for example, is identified by the combination of
MOVIE, THEATER, and DATE.

MOVIE	THEATER	DATE	REVENUE

The primary key is therefore MOVIE + THEATER + DATE.

The primary key is defined as that data item or combination of data
items used to *uniquely* identify one record or group. The primary key is of
great importance because it is used by the computer in locating the record,
by means of an index or other addressing technique.

VALUE   The attributes values need not necessarily be stored
REDUNDANCY   alongside the key values as in Fig. 5.3. There is
                     almost always substantial redundancy of attribute
values if they are stored as in Fig. 5.3. To avoid the redundancy the attribute
values could be stored separately with pointers to them from the keys.
Figure 5.4 illustrates the two ways of storing the attribute values. The value
redundancy in the top half of the figure is removed in the bottom half.

The decision of whether to store the attribute values separately or not
is really a decision concerning physical implementation. It need not—in fact
should not—be included in the *logical* view of the data.

SECONDARY   The computer may also use a key which does not
KEYS   identify a unique record or tuple but which
                     identifies all those which have certain property.
This is referred to as a *secondary key.* A value of the attribute COLOR may
be used as a secondary key, for example, BLUE. This key could be used to
identify those entities which are blue or those tuples for which the data-item
COLOR has the value BLUE. Sometimes a file has many secondary keys
which are used to search for records with given properties. Figure 5.3 shows
one primary key and two secondary keys.

Secondary keys were originally of little concern in the world of batch
processing. Records were usually referred to by their primary key. Often a

1. A conventional record contains value redundancy:

Key	Attribute
123	PRINCE CHARLES HOTEL, WARWICK
410	ST. GEORGE AND THE DRAGON, MANCHESTER
411	TAVERN-ON-THE-GREEN, LONDON
420	PRINCE CHARLES HOTEL, WARWICK
700	PRINCE CHARLES HOTEL, WARWICK
714	ST. GEORGE AND THE DRAGON, MANCHESTER
760	ST. GEORGE AND THE DRAGON, MANCHESTER
800	TAVERN-ON-THE-GREEN, LONDON
802	PRINCE CHARLES HOTEL, WARWICK
804	TAVERN-ON-THE-GREEN, LONDON

2. To avoid value redundancy the value may be stored separately and a pointer to them stored with the key:

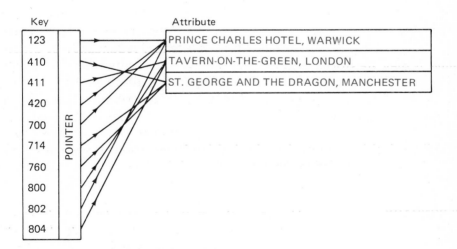

Figure 5.4   Two ways to store attribute values.

file of records would be sorted into a different sequence using one or more attributes as the basis of the sort. In interactive systems these same attributes may form a secondary key. There is not enough time to carry out sorts in interactive systems.

The path from the secondary key to the data items or groups to which it is related may be made in a variety of different ways which we discuss in Part II of this book. One of the ways is to use a *secondary index.* A secondary index uses the secondary key as input and provides a primary key as output so that a record can be identified.

An elementary form of secondary index is an *inverted list.* An inverted list contains all the values of a secondary key, and stores with each value the associated record identifiers. Figure 5.5 shows two inverted lists derived from the file shown in Fig. 5.3. There is one for each secondary key: GRADE and SKILL CODE. The lists do not contain the other attributes shown in Fig. 5.3. They would have to be used in conjunction with the file in Fig. 5.3 to provide information involving the other attributes.

Grade	Employee #
03	51883
	53730
	72921
05	28719
07	41618
	53550
08	36453
11	61903
	79632
13	15971

Skill code	Employee #
02	36453
	53550
07	41618
11	79632
21	61903
43	15971
	28719
73	51883
	53730
93	72921

Figure 5.5   Two inverted lists derived from the secondary key fields in Fig. 5.3.

In this illustration the secondary key points the identifier of the record of which it is a part. In other uses of secondary keys it points to a different record, which itself is associated to the record containing the key. In Fig. 5.6

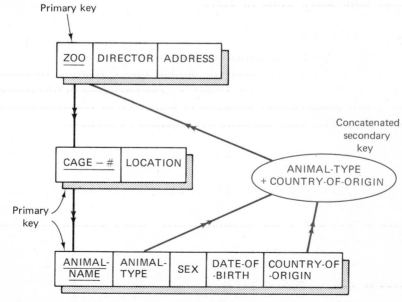

Figure 5.6

a ZOO record is associated with many CAGE records, and CAGE record is associated with one or more ANIMAL records. Two data items in the ANIMAL record are used to form a concatenated secondary key which points to the ZOO record.

If any inverted list were used for implementing the secondary key path, it would list all values of the combined pair of data items ANIMAL-TYPE + COUNTRY-OF-ORIGIN, and with each there would be a pointer to the zoo record.

There are many possible ways of implementing the facilities needed for secondary key searching. In a *logical* description of data we should avoid indicating what technique is used and merely state which are the secondary keys and what association path employs them—the information shown in Fig. 5.6

INVERTED QUERIES

There are two basic ways in which data can be used and organized. The first is the way shown in Fig. 5.3, in which each tuple contains the attribute values of a given entity. The second way is an inversion of the first and is designed so that the entity identifiers associated with a given attribute may be obtained. The first way of storing data is useful for answering the question: What are the properties of a given entity? The second is useful for answering: What entities have a given property?

A completely *inverted* file is one which stores the entity identifiers associated with every value of every attribute. A *partially inverted file* is more common and stores the entity identifiers associated with values of certain attributes but not all attributes. Many systems store a specified collection of secondary key paths such as that in Fig. 5.6.

Figure 5.7 shows six forms of simple query relating to entities, E; attributes, A; and their attribute values, V. The examples in this figure relate to a file giving details about salesmen in which 12 of the attributes are the monthly earnings for each salesman over the last 12 months.

ENTITY, E
ATTRIBUTE, A
VALUE, V

Type 1: $A(E)$ = ? asks: "What is the value of attribute A of entity E?" This is the most common form of inquiry: simply requesting the value of an attribute.

Type 2: $A(?)$ = V is an inverted file inquiry: "What entity, E, has a value of attribute A equal to V?"

Type 3: $?(E)$ = V is less common. It asks "Which attribute, or attributes, of entity E have value V?"

The types with two question marks require a listing as their answers.

Type 4: $?(E)$ = ? requests the values of all attributes of entity E.

Type 5: $A(?)$ = ? requests the value of attribute A for all entities.

Type 6: $?(?) = V$ is also less common. It requests all attributes of all entities having a value V.

	Form	Type of Query	Example
Type 1.	$A(E) = ?$	Common attribute inquiry	How much did Salesman No. 271 earn last month?
Type 2.	$A(?) \begin{smallmatrix} = \\ \neq \\ < \\ > \end{smallmatrix} V$	Which entities have the given value?	Which salesman earned more than $2000 last month?
Type 3.	$?(E) \begin{smallmatrix} = \\ \neq \\ < \\ > \end{smallmatrix} V$	List all attributes having a given set of values for a given entity	Which month's earnings for Salesman No. 271 have exceeded $2000?
Type 4.	$?(E) = ?$	Request for all information about a given entity	List all the information stored about Salesman No. 271
Type 5.	$A(?) = ?$	List the value of a given attribute for every entity	List last month's earnings for every salesman
Type 6.	$?(?) \begin{smallmatrix} = \\ \neq \\ < \\ > \end{smallmatrix} V$	List all entity attributes having a given set of values	For every salesman, list every month when his earnings exceeded $2000

Figure 5.7   Six types of simple query. E means Entity, A means Attribute, and V means Attribute Value. Complex queries consist of combinations of these.

MULTIPLE-KEY
RETRIEVAL
The first three query types can have complex forms. Complex forms are most commonly found with type 2, the inverted file query. The query may specify a group of relationships of the form

$$A \; (?) \; {\substack{= \\ \neq \\ \leq \\ >}} \; V$$

and ask what entities satisfy all of them or what entities satisfy one or more of them, for example, "Which salesmen earned more than $2000 last month AND opened three new accounts?" or "Which salesmen earned more than $2000 in May OR June OR July?" Some complex queries relate to multiple entitles.

Where there are type 2 queries relating to multiple attributes, multiple secondary keys may be defined. A variety of *physical* data organizations of the data is possible to facilitate retrieval or searches based on multiple keys. These are discussed starting in Chapter 26.

REFERENCES

1. A. H. Mealy, "Another Look at Data," in *Proc. AFIPS 1967 Fall Joint Computer Conference,* Vol. 31, AFIPS Press, Montvale, N.J., 1968.

2. R. W. Engles, "A Tutorial on Data Base Organization," *IBM Corporation Technical Report TR.00.2004*, IBM, Poughkeepsie, N.Y., 1970.

6 DATA MODELS: SCHEMAS AND SUBSCHEMAS

D.7

If the function of a data base were merely to store data, its organization would be simple. Most of the complexities arise from the fact that it must also show the associations between the various items of data that are stored.

The most elemental piece of data is the *data item* (field, data element). A data item cannot be subdivided into smaller data types and retain any meaning to the users of the data. It is the atom of data (and is composed of subatomic particles such as bits and bytes). In the diagrams that follow we will use an elipse to represent a data item, and write the name of the data item type in the elipse. Thus:

(SALARY)   *data item*

A data item by itself is not much use. It becomes useful only when it is associated with other data items. Thus:

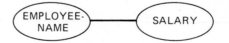

A data base consists of data items and the associations among them. There are a large number of different data-item types and so we need a map showing how they are associated. This map is sometimes called a *data model*.

There are a variety of ways to draw such a map. The map that we use does not show how the data are stored *physically*. It merely shows the *logical* associations between data items. The official map of the London tube system does not bear much relation to the physical layout of the tracks and stations. It does not show bends in the tracks as they are in reality and

60

does not show which are long and which are short links. Like a data-base map, it merely shows the associations between stations. It might be regarded as a *model* of the real world which does not resemble the real world too closely, but which is designed to be as useful a representation as possible to its users.

Before attempting to describe the *physical* layout of data, we must discuss the models of data which the users employ. These models are the *logical* representation of the data. We might think of the London tube as being a *logical* representation of the train system. The authorities could change the physical tracks, taking a track above the Thames instead of below, without changing the logical map.

Before attempting to describe the *physical* representations of relationships between data, we must discuss the way in which the *users* of the data base (terminal users or application programmers) see the relationships. *Logical* data relationships are represented in a variety of ways. Some of these are good ways. Others are confusing and liable to mislead. Others are limited in that they cannot represent some of the relationships that exist in reality. Some are inflexible in that they do not easily permit the view of the data to expand and change in the way a data base ought to develop. This chapter and the following ones discuss *logical* representations of data. Part II concerns itself with *physical* representations.

Given the ability of data management software to separate the physical organization of data from the users' view of data or "logical" organization, the users' view ought, in theory at least, to be formulated *without concern for physical representation*. The user's view of data should be in whatever form is most convenient for him and his associates (present and future), and the data management software should do the translation between this logical organization and whatever physical organization gives efficient performance.

In practice the computer industry has not yet achieved perfect data management software, and so compromises have occurred in the separation of logical and physical data descriptions, as we will see.

THE SCHEMA   It is necessary to describe the organization of the data in a formal manner. The logical and physical data-base descriptions are used by the data-base management software in exacting from the data base those data items which users require.

The overall logical data-base description is referred to as a *schema*.* It

---

*The words *schema* and *subschema* were first brought into wide usage by the CODASYL Data Base Task Group. They are, however, very useful words to describe data descriptions in non-CODASYL data-base systems. They are words of wide applicability.

is sometimes also referred to as an overall *model* of the data, a conceptual model, or a conceptual schema. These terms mean essentially the same thing.

A schema is a chart of the types of data that are used. It gives the names of the entities and attributes, and specifies the relations between them. It is a framework into which the *values* of the data items can be fitted. Like the display at an airport giving arrival and departure information, the schema will remain the same while the values fitted into it change from instant to instant. Figure 5.3 could be regarded as a schema if the attribute values inside the box were removed. When the schema framework is filled in with data-item values, as in Fig. 5.3, it is referred to as *an instance of the schema*.

We must distinguish between a *record type* and an *instance of the record.* When we talk about the "Personnel record," this is really a record type. There are no data values associated with it. Like a schema, it is a framework into which specific data values can be fitted. The "Personnel record for Bill Jones" may more correctly be called a record. There is still not necessarily a set of data values permanently associated with it—the data values may change from time to time. At one moment in time the "Personnel record for Bill Jones" may have the data values shown in the top line in the box in Fig. 5.3. We will refer to this as *an instance of the record*.

A similar distinction applies to data items, data aggregates, and all the other categories of data listed in Fig. 5.1. In the interest of brevity, this book, like other literature, sometimes uses terms such as SALARY data item when it really means SALARY data-item type, SUPPLIER record when it means SUPPLIER record type, and so forth.

The drawings of schemas and records might be thought of as having an extra dimension to them perpendicular to the page, having all the values of each data item.

**RELATIONSHIPS AND
CROSS-REFERENCES**

Schemas* are often drawn in the form of a diagram using blocks. Figure 6.1 shows a typical schema. (Like many of the drawings in this book it has been simplified in that the schema for a purchasing system in real life contains many more items than that in Fig. 6.1.)

The solid lines connecting blocks show associations between the blocks. The PURCHASE-ORDER record is connected to the LINE-ITEM records of which that purchase order is composed. The SUPPLIER record is connected

---

*The classical plural of "*schema*" is "*schemata*." The plural "*schemas*" is used in this book in the belief that most readers are happier with it and that a language should evolve toward more logical forms. After all, we no longer say "dogmata" for the plural of "dogma."

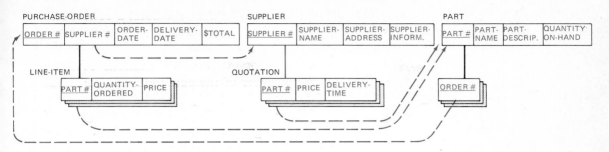

Figure 6.1. A schema. The solid lines between blocks represent relationships; the dashed lines represent cross-references. This is not a well drawn schema, nor it it particularly well designed. We will improve upon it later in the book.

to the QUOTATION records showing the parts that a supplier can provide and the price quotations he has given.

The dashed lines show *cross-references*. The PART-NAME or PART-DESCRIPTION are not in the LINE-ITEM record but in a separate PART record. Similarly, the SUPPLIER-NAME and SUPPLIER-ADDRESS are not in the PURCHASE-ORDER record but in separate SUPPLIER records. In this way it is possible to avoid duplicating SUPPLIER and PART-DESCRIPTION in every LINE-ITEM. Note that the diagram would still represent the information completely if the dashed lines were omitted.

The relationships (solid lines) in the schema can *convey information* which is not inherent in the data items shown in the schema by themselves. There is nothing in the PURCHASE-ORDER record of Fig. 6.1, for example, to say what parts or quantities of parts the order is for. The information is complete only when the LINE-ITEM records are linked to the appropriate PURCHASE-ORDER records. In some data bases the same two record types can be linked with various multiple relationships.

The cross-references, on the other hand, do not convey additional information. The PURCHASE-ORDER record does not contain the supplier's name and address. However, it does contain the supplier number, and using this the name and address can be found from the SUPPLIER file. If the dashed line from SUPPLIER-# to SUPPLIER record were removed, no information would be lost. The cross-reference lines indicate linkages in the file which may enable data to be located more quickly.

THE SUBSCHEMAS   The term *schema* is used to mean an overall chart of all the data-item types and record types stored in a data base. The term *subschema* refers to an application programmer's view of the data he uses. Many different subschemas can be derived from one schema.

The application programmer or terminal user does not need to know about the entire data-base schema. It is often highly complex and we do not want him involved in arguments about that complexity. Sometimes we wish to avoid revealing the entire schema for security reasons. The programmer or terminal user is concerned with his particular applications and the records which they require.

Figure 6.2 shows the subschemas of two application programs. The programmers have very different views of the data, but both are derived from the schema in Fig. 6.1. The PURCHASE-ORDER-MASTER record of programmer A now contains SUPPLIER-NAME and SUPPLIER-ADDRESS, and the PURCHASE-ORDER-DETAIL record contains PART-NAME and PRICE. The ON-ORDER-DETAIL record of programmer B contains data items from three separate records in the schema.

The data-base administrator must ensure that the subschemas they use are derivable from the schema. The data management software assembles the data described in the subschema from the data described in the schema automatically, and gives it to the application program.

THREE DATA
DESCRIPTIONS

Neither the schemas nor the subschemas reflect the way the data are stored physically. As shown in Part II, there are many different forms of physical organization possible for a given logical organization.

There are thus three separate descriptions of the data:

1. The *subschema*—a chart of a portion of the data which is oriented to the needs of one or more application programs—a programmer's file organization.

2. The *global logical data-base description, or schema*—a chart of the entire logical data base. This is the overall view of the data seen by the data-base administrator or those systems analysts who see the entire data base.

3. The *physical data-base description*—a chart of the physical layout of the data on the storage devices. The view seen by the systems programmers and the system designers who are concerned with performance and how data is positioned on the hardware, how it is indexed or located, and what compaction techniques are used.

The subschema is sometimes referred to as a *local view* or LVIEW. One subschema may serve several application programs, and may be defined separately from the application programs as in IBM's IMS system, where it resides in the PSB, program specification block. The term *submodel* is also used for subschema.

The American National Standards Association ANSI X3 SPARC study group on data-base systems published an interim report in 1975 [2] referring

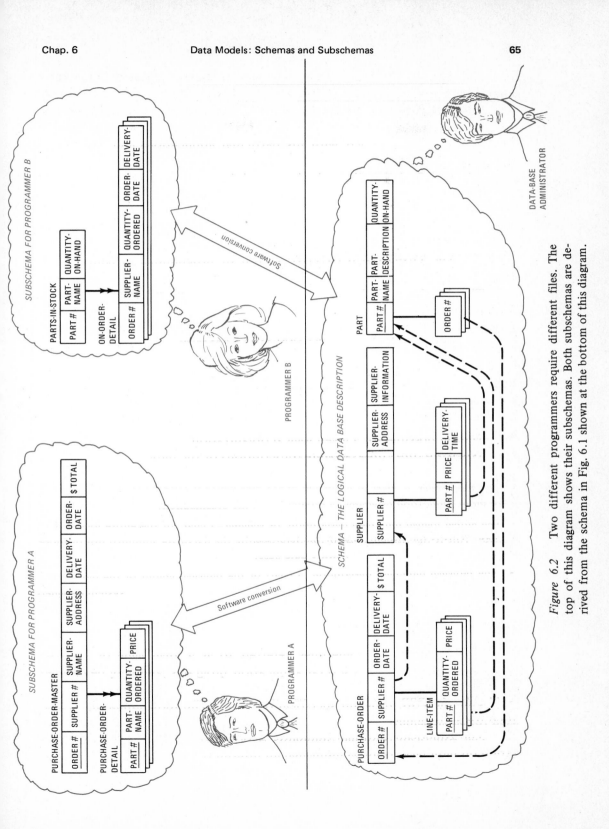

Figure 6.2   Two different programmers require different files. The top of this diagram shows their subschemas. Both subschemas are derived from the schema in Fig. 6.1 shown at the bottom of this diagram.

to the three levels of data description as an *external schema, conceptual schema*, and *internal schema*. These terms are now widely used.

Table 6.1 shows the various terms that are used.

Table 6.1   Alternative terms which describe the views of data. This book uses the words *subschema, schema* and *physical data*, as these are simple, clear terms.

	ANSI X3 SPARC [2]	CODASYL [1]	IBM's DL/I	Other terms
Programmer's view	External schema	Subschema	PSB (Program Specification Block)	Submodel; LVIEW (local view)
Overall logical view	Conceptual schema	Schema	Logical DBD (Data-Base Description)	Model; Conceptual model; Entity set;
Physical view	Internal schema	Physical data	Physical DBD (Data-Base Description)	Entity records

There is often a fourth view of the data—that of the terminal user. Increasingly in the future the terminal user will be a person not trained in the techniques of data processing. The view of the data that he obtains from the system should be as close as possible to the view that is inherent in his job. The way this view is presented to him will depend on the design of the man-computer dialogue that he uses.

Figure 6.3 summarizes these four separate views of the data. Note that the data-base management system does not employ multiple views of the data just for the sake of multiple views. It permits one view to be changed when necessary while the other views are *preserved*. Only in this way can changes be prevented from dragging the entire set of data views with them. In systems without this facility, the attempt to make seemingly trivial changes in data content or organization has proved appallingly expensive, especially on a complex data base.

ASSOCIATIONS BETWEEN DATA   Schemas and subschemas are maps showing the data-item types and associations between them. There are various ways of drawing the associations. The association between two data items can be of two types.

First, there can be a one-to-one mapping from data item *A* to data item *B*. This means that *at every instance in time, each value of A has one and only one value of B associated with it.* There is a one-to-one mapping between EMPLOYEE NAME and SALARY. For each value of EMPLOYEE

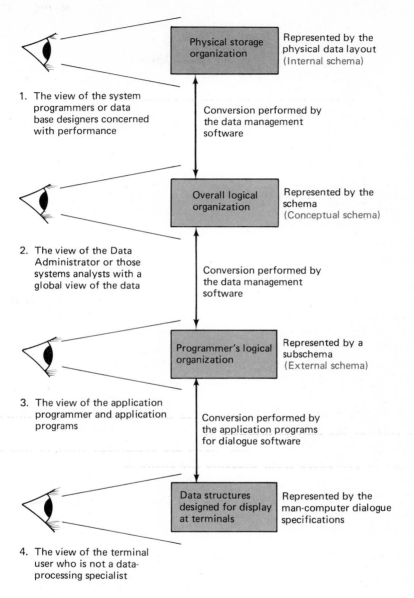

Figure 6.3 Four views of the data.

NAME there is only one value of SALARY. We will draw this as a line with a simple arrow on it connecting *A* to *B*. Thus:

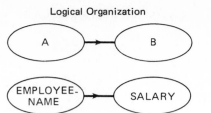

We will refer to this as a 1 association from *A* to *B*. It is said that *A* *identifies B*. If we know the value of *A*, then we can know the associated value of *B*. The single-arrow line is consistent with the notation of mathematical logic in which $A \longrightarrow B$ means *A* *identifies B* (i.e., if *A* has a value *a*, then *B* must have a value *b*).

Second, there can be a one-to-many mapping from data item *A* to data item *B*. This means that *one value of A has zero, one, or many values of B associated with it*. There is a one-to-many mapping between EMPLOYEE NAME and CHILD. For one value of EMPLOYEE NAME, there can be zero, one, or many values of CHILD. We will draw this as a line with a double arrow from *A* to *B* and refer to it as an M association from *A* to *B*. Thus:

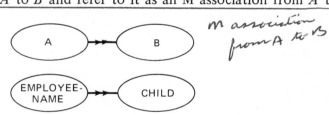

In this case *A* does not identify *B*.

A 1 association is sometimes referred to as a *simple mapping* and an M association as a *complex mapping*. Between any two data items there is a mapping in both directions. We thus have four possibilities for the forward and reverse association, 1:1, 1:M, M:1, and M:M. If the data-item types are MAN and WOMAN, and the relationship between them is called *marriage*, the four possibilities are:

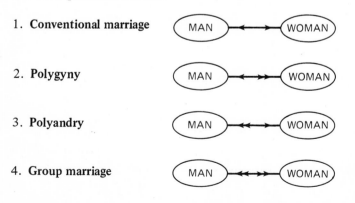

1. **Conventional marriage**

2. **Polygyny**

3. **Polyandry**

4. **Group marriage**

Another type of association which is sometimes distinguished is a *conditional mapping* from *A* to *B*. This means that *each value of A may have one or zero values of B associated with it*. Thus if conventional marriage is assumed, an EMPLOYEE NAME may or may not have an associated SPOUSE NAME. We refer to conditional mapping as a C association. We will draw it as an arrow with a letter C by the arrow, thus:

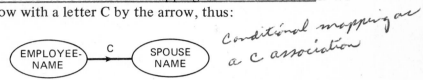

Note that it is a special case of the M association. Nevertheless, it is often treated as a 1 association in which there could be a null value of the associated data item. Figure 6.4 gives an illustration of 1, M, and C mapping between data items.

BUBBLE CHARTS

A schema or a subschema can be represented by drawing each of its data items and drawing the associations between them which are of interest.

Thus:

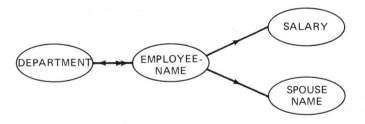

Such a drawing is sometimes referred to as a bubble chart.

Note that not all the possible associations have been drawn. There is no arrow from SPOUSE NAME to EMPLOYEE NAME because no user wants to ask such questions as: "What employees have a spouse named Fred?" If a user wanted to ask, "What employees have a salary over $25,000?" we might include a double arrow from SALARY to EMPLOYEE NAME.

In designing a data base we may start with a collection of user views of data—subschemas—and combine these a step at a time to form a schema from which all the user views can be derived. This design process is illustrated in Chapter 15.

A has a "1" association to B:

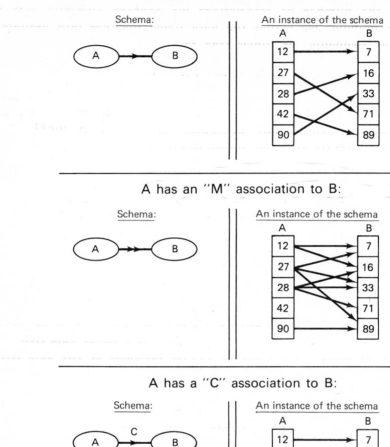

A has an "M" association to B:

A has a "C" association to B:

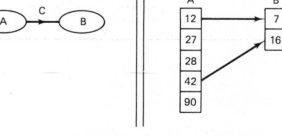

Figure 6.4   1, M, and C associations.

**GROUPINGS OF
DATA ITEMS**

A commercial data base often has hundreds or even thousands of types of data items. A bubble chart would rapidly get out of hand as a means of representing such a data base. Between N data-item types there are $N(N-1)$ possible associations. A large data base has more than 1 million *possible* associations.

To cut the number of associations we concern ourselves with to a reasonable number, we gather the data items together into groupings called records, segments, or tuples (the terminology differing from one manufacturer or software product to another). We then refer to associations between the groupings, as was done in Fig. 6.2. *pg 51*

A basic grouping of data items—let us use the term "record"—has a structure like that in Fig. 5.3. It has a *key* data item which *identifies* the other data items, which we call "attributes" of the key. A bubble chart of a simple record has the structure shown in Fig. 6.5.

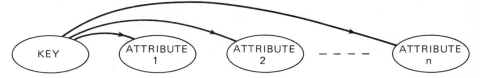

Figure 6.5. The bubble chart of a basic record structure such as that in Fig. 5.3.

As we discussed earlier the primary key of a record sometimes consists of more than one data item, for example, FLIGHT-NUMBER and DATE in an airline reservation system. Such a key is referred to as a *concatenated key*. A concatenated key behaves and is treated as a single data item. We will therefore normally draw them on bubble diagrams as one data item, occupying one bubble. The symbol + is used to connect the components of a concatenated key. Thus:

A portion of a concatenated key may itself be a key to another record. Thus:

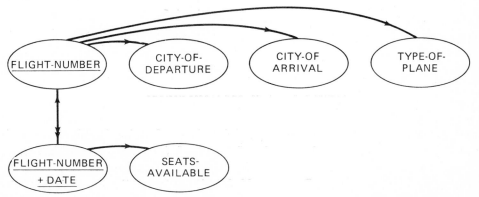

A basic grouping of data items is drawn as an elongated box in this book. The boxes may simply be labeled with the name of the record (or segment) or may have the names of the included data items as in Figure 6.2.

In some cases the records, or basic groupings of data items in a data base, have a structure more complex than that in Fig. 6.5. Later in the book we will question the wisdom of having a basic grouping of data items more complex than Fig. 6.5.

ASSOCIATIONS AMONG RECORDS   Just as data items have 1, M, or C associations among them, so also do the records or groupings with single, double, and occasionally C arrows linking the boxes which represent records (segments). For example:

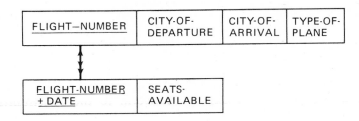

The key of each record should be indicated on the schema and sub-schema drawings. We will *underline* the key in all such diagrams.

The arrow linkage between the records is the same as the arrow linkage between the *keys* in the bubble charts. In bubble charts a primary key may be defined as *any data item which has one or more single-arrow links leaving it*. All data items which are not keys are *attributes*. An attribute in the bubble charts is *any data item which has no single-arrow links leaving it*.

Grouping the data items into records greatly reduces the number of associations that are shown in a schema. Even so, it is still not practical to show all the possible linkages between records in a large data base. Instead, the records (segments) tend to be grouped into structures which are small enough to be manageable. There are few linkages and sometimes no linkages between these structures. Chapters 8 and 9 discuss typical structures of groups of records.

The drawing of the schema will differ somewhat from one data-base management system to another, depending upon the constraints and facilities of the system. It is often useful to design the schemas independently of any software consideration. To do so can give a clearer understanding of the inherent structure of the data. This is discussed in Chapter 15. A software-independent schema may be drawn with the following rules:

1. Each record has the simple structure of Fig. 6.5, some records having a concatenated key.

2. The schema gives the name of the record and the name of the data items in it.

3. No two data items or records may have the same name.

4. The associations between records which will be used are drawn indicating whether they are 1, M, or possibly C associations.

5. The primary key of each record is marked.

6. Secondary key associations are marked on the schema.

7. The schema attempts to represent the inherent properties of the data, and hence is as stable as possible.

Sometimes the term "canonical structure" is used to refer to a schema which integrates multiple user views of data into a minimal data structure in the preceding form. In Chapter 15 we will show how such a schema can be designed.

Some specific software packages do not offer the full functional capability to implement the canonical structure and derive the requisite user views from it. In this case either the canonical structure or the user views of data have to be modified to conform to the constraints of the software.

HOW TO DRAW
A SCHEMA
A badly drawn schema can confuse rather than clarify. Figure 6.6 shows a type of schema diagram that is used in some current publications. It has several confusing aspects. First, the name of a portion of the schema is a block identical to the block containing the name of a data item. SALARY and SKILL, for example, are side by side in identical blocks, but SALARY is a data item and SKILL is not. SKILL is the name of the group of data items containing CODE and TITLE. Second, the diagram does not distinguish between attributes and entities. BIRTH-DATE is drawn from a group of blocks similar to CHILD. BIRTH-DATE is simply an attribute

Example of Poor Drawing

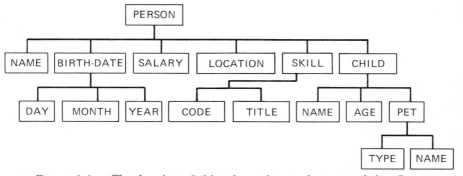

Figure 6.6   The drawing of this schema is not clear enough (see Box 6.1). In some documents, however, schemas are commonly drawn like this.

of PERSON, whereas CHILD is a separate entity. CHILD may be stored in a separate file to PERSON, but BIRTH-DATE may not be. Third, the diagram gives no indications which are one-to-one relationships and which are one-to-many. We know that a PERSON can have more than one CHILD and that a CHILD can have more than one PET, so these are one-to-many relationships. A PERSON has only one BIRTH-DATE, so this is a one-to-one relationship. We do not know whether a PERSON can have more than one SKILL. This is an important fact about the data base, but the diagram gives no clue.

Further, the diagram does not make clear which groups of data items are *record types* and which are *data-aggregate types*. The difference between a record type and a data-aggregate type is that there can be an arbitrary number of occurrences of the former but a limited number of occurrences of the latter. A data aggregate is usually addressed via the record of which it is a part, whereas a record must have its own means of addressing. Some major data-base management systems do not distinguish between data aggregates and records. For example, IBM's IMS and CICS data-base

Box 6.1 Rules for Drawing a Schema
(Compare Figs. 6.6 and 6.7)

1. The gathering of data items into groups (records, segments, tuples) should be made clear.

2. If *data aggregates* are used within a record, as in the CODASYL representation of data, they should be clearly distinguished.

3. The diagram should distinguish clearly between the names of data items, data aggregates, and records, segments, or tuples.

4. Duplicate names should not be used.

5. The primary keys (record identifiers) should be made clear.

6. Where secondary keys are an important part of the schema, these should be made clear.

7. The diagram should make it clear which one-to-one and which one-to-many associations are represented in the schema.

8. If the associations between records are given names (as with CODASYL *sets*, explained later), these should be on the diagram.

An abbreviated schema may be drawn which shows only records or segments and associations between them and does not show data items or keys.

management systems refer to an individually addressable group of data items ("fields") as a *segment*. Where records and data aggregates are distinguished as in the CODASYL-based products, the schema drawing should show which is which. A further fault in Fig. 6.6 is that some of the blocks have identical names.

We suggest that schema diagrams should be drawn with the rules listed in Box 6.1. Figure 6.7 shows one way of redrawing Fig. 6.6 to conform with these rules. Record (segment) names are written outside the boxes, data-item names inside. This drawing does not distinguish between repeating groups (data aggregates) within a record and the records themselves. If data-aggregate representation is used, this should be distinguished in some way, possibly by using dotted boxes. The primary keys are underlined. The secondary key is shown with a double-arrow link indicating what it points to.

Note that Fig. 6.7 does not show all the associations between records (segments). It does not show an upward arrow from PET to CHILD or from CHILD to PERSON, because this *path* is not intended to be used. The upward link from SKILL to PERSON would be a double-arrow link if it were shown. As we will see later, there are problems associated with links which have double arrows in both directions. The schema in Fig. 6.7 is problem-free as long as we do not represent or use a link from SKILL to PERSON.

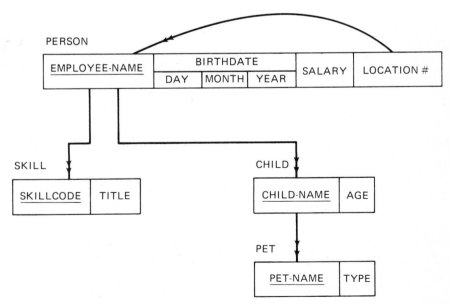

Figure 6.7 One way to redraw the schema of Fig. 6.6 to conform with the rule given. The double-arrow link from LOCATION # indicates that this data item is used as a secondary Key associated with EMPLOYEE-NAME.

MULTIPLE
ASSOCIATIONS
In certain cases there are more than one association between the same data types. For example, if we have MAN records and WOMAN records there could be associations called ENGAGED, MARRIED, and DIVORCED, as shown in Fig. 6.8.

In such a case the association itself needs to be labeled. Note that the label is a form of data. If we removed the label, valuable information would be lost. Different software uses different methods of handling multiple associations such as these in Fig. 6.8, and some cannot handle them.

Schema: An instance of the schema:

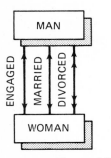
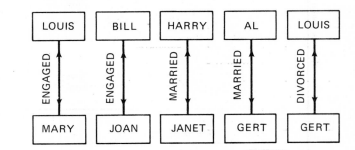

Figure 6.8   Three different associations between the same two data
types.

A MORE
COMPLEX
EXAMPLE

As records or segments become associated in more complex ways, clarity in drawing schemas becomes more important. Figure 6.9 shows five such groups with eight associations between them. Like Fig. 6.1, it is for a purchasing data base, but the mapping is more complex.

Purchase orders are sent out to suppliers. The ORDER and PUR-CHASE-ITEM records together represent the purchase order. Each purchase order can be for several items, each with its own PART-#. They are two one-to-many associations from SUPPLIER to PURCHASE-ITEM. One is for *outstanding* orders and the other for *late* orders. Similarly, there are two one-to-many links from SUPPLIER to QUOTATION, one for *actual* and one for *candidate* suppliers. These two links are bidirectional, as shown. A PART record is linked to QUOTATION records for each part and to PURCHASE-ITEM records. These links are also bidirectional. There is also a bidirectional link from SUPPLIER to ORDER.

This schema will be represented differently using different software methods of representing data. Figures 11.9, 12.11, and 13.5 are illustrations of its representation.

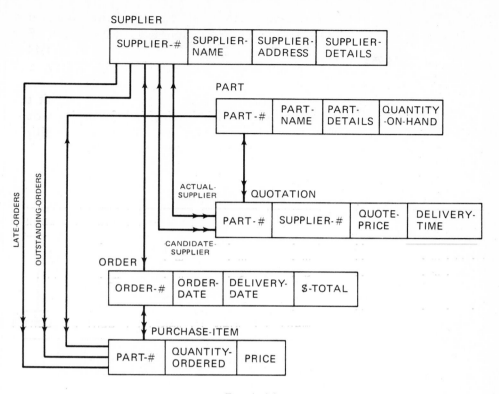

Figure 6.9

Some software cannot represent data structures of the complexity of that in Fig. 6.9. In commercial data bases it is likely that new data and new associations will be added, building up the need to handle more elaborate structures. Commercial data bases often complicate the requirement still further, with the need for secondary keys.

In Chapters 8 and 9 we will characterize the types of schema structures. In Chapter 15 we discuss a design technique for arriving at a schema that is likely to be as trouble-free as possible and meet the needs of multiple users who view the data differently.

BINARY REPRESENTATION   The most basic way of representing a schema or subschema is as a list of binary associations, a list of the links on a bubble chart. Figure 6.10 redraws the schema of Fig. 6.7 in the form of a bubble chart, and then represents it as a list of binary associations.

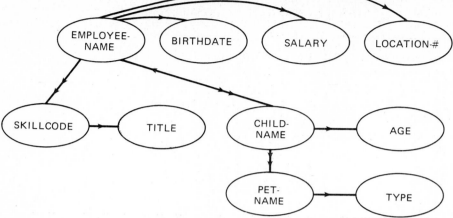

This bubble chart of the schema in Fig 6.7 can be represented as a list of binary associations as follows:

From	To	Association Type
EMPLOYEE-NAME	BIRTHDATE	1
EMPLOYEE-NAME	SALARY	1
EMPLOYEE-NAME	LOCATION - #	1
EMPLOYEE-NAME	SKILL-CODE	M
EMPLOYEE-NAME	CHILD-NAME	M
SKILL-CODE	TITLE	1
CHILD-NAME	EMPLOYEE-NAME	1
CHILD-NAME	AGE	1
CHILD-NAME	PET-NAME	M
PET-NAME	TYPE	1
LOCATION - #	EMPLOYEE-NAME	M

Figure 6.10   A basic way to represent a schema or subschema is as a list of binary associations equivalent to a bubble chart. The chart and list here are for the schema shown in Fig. 6.7. Such a list could be associated with a data dictionary and possibly statements describing the meaning of associations.

Some authorities have claimed that the best way to build an information system which can respond to spontaneous unanticipated requests for information is to use such a schema [3,4,5]. Binary associations represent the ultimate decomposition of a data base and as such give the ultimate flexibility, and data independence. Some tools for the design of conventional data-base schemas start from a description of all the binary associations like that in Fig. 6.10.

In some physical file structures (Chapters 28 and 36) there are advantages to storing binary pairs of items. We will return to discussion of binary structures in Chapter 28. At the time of writing, the only data-base management systems designed to handle binary structures are experimental in nature.

'75

SCHEMAS FOR THE FUTURE   Data-base planning often runs far ahead of current IMPLEMENTATION. It has been suggested that data-base management systems should be designed to contain future schemas which describe, with the aid of a data dictionary, data structures which are not yet in the system. The future data would then be mapped out, and applications could grow to fill out the data plan. A program requesting data not yet in the system would receive an error indication. This idea might be particularly valuable on systems in which the data is generated by means of high-level data-base languages which are linked to the schemas.

INTELLIGENT SCHEMAS   The schemas we use in today's data-base management systems are concerned with how we store the data. The schema in Fig. 6.10 and the earlier figures in this chapter enable us to represent data on physical recording media without excessive redundancy in the storage of data-items.

A fascinating development of the idea of a schema is that it could tell us not merely that data item A is associated with one or many values of data item B, but could also say something about the *meaning* of the association.

Computational linguistics uses graphs somewhat similar to the bubble chart of Fig. 6.10 except that the links are labeled not merely 1 or M, but with words which formally describe the conceptual relationship of the items linked. Data item A might be defined, for example, as a *goal*, a *subset*, a *time*, a *name*, an *agent*, or an *argument* of data item B. There are many possible definitions of the relationships between data items or groups of data items.

Such a schema may be employed along with a data dictionary to tell a user what is in a data base. More interestingly, it may be used to formally support dialogue and prompting facilities which enable a largely untrained user to employ the data base. It may impose constraints on the user of the data which preserve its integrity. It may eventually form a basis for automated programming techniques.

REFERENCES

1. CODASYL Systems Committee, Technical Report, ACM (Association for Computing Machinery), New York, London, and Amsterdam, May 1971.

2. ANSI X3 SPARC/DBMS, Study Group report, published by the American National Standards Institute, Washington, D.C., 1975.

3. J. A. Feldman and P. D. Rovner, "An ALGOL-Based Associative Language," *Comm. ACM 12*, No. 8, Aug. 1968, 439-449.

4. A. J. Symonds, "Use of Relational Programming to Manipulate a Structure in a Software Associative Memory," *ACM/SIAM/EEE Conference on Mathematical Computer Aids to Design*, Oct. 1969.

5. W. Ash and E. H. Sibley, "TRAMP: An Interpretive Associative Processor with Deductive Capabilities," *Proc. ACM 23rd Nat. Conf.* (1968), ACM, New York, London, and Amsterdam, 1968.

BOOK STRUCTURE

An introduction to data-base software:

7 DATA-BASE MANAGEMENT SYSTEMS

The schema and the subschemas are both used by the data-base management system, the primary function of which is to serve the application programs by executing their data operations.

The main events that occur when an application program reads a record by means of a data-base management system are shown in Fig. 7.1. A number of other events also occur, depending on the details of the software, and we will discuss these later. The 11 events below are the essential ones and are numbered in Fig. 7.1:

1. Application program A issues a call to the data-base management system to read a record. The program states the programmer's name for the data type and gives the value of the key of the segment or record in question.

2. The data-base management system obtains the subschema (or program data description) that is used by application program A and looks up the description of the data in question.

3. The data-base management system obtains the schema (or global logical data description) and determines which logical data type or types are needed.

4. The data-base management system examines the physical data-base description and determines which physical record or records to read.

5. The data-base management system issues a command to the computer operating system, instructing it to read the requisite record(s).

6. The operating system interacts with the physical storage where the data are kept.

7. The required data are transferred between the storage and the system buffers.

8. Comparing the subschema and schema, the data-base management system derives from the data the logical record needed by the application program. Any data

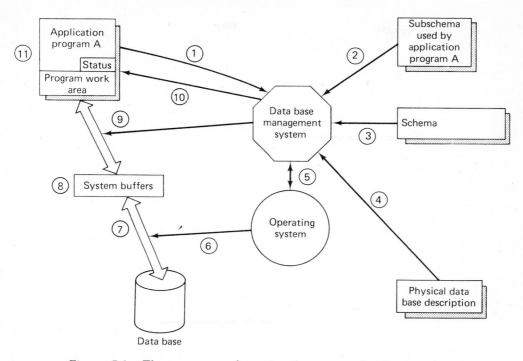

Figure 7.1   The sequence of events when an application program
needs a record, using a data-base management system.

transformations between the data as declared in the subschema and the data as
declared in the schema are made by the data-base management system.

9. The data-base management system transfers the data from the system buffers to the
   work area of application program **A**.

10. The data-base management system provides status information to the application
    program on the outcome of its call, including any error indications.

11. The application program can then operate with the data in its work area.

   If the application program *updates* a record, the sequence of events is ~~Update~~
similar. It will normally read it first, modify it in the program work area, and
then issue an instruction to the data-base management system to write back
the modified data. The data-base management system will make any
necessary conversions in the system buffers—the converse of the conversions
made when the data were read. The data-base management system then
issues the appropriate WRITE command to the operating system.

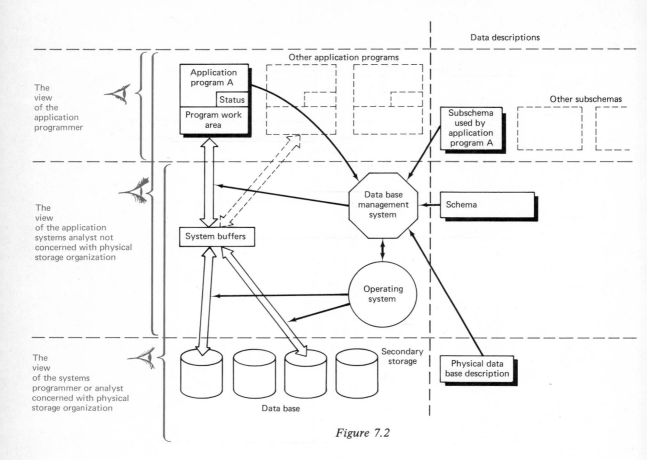

Figure 7.2

VIEWS OF   A data-base management system will usually be
THE SYSTEM   handling multiple data calls concurrently. It must
                 organize its system buffers so that different data
operations can be in process together. Multiple application programs may be
in operation, and these may use many different subschemas (Fig. 7.2).

The system should be organized so that the view of the application
programmer is restricted to the application program, its work area, and
subschema—the top third of Fig. 7.2. Anything in the bottom two-thirds of
Fig. 7.2 should be changeable without changing the application programs or
their subschemas. Many systems analysts may be familiar with the schema,
but their view should be restricted so that they do not concern themselves
with the physical structures. Anything in the bottom third of Fig. 7.2 should

be changeable without changing the schema or application-oriented analyst's view.

On the other hand, a systems programmer or other specialist may be concerned with the physical organization of data. His view may be restricted so that he is unaffected by those changes in the top third of Fig. 7.2—the application programs and subschemas—which do not require a new schema.

Figures 7.1 and 7.2 are generic diagrams which could apply to a variety of data-base management systems using widely different techniques for accomplishing the steps described. Some of the systems in use do not distinguish in a clear-cut fashion among the subschema, the schema, and the physical data-base descriptions. Such systems do not achieve full data independence but are often useful for simple or special-purpose data basis of limited growth potential.

Some systems handle data transmissions as well as data-base operations. These are referred to as *data-base data communications* (DBDC) systems. (See Fig. 7.3.)

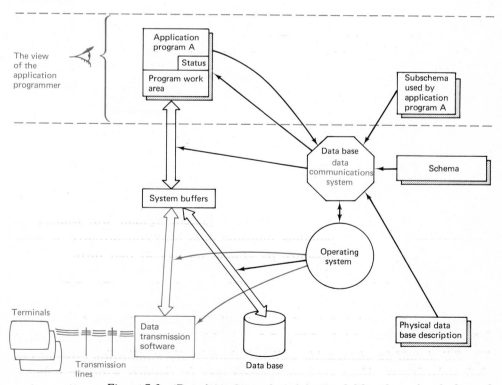

Figure 7.3   Data-base data-communication software.

ADDRESSING
AND SEARCHING
The events we have described are complicated by the fact that the required record usually cannot be located directly from the *key* that is provided by the application program. The record address must be obtained before the input/output routines of the operating system can read or write the record.

Many ways in which the record might be found are discussed in Part II. In one type of method a calculation is performed to convert the key into the requisite record address. This calculation may be performed by a programmed routine which can be called into use by the data-base management system.

In another type of method an index is used. One or more index records must be read or inspected to find the address of the record required by the application program. The program which reads the index records and finds the address may be a part of the operating system. It may be a programmed routine which can be called into use by the data-base management system. Or it may be a routine written by an application programmer which is called and used by the application programs.

Whatever the technique for addressing or locating a record, the program for accomplishing it can be one of three categories, as shown in Fig. 7.4:

1. It may be a routine called into use by application programs.
2. It may be a routine called into use by the data-base management system.
3. It may be a facility of the operating system commonly called an operating system access method.

If it is an application program, this loses some measure of data independence because when the data base is reorganized the program will have to be changed. It is better that the application programmer's view be unaffected by data-base reorganizations. If an operating system access method is relied upon exclusively, this limits the range of options possible to the data administrator in optimizing his physical data organization. In many cases the options offered by the access methods are quite adequate. They may be inadequate, however, where secondary keys are used, inverted lists or inverted files are needed, or some elaborate searching operation is required. In such cases it is desirable that the addressing or searching routines be available to the data-base management system.

In some cases the data-base management system may have to examine many records before it obtains the one which the application program requested. It will read such records into its system buffers (8 in Fig. 7.1).

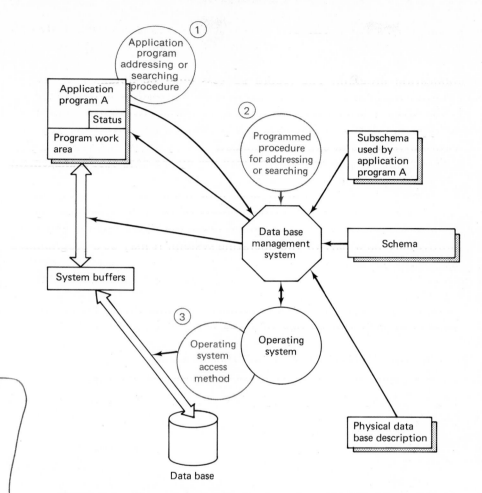

Figure 7.4   The programmed procedure for addressing a record or searching for a record can reside in one of three places (with different effects on data independence).

The application program will not see them. Control will be passed back to the application program only when the record it requested has been found and transferred to that application program's work area or alternatively when the data-base management system has determined that the request cannot be satisfactorily complied with. In the latter case the data-base management system will set an indicator in the STATUS area of that application program (10 in Fig. 7.1).

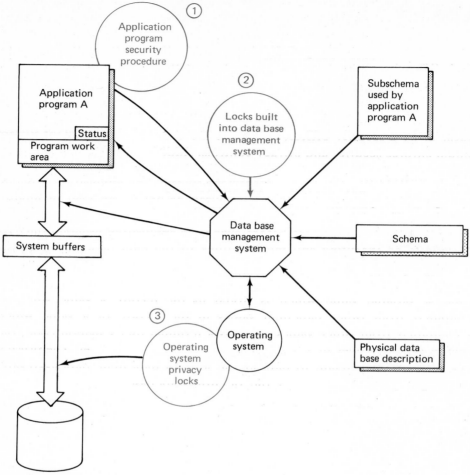

Figure 7.5 Privacy controls may be an application program procedure, a data-base management system procedure, a facility of the operating system, or a combination of these.

PRIVACY CONTROLS

In the multi-user environment of a data base, privacy controls are necessary to ensure that an unauthorized person or program does not read, modify, or damage somebody else's data. The privacy controls range from being very simple, such as passwords on files, to highly elaborate programmed procedures, such as controls on the use of a statistical data base [1].

Like addressing and searching techniques, privacy controls may be incorporated into an *application program routine*, into a *data-base management system routine*, or into privacy lock mechanisms of the *operating system* if it has them (Fig. 7.5). Any combination of these three may be used. Often it will be desirable to supplement the operating system security facilities with procedures incorporated into both the application programs and the data-base management system. In most installations it is highly desirable that security be controlled centrally either by the data administrator or by a security officer, and hence the data-base management system should enforce security and privacy controls. Additional application program may be employed to make the system auditable.

In CODASYL data-base management systems the application program must provide a *privacy key* that is required before it can read or modify any data. The data-base management system (or operating system) will check that the key is correct before giving the application program the data it requests or executing any modifications to the data base. To make the check, the key will be compared with a *privacy lock*—a data-item type which should be declared in the schema. The privacy lock may have a constant *alternatives* value, a variable value which is stored in the record, a value which is computed from other data-item values in the record, or a value which is computed from other values, such as a terminal user's sign-on code, the time of day, or values in a record relating to the terminal user. The privacy lock and key may relate to data at the level of data item, data aggregate, record, group of related records, file, or entire data base.

There are other (and better) ways to provide control of security and privacy, and these may or may not be provided by the data-base management system.

OTHER PROGRAMMED PROCESSES   Just as programmed processes for addressing, searching, or security can reside in the three places shown in Figs. 7.4 and 7.5, so other programmed processes which are used in data-base operations can reside in one of these three positions.

Four categories of program, all of which are likely to be routines accessible to the data-base management system, are

1. Programs for monitoring data-base activity or other forms of *systems instrumentation.*

2. Programs for compressing data so that they can be stored more economically (discussed in Chapter 32).

3. Programs for computing the values of data items in a subschema from other data items in a schema or for computing schema data items from different physical representations.

4. Programs for checking that data are valid (which may be application programs or data-base management programs).

LANGUAGES   To accomplish the objectives of a data-base management system, several languages are needed:

1. Programming Languages

First, there are the languages which the application programmer must use. He will write his programs in a conventional programming language, such as COBOL, FORTRAN, PL/I, or possibly assembler language.

2. Data Manipulation Language

The application program must give instructions to the data-base management system and have a means of interpreting the status messages with which it replies, saying whether the request has been satisfactorily accomplished (events 1 and 10 in Fig. 7.1). For these purposes the data-base management system will provide a set of macroinstructions or call statements for the application programmer. These may be regarded as an extension of the application programming language, as a separate sublanguage, or merely as a set of call statements provided by a particular data-base management system.

If they are an extension of a programming language, they could be independent of any particular data-base management system. If they are facilities of a data-base management system, they could be basically independent of any programming language. If a separate sublanguage forms the interface between the application programs and the data-base management system, it could, in principle, be independent of either.

Some data-base management systems provide an interface which is application-program-independent. The CODASYL Data Base Task Group has proposed an extension of COBOL, called a *data manipulation language* (DML), which it claims could be implemented for a wide variety of data-base management systems [2]. It is highly desirable that any such sublanguage permit full data independence, and the CODASYL DML has been criticized on the grounds that it does not do so [3]. We will summarize the features of the DML on p. 91.

2

3. Subschema Description Language

The application programmer must be able to describe the data that he uses (i.e., declare his subschema). Again, one of three types of facility may be employed for this:

1. A data declaration facility in the application programming language.
2. A facility provided by the data-base management system.
3. An independent data description language.

Probably the most commonly used and convenient approach will be a data declaration facility in the programming language, such as the data division of COBOL or the DECLARE statements of PL/I. It may be necessary to enhance such facilities so that data relationships can be better described.

4. Schema Description Language

The data administrator must be able to describe the global logical data description—the schema. He will sometimes have to describe types of relationships or data characteristics which the application programmer does not describe. For this purpose a *schema data description language* is needed.

Again this language could be a programming language extension, a facility of the data-base management system or an independent language. In practice different data-base management systems have widely differing facilities for describing schemas. There is a strong case for having an independent language for the schema descriptions because it is desirable that they not have to be rewritten when the data-base management software, or hardware, is changed. It is also desirable that they be accessible in various programming languages. The schema descriptions become the foundations of an organization's data processing, steadily increasing in complexity and scope. An organization which builds them so that they will have to be changed when data-base software or hardware changes, or when different programming languages are used, is like a man who builds his house upon the sand.

We will discuss schema description languages in later chapters.

5. Physical Data Description Language

The global logical data description must be mapped into physical storage. Some form of *physical data description language* may be used to describe the mapping. The CODASYL Data Base Task Group refers to a language for this purpose as a *device/media control language*. Such a language would specify the assignment of data to devices and media space; would specify how buffering, paging, and overflow is controlled; and would specify addressing and searching techniques such as indexing and chaining. Today different data-base management systems use widely different techniques for specifying the mapping of logical data to physical storage.

At some future time systems may become clever enough to do the logical-to-physical mapping entirely automatically. However, the state of the art is far from that capability at present.

THE DATA MANIPULATION LANGUAGE   The interface between the application program and the data-base management system, referred to as the *data manipulation language*, is embedded in a *host language* such as COBOL. It is desirable that it should have a syntax compatible with the host language because the application program has host language and data manipulation language statements intimately mixed. In fact, it should appear to the programmer as though he is using a single language. There should be no *enter* or *exit* requirements from one language to the other.

When the data manipulation language requests a given record, this record is delivered to the work area of the application program, from which the application program can manipulate it. Similarly, when a record is to be inserted into the data base, the application program places it in a work area and gives the appropriate command in the data manipulation language.

Typical commands in a data manipulation language are the following (which are taken from the CODASYL language):

1. OPEN: A file or set of records is opened, i.e., made available for an application program to use.

2. CLOSE: A file or set of records is closed, i.e., made unavailable to that application program.

3. FIND: The data-base management system locates a specified occurrence of a named record type. It may have to search through several records to find it. The record becomes the *current* record of the application program in question.

4. GET: The contents of specified data items of a specified record occurrence are transferred to the program work area.

5. MODIFY: The values of specified data items of a specified record occurrence are replaced with values in the program work area.

6. INSERT: The record in the program work area is inserted into one or more named groups of records (*sets* of records in the DBTG language—a set will be described later).

Condition Command	Close	Delete	Find	Free	Get	Keep	Insert	Modify	Open	Order	Remove	Store
Area not open	01	01	01	—	—	—	—	—	—	01	—	01
Database-key inconsistent with area-name	—	—	02	—	—	—	—	02	—	—	—	02
Data-items invalid or inconsistent	—	—	04	—	—	—	—	04	—	—	—	—
Violation of DUPLICATES NOT ALLOWED clause	—	—	—	—	—	—	05	05	—	—	—	05
Current or set, area, or record-name not known	—	—	06	—	—	—	06	—	—	06	—	—
End of set or area	—	—	07	—	—	—	—	—	—	—	—	—
Referenced record or set-name not in sub-schema	—	08	—	—	—	—	—	—	—	—	—	—
Incorrect usage mode for area	—	09	—	—	—	—	09	09	—	09	09	09
Privacy breach attempted	—	10	10	—	10	—	10	10	10	10	10	10
Media space not available	—	—	—	—	—	—	—	—	—	—	—	11
Database-key not available	—	—	—	—	—	—	—	—	—	—	—	12
No current record of run-unit	—	13	—	13	13	13	13	13	—	—	13	—
Object record is mandatory in named set	—	—	—	—	—	—	—	—	—	—	15	—
Record already a member of named set	—	—	—	—	—	—	16	—	—	—	—	—
Deleted record involved	—	—	17	—	—	—	—	—	—	—	—	—
Implicitly referenced area not available	—	18	18	—	—	—	18	18	—	—	18	18
Conversion of value of data-item not possible	—	—	—	—	19	—	—	19	—	—	—	19
Current record of run-unit not of record-name	—	20	—	—	20	—	20	20	—	—	20	—
Affected area not open	—	21	—	—	—	—	21	21	—	—	21	21
Record not current member of named or implied set	—	—	22	—	—	—	—	22	—	—	22	—
Illegal area-name	—	—	23	—	—	—	—	23	—	—	—	23
No set occurrence satisfies argument values	—	—	—	—	—	—	—	25	—	—	—	25
Area already open	—	—	—	—	—	—	—	—	28	—	—	—
Violation of optional deadlock protection rule	—	—	—	—	—	—	—	—	29	—	—	—
Unqualified DELETE attempted on non-empty set	—	30	—	—	—	—	—	—	—	—	—	—
Removed record involved	—	—	50	—	—	—	—	50	—	—	—	—
Deleted record involved	—	—	51	—	—	—	—	51	—	—	—	—
Value of string data-item truncated in program work area	—	—	—	—	54	—	—	—	—	—	—	—

Figure 7.6   Typical error-condition codes which the data-base management system returns to the application program run-unit (event 10 in Fig. 7.1). (Reproduced from Reference 2.)

7. REMOVE: A specified record occurrence is canceled from the membership of one or more named groups of records (*sets* again in the DBTG language).

8. STORE: A new record occurrence is stored in the data base, and all the necessary relationship linkages and addressing facilities are created.

9. DELETE: A specified record occurrence is removed from the data base, and relationships involving it are deleted.

10. KEEP: When an application program has accessed a record, it may use a KEEP statement to notify the data-base management system that it will access it again. The system may then keep the access mechanism in position for that record.

11. FREE: A FREE statement cancels the effect of a KEEP.

12. ORDER: All or specified member records in a named group of records (a file or *set*) are logically reordered in ascending or descending sequence of a specified key.

ERROR
CONDITIONS
A variety of error conditions can occur when a data-base management system attempts to execute the commands which an application program gives it. It will return an error code to the application program to inform it of the status. Figure 7.6 shows some typical error codes for the commands described above. (*Run-unit* in Fig. 7.6 is the CODASYL word for a single application program execution or *task*. *Area* is a named grouping of records which could be independent of the schema.)

REFERENCES

1. James Martin, *Security*, *Accuracy and Privacy in Computer Systems*, Prentice-Hall, Inc., Englewood Cliffs, N.J., 1974.

2. The proposed CODASYL specifications for a Data Manipulation Language: Proposal DBLTG-73001,00, available from Technical Services Branch, Dept. of Supply and Service, 88 Metcalfe Street, Ottawa, Ontario, Canada KIA055.

3. R. W. Engles, "An Analysis of the April 1971 Date Base Task Group Report," in *Proceedings of the ACM SIGFIDET Workshop on Data Description, Access and Control*. ACM (Association for Computing Machinery), New York, London, and Amsterdam, 1972.

4. *Information Management System Virtual Storage (IMS/VS) General Information Manual GH20-1260*, IBM, White Plains, N.Y., 1974.

5. *Data Base Management System Requirements*, a report of the Joint GUIDE-SHARE Data Base Requirements Group, Nov. 1971, available from GUIDE or SHARE, New York.

6. *EDP Analyzer*, March 1972, *The Debate on Data Base Management* (the whole issue), Canning Publications, Inc., California.

7. *EDP Analyzer*, Feb. 1974, *The Current Status of Data Management* (the whole issue), Canning Publications, Inc., California.

8. *EDP Analyzer*, March 1974, *Problem Areas in Data Management* (the whole issue), Canning Publications, Inc., California.

BOOK STRUCTURE

There are three types of approaches to data base structures known as:

i. The hierarchical approach (tree structures)

Chapter 8   Tree Structures
Chapter 24   Physical Representation of Tree
              Structures

ii. The network approach (plex structures)

Chapter 9   Plex Structures
Chapter 25   Physical Representation of Plex
              Structures

and iii. The relational approach (normalized structures).

Chapter 13   Relational Data Bases
Chapter 14   Third Normal Form

8 TREE STRUCTURES

In this chapter and the next we will discuss the types of structures that are found in data-base relationships. We will then illustrate how these structures can be described in formal languages.

We described the data layout in Fig. 5.3 as a *flat* file. Each record has a similar set of fields, and hence the file can be represented by a two-dimensional matrix. Many logical file structures are used which are not "flat." They are described with words such as *hierarchical files, CODASYL sets, tree structures,* and *plex structures.* All these types of structure can be classed as either *trees* or *networks.* We will discuss trees in this chapter and networks in the following chapter. In Chapters 24 and 25 we will discuss the *physical* representations of trees and networks.

It may be noted before we begin discussing trees and networks that these more complicated file structures can be broken down into groups of flat files with *redundant* data items. As we will see later, trees and networks may not be the best methods of logical representation of a data base. However, they are the methods in most common use today.

Some authorities categorize the approaches to data-base representation as *hierarchical* (meaning tree-structured), *network* (meaning plex-structured and often having the specific meaning of having the CODASYL network structure discussed in Chapter 11), and *relational* (with flat files which can be joined to form associations). We discuss these approaches in this and the following chapters.

TREES

Figure 8.1 shows a tree. A tree is composed of a hierarchy of elements, called *nodes*. The uppermost level of the hierarchy has only one node, called the *root*. With the

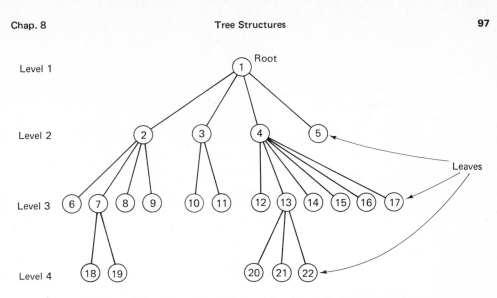

Figure 8.1   A tree: no element has more than one parent.

exception of the root, every node has one node related to it at a higher level, and this is called its *parent*. No element can have more than one parent. Each element can have one or more elements related to it at a lower level. These are called *children*. (The terms *father* and *son* nodes were used in the days before women's liberation.) Elements at the end of the branches (i.e., with no children) are called leaves. (The computer industry likes to mix its metaphors.)

In Fig. 8.1, element 1 is the *root*. Elements 5, 6, 8 through 12, and 14 through 22 are *leaves*. Trees are normally drawn upside down, with the root at the top and the leaves at the bottom.

Trees, such as that in Fig. 8.1, are used in both logical and physical data descriptions. In logical data descriptions they are used to describe relations between segment types or record types. In physical data organization they are used to describe sets of pointers and relations between entries in indices.

A tree can be defined as a hierarchy of nodes with binodal relationships such that

1. The highest level in the hierarchy has one node called a *root*.
2. All nodes except the root are related to one and only one node on a higher level than themselves.

Knuth [1] defines a tree with a recursive definition as follows: "a finite set *T* of one or more nodes such that

1. There is one specially designated node called the *root* of the tree.
2. The remaining nodes are partitioned into $m \geqslant 0$ disjoint (i.e., not connected) sets $T_1, \ldots, T_m$, and each of these sets in turn is a tree. The trees $T_1, \ldots, T_m$ are called the *subtrees* of the root.

Knuth claims that defining trees in terms of trees seems most appropriate since recursion is an innate characteristic of tree structures. Any node can grow a subtree, and its nodes in turn can sprout, just as buds in nature grow subtrees with buds of their own, etc.

Figure 8.2 shows the common terms that are used to describe trees.

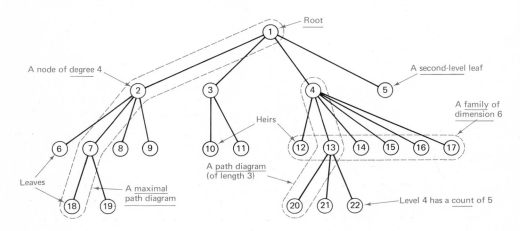

This tree diagram has
height 4   (number of levels)
moment 22 (number of nodes)
weight 16 (number of leaves)
radix 1   (number of roots)

Figure 8.2   Terms used for describing trees.

**BALANCED AND
BINARY TREES**

The term *balanced tree* is sometimes used. In a balanced tree each node can have the same number of branches, and the branching capacity of the tree is filled starting at the top and working down, progressing from left to right in each row. Figure 8.3 shows balanced and unbalanced trees. It is somewhat easier to implement a physical data organization for a tree with a fixed number of branches than for one with a variable number. Most logical data organizations, however, do not fit naturally into a balanced tree structure

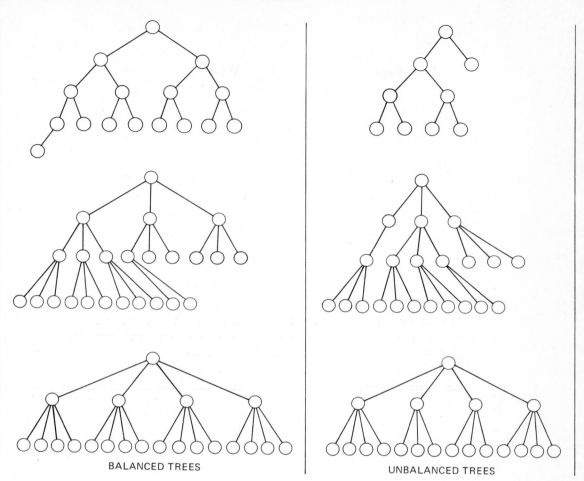

BALANCED TREES   UNBALANCED TREES

Figure 8.3

but require a variable number of branches per node. Indices and search algorithms can fit naturally into balanced tree structures, as will be discussed in Chapter 30.

A special category of balanced tree structure is one which permits up to two branches per node. This is called a *binary tree*. Figure 8.4 shows an unbalanced binary tree. Any tree relationship can be represented as a binary tree in the manner shown in Fig. 8.5. A few logical data organizations fit naturally into binary tree structures. A dog's pedigree, for example, could be represented as a binary tree. Binary trees, like other balanced trees, are mainly of interest in the *physical* representation of data, not the logical representation.

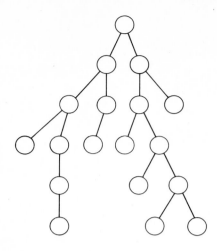

Figure 8.4   A binary tree (unbalanced).

SIMPLE AND   Figures 8.6 and 8.9 show examples of tree struc-
COMPLEX MAPPING   tures, the nodes being data aggregates, segments, or
records.

Figure 8.6 shows a family tree. It can only be described as a tree structure because each item is shown as having only one parent. If two parents
were shown, it would be a more complex structure.

A tree structure implies that there is simple mapping from child to
parent (i.e., a child has one parent) and that the inverse map is usually
complex (one-to-many), as in Fig. 8.7. Figure 8.7 shows a schema and an
instance of that schema for a simple two-level tree structure.

Occasionally there is a simple mapping in both directions as in Fig. 8.8,
where the tree structure relates to records concerning the same entity, which
are stored separately.

HIERARCHICAL   The term *hierarchical file* refers to a file with a
FILES   tree-structure relationship between the records.
Figure 8.7 shows a master-detail file—a common
type of hierarchical file with two record types. Figure 8.11 shows a four-level
hierarchical file.

Data tend to break down into hierarchical categories. One category of
data is a subset of another. A wine merchant stocks wine from many regions,
such as Bordeau and Burgundy. For each region there are many wine
types—St. Emilion, Pomerol, Medoc. For each wine type there are many
years, some better than others. For wine type and year there are several bottle

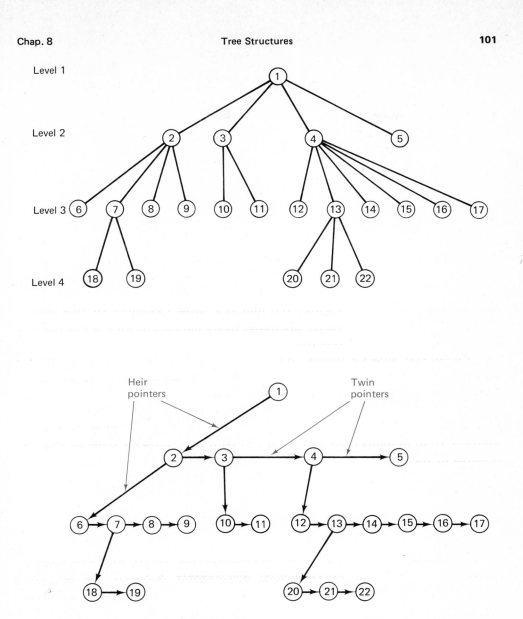

Figure 8.5   Any tree relationship can be represented by a binary tree in which each element can have an heir and a twin pointer.

numbers—the 1971 St. Emilion shipped by Austin Nichols, by Dreyfus Ashby, and so on. The organization of those wine data may be related to the hierarchical categories:

Queries about the wine may relate to the hierarchical structure: "What were good years for Nuits St. Georges?" "What priced bottles do you have for 1970 Chateau Palmer?"

Some data-base software is designed to handle only hierarchical data structures. As we shall see later, hierarchical structures are relatively easy to represent and maintain. This is satisfactory for some applications, but many data are not tree-structured in nature. In many data structures one record needs to have more than one present. In Chapter 15 we discuss how different user views of data should be merged into one data-base schema. The result is usually more complex than a tree structure. Hence software designed to handle only disjoint tree structures is limited in its usefulness and will often severely restrict the growth and evolution of a data base. If tree structures are used, there is a need for records (segments) to become members of more than one tree.

CODASYL SETS

The CODASYL Data Base Task Group makes much use of a relationship called a *set*. A set is a two-level tree of records. A file of sets all of the same type is a two-level hierarchical file. The parent record type is referred to as the *owner* record type and the children as *member* record types. Figures 8.7 and 8.9 both show sets. Each set type is given a name. A multilevel hierarchical file can be regarded as being composed of multiple sets. Figure 8.11 can be regarded as being composed of three, four, or five sets. A record can be a member of multiple sets. We will discuss CODASYL sets in detail in Chapter 11.

HOMOGENEOUS STRUCTURES

The family tree of Fig. 8.6 is fundamentally different in structure from the trees in the subsequent figures. Each node of the family tree could

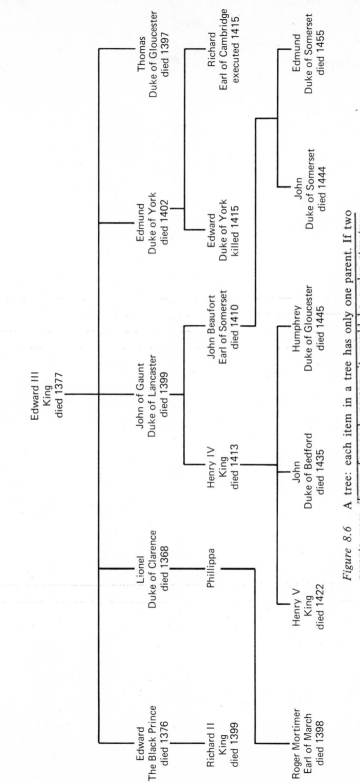

Figure 8.6 A tree: each item in a tree has only one parent. If two parents were shown for each person, it would be a plex structure. Note: this figure shows a homogeneous tree structure of variable depth, whereas the following figures show heterogeneous structures of fixed depth. Different techniques of physical representation are applicable to homogeneous structures.

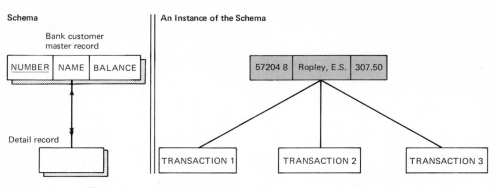

Figure 8.7   A hierarchical file with only two record-types.

be of the same record type. In the other diagrams each node is a different record type (or segment type). Figure 8.6 thus shows a homogeneous tree of variable depth, whereas the subsequent figures show heterogeneous trees of fixed depth. Most data-base software is designed to handle heterogeneous trees of stated depth. A different physical representation could be used to represent a homogeneous tree.

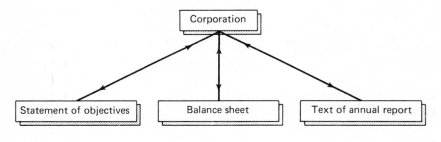

Figure 8.8

If we employ the conventional type of schema used throughout this book to represent Fig. 8.6, it would be that in Fig. 8.10. Figure 8.6 is an instance of the schema in Fig. 8.10.

The distinction between homogeneous and heterogeneous structures is important in Chapter 9 as well, where plex structures are discussed. An important example of a homogeneous plex structure is a bill-of-materials data base used in a manufacturing operation, showing the components and subcomponents in each product, as illustrated in Fig. 9.13.

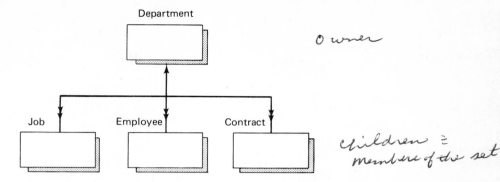

Owner

children =
members of the set

Figure 8.9   DBTG set (CODASYL definition) is a two-level tree of records. The parent record is referred to as the owner; the children records are referred to as members of the set.

Figure 8.10   A tree-structured loop. Figure 8.6 is an instance of this schema.

PATH DEPENDENCY   The lower records (segments) in a tree may be incomplete in meaning without their parents. In Fig. 8.11, for example, the JOB HISTORY record is of no value by itself. To have meaning it must be associated with its parent, EMPLOYEE record. The data item TITLE is not *identified* by the associated key JOB DATE alone. It is identified by the combination of keys EMPLOYEE # and JOB DATE. Consequently, it is said that there is a *path dependency* from EMPLOYEE to JOB HISTORY in this tree.

On the other hand, the EMPLOYEE record in the tree is *not* dependent on its parent. Its key EMPLOYEE # identifies it completely.

SALARY HISTORY is not dependent on its parent but upon its grandparent EMPLOYEE. A combination of the keys EMPLOYEE # and SALARY-DATE are needed to identify the associated data item SALARY.

We cannot tell by looking at Fig. 8.11 whether the JOB record is self-sufficient. We do not have enough information about the nature of JOB #. Let us suppose that JOB # is not a corporate-wide identifier but that each

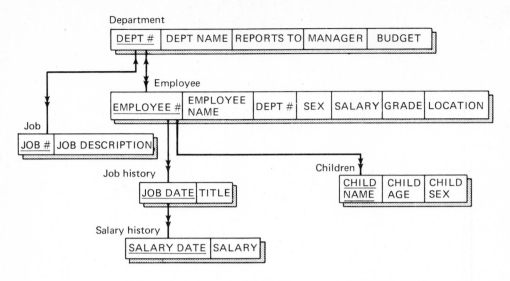

Figure 8.11   A schema for a multilevel hierarchical file.

department can have its own set of job numbers. The JOB record is then dependent upon the DEPARTMENT record. The combined keys DEPT # and JOB # are needed to identify JOB DESCRIPTION.

Figure 8.12 shows the path dependencies in this schema. Note that the same structure could be drawn with no path dependencies by introducing appropriate concatenated keys. This is done in Fig. 8.13, where each record is self-sufficient and not dependent on its parent. Other schema can be adjusted in a similar fashion to make their records non-path-dependent, including the more complex schemas discussed in Chapter 9.

REFERENCE

1. Knuth, Donald E., *The Art of Computer Programming; Volume 1, Fundamental Algorithms.* Addison-Wesley, Reading, Mass., 1968.

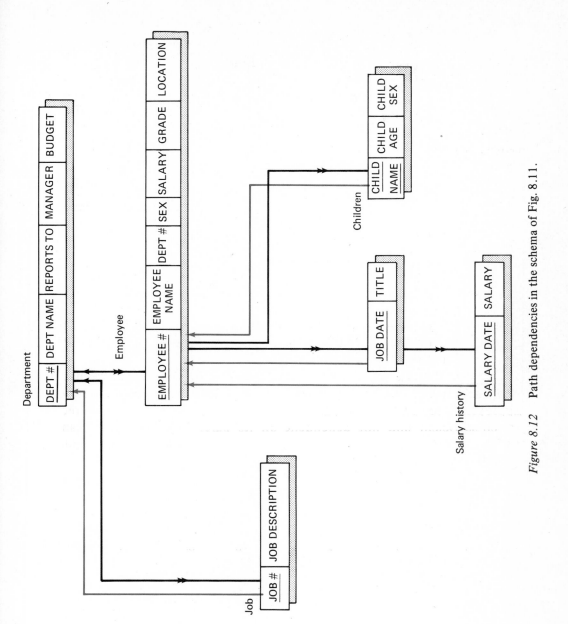

Figure 8.12 Path dependencies in the schema of Fig. 8.11.

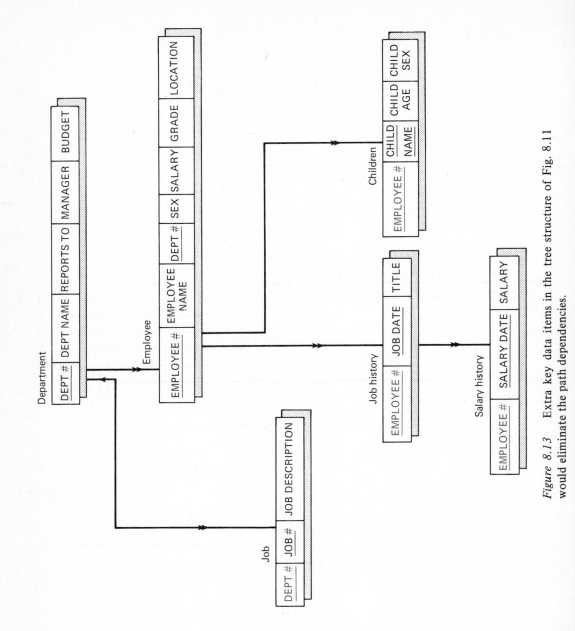

Figure 8.13 Extra key data items in the tree structure of Fig. 8.11 would eliminate the path dependencies.

BOOK STRUCTURE

Chapters 8, 9, and 13 discuss forms of data-base schema.

Chapter 8   Tree Structures
Chapter 9   Plex Structures
Chapter 13   Relational Data Bases

Chapter 25 shows the physical representations of the plex structures discussed in Chapter 9:

Chapter 9   Plex Structures
Chapter 25   Physical Representation of Plex
             Structures

9 PLEX STRUCTURES

If a child in a data relationship has more than one parent, the relationship cannot be described as a tree or hierarchical structure. Instead it is described as a *network* or *plex structure*. As the term *network* is over-worked in the data-communications world, we will use *plex structure*. The term *network* structure is also used sometimes to imply a CODASYL data base structure described in Chapter 11.

Any item in a plex structure can be linked to any other item. Figure 9.1 shows some examples of plex structures. As with a tree structure, a plex structure can be described in terms of children and parents and drawn in such a way that the children are lower than the parents. In a plex structure, a child can have more than one parent. In the first example in Fig. 9.1 each child has two parents. In the second example no indication

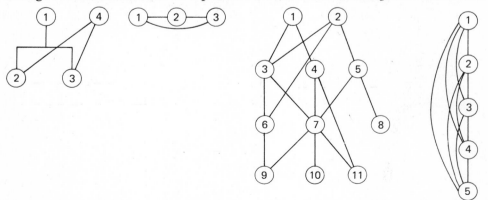

Figure 9.1 Examples of plex structures (networks). One or more nodes have multiple parents.

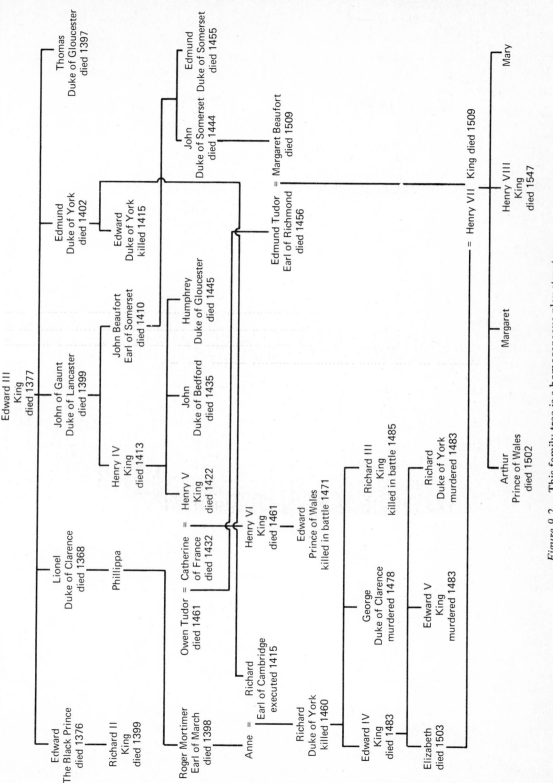

Figure 9.2   This family tree is a homogeneous plex structure.

is given of what the child-parent relationships are. Whichever is the lowest node has two parents. In the fourth example the lowest node has four parents.

In some plex structures it is natural to refer to levels, as with a tree structure. The examples in Fig. 9.1 have two, three, four, and five levels, respectively.

The family tree of Fig. 8.6 is a tree structure only because it does not include women. Each person has two parents, and if they were both shown in the diagram, it would be a plex structure.

Indeed, if we include a few more generations, even the men-only diagram of Fig. 8.6 ceases to be a tree structure because of intermarriages, as shown in Fig. 9.2. Figure 9.2 is a *homogeneous* plex structure.

SIMPLE AND COMPLEX PLEX STRUCTURES   In many plex structures showing the relationships between record types or data-aggregate types, the mapping between parents and children is similar to that in a tree: The parent-to-child mapping is complex and the child-to-parent mapping is simple.

Figure 9.3 shows such a heterogeneous plex structure with five record types. None of the lines joining the record types has double arrows in both directions. Each relationship can be regarded as a parent-child relationship. The PURCHASE-ORDER record type is a child of the PART record type and a parent of the PURCHASE-ITEM record type.

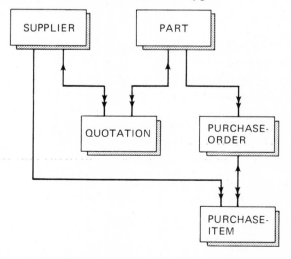

Figure 9.3   A plex structure of five record-types used for a purchasing application.

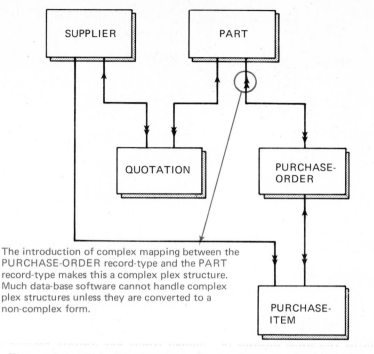

The introduction of complex mapping between the
PURCHASE-ORDER record-type and the PART
record-type makes this a complex plex structure.
Much data-base software cannot handle complex
plex structures unless they are converted to a
non-complex form.

Figure 9.4 The introduction of complex mapping between the
PURCHASE-ORDER record-type and the PART record-type makes
this a complex plex structure. Much data-base software cannot handle
complex plex structures unless they are converted to a non-complex
form.

It is desirable to distinguish between a structure in which the child-to-
parent mapping is simple or unused and one in which the mapping between
any two data types is complex in both directions. In the latter case one of
the lines on the schema will have double arrows going in both directions. We
will refer to this type of schema as a *complex* plex structure. A schema in
which no line has double arrows in both directions will be called a *simple*
plex structure. Figure 9.3 shows a simple plex structure. It becomes a
complex plex structure if the mapping from PURCHASE-ORDER to PART
is used, because one purchase order can be for many parts. Figure 9.4 shows
the schema redrawn as a complex plex structure.

The reason for making the distinction between simple and complex
plex structures is that the latter need more elaborate methods for representing them *physically*. Some data-base management software can handle
simple but not complex plex structures. The data description language
proposed by the CODASYL Data Base Task Group can describe simple plex

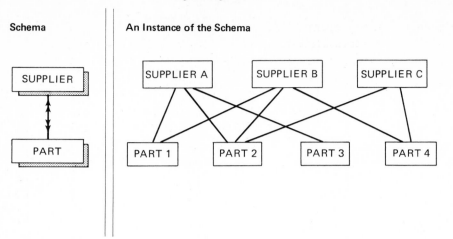

Schema   An Instance of the Schema

Figure 9.5   A "complex" plex structure with only two record-types.
The one relationship has complex mapping in both directions.

structures but not complex ones. This is not necessarily a disadvantage because the complex plex structure can be modified to a simple form, and in most cases *should* be. We will discuss the CODASYL language in Chapter 11.

A complex plex structure can exist with only two record types. Figure 9.5 shows an example. A SUPPLIER record can have more than one child because the supplier can supply more than one type of part. A PART record can have more than one parent because the part can be supplied by different suppliers.

**INTERSECTION
DATA**   In some cases data can be related to the *association* between data items. A part, for example, may be supplied by several vendors who each charge a different price for it. The data item PRICE cannot be associated with the PART record alone or with the SUPPLIER record alone. It can only be associated with the combination of the two. Such information is sometimes called *intersection data*—data associated with the association between records.

Figure 9.6 shows a more complex example of intersection data. Products made by a factory are composed of subassemblies and parts. In the factory data base are records called PRODUCT, SUBASSEMBLY, and PART. These records are different in composition. They might be linked as shown in the schema of Fig. 9.6. Associated with each link is a number which tells how many of a given part is in a given subassembly or product, and how many subassemblies are in a product. For example, product 1001 contains 1 of subassembly X, 2 of subassembly Y, and 4 of part 610. In general, a structure something like that in Fig. 9.6 gives a *bill of materials* showing a breakdown of the products for manufacturing purposes.

**M:M
ASSOCIATIONS**

There are two problems surrounding M:M associations between records—links with double arrows in both directions. The first relates to physical representation. As we shall see in Chapter 24, there are various straightforward ways of representing a 1:M association. Commonly the association $A \longleftrightarrow B$ is represented by the child records, B, following their parent, A. A_1 is followed by its associated B records, then A_2 is followed by *its* B records, and so on. Alternatively, a chain of pointers may be used, linking each A record to its associated B records.

These simple methods cannot be used with the M:M mapping $A \longleftrightarrow B$. Instead, there may be a file of A records and a file of B records, and separate information showing how they are related. Figure 9.7 shows two ways of handling an M:M association between records with keys A and

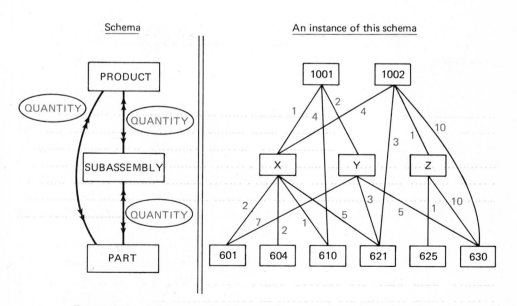

Figure 9.6 A bill-of-materials data base. In this illustration there is much intersection data. Extra records (segments) can be created to store intersection data, as in Fig. 9.8.

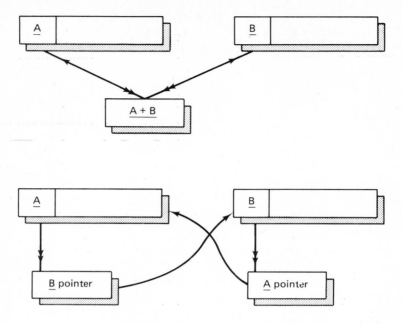

Figure 9.7   Two ways of handling an M:M association $A \leftarrow\!\!\!\!\rightarrow B$.

B. In both cases the effective key to the intersection information is $A+B$. In the lower example half of this key is not explicitly shown, because of the path dependency.

2 A second problem is that *in practice when an M:M association is needed, there will often be intersection data.* If there are no intersection data to start with, they are likely to be added later *as the data-base usage evolves.* If intersection data are associated with records having keys A and B, those data are identified by a concatenated key $A+B$. Figure 9.8 shows two examples of intersection data and how they might be handled.

 Because of the likelihood of adding intersection data, it is usually best to avoid a $A \leftarrow\!\!\!\!\rightarrow B$ link in a schema and instead create an extra record or segment having the concatenated key $A+B$. This avoids later restructuring with the consequent rewriting of programs.

CYCLES   Some structures contain cycles. A cycle refers to a situation where a node has as its descendant an ancestor of the node. The parent-child relationships can be followed around in a closed loop. In the schema diagram double-arrow lines form a continuous path, as in Fig. 9.9.

Two examples of intersection data:

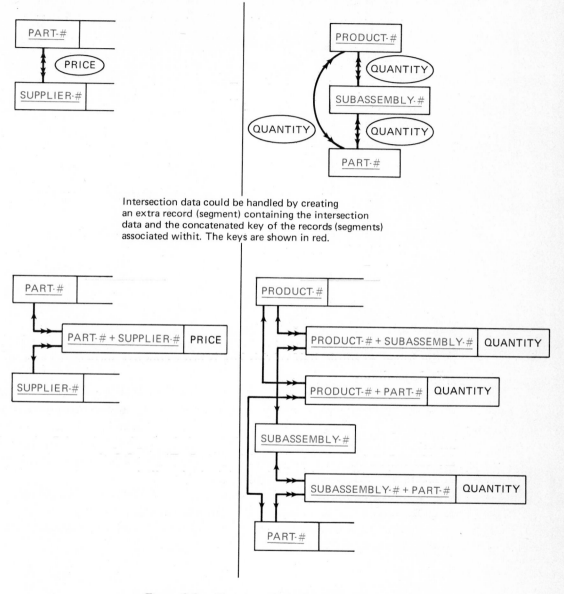

Intersection data could be handled by creating
an extra record (segment) containing the intersection
data and the concatenated key of the records (segments)
associated with it. The keys are shown in red.

Figure 9.8   Two examples of intersection data.

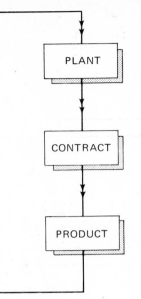

Figure 9.9   A cycle. Some plex structures have multiple cycles.

Figure 9.9 shows a cycle. A plant makes many products. Some products
may be subcontracted out to other plants. One contract may relate to several
products. Representing these relationships gives a cycle. Complicated plex
structures occasionally contain multiple cycles. Some data-base software can
represent cycles, and some cannot.

LOOPS   Sometimes records in a file are associated with
                        other records in the same file. This situation is
referred to as a *loop*. In a loop there is only one record type. The child
record type is the same as the parent. Figure 9.10 shows a loop.

The homogeneous plex structure of Fig. 9.2 is represented by a loop in
Fig. 9.11. Unlike the family tree in Fig. 8.10, it uses M:M mapping. Most
other homogeneous structures can be simplified similarly.

Figure 9.12 shows two of the common situations where loops can be
employed. In a personnel file some employees have specified associations

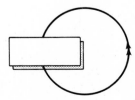

Figure 9.10   A loop.

Figure 9.11   The homogenous plex structure of Fig. 9.2 is an instance of this schema. Unlike that in Fig. 8.10 it has an M:M (complex/complex) mapping.

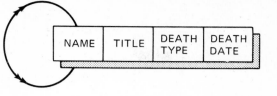

with other employees. In the bill of materials data base of Fig. 9.12 there is often an added complication; some of the subassemblies themselves contain subassemblies.

Some software cannot handle loops. A loop is often an M:M association. This is the case in Fig. 9.11. It is likely that the loop in Fig. 9.12 will evolve into an M:M association because the users of the bill-of-materials data base will want to ask not only "What is the subassembly composed of?" but also "What is this subassembly used in?"

We believe that M:M associations should generally be avoided. Group marriages get you in trouble. The main reason is that intersection data are

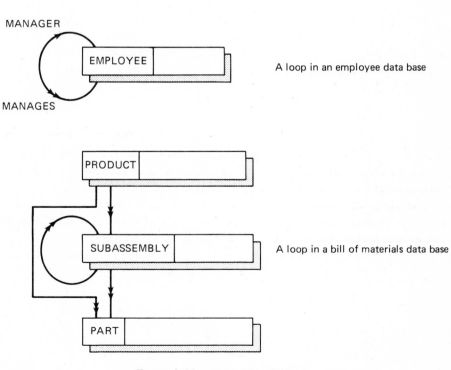

Figure 9.12   Example of loops.

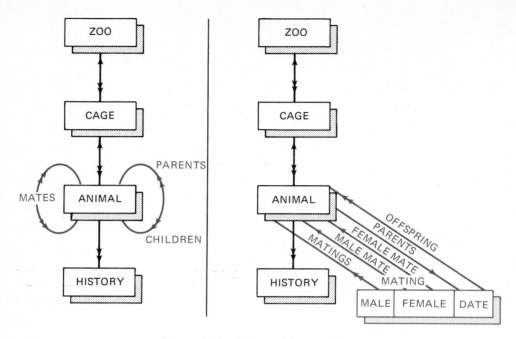

Figure 9.13   The avoidance of loops.

Martin (4) 9-13

likely to be added as the data base evolves and will force a splitting of the M:M association.

The left side of Fig. 9.13 shows the zoo data base of Fig. 5.6 drawn with two loops which show the associations between animals. One purpose of such a data base may be to keep track of mating and parentage, and to help find prospective mates—computer dating for animals.

An animal may have many mates, hence the MATES loop is M:M. It may have two parents and many offspring, hence the PARENTS & CHILDREN loop is M:M. It may become desirable to record the date of a mating. If so, these are intersection data, and a new data-item group is needed. Figure 9.13 shows an extra group (record, segment) used to avoid the loops.

We will leave the reader with a few questions about the right-hand side of Fig. 9.13. First, how could *prospective* mates be added to the data base? Second, there is still an M:M mapping between the ANIMAL and MATING records: MATINGS in one direction, and OFFSPRING in the other. How could this be avoided? Is it worth trying to avoid it?

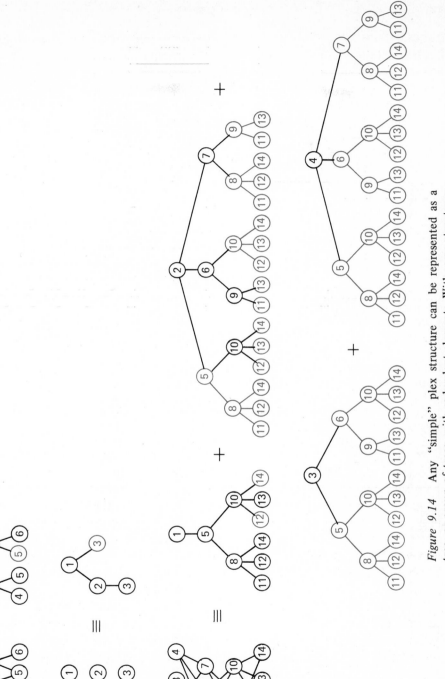

Figure 9.14 Any "simple" plex structure can be represented as a tree, or group of trees, with redundant elements. With some structures the amount of redundancy can be tolerated; with others it is excessive.

DECOMPOSITION
INTO SIMPLER
FORMS

Any plex structure can be reduced to a simpler form by introducing redundancy. Figure 9.14 shows how three simple plex structures may be represented as equivalent tree structures. In some cases the redundancy involved in doing so is small and might be tolerated. In other cases it is excessive. The family network of Fig. 9.2 can be redrawn as

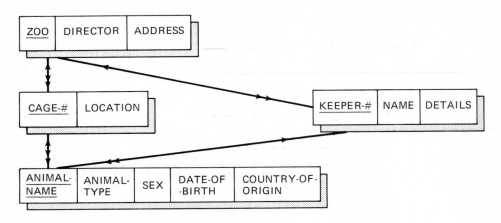

This plex structure can be converted to a tree
structure by adding the data items shown in red

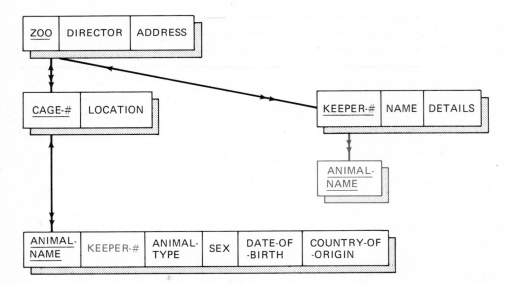

Figure 9.15   In general, plex data structures can be converted to tree structures by adding redundant *key* data items. This can be satisfactory with a data-base management system which can index to records which are not the root of the tree.

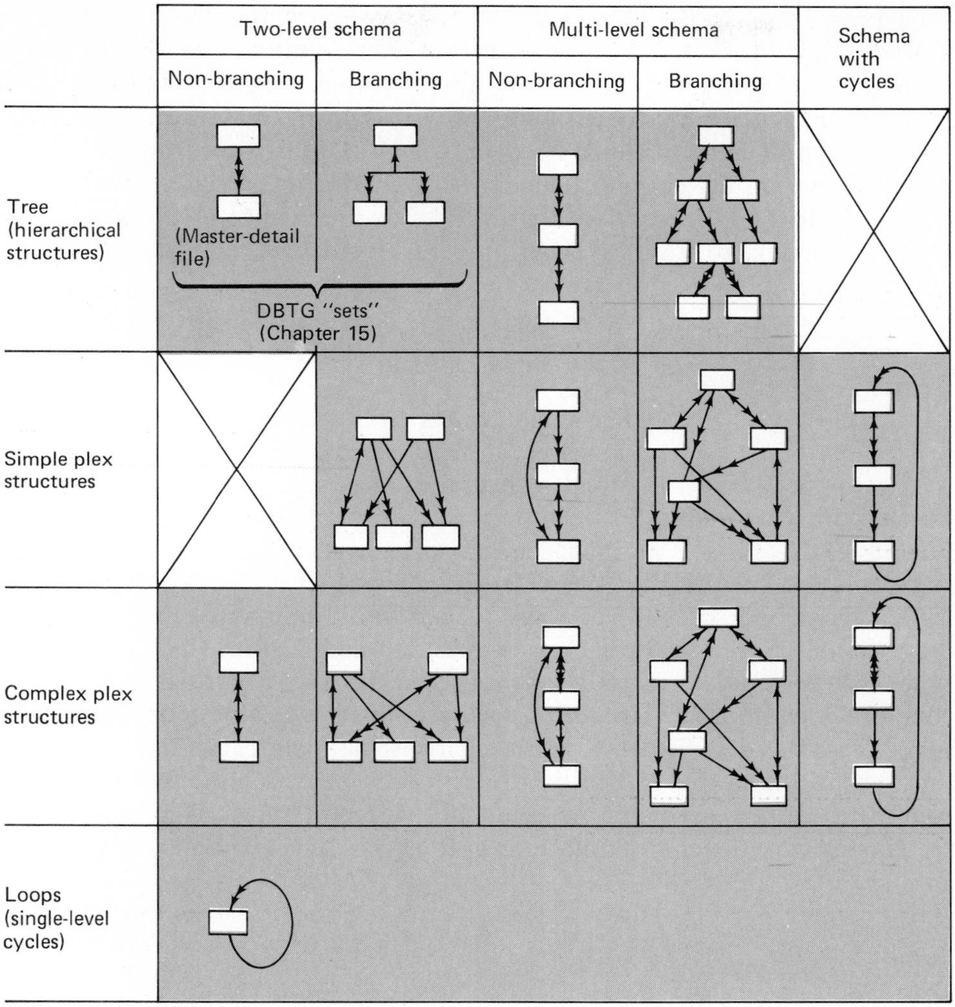

Figure 9.16 Categories of schema. Data-base management systems and languages differ in which of these structures they can handle. Some can handle hierarchical structures but not plex structures. Some can handle simple plex structures but not complex ones. The number of levels that can be handled differs from one system to another. Few (if any) can handle loops.

a tree by including some of the names twice. To do so, however, would probably be misleading to a person looking at the diagram.

The redundancy introduced does not apply to the whole record, only to its primary key or means of identifying it. Figure 9.15 shows the conversion of a simple plex structure to a tree structure. The key of the KEEPER record is added to the ANIMAL record and the KEEPER record is given a child containing merely the key ANIMAL NAME. The path from ANIMAL to KEEPER or from KEEPER to ANIMAL may then be followed even though there is no link between the ANIMAL record and KEEPER record drawn on the schema. The data-base management system would have to be able to find a record with a given key which is not at the root of the tree. An index to the ANIMAL records would be one such method. Similarly, complex plex structures be converted to tree structures by adding key redundancy.

CATEGORIES OF SCHEMA

The main reason for concern about whether relationships are represented by trees or plex structures is that most types of physical data layouts which work well with trees do not work with plex structures (Chapter 25). Consequently, some data management software can handle plex structures and some can handle only trees. The number of levels that can be handled differs from one software package to another. Some software can handle only simple relationships, such as a master-detail file, in which one record type can be related to only one other record type. Others can handle compound relationships in which each record type can be related to many other record types. Figure 9.16 summarizes the main categories of schema that may be permitted. When we discuss the *physical* representation of trees and plex structures, it will be seen that different physical representation techniques have different limitations in the types of schema they can handle.

BOOK STRUCTURE

Chapter 10 discusses data description languages. Chapters 11 to 13 discuss specific examples of such languages.

10 DATA DESCRIPTION LANGUAGES

It is necessary for both the programmers and the data-base administrator to be able to describe their data precisely, specifying data structures such as those in the previous two chapters. They do so by means of *data description languages*. A data description language is the means of declaring to the data-base management system what data structures will be used.

The computer industry is devoting considerable energy to the techniques of data description. Computer manufacturers have specified data description languages and cast them into software. Computer users and vendors have formed manufacturer-independent groups to study the subject—notably the CODASYL committees working on data description languages and the ACM (Association for Computing Machinery) Special Interest Group on File Definition and Translation.

The following chapters discuss different types of data description languages.

WHAT DOES A DATA DESCRIPTION LANGUAGE DO? A data description language giving a *logical* data description should perform the following functions. (*Note:* In a relational data base, discussed later, some of these functions become unnecessary.)

1. It should identify the types of data subdivision such as data item, segment, record, and data-base file. (The types of data subdivision differ from one language to another.)

2. It should give a unique name to each data-item type, record type, file type, data base, and other data subdivision.

3. It should specify which data-item types are in a data-aggregate type, record type, or other subdivision, showing any repeating groups, and must specify their sequence.

4. It should specify which data-item types, parts of data-item types, or combinations of data-item types are used as keys.

5. It should specify how the segment types or record types are related to make structures such as those in the previous two chapters.

6. It should give names to the relationships between segment types or record types (i.e., names to the lines connecting blocks on the schema and subschema diagrams).

7. It may define the type of encoding the program uses in the data items (binary, character, bit string, etc.). This should not be confused with the encoding employed in the physical representation.

8. It may define the length of the data items.

9. It may define the range of values that a data item can assume.

10. It may specify the number of data items that compose a vector, specify the number of dimensions and size of a matrix, or specify the number of data aggregates in a repeating group.

11. It may specify the sequence of records in a file or the sequence of groups of records in the data base.

12. It may specify means of checking for errors in the data.

13. It may specify privacy locks for preventing unauthorized reading or modification of the data. These may operate at the data-item, segment, record, file, or data-base level, and if necessary may be extended to the contents (value) of individual data items. The authorization may, on the other hand, be separately defined. It probably should be, because it is more subject to change than the data structures, and changes in authorization procedures should not force changes in application programs.

14. A *logical* data description should *not* specify addressing, indexing, or searching techniques or specify the placement of data on the storage units, because these topics are in the domain of physical, not logical, organization. It may give an indication of how the data will be used or of searching requirements, so that the physical techniques can be selected optimally, but such indications should not be logically limiting.

THREE TYPES OF DATA DESCRIPTION

As we have seen, the application programmer's view of the data is represented by a subschema and is often different from that represented by the overall schema. Furthermore, the view represented by the overall schema is different from the physical layout of the data. The data therefore need to be described in three ways:

1. From the application programmer's viewpoint—a description of the subschema.
2. From the global logical viewpoint—a description of the schema.
3. From the physical viewpoint—a description of the physical records and their linkages.

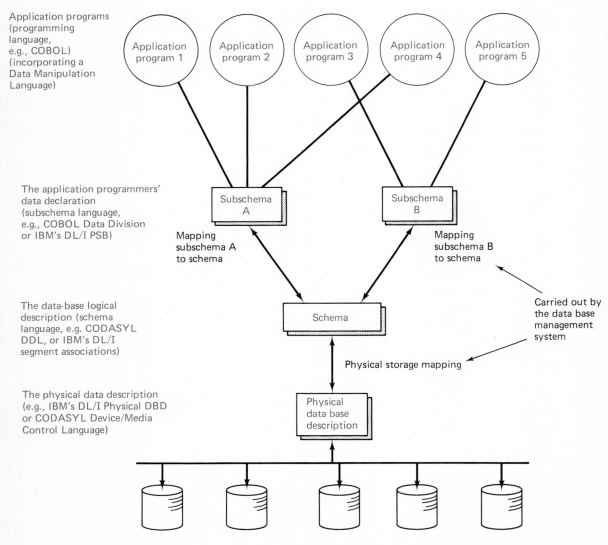

Figure 10.1

Figure 10.1 illustrates the relationships among the three data descriptions. The data-base management system uses the data descriptions. The data-base management system uses the data descriptions as shown in Figure 7.2 to derive the global logical records from the physical records and to derive the records required by the application programs from the global logical records.

SUBSCHEMA LANGUAGES

In many data-base systems today the language which a programmer used to describe his data is different from that which a data administrator uses.

The most common language for describing data from a programmer's viewpoint is the COBOL Data Division. Each program written in COBOL contains a description of the data it uses. The description is concerned only with the data for that program and is compiled along with the other statements in the program. In COBOL, as in other programming languages, there is no concept of data definition as an independent operation. The Data Division statements are always part of a specific program.

Figure 10.2 shows a COBOL description of Programmer A's subschema in Fig. 6.2.

It would be helpful if the programmer's description of data could be of the same form as the data administrator's description of the same data. Unfortunately, with some of today's data-base systems the two descriptions are written in a widely differing manner. Both descriptions are compiled ready for use, and the data-item types, segment types, and other data types are correlated.

SCHEMA LANGUAGES

Most data-base management systems have their own languages for defining the schemas that are used. In most cases these *data description languages* are different from the COBOL Data Division or other programming languages. COBOL, like other programming languages, does not have the capability to define the variety of relationships that may exist in the schemas.

IBM's Information Management System, IMS, uses a language called DL/I (Data Language One), discussed in Chapter 12. This language is used to write both a logical and physical data-base description. The three data descriptions illustrated in Fig. 10.1 are written as follows:

```
DATA DIVISION.
FILE SECTION.
FD PODATA
01 PURCHASE-ORDER-MASTER ; ASCENDING KEY IS ORDER#
    02 ORDER-# ; PICTURE IS 9999
    02 SUPPLIER-# ; PICTURE IS 9999
    02 SUPPLIER-NAME ; PIC A(30)
    02 SUPPLIER-ADDRESS ; PIC A(40)
    02 DELIVERY-DATE ; PIC 9999
    02 ORDER-DATE ; PIC 9999
    02 $TOTAL ; PIC Z(8)
    02 PURCHASE-ORDER-DETAIL ; OCCURS 1 TO 50 TIMES KEY IS PART#
        03 PART-# ; PIC X(8)
        03 PART-NAME ; PIC A(30)
        03 QUANTITY-ORDERED ; PIC 9999
        03 PRICE ; PIC Z(6)
```

Figure 10.2 The subschema for programmer A in Fig. 6.2 coded in COBOL. This subschema is used in conjunction with the schema of Fig. 6.1.

1. Application programmer's viewpoint: *a program specification block* (PSB) describing the data the programmer uses.

2. Global logical viewpoint: embedded in the DL/I data base description from wich subset hierarchical "logical data bases" can be derived with a coded *logical data base description* (logical **DBD**).

3. Physical viewpoint: DL/I *physical data base description* (physical **DBD**), which incorporates physical access methods.

These are illustrated in Figs. 12.6 to 12.8.

Box 10.1 Variations Between Schema and Subschema Descriptions

The subschema data description may differ from the schema data description in the following ways:

1. The subschema may omit descriptions of certain data that are in the schema. It may omit data items, data aggregates, records, or entire files.

2. The characteristics of data items may be changed. For example, a numeric data item may be in BCD code in the subschema data description but in binary code in the schema data description.

3. The sequence of data items in a data aggregate or record or other subdivision may be different.

4. The sequence of records in a file may be different.

5. Vectors may be redefined as multidimensional arrays.

6. The schema may define relationships different from those in the subschema.

7. Different record types may be described which are composed from data items or other record types.

8. Different data aggregates may be described which are composed from data items in other data aggregates or record types.

9. The privacy locks may be changed.

STANDARDIZATION　　　　Just as it is desirable that programming languages should be standardized and independent of specific machines, so also it is desirable that data description languages should be standardized. The data description languages in use today take a variety of forms. Appendix B shows a schema defined in various current data description languages, and the reader may observe how diverse they are in form.

COBOL, FORTRAN, and PL/I are standardized programming languages. It is the stated intent of CODASYL that their Data Description Language should be accepted throughout industry and that all common programming languages should interface with it (see Chapter 11). This language is independent of any programming language, but in many ways is similar to COBOL. Some authorities consider it unsuitable for the awesome responsibility of being an industry standard; controversy over this issue is likely to continue. IBM's Data Language/I is also independent of the program languages it is used with (see Chapter 12), and likewise the proposals for relational data-base systems (Chapter 13). In the long run the relational approach may prove to give the best form of independent data description.

Several major benefits would accrue from having an industry-wide data description language. Conversion problems would be eased. One programmer or data administrator would more easily be able to understand and discuss another's data descriptions. It would be easier to merge or link data bases. It would lessen the need to describe data twice in different languages, as often happens today. The future development of functionally compatible data-base management systems would be enhanced.

Many corporations will be carrying out the lengthy job over the next 10 years of defining the thousands of data-item types they use and constructing, step by step, suitable schemas from which their data bases will be built. The description of this large quantity of data will be an arduous task involving much argument between different interested parties. Eventually the massive data bases that develop will become one of the corporation's major assets. The task of defining the data and agreeing upon suitable schemas which will grow and interlink as time goes by, will be eased if a standard schema description language can be used throughout the corporation. *Whether or not an industry standard exists, it is important that a corporation should adopt its own standard.*

The *disadvantage* of the computer industry standardizing a data description language at this time is that it may restrict the industry to certain classes of data structures and inhibit the development of better forms of structure. As we will discuss in Chapters 13 and 14, it is likely that the data structures in common use at the present time—indeed all the data structures in the previous two chapters—are not the best for the industry. Premature standardization has an inhibiting effect on development.

INDEPENDENCE   We have stressed how important it is that the schemas used be independent of the physical storage and organization of data. Both the layout of data and the machines for storing data are likely to change. In some computer installations the physical organization of data is changed frequently as the system is tuned. For this reason a standardized schema description language should be independent of the physical organization of data. There should be no statements in the schema description language which relate to physical storage organization because such statements would destroy the data independence and would make it necessary to change the logical data descriptions when the physical organization is changed. This could cause great expenditure in rewriting programs.

Similarly, the subschema description language should be independent of the schema description language. The data-base administrator should be free to serve the data users as efficiently as possible by modifying the schemas and access methods when the change can give an improvement, but such changes should not necessitate any reprogramming of application programs or modification of subschemas.

The CODASYL Data Description Language is intended to be a language for defining schemas. It would provide a data structure suitable for many host languages and data manipulation languages. CODASYL has also proposed its own data manipulation language.

The wide acceptance of a common data description language should lay the foundation for common subschema languages, device/media control languages, and data manipulation languages. In the words of the Data Base Task Group: *"It is expected that the schema Data Description Language will have a significant impact on the development of functionally compatible data-base management systems and will increase the portability of programs between different computer systems."*

**NONCOMPLETE
INDEPENDENCE**   One area in which it has proved difficult to separate completely the logical and physical views of data is that of addressing and searching the data base. The logical description should probably make some statement about information accessing and search requirements so that they can be performed efficiently, but should not specify techniques to be used because these will change.

How the system locates a record or performs a search should not, in theory, concern the designer of the *logical* data base. This question is the concern of the designer of the physical storage layout. If the data management software performed its functions perfectly, the logical data-base designer could ignore questions of how records are located or files are searched. Unfortunately, in many cases today he finds it necessary to specify data organizations which speed up addressing or searching.

Consider the plex structure shown in Fig. 10.3, and imagine that one of the application programs which uses such a data base needs a file of the kings of England in order of their succession to the throne. It requires the following subschema, with the records in sequence by DATE OF SUCCESSION:

KINGS OF ENGLAND

NAME	DATE OF SUCCESSION	TYPE OF DEATH

There are several techniques by which this subschema could be derived from the global logical schema. One would be to use an inverted list of kings. Another would be to use a secondary index (discussed later). A third would be to use a *chain* which links together the groups containing kings in the required sequence. Figure 10.3 shows such a chain. In a complex commercial data base, many chains may be used linking together items related in different ways. A second chain, in Fig. 10.4, could link those individuals who died a violent death.

In Chapter 23 we will discuss the subject of chains. The point we wish to make here is that the use of a chain such as that in Fig. 10.3 is a statement about the *physical* organization of data and as such should not be necessary to the logical description of the data. The logical description should merely state the requirements for the kings subschema and not concern itself with how the subschema is derived from the stored data.

Some of today's logical data descriptions invade the realm of physical descriptions by specifying pointers, chains, secondary indices, or other techniques for physical implementation. Unfortunately, as the data base grows, or the hardware or software changes, the physical implementation will change. If the logical data description is entangled with the physical description in any way, then the users or application programmers' view of the data will probably have to change. The application programs may have to be rewritten.

To avoid the high *maintenance* costs that are associated with a data base undergoing the changes that are inevitable in a typical commercial environment, the logical data descriptions should be entirely unaffected by changes in physical storage organizations. Hence, statements about chains or other secondary key-retrieval methods should be excluded from logical data descriptions.

Complicated data descriptions which are truly impervious to future changes are difficult to achieve with the tree and plex structures that we

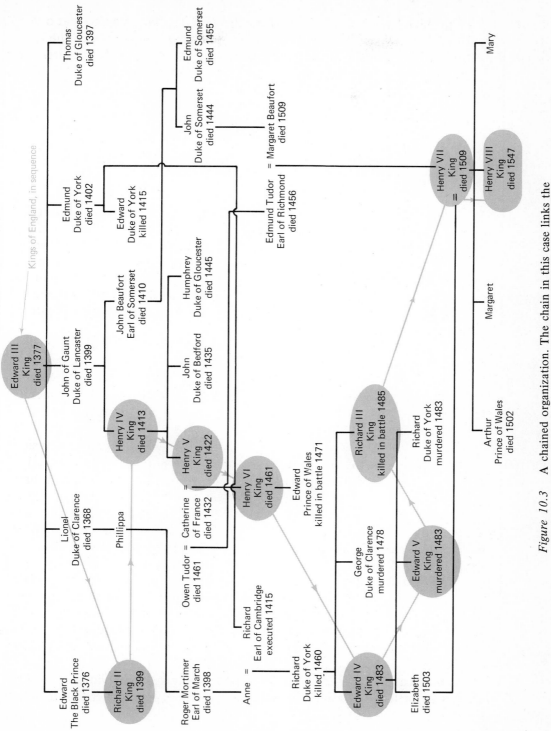

Figure 10.3 A chained organization. The chain in this case links the Kings of England in their order of succession to the throne. When a logical file designer specifies a chain he is going beyond the logical description into a description of the physical organization.

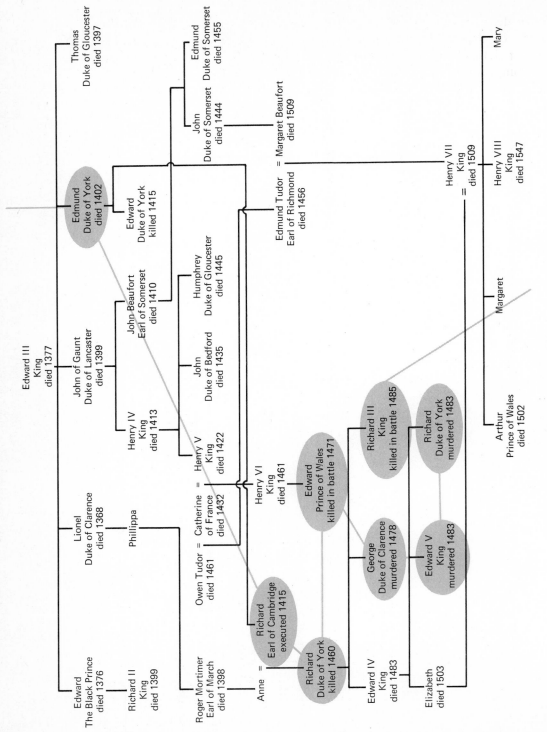

Figure 10.4   A chain linking individuals who die a violent death.

have described or, indeed, with any data descriptions which involve collections of directed links. However, better types of data descriptions need better data management software. With much of today's software, we have to compromise.

BOOK STRUCTURE

Chapter 11 gives one example of a data description language.

11 THE CODASYL DATA DESCRIPTION LANGUAGE

Since 1969 the Conference on Data Description Languages (CODASYL) has been active in the development of a common Data Description Language (DDL) for defining schemas. The current activity within CODASYL on the development of the DDL is being conducted by the Data Description Language Committee (DDLC) composed of voluntary representatives from computer manufacturers and users in industry and federal government.

In this chapter we will summarize the main features of the CODASYL Data Description Language. For a complete description of it the reader should obtain the original CODASYL specification in Reference 1.

FOUR TYPES OF ENTRY
A schema written in the CODASYL Date Description Language contains four types of entries:

1. *One schema entry*, which identifies the schema.
2. *One or more area entries*, which define the grouping of records into areas, as we will discuss below.
3. *Record entries*, which define record types specifying details of their data items and data aggregates.
4. *Set entries* which define the grouping of record types into CODASYL set types (which we describe shortly).

The entries are written in the sequence above. Figure 11.2 gives an example of the resulting code showing the four types of entries used to define the schema in Fig. 11.1.

Schema name: ORGDATA

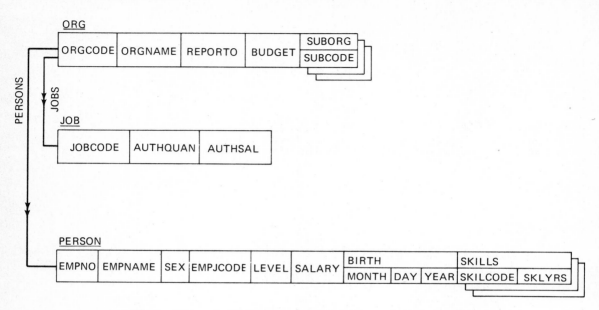

Figure 11.1   A CODASYL Data Desciption Language encoding of this schema is shown in Fig. 11.2. The schema contains three record types: ORG, JOB, and PERSON. The relationships between them are expressed in to sets: PERSONS and JOBS.

The entries consist of English-like statements similar in their form to the COBOL Data Division. Certain words, such as NAME, PICTURE, RECORD, and PRIVACY, are reserved, as in COBOL, for language use. A typical statement is that giving the name of the schema at the top of Fig. 11.2: SCHEMA NAME IS ORGDATA.

RECORD ENTRIES

A record entry states the name of the record and then lists all the data items in a record. The record type PERSON at the bottom of Fig. 11.2 contains two data-aggregate types: BIRTH and SKILLS. SKILLS can occur multiple times in the record. This record type can be described in the language as follows on page 142.

The data items and data aggregates are described in a fashion similar to COBOL. The first data item is EMPNO. The PICTURE clause gives the format of the item, indicating, for example, that EMPNO consists of five digits. (A "9" in the PICTURE statement means a digit. "9(5)" mean five

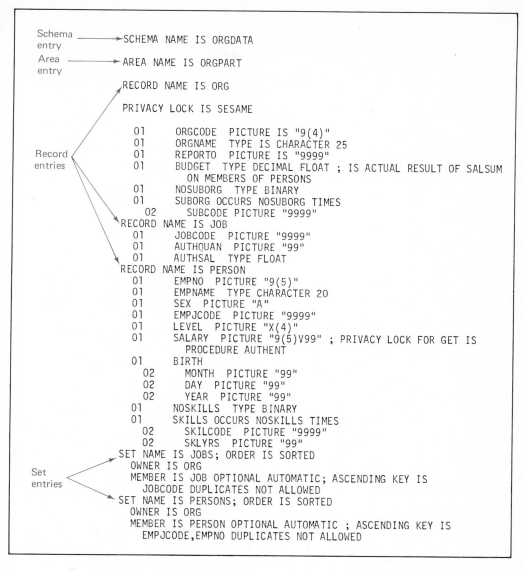

```
Schema ──────→ SCHEMA NAME IS ORGDATA
entry

Area ──────→ AREA NAME IS ORGPART
entry

              RECORD NAME IS ORG

              PRIVACY LOCK IS SESAME

                 01      ORGCODE   PICTURE IS "9(4)"
                 01      ORGNAME   TYPE IS CHARACTER 25
                 01      REPORTO   PICTURE IS "9999"
                 01      BUDGET   TYPE DECIMAL FLOAT ; IS ACTUAL RESULT OF SALSUM
                              ON MEMBERS OF PERSONS
Record           01      NOSUBORG   TYPE BINARY
entries          01      SUBORG OCCURS NOSUBORG TIMES
                    02       SUBCODE PICTURE "9999"
              RECORD NAME IS JOB
                 01      JOBCODE   PICTURE "9999"
                 01      AUTHQUAN  PICTURE "99"
                 01      AUTHSAL   TYPE FLOAT
              RECORD NAME IS PERSON
                 01      EMPNO  PICTURE "9(5)"
                 01      EMPNAME   TYPE CHARACTER 20
                 01      SEX  PICTURE "A"
                 01      EMPJCODE   PICTURE "9999"
                 01      LEVEL  PICTURE "X(4)"
                 01      SALARY   PICTURE "9(5)V99" ; PRIVACY LOCK FOR GET IS
                              PROCEDURE AUTHENT
                 01      BIRTH
                    02     MONTH  PICTURE "99"
                    02     DAY  PICTURE "99"
                    02     YEAR  PICTURE "99"
                 01      NOSKILLS   TYPE BINARY
                 01      SKILLS OCCURS NOSKILLS TIMES
                    02     SKILCODE   PICTURE "9999"
                    02     SKLYRS   PICTURE "99"
              SET NAME IS JOBS; ORDER IS SORTED
                 OWNER IS ORG
Set              MEMBER IS JOB OPTIONAL AUTOMATIC; ASCENDING KEY IS
entries              JOBCODE DUPLICATES NOT ALLOWED
              SET NAME IS PERSONS; ORDER IS SORTED
                 OWNER IS ORG
                 MEMBER IS PERSON OPTIONAL AUTOMATIC ; ASCENDING KEY IS
                     EMPJCODE,EMPNO DUPLICATES NOT ALLOWED
```

Figure 11.2 A description of the schema shown in Fig. 11.1 written in the CODASYL Data Description Language. Reproduced with permission from Reference 2.

digits.) The second data item is EMPNAME, and the TYPE clause indicates that this item consists of 20 characters. A data item can be specified as a bit string, a character string, or arithmetic data, which are decimal or binary, fixed-point or floating-point, and real or complex. It can be specified with a PICTURE clause showing the numbers and types of characters, as in

```
RECORD NAME IS PERSON
    01      EMPNO PICTURE "9(5)"
    01      EMPNAME TYPE CHARACTER 20
    01      SEX PICTURE "A"
    01      EMPJCODE PICTURE "9999"
    01      LEVEL PICTURE "X(4)"
    01      SALARY PICTURE "9(5)V99"
    01      BIRTH
        02      MONTH PICTURE "99"
        02      DAY
        02      YEAR PICTURE "99"
    01      NOSKILLS TYPE BINARY
    01      SKILLS OCCURS NOSKILLS TIMES
        02      SKILCODE PICTURE "9999"
        02      SKYLYRS PICTURE "99"
```

COBOL. In the example above, "9999" means four decimal digits; "9(5)V99" means seven decimal digits, five before and two after the decimal point; "A" means one alphabetic character; "X(4)" means four alphanumeric characters. The data item can also be specified to be of a type to be declared by the implementor. It can be declared to be a data-base *key* with which the record is uniquely identified.

DATA AGGREGATES   The *subentry* which describes a data item can be given a level number; the level number is higher for data items which are components of a data aggregate. The first six data items in the example above have a level number 01. The next subentry, also level 01, is the name of a data aggregate. The subentries following, of level 02, are the data items which compose the data aggregate. As with group items in COBOL, the data aggregates can themselves contain data aggregates, and this would be indicated by higher-level numbers. A data aggregate can be a group of single data items, a vector (i.e., a one-dimensional sequence of data items all of which have identical characters), or a repeating group (a group of data items which is repeated a specified number of times).

CODASYL   The basic construct of the language is called a *set*.
SETS   A *set* is a new but simple concept. It is, in essence, a named two-level tree as shown in Figs. 11.3 and 11.4. Multilevel trees and certain plex structures can be built up from

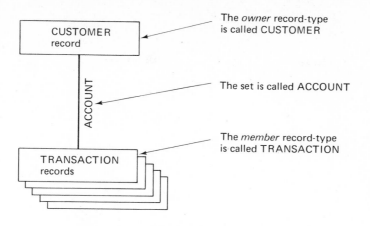

Figure 11.3   An occurrence of a set.

multiple two-level trees. A CODASYL data base is thus composed of multiple sets. A systems analyst can design highly complex structures from many of these two-level linkages, like building bridges with a toy erector kit.

Note: The CODASYL use of the word "set" should not be confused with the conventional set-theory use of the word, which is also employed in data-base discussion.

A *set* is an occurrence of a named collection of records, and each set type can represent a relationship between two or more record types. Each

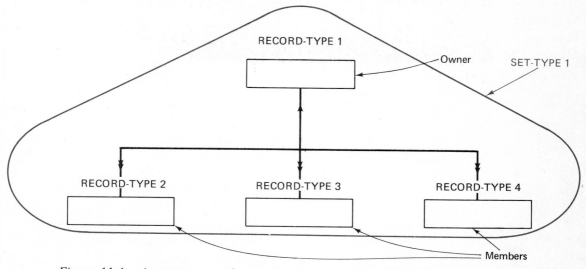

Figure 11.4   A set-type can have only one owner record-type but multiple member record-types.

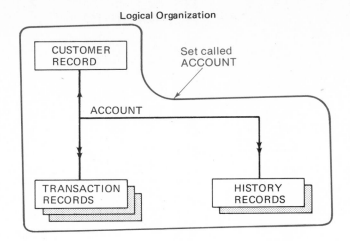

Figure 11.5   A new member record-type added to the set in Fig. 11.3.

set type can have one record type declared as its *owner* and one or more other record types declared as its *members*. Each set *must* contain one occurrence of its owner record type and may contain any number of occurrences of its member record types.

For example, a set may be used for customer transaction records. The set type may be called ACCOUNT and its owner record type called CUSTOMER (see Fig. 11.3). The CUSTOMER records may contain details of a customer's name, address, and account balance. The member record type may be called TRANSACTION. There would be an arbitrary number of TRANSACTION records in one ACCOUNT set giving details of the transactions that have occurred since that customer was last billed. There could be zero transactions, in which case the set occurrence would contain only one record occurrence—that of the owner, CUSTOMER, record.

The set type may contain multiple member record types, as shown in Fig. 11.4. There is a one-to-many relationship between the owner record and the member records, as shown by the double and single arrows in Fig. 11.4. A set thus represents a two-level tree.

In a data base, new record types may be added to a set at a time after the set was originally established. Thus, HISTORY records might be added to the ACCOUNT set in Fig. 11.3 showing a summary of customer purchases. This addition is shown in Fig. 11.5. Although here a new record type was described as becoming a member of an existing set type, alternatively a new set type could have been formed. Figure 11.1 has two set types called JOBS and PERSONS, in a two-level tree.

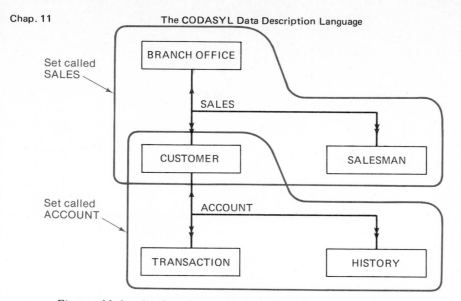

Figure 11.6 A three-level tree requires two sets to describe it. CUSTOMER record-type is here both an owner of the ACCOUNT set and a member of the SALES set.

MULTILEVEL TREES

To represent a multilevel tree, more than one set is necessary. A record type which is declared an *owner* at a lower level in the tree is also declared as *a member* of a higher-level set.

Figure 11.6 shows a three-level tree. Any *N*-level tree requires at least *N*-1 sets to describe it. Two sets are used in Fig. 11.6: SALES and ACCOUNT. In this manner, complex multilevel tree structures can be described.

SIMPLE FILES

A *singular set* is a special type of CODASYL set for which the owner is described as "SYSTEM." There can be only one occurrence of any declared singular set. A singular set is used to create traditional files containing records of the same type. Different record types can be members of the same singular set, owned jointly by "SYSTEM." A data base can have many singular sets, or files, and they are frequently used.

Any record type can be described as being a member of a singular set at the same time as being a member of other more complex sets. The CUSTOMER record type in Fig. 11.6, for example, could be declared a member of a singular set, as shown in Fig. 11.7. The sequence of the records in a singular set may be defined to be a sequence different from that of the same records when they form part of a different set, as will be described shortly.

PLEX	Every *member* record type has one and only one
STRUCTURES	parent in the same set—its *owner* record type. A

member can, however, have more than one parent if each parent is in a different set. In other words, a record can be a member of multiple sets; it can have more than one owner. Consequently, a simple plex structure can be described straightforwardly in the language.

Figure 11.8 illustrates a simple plex structure showing the owners and members of the three sets. Record 6 is a member of two sets.

It is permissible to have *different* sets linking the *same* record types. In this way *different* associations between the same records can be represented:

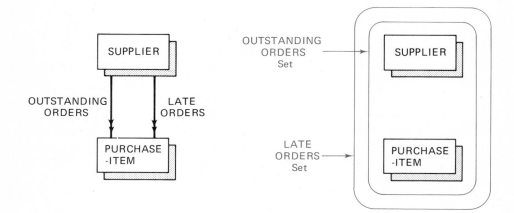

The plex structure of Fig. 6.9 is redrawn in Fig. 11.9, showing the eight associations represented as seven sets. The seven sets have the names OUTSTANDING-ORDERS, LATE-ORDERS, ACTUAL-SUPPLIER-QUOTATION, CANDIDATE-SUPPLIER-QUOTATION, SUPPLIER-ORDER, PURCHASE-ORDER, and PARTS.

While the data description language has no difficulty describing a simple plex structure, it cannot describe a complex plex structure without converting it to a simpler form. An M:M association between records (group marriage association) cannot be represented as such. This is not a serious disadvantage of CODASYL. We have stressed that in general a well-designed

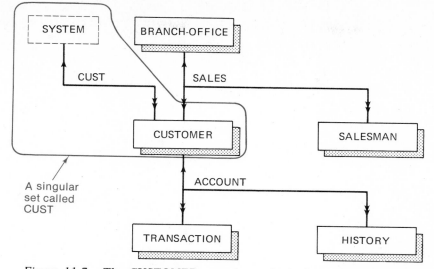

Figure 11.7   The CUSTOMER record-type is declared a member of a singular set called CUST. This declaration enables the CUSTOMER records to be treated as a single simple file.

schema should not contain M:M associations between groups of data items. They should be replaced by adding an extra group with a concatenated key. This is illustrated in Fig. 11.10.

Figure 11.10 shows a schema of a plex structure intended to show which suppliers supply which parts. One supplier can supply many parts, and one part can be supplied by more than one supplier. To convert this plex record type, an intermediate record type may be created containing pairs of data items—a part number and a supplier number. There are then two *sets*, which in Fig. 11.10 are called SUPPLIES and SUPPLIED-BY.

LOOPS   Cycles such as that in Fig. 9.6 are permitted in a CODASYL schema; an owner record, high in a hierarchy or plex structure, can be a member of a set at a lower level. However, loops, such as that in Fig. 9.8 are not permitted because no record can be both a member and owner of the same set.

TYPES OF   A record occurrence can participate in a set in
MEMBERSHIP   several different ways. These are referred to as *types of set membership*. First, the membership can be *mandatory* or *optional*. *Mandatory* membership means that a record

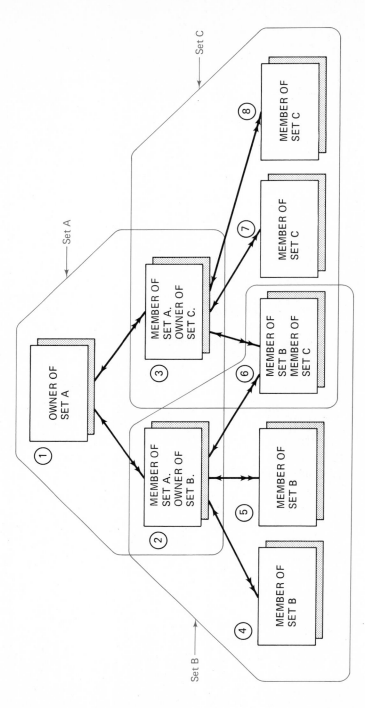

Figure 11.8 A plex structure in the CODASYL language. Record 6 is a member of two different sets. It may be described as having its record occurrences in a different *sequence* in each set. The sequencing will then have to be done by the data-base management system.

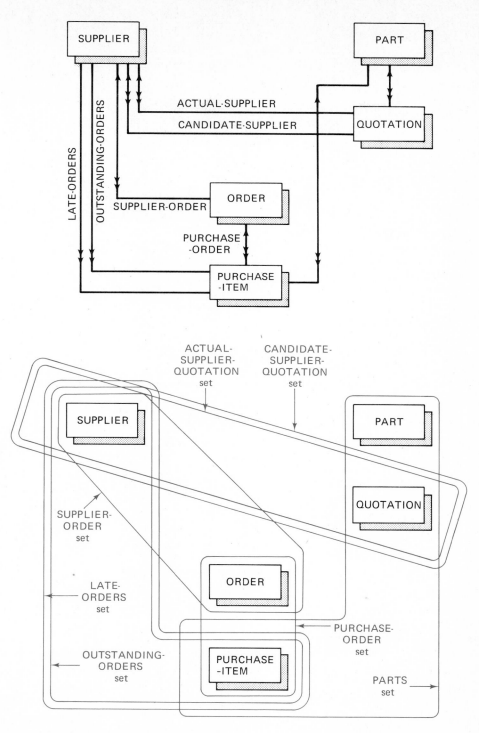

Figure 11.9 The plex structure of Fig. 6.9 can be described in a straightforward manner with seven CODASYL Sets:

An M : M association (complex/complex mapping) between records is not represented directly in the CODASYL Data Description Language. Instead an extra record is introduced so that 1 : M associations can be used:

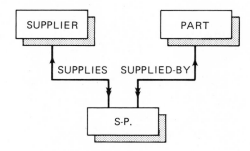

This requires two sets, the details of which are shown below. The key data items are underlined:

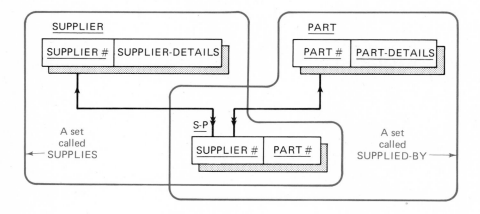

Figure 11.10

is a permanent member of a set once it is included. It can be updated with a MODIFY command but cannot be deleted. *Optional* membership means that a record occurrence can be removed from the set or deleted from the data base.

Second, the membership can be *automatic* or *manual*. *Automatic* membership means that when a record occurrence is stored in the data base, it will be automatically included in the relevant set. *Manual* means that set membership must be established by an application program using an INSERT command. A record may be a manual member of one set and an automatic member of another.

DYNAMIC
SETS

A *dynamic set* is one which can have *no member records declared for it in the schema.* Instead, any record can be made a member of it, or removed from it, by executing in the application program an appropriate command from the Data Manipulation Language.

SECONDARY
KEYS

Secondary keys and secondary indices are becoming increasingly important in today's usage of data bases. Secondary keys were illustrated in Figs. 5.3 and 5.6. In the CODASYL language they are referred to as *search keys.* A search key consists of one or more data items from a member record of a set. The declaration of a search key causes the data-base management system to build some form of indexing using the search key. An index, in the CODASYL vocabulary, consists of *any* means of finding the set occurrences in which the specified data item or items have specified values. This could be a conventional index (discussed in Part II of the book) or any other equivalent mechanism which does not require a complete scan of all the member records involved.

The primary key (record identified) as well as any other data item could be declared as a search key.

THE ORDERING
OF SETS

Each set declared to be part of the data base must have an ORDER specified for its member records starting in what sequence they are to be maintained. The data-base management system will then automatically insert member records into the set in such a way that the *logical* order is maintained. The logical sequence of records (the sequence in which the programmer thinks they are stored) may be quite different from the physical sequence in which they are actually stored. Indeed, *the same records may be members of more than one set and may be declared to be in a different order in each set*, as indicated in Fig. 11.8.

There are many ways in which a set can be represented physically, as will be discussed in Part II. The designers of the schema should not be concerned with the question. One way of representing the sequence of records is by means of a chain which links them, such as the chain linking kings in Fig. 10.4. In an earlier version of the data description language the user could state that he wanted records to be ordered by means of chaining. He could write ORDER IS CHAIN. It was pointed out that such a statement destroys data independence [2]. The physical methods of ordering might be changed, and the change should not cause the schema or subschemas to have to be changed. In the current version of the language the user cannot specify a *technique* such as chaining. The specification of physical techniques is carried out independently of the schema definition. The word CHAIN and similar technique-oriented words are no longer in the DDL vocabulary of reserved words.

Only *member* records can have an order specified for them. An ordering cannot be associated with owner records *as owners*. If these records are also members of a set, they can be ordered.

The member records can be ordered in one of several different ways as follows:

1. The order may be immaterial, and the records can be in whatever sequence is convenient for the data-base management system. The user writes ORDER IS IMMATERIAL or ORDER IMMATERIAL.

2. The order may result from inserting new member records into the set. They may be inserted last in the sequence of member records; the user writes ORDER IS LAST. They may be inserted first in the sequence—ORDER IS FIRST. They may be inserted prior to or after another record selected by the application program—ORDER IS PRIOR or ORDER IS NEXT.

3. A key may be specified, and the records are inserted in ascending or descending sequence of the key value. The user writes ORDER IS SORTED and specifies the key. For example, the bottom two lines of Fig. 11.2 say ASCENDING KEY IS EMPJCODE, EMPNO and then DUPLICATES NOT ALLOWED, stating that no member records are permitted to have the same values for these two data items which together form the key. Sometimes the primary key of the record is used and sometimes a different data item or data items may be specified as the keys for sequencing.

Set characteristics are summarized in Box 11.1.

Box 11.1 Summary of DLL Set Characteristics

The following passage from the Data Description Language Journal of Development summarizes the characteristics and restrictions of sets [1] :

- A set type is a named relationship between record types.
- An arbitrary number of set types may be declared in a schema.
- Each set type must be named and must have one owner record type. However, a special type of set which has exactly one occurrence and for which the system is the owner may be declared. For convenience, this is known as a singular set.
- Each set type must have one or more member record types declared for it in the schema. This does not apply to set types specified to be dynamic.
- Each set type must have an order specified for it in the schema.
- Any record type may be declared in the schema as the owner of one or more set types.
- Any record type may be declared in the schema as a member of one or more set types.
- Any record type may be specified as both an owner of one or more set types and a member in one or more different set types.
- The capability for a record type to participate as both owner and member in the same set type is not supported by the data description language (loops).
- A set consists of an owner record and its member records if any.
- A record cannot be in more than one occurrence of the same set type.
- A set includes exactly one occurrence of its owner. In fact, the existence of the owner record in the data base establishes the set.
- A set which contains only an occurrence of its owner record is known as an empty set.
- A set may have an arbitrary number of occurrences of each of the member record types declared for it in the schema.

PLACEMENT
CONTROLS
One of the claimed disadvantages of making the schema description entirely independent of the physical organization and placement of data is that it may not be possible to use the schema description for optimizing the physical organization. Some authorities say that it need not be used for physical optimization and that, indeed, it should not because to do so destroys data independence [2]. Physical optimization is a localized operation that should not affect the logical data description. How the optimization is carried out should not be governed by statements in logical data description *but by much more complete information, which comes from monitoring the system usage or from design estimates of how frequently the data paths will be traversed and whether they are traversed in real time.*

On most systems it is highly desirable that some optimization of physical positioning occur in order to minimize the response times, maximize the throughput, and shorten the time needed to search the data base. On systems which have not been concerned with data independence (almost all systems during the 1960s and many small, or specialized, or ill-designed systems during the 1970s) the physical layout of data has often been carefully tailored to sizes of disk tracks and patterns of accessing the records. It is precisely such tailoring that causes the programs to have to be rewritten when the hardware or record contents is changed.

Among the types of optimization that are desirable are the following:

1. Records which are commonly accessed together should be placed in close proximity so that there is as little *seek* time as possible between accessing the first one and the subsequent ones.

2. Where paging is used, records which are commonly referred to together should be placed in the same page to minimize the amount of page switching (thrashing).

3. In a storage device which operates by loading cartridges or other storage cells, records which are accessed together should be placed in the same cell, to minimize the time spent changing cells.

4. Frequently referenced items should be stored in an area of the file which can be accessed quickly, whereas infrequently referenced items may be stored in areas needing longer seek times.

A variety of other examples of physical optimization will be discussed in Part II.

In the contested CODASYL view, it is desirable to make some statements in the schema description which can provide advice for physical optimization. These statements should not presume any knowledge of device characteristics or physical organization techniques or independence, will be lost. The schemas should not have to be changed when device characteristics or physical organization techniques change.

To achieve this compromise objective, the Data Description Language Committee introduced the concept of *areas*. An area (later called *realm*) in the DDLC data description language is a named subdivision of a data base to which records may be assigned independently of their membership of sets. There may be any number of areas in a schema. The schema described in Fig. 10.4 has only one area, and that area is named ORGPART. It is described with the area entry

AREA NAME IS ORGPART

No record may be assigned to more than one area, and once assigned the record may not change areas. A record type or set type may, however, have occurrences in multiple areas. A set may span many areas.

An area may be either *permanent* or *temporary*. If it is temporary, it is associated with the execution of one particular program (*task* in IBM language, *run-unit* in DBTG language).

The concept of areas is intended to permit the data-base administrator to subdivide a data base in ways that may be used to enhance system efficiency without introducing any statements which are device-dependent or technique-dependent. A data-base management system or a physical data-base designer may control the placement of an entire area so as to minimize seek times or to confine the area to a given page or hardware zone. Infrequently referenced or archival portions of the data may be suitably placed. A program (task, run-unit) may open certain areas and thus indicate that it is confining its attention to a relatively small portion of the data base. This action may permit the optimization of accesses for that program. Areas may also be used as a convenient unit for fallback. Certain areas may be stored in duplicate or periodically copied.

To indicate that a record is within an area previously named ORGPART, a WITHIN clause is written in the record description as

WITHIN AREA ORGPART

or simply WITHIN ORGPART. If the record is to be in the same area as its owner, the description says

WITHIN AREA OF OWNER

or simply WITHIN OWNER. The area name may be defined as a variable or established by a procedure.

Area characteristics are summarized in Box 11.2.

Box 11.2 Summary of DDL Area Characteristics

> The following passage from the DDLC Journal of Development summarizes the characteristics of areas [1].
>
> - An area is a named subdivision of a data base.
> - An arbitrary number of areas may be declared in a schema.
> - Each area must be named.
> - An area may be either permanent, or temporary and local to a run-unit (task).
> - Records may be assigned to areas independently of their set associations. A given record type or set type may have occurrences in multiple areas, and a set may span areas.
> - Each record must be associated with one and only one area. This association is permanent, and in that a record may not change areas.
>
> The concept of area is one of the most controversial of the current Data Description Language. There is a strong case to be made out that all physical positioning and optimization of data should be carried out quite separately from the description of data by a group who utilize knowledge of how the data are employed. How the data are employed may change frequently, but the logical data description should be independent of such changes.

SEARCHING AND INDEXING

The word SEARCH in the data description declares that a serarch must be made for certain occurrences of a given record type. The search may or may not employ an index. As we will discuss in Part II, there are many ways of searching a data base. As we commented, the word INDEX is used in the DDLC language in a broader way than to mean *any possible* means of searching the member records of a set that does not employ a serial scan of them. The implementor is free to choose and to change the searching techniques. The use of the word INDEX does not conform to the conventional narrower concept of an index.

The user may name an index and could thus write SEARCH USING INDEX NAME DIRECTORY1. He could also name a programmed search procedure: SEARCH USING PROCEDURE S12. If the search is carried out using a secondary key, he could write, for example, SEARCH KEY IS JONES. He might write SEARCH KEY JONES USING INDEX NAME DIRECTORY1.

SET
SELECTION　Usually there will be many occurrences of a given set type in a data base. It is necessary to provide a means of identifying and locating the required set when it is to be retrieved and of determining where to place it when it is to be stored. The techniques for *addressing* records or sets are discussed in Chapter 19. The schema should not be concerned with details of these techniques because they relate to *physical* data-base organization. The schema may, however, specify the general form of set addressing, indicating whether an application program routine is used, whether a key is used, or whether the technique involves the use of another set. Addressing is referred to as *set selection*, and the following types of set selection may be specified:

1. The selection may be performed by means of a named program procedure. This is specified by writing a clause such as SET SELECTION IS BY PROCEDURE Z18, or simply SELECTION PROCEDURE Z18.

2. The selection may be performed using a *key*. The application program provides the key of the required owner record, and the data-base management system uses this key to locate the owner record of the set. This type of addressing may be specified by a clause such as SET SELECTION IS THRU OWNER IDENTIFIED BY DATA-BASE-KEY EQUAL TO JONES, or simply SELECTION THRU DATA-BASE-KEY JONES.

3. The address of the required set is found by means of a calculation using a given data-base key, for example, SET SELECTION IS THRU CALC-KEY EQUAL TO JONES, or simply SELECTION THRU CALC-KEY JONES.

4. The selection may be by means of another set, for example, SET SELECTION IS THRU EMPLOYEE, where EMPLOYEE is a set type used for addressing the required set. In some cases the set selection will be by means of multiple other sets, for example, SET SELECTION IS THRU DEPARTMENT OWNER IDENTIFIED BY DATA-BASE-KEY IS MAIL-ORDER THEN THRU EMPLOYEE.

PRIVACY　The schema description can specify the privacy locks which are used for protecting the data. A *privacy lock* is a value against which a *privacy key* value must be matched before the data in question can be used. Privacy locks can be declared at data-item, data-aggregate, record, set, member, area, and schema levels for protecting any of them. At each of these levels the locks relate to specific functions, such as reading or modifying the data items or inserting new records. A program cannot execute the function in question without providing the correct *privacy key* to the lock.

The privacy lock is a single value. It may be a constant, the value of a variable, or the result of a programmed procedure. It is declared by a clause appended to a data description statement, such as PRIVACY LOCK FOR MODIFY IS HIPPOPOTAMUS or PRIVACY LOCK FOR GET IS PROCEDURE K24. The privacy key which a program must produce as a result of such a declaration is also a single-valued constant, variable, or result of a programmed procedure.

The locks which apply to the use of a record type can relate to one or more of the following functions: INSERT, REMOVE, STORE, DELETE, GET, MODIFY, or FIND. If no such function is mentioned in the privacy declaration for a record, the lock given applies to all these functions, for example, PRIVACY LOCK IS 3274 or simply PRIVACY 3274. On the other hand, a different lock could be used for different functions: PRIVACY LOCK FOR GET FIND IS 3274; PRIVACY LOCK FOR INSERT REMOVE STORE DELETE IS 7493; PRIVACY LOCK FOR MODIFY IS 9105.

CODING   The language used to code the CODASYL data descriptions resembles COBOL, although it is intended that such descriptions should be employed by application programs written in any language. As in COBOL, a list of *reserved words* is employed by the software. These words, shown in Box 11.3, when written in the data description or application programs have precise meanings for the compiler and data-base management system. The words are intended to give a *logical* description of the data and any physical description should be avoided in order to preserve physical data independence. Words with physical connotations such as CHAIN, RING, or LIST, or excluded from the vocabulary, and words such as INDEX which previously had physical meaning are redefined to avoid implying physical meaning techniques.

The following pages show that the types of statements are used in the data descriptions. For more detail the reader should obtain the CODASYL DDL Journal of Development (1).

In the syntactical descriptions that follow, uppercase words are from the vocabulary of Box 11.3 and are written on the system designer's coding

Box 11.3   Reserved Words Used in the CODASYL Data
Description Language and Data Manipulation Language [1]

ACTUAL	IS	THRU
ALL	KEY	TIMES
ALLOWED	KEYS	TO
ALTER	LAST	TYPE
ALWAYS	LINKED	UPDATE
AND	LOCATION (LOC)	USING
ARE	LOCK	VALUE
AREA	LOCKS	VIA
AREA-ID	MANDATORY (MAND)	VIRTUAL
ASCENDING (ASC)	MANUAL	WHERE
AUTOMATIC (AUTO)	MEMBER	WITHIN
BINARY (BIN)	MEMBERS	
BIT	MODE	
BY	MODIFY	
CALC	NAME	
CALC-KEY	NEXT	
CALL	NONEXCLUSIVE (NEXCL)	
CHARACTER (CHAR)	NOT	
CHECK	NULL	
CLOSE	OCCURS	
COMMENT	OF	
COMPLEX	ON	
COPY	OPEN	
CURRENT	OPTIONAL (OPT)	
DATA-EASE-KEY (DBKEY)	OR	
DECIMAL (DEC)	ORDER	
DECODING	OWNER	
DEFINED	PERMANENT	
DELETE	PICTURE (PIC)	
DESCENDING (DESC)	PRIOR	
DIRECT	PRIVACY	
DISPLAY	PROCEDURE (PROC)	
DUPLICATES (DUP)	PROCESSABLE	
DURING	PROTECTED (PROT)	
DYNAMIC	RANGE	
ENCODING	REAL	
EQUAL	RECORD	
ERROR	RECORD-NAME	
EXCLUSIVE (EXCL)	REMOVE	
FIND	RESULT	
FIRST	RETRIEVAL (RETR)	
FIXED	SCHEMA	
FLOAT	SEARCH	
FOR	SELECTION	
GET	SET	
IDENTIFIED	SORTED	
IMMATERIAL	SOURCE	
IN	STORE	
INDEX	SYSTEM	
INDEXED	TEMPORARY (TEMP)	
INSERT	THEN	
INSERTION	THIS	

sheet. Lowercase words are generic terms which are replaced on the coding sheet by names or values selected by the programmer.

The underlined words are *required* when the format of which they are a part is used. The nonunderlined words are *optional* and may be omitted.

When square brackets are used around items listed one above the other, *one or zero* of the items may be used. Square brackets thus represent an option.

$$\begin{bmatrix} A \\ B \\ C \end{bmatrix}$$ *Option:* A, B, C, or none of these may be used.

When curved brackets are used, one and only one of the enclosed items must be used. Curved brackets thus represent a selection:

$$\begin{Bmatrix} A \\ B \\ C \end{Bmatrix}$$ *Selection:* A, B, or C must be used.

Double-line brackets represent a multiple selection. At least one of items listed one above the other must be used, and more than one can be used:

$$\left\Vert \begin{matrix} A \\ B \\ C \end{matrix} \right\Vert$$ *Multiple selection:* A, B, or C must be used and more than one of these can be used.

Three periods in succession indicate that the preceding syntactical unit, in brackets or not, may be repeated.

[, A] . . .   *Repetition:* A, A, A may be used.

Several words used in the Data Description Language refer to basic functions which can be performed on the data by a Data Manipulation Language. These words include the following:

For retrieval functions:

F IND	(locate a record)
GET	(fetch data from a record)

For update functions:

MODIFY	(change data in a record)
STORE	(a record into a data base)
DELETE	(a record from a data base)
INSERT	(a record into a set)
REMOVE	(a record from a set)
ORDER	(reorder the records in a set logically)

For control functions:

OPEN	(make parts of the data base available for user processing)
CLOSE	(make parts of the data base unavailable for user processing)

SCHEMA ENTRY   The entry describing a *schema* will be the first entry. There is only one such entry in a schema. The schema entry can have three clauses, a schema NAME clause, a PRIVACY clause, and an ON clause saying what the data-base management system should do when an error is detected.

SCHEMA NAME IS schema-name-1

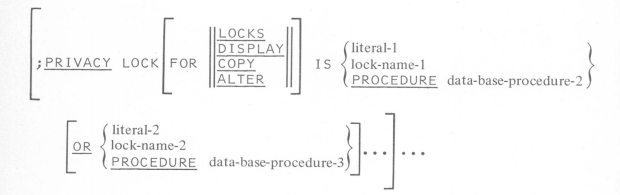

Only the first of these three clauses is mandatory (as indicated by the square brackets). The coding illustration in Fig. 11.2 uses only the first clause of the schema entry.

Both the ON and the PRIVACY clause refer to four operations on the data base which are intended to be performed only by the data-base administrator: ALTER, COPY, DISPLAY, and LOCKS. These operations permit the data-base administrator to organize, monitor, reorganize, and restructure the data base as its requirements change, and to maintain and develop each schema. The four operations are described as follows:

1. ALTER: This operation permits the alternation of all the schema, with the exception of the privacy lock clauses.

2. COPY: This operation permits the extraction of information from the schema for the purpose of constructing a subschema.

3. DISPLAY: This operation permits viewing of the schema with the exception of the privacy locks.

4. LOCKS: This operation allows the viewing, creating, or changing of privacy locks.

AREA
ENTRY

In defining an *area* there are four possible clauses. Only that which names the area is mandatory:

AREA NAME IS area-name-1

[;AREA IS TEMPORARY]

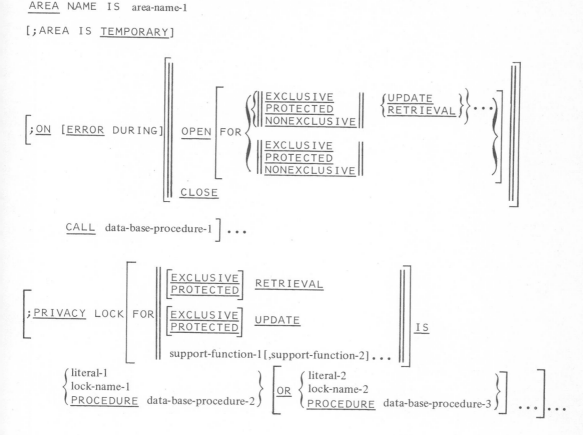

As is often the case, the program in Fig. 11.2 uses only the first of these clauses.

The ON clause specifies the procedure to be executed when an area is opened or closed. There may be a separate ON clause for each type of OPEN and for the CLOSE function.

If the area is to be associated with the execution of only certain run-units (tasks), then the clause [AREA IS TEMPORARY] is used. A run-unit which refers to that area is then allocated a private, unique occurrence of the area.

RECORD ENTRY
The record description has two components. First there is a record subentry for the record as a whole. Second, there are data subentries for the data items and data aggregates in the record.

The record subentry has the following format:

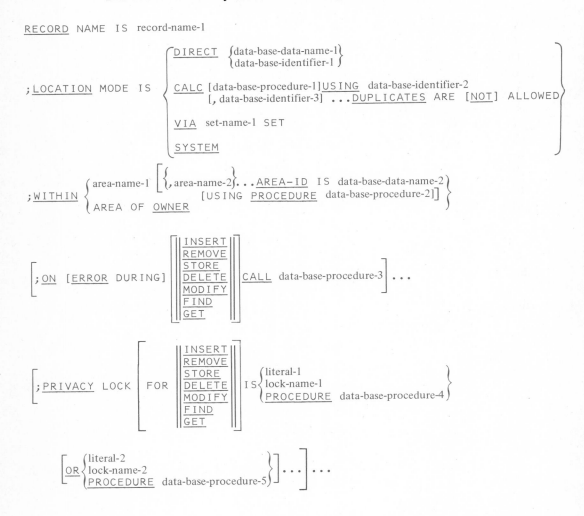

The LOCATION clause specifies the means of assigning keys to records, these keys being used by the data-base management system to locate a record occurrence or to place a record occurrence in the data base. There are four types of location mode: DIRECT, CALC, VIA, and SYSTEM. The DIRECT mode uses a data name, and the data-base management system has some means, for example an index, of using this to locate or place the record. The CALC mode uses a procedure—an algorithm—which may be named in the LOCATION clause. The procedure can operate on a data-base key (identifier) to locate to the record. The VIA mode implies that the record is found by means of its set occurrence. The SYSTEM mode implies that the owner of the record is SYSTEM as in Fig. 11.7, and the location of the record is determined by the ordering of this singular set.

The WITHIN clause can indicate which *areas* a record is a member of.

The ON clause can specify what procedures are used when errors occur in handling the record.

The PRIVACY clause specifies privacy procedures which apply to the record as a whole. Separate privacy procedures can be declared in the *data subentries* applying the data items or data aggregates within the record.

THE DATA SUBENTRY

The data subentry describes the data items and data aggregates within a record in a similar fashion to the Data Division of a COBOL program. The details are as follows:

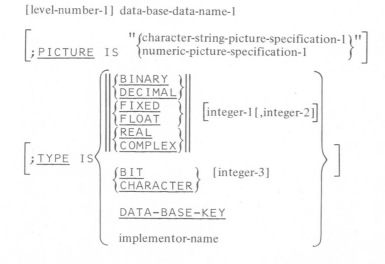

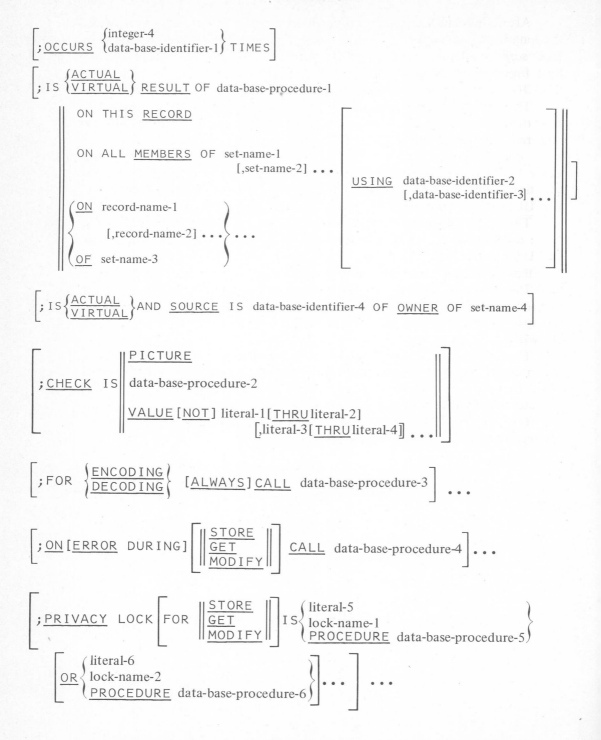

$$\left[;\underline{OCCURS}\ \left\{ \begin{array}{l} \text{integer-4} \\ \text{data-base-identifier-1} \end{array} \right\}\ TIMES \right]$$

$$\left[;\ IS\ \left\{ \begin{array}{l} \underline{ACTUAL} \\ \underline{VIRTUAL} \end{array} \right\}\ \underline{RESULT}\ OF\ \text{data-base-procedure-1} \right.$$

ON THIS <u>RECORD</u>

ON ALL <u>MEMBERS</u> OF set-name-1
               [,set-name-2] ...

$$\left\{ \begin{array}{l} \underline{ON}\ \text{record-name-1} \\ \qquad [,\text{record-name-2}]\ ... \\ \underline{OF}\ \text{set-name-3} \end{array} \right\} ...$$

<u>USING</u> data-base-identifier-2
         [,data-base-identifier-3] ...

$$\left[;\ IS\ \left\{ \begin{array}{l} \underline{ACTUAL} \\ \underline{VIRTUAL} \end{array} \right\} AND\ \underline{SOURCE}\ IS\ \text{data-base-identifier-4}\ OF\ \underline{OWNER}\ OF\ \text{set-name-4} \right]$$

$$\left[;\underline{CHECK}\ IS \left| \begin{array}{l} \underline{PICTURE} \\ \text{data-base-procedure-2} \\ \underline{VALUE}\ [\underline{NOT}]\ \text{literal-1}[\underline{THRU}\ \text{literal-2}] \\ \qquad\qquad [,\text{literal-3}[\underline{THRU}\ \text{literal-4}]]\ ... \end{array} \right| \right]$$

$$\left[;FOR\ \left\{ \begin{array}{l} \underline{ENCODING} \\ \underline{DECODING} \end{array} \right\}\ [\underline{ALWAYS}]\underline{CALL}\ \text{data-base-procedure-3} \right] ...$$

$$\left[;\underline{ON}\ [\underline{ERROR}\ DURING] \left[\left| \begin{array}{l} \underline{STORE} \\ \underline{GET} \\ \underline{MODIFY} \end{array} \right| \right] \underline{CALL}\ \text{data-base-procedure-4} \right] ...$$

$$\left[;\underline{PRIVACY}\ LOCK \left[FOR\ \left| \begin{array}{l} \underline{STORE} \\ \underline{GET} \\ \underline{MODIFY} \end{array} \right| \right] IS \left\{ \begin{array}{l} \text{literal-5} \\ \text{lock-name-1} \\ \underline{PROCEDURE}\ \text{data-base-procedure-5} \end{array} \right\} \right.$$

$$\left. \left[\underline{OR} \left\{ \begin{array}{l} \text{literal-6} \\ \text{lock-name-2} \\ \underline{PROCEDURE}\ \text{data-base-procedure-6} \end{array} \right\} ... \right] ... \right]$$

After the mandatory *data name* clause, the PICTURE clause describes the length and structure of the data item, and the TYPE clause specifies the base, scale, mode, and precision of the data item. An OCCURS clause is used to define a repeating group, saying how many times it occurs. The result is a COBOL-like record description like that on page 142 of this chapter.

The data-item value that a programmer wants may be the result of the execution of a programmed procedure. If this value is maintained in its required form at all times by the data-base management system, it is referred to as the ACTUAL RESULT of a named data-based procedure. If, on the other hand, the value is established by the procedure only when a GET function is executed for that data item, then it is referred to as a VIRTUAL RESULT of the procedure.

The SOURCE clause is used to specify that the value of a data item is to be the same as the value of another specified data item. Again the words ACTUAL OR VIRTUAL determine whether it is kept constantly updated or updated only when a GET function is executed.

The CHECK clause is used to specify a validity-checking procedure to be used whenever the value of a data item is changed or added to the base. It can specify that the value must conform to a specified PICTURE, or that it lies within certain value ranges, or that it is checked by a named procedure.

The ENCODING/DECODING clause specifies that whenever a given data item is retrieved or updated, a named conversion procedure must be used. This may be because the data item is stored in a compacted form to save storage, or an enciphered form for security.

The ON and PRIVACY clauses can be applied to specific data items or data aggregates.

SET
ENTRY
The entry describing a *set* has two major components: a *set subentry* describing characteristics of the set as a whole, and a *member subentry* de-

```
SET NAME IS set-name-1

               ⎧record-name-1⎫
; OWNER IS     ⎨SYSTEM        ⎬
               ⎩             ⎭

⎡        ‖DYNAMIC            ‖⎤
⎢; SET IS ‖PRIOR PROCESSABLE ‖⎥
⎣        ‖                   ‖⎦
```

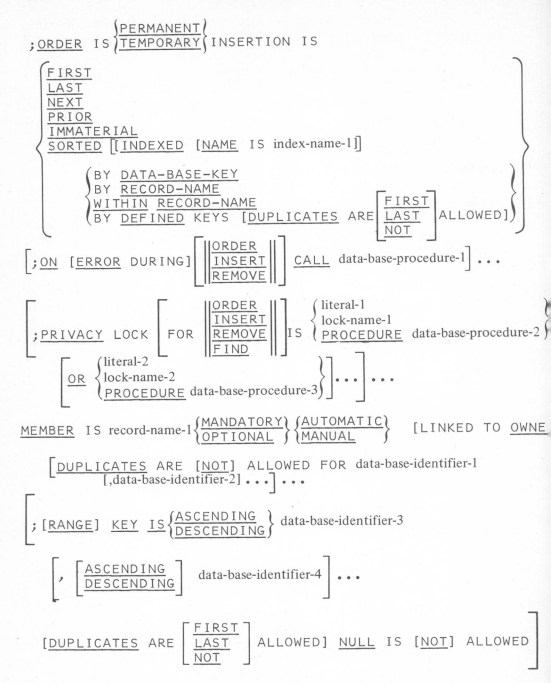

```
               ⎧PERMANENT⎫
;ORDER IS      ⎨TEMPORARY⎬ INSERTION IS
               ⎩         ⎭

  ⎧FIRST                                                                    ⎫
  ⎪LAST                                                                     ⎪
  ⎪NEXT                                                                     ⎪
  ⎪PRIOR                                                                    ⎬
  ⎨IMMATERIAL                                                               ⎪
  ⎪SORTED [[INDEXED [NAME IS index-name-1]]                                 ⎪
  ⎪                                                                         ⎪
  ⎪      ⎧BY DATA-BASE-KEY                                            ⎫     ⎪
  ⎪      ⎪BY RECORD-NAME                                             ⎪      ⎪
  ⎩      ⎨WITHIN RECORD-NAME                                         ⎬      ⎭
         ⎪                           ⎡FIRST⎤                         ⎪
         ⎩BY DEFINED KEYS [DUPLICATES ARE⎢LAST ⎥ ALLOWED]⎭
                                        ⎣NOT  ⎦

          ⎡⎢⎢ORDER ⎢⎢⎤
[;ON [ERROR DURING]⎢⎢⎢INSERT⎢⎢⎢ CALL data-base-procedure-1] ...
          ⎣⎢⎢REMOVE⎢⎢⎦

  ⎡                    ⎢⎢ORDER ⎢⎢      ⎧literal-1                        ⎫
  ⎢;PRIVACY LOCK ⎡FOR ⎢⎢INSERT⎢⎢⎤IS    ⎨lock-name-1                      ⎬
  ⎢                   ⎢⎢REMOVE⎢⎢       ⎩PROCEDURE data-base-procedure-2  ⎭
                     ⎣⎢⎢FIND  ⎢⎢⎦
       ⎡    ⎧literal-2                         ⎫ ⎤
       ⎢OR  ⎨lock-name-2                       ⎬ ⎥ ... ⎥ ...
       ⎣    ⎩PROCEDURE data-base-procedure-3   ⎭ ⎦

                        ⎧MANDATORY⎫ ⎧AUTOMATIC⎫
MEMBER IS record-name-1 ⎨OPTIONAL ⎬ ⎨MANUAL   ⎬   [LINKED TO OWNE
                        ⎩         ⎭ ⎩         ⎭

  ⎡[DUPLICATES ARE [NOT] ALLOWED FOR data-base-identifier-1
  ⎢   [,data-base-identifier-2] ... ] ...

  ⎡                      ⎧ASCENDING ⎫
  ⎢; [RANGE] KEY IS      ⎨DESCENDING⎬ data-base-identifier-3
  ⎣                      ⎩          ⎭

     ⎡  ⎡ASCENDING ⎤                           ⎤
     ⎢, ⎢DESCENDING⎥ data-base-identifier-4   ⎥ ...
     ⎣  ⎣          ⎦                           ⎦

                     ⎡FIRST⎤
   [DUPLICATES ARE   ⎢LAST ⎥ ALLOWED] NULL IS [NOT] ALLOWED
                     ⎣NOT  ⎦
```

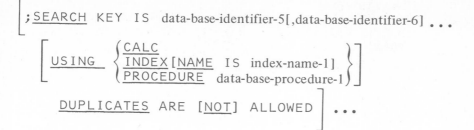

```
[
;SEARCH KEY IS data-base-identifier-5[,data-base-identifier-6] ...

    [          ( CALC                                )]
    | USING   < INDEX [NAME IS index-name-1]         >|
    [          ( PROCEDURE data-base-procedure-1     )]

        DUPLICATES ARE [NOT] ALLOWED ] ...
```

Format 1:

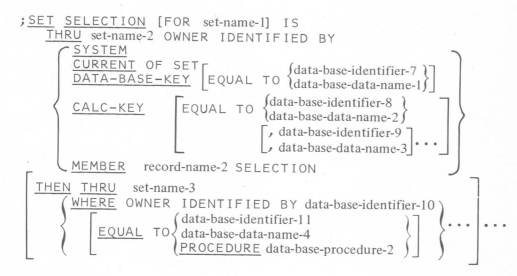

```
;SET SELECTION [FOR set-name-1] IS
     THRU set-name-2 OWNER IDENTIFIED BY
         ( SYSTEM
         | CURRENT OF SET
         | DATA-BASE-KEY [EQUAL TO { data-base-identifier-7  }]
         |                         { data-base-data-name-1   }
         < CALC-KEY     [EQUAL TO { data-base-identifier-8 }
                                  { data-base-data-name-2  }
                                  [, data-base-identifier-9 ] ... ]
                                  [, data-base-data-name-3  ]
         ( MEMBER record-name-2 SELECTION
    [ THEN THRU set-name-3
    | ( WHERE OWNER IDENTIFIED BY data-base-identifier-10 )
    | <              { data-base-identifier-11             > ... ] ...
    | [ EQUAL TO     { data-base-data-name-4               ]
      (              ( PROCEDURE data-base-procedure-2 )   )
```

Format 2:

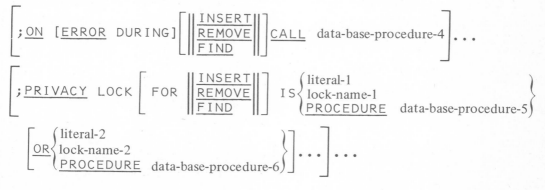

```
;SET SELECTION IS BY PROCEDURE data-base-procedure-3

[                       [||INSERT||]                              ]
|;ON [ERROR DURING]     [||REMOVE|| CALL data-base-procedure-4    ] ...
[                       [||FIND  ||]                              ]

[                   [||INSERT||]       ( literal-1                          )
|;PRIVACY LOCK [ FOR||REMOVE||]  IS   < lock-name-1                         >
[                   [||FIND  ||]       ( PROCEDURE data-base-procedure-5    )

    [  ( literal-2                              )]
    | OR< lock-name-2                           >| ... ] ...
    [  ( PROCEDURE data-base-procedure-6        )]
```

The description gives the set name and the name of its owner. If the set is declared to be DYNAMIC, then no member records can be declared for it. If it is declared to be <u>PRIOR</u> PROCESSABLE, then the data-base management system will select an implementable method which allows the set to be processed as efficiently in a *backward* direction as in a forward direction. (There might be backward-linked pointers between member records, for example, as well as forward-linked pointers.)

The ORDER clause specifies where a record occurrence will be inserted into a set occurrence, for example:

FIRST:	Immediately following the owner record.
LAST:	Immediately preceding the owner record.
NEXT:	Immediately following the member record most recently selected.
PRIOR:	Immediately preceding the member record most recently selected.
IMMATERIAL:	Don't care.
SORTED:	So as to preserve a sort sequence among the member records, based on record name (record type), primary-key or secondary-key data items, or key within record name.

SET MEMBERS In addition to describing the set as a whole, the system designer writes a subentry relating to members of the set. The following clauses may be used.

The first clause gives the name of the member record type and can indicate whether its membership is MANDATORY or OPTIONAL and AUTOMATIC or MANUAL.

The primary KEY of the record (data-base identifier) is specified, and where the member records are to be kept in a sorted sequence, a clause states whether the order is ASCENDING or DESCENDING by key value. Another clause indicates whether DUPLICATE key values or NULL key values are allowed.

One or more secondary keys (SEARCH KEY) may also be specified, and the method of searching can be indicated—CALC, INDEX, or PROCEDURE.

The record in Fig. 5.3 might be declared to be a member of a set, with an ascending primary key and two secondary indices, as follows:

```
MEMBER IS EMPLOYEE MANDATORY AUTOMATIC; KEY IS
ASCENDING EMPLOYEE-NUMBER DUPLICATES NOT ALLOWED;
SEARCH KEY IS GRADE USING INDEX; SEARCH KEY IS
SKILL-CODE USING INDEX.
```

A clause may be used to define rules for selection of the occurrence of a set for the purpose of inserting or accessing a member record. There are two formats for SELECTION. Format 2 simply names a procedure to be used:

SET SELECTION IS BY PROCEDURE XYZ

Format 1 selection contains a variety of options as shown. One use of it is when the selection process is done by using a *path* through several sets. This is illustrated in Fig. 11.11.

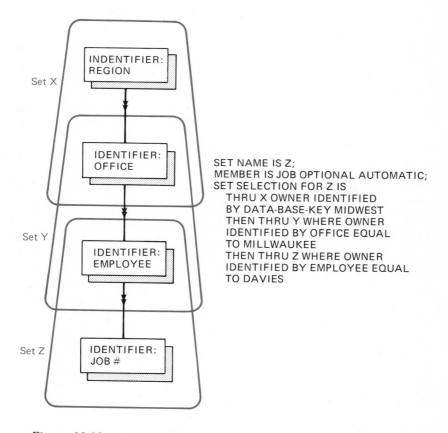

SET NAME IS Z;
MEMBER IS JOB OPTIONAL AUTOMATIC;
SET SELECTION FOR Z IS
   THRU X OWNER IDENTIFIED
   BY DATA-BASE-KEY MIDWEST
   THEN THRU Y WHERE OWNER
   IDENTIFIED BY OFFICE EQUAL
   TO MILLWAUKEE
   THEN THRU Z WHERE OWNER
   IDENTIFIED BY EMPLOYEE EQUAL
   TO DAVIES

Figure 11.11   An example of SET SELECTION format 1 used to locate a JOB record in the above schema. This selection involves a *path* through several sets.

SUBSCHEMAS   When an application programmer uses a CODASYL data base, like any other data base, he must describe, or have described for him, a local view of the data—a subschema. In a CODASYL system it seems natural that the subschema should be described in the COBOL language, or a natural extension of COBOL. Much CODASYL software is designed to this end. However, the CODASYL authorities stress that a CODASYL data base is intended to be used by a variety of programming languages.

Of rapidly increasing importance are languages which are designed for problem solving or other interaction at a terminal—languages such as BASIC and APL, and to some users PL/I, the higher-level data manipulation languages. Terminal users employing such languages often need access to a data base and hence need subschemas. These subschemas need be created for them with statements that look like a subset of the CODASYL DDL which we have described.

REFERENCES

1. National Bureau of Standards Handbook 113, *CODASYL Data Description Language Journal of Development*, U.S. Department of Commerce, National Bureau of Standards. Washington, D.C., 1974.

2. R.W. Engles, "An Analysis of the April 1971 Data Base Task Group Report," *Proc. ACM SIGFIDET Workshop on Data Description, Access and Control, 1971.*

BOOK STRUCTURE

Chapter 12 gives a second example of a data description language.

12 IBM'S DATA LANGUAGE/I

The data description language on which IBM is basing its main data-base products is DL/I (Data Language/I) [1]. This language is used in the data-base management system IMS (Information Management System) [2, 3, 4], and CICS (Customer Information Control System) can be used with a DL/I data base [5]. Some products of independent software houses can also work with DL/I structured data, for example, the Informatics MARK IV data-base management system.

DL/I is used to specify both the logical representation of the data base (schema) and the physical representation. The physical representation is described in terms of a number of standard techniques for physical storage layout, each with their own addressing techniques, and these are referred to as *access methods*. We will discuss access methods in Part II. The logical data description is written separately from the physical description. Nevertheless, it is dependent on the physical description and does not describe the data completely unless the physical description also exists. Changes can be made in the physical description (and hence the physical storage layout) without changing the logical description.

DL/I
VOCABULARY
When discussing specific data-base software it is often necessary to modify our vocabulary to conform to that used with the software. Figure 12.1 compares the terms used in DL/I with those used in the CODASYL language.

A *field* in DL/I is equivalent to a *data item* in the CODASYL language. A *record* and a *data aggregate* as defined in the CODASYL language are both

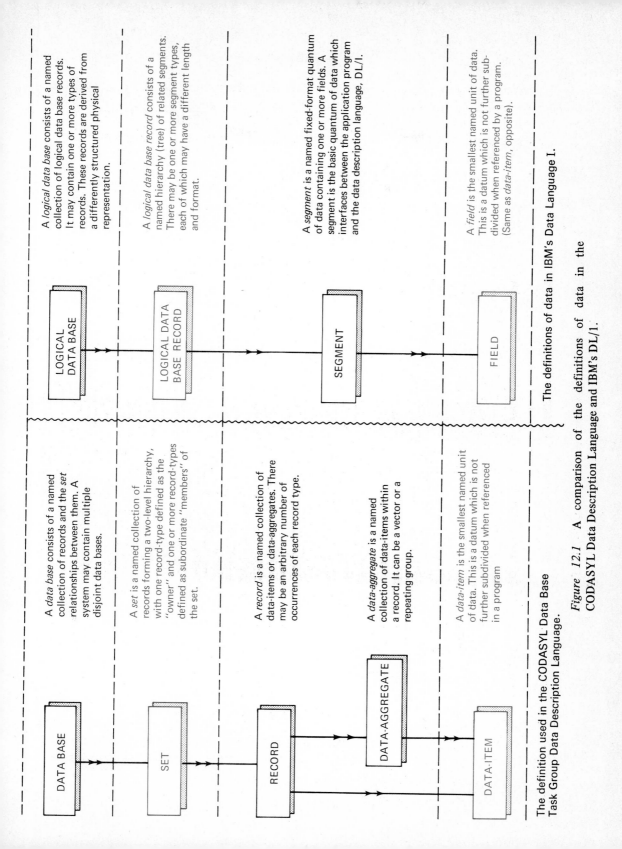

A *logical data base* consists of a named collection of logical data base records. It may contain one or more types of records. These records are derived from a differently structured physical representation.

A *logical data base record* consists of a named hierarchy (tree) of related segments. There may be one or more segment types, each of which may have a different length and format.

A *segment* is a named fixed-format quantum of data containing one or more fields. A segment is the basic quantum of data which interfaces between the application program and the data description language, DL/I.

A *field* is the smallest named unit of data. This is a datum which is not further sub-divided when referenced by a program. (Same as *data-item*, opposite).

LOGICAL DATA BASE

LOGICAL DATA BASE RECORD

SEGMENT

FIELD

The definitions of data in IBM's Data Language I.

A *data base* consists of a named collection of records and the *set* relationships between them. A system may contain multiple disjoint data bases.

A *set* is a named collection of records forming a two-level hierarchy, with one record-type defined as the "owner" and one or more record-types defined as subordinate "members" of the set.

A *record* is a named collection of data-items or data-aggregates. There may be an arbitrary number of occurrences of each record type.

A *data-aggregate* is a named collection of data-items within a record. It can be a vector or a repeating group.

A *data-item* is the smallest named unit of data. This is a datum which is not further subdivided when referenced in a program

DATA BASE

SET

RECORD

DATA-AGGREGATE

DATA-ITEM

The definition used in the CODASYL Data Base Task Group Data Description Language.

Figure 12.1 A comparison of the definitions of data in the CODASYL Data Description Language and IBM's DL/1.

regarded as a named collection of data items which can have an arbitrary number of occurrences, and both are called a *segment* in DL/I. A *segment*, unlike a *data aggregate*, is individually addressable and all data are stored in segments. DL/I has no need to distinguish between a "data aggregate" and a record; both are segments.

A *logical data-base record* in DL/I is a hierarchically related collection of segments. A *logical data base* is a collection of logical data-base records. A data-base record in DL/I might be thought of as corresponding roughly to a *set* in the CODASYL, but, as we will see, the differences are more fundamental than the similarities.

A COLLECTION OF TREES   Whereas the basic construct of the CODASYL language is a *set* and complicated structures can be built from sets, the basic construct of DL/I is a tree. A DL/I data base consists of a collection of trees of segments such as that in Fig. 8.11. Each tree is laid out physically on the file units, the details of the layout being governed by one of the standard DL/I access methods. There can be *logical* linkages between trees. Two of the access methods (HSAM and HISAM) lay out the tree of segments serially, as on tape, for example. Two of the access methods (HDAM and HIDAM) lay out the tree so that there can be direct access to any segments, as on disk or other direct access storage device. The letter I in the abbreviation for the access method means that the index is used. The letter H means that the structure is hierarchical or in the form of a tree. The four methods of layout of the trees physically are thus

HSAM: Hierarchical sequential-access method

HISAM: Hierarchical index sequential-access method

HDAM: Hierarchical direct-access method

HIDAM: Hierarchical indexed direct-access method

We will discuss these access methods in Part II.

A tree can have up to 15 levels. Each level can have multiple segment types. Sometimes only one level (i.e., a solitary root segment) exists. A data base may consist of many of these physical trees.

LOGICAL CHILDREN   In constructing the trees, pointers are used to avoid duplicating the same segment in different trees. In Fig. 12.2, for example, an EMPLOYEE segment

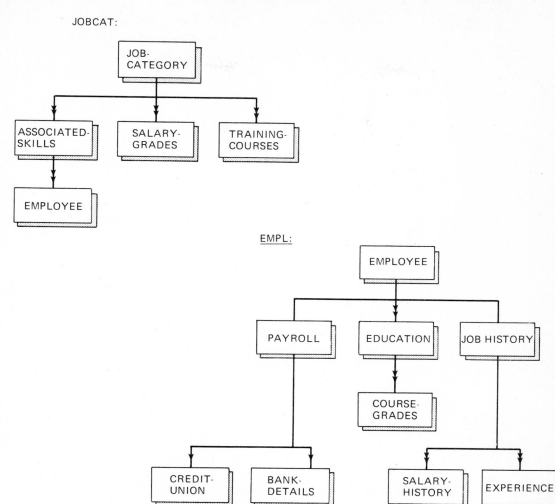

Figure 12.2   Two physical tree structures. A variety of different logical structures may be derived from this physical structure using DL/I.

appears in two separate trees. If the trees were constructed in this form, there would be redundancy between them in the EMPLOYEE segment. The EMPLOYEE segment in the JOBCAT tree is therefore replaced by the pointer segment shown in Fig. 12.3. The pointer segment gives the addresses of the relevant EMPLOYEE segments.

The EMPLOYEE segment in the EMPL tree then becomes, *in effect*, a child of the ASSOCIATED SKILLS segment in the JOBCAT tree. It is referred to as a *logical child* because the trees still remain separate physically.

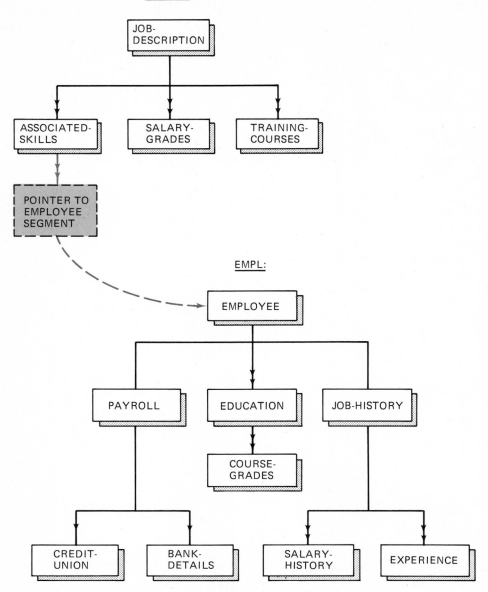

Figure 12.3 The two employee segments in Fig. 12.2 are redundant. One of them is therefore replaced with a pointer segment.

The pointers are referred to as *logical child pointers*. In a DL/I data base, many logical child pointers may be used. As well as being used to avoid physical redundancy, they make it possible to derive multiple logical structures from the physical trees.

THE LOGICAL
DATA-BASE RECORD
The organization perceived by an application programmer is also a *tree* of segments. However, it may be different from any tree that exists *physically*. The tree which the application programmer perceives is referred to as a *logical data-base* structure. Figure 12.4 shows a logical data base. This tree will be derived from the physical tree, EMPL, in Fig. 12.3.

The segments in a logical data-base structure will be presented to the application program starting with the root segment and progressing through its subtrees from left to right. Each subtree will be presented starting with *its* root segment and progressing through *its* subtrees from left to right. Thus, the logical data-base structure shown in Fig. 12.4 would be presented in the sequence shown in Fig. 12.5.

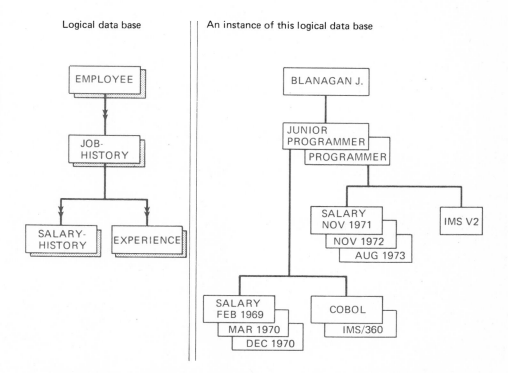

Logical data base | An instance of this logical data base

Figure 12.4   One of the many logical data-base structures which can be derived from the physical structure in Fig. 12.3.

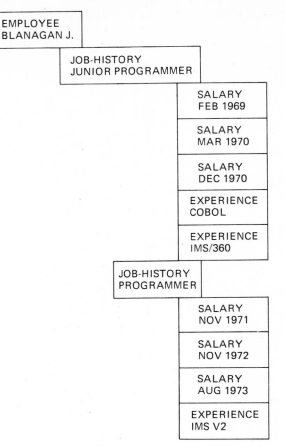

Figure 12.5 The sequence in which the segments in Fig. 12.4 are presented to the application program when used sequentially.

The programmer may read the segments in a logical data base with the following types of call statements:

1. GET UNIQUE (GU): To retrieve a named segment within the data base.

2. GET NEXT (GN): To retrieve the next segment in the sequence shown in Fig. 12.5.

3. GET NEXT WITHIN PARENT (GNP): To retrieve the lower-level segments of a parent segment which is established by looking back to the previous GET UNIQUE or GET NEXT call which was successfully completed. If no further segment exists with that percentage, a NOT FOUND status code is returned.

4. GET HOLD UNIQUE (GHU).

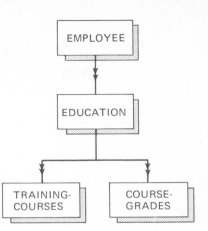

Figure 12.6   To derive this logical data base from the physical trees in Fig. 12.3, a pointer segment is needed connecting the trees as shown in Fig. 12.7.

5. GET HOLD NEXT (GHN).

6. GET HOLD NEXT WITHIN PARENT (GHNP): Calls 4, 5, and 6 are the same as calls 1, 2, and 3 except that they indicate that the segment is to be updated or deleted. No other operation may proceed on the segment until the HOLD condition is cleared.

7. REPLACE (REPL): This call is used after one of the previous three GET HOLD calls to update a segment.

8. DELETE (DLET): This call is used after one of the three GET HOLD calls to delete a segment. The segment may not be *physically* deleted until the data base is reorganized; it may merely be flagged to indicate deletion.

9. INSERT (ISRT): This call is used to insert new occurrences of a segment type into a data base.

When any of these operations are performed on a logical data base, appropriate status or error messages are returned to the application program.

POINTERS BETWEEN TREES   The logical data-base structure in Fig. 12.4 is derived from one physical tree. Sometimes they are derived from multiple physical trees by means of pointers connecting the trees. Figure 12.6 shows a logical data base which contains segments from both of the trees in Fig. 12.3. To construct it, a *logical child* pointer segment is added under the EDUCATION segment in the EMPL tree, pointing to the TRAINING COURSES segment in the JOBCAT tree, as shown in Fig. 12.7.

Logical parent or *logical twin* pointers may be used similarly, either within a physical tree or spanning different trees. For example, if each of the TRAINING COURSES is part of a particular EDUCATION program, the EDUCATION segment in the EMPL tree can be made the *logical parent* of the TRAINING COURSES segment in the JOBCAT tree. The pointers

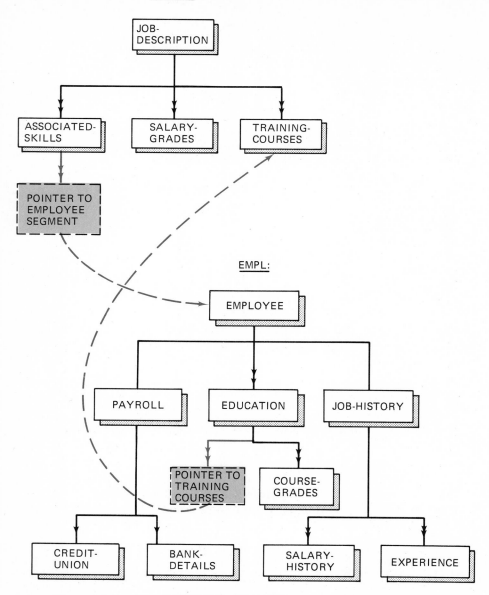

Figure 12.7 The TRAINING COURSES segment is made a logical child of the EDUCATION segment in order to produce the logical data base shown in Fig. 12.6. There can be many logical linkages between the tree-structured physical data bases of DL/I.

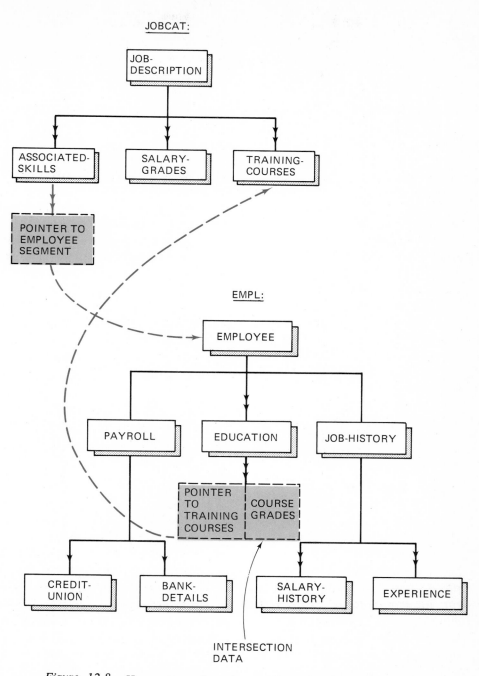

JOBCAT:

JOB-DESCRIPTION

ASSOCIATED-SKILLS

SALARY-GRADES

TRAINING-COURSES

POINTER TO EMPLOYEE SEGMENT

EMPL:

EMPLOYEE

PAYROLL

EDUCATION

JOB-HISTORY

POINTER TO TRAINING COURSES

COURSE GRADES

CREDIT-UNION

BANK-DETAILS

SALARY-HISTORY

EXPERIENCE

INTERSECTION DATA

Figure 12.8 Here an employee's course grades for given training courses are treated as *intersection data*.

between the EDUCATION and TRAINING COURSES segments can then be declared as *bidirectional* pointers.

Again, segments relating to similar entities may exist in different data bases. For example, both a factory data base and a research data base may contain EMPLOYEE segments. A *logical data base* may combine these separate segments if they are interconnected with *logical twin* pointers.

INTERSECTION   In some cases when a relationship exists between
DATA   two segments, there can be data which are relevant
                          to the relationship but not relevant to either
segment by itself. In DL/I terms such data are called *intersection data*.

Figure 9.12 showed different relationships between a MAN segment and a WOMAN segment. The relationship could be called "married," "engaged," "divorced" (or possibly other things). The nature of the relationship could be stored as *intersection data* in a DL/I representation. Again, in Fig. 9.13 each relationship is labeled with a number showing, for example, how many subassemblies are in a product. The number is meaningless if attached to one segment. It has meaning only when it relates to the pair of segments. Such numbers could form intersection data. In each case the information is incomplete without the intersection data associated with the relationship.

The COURSE GRADES in Fig. 12.7 might be better represented as intersection data if they are dependent on the relationship between the employee and his training courses. Figure 12.8 shows them represented as intersection data.

PLEX   As discussed in previous chapters, not all data
STRUCTURES   structures are in the form of trees. DL/I in
                          principle can handle any form of plex structure;
however, it has to do so by establishing logical relationships between the physical tree structures. Many DL/I data bases do this in practice. Some of the implementations of DL/I have restrictions which prevent certain less common plex structures being handled without modification. Usually there is more than one method of representing a plex structure. The designer should choose which method he prefers on the basis of such factors as which access paths are the most frequently used, which need fast response times, which data need efficient disk space utilization, and which need frequent reorganization.

Figure 12.8, for example, represents a plex structure in which

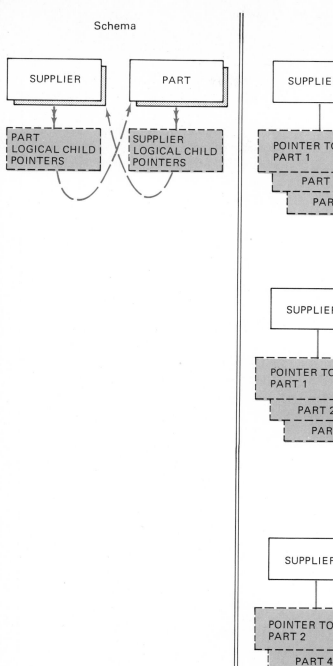
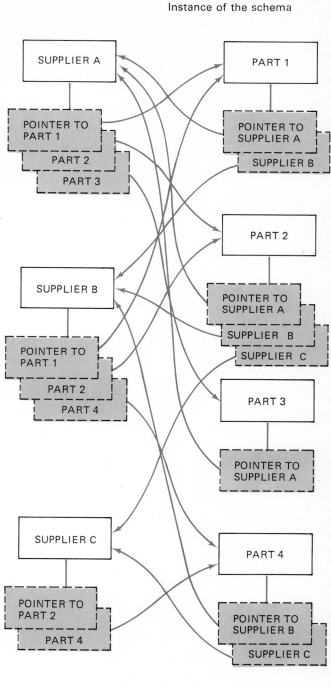

Schema

Instance of the schema

Figure 12.9 An M:M association between segments in separate physical data bases.

TRAINING-COURSES has two parents. One is a physical parent, JOB DESCRIPTION, and the other is a *logical parent*, EDUCATION.

A complex plex structure, like a simple plex structure, can be handled with logical child and logical parent pointers.

MANY-TO-MANY ASSOCIATIONS   A many-to-many association between segments requires two sets of logical-child pointers. The association between suppliers and parts is shown in Fig. 12.9. SUPPLIER is a logical child of PART, and PART is a logical child of SUPPLIER. An instance of the structure is illustrated:

The reader might compare the schema in Fig. 12.9 with that for CODASYL DBTG in Fig. 11.10.

PAIRING   As we commented earlier, when a many-to-many association is used, there are often data related to that association. For example, the PRICE which a given supplier charges for a given part could be linked to the association SUPPLIER ⟷ PART. This could be treated as *intersection data* and placed in a pointer segment. In Fig. 12.9 any intersection data could be placed in either the SUPPLIER logical child or the PART logical child. It might be needed when using either the path from SUPPLIER to PART or that from PART to SUPPLIER. DL/I handles this dual need for intersection data with a technique called *pairing*.

There are two types of pairing—physical pairing and virtual pairing. *Physical pairing* stores the intersection data in *both* pointer segments and automatically updates both. When a new intersection segment is created, it will be automatically created for both; similarly when a segment is deleted or updated.

Physical pairing takes up unnecessary storage because the intersection data are stored twice. *Virtual pairing* avoids this redundancy by storing the data once with pointer linkages to it. Physical pairing is sometimes still used because it gives faster access from one of the parents to the intersection data. Figure 12.10 illustrates the two pairing methods.

In Fig. 12.11 the plex structure of Fig. 6.9 is drawn in a DL/I form using five virtual bidirectional logical relationships. For convenience the virtual bidirectional relationship is shown as one segment with a concatenated key. It is linked by a solid line to its physical parent and by a dotted

Physical bidirectional pairing:

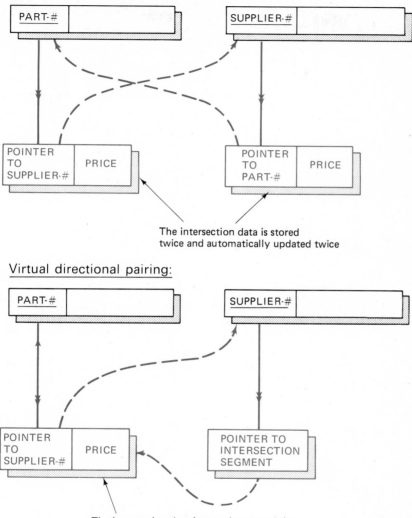

PART-#

SUPPLIER-#

POINTER
TO
SUPPLIER-#   PRICE

POINTER
TO
PART-#   PRICE

The intersection data is stored
twice and automatically updated twice

Virtual directional pairing:

PART-#

SUPPLIER-#

POINTER
TO
SUPPLIER-#   PRICE

POINTER TO
INTERSECTION
SEGMENT

The intersection data is stored once and the
pointers are automatically updated

Figure 12.10   Two methods of *pairing* in DL/I, permitting a bidirectional complex relationship between segments, with intersection
data.

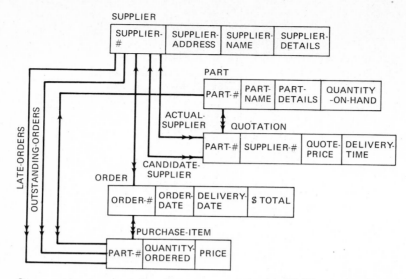

One way to represent the above structure in the DL/I language is as follows:

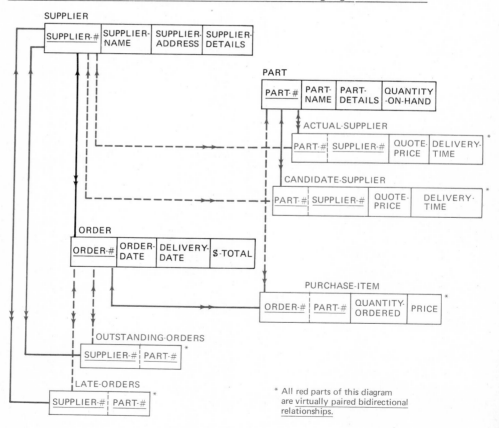

* All red parts of this diagram
  are <u>virtually paired bidirectional
  relationships.</u>

Figure 12.11

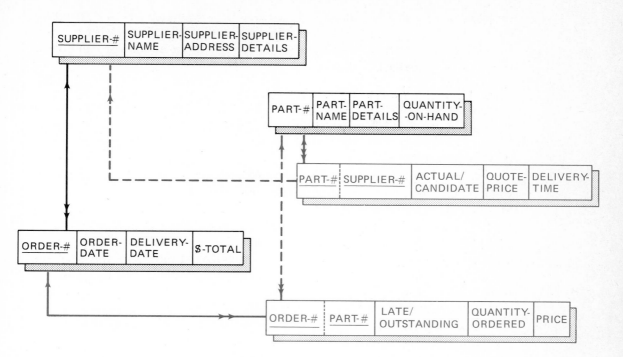

Figure 12.12

line to its logical parent. Three of these segments contain intersection data. The ACTUAL SUPPLIER and CANDIDATE SUPPLIER segments both contain QUOTE PRICE and DELIVERY TIME, but these are not redundant because they are for different suppliers.

　　The link from ORDER to PURCHASE-ITEM is used more frequently than the link from PART to PURCHASE-ITEM; hence the former is made a physical link and the latter a logical link. Similarly, the links from PART to ACTUAL SUPPLIER and CANDIDATE SUPPLIER are made physical.

　　There are several different ways in which the plex structure of Fig. 12.11 could be represented in DL/I. Figure 12.12 shows an alternative, and somewhat simple, way. The indication of whether a QUOTATION is from an actual or candidate supplier is placed in the QUOTATION segment. Similarly, the indication of whether a PURCHASE-ITEM is late or outstanding is placed in the PURCHASE-ITEM segment. This lessens the number of segments and links that are needed. However, it has the disadvantage that when the late (or outstanding) purchase items from a given supplier are needed, all the PURCHASE-ITEM segments for that supplier must be examined. Similarly, all the QUOTATION segments for a given part must be examined to find the quotations of an actual (or candidate) supplier.

SECONDARY
INDICES

Any field (data item) or a group of up to five fields within a segment, not necessarily contiguous, may be declared to be a secondary key, or the basis of a secondary index operation.

A secondary key normally has an M association to some primary key. Figure 12.13 gives two illustrations. In the top one, ANIMAL-TYPE has an M association to ANIMAL-NAME—the double-arrow link. Using this link we might request that the names of all the bears in the data base be listed. In order to follow the link, the DL/I designer can define an index pointer segment. The key of this segment is ANIMAL-TYPE and the segment contains a pointer to the ANIMAL segment. Once the ANIMAL segment is found, any attribute, such as KEEPER or parent pointers, can be used to CAGE-# or ZOO.

The segment containing the secondary key is called the *source segment* and the segment pointed to is called the *target segment*. In the first illustration the source segment and target segment are the same. In the second illustration the target segment is higher in the tree.

In the second illustration two fields are used as secondary keys, ANIMAL-TYPE and COUNTRY-OF-ORIGIN. The index pointer segment therefore has a concatenated key ANIMAL-TYPE + COUNTRY-OF-ORIGIN. We may thus make queries like: "What zoos have Chinese bears?" or using the segments beneath the zoo segment: "What are the cage numbers of Chinese bears and who are their keepers?" The application programmer might request the following user view of information about Chinese bears:

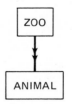

This is a logical data base, derived from the physical data base of Fig. 12.13, and accessed by a secondary index.

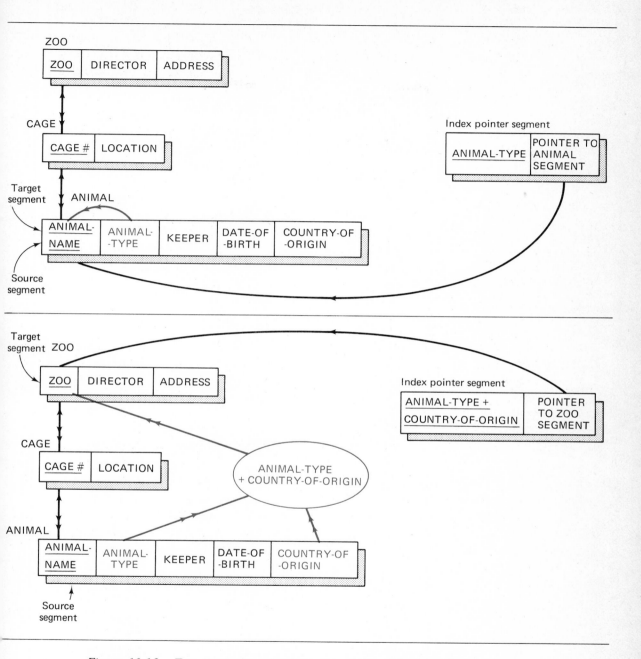

Figure 12.13 Two examples of a secondary index. The secondary keys are shown in red. A secondary index may point to the segment containing the keys or any segment higher in the same physical tree.

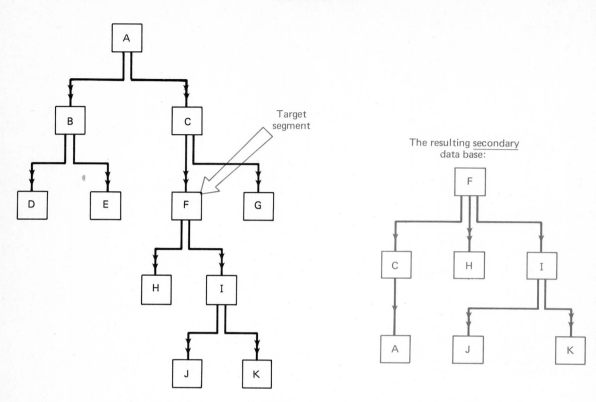

Figure 12.14 The secondary index gives a secondary data-base structure as shown here. The normal DL/I tree-structure processing sequence applies to this secondary structure.

In some cases the target segment is in the middle of a DL/I tree. In that case the segment pointed to is treated as the root of a *secondary data base*. The segments beneath the root of the secondary data base are those that were beneath it in the original plus, to the left, those that were above it. This is shown in Fig. 12.14. The segments in the secondary data base will be presented to the application program in the normal top-bottom, left-right sequence of Fig. 12.5. A secondary index can thus be used for changing the processing or presentation sequence of a data base if that is desirable.

Secondary indices are themselves a data base. They are maintained as such, and they may be processed. Secondary indices may be merged or matched, or specified occurrences selected from them, before they form the entry of a search.

The secondary index must be updated when the source segment is updated. Often this will necessitate the insertion or deletion of index pointer

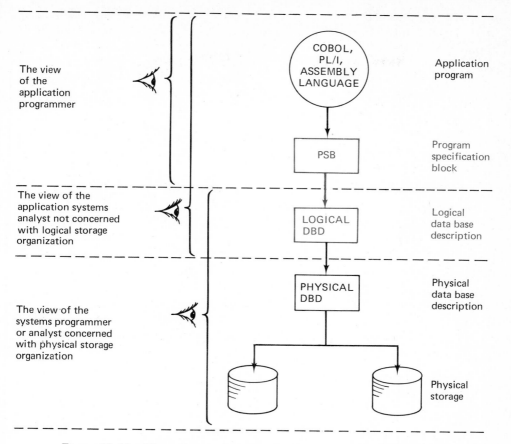

Figure 12.15 Three descriptions which define the data when DL/I is used.

segment occurrences. This maintenance is performed automatically in DL/I systems which use secondary indices.

APPLICATION
PROGRAM
SENSITIVITY

One application program may see one or more types of logical data-base record. For example, an application program using the data base in Fig. 12.3 may perceive only segments of the type in Fig. 12.4. It cannot read the other segments in the data base. Another application program may perceive quite different segments in the same data base. This concept of separation of viewpoints, an essential step toward data independence, is referred to in DL/I circles as *sensitivity*. An application program is defined as being *sensitive* to certain segments. This definition is incorporated into a *program specification block*, which is used by each application program.

There are thus three descriptions of data which form part of a system employing DL/I. They are shown in Fig. 12.15. All three descriptions are coded in DL/I language and are illustrated in Figs. 12.16, 12.17, and 12.18.

PHYSICAL
DATA-BASE
DESCRIPTION

The physical data-base description (DBD) is the only one of the three which gives details of the fields within a segment. The other two describe data at the segment level. Figure 12.16 shows the code which describes the physical tree JOBCAT of Fig. 12.3. The FIELD statements give the name, length, type of representation, and position in the segment of each field. For fields which are a segment *key*, the field name is followed by the phrase SEG, U, meaning that the field is *sequenced* (i.e., a key) and *unique* (i.e., no two occurrences of the key can have the same value). Thus, in the JOBDESCR segment, FIELD NAME = (JOBCODE, SEQ, U) means that JOBCODE is the key and can have only unique values. If the statement had read NAME = (JOBCODE, SEQ, M), multiple occurrences of the key JOBCODE could have had the same value.

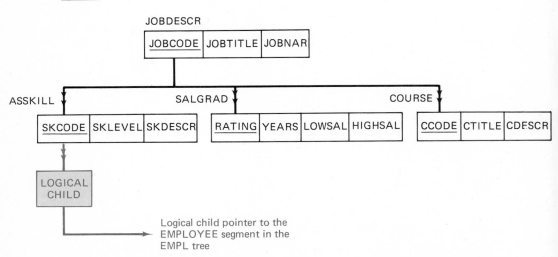

Figure 12.16   Physical data-base description. This is the JOBCAT tree of Fig. 12.3 showing the coded names of segments and fields. It is described in a DL/I physical data-base description as shown opposite.

Figure 12.16 (a physical database description coded on a programming form):

```
DBD      NAME=JOBCAT,ACCESS=HDAM,RMNAME=(RAMDMODL,1,500,824)
DATASET  DD1=JCHDAM,DEVICE=3330,BLOCK=1,SCAN=5
SEGM     NAME=JOBDESCR,BYTES=340,FREQ=1000,PTR=T,PARENT=0
FIELD    NAME=(JOBCODE,SEQ,U),BYTES=3,START=1,TYPE=C
FIELD    NAME=JOBTITLE,BYTES=40,START=4,TYPE=C
FIELD    NAME=JOBNAR,BYTES=300,START=44,TYPE=C
SEGM     NAME=SKILDESC,BYTES=80,FREQ=10,PTR=T,PARENT=JOBDESCR
LCHILD   NAME=(EMPLOYEE,SKILL)
FIELD    NAME=SKILLEVEL,BYTES=2,START=3,TYPE=C
FIELD    NAME=SKILDESCR,BYTES=60,START=5,TYPE=C
SEGM     NAME=SALGRAD,BYTES=16,FREQ=8,PTR=P,PARENT=JOBDESCR
FIELD    NAME=(RATING,SEQ),BYTES=2,START=1,TYPE=P
FIELD    NAME=YEARS,BYTES=2,START=3,TYPE=P
FIELD    NAME=LOWSAL,BYTES=4,START=9,TYPE=P
FIELD    NAME=HIGHSAL,BYTES=4,START=13,TYPE=P
SEGM     NAME=COURSE,BYTES=35,FREQ=30,PTR=T,PARENT=JOBDESCR
FIELD    NAME=(CCODE,SEQ,U),BYTES=3,START=1,TYPE=C
FIELD    NAME=CTITLE,BYTES=4,START=4,TYPE=C
FIELD    NAME=CDESCR,BYTES=50,START=5,TYPE=C
DBDGEN
FINISH
END
```

Annotations on the form:
- Physical details of the access method and storage device
- C means data in the form of characters
- P means packed decimal data
- Can occur up to 30 times
- SEQ indicates the key (sequenced) field

Figure 12.16 (cont.)

The SEGM statements give the name and size of each segment and the maximum number of times that segment can occur in the data base. Thus, SEGM NAME = JOBDESCR, BYTES = 343, FREQ = 1000 means that segment JOBDESCR is 343 bytes in length and can occur up to 1000 times in the physical data base. The segment statements also define the structure of the physical tree. SEGM NAME = ASSKILL ... PARENT = JOBDESCR indicates that JOBDESCR is the physical parent of ASSKILL. Only the root segment does not have a PARENT clause.

The SEGM statement may also include information about how the tree is structured physically. PTR = T in Fig. 12.16 means that *twin* pointers are used in the physical structure. The physical structure will be discussed in Chapter 24.

The LCHILD statement with NAME = (EMPLOYEE, EMPL) describes the logical child segment which points to the EMPLOYEE segment in a separate physical tree called EMPL (Fig. 12.3).

The top line of code in Fig. 12.16 gives the type of physical data-base organization, HDAM (hierarchical direct-access method) in this case. The second line describes the nature of the data set, indicating the block size it uses and the type of storage device. We will discuss these descriptions of physical organization later.

The last three statements in Fig. 12.16 are DBDGEN, which signifies the end of the DBD generation control cards for this data base; FINISH, which is an instruction to the link-edit program; and END, which indicates the end-of-input card to the operating system assembler.

LOGICAL DATA-BASE DESCRIPTION

Figure 12.17 shows a description of one of the many logical data bases which can be derived from the two physical trees in Fig. 12.8.

The top line gives the name of this data base, NAME = SKILLDB, and indicates that it is a logical data base, ACCESS = LOGICAL.

The SEGM statements again show the parent-child relationship between the segments. For example, the SKILL segment is the parent of the EMPLOYEE segment, and so SEGM NAME = EMPLOYEE, PARENT = SKILL is written.

Each SEGM statement shows the physical derivation of the segment in a SOURCE clause. The SKILL segment has the clause SOURCE = ((ASSKILL,,JOBCAT)), showing that this segment is the ASSKILL segment in the physical tree called JOBCAT. In some cases the segment could contain only the key field from the physical segment. In this case the work KEY

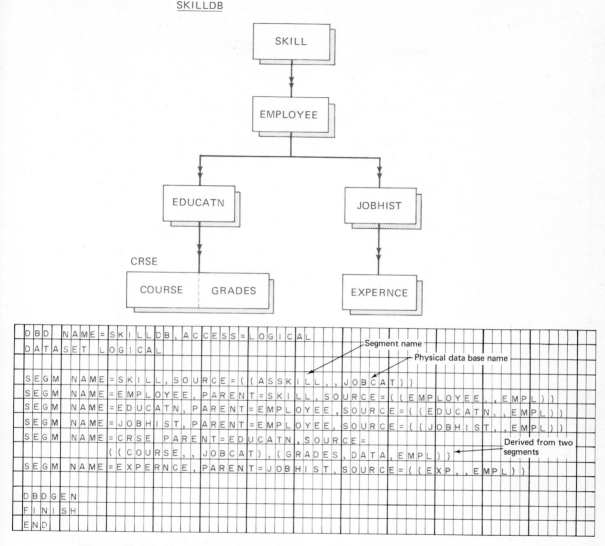

Figure 12.17 Logical data-base description. This logical data base, called SKILLDB, is derived from the physical data base of Fig. 12.8. It is described in DL/I as shown.

would be included in the SOURCE clause, e.g., SOURCE = ((ASSKILL, KEY, JOBCAT)).

The segment named CRSE is derived from two physical segments in Fig. 12.8. It combines the training course segment from the JOBCAT tree and the intersection data, giving course grades from the EMPL tree. The

SOURCE statement therefore reads SOURCE = ((COURSE,,JOBCAT), (GRADE, DATA, EMPL)).

The data-base description ends, as before, with DBDGEN, FINISH, and END.

**PROGRAM
SPECIFICATION
BLOCK DESCRIPTION**

Various different subschemas can be derived from the schema of Fig. 12.17. Fig. 12.18 shows one of them and gives the coding of its *program specification block.* The application program which

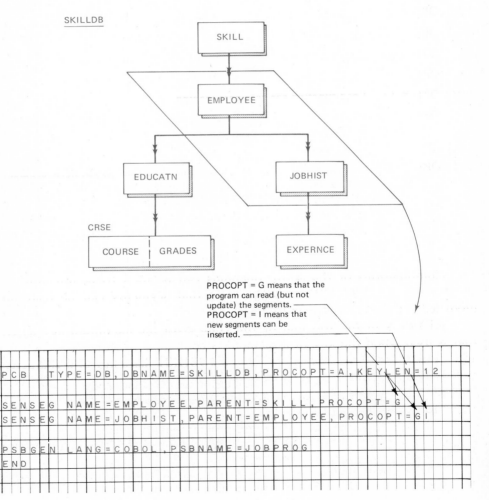

Figure 12.18

employs this program specification is sensitized to the EMPLOYEE and JOBHIST segments only, EMPLOYEE being the parent of JOBHIST.

The PROCOPT clauses say what kind of processing is permitted when the subschema is used. They are employed to limit the programmer's activity when accessing the data base. PROCOPT = G, for example, means that the program can GET (i.e., read) the segment or data base in question but cannot change or delete the data or insert new segments. The PROCOPT operands include the following:

PROCOPT = G: Get.

PROCOPT = R: Replace (i.e., modify the segment).

PROCOPT = I: Insert new segments.

PROCOPT = D: Delete segments.

PROCOPT = A: Any or all of the functions above.

PROCOPT = L: Load function for data-base loading.

PROCOPT = xS: Where x is one of the above operands (G, R, I, D, A, or L) and S means that the segments can be read, inserted, or written in ascending sequence only.

PROCOPT = K: Key only. The segment is not moved to the application program's work area. In the subschema of Fig. 12.18, if PROCOPT = K were written in the EMPLOYEE segment, the program could not read the data in that segment but could give a GET NEXT command to read the JOBHIST segments relating to the EMPLOYEE.

Combinations of the above operands can be used to permit multiple functions; e.g., PROCOPT = GRI means that segments can be read and modified and that new segments can be inserted.

KEYLEN in the top line of the code gives the maximum key length that is used when the key of a segment is combined with that of its parent and ancestors in the subschema. Thus, if JOBHIST has a key of 5 characters and EMPLOYEE has a key of 7, KEYLEN = 12 is written. The concatenated key which defines the lowest segment can have this number of characters.

The PSBGEN line states that the program which uses the subschema in Fig. 12.18 is written in COBOL and that the PBSNAME is JOBPROG. Multiple programs can use the JOBPROG subschema.

REFERENCES

1. *Data Language/I – System/370 DOS/VS, General Information Manual GH20–1246,* IBM, White Plains, N.Y., 1974.

2. *Information Management System Virtual Storage (IMS/VS), General Information Manual GH20–1260,* IBM, White Plains, N.Y., 1974.

3. *Information Management System/360, Version 2, Application Programming Reference Manual SH20–0912,* IBM, White Plains, N.Y., 1974.

4. *Information Management System/360, Version 2, System Programming Reference Manual SH20–0911,* IBM, White Plains, N.Y., 1974.

5. *Interactive Query Facility (IQF) for IMS/360 Version 2, General Information Manual GH20–1074,* IBM, White Plains, N.Y., 1974.

BOOK STRUCTURE

Chapter 13 illustrates a third form of logical data structure:

or a third type of language for the logical description of data:

Tuple - a related set of values pg. 53

from 228

13 RELATIONAL DATA BASES

Throughout the history of engineering a principle seems to emerge: *Great engineering is simple engineering.* Ideas which become too cumbersome, inflexible, and problematic tend to be replaced with newer, conceptually cleaner ideas which, compared to the old, are aesthetic in their simplicity. When a programmer's block diagram looks like a tangled cobweb, the time has come to rethink the entire program.

Data-base systems run the danger of becoming cumbersome, inflexible, and problematic. The logical linkages tend to multiply as new applications are added and as users request that new forms of query be answerable with the data. A high level of complexity will build up in many data-base systems. Unless the designers have conceptual clarity they will weave a tangled web.

It is possible to avoid the entanglements that build up in tree and plex structures, by a technique called *normalization*. Normalization techniques have been designed and much advocated by E. F. Codd [1, 2, 3, 4]. This chapter and the next are about the principles that Codd would employ in the design of data bases. These principles relate to the user's view of the data or to the *logical* description of the data. It is very important to note that they do not apply directly to its physical representation. There are many ways in which a Codd data base could be *physically* structured.

By means of data management software the user's view of data can be kept entirely separate from the physical representation of data, and the physical representation and the hardware can be changed, if necessary, without changing the user's *logical* description of the data. Given this independence, one consideration is of overriding importance in the logical data description: *the convenience of the majority of application programmers and users.* We must search for a way of describing the data that

(1) can be understood easily by users with no training in programming; (2) makes it possible to add new data items, records, and associations to the data base without changing the existing subschemas and hence changing the application programs; and (3) permits the maximum flexibility in handling unanticipated uses of data or spontaneous inquiries at terminals.

As we will indicate, tree, plex-structured, and pointer-linked logical data representations in general can inhibit many changes to data that may be needed as a data base grows, and the growth can *play havoc* with ill-founded logical representations of data and hence with the application programs.

**TABULAR
REPRESENTATION**

Often the most natural way to represent data to a nonprogramming user is with a two-dimensional table such as that in Fig. 5.3. The user is familiar with and can understand, remember, and visualize two-dimensional tables. Just as a plex structure representation can be reduced to a tree representation with some redundancy (Fig. 9.9), so *any* representation can be reduced to a group of two-dimensional flat files with some redundancy. *Normalization* is a step-by-step process for replacing associations between data such as those in the previous two chapters with associations in a two-dimensional tabular form. The tables must be set up in such a way that no information about the associations between data items is lost.

The tables in question are rectangular arrays which can be described mathematically. As with the table in Fig. 5.3, they have the following properties:

1. Each entry in a table represents one data item; there are no repeating groups.

2. They are column-homogeneous; that is, in any column all items are of the same kind.

3. Each column is assigned a distinct name.

4. All rows are distinct; duplicate rows are not allowed.

5. Both the rows and the columns can be viewed in any sequence at any time without affecting either the information content or the semantics of any function using the table.

**RELATIONAL
DATA BASES**

The enthusiasts of normalization have a vocabulary of their own and a tendency to dress up a basically simple subject in confusing language. The table, like that in Fig. 5.3, is referred to as a *relation*. A data base constructed using relations is referred to as a *relational data base*. A relational data base is thus one constructed from "flat" arrangements of data items.

The relational approach is based on the mathematical theory of relations, and the vocabulary used is taken from this branch of mathematics. The results of relational mathematics can be applied directly to relational data bases, and hence operations on data can be described with precision.

The relation, or table, is a set of *tuples*. If they are n-tuples (i.e., if the table has n columns), the relation is said to be of *degree n*. Relations of degree 2 are called *binary*, degree 3 are called *ternary*, and degree n are *n-ary*.

A set of values of one data-item type (i.e., one column in a relation) is referred to as a *domain*. The jth column is referred to as the jth *domain* of the relation.

In mathematical language, given sets $S_1, S_2, \ldots, S_n$ (not necessarily distinct), R is a *relation* on these n sets if it is a set of n-tuples each of which has its first element from S_1, its second element from S_2, and so forth.

Mathematical notations exist, based on relational algebra or relational calculus, for describing such relations and operations between them. Codd has devised a mathematical sublanguage for manipulating such a data base [4]. A more conventional man-computer dialogue could be translated into this sublanguage. We will use nonmathematical language to describe the way the tables may be manipulated.

Different users of the same data base will perceive different sets of data items and different relationships between them. It is therefore necessary to extract subsets of the table columns for some users, creating tables of smaller degree, and to join tables together for other users, creating tables of larger degree. Codd's sublanguage carries out these operations. As some of the tables may have many rows and columns, the ability to extract subsets is important. These cutting and pasting operations give a degree of flexibility that is not possible with most tree structures and plex structures.

The logical view of the data base can thus consist of sets of two-dimensional tables with operations for extracting columns and joining them. In Codd's words: "Both the application programmer and the interactive user view the data base as a time-varying collection of normalized relations of assorted degrees" [2].

| PIONEERING IMPLEMENTATIONS | There have been a number of implementations of relational data bases. References 8 to 11 discuss some of the earliest (predating Codd's) work. |

References 12 to 18 discuss more recent implementations.

The implementations in references 8, 9, 10, and 12 use binary relations (i.e., relations with only two domains). Although it has been argued that binary relations give the ultimate in flexibility, relations of variable degree seem desirable for most commercial applications. Most data bases using binary relations were designed for applications with data less cumbersome than a typical commercial data base.

REPEATING GROUPS

It sometimes comes as rather a shock to the database specialist steeped in tree and plex structures to hear that *all such structures can be represented as flat files.* He sometimes finds this difficult to believe. We had better consider some examples.

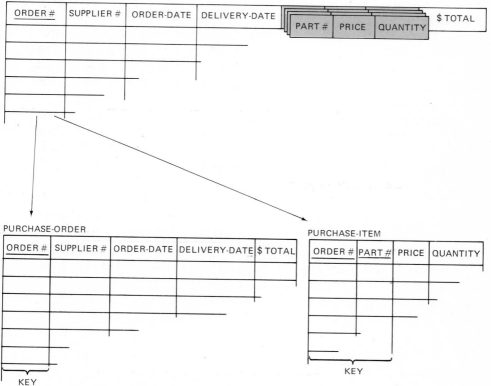

Figure 13.1 A repeating group is removed by splitting the file into two relations.

First, a file which is "flat" except for a repeating group can be normalized by removing the repeating group into a separate table or flat file, as shown in Fig. 13.1. The new file or *relation* so formed is given a name. The tuples in it must have keys which uniquely identify them. The data item ORDER-# is repeated in the PURCHASE-ITEM file and is combined with PART-# to form a unique identifier.

It might be objected that redundancy is increased because the data item ORDER-# appears twice. Normalization does require that some data items appear in more than one record in order to identify the records. This duplication does not necessarily imply an increase in storage requirements because normalization is concerned with *logical* structures—the user's view of data—and not with the way they are *physically* represented in storage.

If repeating groups are not separated out in this way when a data base is initially designed, there is a danger that subsequent evolution in the way the data base is used will necessitate their separation. For example, programs may have to be added in the future in which the individual PURCHASE-ITEM tuples in Fig. 13.1 are associated with a different record. The PURCHASE-ORDER data base may evolve as shown in Fig. 6.8 so that an association between SUPPLIER records and the PURCHASE-ITEM tuples is used. In Fig. 6.8 the PURCHASE-ITEM tuple must be a separate record rather than a repeating group of the PURCHASE-ORDER record. If repeating groups have to be separated out at a time after application programs have been written using them, then these application programs must be substantially modified and retested. Normalization coupled with data independence in the software will avoid this maintenance cost.

KEYS   Each tuple must have a key with which it can be identified. The tuple may be identifiable by means of one attribute. ORDER-# in Fig. 13.1 identifies a PURCHASE-ORDER tuple. Often, however, more than one attribute is necessary to identify the tuple. No single attribute is sufficient to identify a PURCHASE-ITEM tuple in Fig. 13.1, so the key would consist of the two attributes ORDER-# and PART-#.

The key must have two properties:

1. *Unique identification:* In each tuple of a relation, the value of the key must uniquely identify that tuple.

2. *Nonredundancy:* No attribute in the key can be discarded without destroying the property of unique identification.

There may be more than one set of attributes in each tuple which have the above two properties. Such sets are referred to as *candidate keys*, and one of them must be designated the *primary key*, which will in fact be used to identify the record. Where there is a choice, the attributes in the primary key should be chosen, first, so that none of them has an undefined value and, second, so that the number of attributes will be as small as possible.

To avoid having to draw tables like Fig. 13.1 we will use notations such as the following:

PURCHASE–ORDER (ORDER–#, SUPPLIER–#, ORDER–DATE, DELIVERY–DATE, $–TOTAL)
PURCHASE–ITEM (ORDER–#, PART–#, PRICE, QUANTITY)

The item prior to the parentheses is the name of the relation. The items inside the parentheses are the names of the domains. The underlined items are the keys which are necessary to identify the tuples (i.e., the primary keys).

TREE STRUCTURES

A tree structure can be normalized in a similar fashion. Figure 13.2 illustrates a four-level tree and shows how it is replaced by six relations. The key of a relation may incorporate the key of the relation immediately above it in the tree. JOB-HISTORY, for example, has a key (EMPLOYEE-#, JOB DATE) which incorporates the key of the item above it (EMPLOYEE-#). The EMPLOYEE relation, however, has a key of its own (EMPLOYEE-#), which *uniquely* identifies the EMPLOYEE tuples and so does not need to incorporate the key of the relation above it.

Note that the concatenated keys are the same as those we use in an unnormalized structure if we eliminate *path dependencies*, as was discussed in Chapter 8 (Fig. 8.12). The tuple structures of the normalized version in Fig. 13.2 are the same as the record structures in Fig. 8.13.

The links with arrows on a conventional schema represent *paths* that will be followed when employing the data base for certain applications. There must be some means of following all such paths with the normalized schema. In Fig. 13.2, the paths from EMPLOYEE to CHILDREN, JOB-HISTORY, and SALARY-HISTORY can be followed because these three tuples each contain the data item EMPLOYEE-#. The path from the EMPLOYEE to DEPARTMENT tuple can be followed because the EMPLOYEE tuple contains the data item DEPT-#. The path from DEPARTMENT to EMPLOYEE also requires that the field DEPT-# be

A schema for a tree structure:

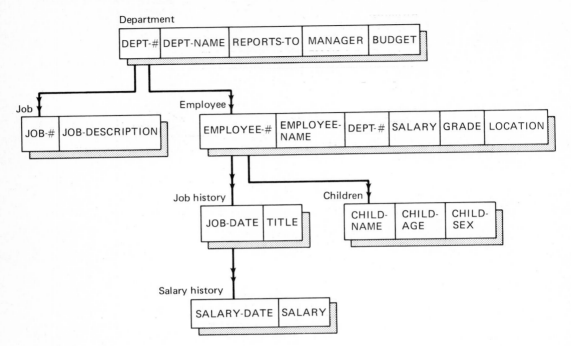

A normalized form of this schema:

```
DEPARTMENT (DEPT-#, DEPT-NAME, REPORTS-TO, MANAGER, BUDGET,
JOB (DEPT-#, JOB-#, JOB-DESCRIPTION)
EMPLOYEE (EMPLOYEE-#, EMPLOYEE-NAME, DEPT-#, SALARY, GRADE, LOCATION)
JOB-HISTORY (EMPLOYEE-#, JOB-DATE, TITLE)
SALARY-HISTORY (EMPLOYEE-#, SALARY-DATE, SALARY)
CHILDREN (EMPLOYEE-#, CHILD-NAME, CHILD-AGE, CHILD-SEX)
```

Figure 13.2 To convert this tree structure to a normalized structure the path dependencies are removed by adding extra key data items (shown in red).

used. DEPT-# is now employed as though it were a secondary key. This can be done with any of the various mechanisms. For noninteractive systems the EMPLOYEE tuple could be sorted on the DEPT-# data item.

In normalizing a structure, extra data items may be added for two reasons. First, *primary-key* data items may be added, as above, to make the resulting concatenated key identify the tuple uniquely. The tuple must be self-contained. Second, *attribute* data items may be added to represent

Schema:

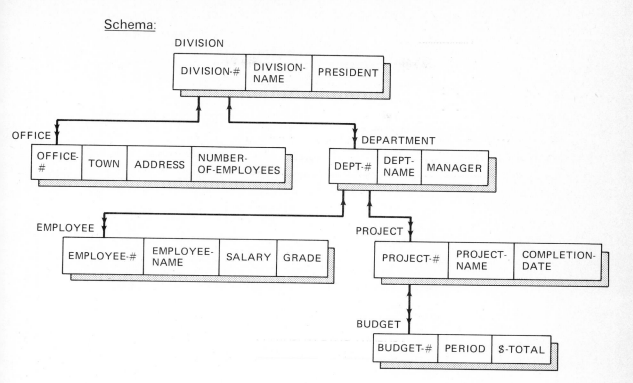

A normalized version of this schema:

DIVISION (DIVISION-#, DIVISION-NAME, PRESIDENT)
OFFICE (OFFICE-#, DIVISION-#, TOWN, ADDRESS, NUMBER-OF-EMPLOYEES)
DEPARTMENT (DEPT-#, DIVISION-#, DEPT-NAME, MANAGER)
EMPLOYEE (EMPLOYEE-#, DEPT-#, EMPLOYEE-NAME, SALARY, GRADE)
PROJECT (PROJECT-#, DEPT-#, PROJECT-NAME, COMPLETION-DATE)
BUDGET (BUDGET-#, PROJECT-#, PERIOD, $-TOTAL)

Figure 13.3   To convert this tree structure to a normalized structure extra *attributes* are added to represent the upward paths. These are shown in red. To follow the double-arrow links in such data bases secondary key operations are needed (such as sorting, chains or secondary indices).

the paths that we draw with lines and arrows on conventional schemas. Double-arrow lines may require secondary-key operations to be performed. These range from sorting to secondary indices and are discussed in Part II of the book.

Schema:

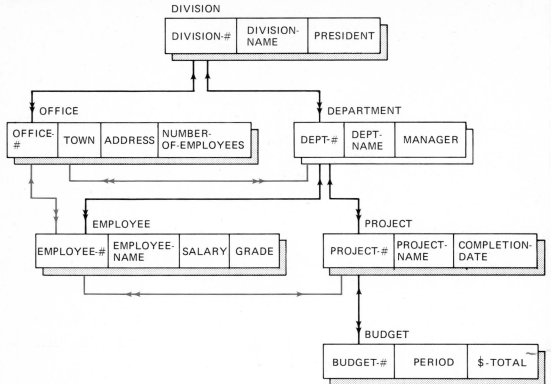

A normalized version of this schema:

    DIVISION (DIVISION-#, DIVISION-NAME, PRESIDENT)
    OFFICE (OFFICE-#, DIVISION-#, TOWN, ADDRESS, NUMBER-OF-EMPLOYEES)
    DEPARTMENT (DEPT-#, DIVISION-#, DEPT-NAME, MANAGER)
    EMPLOYEE (EMPLOYEE-#, DEPT-#, OFFICE-#, PROJECT-#, EMPLOYEE-NAME,
    SALARY, GRADE)
    PROJECT (PROJECT-#, DEPT-#, PROJECT-NAME, COMPLETION-DATE)
    BUDGET (BUDGET-#, PROJECT-#, PERIOD, $-TOTAL
    LOCATION (OFFICE-#, DEPT-#)

> *Figure 13.4* This diagram shows extra links added to the tree
> structure of Fig. 13.3, making it a plex structure. The added links are
> handled simply by adding two extra attribute data items to the tuples,
> and creating one new tuple.

The schema drawn in Fig. 13.3 does not need any primary-key data
items adding when normalized. Each key uniquely identifies its tuple.
Extra attributes are added, however, to enable a user to follow the paths
pointing upward.

ADDING TO A NORMALIZED SCHEMA

A relational data base would normally be designed so that new data items can be added to existing tuples when new applications or user views require them. New links between existing relations can also be added, either by adding new data items, or, occasionally by creating a new relation.

Figure 13.4 shows some new links added to the tree structure of Fig. 13.3, converting it into a plex structure. The link between EMPLOYEE and OFFICE can be added by including the data item OFFICE-# in the EMPLOYEE tuple. The link between EMPLOYEE and PROJECT can be added by including PROJECT-# in the EMPLOYEE tuple.

Describe Fig. 13.4

The link between OFFICE and DEPARTMENT is slightly more complex. It is an M:M association (a group-marriage association). One office can house more than one department, and one department can occupy more than one office location. If we added the data item DEPARTMENT-# to the OFFICE tuple, we would have to repeat the tuple for one office several times. This is wasteful, so, as in the CODASYL illustration in Fig. 11.10, we create a new tuple consisting simply of the data item OFFICE-# and DEPARTMENT-#. This makes it possible to find the office locations of a given department and what departments a given office houses.

In general, a relational data base should be able to absorb new data items and new associations, so that previous subschemas need not be disrupted.

PLEX STRUCTURES

Figure 13.4 is a plex structure. A plex structure can be normalized as easily as a tree structure. Figure 13.5 shows a plex structure used earlier and gives one of several normalized forms of it. As before, the tuples have keys which uniquely identify them, and have data items which permit every path on the plex structure to be followed.

Some of the groups of data items in Fig. 13.5 have two associations joining them. The links between SUPPLIER and QUOTATION indicate whether the supplier actually supplies the part in the QUOTATION record or is merely a candidate to supply it. The links from SUPPLIER to PURCHASE-ITEM show the outstanding and late orders for each supplier.

Figure 11.9 shows the same plex structure represented as CODASYL sets, and Figure 12.11 shows it in DL/I.

A schema for a plex structure:

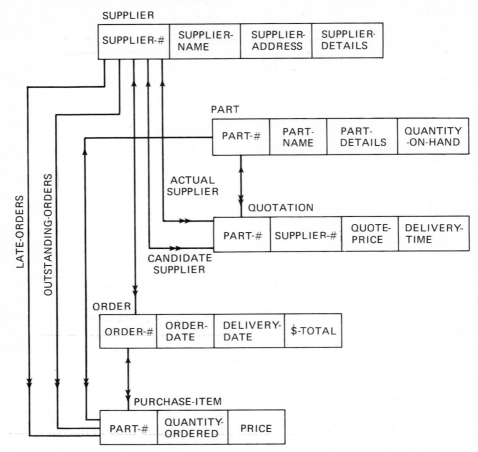

A normalized form of this schema:

SUPPLIER (SUPPLIER-#, SUPPLIER-NAME, SUPPLIER-ADDRESS)
PART (PART-#, PART-NAME, PART-DETAILS, QUANTITY-ON-HAND)
ACTUAL-SUPPLIER (PART-#, SUPPLIER-#, QUOTE-PRICE, DELIVERY-TIME)
CANDIDATE-SUPPLIER (PART-#, SUPPLIER-#, QUOTE-PRICE, DELIVERY-TIME)
ORDER (ORDER-#, SUPPLIER-#, ORDER-DATE, DELIVERY-DATE, $-TOTAL
PURCHASE-ITEM (ORDER-#, PART-#, QUANTITY-ORDERED, PRICE)
OUTSTANDING-ORDERS (SUPPLIER-#, PART-#, LATE?)

Figure 13.5

**PROBLEMS WITH
DIRECTED LINKS**
In the view of the relational enthusiasts, there is no need at all for directed links, such as those in Fig. 13.5, in the users' or application programmers' description of the data. They tend to confuse rather than to clarify.

Some of the links in Fig. 13.5 could be said to be *unnecessary*. The links between PART and PURCHASE-ITEM are not strictly necessary because both of them have the key PART-#. The links from QUOTATION to SUPPLIER are unnecessary because the QUOTATION group contains the data item SUPPLIER-#.

In some schema drawings the directed links are really a statement about the *physical* representation of data in which a physical pointer might be used.

In a large data base with diverse interactive usage, if links were drawn showing all the paths used between data items or groups, an impossibly tangled web of interconnections would result.

In data-base systems designed to handle tree structures, the natural growth illustrated by Fig. 13.4 cannot occur. Even systems designed to handle plex structures have various restrictions about what links are permissible.

The links drawn on schema diagrams generally represent a relation of degree 2 (a relation with two domains). Such links imply a different treatment of relations of degree 2 to relations of higher degree, whereas, in fact, they may be treated identically. If they *are* treated differently by the computer, for example, with different addressing methods, this difference should be the concern of the designer of the *physical* data structure, not the designer of the *logical* structure.

As the data base grows, a relation which is at one time of degree 2 may become a relation of higher degree. If the degree 2 relations are lines with arrows in the logical data description, this growth is difficult to represent. It entails replacing a linkage in the logical schema by a new relation, thus disrupting some application programs.

Where lines with arrows are drawn from one block to another and then to a succeeding block, the user tends to follow these lines and assume that they represent a ternary relation. Drawing such lines offers the temptation to represent a ternary relation as two binary relations, but to do so may be invalid. Codd refers to this as "the connection trap" [1]. Consider case 1 in Fig. 13.6. Arrows go from PART 4 to SUBASSEMBLY C and from SUBASSEMBLY C to PRODUCT 5. A casual user may draw the implication from the arrows that PRODUCT 5 contains PART 4, and he would be correct. Now, however, consider case 2 in Fig. 13.6. This case is identical to case 1 except that the left-hand column is now headed "SUPPLIER" instead

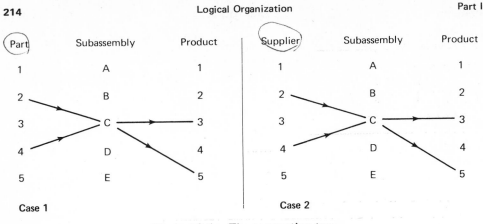

Figure 13.6   The connection trap.

of "PART." Arrows go from SUPPLIER 4 to SUBASSEMBLY C and from SUBASSEMBLY C to PRODUCT 5. The user may draw the implication from the arrows that PRODUCT 5 has SUPPLIER 4 as one of its suppliers. This time he may be wrong. The SUBASSEMBLY C used in PRODUCT 5 may be supplied by SUPPLIER 2, not SUPPLIER 4; that in PRODUCT 3 alone may be supplied by SUPPLIER 4.

Ternary relations are needed to clarify the situation, as follows:

Case 1			Case 2		
Part	Subassembly	Product	Supplier	Subassembly	Product
2	C	3	2	C	5
2	C	5	4	C	3
4	C	3			
4	C	5			

In general, lines with arrows offer the designer of the logical data base the temptation to draw structures which are inflexible, misleading, and sometimes invalid. A relational representation can be flexible, easily comprehensible, and mathematically rigorous. Nevertheless, incautious manipulation of relations can also create difficulties similar to the above correction trap.

BILL-OF-MATERIALS NORMALIZATION   In many cases the normalized form appears much simpler than a conventional schema. This is the case with the bill-of-materials schema shown in Fig. 13.7. The products made by a factory consist of parts such as screws or rods and subassemblies such as drive units and door catches. A subassembly may

A schema for a bill-of-materials file:

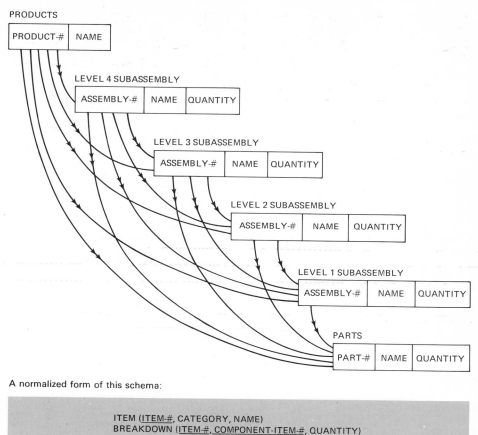

A normalized form of this schema:

ITEM (ITEM-#, CATEGORY, NAME)
BREAKDOWN (ITEM-#, COMPONENT-ITEM-#, QUANTITY)

Figure 13.7   In some cases the normalized form can be much simpler than unnormalized schemas. The more complex the relationships the more the user needs normalization to keep his head straight.

itself be composed of parts and other subassemblies. Level 4 subassemblies may contain level 3 subassemblies, which may contain level 2 subassemblies, and so forth. The bill-of-materials file shows what the products and subassemblies are composed of.

The normalized form of this file contains two relations: (1) an ITEM relation which contains the ITEM-#, NAME, and an attribute saying whether the item is a product, part, or level 1, 2, 3, or 4 subassembly, and

(2) a BREAKDOWN relation giving the quantity of each item that is a component of another item.

It is a characteristic of many bill-of-materials files that engineering changes occur frequently. The product breakdown both before and after the engineering change will be stored. If the file is represented by a plex structure, the addition of engineering changes will be complex. In the normalized form of the file it is simple. Any new items introduced by the change are added to existing ITEM and BREAKDOWN relations, and a third relation is used: ENG CHANGE (ENG-CHANGE-#, ITEM-#).

MANIPULATION OF RELATIONS

The key to flexibility in a relational data base lies in the ease with which relations can be manipulated. The terminal user or application programmer will often employ different relations to those in the schema. In other language: the user's model is different from the conceptual model. The user's relations must be derived from the schema relations.

Relational mathematics defines a variety of operators with which relations may be manipulated to achieve any desired tabular representation of the data. We will describe two operations which are particularly useful: *project* and *join*. These two operations enable us to cut and paste the columns in the relational tables to form new relations. This gives an elegant flexibility in manipulating relations. The relations which the end user perceives can be simply created from the global relational schema. The *project* and *join* operations must, however, be used with certain rules to prevent invalid views of the data being created.

PROJECTION

The operator *project* enables a user to select what columns he wants from a relation, and to specify what order he wants them in. Projection is illustrated in Fig. 13.8. The symbol Π is used as the projection operator.

Fig. 13.8 shows two projections of the relation ENGINEER. One has been called DEPT and contains the data items DEPT-# and LOCATION. To achieve this we write

```
DEPT = Π ENGINEER (DEPT-#, LOCATION)
```

The other projection has been called EMP and is created with the statement

ENGINEER

EMPLOYEE-#	EMPLOYEE-NAME	DEPT-#	SALARY	LOCATION
53702	BLANAGAN J E	721	1200	NEW YORK
53703	ROPLEY E S	721	2300	NEW YORK
53791	MUSSOLINI M	007	5000	DETROIT
53800	FRANKENSTEIN W	402	1100	MIAMI
53805	DUNNE J	721	1900	NEWYORK
53806	JONES P L	402	1000	MIAMI

EMP = Π ENGINEER (EMPLOYEE-NAME, EMPLOYEE-#, LOCATION, SALARY)

DEPT = Π ENGINEER (DEPT-#, LOCATION)

EMP

EMPLOYEE-NAME	EMPLOYEE-#	LOCATION	SALARY
BLANAGAN J E	53702	NEW YORK	1200
ROPLEY E S	53703	NEW YORK	2300
MUSSOLINI M	53791	DETROIT	5000
FRANKENSTEIN W	53800	MIAMI	1100
DUNNE J	53805	NEW YORK	1900
JONES P L	53806	MIAMI	1000

DEPT

DEPT-#	LOCATION
721	NEW YORK
007	DETROIT
402	MIAMI

Figure 13.8   Two projections of the relation ENGINEER.

EMP = Π ENGINEER (EMPLOYEE NAME, EMPLOYEE #, LOCATION, SALARY)

No duplicate tuples exist in a relation. Consequently, there may be fewer tuples in a projection of a relation than in the original. This is so with DEPT in Fig. 13.8.

The projection operation contains no information about the sort sequence of the tuples. They could be in any sequence. Sorting is not generally listed as one of the basic relational algebra operations because it does not change the information content of a relation. *Physical* handling of a relation in a batch-processing system may require sorting to be performed.

JOIN   When two relations share a common data-item type
                    they might be *joined*. The *projection* operation
splits relations, selecting certain columns. The *join* operation puts together
columns from different relations.

✻ is the symbol used as the join operator. The statement EMPLOYEE
= EMP ✻ DEPT does the opposite of the operation shown in Fig. 13.8 and
forms the relation EMPLOYEE from the relations EMP and DEPT.

A user may wish to form a relation out of two or more separate
relations, which does not use all the attributes of these relations. For
example, in joining EMP and DEPT he may wish to create a relation which
gives only the employees' names and locations. This can be done with the
statement

```
EMPLOC = EMP ✻ DEPT (EMPLOYEE NAME, LOCATION)
```

Figure 13.9 shows several join operations on two relations. The
relations in this illustration have the domain B in common. Figure 13.10
shows a join on three relations.

When relations are joined on a given data-item type, only those tuples
which share the same value of that data item appear in the result. Consequently, the resulting relation may contain fewer tuples than either of the
original relations. This is seen in Figs. 13.9 and 13.10. The reduction effect
may be used to isolate certain tuples in response to queries. A relation
with only one domain, and possibly only one data item, may be joined to
other relations to extract a restricted set of the tuples. In Fig. 13.9 for
example, the relation R_3 contains only one data item, E, and only one
value of that data item, T. When it is joined with R_2 it produces an answer
to the query "What tuples in R_2 have a value of data item E equal to T?"

The join we have described, joining on the basis of equal data-item
values in shared domains and not duplicating the shared domain in the
result, is called a *natural join*. Other types of joins are possible, including
ones which search a domain for values *not equal*, *greater than*, or *less than*
those in a given domain.

A variety of other operations, less useful than joins and projections,
can be employed to manipulate relations. A complete set of relational
algebra operations is described in Reference 3.

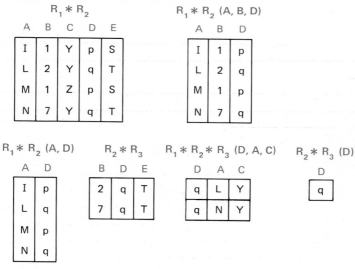

Figure 13.9   Examples of natural joins.

DANGERS IN
MANIPULATING
RELATIONS

It must be noted that there are dangers in indiscriminate manipulation of relations. A projection or a join can produce invalid results in some circumstances.

Consider the projection in Fig. 13.8 which creates the relation DEPT (DEPT-#, LOCATION) from the ENGINEER relation.

If the association between DEPT-# and LOCATION is a 1 association,

A117

IDENTIFIC-ATION-#	NAME	ADDRESS	ZIP-CODE
817.53711	JENKINS L	10.E.51	10017
817.42815	SMITH A	24.E.51	10017
817.60712	ROPLEY ES	201.E.51	10017
817.31179	ELIOT K	402.E.51	10017
817.44051	DOE J	497.E.51	10017

A125

IDENTIFIC-ATION-#	NAME	PROFESSION	INCOME-RANGE
817.42815	SMITH A	ACCOUNTANT	10 000
817.77112	WILLIAMS S	REALTOR	30 000
817.73119	NELSON H	SAILOR	10 000
817.44051	DOE J	DIPLOMAT	50 000
817.91254	MARTIN P	PROGRAMMER	10 000

P123

IDENTIFIC-ATION-#	CONVICTION-DATE	CONVICTION-TYPE	CONVICTION-LENGTH
817.42315	1.12.75	RAPE	12
817.42815	2.2.76	THEFT	24
817.43001	10.12.73	THEFT	36
817.44051	11.1.76	DRUGS	LIFE
817.46172	3.5.75	RAPE	363

k = P123*A117*A125 (NAME,ZIP-CODE,PROFESSION,CONVICTION-TYPE, CONVICTION-DATE)

NAME	ZIP-CODE	PROFESSION	CONVICTION-TYPE	CONVICTION-DATE
SMITH A	10017	ACCOUNTANT	THEFT	2.2.76
DOE J	10017	DIPLOMAT	DRUGS	11.1.76

Figure 13.10   A *join* operation on three relations.

the projection is valid. We have the following associations:

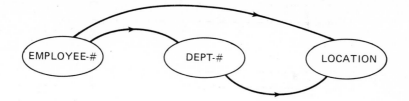

However, it may not be valid if the association between DEPT-# and LOCATION is an M association (i.e., a department can have more than one location), thus:

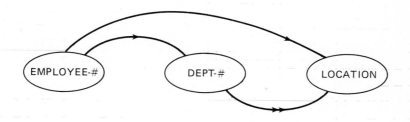

Dept. 721 in Fig. 13.8 might have an office in Detroit as well as New York for all we know, and the Detroit office has no engineers.

A similar argument applies to *join* operations. Suppose that two relations were joined as follows:

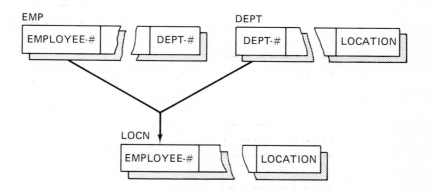

This join is valid if there is a 1 association between DEPT-# and LOCATION. It is not valid if there is an M association between DEPT-# and LOCATION, because although a department can have more than one location, an employee works in only one location. Thus:

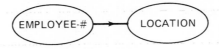

SEMANTIC
INTEGRITY

The term *semantic disintegrity* is applied to operations which create invalid combinations of data items in this way. To achieve semantic integrity, rules are needed about which operations are permissible, and these rules should be governed by the associations between data items. It is inadvisable to mix domains indiscriminately using join and project operations, but some of the query software written for relational data bases permits this. Such software can give a user invalid results.

The following two chapters discuss the issue of what items should be grouped together to form a tuple (segment, or record), and further discuss the semantic integrity problem.

RELATIONAL
CALCULUS VERSUS
ALGEBRA

Notation such as the above for manipulating relations is called a *relational algebra*. A relational algebra operation is one which takes one or more relations as its operand(s) and manipulates them to form a new relation. To obtain a particular result a user may specify a sequence of relational algebra operations.

A more automatic approach is to use what is called a *relational calculus*. With a relational calculus the user simply defines the result he wants and leaves the system to decide what operations are necessary to extract that result from the data base. A relational calculus is a notation for defining a relation which is to be derived from the existing relations in the data base.

Figure 13.11 lists symbols which may be employed in a relational calculus. The following are some typical examples of the use of such a calculus:

1. Using the ENGINEER relation of Fig. 13.8, produce a relation, called Q, which contains a set of EMPLOYEE NAME values for every employee in department #721:

```
Q (ENGINEER.EMPLOYEE NAME): ENGINEER. DEPT# = 721
```

2. Using the same ENGINEER relation, produce a relation Q which contains the domains EMPLOYEE NAME and SALARY for every employee in department #721 with a salary greater than 2000:

```
Q (ENGINEER. EMPLOYEE NAME, ENGINEER. SALARY):
    ENGINEER. DEPT# = 721 ∧  ENGINEER.SALARY >2000
```

3. Using the relations P123 and A125 in Fig. 13.10, produce a relation, Q, showing CONVICTION TYPE AND CONVICTION LENGTH for persons whose profession is ACCOUNTANT:

```
Q (P123.CONVICTION TYPE,P123.CONVICTION LENGTH): ∃
     A125 (A125.PROFESSION = 'ACCOUNTANT' ∧
     A125.IDENTIFICATION# = P123.IDENTIFICATION#)
```

4. Using the relations

```
    STUDENT (STUD#, STUD-NAME, STUD-DETAILS)
    INSTRUCTOR (INST#, INST-NAME, INST-DETAILS)
    S-I (STUD#, INST#)
```

produce a relation showing which students are taught by *every* instructor:

```
Q (STUDENT.STUD#, STUDENT.STUDENT NAME): ∀ INSTRUCTOR
    ∃ (S-I. STUD# = STUDENT. STUD# ∧ S-I. INST#
    = INSTRUCTOR.INST#)
```

Symbol	Explanation
$x \cdot v$	The set of values of the data items in domain y of relation x.
$A (x_1 \cdot y_1, x_2 \cdot y_2, ...)$	A relation called A consisting of domains containing the sets of values $x_1 \cdot y_1, x_2 \cdot y_2, ...$.
:	"Such that." The expression on the left of the colon indicates what is to be retrieved, and the expression on the right of the colon is a qualifier.
∃	"There exists."
∀	"For all."
∧	"And." The conditions on the left and right of the symbol both apply.
∨	"Or." Either the condition on the left or that on the right of the symbol applies.
⌐	"Not." The condition on the right of the symbol does not apply.
$=, \neq, <, >$.	Equal to, not equal to, less than, greater than.
$'x'$	The literal value of x.

Figure 13.11   Symbols used in a relational calculus.

There are many possible forms a relational calculus could take. It can have several advantages over a relational algebra. First, the user makes no statement about *how* the system obtains the desired result; hence the system is left free to optimize the method. Second, it could permit more discriminating security procedures because these procedures can be based on a definition of the properties of the data requested rather than on a stated procedure for retrieving the data. Third, requesting data by its properties is more natural to a nonprogramming data-base user than requesting it by specifying a sequence of operations. The user will not enter statements in the form above, but in the form of a psychologically planned dialogue which the machine translates into a formal data-base calculus. Some dialogues which perform the functions of a relational calculus are remarkably elegant and simple to use [19].

The disadvantage of a calculus rather than an algebra is that it is more complex to implement. It represents a higher level of automation.

A calculus, like an algebra, can produce invalid results (semantic disintegrity) if not used with rules about associations between data items.

References 10, 12, 16, 17, and 19 discuss implementations of relational calculi. References 3, 4, and 5 discuss the theory of using a relational calculus.

THREE LEVELS OF AUTOMATION

Three levels of automation are to be found in data-base sublanguages:

1. *Calculus.* The highest level of automation. The user states what he needs and the system obtains it.

2. *Algebra.* The user states a set of high-level operations to be performed on relations (or other groupings of data items).

3. *A tuple at a time.* The lowest level. A programmer proceeds a record or tuple at a time.

The phrase "navigation by a programmer" became popular for describing a programmer finding his way through a data base a record or segment at a time. Users of data-base systems without an algebra or calculus (or high-level data manipulation capability) can only proceed by programmer navigation. Programmers are necessary as middlemen to translate a user's request into a set of programming steps.

The use of a calculus can be compared to telling a taxi driver, "Take me to the Plaza Hotel." Navigation by a programmer can be compared to having a middleman in the taxi who interprets the passenger's request and tells the

driver "Turn left; go three blocks; turn right. . . . "

The industry should strive toward automatic navigation, as with a relational calculus. The use of high-level operators or automatic navigation would be much more complex on a data base with tree or plex structures or with repeating groups than on a relational data base. The advocates of relation bases therefore see normalization as the key to a further level of automation in data-base management software.

DISADVANTAGE   A disadvantage sometimes cited for relational
                         data bases is machine performance. With present-
day hardware the JOIN operation is likely to take substantial machine time. It may be feasible with small relations, but some commercial files are hundreds of millions of bytes long.

In understanding the performance issue it is important to remember that the relations and the operations on them such as JOIN are a *logical* view. With interactive systems it is unlikely that the JOIN will ever take place *physically*. Instead, equivalent results will be produced by means of pointer structures or indices. With batch-processing systems a physical JOIN may be permitted and should be regarded as the equivalent of a *merge* operation on tape.

The physical data layout of the relational system will be chosen so as to give good performance to the most frequently run operations. The least frequently run operations may suffer accordingly, just as they do on other types of data-base systems.

A relational data-base design is sometimes depicted as not being "driven" by user views of data. A new unanticipated user view can be handled with ease if the data it needs are stored. Although this is true in connection with the *logical* structure of the data, the new user view may not be handled with good machine performance because the *physical* structure of the data was designed to best serve the most common applications. The physical structure is user-"driven" even if the logical structure is not.

The performance of a relational data-base system will depend very much on the physical techniques that are employed. If these are well selected and tailored to usage patterns, the performance should be comparable to that of other systems.

SUMMARY OF   The following are the advantages of representing
ADVANTAGES   data in a normalized form, particularly in third
                         normal form, which is described in Chapter 14:

1. *Ease of use.* The easiest way to represent most data to users not trained or talented in the techniques of data processing is with two-dimensional tables.

2. *Flexibility.* Operations such as PROJECTION and JOIN permit cutting and pasting of relations so that the different logical files wanted by different application programmers can be given to them in the form they want them.

3. *Precision.* The directed links which are common today in some logical data representations can sometimes be misleading, as in Fig. 13.6. The precise results of relational mathematics can be applied to the manipulation of relations.

4. *Security.* Security controls can be more easily implemented. Security authorizations will relate to relations. Sensitive attributes, such as SALARY in an employee file, could, for example, be moved into a separate relation with its own authorization controls. If the authorization requirements are met, SALARY will be JOINed back to the other employee attributes [6].

5. *Relatability.* The maximum flexibility is possible in relating attributes from different sets of tuples, or different "files."

6. *Ease of implementation.* As we will see in Part II, the physical storage of flat files can be less complex than the physical storage of tree and plex structures. As more elaborate physical techniques come into use, such as storage hierarchies (Chapter 33) and associative memories (Chapter 36), the simplification offered by normalization pays major dividends. Hardware devices to assist in rapid file searching are more feasible with files which avoid complex pointer linkages.

7. *Data independence.* There will be need for most data bases to grow by adding new attributes and new relations. The data will be used in new ways. Tuples will be added and deleted. New data-item types will be added and old ones deleted. New associations will be added as in Fig. 13.4. If the data base is in a normalized form with data independence in the software, the data can be restructured, and the data base can grow without, in most cases, forcing the rewriting of application programs. This is important because of the excessive and growing costs of maintaining an organization's application programs and its data from the disrupting effects of data-base growth. As the quantity of application programs increases, the cost of maintaining them without data independence will rise to prohibitive levels. Good data independence can probably be achieved more easily with normalized logical structures than with tree or plex structures.

8. *Data manipulation language.* A data manipulation sublanguage can be based on relational algebra or relational calculus. If the data were organized so that a variety of nonflat structures were permitted, the data sublanguage would either be unnecessarily complex for the user or else be limited in its capability.

9. *Clarity.* The logical data-base representations using arrows, such as those in Fig. 6.1 or 6.8, may be clear as long as the number of records is low. The ultimate objective of data-base growth, however, is to produce data bases which encompass many related activities of an organization. Figure 13.12 shows, for example, in a highly simplified

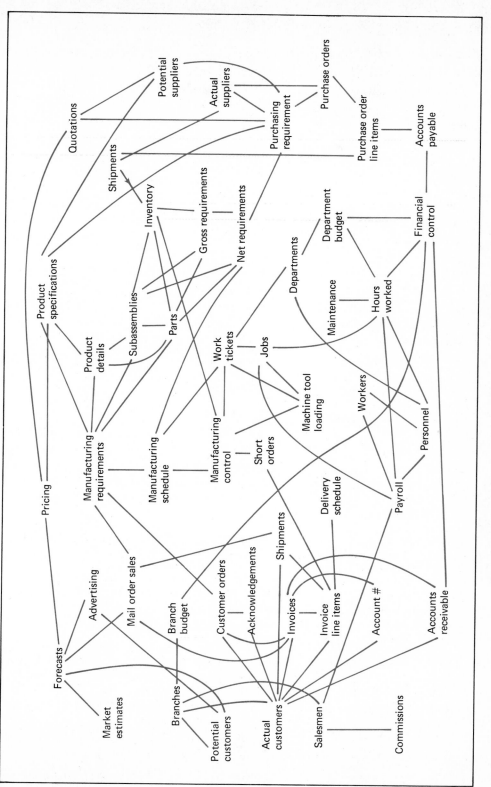

Figure 13.12 As the data bases in an organization grow the number of interrelations become too numerous and too entangled to represent clearly by schemas with directed links. The constant requirement for growth and change make it desirable to use normalized data structures.

fashion, some of the files in a corporation that may be interrelated. An attempt to represent the details of the interrelations of the files using schemas with arrows would produce an unholy mess. As data bases grow to encompass more and more activities, it is essential that we break away from logical representations using pointers to pointers to pointers. Relational data bases seem the best alternative.

Eventually, one hopes, data management software will be designed around normalized data structures. The data-base management systems shown in Figs. 7.1 to 7.5 could work well if the schema were in a normalized form. Most of today's data management software can be used to implement normalized data bases, and for some organizations this would be a worthwhile course.

REFERENCES

1. E. F. Codd, "A Relational Model of Data for Large Shared Data Banks," *Comm. ACM 13*, No. 6, ACM (Association for Computing Machinery), New York, London, and Amsterdam, June 1970, 377-387.

2. E. F. Codd, "Further Normalization of the Data Base Relational Model," in *Courant Computer Science Symposia*, Vol. 6: "Data Base Systems," edited by R. Rustin, Prentice-Hall, Inc., Englewood Cliffs, N.J., 1972.

3. E. F. Codd, "Relational Completeness of Data Base Sublanguages," in *Courant Computer Science Symposia*, Vol. 6: "Data Base Systems," edited by R. Rustin, Prentice-Hall, Inc., Englewood Cliffs, N.J., 1972.

4. E. F. Codd, "A Data Base Sublanguage Founded on the Relational Calculus," in *Proceedings of the 1971 ACM-SIGFIDET Workshop on Data Description, Access and Control*. ACM (Association for Computing Machinery), New York, London, and Amsterdam, 1972.

5. C. J. Date and E. F. Codd, "The Relational and Network Approaches: Comparison of the Application Programming Interfaces," *Proceedings of the 1974 ACM-SIGFIDET Workshop*, ACM, New York, London, and Amsterdam, 1974.

6. E. F. Codd, "Access Control for Relational Data Base Systems," Presented at BCS Symposium on Relational Database Concepts, April 1973, British Computer Society, London, 1973.

7. E. F. Codd, "Recent Investigations in Relational Data Base Systems," *Information Processing '74*, North-Holland, Amsterdam, 1974.

8. J. A. Feldman and P. D. Rovner, "An Algol-Based Associative Language," *Comm. ACM 12*, No. 8, ACM, New York, London, and Amsterdam, Aug. 1969.

9. W. Ash and E. H. Sibley, "TRAMP: An Interpretive Associative Processor with Deductive Capabilities," *Proc. ACM 23rd Nat. Conf.* (1968), ACM, New York, London, and Amsterdam, 1968.

10. R. E. Levein and M. E. Maron, "A Computer System for Inference Execution and Data Retrieval," *Comm. ACM 10*, No. 11, ACM, New York, London, and Amsterdam, 1967.

11. D. L. Childs, "Description of a Set-Theoretic Data Structure," *Proc. FJCC*, AFIPS (American Federation of Information Processing Societies), New York, 1968.

12. M. F. Crick, R. A. Lorie, E. J. Mosher, and A. J. Symonds, *A Data Base System for Interactive Applications*, IBM Technical Report G320–2058 (July 1970), IBM Scientific Center, 545 Technology Square, Cambridge, Mass. 02139.

13. R. C. Goldstein and A. J. Strand, "The MacAIMS Data Management System," *Proc. ACM SIGFIDET Workshop in Data Description and Access*, ACM, New York, London, and Amsterdam, 1970.

14. A. J. Strand, "The Relational Approach to the Management of Data Bases," *Proc. IFIP Congress*, North-Holland, Amsterdam, and AFIPS, Montvale, N.J., 1971.

15. M. G. Notley, *The Peterlee IS/1 System*, IBM (UK) Scientific Centre Report UKSC-0018 (March 1972), IBM (UK) Scientific Centre, Neville Rd., Peterlee, Co. Durham, England HA2 7HH.

16. G. Pracchi, A. Fedeli, and P. Paolini, *A Relational Data Base Management System*, Internal Report No. 72-5, Laboratorio di Calcolatori, Istituto di Elettrotecnica ed Elettronica, Politechnico di Milano, Italy (Feb. 1972).

17. G. Bracchi, A. Fedeli, and P. Paolini, "A Language for a Relational Data Base Management System," presented at 6th Annual Princeton Conference on Information Sciences and Systems, Princeton University, March 1972.

18. V. K. M. Whitney, "Relational Data Management Implementation Techniques," *Proc. 1974 ACM-SIGFIDET Workshop*, ACM, New York, London, and Amsterdam, 1974.

19. Moshe M. Zloof, "Query-by-Example," *International Conference of Very Large Data Bases*, Framingham, Mass., ACM, New York, London, and Amsterdam, 1975.

BOOK STRUCTURE

Chapters 14 and 15 are important chapters for data-base designers. How should data items be grouped into data structures?

14 THIRD NORMAL FORM

An issue of concern to most data-base designers is what data items should be grouped together into records, segments, or tuples. There are many different ways the hundreds or thousands of data items can be grouped, and some ways are better than others. Some will lead to subtle problems in the future.

As we have stressed, most data bases constantly change. New data items and new associations between data items are added frequently and new usage patterns occur. As we change the data base, we must preserve the old user views of data so as to avoid having to rewrite programs. There are, however, certain changes in data associations or usage which could force modification of programs. For example, we may have to split a record (segment) into two, or change the key that is used for certain data items. Such changes can be extremely disruptive. If the grouping of data items and keys is well thought out originally, we can make such disruption unlikely to happen.

Again, the indiscriminate grouping of data items can lead to the semantic disintegrity problems which we discussed in Chapter 13. These can occur when powerful query facilities are used either with relation data bases or with pointer-structured data.

This chapter and the following one are concerned with the best grouping of data items into records, segments, or tuples. The ideas in these chapters may be tedious for some readers to grasp, but once learned become a fundamental part of a systems analyst's understanding of the data. They are important for the design of stable data structures that will minimize the probability of future disruption.

The wording used in this chapter is that of relational data bases. The ideas described, however, can and ought to be applied to nonrelational data bases, including those using CODASYL, DL/I, or other structures. Some software vendors of nonrelational systems recommend that the data should be in *third normal form*.

To simplify the wording, we will avoid the use of the word *tuple* and call it a *segment* or *record* instead.

The normalization process described so far removes all nonsimple domains, converting the data into the form of two-dimensional tables. This is referred to as *first normal form*. The futher normalization process described in this chapter examines the relations in first normal form and may split some of them into still simpler relations. The process proceeds in two steps. The first reduces the data to *second normal form* and the final step to *third normal form*. The basic ideas behind second and third normal forms are simple, but the ramifications of this normalization are many and subtle and vary from one type of data-base usage to another [1].

As with the first normalization process, this further normalization says nothing about the physical layout of the data. It is concerned only with the user's view and the global logical view of the data.

FUNCTIONAL DEPENDENCE

In attempting to lay out the relationships between data items, the designer must concern himself with which attributes are dependent on which others. The phrase *functionally dependent* is defined as follows: *Attribute B of a relation R is functionally dependent on attribute A of R if, at every instant of time, each value in A has no more than one value in B associated with it in relation R* [1].

Saying that *B* is functionally dependent on *A* is equivalent to saying that *A identifies B*. This is the condition we have represented throughout the book with a single-arrow link from *A* to *B*. In other words, if at one instant in time the value of *A* is known, then the value of *B* is determined.

Consider the relation

```
EMPLOYEE (EMPLOYEE-#, EMPLOYEE-NAME, SALARY, PROJECT-#,
          COMPLETION-DATE)
```

The functional dependencies in this relation are as follows:

EMPLOYEE-#	is dependent on	EMPLOYEE-NAME
EMPLOYEE-NAME	is dependent on	EMPLOYEE-#
SALARY	is dependent on	either EMPLOYEE-NAME or EMPLOYEE-#
PROJECT-#	is dependent on	either EMPLOYEE-NAME or EMPLOYEE-#
COMPLETION-DATE	is dependent on	EMPLOYEE-NAME, EMPLOYEE-# or PROJECT-#

EMPLOYEE-# is not functionally dependent on SALARY because more than one employee could have the same salary. Similarly, EM-PLOYEE-# is not functionally dependent on PROJECT-# but COMPLE-TION DATE is. No other attribute in the relation is fully dependent on PROJECT-#.

Functional dependencies are more clearly shown in a diagram. Figure 14.1 shows the above dependencies. If B is functionally dependent on A, we show an arrow going from A to B. The asterisks following the attribute names in this drawing mark the *prime attributes* (attributes which are members of at least one candidate key).

An attribute can be functionally dependent on a group of attributes rather than a single attribute. Consider, for example, the following relation, which shows how programmers spent their time:

PROGRAMMER-ACTIVITY (PROGRAMMER-#, PACKAGE-#, PROGRAMMER-NAME, PACKAGE NAME, TOTAL-HOURS-WORKED)

TOTAL-HOURS-WORKED is functionally dependent on the concate-nated key (PROGRAMMER-#, PACKAGE-#) or on any of the candidate keys (PROGRAMMER-#, PACKAGE-NAME), (PROGRAMMER-NAME, PACKAGE-#), or (PROGRAMMER-NAME, PACKAGE-NAME). (This assumes that no two programmers and no two packages have the same name.)

The functional dependencies in this relation can be drawn as in Fig. 14.2.

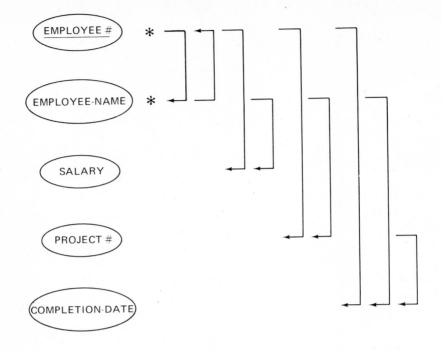

An instance of the above relation:

EMPLOYEE #	EMPLOYEE NAME	SALARY	PROJECT #	COMPLETION DATE
120	JONES	2000	x	17.7.81
121	HARPO	1700	x	17.7.81
270	GARFUNKAL	1800	y	12.1.84
273	SELSI	3600	x	17.7.81
274	ABRAHMS	3000	z	21.3.82
279	HIGGINS	2400	y	12.1.84
301	FLANNEL	1800	z	21.3.82
306	MCGRAW	2100	z	21.3.82
310	ENSON	3000	z	21.3.82
315	GOLDSTEIN	3100	x	17.7.81
317	PUORRO	2700	y	12.1.84
320	MANSINI	1700	y	12.1.84
321	SPOTO	2900	x	17.7.81
340	SCHAFT	3100	x	17.7.81
349	GOLD	1900	z	21.3.82

Figure 14.1 Functional dependencies in the relation **EMPLOYEE (EMPLOYEE-#, EMPLOYEE-NAME, SALARY, PROJECT-#, COMPLETION-DATE).** The asterisks indicate the prime attributes (members of candidate keys).

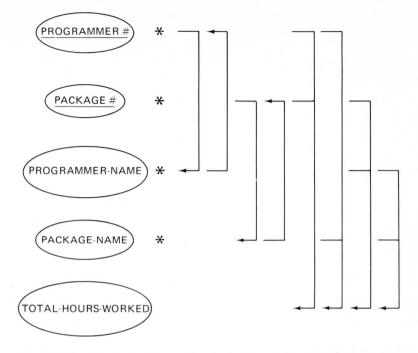

Figure 14.2　Functional dependencies in the relation PROGRAMMER-
ACTIVITY (PROGRAMMER-#, PACKAGE-$, PROGRAMMER-NAME,
PACKAGE-NAME, TOTAL-HOURS-WORKED) . . . The asterisks mark
the prime attributes (members of candidate keys).

**FULL FUNCTIONAL
DEPENDENCY**
An attribute or a collection of attributes, *B*, of a
relation *R* can be said to be *fully functionally
dependent* on another collection of attributes, *A*,
of relation *R* if *B* is functionally dependent on the whole of *A* but not on
any subset of *A*.

For example, in the relation PROGRAMMER-ACTIVITY (Fig. 14.2)
above, TOTAL-HOURS-WORKED is fully functionally dependent on the
concatenated key (PROGRAMMER-#, PACKAGE-#) because it refers to
how many hours a given programmer has worked on a given package. Neither
PROGRAMMER-# alone nor PACKAGE-# alone identifies TOTAL-
HOURS-WORKED.

TOTAL-HOURS-WORKED, however, is the *only* attribute which is
fully functionally dependent on the concatenated key. PROGRAMMER-
NAME is fully functionally dependent on PROGRAMMER-# alone, and
PACKAGE-NAME is fully functionally dependent on PACKAGE-# alone.
The arrows in Fig. 14.2 make these dependencies clear.

**SECOND
NORMAL FORM**
We are now in a position to define second normal form: *A relation R is in second normal form if it is in first normal form and every nonprime attribute of R is fully functionally dependent on each candidate key of R* [1].

In a relation such as that in Fig. 14.1 the candidate keys have only one attribute, and hence the relation is always in second normal form because the nonprime attributes must be fully dependent on the candidate keys. Where the candidate keys consist of more than one attribute, a first-normal-form relation may not be in second normal form.

The relation in Fig. 14.2 is in second normal form because its solitary nonprime attribute, TOTAL-HOURS-WORKED, is fully functionally dependent on each candidate key.

The following relation is not in second normal form:

```
SUPPLY-SOURCE (SUPPLIER-#, PART-#, SUPPLIER-NAME,
               SUPPLIER-DETAILS, PRICE)
```

This relation has only one candidate key. SUPPLIER-NAME does not participate in a candidate key because the same supplying firm at different locations has different supplier numbers. SUPPLIER-NAME does not identify SUPPLIER-#. As can be seen in Fig. 14.3, the nonprime attributes SUPPLIER-NAME and SUPPLIER-DETAILS are functionally dependent on SUPPLIER-#, not on the whole concatenated key.

There are a few problems that can result from its not being in second normal form:

1. We cannot enter details about a supplier until that supplier supplies a part. If the supplier does not supply a part, there is no key.

2. If a supplier should temporarily cease to supply any part, then the deletion of the last segment (record, tuple) containing that SUPPLIER-# will also delete the details of the supplier. It would normally be desirable that SUPPLIER-DETAILS be preserved.

3. We have problems when we attempt to update the supplier details. We must search for every segment which contains that supplier as part of the key. If a supplier supplies many parts, much redundant updating of supplier details will be needed.

These types of irregularities can be removed by splitting the relation into two relations in second normal form, as shown in Fig. 14.4. Only PRICE is fully functionally dependent on the concatenated key, so all other attributes are removed to the separate relation on the left which has SUPPLIER-NUMBER only as its key.

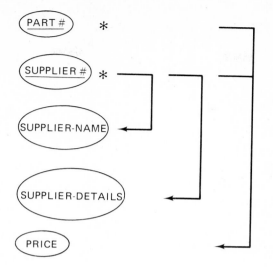

An instance of this relation:

PART #	SUPPLIER #	SUPPLIER -NAME	SUPPLIER DETAILS	PRICE
1	1000	JONES	x	20
1	1500	ABC	x	28
1	2050	XYZ	y	22
1	1900	P—H	z	30
2	3100	ALLEN	z	520
2	1000	JONES	x	500
2	2050	XYZ	y	590
3	2050	XYZ	y	1000
4	1000	JONES	x	80
4	3100	ALLEN	z	90
4	1900	P—H	z	95
5	1500	ABC	x	160
5	1000	JONES	x	140

Figure 14.3   The functional dependencies in a relation which is not in second normal form.

Splitting to second normal form is the type of splitting that natural data-base growth tends to force, so it might as well be anticipated when the data base is first set up. In general, every attribute in a relation should be dependent on the *entire* key; otherwise, it should be removed to a separate relation.

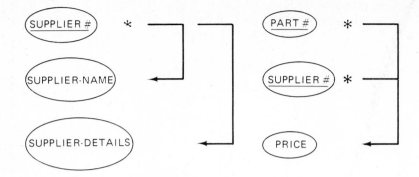

An instance of the above pair of relations:

SUPPLIER #	SUPPLIER NAME	SUPPLIER DETAILS
1000	JONES	x
1500	ABC	x
2050	XYZ	y
1900	P—H	z
3100	ALLEN	z

PART #	SUPPLIER #	PRICE
1	1000	20
1	1500	28
1	2050	22
1	1900	30
2	3100	520
2	1000	500
2	2050	590
3	2050	1000
4	1000	80
4	3100	90
4	1900	95
5	1500	160
5	1000	140

Figure 14.4   To convert the relation in Fig. 14.3 into second normal form, it is split into these two relations.

THIRD NORMAL FORM

Anomalies similar to the three described above can occasionally occur in a relation which is in second normal form. To remove them the last normalization step is used, which converts second normal form to third normal form. This step removes what is referred to as *transitive dependence*.

Suppose that A, B, and C are three attributes or distinct collections of attributes of a relation R. If C is functionally dependent on B and B is functionally dependent on A, then C is functionally dependent on A. If the inverse mapping is nonsimple (i.e., if A is not functionally dependent on B *or* B is not functionally dependent on C), then C is said to be *transitively dependent* on A.

In a diagram C is transitively dependent on A if

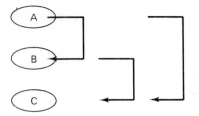

Conversion to third normal form removes this transitive dependence by splitting the relation into two:

In Fig. 14.1, for example, COMPLETION DATE is functionally dependent on PROJECT-#, and PROJECT-# is functionally dependent on EMPLOYEE-#. COMPLETION DATE is therefore transitively dependent on EMPLOYEE-#. The relation in Fig. 14.1 can be converted to third normal form by splitting it as in Fig. 14.5.

```
EMPLOYEE (EMPLOYEE-#, EMPLOYEE-NAME, SALARY
          PROJECT-#)
PROJECT (PROJECT-#, COMPLETION DATE)
```

The pair of relations in Fig. 14.5 is preferable because information about projects will be needed independently of the employee information, and COMPLETION DATE is primarily a fact about a project rather than about the employee.

A few problems might result from the relation in Fig. 14.1 not being in third normal form.

1. Before any employees are recruited for a project the completion date of the project cannot be recorded in the relation in Fig. 14.1.

2. If all the employees should leave the project so that the project has no employees until others are recruited, all segments (records) containing the completion date would be deleted. This may be thought an unlikely occurrence, but on other files a similar danger of loss of information can be less improbable.

3. If the completion date is changed, it will be necessary to search for all segments containing that completion date, and update them all.

   Third normal form is defined as follows: *A relation R is in third normal form if it is in second normal form and every nonprime attribute of R is nontransitively dependent on each candidate key of R.*

   As can be seen from the arrows in Fig. 14.5, the pair of relations in third normal form contains no transitive or nonfull dependencies.

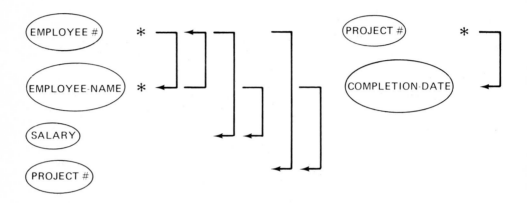

An instance of the above pair of relations:

EMPLOYEE #	EMPLOYEE	SALARY	PROJECT #		PROJECT #	COMPLETION DATE
120	JONES	2000	x		x	17.7.81
120	HARPO	1700	x		y	12.1.84
270	GARFUNKAL	1800	y		z	21.3.82
273	SELSI	3600	x			
274	ABRAHMS	3000	z			
279	HIGGINS	2400	y			
301	FLANNEL	1800	z			
306	MCGRAW	2100	z			
310	ENSON	3000	z			
315	GOLDSTEIN	3100	x			
317	PUORRO	2700	y			
320	MANSINI	1700	y			
321	SPOTO	2900	x			
340	SCHAFT	3100	x			
349	GOLD	1900	z			

Figure 14.5   To convert the relation in Fig. 14.1 into third normal form, it is split into these two relations.

**THREE
NORMALIZATION
STEPS**

There are thus three steps in the normalization process. They are summarized in Box 14.1.

Once the data items and their interdependencies are defined, the three normalization steps could be carried out automatically by an algorithm. The physical mapping of third-normal-form data into physical storage may also be done automatically at some time in the future. If such is the case, the problems of data-base design will lie primarily in the identification of the attributes which are to be stored and their interdependencies.

There is scope for some variation in the way the interdependencies are defined. Several first-normal-form versions of the schema in Fig. 13.5 are possible, for example, besides that which is shown. ACTUAL/CANDIDATE could be defined to be an attribute. There could be a separate relation for late orders. Where there is a choice the analyst should choose those attributes and relations which are least likely to be disrupted by future additions or future changes in the way the data are used.

Caution is needed with the candidate keys. It is probably undesirable with the relation in Fig. 14.2, for example, to treat either PROGRAMMER-NAME or PACKAGE-NAME as candidate keys, because at some time in the future there might conceivably be two packages with the same name or two programmers with the same name. Furthermore, if a given package has no programmer working on it at some time in the future, then the package name would be deleted. Similarly, if a programmer goes on a course and is working on no packages, then his name would be deleted. If the asterisks are removed from PROGRAMMER-NAME and PACKAGE-NAME in Fig. 14.2, then the relation is no longer in second normal form. In practice the information in it would be more likely to be stored along with programmer and package details as follows:

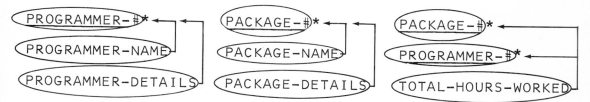

A user describing the attributes to be stored should not therefore assume that PROGRAMMER-NAME identifies PROGRAMMER-# or that PACKAGE-NAME identifies PACKAGE-#, although at first sight it may appear so.

When invoices are filed, for example, an invoice number is usually used as the primary key. The designer may, however, consider other candidate

Box 14.1 Steps in the Normalization Process [1]

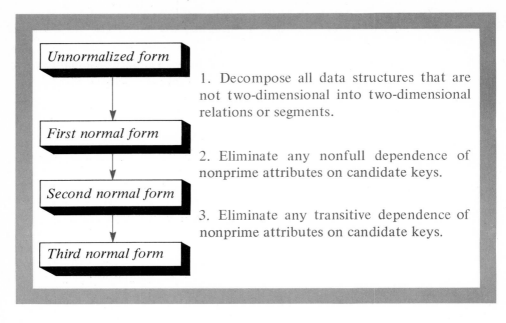

Unnormalized form

1. Decompose all data structures that are not two-dimensional into two-dimensional relations or segments.

First normal form

2. Eliminate any nonfull dependence of nonprime attributes on candidate keys.

Second normal form

3. Eliminate any transitive dependence of nonprime attributes on candidate keys.

Third normal form

keys. If not more than one invoice preparation run is performed per day, the customer number and invoice date may uniquely identify the invoice and hence form a candidate key. The customer name and invoice date may then also form a candidate key. If there can be two customers with the same name but not with the same name and address, then the customer name, customer address, and invoice date form a candidate key. One of the data items in the invoice record is the customer order number. The invoicing operation may be such that no invoice relates to more than one customer order number. When the goods are dispatched a shipment number is used, uniquely identifying the shipment. If there is never more than one shipment per invoice, then SHIPMENT-# is a candidate key. In reality, however, *it would be better to avoid the use of any of these candidate keys* because of possible changes that may occur in the future, such as duplicate customer order numbers, multiple shipments per invoice, or more than one invoicing run per day.

If we forget about candidate keys the concept of third normal form might be summarized as follows: All data items in a logical record are functionally dependent on the key of that record, the whole key, and nothing but the key.

Box 14.1 *continued*

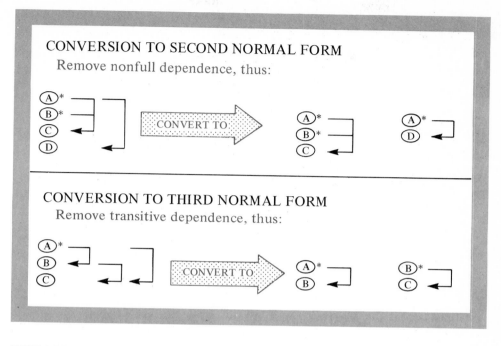

CONVERSION TO SECOND NORMAL FORM
Remove nonfull dependence, thus:

CONVERSION TO THIRD NORMAL FORM
Remove transitive dependence, thus:

STORAGE AND PERFORMANCE

Objections to third normal form are occasionally heard on grounds that it requires more storage because of key duplication, or needs more machine time because there are more records.

In fact, it needs less storage in most cases because there is less duplication of data item values. This can be seen in comparing Figs. 14.1 and 14.5, and Figs. 14.3 and 14.4. Also it is often better for machine performance because when a data item is updated, many tuples may have to be read and written if not in third normal form. Consider the completion date of project x being changed to 1.10.81 in Fig. 14.1, or the **SUPPLIER-DETAILS** of supplier JONES being changed in Fig. 14.3.

There are exceptions to this, and on rare occasions a designer may consciously design non-third-normal-form records.

SEMANTIC INTEGRITY

Let us now return to the question of semantic integrity which we left in Chapter 13. *If relations are in third normal form*, some simple rules enable us to maintain semantic integrity during *projection* and *join* operations:

1. *Projection* is permitted if the resulting segment (record) contains the same key or an equivalent candidate key.

2. Segment A may be *joined* to segment B if
   a. The key of B is a data item or group of data items in A.
   b. The key of B is uniquely identified by a data item or group of data items in A.

3. If the join also includes a projection, then both of the above rules apply.

The two examples of semantic disintegrity given in Chapter 13 are repeated in Fig. 14.6, with the associations between data items shown. They do not follow the rules above. The reader might now reexamine Fig. 13.9 and ask himself what assumptions have been made if the examples of join operations shown are valid.

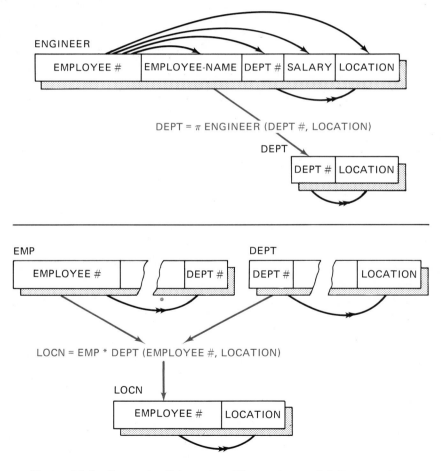

Figure 14.6 Semantic disintegrity. The *project* and *join* operations shown here do not follow the rules given in this chapter and give results which are likely to be invalid.

SUMMARY   The concept of third normal form applies not only to relational data bases but to all data bases. Experience has shown that the records of a CODASYL system, the segments of a DL/I system, or the group of data items in other systems can benefit from being in third normal form.

We believe that the ability to spot that a record is not in third normal form should be part of a systems analyst's instinct when he deals with data. He may sometimes choose to allow a record or segment to be stored *not* in third normal form, but when this is so, he should at least know what he is doing, understand his reasons, and understand the possible consequences when new data items and associations are added. A record not in third normal form may occasionally be used for performance reasons.

A record in third normal form has the simple structure shown in Fig. 6.5. If it has a concatenated key, the key may use multiple data items rather than the single data item of Fig. 6.5. On the other hand, the concatenated key may be treated as a single data item. There are no hidden single-arrow associations in the record (no transitive dependencies). If a concatenated key is used, all data items are dependent on the entire key.

This clean, simple, data grouping is easy to implement and to use. There may be complications in store in the future if more complex record structures are used. The next chapter gives a method for arriving at a clean simple schema.

The concept of semantic disintegrity applies not only to relational systems but to all data bases in which an inquiry language may divide or join groups of data items. If all records (segments) are in third normal form, the inquiry processor can be designed to enforce the rules given above or at least to warn the users that an operation they request is questionable. The alternative is for the inquiry processor to know all the associations between all data items.

For the data-base administrator, third normal form is an aid to precise thinking. A data base in third normal form can grow and evolve naturally. The updating rules are straightforward. A third-normal-form record type can have records added to it or can have records deleted without the problems that could occur with non-third-normal-form record types. Consequently, third-normal-form structuring gives a simple view of data to the programmers and users, and makes them less likely to perform invalid operations.

A SUGGESTED   Probably the best way for a data-processing user to
EXERCISE   become convinced of the value (or otherwise) of normalization is to take a section of his files and

write down what third-normal-form relations would be used to represent them. A group of systems analysts should then list all the plausible changes that might occur to the files as data processing evolves in the years ahead, and see how many of these changes would necessitate restructuring the relations in such a way that previously written application programs would have to be changed. Compare this with what reprogramming would be needed if the same changes were applied to the existing records.

REFERENCE

1. E. F. Codd, "Further Normalization of the Data Base Relational Model," in *Courant Computer Science Symposia*, Vol. 6: "Data Base Systems," edited by R. Rustin, Prentice-Hall, Inc., Englewood Cliffs, N.J., 1972.

Note: To become comfortable with normalization and third normal form, it is suggested that the reader does the exercises for Chapters 13 and 14 at the end of the book.

BOOK STRUCTURE

Chapter 14 discussed how data items should be grouped into records, or segments. Chapter 15 discusses the overall logical data-base design.

15 CANONICAL DATA STRUCTURES

There are many different ways in which a collection of data items can be associated to form a logical data base. The data-base administrator has to design a *model* or logical structure of data that will best serve the needs of its users.

CANONICAL
SCHEMA

Is there any one grouping of data which is the best for a given group of end users? Attempts have been made to find a procedure which will give a near-optimal grouping of data. The resulting minimal structure of the data is sometimes referred to as a *canonical* schema, a term used by Hubbard and Raver [1].

The ideas of canonical structuring are important in the design of data bases using today's software. They provide a design technique which the data-base administrator can and should apply in designing the schemas.

Chapter 14 discussed the groupings of data items into records (segments). This chapter discusses the linking of these groups into a schema. Both the ideas of third normal form and the ideas of canonical structuring are an aid to clear thinking about data. The systems analyst should make himself sufficiently at ease with both sets of ideas to apply them freely.

We will define a canonical schema as *a model of data which represents the inherent structure of that data and hence is independent of individual applications of the data and also of the software or hardware mechanisms which are employed in representing and using the data.*

It is desirable to step away from the current software for a moment and ask the question, "Are there any inherent properties in the data which should lead to data items being grouped and groups being interconnected in a particular structure?" The design procedure described in this chapter makes such structures clear. We refer to them as canonical structures. To be inherently stable, and be able to evolve naturally to meet the needs of new applications, a data base should have a canonical structure. This gives it the best chance of surviving future changes. It minimizes the risk of having to rewrite application programs because of data-base changes.

A DESIGN PROCEDURE   A procedure is described in this chapter by means of which a canonical schema can be derived, starting from a number of end user's views of data. Such a procedure is of value to the data-base administrator or logical data-base designer.

As we have stressed, most data bases will be changed frequently as new applications are added and new user views incorporated. It is therefore of value if the procedure can be an incremental one as to observe the effect on an existing schema of incorporating a new subschema.

The canonical form of data which we derive in this chapter is independent of whether the data will eventually be represented by means of hierarchical, CODASYL, relational, or other structures. An additional step in deriving a workable schema is to convert the canonical form of the data into a structure that can be supported by whatever software is being used. This is a relatively straightforward step.

In first deriving the canonical form of the data we will ignore the question of machine performance. Infrequently used linkages between data will be treated in the same way as linkages of high usage. The resulting minimal data structure will then be reexamined to distinguish between the high-usage and low-usage paths, or paths which are used in real-time operation. It will often be necessary to deviate from the minimal structure because of constraints in the software that is used.

It should be noted that not all software packages are able to represent the canonical data structures we derive. If software is used which cannot handle canonical structures, it may prevent desirable future evolution of the data base. The canonical data structure derived for a set of applications may be used as one means of comparing available software packages.

USAGE PATHS   A data base containing a certain collection of data could be designed *independently of how that data will be used*. In reality today, because of performance considerations, data-base design will normally be done by considering the data applications and constructing a data model which satisfies those applications. That is how we will proceed in this chapter. Although the data structure is designed with applications in mind, it is independent of *any one application* and represents inherent properties of the data. The structure which results from the design procedure may be adjusted in anticipation of possible new applications of the data not yet specified.

The relational model does not take into consideration the *usage paths* of the data. It does not say, for example, that when we print the purchase order header we will also want the purchase order details:

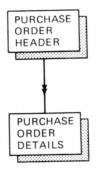

Relational enthusiasts claim that it is an advantage to exclude the usage paths from the logical data model because then that model can satisfy any type of usage in the future. However, to implement a relational data base and achieve a reasonable performance, knowledge is needed of what paths are used from one type of tuple to another.

There are two possibilities, then. A logical data representation could include or exclude information about the usage paths between groups of data items (segments, records). Most of today's software *includes* it, by means of tree structures, plex structures, sets, and so on. If the *logical* representation excludes it, as in a relational data base, the physical representation must normally include it for performance reasons.

The associations between groups of data items are an essential part of the data structures we derive in this chapter.

CANONICAL RECORD (SEGMENT) STRUCTURE   As discussed earlier, a data-base schema or sub-schema can be represented by a bubble chart—a graph consisting of directed links between data-item types.

The simplest grouping of data items is a record consisting of one key which identifies *n* attributes:

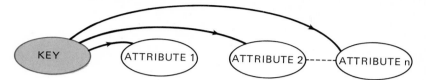

The record has no transitive dependencies, and if a concatenated key is used it is regarded as one data item. The key that is used completely identifies the attributes; *there are no path dependencies*. Such a record is in third normal form. We will refer to this as a *canonical* record (or segment) structure.

COMBINING
BUBBLE
CHARTS

The procedure we describe takes any number of logical views of data (subschemas) and combines them into a schema—a minimal set of canonical records with the requisite links between records.

The subschemas may be current user view, records, documents, or displays used in current applications, or views of how the data may be used in the future. We will represent these views of data, by means of bubble charts and will combine them, a step at a time, eliminating redundancies. Unlike Chapter 14, we will not include every possible link between the data items, but only those which end users or application programs employ. The procedure is tedious to do by hand but it is easy to do by computer.

ELIMINATION
OF REDUNDANCIES

Where single arrows are used, we can eliminate those which are redundant. In the following grouping of data items, the arrow from X to Z is probably redundant:

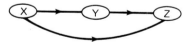

If we know that $X \longrightarrow Y$ and $Y \longrightarrow Z$, this implies that $X \longrightarrow Z$ (i.e., there is one value of Z for each value of X). In the wording of Chapter 14, X identifies Y; Y identifies Z; therefore, X identifies Z.

Why did we say that the arrow from X to Z is "probably" redundant? Is it not *always* redundant?

Unfortunately, we cannot be absolutely sure unless we know the meaning of the association. As we have illustrated earlier, it is possible to have more than one association between the same two data items:

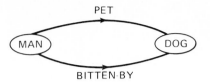

Therefore, before we delete $X \longrightarrow Z$ we must examine the meaning of the associations to be sure that $X \longrightarrow Z$ is *really* implied by $X \longrightarrow Y$ and $Y \longrightarrow Z$.

In the following case we could not delete it. An employee has a telephone number:

The employee reports to a manager:

The manager also has a telephone number:

Combining these:

It would not be valid to assume that EMPLOYEE $\longrightarrow$ TELE-PHONE-# is redundant and delete it. The employee's telephone number is different from the manager's and we want both:

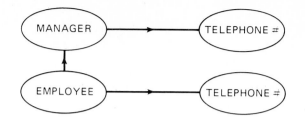

Because TELEPHONE-# is an attribute, we can have a separate data item with this name associated with both EMPLOYEE and MANAGER.

The same pattern of associations could have occurred if all the data items in question had been keys:

In this case the links between the three key data items would be left as shown.

Nevertheless, the situation when we have

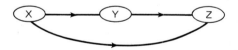

and cannot delete $X \longrightarrow Z$ is the exception rather than the rule. We have trouble in the case above because of muddled thinking: MANAGER and EMPLOYEE are really the same type of data item—a manager is an employee. We will use the rule that single-arrow redundancies can be removed, but each time we use this rule we must look carefully to ensure that we have a genuine redundancy.

Sometimes redundancies can be removed in longer strings of links. Thus, in the case

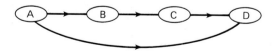

$A \longrightarrow D$ is a candidate for removal.

**COMBINING
USER VIEWS**
In the procedure that we recommend, the first user view is drawn as a bubble chart. The other user views are then added to it one at a time. As each new user view is added, the combined diagram is inspected to see whether any single-arrow links can be removed.

The process is illustrated in Box 15.1.

**KEYS AND
ATTRIBUTES**
The data items on the graph can be divided into two categories: those which are *primary keys* and those which are not. Because a primary key is a data item which *uniquely* identifies one or more other data items, we can define it simply in terms of the graph.

A primary key is a node with one or more single arrows leaving it.

There is one exception to this definition—the situation in which we have more than one *candidate key*; more than one data item identify the other data items in a group. Thus:

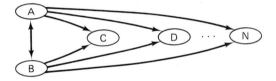

A and *B* in this case are equivalent. Each identifies the other; hence both identify $C, D, \ldots, N$. There is redundancy in this diagram. We could remove $A \longrightarrow C, A \longrightarrow D, \ldots, A \longrightarrow N$. Alternatively, we could remove $B \longrightarrow C, B \longrightarrow D, \ldots, B \longrightarrow N$.

The designer might decide that *A* is the candidate key which he wants to employ. *A*, for example, might be EMPLOYEE-# and *B* is EMPLOYEE-NAME. The designer then deletes the links $B \longrightarrow C, B \longrightarrow D, \ldots, B \longrightarrow N$:

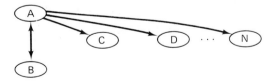

Candidate keys are not as common as this example or those in Chapter 14 might suggest. EMPLOYEE-NAME would not normally be represented as identifying EMPLOYEE-# because two employees could have the same name. EMPLOYEE-# is the unique identifier. Occasionally, there is a

First User View:

Second User View:

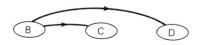

These two views are combined. *A* and *B* are colored because they are keys:

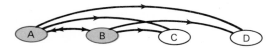

The links $A \longrightarrow C$ and $A \longrightarrow D$ are now redundant and are removed:

Third User View:

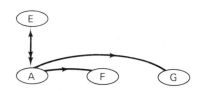

This view is merged into the diagram. There are no redundancies created:

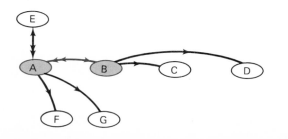

Box 15.1 *continued*

Fourth User View:

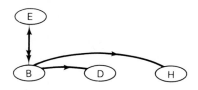

This view is merged into the diagram:

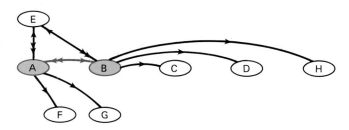

The link $A \longrightarrow E$ is now redundant and is removed. The 1:M link from E to A remains, however.

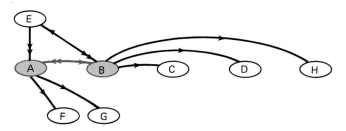

The diagram now has two primary keys, A and B. B is the root key. The diagram is redrawn with the root key at the top:

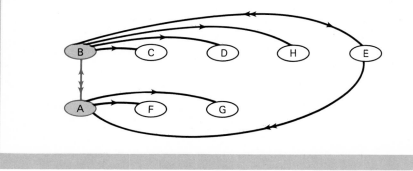

Box 15.1 *continued*

The data items may now be grouped in records (segments):

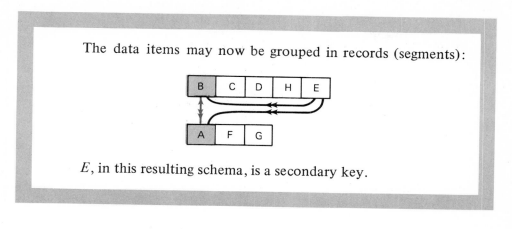

E, in this resulting schema, is a secondary key.

genuine $A \longleftrightarrow B$ relationship which should be left in the graph, for example EMPLOYEE-# $\longleftrightarrow$ SOCIAL-SECURITY-#. The designer must make a decision about which redundant links are deleted.

Data items which are not keys are referred to as *attributes*. If only single arrows are used on the graph, its terminal nodes are attributes. We can define the attributes simply: *An attribute is a node with no single arrows leaving it*.

Some of the primary keys themselves identify other primary keys; i.e., they have single arrows going to other "parent" primary keys. We suggest that, for clarity, the parent keys should be drawn *above* their associated child keys. In other words, the single arrows between keys should point upward whenever possible, as in common tree or plex structure diagrams. The uppermost key in the final graph is sometimes referred to as a *root key*. We can define a root key: *A root key is a primary key with no single arrows leaving it to another primary key.*

A key with no single-arrow links entering it is called an *initial key*. All nodes in the graph except the initial keys have a single-arrow link entering them. In Box 15.1, *A* is an initial key and *B* is a root key.

Box 15.1 shows the resulting graph drawn with the root key at the top.

To make the structure of a complex graph as clear as possible to the systems analyst, the single-arrow linkages between keys may be isolated—drawn in a different color or on a different sheet. In Box 15.1, and elsewhere in this chapter, primary keys and linkages between primary keys are drawn in red.

SECONDARY
KEYS

A secondary key does not uniquely identify another data item; one value of a secondary-key data item is associated with zero, one, or multiple values of a related data item. An attribute with a double-arrow link leaving it is referred to as a *secondary key* (or *search key*).

In the resulting schema of Box 15.1, data item *E* is a secondary key. As in Fig. 5.6, secondary keys can also consist of concatenated data items. Note that secondary keys do not give information about the *structure* of data. They give information about how it is used.

TRANSITIVE
DEPENDENCIES

The user views of data, for example the records which application programmers employ, often contain hidden transitive dependencies.

In Fig. 6.2, for example, programmer *A* used a purchase-order master record of the following structure:

ORDER #	SUPPLIER #	SUPPLIER -NAME	SUPPLIER -ADDRESS	DELIVERY- DATE	ORDER- DATE	$-TOTAL

ORDER-# is the key. It might be tempting to diagram this record as

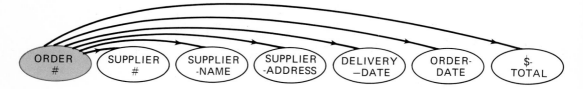

However, SUPPLIER-NAME and SUPPLIER-ADDRESS are identified by SUPPLIER-#. The record is therefore better diagrammed as in Box 15.2.

This process of removing transitive dependencies is essentially equivalent to the conversion to *third normal form* discussed in Chapter 14.

In the design technique discussed in this chapter, transitive dependencies will be removed from user's views when they are diagrammed, making all the user's attributes directly, not transitively, dependent on a key.

CONCATENATED
KEYS

Some data items may not be identified by one single data item in a user's view. In our earlier example, several suppliers may supply a part, and each charge a different price for it. The key SUPPLIER-# is used for

Box 15.2 The Avoidance of Hidden Transitive Dependencies in the Representation of User Views of Data

The record below, taken from a user's view of data in Fig. 6.2, contains a hidden transitive dependency:

ORDER #	SUPPLIER #	SUPPLIER NAME	SUPPLIER ADDRESS	ORDER DATE	DELIVERY DATE	$ TOTAL

It might be tempting to diagram it thus:

However, **SUPPLIER NAME** and **SUPPLIER ADDRESS** are identified by **SUPPLIER #**. The record should then be diagrammed as follows:

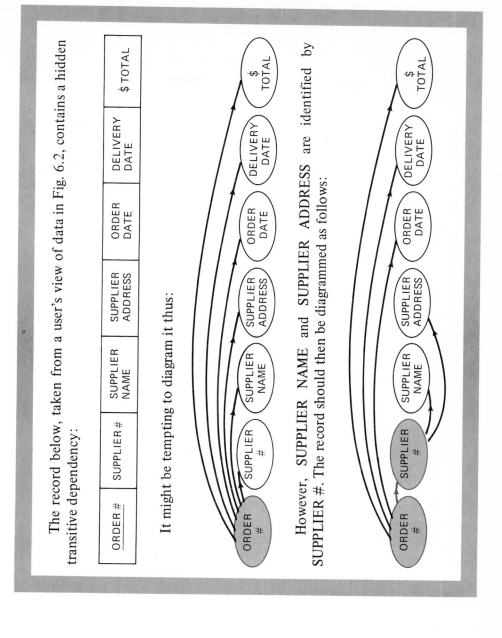

identifying information about a *supplier*. The key PART-# is used for identifying information about a *part*. Neither of those keys is sufficient for identifying the *price*. The price is dependent on both the supplier and the part. As before in the book, we create a new key to identify the price, which consists of SUPPLIER-# and PART-# joined together (concatenated).

We draw this as one bubble: ⟨ SUPPLIER-# + PART-#. ⟩

The concatenated key has single-arrow links to the keys SUPPLIER-# and PART-#. The resulting graph is as follows:

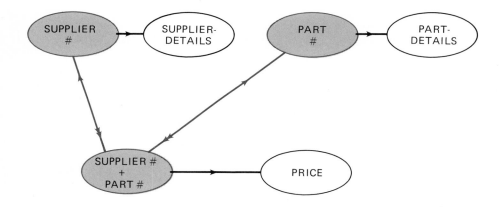

By introducing this form of concatenated key into the logical view of data, we make each data item dependent on *one* key data item.

Whenever a concatenated key is introduced, the designer should ensure that the items it identifies are dependent on the whole key, not on a portion of it only. Concatenated keys enable us to represent all records (segments) in the simple canonical form with one *key* bubble.

In practice it is sometimes necessary to join together *more than two* data items in a concatenated key.

For example, a company supplies a product to domestic and industrial customers. It charges a different price to different *types of customers*, and also the price varies from one *state* to another. There is a *discount* giving different price reductions for different quantities purchased. The *price* is identified by a combination of CUSTOMER-TYPE, STATE, DISCOUNT, and PRODUCT.

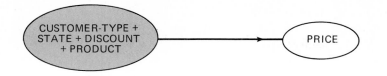

A schema relating to this component key might be:

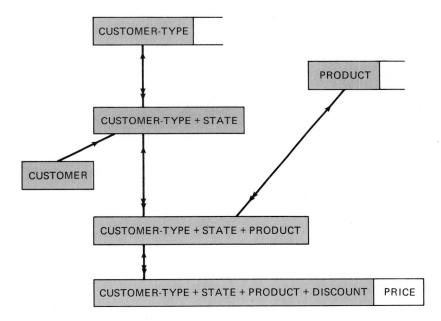

MAPPING
BETWEEN
KEYS

As we have commented earlier in the book, M:M (group marriage) mappings between records cause problems and should be avoided. The canonical schema will contain no M:M mapping between primary keys. Furthermore, it should be designed so that such a mapping will not appear in the future as the data base evolves.

When a concatenated-key bubble is used on the bubble chart, separate bubbles will be drawn for each of the data items which are components of the concatenated key, as shown in Fig. 15.1. The components CUSTOMER-TYPE, STATE, PRODUCT, and DISCOUNT could have been linked directly to the four-part concatenated key if the other concatenated keys had not existed on the diagram.

It is possible that some of the data items which compose a concatenated key will not themselves be keys on the final graph. DISCOUNT in

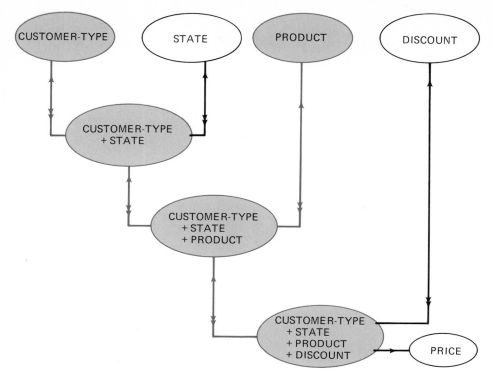

Figure 15.1   When a concatenated key is used the components of the
key will be drawn as separate bubbles on the chart. Some of these
components may not themselves be keys.

Fig. 15.1, for example, might remain as attribute rather than a key. So might
STATE. On the other hand, a discount structure might be used for which
DISCOUNT will be a key, or state tax information might be added for
which STATE is the key. If on the final graph DISCOUNT or STATE is not
a key, these bubbles and the links to them can be deleted.

       To avoid this problem, when the design procedure gives a mapping
between keys in one direction, we will add the equivalent mapping in the
opposite direction. In other words, the line between keys has arrows drawn
in both directions. If we then have an M:M mapping between two keys *A*
and *B*,

and the path in either direction might conceivably be traversed, we introduce
a third key $A + B$ as follows:

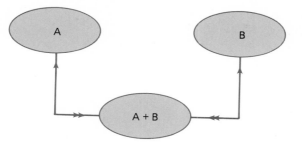

Because we use this procedure the canonical schema we create will
have no M:M links between keys unless the association could *never* be used
in one direction.

INTERSECTING   The graph which results from combining the user
ATTRIBUTES   views could contain *intersecting attributes*. An
                           intersecting attribute is an attribute which is
attached to more than one key, i.e., an attribute bubble which has more
than one arrow pointing to it.

Box 15.3 illustrates an intersecting attribute and shows three ways
of dealing with it. There should be no intersecting attributes on the final
canonical graph.

ISOLATED   An isolated attribute is an attribute which is not
ATTRIBUTES   identified by a primary key. It is a bubble with no
                           single arrows entering or leaving it, although there
will be double-arrow links.

An isolated attribute should be treated in one of the following ways:

1. It may be implemented as a repeating attribute in a variable-length record.

2. It may be treated as a solitary key—a one-data-item record.

Often it results from an error in interpretation of the user's data, and
so the meaning related to it should be carefully checked.

Box 15.3 Intersecting Attributes Must Be Reorganized

The following graph contains an intersecting attribute:

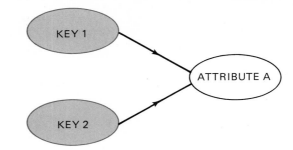

An intersecting attribute can be avoided in one of the following three ways:

1. All but one link to it may be replaced with equivalent links via an existing key:

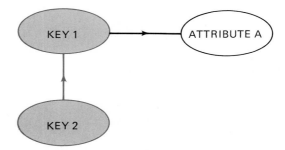

2. Redundant versions of it may be connected to each associated key:

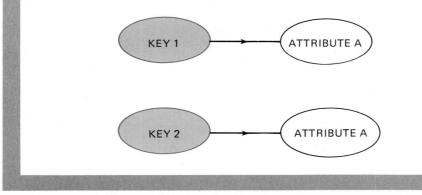

Box 15.3 *continued*

3. It may be made into a key with no attributes:

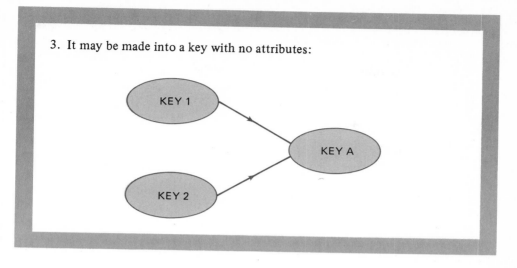

RECORD
SEQUENCE

In certain user views the *sequence* in which the data are presented to the application program, or displayed on a terminal, is critical. However, the canonical schema does not indicate the sequence in which records are stored. *In general, it is undesirable to state a record sequence in the canonical schema because different applications of the data might require the records in a different sequence.*

In a data base of book titles, for example, one application might want a logical file of book titles in alphabetical order, another might want them ordered by author, another by Library of Congress number. The different sequencing can be indicated by secondary keys—bubbles with a double-arrow link to BOOK-TITLE.

When the canonical schema is converted to a physical representation, it is necessary to state the record sequencing. This is a statement that should be part of the physical, rather than the logical, description of data. Some *logical* data description languages require statements about the order of records. This information must then be added when the canonical schema is converted to the software logical schema. The enthusiasts of *relational* data bases stress that the sequencing of the tuples should not be part of the *logical* data description.

EXAMPLE 1

We will now step through an example of our database design procedure.

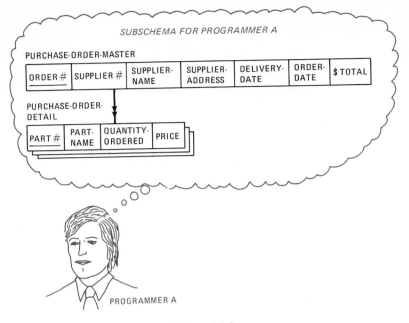

Figure 15.2

Consider the data base illustrated at the bottom of Fig. 6.2. Could that be designed in a cleaner fashion?

We start with the view of programmer *A*, drawn again for convenience in Fig. 15.2. Caution is needed in interpretation. Neither of programmer *A*'s records are in the simple canonical form we have described. The purchase-order-master record contains the transitive dependency shown. The purchase-order-detail record contains QUANTITY-ORDERED, which depends not merely on PART-# but also on ORDER-#. We therefore have to introduce a concatenated key PART-# + ORDER-#. What the programmer means by PRICE needs to be clarified. Probably he means the total price of the quantity ordered of a given part. PRICE is then also identified by PART-# + ORDER-#.

Figure 15.3 shows the resulting graph. The keys and associations between them are in red.

The completed mapping between keys does not introduce any M:M association.

The view of programmer *B*, shown in Fig. 15.4 may now be added to the graph. It introduces only one new data item, QUANTITY-ON-HAND, but two new associations between existing data items, shown in Fig. 15.5.

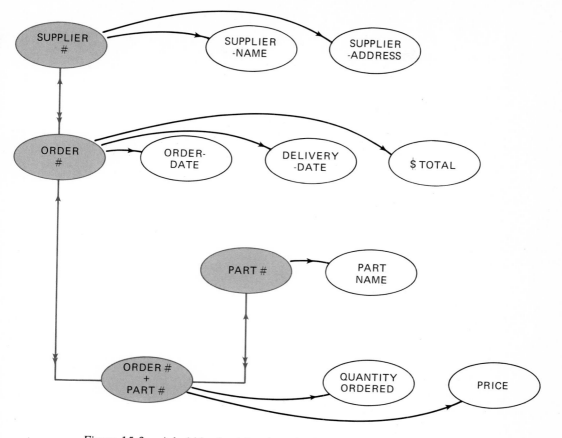

Figure 15.3   A bubble chart for the subschema in Fig. 15.2.

The new link between ORDER-# and SUPPLIER-NAME is redundant and is deleted. The link between ORDER-# and PART-# is an M:M association between keys and hence is not permitted.

The concatenated key we need to avoid this M:M link already exists, ORDER-# + PART-#. The link between ORDER-# and PART-# is therefore deleted.

ESTABLISHING
PRECISION
To draw this graph correctly, the data-base designer needs to have a precise understanding of the meaning of the data items and the associations between them. Often in practice the designer's initial understanding of the

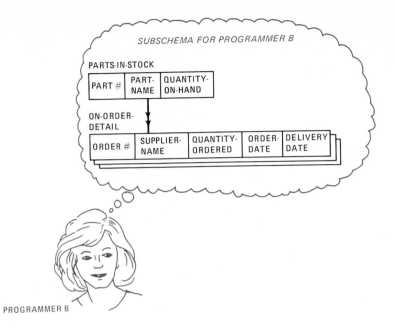

Figure 15.4

data is insufficiently precise. Sometimes two data items with different names in different user views are really the same. More often two data items with the same name are really different. The latter are called *homonyms*, the former *synonyms*. In this book the terms DATA ITEM and FIELD are synonyms. In Fig. 6.2 the data items labeled PRICE are homonyms. The data item called PRICE in the QUOTATION record is a quotation price. It is a different data item to PRICE on the purchase order. Homonyms frequently occur with data items having labels such as QUANTITY or TOTAL. When a homonym is encountered, the name of one of the data items should be changed. In this case we will change PRICE in the QUOTATION record to QUOTE-PRICE.

In Fig. 6.2, there are no arrows on the association between the records SUPPLIER and QUOTATION. The mapping between the keys PART-# and SUPPLIER-# is therefore uncertain. In the earlier illustrations in this book we have assumed an M:M mapping between PART-# and SUPPLIER-#, but this is not necessarily the case. It depends on the nature of PART-#. PART-# might be the supplier's unique number for a part, in which case the mapping is PART-# ◄───► SUPPLIER-#. On the other hand, it might be the purchasing firm's number in which case we have: PART-# ◄───►► SUPPLIER-#.

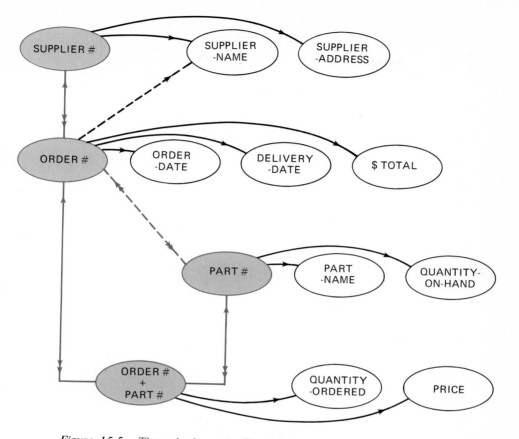

Figure 15.5 The subschema in Fig. 15.4 is merged into the bubble chart of Fig. 15.3. The dotted line between ORDER-# and SUPPLIER-NAME is redundant and can be deleted.

The dotted link between ORDER-# and PART-# is an M:M association between keys and hence is not permitted.

We will assume the latter. In that case the QUOTATION record is identified by the concatenated key PART-# + SUPPLIER-#. We need to introduce this new key to identify QUOTE-PRICE and DELIVERY-TIME. The data-base administrator's view in Fig. 6.2 also introduces two new data items: SUPPLIER-INFORMATION identified by SUPPLIER-#, and PART-DESCRIPTION identified by PART-#.

The resulting graph is shown in Fig. 15.6.

It is possible that other *paths* will be required which are not yet represented on the schema. Before completing the canonical schema, the

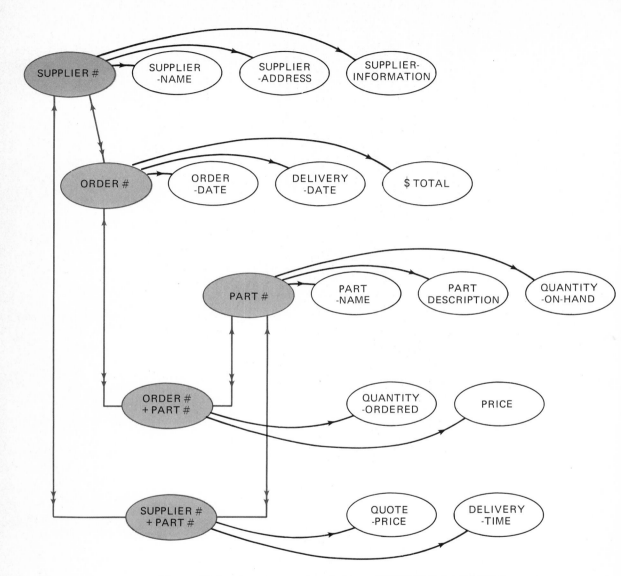

Figure 15.6   A new concatenated key, SUPPLIER-# + PART-#, must
be introduced to identify the data items QUOTE-PRICE and DELIV-
ERY-TIME. This canonical schema is redrawn in Fig. 15.7 showing the
resulting records or segments.

paths between keys may be examined to see whether any other key-to-key
association should be added, because it is likely to be needed in a user
view not yet considered.

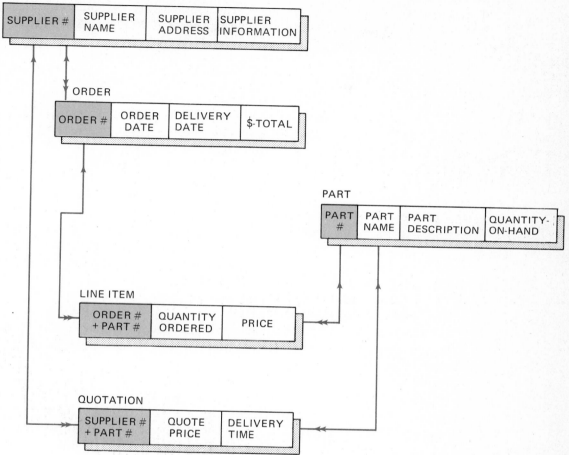

Figure 15.7 A canonical structure of the data base in Fig. 6.2. It can be converted simply to the data structures used by specific software such as CODASYL, DL/I, or relational systems. Each arrow, single and double, should have a number associated with it giving the frequency of usage of that path, and an indication whether it is used interactively. These numbers will be used in selecting the particular software schema.

CONVERSION TO OTHER STRUCTURES   It is generally easy to convert the canonical data base into a data base related to a particular software view, provided that software has the requisite functions.

The schema in Fig. 15.7 is representable as three CODASYL sets whose owners are SUPPLIER record, ORDER record, and PART record. It is representable as two DL/I physical data-base records with two logical connections between them. Third, the record structure is already in third normal form, and the single-arrow links indicate where extra identifier data items need to be added to the relations. SUPPLIER-# would be added to the ORDER-# relation to provide the path from ORDER to SUPPLIER.

A relational version of this schema would therefore have the following structure:

```
SUPPLIER (SUPPLIER-#, SUPPLIER-NAME, SUPPLIER-ADDRESS,
     SUPPLIER-INFORMATION)
PART (PART-#, PART-NAME, PART-DESCRIPTION, QUANTITY-ON-HAND)
QUOTATION (SUPPLIER-#, PART-#, QUOTE-PRICE, DELIVERY-TIME)
ORDER (ORDER-#, SUPPLIER-#, ORDER-DATE, DELIVERY-DATE, $-TOTAL)
LINE-ITEM (ORDER-#, PART-#, QUANTITY-ORDERED, PRICE)
```

PERFORMANCE CONSIDERATIONS   Whereas a canonical data structure is not concerned with machine performance, a DL/I or CODASYL structure needs to take into consideration which are the frequently used paths or paths used in fast-response operation. It may also need to take into consideration the lengths of records (segments). Inasfar as these considerations are necessary, it could be said that DL/I and CODASYL data descriptions (and those of most other database software) are not completely machine-independent.

In representing Fig. 15.7 in DL/I, there is more than one way to group the segments into physical trees. Figure 15.8 shows two ways.

The logical links between the trees, shown as dashed lines, normally take more machine time to follow than the paths which constitute the physical trees. Often the logical paths require a seek, whereas the physical paths do not. The frequently used paths should therefore be physical rather than logical. In Fig. 15.7 the path from ORDER to LINE ITEM may be far more frequently used than any other path. In this case the right-hand structure of Fig. 15.8 is the better of the two.

The canonical structure has two-way mapping between all associated keys. In practice certain paths between keys (i.e., between records or segments) may not be traversed in both directions. If a path is never traversed, the pointers or other mechanisms in the physical data base that would be required for that path will be omitted.

AUTOMATING THE PROCEDURE   The procedure we have described is tedious. However, automation can help. An interactive design tool could be programmed in which the designer enters one user view at a time, checks that it appears correct in its own right, has it merged into the data base, and inspects the results. When

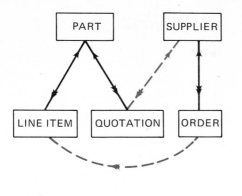
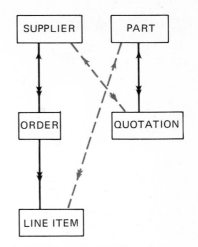

Figure 15.8　　Two ways of representing the canonical schema of Fig. 15.7 by physical tree structures with links spanning the trees. If ORDER to LINE ITEM is by far the most frequently used path, the right-hand way is better. This could be the schema for DL/I or TOTAL software.

the program deletes an apparently redundant association, it should ask the designer if he considers it to be *genuinely* redundant. This tool would be valuable for a data-base administrator. Each time a programmer or user wants to add new data types or use the data base in a new way, the data-base administrator could enter the new user view and see what effect it has on the existing data base.

It is desirable to consider the effect of different data structures on machine performance. To do this, the frequency of use of each user's view should be estimated. From these estimates the frequency of traversing each association path may be added up—again a tedious task which can be automated. A graph showing frequency of traverse of each link may have a major effect on how a designer converts his canonical schema into a working software schema. As well as showing the frequency of traverse, the graph should show which associations are used interactively with fast-response requirements.

We will discuss performance considerations again later in the chapter.

Box 15.4 summarizes a procedure for canonical schema design. Several of the steps in this procedure require intelligent human consideration and hence the procedure is probably best programmed as an interactive operation in which the designer feeds in one data view at a time.

Programs have been written to automate logical file design for certain data-base management systems [1, 2].

Box 15.4 A Procedure for Canonical Data-Base Design

1. Take the first user's view of data and draw it in the form of a bubble chart—a graph with point-to-point directed links between single data items, representing associations of the two types: 1 and M.

    Where a concatenated key is used, draw this as one bubble, and draw the component data items of the concatenated key as separate bubbles, thus:

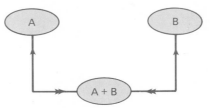

    Check that the representation avoids hidden transitive dependencies (see Box 15.2). Where a concatenated key data item has to be used, ensure that all single-arrow links from it go to data items which are dependent on the *full* concatenated key, not merely part of it. In other words, ensure that the representation of the user's view is in third normal form.

    Otherwise draw only the associations which concern this user.

2. Take the next user's view, representing it as above. Merge it into the graph. Check for any synonyms or homonyms, removing them if they appear.

3. In the resulting graph distinguish between the attribute nodes and the primary key nodes. (A primary key node has one or more single-arrow links leaving it.) Mark the primary keys in some way, e.g. red color.

4. For each association *between keys*, add the inverse association if it is not already on the graph. If this results in an M:M link between keys, determine whether the inverse association would ever be used in reality. If it could be used at any time in the future, replace it by introducing an extra concatenated key incorporating the key data items that were linked.

5. Examine the associations and identify any that appear redundant. For any associations that are candidates for removal, check carefully that their meaning is *genuinely* redundant; if so, remove them.

6. Repeat the previous four steps until all user views are merged into the graph.

Box 15.4 *continued*

7. Identify the root keys. (A root key is a primary key with no single arrow leaving it *to another key*.)

    For pictorial clarity the diagram should be rearranged with the root keys at the top. The single-arrow links between keys should point upward where possible. The links between primary keys may be marked in color.

8. Observe whether the graph contains any isolated attributes. An isolated attribute is a node with no single-arrow links entering or leaving it (only double-arrow links). An isolated attribute could be treated in one of three ways:

    a. It may be implemented as a repeating attribute in a variable-length record.
    b. It may be treated as a solitary key—a one-data-item record.
    c. It may be the result of an error in interpretation of the user's data, in which case the error is corrected.

9. Adjust the graph to avoid any intersecting attributes. (An intersecting attribute is an attribute with more than one single-arrow link entering it.) An intersecting attribute can be avoided as in Box 15.3 by:

    a. Replacing one or more links to it with equivalent links via an existing key.
    b. Duplicating the data item in question.
    c. Treating it as a solitary key—a one-data-item record.

10. Redraw the data items arranged into groups (records, segments, tuples), each having one primary key and its associated attributes. A group may now be drawn as a box.

11. Identify all secondary keys. (A secondary key is an attribute with one or more double-arrow links leaving it.) Draw the secondary-key links between the boxes.

12. The unconstrained "canonical" schema may now be converted into the more constrained view associated with a particular software package. It is generally a simple step to convert the canonical schema into a CODASYL, DL/I, or relational schema. Some software, however, has constraints that would require a major deviation from, or splitting of, the canonical view. Some software will simply not be able to handle it.

    In converting the canonical schema to a particular software schema, performance considerations associated with high-usage and fast-response paths should be examined. We suggest the following steps:

Box 15.4 *continued*

a. Mark all paths which are used in interactive systems and which need fast response time.

b. Estimate the number of times per month each user path will be traversed. Add up how often each association will be traversed (in each direction when applicable).

c. Estimate the length of each group.

d. For each M association, estimate the size of M, i.e., how many values on average are associated with one value, or how many "child" groups are associated with a 'parent" group.

   The information above may affect the choice of structure and may cause the designer to modify the schema. In some cases a group may be split because it contains a mixture of frequently used and rarely used data, or is too long. In some cases a schema will be split to avoid complexity.

13. With the software schema designed, return to the original user views and ensure that they can be handled by it. In some cases the performance cost of handling a particular user view is sufficiently great that it is worthwhile completely modifying that user view.

EXAMPLE 2   Now we will examine a slightly more complex example—although still highly simplified from reality. For ease of tutorial diagramming, many *attributes* have been combined or omitted.

The application relates to the movement of cargo by sea. A company operates a fleet of cargo ships which visit many ports. Box 15.5 shows the views of data which various application designers require.

We will assemble these user views into a canonical schema. As always we should be cautious when taking the user views and translating them into bubble charts.

Figures 15.9 to 15.17 illustrate the process.

Figure 15.9

Box 15.5 Example 2: 7 User Views

First User View:

Information is stored about each ship, including the volume of its cargo storage capacity. The key is VESSEL.

VESSEL	CARGO-VOLUME	DETAILS

Second User View:

A ship stops at many ports and it is necessary to print out its itinerary:

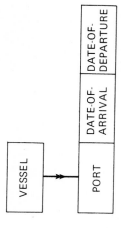

Third User View:

Persons who ship goods are referred to as consignees. Their goods must be crated or stored in shipping containers. These are given a container identification number. A list can be obtained, when requested, of what containers have been sent by a consignee:

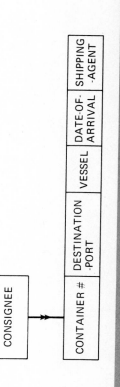

Box 15.5 *continued*

Fourth User View:

The shipments are all handled by shipping agents. A shipping-agent report must be generated, listing all the containers that a given agent is handling and giving their waybill numbers:

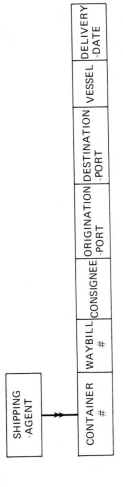

| SHIPPING -AGENT |

| CONTAINER # | WAYBILL # | CONSIGNEE | ORIGINATION -PORT | DESTINATION -PORT | VESSEL | DELIVERY -DATE |

Fifth User View:

The fifth user view is the waybill. A waybill relates to a shipment of goods between two ports on a specified vessel. The shipment may consist of one or more containers:

| WAYBILL # | ORIGINATION -PORT | DESTINATION -PORT | CONSIGNEE | DATE-OF- DEPART. | DELIVERY -DATE | VESSEL | SHIPPING -AGENT |

| CONTAINER # | CONTENTS | HANDLING- INSTRUCTIONS | SIZE |

Sixth User View:

For a given vessel a list is required of what containers should be off-loaded at each port:

Box 15.5 *continued*

Seventh User View:

For a given vessel a list is required of what containers are to be loaded at each port. Details of the container size, handling instructions, and destination port are needed for loading purposes:

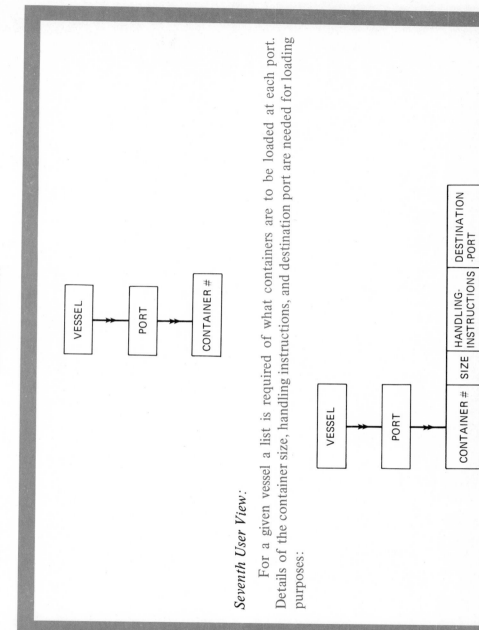

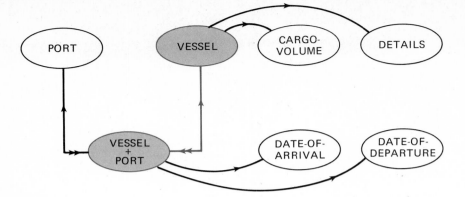

Figure 15.10 When the second user view is added, a concatenated key is needed, VESSEL + PORT. The components of such a key are drawn on the graph (in this case adding the data-item PORT).

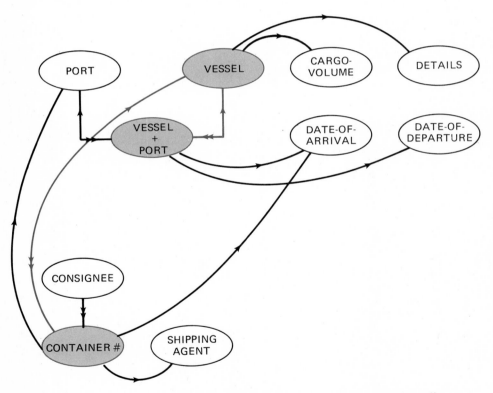

Figure 15.11 DESTINATION PORT in the third user view is really the same data item as PORT in the previous graph. This causes PORT to become an intersecting attribute when the third user view is merged into the graph. DATE-OF-ARRIVAL also becomes an intersecting attribute. We could take action at this stage to avoid the intersecting attributes. However, we will leave them until the remaining user views are merged into the graph, because they might disappear.

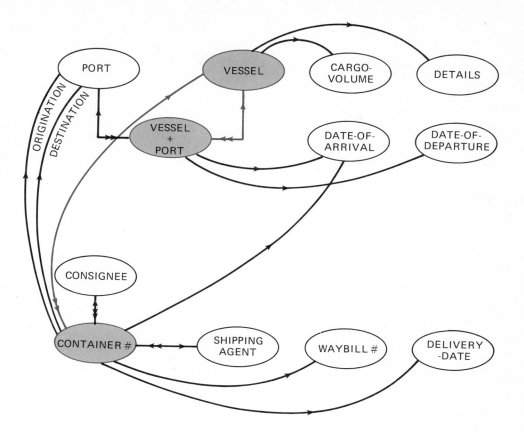

Figure 15.12 The fourth user view introduces two new data-items, WAYBILL-# and DELIVERY-DATE. The designer should find out whether DELIVERY-DATE is really the same as DATE-OF-ARRIVAL. In fact it is not. DATE-OF-ARRIVAL is the scheduled docking data of the vessel, and DELIVERY-DATE is the estimated date of delivery to the customer. There are also some new associations. There are two associations between CONTAINER-# and PORT. It is perfectly acceptable to draw multiple links between the same data items. When this is done, the links must be labeled to indicate their meaning.

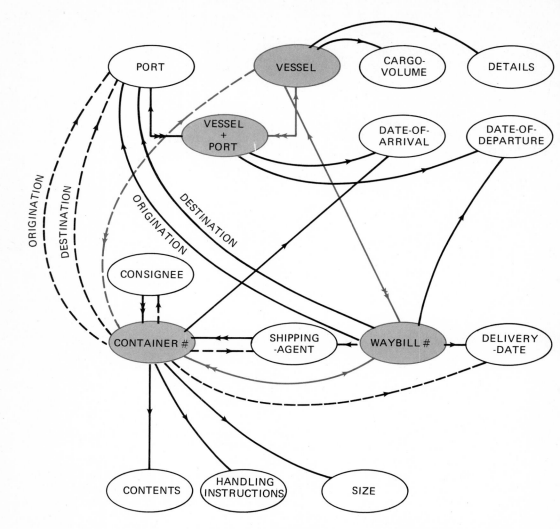

Figure 15.13 The fifth user view adds three more data-items which are attributes of CONTAINER-#. It adds several new associations and creates six possible redundancies in the associations. The redundancies are drawn here as dashed lines.

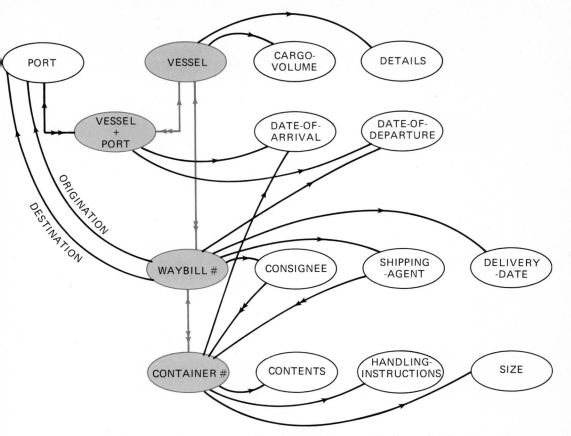

Figure 15.14   This Figure is Fig. 15.13 redrawn with the redundant associations removed, and the primary keys arranged so that the single arrows between them are pointing upwards for visual clarity. There are three *intersecting* attributes in this graph: PORT, DATE-OF-ARRIVAL, and DATE-OF-DEPARTURE. We should not attempt to deal with them (as in Box 15.3) until all user views have been merged into the graph. New user views might change their situation.

VALIDATION   Once again, the structure derived by this method must be converted into a structure which meets the constraints of a given software package. The structure in Fig. 15.17 can be represented by four CODASYL sets as in Fig. 15.18 or by a DL/I data base with one physical tree and a logical child and parent linkage as shown in Fig. 15.19. SHIPPING AGENT and CONSIGNEE are secondary keys, both pointing to CONTAINER-#. These could be represented with secondary indices in CODASYL or DL/I.

Figure 15.20 shows a relational version of the schema.

When a software schema is created in this way, it should be validated by returning to the original user views and checking to see whether each view can be handled satisfactorily. If some of them cannot, this may indicate either that the user views were misinterpreted in the design process, or that the software does not contain adequate facilities for handling a canonical structure.

When the software is not adequate, it is usually possible to back away from the canonical structure by introducing redundancy. Some software, for example, cannot handle the secondary keys of Fig. 15.17. Additional records, sets, or segments may be added to avoid the need for secondary-key mechanisms. In general, however, such deviation from the canonical structure may cause the future needs for program conversion that we seek to avoid.

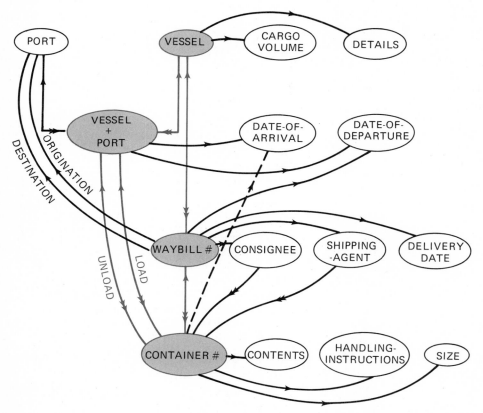

Figure 15.15 The sixth and seventh user views are merged into the graph. The association between CONTAINER-# and DATE-OF ARRIVAL becomes a candidate for removal. Caution is needed because there are two paths which are possibly equivalent from CONTAINER-# to VESSEL + PORT to DATE-OF-ARRIVAL. In fact it is a genuine redundancy and so is removed.

In practice, given today's software and hardware, there may be several reasons for deviating from the canonical structure:

1. Software limitations make it necessary to modify the structure, often by adding redundant records, sets, or segments.

2. A record may be split because it is excessively long, and performance can be improved by dividing it.

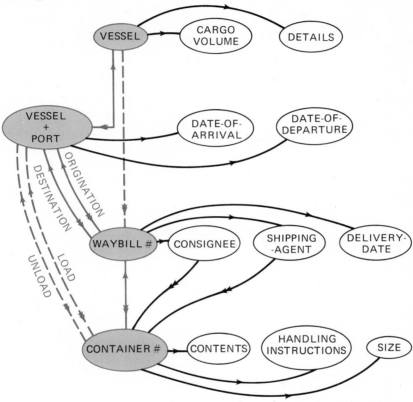

Figure 15.16   We now deal with the intersecting attributes. The problem with DATE-OF-ARRIVAL disappeared in the previous figure. Two intersecting attributes remain: PORT and DATE-OF-DEPARTURE.

DATE-OF-DEPARTURE is identified by VESSEL + PORT. We therefore substitute WAYBILL-# → VESSEL + PORT for WAYBILL-# → DATE-OF-DEPARTURE. This causes the key association WAYBILL-#→VESSEL to become redundant, and be removed.

Similarly PORT is identified by VESSEL + PORT. We there substitute two WAYBILL-# → VESSEL + PORT links for the WAYBILL-# → PORT links. There is then no need for the separate attribute PORT. The links from CONTAINER-# to VESSEL + PORT then appear redundant, and can in fact be removed. The three dashed lines represent single-arrow linkages which can be removed, and also double-arrow linkages which should never by *automatically* removed. Here, however their double-arrow meanings are also redundant and so are removed.

3. A data base may be split to avoid excessive complexity or size, or to improve machine performance.

4. Frequently used or fast-response paths may be separated from infrequently used paths to improve machine performance.

5. A record or data base may be split for secondary reasons.

6. In certain applications high availability may be exceptionally critical. The data for those applications may be isolated from the overall schema so that if a failure occurs relating to other less critical data, it does not knock out the critical applications.

SUMMARY   A canonical data-base structure is a minimal conceptual schema. Its records are in third normal form and there is no M:M mapping between records. It can be derived by a step-by-step procedure of combining the user views of data.

When implemented with an appropriate data-base management system, it will provide the best protection from the future that can be reasonably expected. In the future the requirements for, and usage of, data will change, and in most cases such change can be accommodated by incremental growth of a canonical schema, without drastic restructuring.

It is recommended that a data-base designer should design a canonical schema and then represent it in the software structure of his choice,

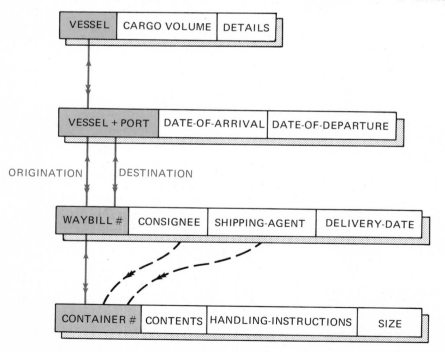

Figure 15.17   A canonical schema encompassing the subschemas of Box. 15.5. This is Fig. 15.16 redrawn in a more conventional form.

carefully examining the performance considerations. A canonical schema can be represented in CODASYL DBTG-based software, in DL/I-based software, as a relational data base or in some other data-base software structures. When viewed in this way, *the similarity between these three forms of data base is perhaps more striking than the differences.* Whichever approach is used, a variety of *physical* organization techniques can be applied. The choice of physical organization greatly affects the machine performance, and the alternatives are similar whichever logical representation is used.

The design process is illustrated in Fig. 15.21. Both stated end-user requirements and assumptions about how data will be employed in the future may be used in assembling the canonical schema. This schema will then be converted into the logical data description facilities of a given software package, and a physical data organization will be designed.

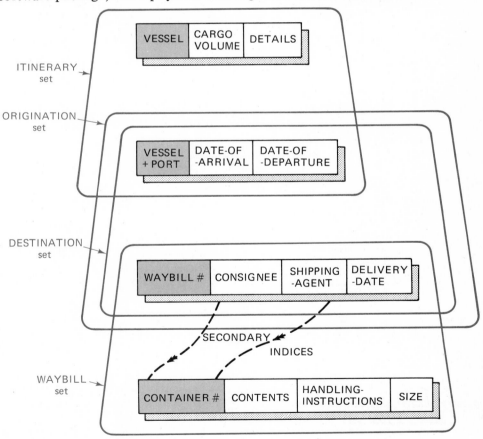

Figure 15.18   A CODASYL representation of the canonical schema of Fig. 15.17.

VESSEL
VESSEL
CARGO-VOLUME
DETAILS
PORT
PORT
DATE-OF-ARRIVAL
DATE-OF-DEPARTURE
DESTINATION
LOGICAL CHILD AND PARENT LINKAGE
WAYBILL
WAYBILL #
CONSIGNEE
SHIPPING-AGENT
DELIVERY-DATE
SECONDARY KEYS
CONTAINER
CONTAINER #
CONTENTS
HANDLING-INSTRUCTIONS
SIZE

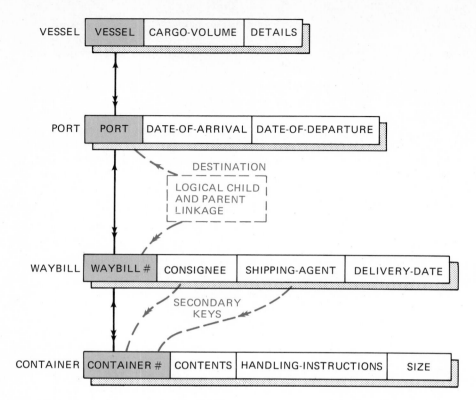

Figure 15.19 A DL/I representation of the canonical schema of Fig. 15.17.

VESSEL
CARGO VOLUME
DETAILS
VESSEL
PORT
DATE-OF-ARRIVAL
DATE-OF-DEPARTURE
WAYBILL #
VESSEL
ORIGINATION -PORT
DESTINATION -PORT
CONSIGNEE
SHIPPING -AGENT
DELIVERY -DATE
CONTAINER #
WAYBILL #
CONTENTS
HANDLING-INSTRUCTIONS
SIZE

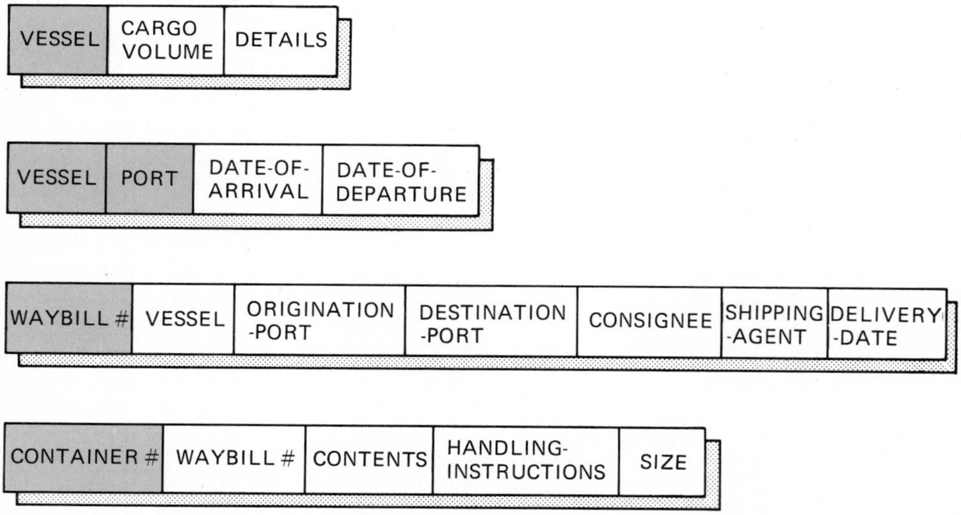

Figure 15.20 A relational representation of the canonical schema of Fig. 15.17. An optimum physical structure used to implement this schema could be similar to that used to implement the schemas of Fig. 15.18 or Fig. 15.19.

Changes will occur in the future as illustrated by the red parts of Fig. 15.21. New uses of the data will crop up. Design feedback from the operational system will cause modification to the physical organization and possibly also to the software logical data description.

High-level languages for querying, searching, or updating data can be based on a canonical data structure. Such languages could employ the *join* and *project* operations or a relational calculus such as that discussed in Chapter 13 and hence could give a high flexibility in using the data. They could employ dialogue techniques designed to be as easy as possible for the nonprogramming user. Such facilities could operate whether the data base uses a relational, CODASYL, DL/I, or some other canonical schema.

It is clear that end-user languages of this type are beginning to emerge which are both very powerful and easy to use [3]. It is likely that much of the future of commercial data processing will employ data-base interrogation and manipulation languages and report generators, *which bypass the need for application programming*. Such facilities will be easier to create if they are based on clean data structures in third normal form and without M:M associations. Powerful, easy-to-use facilities will always run the risk of creating results with semantic disintegrity, and to control this problem conceptually clean data structures are needed in third normal form.

We noted that some data-base management systems cannot in general handle canonical structures. These, in the long run, will be of limited application. In the author's view, new data-base software should be designed to handle canonical structures, and the hardware should be designed to assist. Future hardware could assist in locating and searching data, possibly with automated facilities for primary or secondary indexing or with associative memory modules, which are discussed in Part II.

REFERENCES

1. G. Hubbard and N. Raver, "Automating Logical File Design," *Proc. International Conference on Very Large Data Bases, Framingham, Mass., 1975,* ACM, New York, London, and Amsterdam, 1975.

2. *Data Base Design Aid, Designer's Guide, IBM Manual GH20-1620,* a manual on an IMS (DL/I) design program, IBM, White Plains, N.Y., 1976.

3. Moshé M. Zloof, "Query-by-Example: The Invocation and Definition of Tables and Forms," *Proc. International Conference on Very Large Data Bases, Framingham, Mass., 1975,* ACM, New York, London, and Amsterdam, 1975.

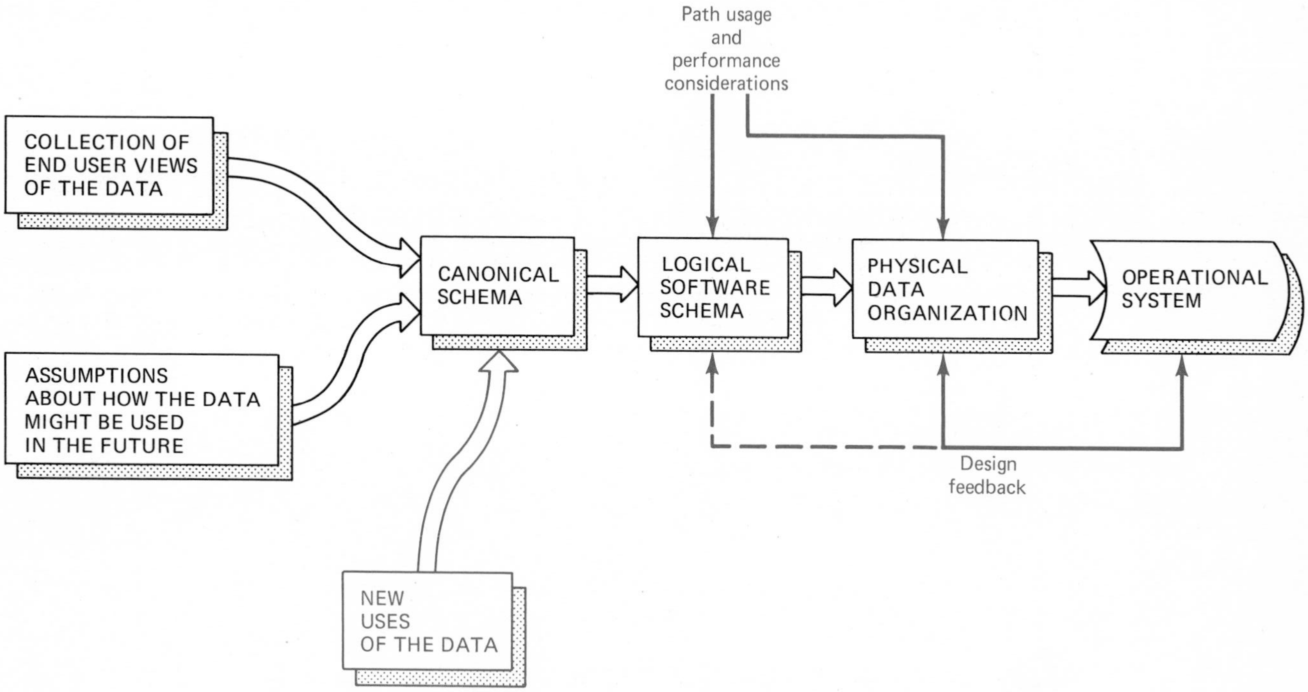

Figure 15.21 **The design process.**

16 VARIETIES OF DATA INDEPENDENCE

We have stressed that data independence is one of the main reasons for complications in data-base management systems. There are, however, several varieties of data independence which differ in cost. Data-base systems in practice range from having effectively no data independence to having extremely elaborate software for converting data items and structures as the application programs are being executed.

The advantage of the former is that less main memory and instruction cycles are needed, and the data structures can be tailored to maximize throughput or minimize response times. Indeed, on many real-time systems demanding response times of 2 seconds or so, one finds that data independence has been thrown to the winds. Such systems impose a straitjacket on application developers. Often in the long run these systems cost much more in maintenance than the original implementation cost.

In a few rare cases an application is so well defined and insulated from other applications that the data base will not change. Most of the time in practice, however, an initial appearance of stability has proved to be deceptive. Change has come in unanticipated ways from unexpected quarters, and often the modifications have been horrifyingly expensive. In the light of such experience a major principle of data processing must be that *you can never tell how the application of stored data will eventually evolve.* Furthermore, *in most cases the data changes before the system is installed.* The data-base installation and management techniques must be designed for change.

Some data-base management systems are designed around these principles. Others are not designed to facilitate change and do not provide for the processing of data in a manner other than that in which they are organized.

The latter systems do not permit data to be restructured without consequent upheavals in the programs that use them.

CANONICAL
SCHEMA

The canonical schema that we described in Chapter 15 is an attempt to make a statement about the *inherent properties of the data*. Those properties remain no matter what hardware or software is used to represent the data.

If the data-base management system employed a canonical schema and that schema remained intact no matter what software, hardware, or physical structuring was used, *then we would have true data independence*. Most data-base management systems today, however, do not use a canonical schema. The canonical schema in Fig. 15.21 was not described as being part of a data-base management system, but rather as being a design tool external to such a system. The canonical schema has to be converted to the logical schema of the software, and this contains information other than that which is *inherent in the nature of the data*.

Certain types of information probably should not be in the canonical schema because they do not describe the inherent proportion of the data but describe how it is used or how it is represented in machines. How it is used and how it is represented will change, and sometimes change fast and substantially. The canonical schema should therefore not contain:

1. Information about volume of path usage, throughput, or response-time requirements.
2. Structures derived from a knowledge of the above.
3. Details of the sequence in which records will be read. Different users may want the records in a different sequence.
4. Information about accessing techniques used to obtain the records.

This implies that the canonical description of data should not use phrases such as the following from the CODASYL Data Description Language:

```
LOCATION MODE IS CALC PROCEDURE ABC

ORDER IS PERMANENT INSERTION IS PRIOR

SET SELECTION THRU CALC-KEY EQUAL TO PARTCODE

WITHIN AREA OF EMPLOYEE
```

```
FOR DECODING CALL PROCEDURE XYZ

OWNER IDENTIFIED BY CURRENT OF SET

SORTED BY SUPPLIER WITHIN CODE WITHIN REGION

USING INDEX NAME FRED
```

The use of such phrases violates the principle of data independence and introduces elements into the data description which are likely to be changed in the long-term future, thereby necessitating application program rewriting. Furthermore, they make the logical data description unnecessarily complex. A canonical data description ought to be easily understood by a non-programming layman who wants to use the data (with the help of a data dictionary).

A data-base management system employing canonical conceptual schemas should have the structure shown in Fig. 16.1. The design of the *physical* data description should take into consideration performance requirements, response-time requirements, path-usage volumes, and recovery considerations—all of which are deliberately excluded from the design of the conceptual schema. The physical data description will be concerned with the sequence of records, with the access methods, and with security techniques.

When the system is running, usage data relevant to the design of the physical schema should be collected automatically. There is thus *design feedback* which permits the physical schema to be constantly tuned or restructured, but this process does not change the canonical schema. The design feedback could be handled manually by the data-base administrator staff. Future systems might have sufficient capability to adjust the physical positioning or organization of data automatically, a dynamic response to the usage of the data.

A canonical schema and its associated data description language could take a variety of forms—all of them simpler than the CODASYL or DL/I methods of logical data description. Possibly the best form is that of a relational data base.

BINDING

The process of converting one view of data into another is called *binding*. Where there are the three views of data we have described, the programmer's logical view must be "bound" to the global logical view and the global logical view must be "bound" to the physical view before an application program can use the

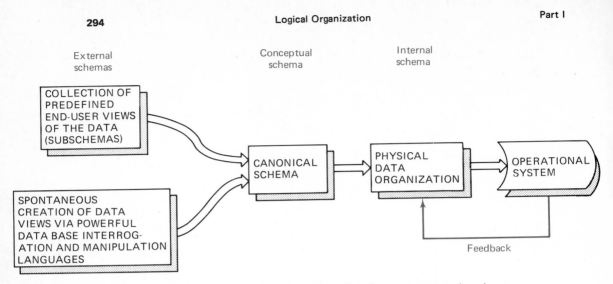

External schemas   Conceptual schema   Internal schema

Figure 16.1   A structure for future data base management systems.

data. The binding associates the data and relationships in one view with those in another.

Suppose, for example, that an application programmer writes statements requesting the records shown in Fig. 6.2. At some time prior to execution, these statements must be converted into statements requesting the relevant records from the global view of data in Fig. 6.1 (or a canonical equivalent) and reshuffling the data items to form the two record types that constitute the programmer's view. These resulting statements must then be converted into statements instructing the machine how to locate the physical records that are needed (which may require the examination of index records or other intermediate records) and how to deblock or otherwise convert the physical records into the form described in the schema description language. We will call the first of these two conversions *logical binding* and the second *physical binding*.

There are several places at which binding could be accomplished. Logical and physical binding may occur separately. Binding can occur at one of the following times:

1. When the application program is compiled.

2. When the compiled (object) program is linked, with precompiled table or routines containing data descriptors.

3. When the application program is loaded into the computer.

4. When the file is opened.

5. When the data are accessed.

Once binding has occurred, the application program is no longer independent of the physical data. In the list of binding times above the interval between binding and using the data varies from long to short. If binding occurs when the data are accessed, the period of data dependence is very short. If binding occurs when the application program is compiled, the interval could be very long. If *logical* binding occurs when the program is compiled, the schema must not be changed between compilation time and the time when the program is run. If *physical* binding occurs when the program is compiled, the physical data organization must not be changed between compilation time and the time when the program is run.

STATIC AND DYNAMIC DATA INDEPENDENCE Binding when the data are accessed gives maximum flexibility; the schema or physical organization can be modified at any time. We will refer to this as *dynamic binding*. Dynamic binding gives *dynamic data independence*. Binding at any time prior to the usage of the application program will be called *static binding*, and this gives *static data independence*.

Static data independence implies that when a change is made either to the schema, subschema, or physical representation, all the necessary conversions must be completed before any application program using the modified data can be executed. The program must be recompiled and link-edited; the physical data and the indices, pointers, or other means of addressing them must all be consistent with the new format. The recompilation and conversion that is necessary may take some time.

Dynamic data independence implies that separate forms of representation of the same data can coexist. The different forms may employ different indexing or addressing schemes, different types of coding, different sequences of data items, different privacy locks, and so forth. The application programs need not be recompiled before execution. The application program is matched to the data, whatever the form of the data, at the time the data are read.

Dynamic data independence is costly in that it consumes extra processing time for each data access and in that the necessary tables must be available to the computer. More main memory is consumed. The software is considerably more complex. Static data independence, requiring binding at compile or linkage time, is relatively inexpensive and will permit greater system throughput or faster response times.

There is no question that in most data-base systems, static data independence is of prime importance. Dynamic data independence is more of a luxury. Its cost may outweigh its advantages. There are some situations, however, in which dynamic independence is worthwhile or essential. First, the user may be a terminal operator who enters program and data management statements which are executed interpretively.

Second, the terminal operator may be a nonprogramming operator, but one who wishes to browse through the data structures in a manner which is not precisely preplanned. This user will have his own view of the data, which may be different from the schema and will almost certainly be different from the physical representation. For such a system, dynamic binding is necessary. Note, however, that the majority of nonprogramming terminal operators today use data structures that are preestablished and statically bound to their programs.

Third, the same data types may have different formats and relationships in different parts of the storage. Such variation is generally undesirable but often occurs in practice because of the way a data base has evolved. Records that have been used for one application are combined in the data base with records that have been used in another but which contain some of the same information. Two locations, each of which has its own data processing, may, for example, be made to share a computer by means of data transmission; their files are combined into one data base, but similar record types have different formats. A seven-character account number has been used for the last 10 years, but now an eight-character account number has come into use. The vast quantities of files with seven-character account numbers are not all rewritten. In such cases the cost of converting the existing files may be greater than the added cost of using dynamic binding, which enables application programs to use the mixture of data formats. The longer systems have been in existence and the more systems or programmer groups that have been merged, the more likely is an installation to have an incompatible mixture of files needing dynamic data independence. Some old installations have many thousands of tapes, containing much redundant data, which are to be merged step by step into a data-base system. Many old tapes may be deliberately left as they are while the new files are created.

Fourth, different versions of a record type may be kept with different physical organizations for performance reasons. Frequently referenced data may be kept with a physical organization that minimizes the access times but is expensive in storage costs, while infrequently referenced data of the same type may be kept in lower-cost storage at the expense of longer access times. In an airline reservation system, for example, records about flights and passengers taking off in the next few days are stored differently from records about those taking off months hence. The programmers may be insulated from such performance-oriented differences by the use of dynamic binding.

THE DEGREE
OF RESOLUTION

The fineness of resolution of data independence differs from one data-base management system to another. Three levels of fineness may be distinguished:

1. *Segment (or other data-item group).* The contents of a named segment, record, or tuple, are defined once. Every programmer who refers to that segment must assume the same contents. Different data bases may be defined from the same collection of segments.

2. *Data item.* The contents of a named data item are defined once. Every programmer who refers to that data item must assume the same data-item contents. However, different programmers can be given segments or records differently composed but derived from the same physical segments or records.

3. *Subdata item.* The contents of a named data item may differ from one application program to another. For example, one program may refer to a seven-digit and another to an eight-digit ACCOUNT NUMBER data item.

Data Language/I, as currently implemented, operates at the segment level. Figures 12.6 to 12.8 illustrate this. The contents of the segment are defined once in the physical data-base description (Fig. 12.6). The schema (Fig. 12.7) and subschema (Fig. 12.8) then refer to the segment by name but cannot redefine its contents.

It would be possible to implement the DBTG Data Description Language specifications so as to operate at the data-item or sub-data-item levels. If the application programs contain data-item declarations, and these are mapped to subschema data-item definitions such as those in Fig. 10.2, then the data items could differ in representation from one application program to another.

Fineness of resolution (e.g., sub-data-item independence) is not so vital as basic data independence and is expensive in machine time. *It is desirable to reach a compromise between achieving every form of data independence that is theoretically possible and obtaining data-base management software that is workable at a reasonable cost and that has suitably good performance.*

HOW
INDEPENDENT?

An application program cannot be independent of *all* changes that could be made to the data it uses.

If the program regards an association as 1 and it changes to M (one-to-many mapping), the program must be modified. For example, a program may have been written using a subschema in which each PART has one SUPPLIER. The business practice may change so that each

PART can have more than one SUPPLIER, as in Fig. 9.5. In general, any change which impacts the program's internal algorithm rather than merely the nature of the data will necessitate program rewriting.

In judging a present-day data-base management system the user must ask not whether it provides complete data independence, but how much. Given the system's facilities, what possible changes in physical organization could necessitate schema modification, and what possible changes in the data format, structures, or location method could necessitate program modification?

Box 16.1 gives a list of possible changes that can occur. It might be used as a checklist to compare the data independence capabilities of different data-base management systems. Which of these changes can they handle without application programs having to be modified?

APPLICATION PROGRAM STANDARDS No data-base management system today provides protection from all these types of changes to data. As data-base software and hardware improve, the degree of data independence available at a realistic cost will increase.

A few of the program maintenance costs which occur because of insufficient data independence could be avoided by appropriate programming standards or systems analysis discipline in an organization.

A *data dictionary* giving the names, lengths, representations, and descriptions of all data items should be used. Programmers should be permitted to use only the names and representations in the dictionary. Most corporations have, or will have, several thousand named data items. The task of standardizing, defining, and naming them is a long and arduous one, especially as the same data item is often named, represented, and defined differently in different departments. Data dictionaries have been automated and may, indeed, form the foundation of effective control of a data-base system. Recognizing that different departments have different names and representations for the same data item, the dictionary may have synonym capabilities.

We commented that no data independence technique is likely to protect a program from certain types of changes in the perception of data. To avoid this problem, programmers may be disciplined never to make assumptions about the number of logical records referenced in data-base operations. They should always operate with files of logical records (or *sets* in CODASYL language) which may contain zero, one, or many record occurrences. Rather than assuming that a PART has only one SUPPLIER,

Box 16.1 A List of Changes to Data That Might Be Necessary

(The list can be used as a checklist to compare to data independence capabilities of different data-base management systems. *Which of these changes can they handle without application programs having to be rewritten?*)

1. *Changes to data items*
   a. *The name of the data item is changed.* Can the names used for the same data item be different in different programs (which may have been written at different times by different groups)?
   b. *The maximum size of the data item is increased.*
   c. *The type, representation, or code of the data items is changed* (BCD, ASCII, COBOL-formatted fixed-point number with a given decimal point position, PL/I-formatted floating-point).
   d. *The scale of unit of measure of the data items is changed* (feet and inches are changed to metric measurements).
   e. *The encoding of the data items is changed.* (IDL representing Idlewild Airport is changed to JFK.)
   f. *The method of derivation of a derived data item is changed.* (TOTAL TAX is not stored. When requested it is derived from STATE, CITY, FIT, and FICA.)
   g. *The method of maintaining privacy of the data item is changed.* (Privacy lock by record may be changed to privacy lock by item for certain critical items.)

2. *Changes to data aggregates, segments, or logical records*
   a. *The name of a data-aggregate type or record type is changed* (possibly as separate applications are combined).
   b. *A new data-item type is introduced.*
   c. *A data-aggregate type or record type is split into two* (possibly as normalization or third normal form is introduced).
   d. *Two data-aggregate types or record types are merged* (a common event as files for separate programs are combined into a data base).
   e. *The sequence of data-item types is changed* (which happens when similar record types from different systems or applications are combined).
   f. *The maximum permitted quantity of a repeating group is changed.*
   g. *The primary key is modified.*
   h. *Secondary keys are introduced.* (New types of queries are to be answered with the data base, requiring new search methods and new keys.)
   i. *The method of maintaining privacy is changed.* (More elaborately structured locks are introduced. Content-dependent privacy locks are introduced.)

Box 16.1 *continued*

3. *Changes to logical structure*
   a. *A relationship name, such as set name, is changed.*
   b. *A new record type is introduced into a structure, such as a set.*
   c. *A one-to-one relationship becomes one-to-many.*
   d. *The number of levels in a hierarchical file increases.*
   e. *A tree structure evolves in a plex structure.*
   f. *A simple plexstructure evolves into a complex plexstructure* (see Fig. 9.11).
   g. *A tree or plex structure is converted to third normal form.*
   h. *The accessing path is changed.* (A cross-reference linkage to a record type, such as the dotted lines in Fig. 6.1, is introduced into a different record type.)
   i. *The method of maintaining privacy is changed.*

4. *Changes to physical structure*
   a. *Record blocking is changed* (the number of logical records in one physical record).
   b. *The physical record length is changed.*
   c. *Fixed-length physical records are changed to variable-length.*
   d. *The relative placement of records is changed to improve access efficiency.*
   e. *The addressing technique is changed* (indexing, algorithm, randomizing, chains; see Chapter 21).
   f. *The method of handling overflow records is changed.*
   g. *The method of handling insertions and deletions is changed.*
   h. *The files are stored on different volumes.*
   i. *The data-set organization is changed.* (ISAM is changed to VSAM; see Chapter 20.)
   j. *Multiple-key indices or chains are introduced.*
   k. *Searching techniques are changed.*
   l. *Inverted files or lists are introduced.*
   m. *The volume is reorganized.*
   n. *The relative or absolute address at which the data are recorded is changed.*
   o. *Compaction techniques are introduced or modified.* (See Chapter 31.)
   p. *An adaptive organization is used.*
   q. *Duplicate storage of the same files is introduced for availability or security reasons.*

5. *Changes to hardware*
   a. *Tapes are replaced with direct-access files.*
   b. *Volume sizes change.*
   c. *Track lengths or cell sizes change.*

Box 16.1   *continued*

d. *The form of physical encoding changes.*
e. *The address of the storage devices changes.*
f. *Removable volumes are replaced with fixed volumes or vice versa.*
g. *The host computer changes.*
h. *The geographical locations change with the use of data transmission or distributed data bases.*

the programmer should leave open the possibility that in the future it could have several suppliers. There are many other ways in which the programmer or systems analyst can leave open an avenue of possible change and thus enhance data independence. Still more important, the systems analysts can avoid data structures which are likely to be difficult to change or which may inhibit the type of evolution in which many separate application data bases become combined.

Probably the best way to acquire stable logical schemas is to have them designed in a canonical fashion by a data-base administrator who knows what to look for in data, and who understands the dangers. The structures used should be as amendable as possible to future evolution. A data description language should be employed which can handle the canonical structures. The same data description language should be used for all data bases in a corporation, to maximize the chances of future interlinking of data structures which were originally separate, and to make it possible to transfer working applications from one part of the corporation to another.

The data-base management system itself may not be able to handle canonical structures without modification to a form such as that of CODASYL or DL/I. In this case the canonical structure should be used as a design aid.

REFERENCES

1. C. J. Date and P. Hopewell, "File Definition and Logical Data Independence," *Proc. ACM SIGFIDET Workshop on Data Description, Access and Control* (Nov. 1971), pp 117-138.

2. C. J. Date and P. Hopewell, "Storage Structure and Physical Data Independence," *Proc. ACM SIGFIDET Workshop on Data Description, Access and Control,* Nov. 1971.

3. R. W. Engles, "An Analysis of the April 1971 Data Base Task Group Report (CODASYL)," *Proc. ACM SIGFIDET Workshop on Data Description, Access and Control,* Nov. 1971.

BOOK STRUCTURE

Part II

A fast path through PART II of the book:

PART  **PHYSICAL ORGANIZATION**

17 CRITERIA AFFECTING PHYSICAL ORGANIZATION

In Part II we will discuss physical storage organizations. We are now no longer concerned with the way the application programmer views the data but with how it is laid out on the storage units.

The set of criteria which determines the choice of physical organization is different from that which determines the choice of logical organization. The selection of physical organization is determined largely by the need for operational efficiency, fast response times, and cost minimization.

Most data storage devices record data as a stream of bits on a magnetic surface. Future devices may use technologies other than magnetic recording but still store *sequential streams of bits*. Such devices may be remote from the computers which use them, at the other end of a transmission line or a satellite link which transmits the data *as a sequential stream of bits*.

The problem to be solved in physical data organization is: How do we represent the data structures in Part I of this book as sequential streams of bits?

There are several aspects to this problem. First: *How do we find a record which a program needs in that mass of stored data?*

The groups of bits which we can read with one machine instruction are called *physical records*. The physical records are stored at locations which are identified by a means of *machine addresses*. A program identifies a logical record or segment by means of a *key*. To find that data for the program we must use the key to identify the machine address of the physical record which contains the data.

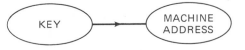

There are, however, a very large number of key values and machine addresses. Therefore, careful attention must be paid to the techniques for associating keys with machine addresses. The technique for using a key to find a record is referred to as *addressing.* Chapter 19 discusses the various methods of addressing. Chapters 20 and 21 discuss in more detail two of the most useful addressing methods. Chapter 36 discusses a possible future technique employing new types of hardware.

The retrieval of data is sometimes not based on the use of a primary key. Secondary keys are used, as discussed in Chapter 15. Queries may be stated in such a way that many records have to be searched to find an answer. In Fig. 5.7 query types 2 and 3 require a searching operation. Sometimes multiple keys are used in expressing a query or a data-base operation. For example, "Which customers in the Detroit area have ordered more than 500 of Item No. 721?" A second problem of physical data organization is then: *How can we organize data so that it can be searched efficiently and so that records can be retrieved on the basis of multiple keys?*

Multiple-key retrieval operations are generally more complex than primary-key operations and involve more intricate physical data organizations. Chapters 26, 27, and 28 discuss multiple-key organizations.

A third aspect to the problem of physical representation is: *How do we represent the tree and plex structures in Part I using data organized as sequential bit streams?*

A variety of techniques are available for physically representing complex structures. These are discussed in Chapters 24 and 25. The techniques differ widely in their effectiveness.

All the techniques for organizing the physical bit streams are complicated by the fact that we have to insert new records into the data base, and also delete records. A fourth aspect to physical organization is therefore: *How do we insert new records into data organized as physical bit streams, delete old records, and still preserve the addressing and searching capabilities and the data structures?*

This theme pervades all the chapters which discuss physical organization techniques. A few applications are characterized by an extremely high rate of inserting new records and deleting old ones. We refer to their files or data bases as highly *volatile.* Chapter 34 discusses techniques for volatile files.

Physical storage is expensive, and therefore the techniques employed should, as far as possible, use it economically. *How do we design the physical storage of data to achieve a high packing density?*

Some techniques for addressing, and representing structures, are more wasteful of storage space than others. We can deliberately attack the packing-density question by means of data-*compaction* techniques, which are discussed in Chapter 32, but these introduce additional processing complexity.

Access times or transaction throughput may be of more concern than storage packing density. Users carrying out dialogues with computer terminals need fast response times. *How do we design the physical storage of data to achieve fast response times or handle a high volume of transactions per second?*

The question of access speed also pervades most of the chapters concerned with physical storage techniques. Chapter 35 summarizes the types of methods that are successful in achieving fast response times.

TRADEOFFS   The system designer is faced with trade-offs between different desirable features. Figure 17.1 illustrates some of the trade-offs in physical data-base organization.

Those techniques which give a high packing density tend to require more time for file addressing or searching. To achieve faster retrieval speeds more expensive storage units are needed. Techniques which provide a high flexibility for searching generally require more storage space or give slower access times.

Techniques which facilitate easy real-time insertion of new records tend to use more storage space. Techniques which use storage space efficiently are often poor from the maintenance point of view needing a reorganization of the storage when new records are inserted.

The achievement of good data independence is done at the expense of machine performance. High performance in storage operations has been achieved at the expense of abandoning some, or most, data-base functions, and sometimes by abandoning data independence.

To achieve a high level of efficiency, fast response times, and tight utilization of storage space generally requires complex techniques. High complexity, however, sometimes has the disadvantage of impairing the ability to recover from failures or losses of data.

FACTORS AFFECTING   The remainder of this chapter lists factors
PHYSICAL ORGANIZATION   which affect the physical organization. Box 17.1 summarizes the differences between logical and physical data organization.

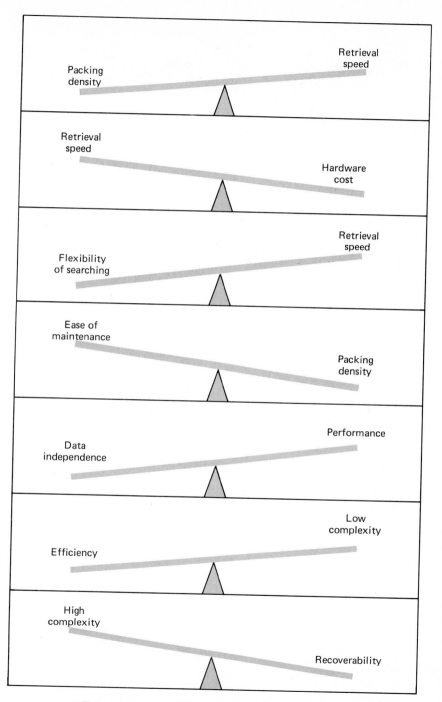

Figure 17.1   Trade-offs in physical organization.

Box 17.1 Differences Between the Logical and Physical Organization of Data

Logical Organization	Physical Organization
Simplicity is important.	*Complex organizations* may be advantageous. The software hides the complexity from the users.
Application program requests correspond to the logical data structure.	*Application program requests* may be for data in a form quite different from that in which the data are actually stored.
Data independence is of prime importance.	*Data independence* is of little concern if facilities are provided for restructuring the physical data without changing the schema.
Efficient use of storage is of little or no concern.	*Efficient use of storage* is a major concern in choosing between different techniques of physical representation and layout.
Efficient timing of data accesses is normally of no concern.	*Speed of access* is a major concern in choosing between different techniques of physical storage organization.
Storage unit characteristics should not affect the logical organization.	*Storage unit characteristics* such as track length and volume size may be a major determinant of storage organization.
A high level of redundancy often exists between logical files.	*Elimination of redundancy* is an objective of physical organization.

Box 17.1 *continued*

Logical Organization	Physical Organization
Insertions and deletions do not normally have an effect on logical structures.	*Insertions and deletions* can have a major effect on physical data layouts, especially for volatile data.
The means of addressing the data does not have a major effect on logical structures.	*Addressing techniques* have the major effect on physical storage layout.
Secondary keys do not have a major effect on logical structures.	*Secondary keys and inverted organizations* may be major considerations in physically structuring the storage layout.
The sequence of records is the primary key sequence, or the sequence in which records are used by an application program.	*The sequence of records* may be selected with other considerations such as shortening access times or reducing index sizes.
Relationships between records or data aggregates may be represented by simple hierarchical pointers.	*Complex sets of pointers* may be used to link physically separate records or data aggregates.
Protection from failures or data loss may not affect the logical organization.	*Restart and recovery techniques* may have special physical storage requirements, such as duplicating parts of the data.
The logical organization must be stable so that application programs do not have to be rewritten.	*The physical layout may be changeable,* designed for periodic reorganizations and tuning and possibly for data migration.

1. Space Saving

A variety of techniques is concerned with maximizing the amount of data that can be stored on the volumes. There are two categories of techniques having this objective. First, there are techniques which group several logical records into one physical record without changing the record contents. We will discuss this *blocking* of records in the next chapter. Second, there are techniques which convert the data into more compact forms. There is a variety of ways of *compacting* data, some of which are complex. Some compaction techniques are dependent on the specific usage of the system, and some are application-independent. In Chapter 32 we will discuss data compaction.

2. Minimization of Redundancy

As we have commented, a high level of data redundancy exists in most systems designed prior to the use of data-base techniques. The *logical* data organizations discussed in Part I do much to remove this redundancy but do not necessarily remove *all* redundant data items. The mapping of the schemas into physical storage may give further elimination of redundancy. For example, instead of storing a *key* data item multiple times in normalized files such as those in Fig. 13.2, a reference or *pointer* to the key may be stored. Some physical data organizations make much use of pointers for eliminating redundancy.

3. Random or Sequential Processing?

Many data-processing jobs are, by their nature, best done sequentially, scanning through a file in a given order. Payroll, for example, involves going through the employee list, extracting relevant information, and making up pay slips. There is no point in doing this other than in a serial computer run. There is no point in incurring lengthy random-access seeks.

Other jobs, however, have traditionally been done serially when a random approach could be of value. Stock updating, for example, is done in many firms by a sequential run that fits into the computer's cycle of sorting and processing and so may come around perhaps once a week. It is of value in some types of business to reduce this cycle time, to be able to check the latest stock position on certain items immediately, to reorder stock quickly when large orders come in or when exceptional circumstances arise, and so forth. This is especially so if the turnover rate is high, if the stock is perishable, if the demand for products fluctuates and is uncertain, or if the competitive situation is especially keen. With in-line processing the stock records may be checked and updated when each order is received. Access to stock records at random is necessary for this. There is not time to scan through a sequential file.

For some computer work, sequential processing cannot be considered. Most real-time jobs fall into this category. When a computer must react within hours to an unanticipated situation, it is usually too time-consuming to load a sequential file and scan through it. In production or operation scheduling, for example, the computer makes up an optimum timetable for the operations. Any unanticipated change, of which there may be many, must be fed to the machine so that it can modify the timetable if necessary. To do this it needs quick access to a variety of different records. Systems for answering inquiries, booking seats, updating savings books at a bank counter, or carrying on a conversation with terminal operators demand quick, and therefore random, access to files.

Records which are always used sequentially, in one given sequence, can be laid out in that sequence. Records which may be referred to in any sequence need more elaborate means of locating a record, and the *addressing* procedures are likely to dominate the record layout. In Chapter 19 we will discuss addressing techniques and their effect on data layout.

4. File-Activity Ratio

In many systems in which records are processed sequentially, not every record is used. On a billing operation, for example, the customer file may be scanned, but only certain customer records are required and these may be a small proportion of the whole.

A file-activity ratio may be defined as

$$\text{File-activity ratio} = \frac{\text{Number of records read and used in one run}}{\text{Number of records scanned in that run}}$$

If the file-activity ratio is large, this run may be done, using a high-speed magnetic tape, in about the same time as using a direct-access device, and magnetic tape is a cheaper storage medium. On the other hand, if the file-activity ratio is low, say 2%, the direct-access device can skip the unwanted records. Most magnetic tape units cannot skip but have to read all records scanned. The direct-access device therefore becomes faster than tape, and it may avoid lengthy scanning operations.

5. Single-Transaction Access or Grouping

On some systems, usually those requiring a fast response time, each transaction must be processed when it arrives. On others the transactions can be saved until a group of them are ready to be processed; the group can then be sorted into the optimum sequence for accessing the records.

6. Frequency of Reference

A record may be referred to many times, or it may be referred to infrequently. In many commercial files a small proportion of the records is referred to frequently, and a large proportion, not very often. For example, 90% of the stock movements may relate to 10% of the items. In an airline 10% of booking records may relate to flights taking off in the next week, but most of the activity—cancelations, rebookings, and inquiries—relates to these flights; 10% of a bank's customers give rise to 90% of the withdrawals and deposits. Similarly, some stock items hardly ever move; some passengers book a year in advance and are never heard of again until the plane takes off; some bank accounts are hardly ever touched.

The selection of the hardware and the placing of the data on it should, where possible, be such that the records used most frequently will be easy and quick to locate. If, in a stockbroker's system, processing is constantly being interrupted by inquiries or transactions relating to certain popular stocks, let these be stored where access to them can be in 20 milliseconds rather than 100 milliseconds.

Certain items on the files may be read very often, for example, programs, index records, and master records. These might be placed on a device with a very short access time.

7. Response-Time Requirements

If an item is referred to frequently, it is generally desirable that the speed of obtaining it should be high. However, speed of reference may also be related to the response time required at terminals. If the system must give its reply in a second or so, possibly because of the demands of the conversation mode, and formulating the reply takes several seeks on channels where the queuing is high, then the seeks must not take long. On the other hand, if a response time of half an hour is good enough, the machine can stack the file requests and make infrequent excursions into the remoter areas of the files, collecting several records while it is there.

Fast response-time requirements can affect both the choice of storage device and the organization of data on it. These choices are especially critical when multiple records have to be searched in order to process certain queries or transactions.

8. Throughput

It is generally desirable that the physical data organization should enhance the transaction throughput. On certain systems the throughput requirements have a major effect on the choice of storage layout. This is so on systems which must handle a high volume of real-time transactions, such as airline reservations systems. On such systems multiple file references must take place in parallel. Various data organizations discussed later in the book will be designed for parallel rather than sequential operations, and the physical data organization will be chosen to minimize seek times.

9. Data Volatility

New records are occasionally added to most files, and old records are deleted. A file with a high rate of record additions and deletions is referred to as *volatile*. Where the records are laid out in some predetermined sequence, new records must somehow be inserted into the sequence. As will be discussed in Chapter 20, there are various techniques for inserting and deleting records. They offer different advantages (or disadvantages) and affect the physical layout of data. When a file is *highly* volatile, additions and deletions become a primary consideration in its physical organization.

Most files in which records are inserted or deleted drift away from an optimum layout and have to be reorganized periodically. The ease or duration of the reorganization process may be a consideration in selecting the physical data organization.

In practice some data organizations which have worked well with static files have had such severe problems with insertions and deletions that they had to be abandoned.

10. Clustered Insertions

If new insertions to a file occur singly and at random, a given data organization may absorb them without difficulty. A special problem occurs when the insertions are clustered. For example, an inventory file may be laid out in sequence of its key: PART NUMBER. The records for parts 217AK300 and 217AK700 are physically adjacent, but a new group of 100 records arrives for parts 217AK400 to 217AK499. All the new additions must be inserted between the records for parts 217AK300 and 217AK700. Some physical organizations can absorb such a cluster without problems. Others do it in such a way that the time to access the records in question is greatly increased. If clustered insertions are to be handled smoothly, an appropriate physical organization is needed.

11. Expandability

There may be more additions than deletions in which case the file grows. In some systems the growth is rapid. A physical organization is needed which can handle the expansion and which is not restricted by volume or cell sizes, sizes of index blocks, or other constraints.

12. Complexity of Logical Structure

As we will see in subsequent chapters, different techniques are needed to represent different logical structures. Plex structures are represented differently from tree structures. The *sets* of the CODASYL DDL are represented differently from the logical relationships and multilevel hierarchy structures of DL/I. Simple logical structures such as those of a normalized data base can be most neatly converted to physical forms.

13. Multiple-Key Retrieval

When records must be retrieved on the basis of more than one key type per record, physical organizations are substantially more complex than for single-key records. For example, the physical sequencing of records or index entries may be based on the primary key, but then the physical sequencing is of no assistance in retrieving records by means of the secondary keys. We will discuss multiple-key retrieval in Chapters 26, 27, and 28.

14. File-Searching Requirements

Inverted files are a special case of multiple-key retrieval, allowing queries of the form

$$A \ (?) \begin{array}{c} \neq \\ = \\ > \\ < \end{array} V$$

to be processed (see Fig. 5.5). The capability to answer such queries or to do searches bases on multiple parameters requires certain types of file layout.

15. Availability

It is important that most real-time systems continue to work as much of their operational time as possible; i.e., they should have a high availability. Storage devices sometimes fail, especially when they have electromechanical components. Critical data may be duplicated so that when one storage device fails a copy of the data is still on-line on another device. Alternatively, the data may be on removable volumes which can be quickly transferred to a working device.

16. Recovery from Data Loss

Data may become accidentally destroyed. It is essential that a procedure should exist for reconstructing any data that are vital. To make reconstruction possible, parts of the files must be copied periodically, and as file updating proceeds certain data items must be logged. Both the copies and the log may be recorded on an inexpensive storage medium, such as tape, which can be stored away from the computer center.

17. Vulnerability

Certain techniques of representing data physically are more susceptible to damage than others. For example, sometimes long strings of pointers are used to provide the means for locating data. Record A has a pointer to record B, record B has a pointer to record C, and so forth. If one pointer in the string is damaged or deleted, for example, by a programming error, then the other records in the string cannot be found unless some means of reconstructing the pointers is provided.

18. Data Independence

One of the most important concerns in the logical organization of data is that of data independence. Data independence is of some concern in physical organization also. It is possible to select a physical organization technique which can be rendered invalid by a change in the data or in their application. For example, an application-oriented compaction technique could become inappropriate if the data compacted are used for a different application. An addressing schema which relies upon a N-digit data item could become invalid if the data item were expanded to $N + 1$ digits. A tree-structured logical relationship could be changed to a plex structure and render the method of physical representation invalid.

Changes which undermine a physical organization are probably less common than changes which undermine a logical organization. Furthermore, if the software used is such that the physical organization is not reflected in the application programs or in the schema description, then the physical organization can be adjusted without the burdensome task of rewriting the application programs or the schema.

19. Tuning

The software should indeed be designed to isolate the physical organization from the logical organization. In many systems, as we commented earlier, the physical data layout is frequently adjusted in attempts to improve the system performance, and hence the physical data layout should be completely severed from the application program's view of the data and from the schema, as illustrated in Fig. 4.1.

18 DIFFERENCES BETWEEN PHYSICAL AND LOGICAL ORGANIZATION

We will discuss many techniques usable in physical data-base organization. Some of them are more efficient than techniques used in today's best-selling software. Often, however, they are more complex. It is acceptable to introduce more complex mechanisms if, and only if, the complexity can be hidden from the data-base users—in othe words, if there is physical data independence (Fig. 18.1).

In this chapter we examine briefly a few of the differences between logical and physical organization.

BLOCKING   To make efficient use of storage devices it is often desirable to avoid storing small physical records. Up to a certain size the larger the physical blocks of data that are employed, the more data can be stored. The application program, on the other hand, may use small logical records. In the early history of computing this difference led to the first dichotomy between logical and physical organization. On magnetic tape, records were stored as in Fig. 18.2. The gap between physical records (the *interrecord gap*) was usually long compared to the space occupied by a logical record, and so the storage space was used inefficiently if each logical record was stored by itself. The logical records were therefore packed together into blocks which formed physical records, and the block length was made sufficiently large so that the space overhead in storing a physical block was a small proportion of the total.

When the program issues a READ instruction, one *physical* record is read. The application program, however, requires one logical record. The

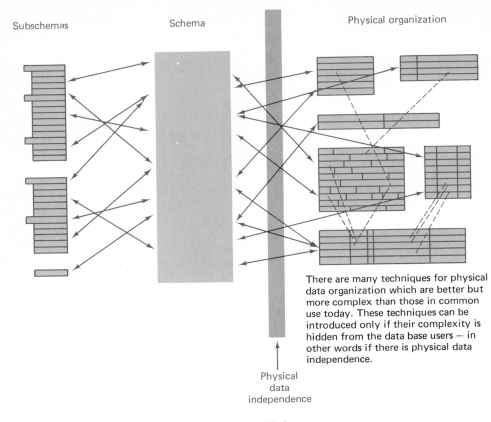

Subschemas   Schema   Physical organization

There are many techniques for physical data organization which are better but more complex than those in common use today. These techniques can be introduced only if their complexity is hidden from the data base users — in other words if there is physical data independence.

Physical
data
independence

Figure 18.1

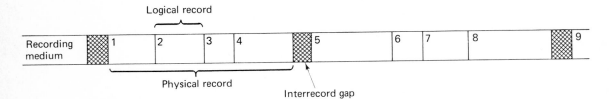

Logical record

Recording medium   1   2   3   4   5   6   7   8   9

Physical record

Interrecord gap

Figure 18.2 The relationship between physical records and logical records in a simple file. A computer READ instruction reads one physical record. An application program requires one logical record at a time.

physical record is therefore deblocked by the software, and the logical record is transferred to the program work area.

VARIABLE-LENGTH RECORDS   The storage organization on some systems is designed so that it can handle only fixed-length physical records. The logical records, on the other hand, may be variable in length. In this case the physical records will be filled with as many logical records as possible, but the filling will usually leave a gap, as in Fig. 18.3 The gap may be filled with meaningless *pad* characters. The greater the ratio of the physical record length to the mean logical record length, the less will be the space that is used for padding. Long physical records lessen the wastage both in padding and in interrecord gaps.

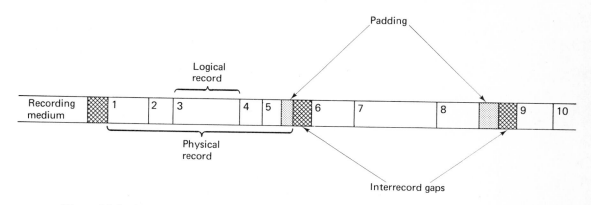

Figure 18.3 An organization in which the physical records are of fixed length but the logical records are of variable length.

THE SEQUENCING OF RECORDS   The application programmer often imagines the records of a file to be laid out in sequence on the storage medium. This is not necessarily the case; the physical sequence of records may be different from the logical sequence.

There can be only one physical sequence of records (unless they are duplicated). It should be chosen to be as useful as possible. The sequence may be selected for one of the following purposes:

1. To speed up frequently executed operations by storing the records in the same sequence as the required output (a customer file in customer-number sequence).

2. To represent relationships, especially master-detail or tree structures (more about that in Chapter 24).

3. To speed up or simplify the means of addressing the file (as with direct addressing or hashing, discussed in Chapter 19).

4. To reduce the size of the index that is used and hence reduce the index-searching time.

5. To shorten average access times by placing the most frequently referenced items in the most quickly accessible locations. (In an airline reservation data base, for example, the most frequently referenced items are gathered together on the innermost cylinders; the least frequently referenced items are at the extremities.)

6. To facilitate insertion and deletion of records and maintenance operations. (On a highly volatile file the ordered sequencing of records may be deliberately avoided.)

Later in the book we will discuss specific examples of the use of physical sequencing of records.

The importance of direct-access storage devices such as disks is that records can be read in any sequence. On a serial-access storage medium such as magnetic tape the records must be read in a fixed sequence unless substantial time is spent skipping from one part of the tape to another. It is rather like comparing music on a jukebox with music on a tape recorder. Records on the jukebox can be selected at random in any sequence, whereas records on the tape recorder must be played in a fixed sequence unless time is spent skipping backward and forward on the tape.

Although records on direct-access storage devices can be read in any sequence, it is much faster to read them in some sequences than others.

1. Conventional serial organization

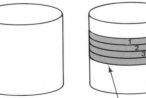

A file of records laid out contiguously on one disk pack in a conventional fashion

2. A parallel cellular organization

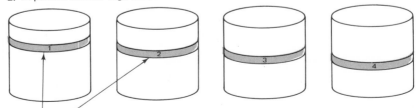

The same file distributed across the available storage devices in order to shorten real-time response times, or achieve a higher throughput

Figure 18.4

Reading sequences which require the access mechanism to be moved backward and forward are time-consuming. With mechanisms which can interchange physical cells or cartridges it is desirable to have reading sequences which do not skip between the cells or cartridges. The choice of physical storage organization is usually highly dependent on timing considerations and hence on the physical sequencing of the records.

PARALLEL   In many systems the requests for records occur at
CELLULAR   random, and queues of items waiting to be serviced
ORGANIZATIONS   build up. The positioning of the records can be
                    arranged to minimize the queue lengths and hence
minimize the overall access time or maximize the throughput. This consideration is particularly important on some real-time systems which

Figure 18.5 If the majority of accesses are to the file in Fig. 18.4, then the queuing times when accessing these records will be greater with the conventional serial organization than with the parallel cellular organization.

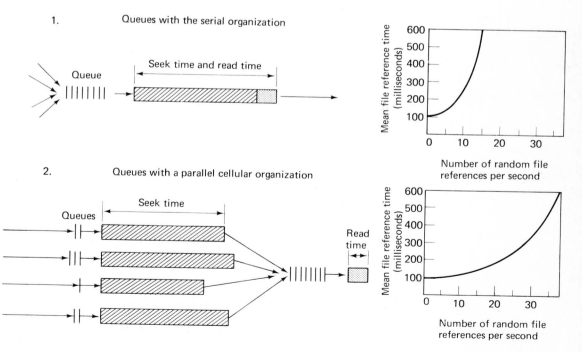

require fast response times.

There are usually several access mechanisms which can operate simultaneously, seeking or reading data. To minimize the queuing times the data should be distributed across the storage units so that as many access mechanisms as possible are likely to be operating at the same time.

For the remainder of this book we will use the word *cell* to mean a track, cylinder, module, or other zone delimited by a natural hardware boundary such that the time required to access data increases by a step function when data extend beyond the cell boundaries. If the cells are such that data can be read from more than one cell at the same time, we will refer to them as *parallel* cells. A storage organization in which a file is spread across several cells and in which the cells are accessed in parallel in order to speed up the locating of data will be called a *parallel cellular organization.*

Figure 18.4 shows a number of disks on which a file is laid out first in a conventional serial fashion and second in a parallel cellular fashion with the record sequence skipping from disk to disk. The access mechanism has one read head per track and can be positioned on one cylinder at a time. If the majority of the storage accesses are to the file shown, then the queuing times will be higher for the serial layout than for the parallel layout. The parallel layout will help in achieving fast responses. A higher transaction throughput will be possible with the parallel organization. Very often today's systems employ the serial organization because it is simpler to have the entire file on one disk pack.

Figure 18.5 shows the queuing situation that exists with the two organizations of the file in Fig. 18.4. It assumes that the four disks are attached to one channel so that *seeks* on each disk can occur simultaneously but *reads* cannot. In the parallel cellular case there are two queues. Transactions must queue first for the access mechanism (the seek operation and rotational delay) and then for the channel (the read operation). The time a transaction occupies the channel is much shorter than the time it occupies the access mechanism. The timing is therefore dominated by the queue for the access mechanism. This queue is much shorter with the parallel organization than with the serial organization. The total time for accessing the record is therefore shorter with the parallel organization, as shown in the two curves. As the throughput is raised, the queue for the access mechanism will be the limiting factor in the serial organization. The throughput will be choked at a lower level than with the parallel organization in which the main transaction stream is distributed between several access mechanisms.

In designing a system it is desirable that the queuing times and maximum throughputs be investigated with queuing theory or simulation. (See the author's *Design of Real-Time Computer Systems*, Section V.)

POSITIONING BY FREQUENCY OF USE   In some storages which are organized in a parallel fashion the data-base management system divides up the storage according to frequency of use of the data. Figure 18.6 illustrates this technique. The most frequently used data are stored on the innermost cylinders of the disks in Fig. 18.6. The least frequently used data are stored on the outermost cylinders. Data with an intermediate frequency of use are stored between these inner and outer zones.

Most airline reservation systems operate in this manner. They have a high transaction throughput and need for fast response times. Some records are referred to very frequently, such as the records giving the availability of seats on today's flights. Some records are referred to very infrequently, such as records giving details of passengers booked on flights many months hence. The file-addressing scheme automatically allocates the records to the appropriate group of cylinders, and the records are spread across the cylinders as in Fig. 18.5.

Sometimes a system uses more than one type of storage device when one type can be accessed more rapidly than another. The frequently used items will be stored on the faster-access device and the infrequently used items on the slow-access device.

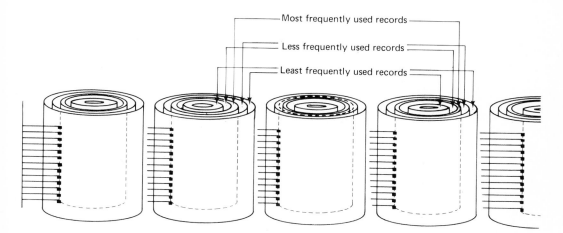

Figure 18.6   An organization in which the most frequently referenced records are kept together on the innermost cylinders. The least frequently referenced records are on the outermost cylinders. The dotted cylinders show the positions of the access mechanism at one instant in time.

If an index to the data is used, the index may be on a fast-access device and the data on a slower-access device. When very infrequently referenced data are kept, they may be stored on a cheap off-line serial medium such as magnetic tape, whereas the more often-used data may be on more expensive direct-access devices. Archival records, for example, are dumped onto magnetic tape.

It seems likely that many complex systems for the near-term future will have at least three levels of storage: (1) solid-state electronic storage with a capacity of millions of bytes (this figure rising rapidly as the cost of large-scale-integration memory drops), (2) disks giving capacities totaling billions of bytes, and (3) tape or direct-access cartridges having much larger capacities than disks but longer access times.

PAGING   Data may be moved between the different levels of storage in fixed-length pages, as in today's virtual memory systems. The page size is a parameter of the system and is not determined by the record lengths used by individual programmers. Where paging is used the data will be logically independent of page size but will have to be physically packaged to fit into the pages.

Where multiple levels of storage hardware are used, blocks of data, like pages, may be passed across the interfaces between the levels. This technique is called *staging* and is discussed in Chapter 33.

Where paging or staging is used, the chains, rings, and indices that compose the physical accessing methods, as we will discuss, may be tailored to page sizes so as to minimize the page swapping that is necessary. A chain, for example, which straggles backward and forward across many pages can seriously degrade the performance of a paging system.

A FINITE SET   Often an attribute can take on one of a finite set of
OF VALUES   values. It is often possible to save storage space by giving each of the attribute *values* a binary number.
The binary number is then stored in the record instead of the attribute value. If there are N possible attribute values, then the binary number has $\lceil \log_2 N \rceil$* bits, and this is often much smaller than the number of bits needed to store the attribute value itself.

---

*When x is not an integer, $\lceil x \rceil$ refers to the next largest integer. Thus $\lceil 2.7 \rceil = 3$. $\lceil \log_2 15 \rceil = 4$.

Employee number	Job category		Employee number	Bits		Bits	Job category
4732	Accountant		4732	001		001	Accountant
3119	Engineer		3119	010		010	Engineer
0604	Clerk		0604	011		011	Clerk
7230	Consultant		7230	100		100	Consultant
6112	Clerk		6112	011		101	Secretary
1147	Secretary		1147	101			
0991	Accountant		0991	001			
1237	Secretary		1237	101			
3743	Engineer		3743	010			
5150	Clerk		5150	011			
1751	Consultant		1751	100			
1296	Engineer		1296	010			
2914	Clerk		2914	011			
2117	Consultant		2117	100			

LOGICAL REPRESENTATION   PHYSICAL REPRESENTATION

Figure 18.7 A data-item-type with a finite set of possible values is replaced with a bit pattern which acts as a pointer to the value in question.

A penalty of storing the attribute values in the form of binary numbers is that a further conversion is needed to obtain the actual attribute value. If N is small enough, the table for converting the binary numbers into attribute values may be in main memory. If it is not small enough for main memory, it will be in a fast-access storage device. The possibility of storing data in this manner can present a trade-off between storage space and time.

The conversion from attribute value to binary number could be performed by the application programmer or by the data-base management software. If it is performed by software, the logical representation of data will contain the normal representation of the attribute value, and the physical representation will contain the binary number. This difference is illustrated in Fig. 18.7. The binary number in this case could be regarded as a *pointer* to the actual attribute value.

VARIABLE-LENGTH ATTRIBUTE LISTS   Sometimes it is necessary to store a variable-length list of values of the same attribute, for example, a list of the part numbers of which an item is composed or a list of the possible suppliers for a given part. If the attribute values in question are from a finite set of possible values, there are two possible methods of storing them. Method 1 stores them as a string of values, possibly values reduced to binary numbers. Method 2 stores them as a bit matrix.

Figure 18.8 illustrates the two methods. It shows the courses which students are registered for. In the top diagram the course numbers for each student are stored as variable-length lists. (The numbers could be reduced to bit patterns as in Fig. 18.7.) In the bottom diagram there is a 1 or 0 bit for

Method 1:   Variable-length lists

Student number	Courses
54381	177, 179, 184, 185, 187
54407	177, 178, 181, 183, 187, 191
54408	176, 184, 189, 191
54503	181, 185, 188
54504	178, 183, 185, 188, 191

Method 2:   A bit matrix

Student number	176	177	178	179	180	181	182	183	184	185	186	187	188	189	190	191
54381	0	1	0	1	0	0	0	0	1	1	0	1	0	0	0	0
54007	0	1	1	0	0	1	0	1	0	0	0	1	0	0	0	1
54408	1	0	0	0	0	0	0	0	1	0	0	0	0	1	0	1
54503	0	0	0	0	0	1	0	0	0	1	0	0	1	0	0	0
54504	0	0	1	0	0	0	0	1	0	1	0	0	1	0	0	1

Figure 18.8 Two methods of physically storing a set of attribute values.

every possible value, the 1 bit indicating that the student takes the course in question and the 0 bit indicating that he does not.

If there are N possible values, method 2 requires simply N bits per entity. If the entity has, on average, a fraction, p, of all the possible attribute values in its variable-length list, then method 1 will need an average of $p \cdot N$ ($\lceil \log_2 N \rceil$) bits per entity.

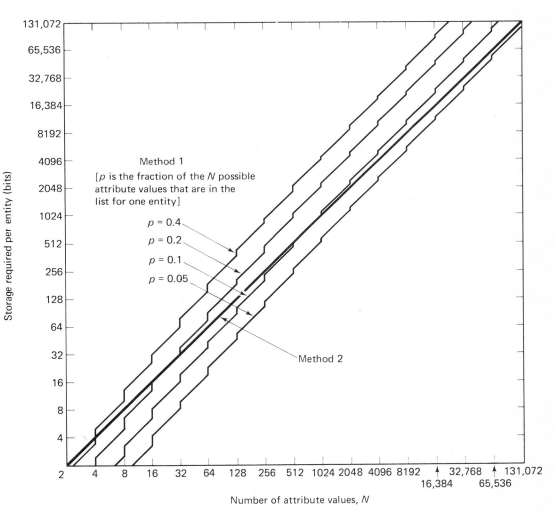

Figure 18.9

Method 1 will take less storage when

$$p \cdot N(\lceil \log_2 N \rceil) < N$$

i.e.,

$$p < \frac{1}{\lceil \log_2 N \rceil}$$

In some situations method 1 will be better; in others, method 2. Figure 18.9 illustrates the relative storage requirements of the two methods.

COMPACTION   The methods of representing data in Fig. 18.7 and
TECHNIQUES   method 2 of Fig. 18.8 are examples of how data
may be compacted so that when they are stored physically, they occupy less space. There is a variety of other compaction techniques,which we will discuss in Chapter 32. Where compaction is used the data-base management system may convert between the compacted physical representation and the noncompacted logical representation.

BOOK STRUCTURE

A primary problem of physical organization is *addressing*. Given a key, how do we find the record which that key refers to? Chapter 19 discusses addressing methods. Chapters 20 and 21 give more detail of two common methods.

19 ADDRESSING TECHNIQUES

Records in a logical file are identified by means of the unique number or group of characters, called a *key*. The key is usually a fixed-length field which is in an identical position in each record. It may be an account number in a bank or a part number in a factory. It may be necessary to join two or more fields together in order to produce a unique key, and this is called a *concatenated key*. For example, the key which identifies the flight record in an airline is a combination of the flight number and date of takeoff. The flight number alone is not unique, as a flight with the same number may take off every day.

In some files the records contain more than one key. A purchased item may have a different supplier's number and user's number, both of which are employed as keys. Many applications need to identify records on the basis of keys which are not unique. *One* key, however, must be unique because that is the key which is used for determining where the record should be located on the file unit and for retrieving the record from the file. This is called the *prime key* or *identifier*.

The basic problem of file addressing is this: *Given a prime key, such as an account number, how does the computer locate the record for that key?* There are several different techniques for addressing records. In the remainder of this chapter we will discuss them and their effect on the organization of the files.

Technique 1: Scanning the File

The simplest and crudest way of locating a record is to scan the file inspecting the key to each record. This method is far too slow for most purposes and is only likely to be used on a batch-processing operation using a serial file, such as tape, in which each record must be read anyway.

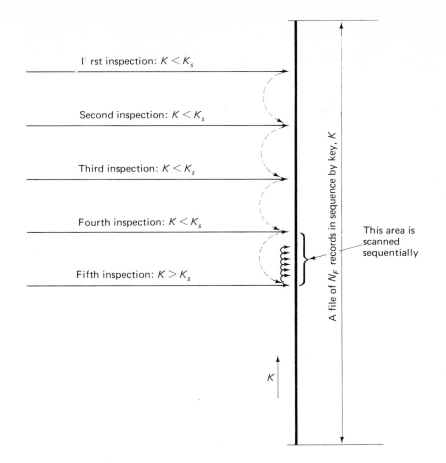

Figure 19.1 A block search. The file is in ascending order of its prime key, K. It is searched for a record with key K_5. The records are grouped into blocks of N_B items. Where a total of N_F items must be searched, the optimum block size is

$$N_B = \sqrt{N_F}.$$

Technique 2: A Block Search

Where the records are sequentially organized by key not every record need be read when scanning the file. The computer might, for example, examine every hundredth record in ascending key sequence (Fig. 19.1). When a record is found with a key higher than the key used for searching, the 99 records that were skipped are then searched. This is called a *block search*, the records being grouped into blocks and each block being inspected once until the correct block is found. It is also sometimes called a *skip search*.

The calculation of the optimum block size in a block search is similar to the calculation of skip length in a skip-searched chain, given in Chapter 23. If there are N_F records in the file, the number of records that must be examined, on average, is a minimum if the block size is $\sqrt{N_F}$. In this case $\sqrt{N_F}$ items, on average, would be examined. (See Box 19.1.)

For a file of 10,000 records, blocks of 100 records might be used, and on average 100 records would be inspected before the required record was found.

In practice no sequential file of 10,000 records is likely to be searched with a block search. However, the technique is important for searching index data sets, as we will discuss in Chapter 30. N_F index items are grouped into blocks of $\sqrt{N_F}$ and are block-searched.

Technique 3: A Binary Search

A binary search goes to the midpoint of the area to be searched and compares the key of that record with the search key. It then halves the search area and repeats the process (Fig. 19.2). The file will be inspected approximately $\log_2 N_F - 1$ times on average, when N_F is large (for an exact calculation, see Appendix A). This is a smaller number than the $\sqrt{N_F}$ inspections of a block search.

A binary search is generally inappropriate for searching a direct-access storage device because it necessitates time-consuming seeks. It cannot be used for searching a chain because the computer has no means of directing the search. It can be useful, however, for searching items in main memory or in a solid-state storage.

A special type of binary search is one in which the items searched are not laid out in sequence but in the form of a binary tree with pointers. The search then proceeds by following the pointers (glance ahead to Fig. 30.2). The advantage of this form of binary search is that new records can be inserted into the file to be searched without having to move aside other items, which would be a time-consuming and clumsy operation.

Binary searching is more likely to be used for searching an index to a file than for searching the file itself. We will postpone further discussion of it until Chapter 30, on index searching.

Technique 4: Indexed Sequential Files

In general, scanning or searching the files to find an item is too time-consuming a process to be used on its own, but it is often used to

Box 19.1 Optimum Block Size for a Block Search

Let N_F be the number of records in a file. Let N_B be the number of records in a block. There are then $\lceil N_F/N_B \rceil$ blocks.

The mean number of blocks that must be examined in order to find the required block is

$$\sum_{k=1}^{N_F/N_B} (k \times \text{Probability that the } k\text{th block examined contains the required record})$$

If the required record is equally likely to be in any block, then the mean number of blocks examined is

$$\sum_{k=1}^{\lceil N_F/N_B \rceil} k \, \frac{1}{\lceil N_F/N_B \rceil} = \frac{\lceil N_F/N_B \rceil + 1}{2}$$

Having found the right block, the search then examines the records in the block. The first record has already been examined. The search must therefore examine between 0 and $N_B - 1$ other records. The mean number of records examined in the block is

$$\sum_{k=0}^{N_B-1} (k \times \text{Probability that the } k\text{th record examined is the one required})$$

If the required record is equally likely to be in any position in the block, then this mean number of records examined is

$$\sum_{k=0}^{N_B-1} k \, \frac{1}{N_B} = \frac{N_B - 1}{2}$$

Let N_P be the number of records that must be examined in total in the search.

Box 19.1 *continued*

The mean number of records that must be examined, $E(N_p)$, is the sum of the mean number of blocks examined and the mean number of records within a block:

$$E(N_P) = \frac{\lceil N_F/N_B \rceil + 1}{2} + \frac{N_B - 1}{2} = \frac{1}{2}\left\lceil \frac{N_F}{N_B} \right\rceil + \frac{N_B}{2} \quad (19.1)$$

We can adjust N_B, the number of records in a block, to give the minimum value of $E(N_P)$:

$$\frac{dE(N_P)}{dN_B} \simeq -\frac{N_B}{2N_B{}^2} + \frac{1}{2}$$

$$= 0 \quad \text{when } \frac{N_F}{2N_B{}^2} = \frac{1}{2} \text{ , i.e. } N_B = \sqrt{N_F} \quad (19.2)$$

Thus, the optimum number of records is a block is $\sqrt{\text{the number of records in the file.}}$

The number of records that must be inspected if there are $\lceil \sqrt{N_F} \rceil$ records in each block is [from Eq. (19.1)]

$$E(N_{P'}) = \frac{1}{2}\left\lceil \frac{N_F}{\lceil \sqrt{N_F} \rceil} \right\rceil + \frac{\lceil \sqrt{N_F} \rceil}{2} \simeq \sqrt{N_F} \quad (19.3)$$

pinpoint an item within a small area when some other technique has found that area. Scanning a disk or drum track can be made to overlap the rotation time and hence is worthwhile.

If a file is in key sequence, the usual method of addressing it is by means of a table called an *index*. The input to the table is the key of the record sought, and the result of the table look-up operation is the relative address or actual address of the record on the file unit.

An index may be defined as *a table which operates with a procedure that accepts information about certain attribute values as input and gives information as output which assists in quickly locating the record or records that have those attribute values.* A primary index is one which uses a record

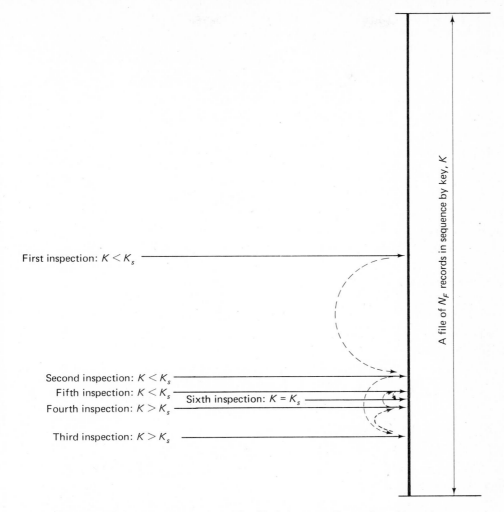

Figure 19.2   A binary search. The file is in ascending order of its prime
key, K. It is searched for a record of key K_5. Each inspection of the file
halves the area to be searched. A binary search may be unsuitable for
searching a file on direct access storage because of the seeks it incurs. It
is commonly used for searching an index which is entirely within the
main memory.

identifier (prime key) as input and gives information concerning the record's
physical location as output. A secondary index is one which uses a secondary
key as input.

An index is sometimes referred to as a *directory*. In this book we will use the word *index* as defined above and use *directory* to refer to a table which gives information about relationships between records, for example, gives the linkages in a plex structure or tree structure, as will be discussed in Chapters 24 and 25.

When an index is used for addressing a file the computer must search the index rather than search the file. A considerable amount of time is saved, but space is needed to store the index. It is rather like the use of a card index in a library. The user looks up the name of the book he wants in the card index, and the index gives the catalogue number, which is like a relative address of the book position on the shelves.

If the file is in key sequence, the index does not normally contain a reference to every record but rather a reference to blocks of records which can be scanned or searched.

Referencing blocks of records rather than individual records substantially reduces the size of the index. Even so the index is often too large to be searched in its entirety, and so an index to the index is used. Figure 19.3 shows two levels of index. Large files have more than two levels.

To save seek time the segments of the lower-level index (Fig. 19.3) may be dispersed among the data records which they refer to. On a disk-file for example, it is normal to have an index track on each cylinder, containing references to the records stored on that cylinder.

Sequential files with indices constitute the most common form of file addressing. In the next chapter we will discuss these in more detail.

Technique 5: Indexed Nonsequential Files

A nonsequential file can be indexed just as can a sequential file. A much larger index is needed, however, because it must contain an entry for every record rather than an entry for every block of records. Furthermore, it must contain *complete* addresses (or relative addresses), whereas an index to a sequential file can truncate the address it contains because the high-order characters of succeeding addresses are the same.

Compared with an indexed nonsequential file, an indexed sequential file is more economical of both index space and the time needed to search the index. Why, then, would a nonsequential file be used? The main reason is that the file may have to be addressed by more than one key. If it is in sequence for one key, then it is out of sequence for another. An index may be used for each key, the index for the sequential key having one entry per block of records and the other being longer, with an entry for every record. The key that is used most frequently for addressing the file is usually the one

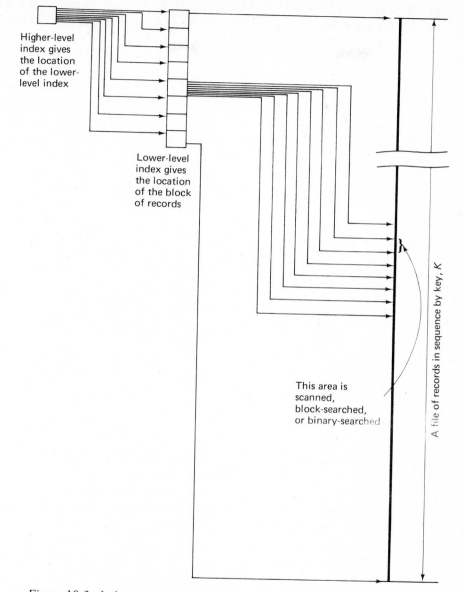

Higher-level index gives the location of the lower-level index

Lower-level index gives the location of the block of records

This area is scanned, block-searched, or binary-searched

A file of records in sequence by key, K

Figure 19.3 Index-sequential addressing. There may be multiple levels of index, as in Fig. 29.2.

that is used for sequencing it because fast access is possible with the short sequential index.

The analogy of a library card index is better suited to an indexed nonsequential file than to an indexed sequential file. Two keys are used in the card index—book title and author's name—and neither key is used for sequencing the books on the nonfiction shelves. There must therefore be an entry for *every* book in both of these indices.

The books are in sequence by catalogue number. When the user has found the catalogue number of the book he wants, he searches through the rows of shelves. Each *row* usually contains a sign giving the beginning and ending numbers of the books in that row. The user compares the catalogue number he has obtained from the index with the numbers posted on the rows. Upon locating the correct row, he searches for the *shelf* that contains the book. When he finds it, he looks at the individual book numbers on the shelf. A computer narrows down its search of the files in a similar way, going, for example, from a master index to a cylinder index and thence to a track index.

The library index does not give the *physical* location of the book on the shelves. Instead, it gives what might be regarded as a *symbolic address*, the catalogue number. The reason the address is symbolic is that the books change their location, and if a physical address were used, the library index would have to be frequently updated. Indexed nonsequential files also sometimes use a symbolic address rather than an actual address for a similar reason. The records change their location as new records are added and old ones deleted. When more than one key is used in the records the index on a nonprime key may give as its output the prime key of the record. The prime key is then used for locating the record using any other addressing technique. This method is slower than if the index gave the physical address of the record, but on files in which the records change their positions frequently symbolic addressing can be worthwhile.

Another reason for using a nonsequential record layout is that the file is highly volatile and the continued insertion and deletion of records into a sequentially ordered file would be too difficult or too time-consuming. If books were stored on the library shelves in alphabetical order, maintenance would be too time-consuming because many books would have to be moved on the shelves each time a new book was inserted.

There is a variety of techniques with which the indices themselves may be structured and employed. We will discuss these techniques in Chapters 29 and 30.

Technique 6: Key-Equals-Address Addressing

There are various methods of converting a key directly into a file address. Where this can be done it provides the fastest means of addressing, and there is no need for file searches or index operations.

The simplest way to solve the addressing problem is to have in the input transaction the relative machine address of the record in question. In some early banking applications the account numbers were changed as that the account number or part of the number was the file address of the account record. The address was equal to the key or derivable from it simply.

In many applications this direct approach is not possible. The item numbers in a factory could not be changed to suit the computer because they have a significance to the firm in question.

Sometimes a *machine reference number* can be used in an input transaction without any need for it to be a customer number or item number. The file address of the account record may, for example, be printed on the passbook of a savings bank customer and keyed in by the teller who operates the terminal. When an airline reservation computer sends a teletype message to another airline it includes, in some cases, a machine reference number of the passenger record. A teletype message received in reply, for example, confirming a reservation, should include the machine reference number so that the passenger record is speedily found.

Such schemes are referred to as *direct addressing*, although this term has been extended to include any algorithm which converts a key directly into a machine address and so includes technique 7 and, sometimes, technique 8.

Technique 7: Algorithm for Key Conversion

Almost as fast as the key-equals-address technique is the use of an algorithm for converting the key into the address. The address on some applications may be computed from entity identifiers such as street location and number or airline flight number and date. This is not possible on the majority of applications, but where it can be done it is a simple and fast method. It is most commonly found on interactive systems where file reference time is critical.

It usually has the disadvantage that it does not completely fill the file. Gaps will be left because the keys do not convert to a continuous set of addresses. An airline may, for example, have 150 flight numbers. The algorithm uses these and the date to calculate the file address. However, not every flight flies on every day; hence, some of the addresses generated will not contain a record.

A situation particularly amenable to a calculation of the file address is one in which the records form a matrix. A corporation may have many distributors, for example. Each distributor handles 200 products, and records are kept about the sales of each product for each distributor for each week of the year. If the records are 100 bytes long, the relative byte address of the record for the Ath distributor, the Bth product, and the Cth week may be calculated to be

$$(A - 1) \times 200 \times 52 \times 100 + (B - 1) \times 52 \times 100 + (C - 1) \times 100 + 1$$

A program would convert this relative address into a machine address.

    A disadvantage of direct addressing schemes is their inflexibility. The machine addresses of the records may change as files expand or are moved to a different unit or merged or modified. To combat the inherent inflexibility, direct addressing is usually carried out in two stages. The first converts the key to an *ordinal number*. The second converts the ordinal number to the machine address (Fig. 19.4). The ordinal numbers used are such that the

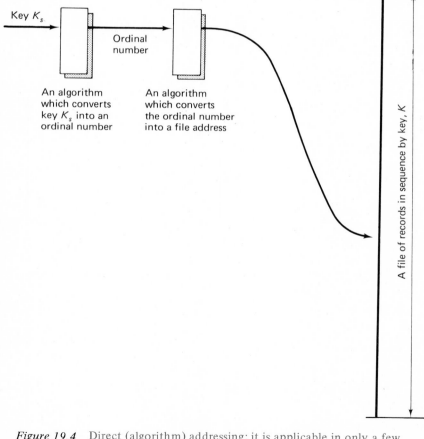

Figure 19.4   Direct (algorithm) addressing; it is applicable in only a few cases.

second stage can be modified easily when the machine addresses of the records are changed.

Technique 8: Hashing

An ingenious and useful form of address calculation technique is called *hashing* (sometimes *randomizing* or *scrambling*). With this technique the item's key is converted into a near-random number, and this number is used to determine where the item is stored. The near-random number could refer to the address where a record is stored. It is more economical, as we will see, for it to refer to an area where a *group* of records is stored, referred to as a *bucket* (sometimes *pocket* or *slot*). See Fig. 19.5. The number of logical records stored in this area is referred to as the *bucket capacity*.

When the file is initially loaded the location in which the records are stored is determined as follows:

1. The key of the record is converted into a near-random number, n, that lies within the range 1 to N, where N is the number of buckets usable for storage. Many hashing algorithms are possible for this operation, and one must be selected that suits the key set of the records in question.

2. The near-random number, n, is converted in the address of the nth bucket, and the physical record which constitutes that bucket is read.

3. If there is space remaining in the bucket, the logical record is stored in the bucket.

4. If the bucket is already full, the record must be stored in an *overflow bucket*. This could be the next sequential bucket, or it could be a bucket in a separate area with a pointer to it.

When records are read from the file the method of finding them is similar; i.e.,

1. The key of the record to be found is converted into a near-random number, n, using the same algorithm.

2. The near-random number, n, is converted into the address of the nth bucket, and that physical record is read.

3. The bucket is searched to find the required logical record.

4. If the required record is not in the bucket, then the overflow bucket is read and searched. It will occasionally be necessary to read more than one overflow bucket to find the record.

Because of the random nature of the algorithm, this technique will not achieve 100% packing density; 80% or 90% packing, however, can be achieved with most files, and no space is needed for indices. Most records

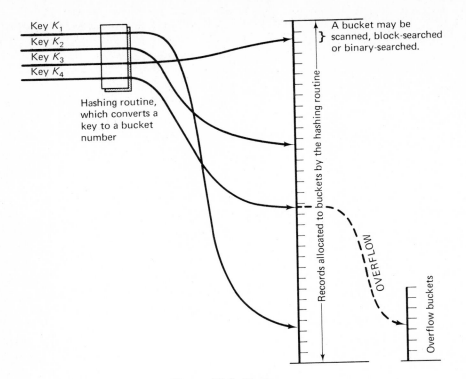

Figure 19.5 Hashing.

will be found with one seek, but some need a second (overflow) seek. A very small proportion need a third or fourth seek. In Chapter 21 we will discuss hash addressing.

INSERTIONS AND DELETIONS

A major concern in the design of file-addressing schemes and their associated record layouts is how new records will be inserted into the file and old ones deleted. Insertions and deletions, and the subsequent maintenance operations they cause, will be discussed when addressing techniques and indices are described in more detail later in the book.

COMBINATIONS OF TECHNIQUES

With some files, combinations of the above techniques are used to address the records. An index, for example, may locate an area of the file, and that area is then scanned or binary-searched. A direct-addressing algorithm may locate a section of an index so that it is not necessary to search the entire index.

An example of combined addressing techniques is the location of the CITY-PAIR records in an airline reservation system, illustrated in Box 19.2.

Box 19.2

The CITY-PAIR records in an airline reservation system give details of what flights fly between any two cities served. Seat availability on the flights is kept in AVAILABILITY records, but all other information necessary for displaying schedules or availability is in the CITY-PAIR records.

The key for addressing a CITY-PAIR record is the combination of two city names. Any city to which the airline flies can be included in the pair. A typical airline may serve up to 255 cities and hence need up to 64,770 (=255 × 254) CITY-PAIR records. However, these records are of fixed length, and some city pairs have so many flights that not all flights can be included in one record, and hence *overflow* records are needed. Some city pairs are not served by the airline and hence need no CITY-PAIR record. To further complicate matters the journey between some city pairs requires more than one flight via one or more connecting cities, and some of these flights could be with another airline.

Figure 19.6 illustrates the addressing mechanism that is used. The first step converts both of the city mnemonics in the terminal operator's input into ordinal numbers. As not more than 255 cities will be served, 1 byte can be used for each ordinal number. The convertion is done by means of a table look-up operation in core. Some of the cities, such as New York, are referred to very frequently, but the majority of the cities are small and referred to much less frequently. The table is scanned serially with the popular cities at the front and the infrequently referenced ones at the back. The same table can be used for converting city ordinal numbers back into city mnemonics.

The pair of city ordinal numbers are then used as a key to locate a CITY-INDEX record. The following algorithm is used:

$$\frac{(\text{CON}_1 \times \text{NC}) + \text{CON}_2}{\text{NI}} = Q + R$$

Box 19.2 *continued*

where CON_1 = ordinal number of the departure city

CON_2 = ordinal number of the arrival city

NC = total number of cities served (including an allowance for expansion)

NI = number of entries in the CITY-INDEX record

Q = quotient of this division

R = remainder of this division

The quotient Q is used for calculating the machine address of the CITY-INDEX record, using an algorithm called the *file address compute program*.

The remainder of the division, R, is used for calculating the field address in the CITY-INDEX record, as follows:

$$BA = R \times NE + NH$$

where NE = number of bytes per entry

NH = number of bytes in the header

BA = relative byte address of the required field in the record

The entry that is located in the CITY-INDEX record is an ordinal number for the *CITY-PAIR*. This number is given to the *file address compute program* to calculate the address of the required CITY-PAIR record. Each CITY-PAIR record contains spaces for pointers to *overflow* CITY-PAIR records.

The files of records are not stored contiguously but are distributed across many disks, as in Fig. 18.5, to maximize the likelihood of simultaneous access, and hence they lower the mean access time. The *file address compute program* converts the ordinal numbers given to it into the correct address of the scattered CITY-INDEX and CITY-PAIR records.

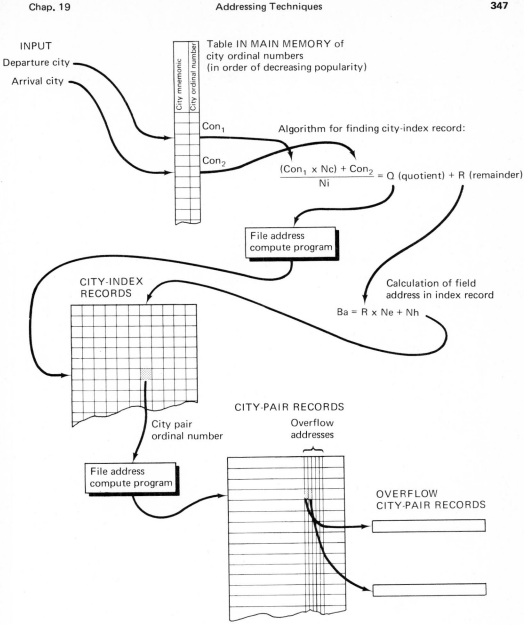

INPUT
Departure city
Arrival city

City mnemonic
City ordinal number

Table IN MAIN MEMORY of
city ordinal numbers
(in order of decreasing popularity)

Con_1

Con_2

Algorithm for finding city-index record:

$$\frac{(Con_1 \times Nc) + Con_2}{Ni} = Q \text{ (quotient)} + R \text{ (remainder)}$$

File address
compute program

CITY-INDEX
RECORDS

Calculation of field
address in index record

$$Ba = R \times Ne + Nh$$

City pair
ordinal number

CITY-PAIR RECORDS
Overflow
addresses

File address
compute program

OVERFLOW
CITY-PAIR RECORDS

Figure 19.6 A combination of direct and indexed nonsequential
addressing tailored for a specific application. (See Box 19.2.)

ASSOCIATIVE   There is a type of storage device with which no
MEMORY   addressing of the types discussed is necessary. It is
                  called *associative* storage. Associative memories are
not accessed by an address but by *content*. Associative storage is not widely
used yet but will be very important one day. It is discussed in Chapter 36.

SUMMARY   Box 19.3 summarizes the file-addressing methods.

Box 19.3   Summary of File - Addressing Methods

Technique	Record Sequence in Storage	
Serial scan	Key sequence	Suitable only for sequential batch processing.
Block search	Key sequence	Not recommended for searching data records; used for searching index entries.
Binary search	Key sequence	Not recommended if it requires time-consuming seeks. Suitable only if the data are in solid-state storage.
Indexed sequential (Chapter 20)	Key sequence	The most commonly used method. *Advantages*: Good storage utilization. Records in key sequence suitable for batch processing. *Disadvantages*: Care needed with the handling of inserted and deleted records. Poor with highly clustered insertions.

Box 19.3 *continued*

Indexed nonsequential	Any sequence	*Advantages*: No problem with insertions. Physical sequence can be employed for some other purpose, e.g., optimizing access time. Useful for secondary-key addressing. *Disadvantage*: Much larger indices than indexed sequential.
Key = address	Key sequence	Very limited. Highly inflexible.
Algorithm	Sequence determined by algorithm	Addressing algorithms tailored to applications can give fast access times but often give poor storage utilization and destroy data independence.
Hashing (Chapter 21)	Sequence determining by hashing transform	Useful and efficient technique. *Advantages*: Faster than indexing. No problem with insertions and deletions. Can take advantage of variations in reference density. *Disadvantages*: May give lower storage utilization than indexed methods. Records not in sequence for batch processing.

BOOK STRUCTURE

Chapter 20 discusses in detail the most common of the addressing methods given in Chapter 19.

20 INDEXED SEQUENTIAL ORGANIZATIONS

Records exist on storage devices in a given physical sequence. This sequencing may be employed for some purpose. The most common purpose is that records are needed in a given sequence by certain data-processing operations, and so they are stored in that sequence. A weekly run may be made, for example, listing the details of all customer accounts in account number order. Different applications may need records in different sequences. In batch-processing operations using tape or card files, much time is spent sorting the files from one sequence to another. On direct-access files the records are stored in one sequence only, and it is desirable to select the most useful sequence.

SEQUENTIAL OR RANDOM PROCESSING? The most common method of ordering records is to have them in sequence by a key—that key which is most commonly used for addressing them. Unless the keys follow a completely regular pattern, direct addressing is not then possible, and an index is required in order to find any record without a lengthy search of the file.

Two types of processing may be used with an indexed sequential file: (1) *sequential processing* in which records will be referred to in the same sequence as their file layout, and (2) *random processing* in which records are accessed in any sequence with no consideration of their physical organization. The ratio of the amount of sequential processing to random processing in the usage of the file may affect the choice of index sequential organization. Some files are used mainly for sequential processing with a small number of random accesses. Other files are addressed predominantly at random. This difference is reflected in the organization techniques that are used. Some are basically sequential organizations with an auxiliary index for random file accesses. Others are designed to maximize the efficiency of accessing at random, with sequential file processing being a secondary consideration.

If the data records are laid out sequentially by key, the index for that key can be much smaller than if they are nonsequential. Figure 20.1 shows an index for sequential records. Figure 20.2 shows an index for the same records laid out randomly (perhaps in order of arrival; perhaps in sequence by some other key). The index for the nonsequential file is more than N times larger than that for the sequential file, where N is the number of entries per index block.

MAINTENANCE   Although the sequential data organization of Fig. 20.1 requires a smaller index, it is more difficult to maintain. When new records are added the file must either be reshuffled to place them in sequence or else they must be placed in a separate location with pointers to them. Figure 20.3 shows four new records added to the sequential file. They are placed in an *overflow* area. The disadvantage of having records in an overflow area is that an extra read operation, and possibly an extra seek, is needed every time they are retrieved. In practice a file with overflows like that in Fig. 20.3 will be reorganized periodically with all the records rewritten in sequence and the index reconstructed. This operation is referred to as *maintenance*. Whereas maintenance of the file in Fig. 20.3 is not too difficult, maintenance of some data-base structures, which we will discuss later in the book, is a serious problem.

Figure 20.4 shows the addition of new records to the nonsequential file of Fig. 20.2. The new records are simply added on at the end of the file. No overflow pointers are needed and no subsequent maintenance run. Some reshuffling of the index entries is necessary, however, when some of the new records are added. If a file is very large or has new records added frequently (is volatile), then the avoidance of maintenance operations is worthwhile, and the data records may be stored nonsequentially.

Another way to lessen the need for overflows and maintenance with a sequential file is to leave empty record positions throughout the file, as shown in Fig. 20.5. This technique lessens the need for overflows or record reshuffling but does not avoid it entirely because some of the insertions will be clustered. The addition of LESLIE and JOAN to the records in Fig. 20.5 causes no problem, but then the addition of JENNIFER cannot be accomplished without either adding an overflow record and pointer or moving records. The record group beginning with KRISTEN could be moved

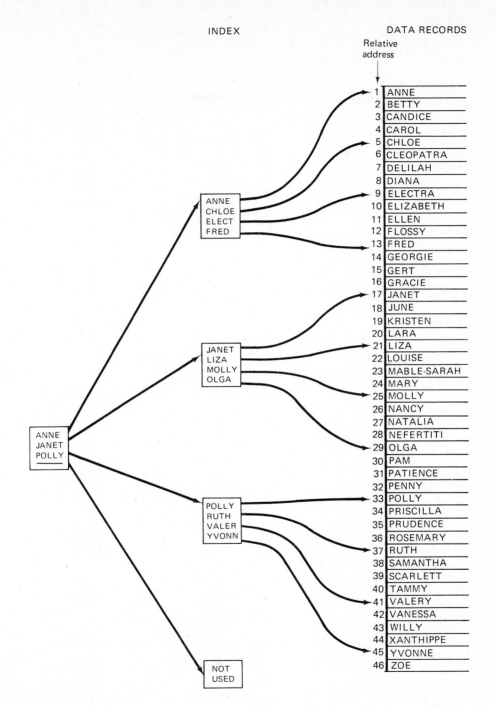

Figure 20.1 An indexed sequential organization. Compare with Fig. 20.2.

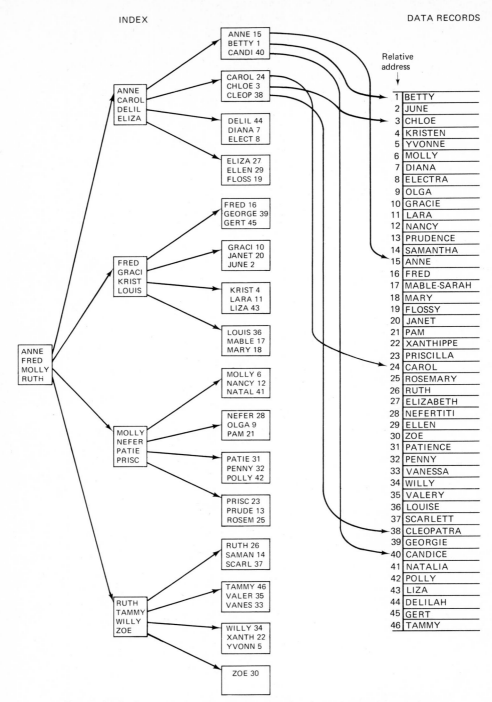

INDEX   DATA RECORDS

Figure 20.2 In an indexed nonsequential organization, a much larger
index is needed than with an indexed sequential organization.

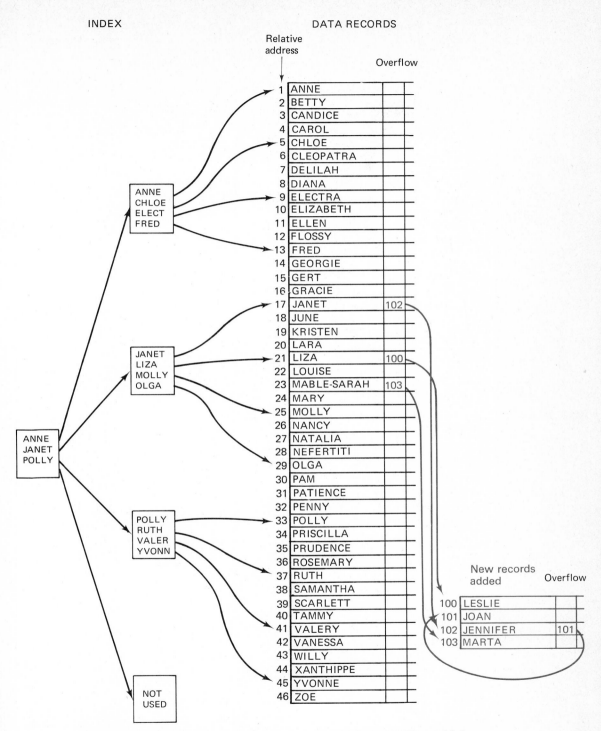

Figure 20.3 Four new records added to the file illustrated in Figure 20.1.

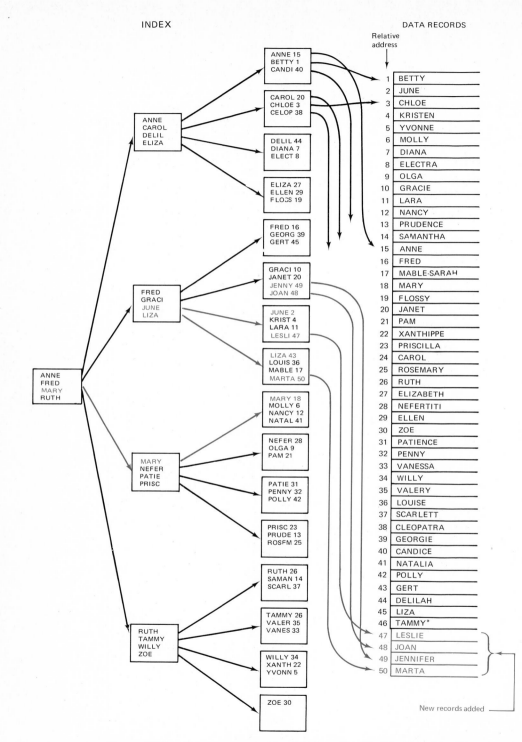

INDEX

DATA RECORDS

Figure 20.4 Four new records added to the file illustrated in Figure 20.3.

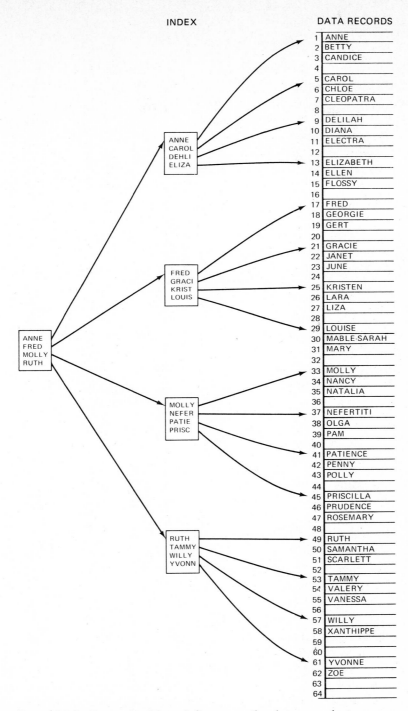

INDEX DATA RECORDS

Figure 20.5 Empty positions left among the data records to accommodate insertions. Clustered insertions will still require overflow records or record reshuffling.

down one position, but this group is now full and so the group beginning with LOUISE would also have to be pushed down one position. Then the addition of MARION would necessitate a further shuffle.

The technique of leaving gaps in the file in anticipation of new items being inserted is called *distributed free space*. Although overflow records could be avoided in this way, a periodic maintenance run would still be desirable to reestablish free space in the file.

HARDWARE CONSIDERATIONS

An indexed sequential organization can be tailored to fit a specific file hardware configuration. To do so saves both access time and storage space. The argument against fitting the organization to the hardware is that the type of storage devices may be changed or the file may be moved from one type of storage device to another. In such cases it is advantageous if the physical organization is hardware-independent.

We will illustrate the differences in indexed sequential organizations by reference to two "access methods" used with the IBM System 370. The first is ISAM (Indexed Sequential Access Method) in which the indexes and blocks are designed to fit specific file units. The second is VSAM (Virtual Storage Access Method), which is hardware-independent.

ISAM

With ISAM files the records are grouped so as to fit onto physical disk tracks, and one track on each cylinder contains an index to the records stored in that cylinder. When new records are inserted after the original sequential file has been set up these are stored in an overflow area. The index track contains pointers both to the prime data area and to the overflow area.

The overflow area, as shown in Fig. 20.6, can be on a track in the same cylinder as the prime data into which the overflow items are inserted. Alternatively, it can be in an entirely separate location. The advantage of the former technique is that it is on the same cylinder as the track index which refers to it. As indicated in the top illustration of Fig. 20.6, one read and no seek is needed to go from the track index to an item in the overflow area. In the bottom illustration of Fig. 20.6, a seek is shown from the track index to the overflow item. However, the overflow items might be on a different module capable of being accessed in parallel with the prime data module. In this case the accessing of the next item could begin while the overflow item is being read.

An overflow track for each cylinder, as in the upper diagram of Fig. 20.6, is commonly used. Unfortunately, however, the overflow track may

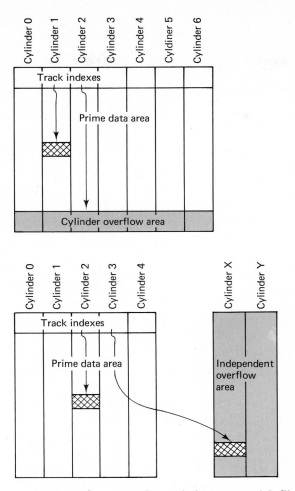

Figure 20.6 The overflow area in an index sequential file can be either on the same cylinders as the prime data area or in an entirely separate part of the file unit. Usually both are used.

become filled with overflow records. There is always a chance that this might happen quite suddenly. Therefore, many ISAM systems use *both* a cylinder overflow area (upper diagram of Fig. 20.6) and an independent overflow area (lower diagram of Fig. 20.6). A track can then be found in the independent overflow area when the cylinder overflow track fills up.

BLOCKING   As discussed in Chapter 18, a sequential file is often blocked, whereas a random file may not be, and the blocking substantially increases the packing density on direct-access devices (Fig. 18.1). When an indexed sequential file is originally loaded the records are usually blocked. If variable-length records are used, they may be stored in fixed-length blocks (Fig. 18.2).

MULTIPLE LEVELS
OF INDEX

Most indexed files need multiple levels of index, i.e., indices to the index as in Fig. 19.3. The lowest level of index is usually dispersed among the data records in order to minimize seek times, as with the track indices in Fig. 20.6.

In ISAM the level of index above the track index is called the *cylinder index*. The track index contains the highest-value key on each track and points to that track. The cylinder index contains the highest-value key on each cylinder and points to the track index of that cylinder. The cylinder index is on a cylinder that is separate from most of the data. It may be on the same module as the data, but the access operations are usually faster if it is on a different module so that seeking the cylinder index can occur while the previous data access is still taking place.

The level of index above the cylinder index is called the *master index*. The cylinder index is organized by track, and the master index contains the highest-value key on each track of the cylinder index, along with a pointer to that track. These indices are shown in Fig. 20.7.

There may be only one level of master index, or there may be up to three levels, as in Fig. 20.7. The master indices, like the cylinder index, are organized by track. The highest level is small enough to fit onto one track; it is this fact which determines how many levels of index are needed.

Let us suppose that a computer using the ISAM files illustrated in Fig. 20.7 is required to read the record whose key is 144.

The sequence of events is as follows:

1. The computer examines the highest level of the master index, which will normally be in main memory. The lowest entry in this index is 30500, which has a pointer to the of the level 2 master index.

2. The computer reads the relevant track of the level 2 master index. The lowest entry is 2100, which points to the first track of the level 1 master index.

3. The computer reads the relevant track of the level 1 master index, which is likely to be on the same cylinder as the level 2 master index in which case no seek is needed. The next highest entry above 144 is 330, which points to the first track of the cylinder index.

4. The computer reads the relevant track of the cylinder index. The next highest entry above 144 is 164. The entry points to the track index of cylinder 3.

5. The computer seeks cylinder 3 and reads the track index. The next highest entry above 144 is 146. This entry points to track 6.

6. The computer reads the relevant block of records into core from track 6 and scans the block to find logical record 144. The ISAM software gives this record to the application program which requested it.

VSAM

The way VSAM reads a record is somewhat similar to ISAM except that, since it is *hardware-independent*, we no longer describe the operation in terms of tracks and cylinders.

Figure 20.8 illustrates VSAM. Instead of cylinders subdivided into tracks, the diagram shows *control areas* subdivided into *control intervals*. The control intervals in one data set are all the same length, and widely varying lengths can be selected. There may be several control intervals per track, or the control interval may spread over several tracks.

Just as ISAM has a track index, so VSAM has a control interval index. It is called a *sequence set*. Just as ISAM has one track index per cylinder, so VSAM has one sequence set index per control area.

The sequence set index is itself indexed by a hierarchy (tree) of indices not unlike the ISAM master indices. These are called the *index set*. The sequence set index contains the highest key value in each control interval and points to that control interval. The lowest level of the index set contains the highest-value key in each control area and points to the sequence set index block for that control area.

To find a record, VSAM starts with the uppermost block of the index set, as did ISAM, and works its way down. The structure of the VSAM index blocks is different from those of ISAM. Index structures are discussed in Chapter 30.

The most important difference between ISAM and VSAM, apart from the question of device independence, is the way they handle the insertion and deletion of records.

INSERTIONS AND DELETIONS

The organization of an indexed sequential file would be a simple matter if no new records had to be added to the file. The handling of insertions and deletions is the main reason for differences in indexed sequential techniques.

In the traditional magnetic tape file, insertion and deletion is no problem. The required changes are sorted into the same key sequence as the

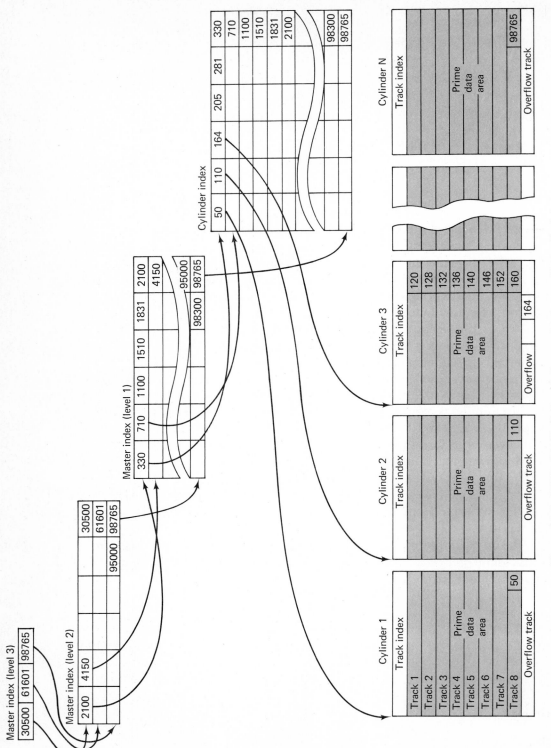

Figure 20.7 IBM's ISAM (Indexed Sequential Access Method). Other illustrations of ISAM are in Figs. 20.1 and 20.3.

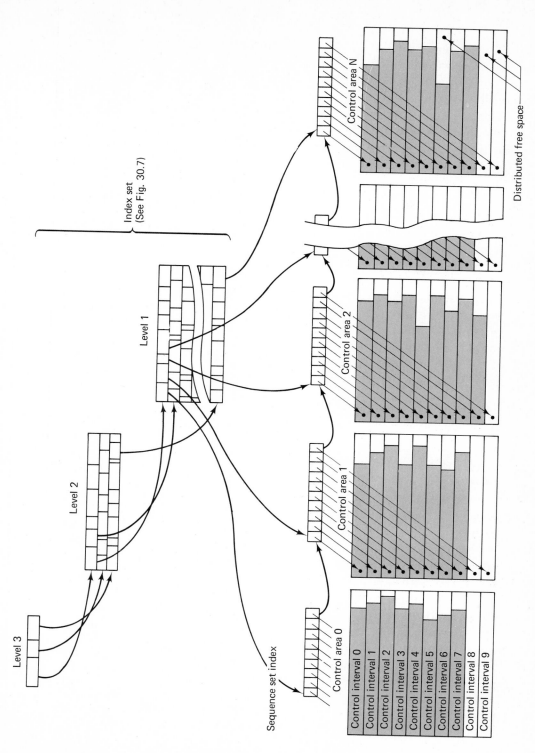

Level 3

Level 2

Index set
(See Fig. 30.7)

Level 1

Sequence set index

Control area 0

Control area 1

Control area 2

Control area N

Control interval 0
Control interval 1
Control interval 2
Control interval 3
Control interval 4
Control interval 5
Control interval 6
Control interval 7
Control interval 8
Control interval 9

Distributed free space

Figure 20.8 IBM's VSAM (Virtual Storage Access Method). See also Fig. 20.5.

file; they are read in with it, and a new file is written with the additions and deletions incorporated.

With a direct-access file it may also be possible to delay the insertions until the end of the day or the end of the month as with batch processing. (There is no need to delay the deletions; a record can be marked to indicate that it is effectively deleted.) Where such delay is permissible the file might be periodically rewritten, like a tape file, to incorporate the changes. This approach is occasionally used, but two snags occur on large and complex files. First, the file may be so large that rewriting it is excessively time-consuming and should be postponed as long as the maintenance and recovery techniques permit. Second, rewriting it may be complex, and hence time-consuming, because the file is structured with multiple pointers, chains, or secondary indices.

Except with very static (nonvolatile) files, it is generally desirable to avoid having to rewrite direct-access files in order to handle insertions. On some systems it is imperative the new records be inserted in real time. This is true on an airline reservation system, for example, but here the files are not sequentially ordered. Where a very high volume of real-time file inserts are needed sequential files are usually avoided. On many, perhaps the majority, of the systems using sequential files, insertions can be made at the end of the day, rather than in real time.

OVERFLOWS   As illustrated earlier, there are two methods of accommodating insertions without having to rewrite the file. First, they may be stored in an area specially reserved for *overflows*, as in Fig. 20.6.

A means of locating the items in the overflow area is needed. The items in it will sometimes be needed in sequence, although they were not inserted into file in sequence. To make matters worse the insertions sometimes arrive in *clusters*. It is always more difficult to devise a satisfactory means to handle clustered insertions than insertions which arrive singly and with random key values. Some applications have *highly* clustered insertions. In a factory, for example, a block of new part numbers may be added whose keys fit between two existing keys. There may be 1000 new part numbers in the insertion. This is a rare circumstance but one which has on occasions played havoc with overflow schemes.

There are three main ways of addressing the overflow area. The ISAM method of addressing the overflow is to use pointers from the track index and then chains to indicate the key sequence of the inserted items. A field exists in the track index for one pointer for each prime data track.

The ISAM overflow procedure is illustrated in Fig. 20.9. The data records have alphabetical keys of which the first three letters are shown. When the file is first loaded the overflow track is empty. The first record to be inserted has a key that begins with the letters ARK. It is therefore fitted into prime data track 1 between APU and ARM. The three records on the track with a key higher in sequence (alphabetical order) than ARK have to be slid to the right. There is then no room for the record ASP on the track, and so it is written on the overflow track. On the index track there is a position for an overflow entry for track 1, and the new address of ASP is written in that position.

Next a cluster of inserts are added: BED, BEG, BEN, and BET. These go onto track 2 with the result that four records, BIN, BIT, BUZ, and CAD, go to the overflow track. The highest key of these four is written in the overflow index entry for track 2, along with the address of BIN, the one with the lowest key. BIN is chained to BIT, BIT to BUZ, and BUZ to CAD.

After three more records have been inserted the overflow track is full, and so the next record to be displaced, BEN, is written on a track in the independent overflow area. It is chained to the other track 2 items on the original cylinder overflow track. The next record cast out to reside in the independent overflow area is ARL, and this is chained to the items from its native track 1.

This scheme is excellent for a not-too-large number of scattered insertions. If there is only one overflow from a prime data track, it can be retrieved as quickly as the items still on the prime data track. If several items have overflowed but still reside on the overflow track of the original cylinder, the chains between them can be quickly followed in core. If, however, there are many clustered overflows scattered around the independent overflow area, following the chains requires repeated reads and seeks and can become time-consuming. There are stories associated with ISAM files about computer operators watching the seek arm clicking away for many minutes while the system waits for the record it is attempting to read.

The second way to address the overflow items avoids the chains between items by having multiple pointers to each of the overflow records. Instead of having one pointer for each prime data track overflow, the index track is designed so that there could be many pointers. This scheme complicates the index track organization and leaves the possibility of running out of space for pointers.

A third way to organize the overflow items is to put them into an independent overflow area which has its own index, as shown in Fig. 20.6. The reading of any overflow record then requires a seek to the overflow cylinder, the reading and inspection of the overflow index, and then the

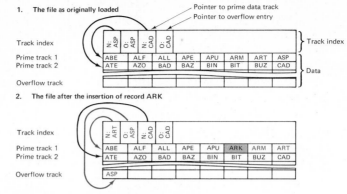

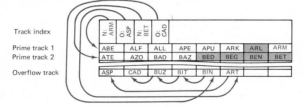

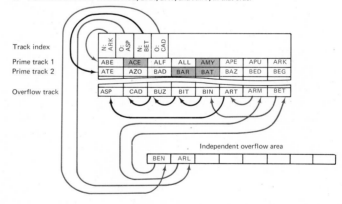

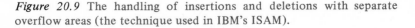

Figure 20.9 The handling of insertions and deletions with separate overflow areas (the technique used in IBM's ISAM).

reading of the track containing the record. This procedure takes longer than reading an ISAM overflow record without chains, but the possibility of having very lengthy chains is avoided.

An ISAM file behaves well as long as the overflow chains are short. A maintenance run is therefore carried out periodically to rewrite the file,

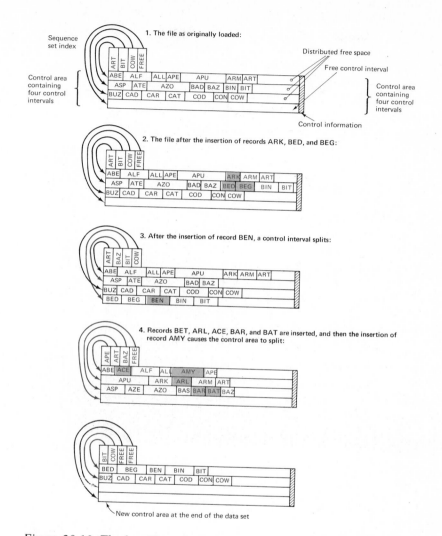

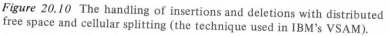

Figure 20.10 The handling of insertions and deletions with distributed free space and cellular splitting (the technique used in IBM's VSAM).

putting all the records on the prime data tracks. If the interval between maintenance runs is too long, performance degradation in the form of lengthy file accesses will occur.

**DISTRIBUTED
FREE SPACE**

The use of overflow areas always increases the access time needed to read some of the inserted records. An alternative is to use *distributed free space*, which incurs little penalty in time. It would not be economical to have gaps between every logical record; therefore, the logical records are arranged into groups (possibly physical records), and a gap is left in each group. Some entire groups may be left empty.

When an item is inserted into the distributed free space this can be done in one of two ways. First, the item could be placed in the gap without reshuffling the other items. To find it then, the entire group would have to be scanned. Second, the other items in the group could be moved when the new item is inserted so that the items in the group as a whole remain in sequence. It takes longer to insert an item because data records are moved, but the subsequent reading of the items will be quicker. As reading occurs far more often than the insertion of new items, the latter approach is the better.

VSAM uses two kinds of distributed free space, as shown in Fig. 20.10. First, each *control interval* is not completely filled with records when the file is set up. Second, some entire *control intervals* within a *control area* are left empty. Each index entry in the sequence sets index points to one control interval, and if that control interval is empty, there will be a *free-space entry* in the index. The systems programmer who sets up a file specifies how much free space and how many empty control intervals that file will have.

When a record is deleted from a VSAM file the remaining records in the control interval are slid to the left. All the empty space in the control interval is then contiguous and so is more easily allocated to new records. If deletion of records empties a control interval entirely, then a free-space entry will be made for that control interval in the index. These processes are referred to as *dynamic space reclamation*.

CELLULAR SPLITTING

If an appropriate amount of free space is left in the control intervals, most new records can be inserted by sliding existing records to the right within the control intervals. Occasionally, however, there will not be enough free space left in a control interval to accommodate the new record. In this case a *control interval split* must take place. The software moves approximately half the records from that control interval into an empty control interval in the same control area. The software finds empty control intervals by means of the free-space entries that are in the index.

Occasionally there will not be a free control interval left in the control area in question. In this case a *control area split* must take place, which is similar to a control interval split. The software establishes a new control area at the end of the data set and moves about half the control intervals from the full control area into it with all their data records. The new control area may be created from space already allocated for it in the data set, or new space may be created by adding an additional *extent* to the data set. When a control interval or control area split occurs the indices are adjusted to reflect it.

The technique of successively splitting groups of records is sometimes called *cellular splitting* There is, perhaps, a certain esthetic appeal to cellular splitting for it enables a file to grow rather like a biological organism splitting its cells. It can be designed so that no periodic maintenance is required. The maintenance is done in effect when the splits occur.

The upper diagram of Fig. 20.10 shows a VSAM file as originally set up with its empty space in the control intervals and, in this case, one empty control interval in each control area. The second diagram shows how the records with keys beginning with ARK, BED, and BEG are inserted without splitting any control intervals. Note that the records can be fully variable in length. An update operation may shorten or lengthen a record, and the record is refitted into the file like an insertion or deletion.

When the record BEN is added to the file in Fig. 20.10, it splits the second control interval. Two new control intervals result, each with five records in key sequence. Before the split the sequence set index indicated that the fourth control interval was free. After the split it gives the value of the highest key in the control interval.

Five more records, BET, ARL, ACE, BAR, and BAT, are inserted with no further splitting. The next record is too long for the first control interval. As no free control interval is left, the control area splits. The control intervals are divided sequentially between the two control areas, and the index blocks are modified to reflect the change.

After a control interval split, the records are in sequence within the control intervals but not within the control area as a whole. They can be retrieved sequentially because the entries in the sequence set index *are* in sequence (third diagram of Fig. 20.10). When the control area splits, the control intervals in the two resulting control areas are in sequence once more. The control area split is in effect a file maintenance operation. After the control area split, however, the control areas are no longer in sequence and neither are the sequence set index records which relate to them. The entries in the lowest level of the index set *are* in sequence.

The file can be left with its control areas out of sequence. This does no harm except to increase the access time for sequential processing very slightly because a seek is needed to go to an inserted control area and back. The sequence set index blocks, each of which relates to a control area, are chained together horizontally as shown in Fig. 20.8. If the control areas are out of sequence, these horizontal pointers will indicate the correct key sequence. Sequential processing takes place *without using the index set* by following the horizontal pointer of the sequence set. The index set is used only for direct accessing.

A VSAM key-sequenced file can thus be left with no periodic maintenance runs.

The use of distributed free space generally results in higher storage requirements than an overflow chaining method. However, it permits much faster retrievals of inserted records. The time taken to retrieve an inserted record with VSAM is the same as the time taken to retrieve one of the original records. The control interval and control area splitting makes possible the accommodation of highly clustered insertions without paying the penalty of either leaving an excessive amount of distributed free space or else having time-consuming overflow chains.

Box 20.1 summarizes the techniques for handling insertions in an indexed sequential file.

**POSITIONING
THE INDICES**

The positioning of the indices on the file units have a considerable effect on the access times with an indexed sequential file.

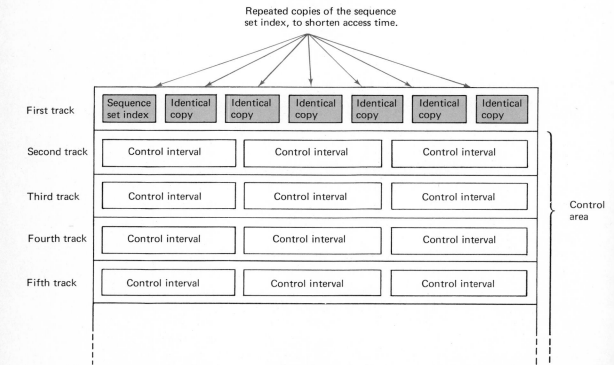

Figure 20.11 The sequence set index record is placed next to the control area it indexes to avoid unnecessary access time, and is replicated several times around a track to lessen the rotational delay.

Box 20.1 A Summary of the Techniques for Handling Insertions
in an Indexed Sequential File

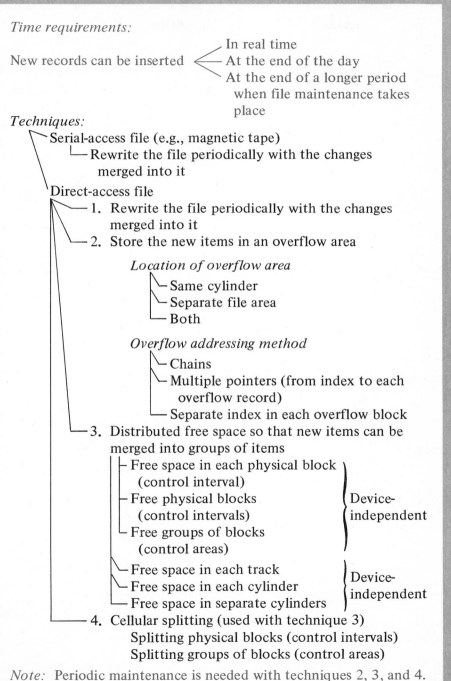

Time requirements:

New records can be inserted ⟨ In real time
At the end of the day
At the end of a longer period
when file maintenance takes
place

Techniques:

Serial-access file (e.g., magnetic tape)
└ Rewrite the file periodically with the changes
merged into it

Direct-access file

1. Rewrite the file periodically with the changes
merged into it
2. Store the new items in an overflow area

Location of overflow area
└ Same cylinder
└ Separate file area
└ Both

Overflow addressing method
└ Chains
└ Multiple pointers (from index to each
overflow record)
└ Separate index in each overflow block

3. Distributed free space so that new items can be
merged into groups of items
├ Free space in each physical block
(control interval)
├ Free physical blocks
(control intervals)
└ Free groups of blocks
(control areas) ⎬ Device-
independent

├ Free space in each track
├ Free space in each cylinder
└ Free space in separate cylinders ⎬ Device-
independent

4. Cellular splitting (used with technique 3)
Splitting physical blocks (control intervals)
Splitting groups of blocks (control areas)

Note: Periodic maintenance is needed with techniques 2, 3, and 4.

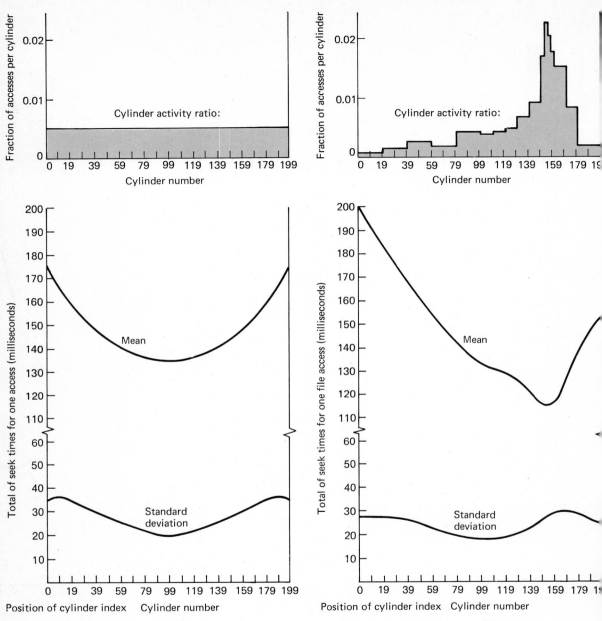

Figure 20.12 The mean record-access time (to access the index and then the record) varies with the positioning of the index in the data. In this illustration the index is on one cylinder of a disk unit, and the data is on another cylinder of the same module. The best cylinder for the index varies with the distribution of file activity.

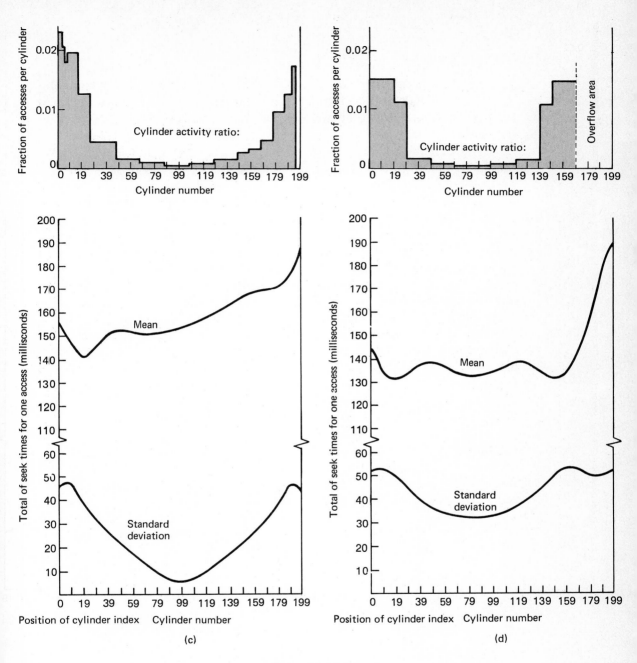

(c)

(d)

Figure 20.12 (cont.)

The lowest-level index (track index or sequence set index) is usually interspersed among the data records so as to avoid seeks in going from this index to the data. In addition, it may be *repeated* several times around a track to minimize the time waiting for track rotation when it is read, as shown in Fig. 20.11.

The cylinder index in ISAM or lowest level of the index set in VSAM should be placed in a position that minimizes both the index seek time and the subsequent data seek time. An effective way to do this is to place the index on a separate module where an access mechanism sits over it doing nothing but index reads. The indices have characteristics different from the data, and there is much to be said for storing them on different types of devices. It is particularly important to do so when the data are on a file with a single access mechanism, such as a data cell drive. It is time-consuming to move the data cell access mechanism backward and forward between the higher levels of index and the data. The higher levels of index should be moved to a separate, smaller, and faster device such as small disk unit.

Often a data set is on one disk pack, and that disk pack contains its own cylinder index (or *virtual* equivalent). The systems programmer usually has a choice of where to position the cylinder index, and he should choose that cylinder which minimizes the seek times. Surprisingly often, the cylinder index has been placed on cylinder 0 and this is usually the worst place for it. If the frequency of reference is evenly distributed across the file, the optimum position for the cylinder index is in the center of data. Often the file has a far from even reference density, and then a calculation may be needed to determine the optimum position for the cylinder index. Figure 20.12 shows two cases. The upper chart for each plots the reference density across the file. The lower chart shows the mean and standard deviation of access time for the two reads (seeking and reading the cylinder index and then seeking and reading the data cylinder). It will be seen that the best cylinder on which to position the index varies with the distribution of file activity.

BOOK STRUCTURE

Chapter 21 discusses in detail one of the most effective addressing methods.

21 HASHING

Hashing (Fig. 19.5) has been used for addressing random-access storages since they first came into existence in the mid-1950s, but nobody had the temerity to use the word *hashing* until 1968. The word *randomizing* was used until it was pointed out that not only did the key conversion process fail to produce a *random* number, but, contrary to early belief, it was undesirable that it should.

Many systems analysts have avoided the use of hashing in the suspicion that it is complicated. In fact it is simple to use and has two important advantages over indexing. First, it finds most records with only one seek, and, second, insertions and deletions can be handled without added complexity. Indexing, however, can be used with a file which is sequential by prime key, and this is an overriding advantage for some batch-processing applications.

There are many variations in the techniques available for hashing. They have been compared in many different studies [1,2,3,], and from these studies we will draw certain guidelines about which are good techniques and which are best avoided.

FACTORS AFFECTING EFFICIENCY The factors which the systems analyst can vary when using hash addressing are as follows:

1. The bucket size.

2. The packing density, i.e., the number of buckets for a file of a given size.

3. The hashing key-to-address transform.

4. The method of handling overflows.

Optimal decisions concerning these factors have a substantial effect on the efficiency of the file organization. We will review them in the above sequence.

BUCKET
SIZE
A certain number of address spaces are made available, called *home buckets*. A bucket can hold one or more records, and the systems analyst can select the bucket capacity. As shown in Fig. 19.5, the hashing routine scatters records into the home buckets somewhat like a roulette wheel tossing balls into its compartments.

Let us suppose that a roulette wheel has 100 balls which it will distribute to its compartments. Each ball represents a record, and each compartment represents a bucket. The wheel's compartments can hold 100 balls in total; however, we can vary the size of the compartments. If a ball is sent to a compartment which is full, it must be removed from the roulette wheel and placed in an overflow area.

If we have 100 compartments which can hold only one ball each, the wheel will often send a ball to a compartment which is already full. There will be a high proportion of overflows. If we have 10 compartments which

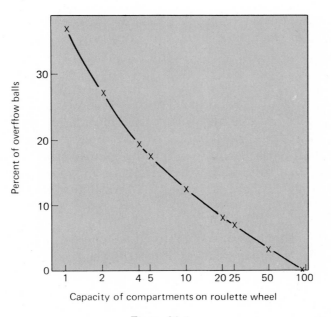

Figure 21.1

can hold 10 balls each, there will be far fewer overflows. It is an exercise in basic statistics to calculate the expected number overflows, and Fig. 21.1 shows the result.

If a systems analyst chooses a small bucket size, he will have a relatively high proportion of overflows, which will necessitate additional bucket reads and possibly additional seeks. A larger bucket capacity will incur fewer overflows, but the larger bucket will have to be read into main memory and searched for the required record.

Figures 21.2 and 21.3 illustrate a simple hashing process with a bucket capacity of 2.

If a direct-access device is used which has a long access time, it is desirable to minimize the numbers of overflows. A bucket capacity of 10 or more should be used to achieve this end.

On the other hand, if the file is stored in a solid-state, or core, storage, the overflow accesses can be carried out as rapidly as the read operations used when searching a bucket. In this case it is desirable to minimize the bucket-searching operation at the expense of more overflows. In such a case a bucket size of 1 is economical. Later we will discuss systems using *paging* in which a page containing many items is read into solid-state storage and hashing is used for finding an item on the page as quickly as possible. A bucket size of 1 is used.

In practice, bucket capacity is often tailored to the hardware characteristics. For example, one track of a disk unit, or half a track, may be made one bucket.

PACKING DENSITY   The proportion of overflows is also affected by the density with which records are packed into the home buckets. If the roulette wheel can hold 100 balls in total and 100 balls are spun into its compartments, there will be a high probability that some balls will overflow—even if the compartments are quite large. If only 80 balls are spun, the probability of overflow will be much lower.

$$\text{Packing density} = \frac{\text{Number of records stored in home buckets}}{\text{Maximum number of records that could be stored in them}}$$

When we use this ratio to refer to the home buckets only, ignoring overflow records, we will call it the *prime packing density*. The above roulette wheel spinning 80 balls is used with a prime packing density of 80%.

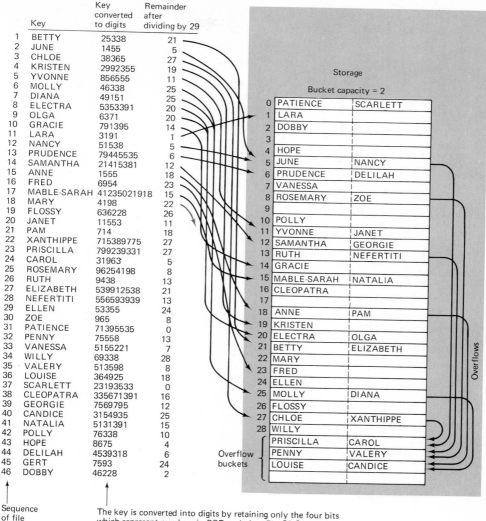

	Key	Key converted to digits	Remainder after dividing by 29
1	BETTY	25338	21
2	JUNE	1455	5
3	CHLOE	38365	27
4	KRISTEN	2992355	19
5	YVONNE	856555	11
6	MOLLY	46338	25
7	DIANA	49151	25
8	ELECTRA	5353391	20
9	OLGA	6371	20
10	GRACIE	791395	14
11	LARA	3191	1
12	NANCY	51538	5
13	PRUDENCE	79445535	6
14	SAMANTHA	21415381	12
15	ANNE	1555	18
16	FRED	6954	23
17	MABLE-SARAH	41235021918	15
18	MARY	4198	22
19	FLOSSY	636228	26
20	JANET	11553	11
21	PAM	714	18
22	XANTHIPPE	715389775	27
23	PRISCILLA	799239331	27
24	CAROL	31963	5
25	ROSEMARY	96254198	8
26	RUTH	9438	13
27	ELIZABETH	539912538	21
28	NEFERTITI	556593939	13
29	ELLEN	53355	24
30	ZOE	965	8
31	PATIENCE	71395535	0
32	PENNY	75558	13
33	VANESSA	5155221	7
34	WILLY	69338	28
35	VALERY	513598	8
36	LOUISE	364925	18
37	SCARLETT	23193533	0
38	CLEOPATRA	335671391	16
39	GEORGIE	7569795	12
40	CANDICE	3154935	25
41	NATALIA	5131391	15
42	POLLY	76338	10
43	HOPE	8675	4
44	DELILAH	4539318	6
45	GERT	7593	24
46	DOBBY	46228	2

Sequence of file loading

Storage

Bucket capacity = 2

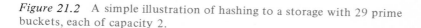

The key is converted into digits by retaining only the four bits which represent numbers in BCD code (see Fig. 32.2). This method should not be used in practice because it throws away information in the key. It is used here to provide an easily-followed illustration.

Figure 21.2 A simple illustration of hashing to a storage with 29 prime buckets, each of capacity 2.

The systems analyst can exercise a trade-off between saving storage and saving time by adjusting the prime packing density. If the key-to-address conversion algorithm scatters the records into buckets at random like the roulette wheel, we could calculate statistically the percentage of overflows

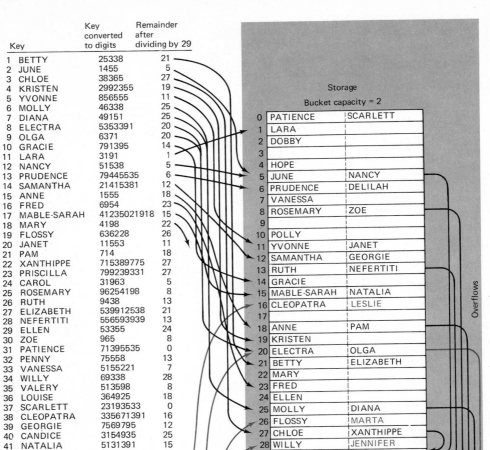

Key	Key converted to digits	Remainder after dividing by 29
1 BETTY	25338	21
2 JUNE	1455	5
3 CHLOE	38365	27
4 KRISTEN	2992355	19
5 YVONNE	856555	11
6 MOLLY	46338	25
7 DIANA	49151	25
8 ELECTRA	5353391	20
9 OLGA	6371	20
10 GRACIE	791395	14
11 LARA	3191	1
12 NANCY	51538	5
13 PRUDENCE	79445535	6
14 SAMANTHA	21415381	12
15 ANNE	1555	18
16 FRED	6954	23
17 MABLE-SARAH	41235021918	15
18 MARY	4198	22
19 FLOSSY	636228	26
20 JANET	11553	11
21 PAM	714	18
22 XANTHIPPE	715389775	27
23 PRISCILLA	799239331	27
24 CAROL	31963	5
25 ROSEMARY	96254198	8
26 RUTH	9438	13
27 ELIZABETH	539912538	21
28 NEFERTITI	556593939	13
29 ELLEN	53355	24
30 ZOE	965	8
31 PATIENCE	71395535	0
32 PENNY	75558	13
33 VANESSA	5155221	7
34 WILLY	69338	28
35 VALERY	513598	8
36 LOUISE	364925	18
37 SCARLETT	23193533	0
38 CLEOPATRA	335671391	16
39 GEORGIE	7569795	12
40 CANDICE	3154935	25
41 NATALIA	5131391	15
42 POLLY	76338	10
43 HOPE	8675	4
44 DELILAH	4539318	6
45 GERT	7593	24
46 DOBBY	46228	2
47 LESLIE	352395	16
48 JOAN	1615	20
49 JENNIFER	15559659	28
50 MARTA	41931	26

Storage

Bucket capacity = 2

0	PATIENCE	SCARLETT
1	LARA	
2	DOBBY	
3		
4	HOPE	
5	JUNE	NANCY
6	PRUDENCE	DELILAH
7	VANESSA	
8	ROSEMARY	ZOE
9		
10	POLLY	
11	YVONNE	JANET
12	SAMANTHA	GEORGIE
13	RUTH	NEFERTITI
14	GRACIE	
15	MABLE-SARAH	NATALIA
16	CLEOPATRA	LESLIE
17		
18	ANNE	PAM
19	KRISTEN	
20	ELECTRA	OLGA
21	BETTY	ELIZABETH
22	MARY	
23	FRED	
24	ELLEN	
25	MOLLY	DIANA
26	FLOSSY	MARTA
27	CHLOE	XANTHIPPE
28	WILLY	JENNIFER
	PRISCILLA	CAROL
	PENNY	VALERY
	LOUISE	CANDICE
	JOAN	

Overflow buckets

Overflows

Figure 21.3 Four new records added to the file in Fig. 21.2.

for different prime packing densities. Box 21.1 shows the calculation, and the curves in Fig. 21.4 give the results of this calculation.

The systems analyst ought to be able to find key-to-address conversion algorithms that do better than the roulette wheel, as we will see. Many are worse. The equations in Box 21.1 and the curves in Fig. 21.4 give a useful guideline to the trade-off among prime packing density, bucket size, and the number of overflows.

Let N = the total number of balls, M = the total number of compartments in the roulette wheel, and C = the capacity of a compartment. Then the prime packing density = N/CM.

Using the binomial distribution, the probability that a given compartment will have x balls sent to it in N spins of the roulette wheel is

$$\text{Prob }(x) = \frac{N!}{x!(N-x)!} \left(\frac{1}{M}\right)^{x} \left(1 - \frac{1}{M}\right)^{n-x}$$

The probability that there will be Y overflows from a given compartment is $P(C + Y)$.

The mean number of overflows from a given compartment is

$$\sum_{Y=1}^{\infty} \text{Prob }(C + Y) \cdot Y$$

The percentage of overflows for the entire roulette wheel is therefore

$$100 \times \frac{M}{N} \cdot \sum_{Y=1}^{\infty} \text{Prob }(C + Y) \cdot Y$$

From this we can explore the relationship between bucket capacity, C, prime packing density, N/CM, and percentage of overflows in a hashed file. The results are plotted in Fig. 21.4.

If the file is on an electromechanical storage with a long access time, the primary concern may be to cut down the number of accesses. The systems analyst may decide to hold the overflow percentage to 1%. As seen in Fig. 21.4, he may do so by having a prime packing density of 70% and a bucket capacity of 20 or more. On the other hand, access time may be of less concern than the efficient use of storage space. He may decide to use a

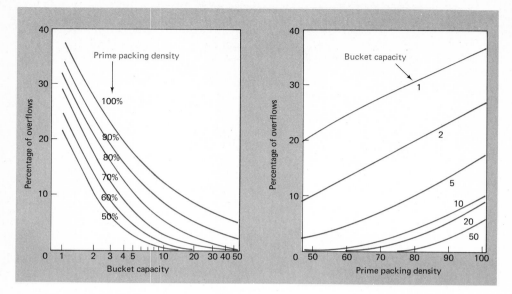

Figure 21.4 The systems analyst can exercise a trade-off between prime packing density, bucket capacity, and percentage of overflows. These curves are drawn from a key-to-address transform which perfectly randomizes the key set, like a roulette wheel. Compare with Fig. 21.7.

prime packing density of 95% and again use a large bucket size to reduce overflows. Conversely, he may want to avoid the computer time needed to search a large bucket. If the file is in solid-state memory so that overflow access is not time-consuming, he may use a bucket capacity of 1 and use a high packing density because this storage is expensive.

KEY-TO-ADDRESS CONVERSION ALGORITHMS

The key-to-address conversion algorithm generally has three steps:

1. If the key is not numeric, it is converted into a numeric form ready for manipulation. The conversion should be done *without losing information* in the key. For example, an alphabetical character should not be converted into *one* digit (as in Fig. 21.2) but into two. Alphanumeric data may be manipulated in the form of binary strings.

2. The keys are operated on by an algorithm which converts them into a spread of numbers of the order of magnitude of the address numbers required. The key set should be distributed *as evenly as possible across this range of addresses.*

3. The resulting numbers are multiplied by a constant which compresses them to the precise range of addresses. The second step may, for example, give four digits when 7000 buckets are to be used. The four-digit number is multiplied by 0.7 to put it in the range 0000 to 6999. This *relative bucket number* is then converted into a machine address of the bucket.

For the second step many transforms have been proposed and tested. It is desirable that the transform distribute the keys as evenly as possible between the available buckets. Realistic transforms distribute the keys very imperfectly, and so overflows result. The following are some of the more useful candidates:

1. Mid-square method

The key is multiplied by itself, and the central digits of the square are taken and adjusted to fit the range of addresses.

Thus, if the records have 6-digit keys and 7000 buckets are used, the key may be squared to form a 12-digit field of which digits 5 to 8 are used. Thus, if the key is 172148, the square is 029634933904. The central four digits are multiplied by 0.7: $3493 \times 0.7 = 2445$. 2445 is used as the bucket address.

This is close to roulette-wheel randomization, and the results are usually found to be close to the theoretical results of Fig. 21.4.

2. Dividing

It is possible to find a method which gives better results than a random number generator. A simple division method is such. The key is divided by a number approximately equal to the number of available addresses, and the remainder is taken as the relative bucket address, as in Fig. 21.2. A prime number or number with no small factors is used.

Thus, if the key is 172148 again and there are 7000 buckets, 172148 might be divided by 6997. The remainder is 4220, and this is taken as the relative bucket address.

One reason division tends to give fewer overflows than a randomizing algorithm is that many key sets have runs of consecutive numbers. The remainder after dividing by, say, 6997 also tends to contain runs of consecutive numbers, thereby distributing the keys to different buckets.

3. Shifting

The outer digits of the key at both ends are shifted inward to overlap by an amount equal to the address length, as shown in Fig. 21.5. The digits

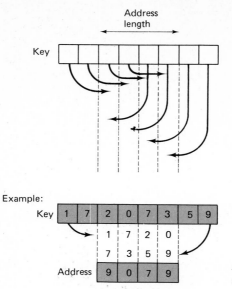

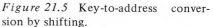

Example:

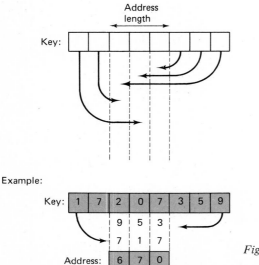

Figure 21.5 Key-to-address conversion by shifting.

are then added, and the result is adjusted to fit the range of bucket addresses.

4. Folding

Digits in the key are folded inward like folding paper, as shown in Fig. 21.6. The digits are then added and adjusted as before. Folding tends to be more appropriate for large keys.

Figure 21.6 Key-to-address conversion by folding.

5. Digit Analysis

Some attempts at achieving an even spread of bucket addresses have analyzed the distribution of values of each digit or character in the key. Those positions having the most skewed distributions are deleted from the key in the hope that any transform applied to the other digits will have a better chance of giving a uniform spread.

6. Radix Conversion

The radix of a number may be converted, for example, to radix 11. The excess high-order digits may then be truncated.

The key 172148 is converted to

$$1 \times 11^5 + 7 \times 11^4 + 2 \times 11^3 + 1 \times 11^2 + 4 \times 11^1 + 8 = 266373$$

and the digits 6373 are multiplied by 0.7 to give the relative bucket address 4461.

Radix 11 conversion can be performed more quickly in a computer by a series of shifts and additions.

7. Lin's Method [9]

In this method a key is expressed in radix p, and the result is taken modulo q^m, where p and q are prime numbers (or numbers without small prime factors) and m is a positive integer.

The key 172148 would first be written as a binary string: 0001 0111 0010 0001 0100 1000. Grouping the string into groups of three bits, we obtain 000 101 110 010 000 101 001 000 = 05620510. This is expressed as a decimal number and divided by a constant q^m. The remainder is used to obtain the relative bucket address.

8. Polynomial Division

Each digit of the key is regarded as a polynomial coefficient; thus, the key 172148 is regarded as $x^5 + 7x^4 + 2x^3 + x^2 + 4x + 8$. The polynomial so obtained is divided by another unchanging polynomial. The coefficient in the remainder forms the basis of the relative bucket address.

CHOICE OF
TRANSFORM

The best way to choose a transform is to take the key set for the file in question and simulate the behavior of many possible transforms. For each transform, all the keys in the file will be converted and the numbers of records in each bucket counted. The percentage of overflows for given bucket sizes will be evaluated.

Several researchers have conducted experiments on typical key sets searching for the ideal transform [3]. Their overall conclusion is that the simple method of *division* seems to the best general transform. Buchholz [1] recommends dividing by a prime slightly smaller than the number of buckets. Lum et al. [3] say that the divisor does not have to be a prime; a nonprime number with no prime factors less than 20 will work as well.

Figure 21.7 shows some typical results. The red curve shows the theoretical behavior of a perfectly randomizing transform like a roulette wheel. The points plotted show the average overflow percentages given by three common transforms on eight widely differing but typical key sets. The mid-square method is close to a theoretical randomizing transform. The division method performs consistently better than the randomizing transform. The folding method is erratic in its performance and so is the shifting method, probably because of the uneven distribution of characters in the key sets. Shifting and folding almost always perform less well than division. The more complex methods such as radix transformation, Lin's method, and polynomial division also perform less well, often because their behavior is close to that of an imperfect random number generator.

The ideal transform is not one which distributes the key set *randomly* but one which distributes it uniformly across the address space.

DESIGN
RECOMMENDATION

The behavior of the good transforms on actual files is usually somewhat better than that of a perfectly randomizing transform but is fairly close to it. A systems analyst who is designing file layouts would therefore be employing a prudently conservative assumption if he used the roulette wheel calculation of Box 21.1 or the curves in Fig. 21.4 for making estimates of file packing density and percentage of overflows. He should use these curves along with knowledge of the hardware characteristics to select appropriate bucket sizes.

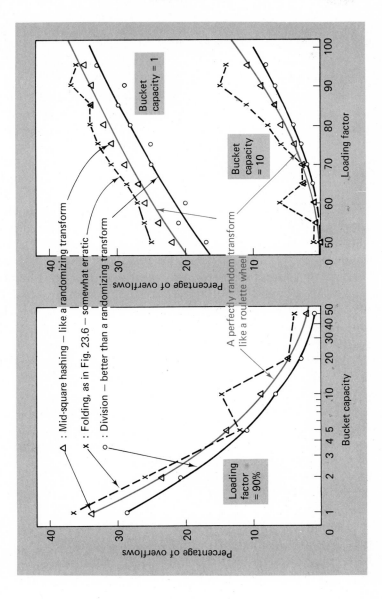

Figure 21.7 A comparison of three popular hashing algorithms with a perfectly random transform. *(Plotted from data averaging the results from eight different files, in Reference 3.)*

387

WHAT SHOULD WE DO   There are two main alternative places to store
WITH OVERFLOWS?   overflows. They may be stored in a separate
                          overflow area or in the prime area. The calculation
of Fig. 21.4 assumes that they are stored separately from the prime area.

If separate space is set aside for overflows the question arises: Should
there be an overflow area for each bucket that overflows or should the
overflows from many buckets be pooled?

There are two primary techniques in use. One is called *overflow
chaining*, and the other we will call *distributed overflow space* because it is
similar to the *distributed free space* discussed in the previous chapter.

OVERFLOW   Overflow chaining is straightforward when the
CHAINING   overflow bucket capacity is 1. If a record has the
                          misfortune to be assigned to a full home bucket, a
free bucket in the overflow area is selected, and the record is stored in that
overflow bucket. Its address is recorded in the home bucket. If another
record is assigned to the same full home bucket, it is stored in another
overflow bucket, and its address is stored in the first overflow bucket. In this
way a chain of overflows from the home bucket is built, as in Fig. 21.8. The
home bucket may have a capacity of one or many records.

If the home bucket size and load factor are selected appropriately, the
mean chain length can be kept low. An overflow chain as long as that in
Fig. 21.8 should be a rarity. Nevertheless, the risk of multiple seeks to find
one record can be reduced if the overflow buckets have a capacity greater
than 1.

In Fig. 21.9 the home and overflow bucket each have the same
capacity, say, 10 records. The first bucket to overflow is assigned a bucket in
the overflow area. It is unlikely to fill that bucket, so the next buckets to
overflow are also assigned the same overflow bucket. The overflow bucket
will be unlikely to overflow itself, but such an event will happen
occasionally. When it does happen, the overflow bucket will be assigned
another overflow bucket just as are the home buckets.

If a record is deleted from the single-record chain in Fig. 21.8, the chain
is reconnected. If a record is deleted from the bucket chain of Fig. 21.9, the
chain cannot be reconnected. Instead the empty record location is left, and
another overflow may fill it at a later time. If the overflow buckets have
many deletions, it may be desirable to reorganize the overflow area
periodically.

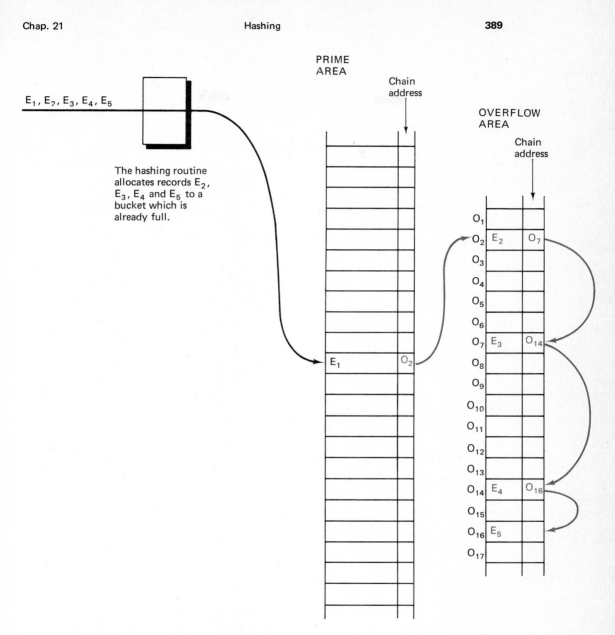

Figure 21.8 Overflow chain with overflow bucket capacities of 1 record.

DISTRIBUTED OVERFLOW SPACE　　In Fig. 21.10 there is no chain. Instead overflow buckets are distributed at regular intervals among the home buckets. If a home bucket overflows, the

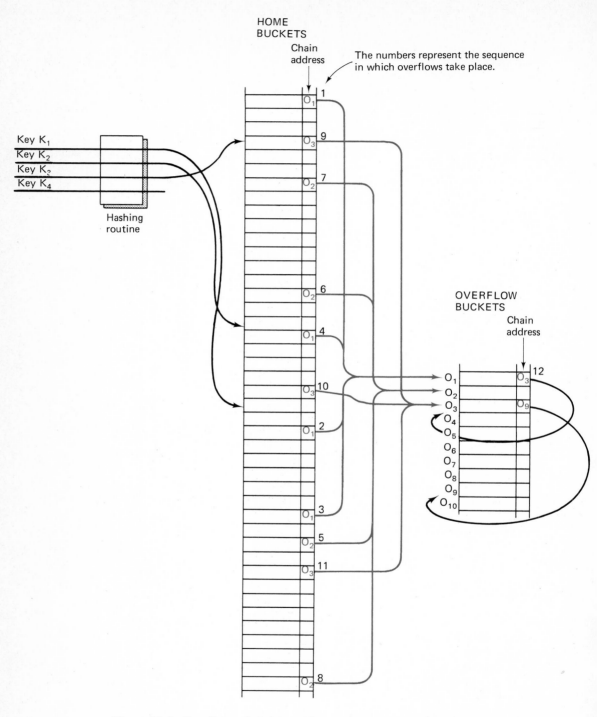

Figure 21.9 Overflow chaining with overflow bucket capacities of many records.

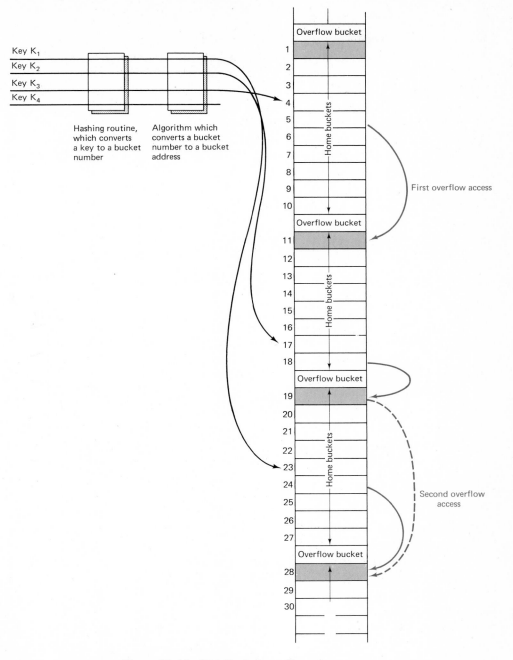

Figure 21.10 Distributed overflow space.

system attempts to store the record in the next overflow bucket. The method has the advantage that the overflow bucket is physically close to the home bucket. No access arm movement should be needed to go from home bucket to overflow bucket, and no chains have to be maintained.

If an overflow bucket itself overflows, the next consecutive overflow bucket is used in Fig. 21.10, requiring a second overflow access as shown.

The hashing routines described address a sequential spread of bucket numbers. An algorithm must therefore be applied to this spread to give the addresses after the overflow buckets have been inserted. Thus, in a byte-addressed device with an overflow bucket in every tenth position as in Fig. 21.10:

$$\text{Bucket address} = B_0 + B\left(N + \left\lceil \frac{N}{9} \right\rceil\right)$$

where B_0 = starting byte
B = number of bytes per bucket
N = sequential bucket number produced by hashing algorithm

PRIME AREA
SPILL METHODS

If overflows are stored *in the prime area* rather than in separate overflow buckets, the easiest way to handle them is the *consecutive spill method* (proposed by Peterson [4] and sometimes called *open addressing*). With this technique the hashing routine allocates a record to a home bucket, and if the bucket is full, it is stored in the next consecutive bucket. If that bucket is full, it is stored in the next bucket, and so forth.

The advantage of the consecutive spill method is that a lengthy seek is not usually needed for overflows. The next-door neighbor's bucket is often not more than one disk rotation away. However, when a neighborhood becomes crowded, many buckets may have to be examined in a search for free space. This is especially so if the buckets are of small capacity. A bucket with only one or two spaces left will find its free space being raided by its neighbors. (The method is sometimes called the bad neighbor policy!)

In general the consecutive spill method is efficient if the bucket capacity is large and inefficient if it is small. It should not be employed when the buckets have a capacity of 10 or less. The effect of bucket size can be seen in Fig. 21.11.

Many files laid out by hashing have clusters of full buckets. When this is the case the consecutive spill method tends to have patches of poor performance in which strings of full buckets must be searched. A variation of the consecutive spill method is the *skip spill method* in which, when a

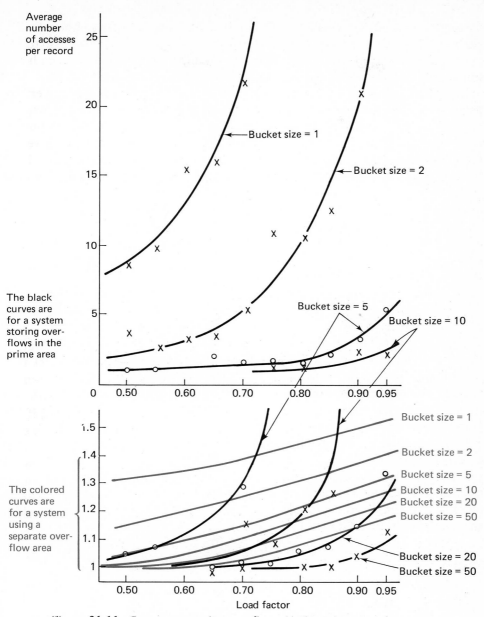

Average number of accesses per record

25

20

Bucket size = 1

15

Bucket size = 2

10

The black curves are for a system storing overflows in the prime area

5

Bucket size = 5

Bucket size = 10

0   0.50   0.60   0.70   0.80   0.90 0.95

1.5

Bucket size = 1

1.4

Bucket size = 2

The colored curves are for a system using a separate overflow area

1.3

Bucket size = 5

Bucket size = 10
Bucket size = 20
Bucket size = 50

1.2

1.1

1

Bucket size = 20

Bucket size = 50

0.50   0.60   0.70   0.80   0.90 0.95

Load factor

Figure 21.11 Curves comparing overflows in the prime area (consecutive spill method) with overflows in a separate area (in red). It is very inefficient to have overflows in the prime area with a small bucket size (say 10 or less). It can be efficient to have overflows in the prime area with a large bucket size (say 20 or greater). (Plotted from empirical data in reference [3].)

record's home bucket is filled, space is searched for by skipping buckets, as defined by a selection rule [5,6]. For a layout which tends to cluster this may be an improvement. In general its performance can be expected to be similar to the consecutive spill method. Either method is likely to be erratic in its behavior when the mean number of spills is allowed to rise either by using a small bucket size or a high load factor.

FREE-SPACE DIRECTORY   A way to store overflows in the prime area without running the risk of having to search many buckets is to use a directory of free space. The directory indicates which buckets have free space. It may or may not say how much free space they have. When a new record is inserted the hashing algorithm is used to select a bucket for that record. If the bucket is full, the directory is examined to find a nearby bucket with free space. The record is stored in that bucket, and a pointer to it is left in the home bucket.

Whenever a record is inserted or deleted the *space directory* must be updated. However, the directory is needed *only* when insertions and deletions occur, so with a file of low volatility it is not read often. The shortest form of space directory is one which lists only the full buckets. When overflows occur no more than two accesses are needed to read a record, and the second access may be short, to a prime bucket nearby.

The snag with the directory method is that pointer lists must be stored in the home bucket saying where the overflows are. In some instances the list of pointers becomes lengthy, consuming the space of one or more records.

The method can be efficient with a large bucket size (say capacity $\geqslant 20$) if the load factor is not too high. The large bucket size both reduces the number of overflows (Fig. 21.4) and reduces the size of the space directory. If the space directory shows only the full buckets, it can be small when the loading is not too high. When the loading increases, above say 90%, the overhead in pointer lists and directory entries builds up fast.

Box 21.2 summarizes the techniques for handling overflows.

OPTIMIZATION   A file addressed by hashing can have its performance optimized in a simple way.

A small proportion of the records will be stored as *overflows*. Because these records will take longer to access than others, they should be records which are accessed *infrequently*. To achieve this when the file is initially loaded, the frequently referenced items should be loaded first, and the infrequently referenced ones last. If possible, the loading should be in order

Box 21.2   Methods for Handling Hash Addressing Overflows

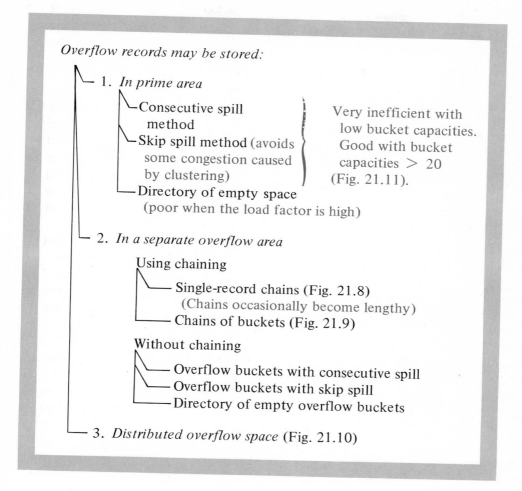

Overflow records may be stored:

1. *In prime area*

   Consecutive spill method

   Skip spill method (avoids some congestion caused by clustering)

   Directory of empty space (poor when the load factor is high)

   > Very inefficient with low bucket capacities. Good with bucket capacities > 20 (Fig. 21.11).

2. *In a separate overflow area*

   Using chaining

   — Single-record chains (Fig. 21.8)
     (Chains occasionally become lengthy)
   — Chains of buckets (Fig. 21.9)

   Without chaining

   — Overflow buckets with consecutive spill
   — Overflow buckets with skip spill
   — Directory of empty overflow buckets

3. *Distributed overflow space* (Fig. 21.10)

of popularity. The most frequently referenced items will go to the home buckets. By the time the overflow positions are being loaded it will be with the less popular items. When the file is used overflows will be less frequent.

Statistics on frequency of reference may be kept while the file is in use, and these statistics may be employed later when the file is reloaded. As with most physical data-base organizations, periodic reorganization can improve performance.

REFERENCES

1. W. Buchholz, "File Organization and Addressing," *IBM Systems J. 2*, June 1963, 86–111.

2. R. Morris, "Scatter Storage Techniques," *Comm. ACM 11*, No. 1, Jan. 1968, 38–44.

3. V. Y. Lum, P. S. T. Yuen, and M. Dodd, "Key-to-Address Transform Techniques: A Fundamental Performance Study on Large Existing Formatted Files." *Comm. ACM 14*, No. 4, April 1971, 228–259.

4. W. W. Peterson, "Addressing for Random-Access Storage," *IBM J. Res. Develop. 1*, No. 2, April 1957, 130–146.

5. C. E. Radke, "The Use of Quadratic Residue Research," *Comm. ACM*, Feb. 1970.

6. J. R. Bell, "The Quadratic Quotient Method: A Hash Code Eliminating Secondary Clustering," *Comm. ACM*, Feb. 1970.

7. J. A. van der Pool, "Optimal Storage Allocation for Initial Loading of a File." *IBM J. Res. Develop. 16*, No. 6, 1972, 579.

8. J. A. van der Pool, "Optimal Storage Allocation for a File in Steady State," *IBM J. Res. Develop. 17*, No. 1, 1973, 27.

9. A. D. Lin, "Key Addressing of Random Access Memories by Radix Transformation," in *Proceedings of the Spring Joint Computer Conference*, 1963.

10. C. A. Olson, "Random Access File Organization for Indirectly Addressed Records," in *Proceedings of the ACM National Conference*, 1969.

BOOK STRUCTURE

Pointers are used in many of the techniques for representing associations between records or segments. Chapter 22 discusses pointers and the following three chapters give methods of representing the associations between data.

22 POINTERS

Many data bases have links between one record and another, called *pointers*. A pointer is a field in one record which indicates where a second record is located on the storage devices. Pointers are drawn in the diagrams of this book as arrows linking the first record to the second.

Pointers also link data aggregates (or segments in DL/I terminology). Whenever we discuss pointers between *records* the reader should assume that we imply pointers between *data aggregates* also.

THREE TYPES OF POINTERS Three types of pointers are in common use. A pointer can be:

1. *The machine address* of the record pointed to.

2. *A relative address* of the record pointed to. The records in a file may be thought of as being sequentially numbered, and the pointers give the sequential number. A program converts the sequential number into the actual machine address. The records need not be contiguously positioned. They may occupy different file extents or may be scattered across the file modules as in Fig. 18.6.

3. *A record identifier*, which must be converted into the file address by whatever addressing technique the file uses, such as an index or an addressing algorithm. (Addressing techniques will be discussed in Chapter 19.)

Using the *actual machine address* as the pointer gives the fastest operation.

Using a *relative address* makes it possible for the entire file to be split or moved, for example, to a different disk unit. When records are moved the pointers do not have to be changed. Instead the algorithm which converts the relative address into actual address is changed. A measure of machine independence is achieved by using relative address pointers. Also, relative address pointers can usually occupy less storage space than machine address pointers. Relative address pointers are particularly important when *paging* is used, moving sections of files from one level of storage hierarchy to another.

A pointer which does not give an address, relative or actual, but gives a record identifier is sometimes called a *symbolic pointer.* Using the record identifier as the pointer makes it possible for individual records to be moved in the file without modifying all the records which point to them. On some files this is very important because many records have to be inserted into the file, and other records are shuffled, as we will see, to make room for them. On a file with many pointers and a high rate of inserting new records, symbolic pointers are much better than address pointers.

This book was written using symbolic pointers. The chapters and figures had alphabetical designations while it was being written. This chapter was Chapter BP, for example. The chapters and figures could then be deleted or reshuffled, and new ones could be added without my changing the cross-references in the text—a great advantage because I make many changes. When the book was published, all the alphabetic designations were changed to the sequential chapter and figure numbers which you now read.

Symbolic pointers are advantageous on many volatile files. However, the time taken to follow symbolic pointers is longer than with address pointers, especially if the addressing method used requires more than one seek. If a high proportion of the time is spent following pointers (as with some of the chain and ring structures discussed in the next chapter), it may be better to use relative address pointers rather than symbolic pointers.

Most chained files use relative address pointers.

Box 22.1 summarizes the advantages and disadvantages of the three types of pointers.

POINTERS TO
REPRESENT
SCHEMAS

Schemas such as that in Fig. 22.1 can be represented physically in a variety of ways, as we will see later. Some of these ways involve pointers. In Fig. 22.2, all the instances of one record type are connected with *twin* pointers and a *child* pointer is used from each parent record to the first instance of each subordinate.

Box 22.1 Advantages and Disadvantages of Three Types of Pointers

Pointers contain	Advantages and Disadvantages		
	Speed	*Independence*	*Other*
1. Machine address	The fastest type of pointer	None. Poor for volatile files	
2. Relative address	Almost as fast	Partial machine independence; essential when files are moved, for example, with paging techniques	Shorter than machine address
3. Record Identifier ("symbolic pointer")	Slower, especially if the record has an addressing method needing more than one seek; may be too slow for use with chains or rings	Machine-independent and independent of records being moved by the insert, delete, or maintenance process	

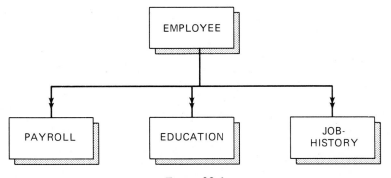

Figure 22.1

PC = Physical child
PT = Physical twin

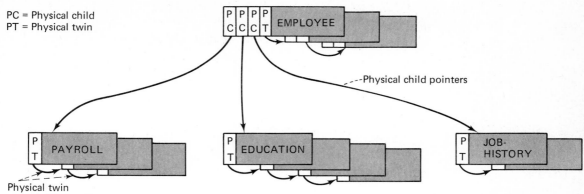

Physical child pointers

Physical twin
pointers (forward)

Figure 22.2 The schema of Fig. 22.1 represented physically with child and twin pointers.

PCF = Physical child (first)
PCL = Physical child (last)
PTF = Physical twin forward
PTB = Physical twin backward

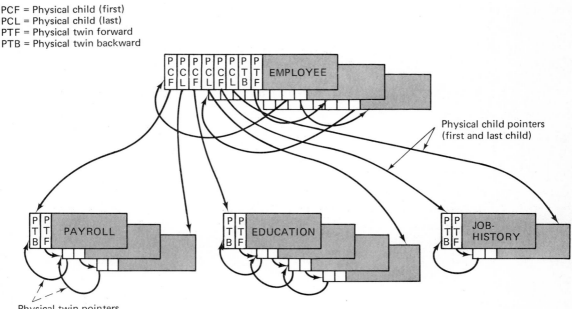

Physical child pointers
(first and last child)

Physical twin pointers
(backwards and forwards)

Figure 22.3 The schema in Fig. 22.1 represented with double child and twin pointers. Forward and backward twin pointers are used, and the child pointers point to the first and last instance of each record (segment) type.

In Fig. 22.3, twice as many pointers are used to represent the same schema. Two child pointers are used to each subordinate record type, one pointing to the first instance of the record type and the other pointing to the last instance. The pointer to the last instance is useful when new records are inserted out of sequence at the end of the group of records and linked to the last instance. The pointer to the last instance enables the new records to be linked up without skipping through the twin pointers to find the right location.

The twin pointers in Fig. 22.3 go in both directions, backward and forward. The backward twin pointers are needed if a record can be located without going through the forward twin pointers and if it is necessary to locate its predecessor. A record, such as an EDUCATION record in Fig. 22.3, might be located without using the pointers in Fig. 22.3 if it is pointed to by some other record not shown in Fig. 22.3. In the terminology of DL/I, an EDUCATION segment might be found because it is the logical child or logical parent of a segment in a different physical data base. It may be retrieved in this way, and its predecessor may be found using the backward twin pointer.

It may be necessary to progress from one of the lower records in Fig. 22.3 to that record's parent. In this case, physical parent pointers may be used as well as the twin pointers shown.

If the relationships shown in Fig. 22.3 are part of a DL/I structure, then logical pointers may be required as well as physical pointers. Figure 22.4 assumes that DEPARTMENT in a separate physical data base has been declared to be the logical parent of EMPLOYEE and that TRAINING-COURSE has been declared to be the logical child of EDUCATION. The EMPLOYEE segment, in addition to its physical pointers, has a *logical parent* pointer to the DEPARTMENT segment, and EDUCATION has a *logical child* pointer to the TRAINING-COURSE segment. If a DL/I schema is more complex, as with that in Fig. 12.7, many pointers may be used to represent it physically in a direct-access fashion. On the other hand, it is possible to use fewer pointers, as we will see in Chapter 24.

Figure 22.5 shows the format of the EMPLOYEE segment of Fig. 22.4 in a DL/I data base. A prefix to the data contains the pointers. It also contains a segment code giving the type of segment; a delete flag, which may indicate that the segment has been deleted; and an optional count, which is used to keep track of active logical relationships.

The pointers to be used in DL/I are specified in the physical data-base description (DBD). That in Figure 12.12 contains the clause PTR = T in each segment, meaning forward twin pointers; the child pointers would be assumed, as in Fig. 22.2. More complex pointers as in the EMPLOYEE

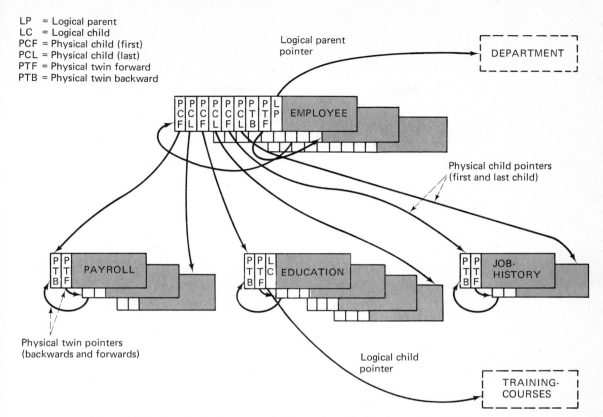

LP = Logical parent
LC = Logical child
PCF = Physical child (first)
PCL = Physical child (last)
PTF = Physical twin forward
PTB = Physical twin backward

Logical parent pointer

DEPARTMENT

Physical child pointers
(first and last child)

Physical twin pointers
(backwards and forwards)

Logical child pointer

TRAINING-COURSES

Figure 22.4 A physical representation of a DL/I schema in which
DEPARTMENT in a different physical data base is the logical parent of
EMPLOYEE, and TRAINING COURSES the the logical child of
EDUCATION.

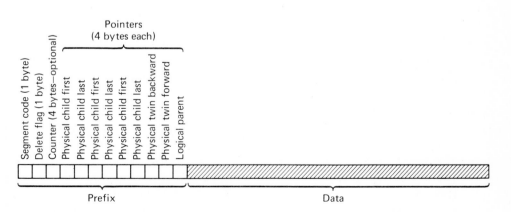

Figure 22.5 A typical DL/I segment format. This is the format of the
EMPLOYEE segment in Fig. 22.4. Fewer pointers could be used, but at
the price of less speedy direct-access operations.

segment of Fig. 22.4 could be defined: PTR = (LPARNT, DBLE, TWNBWD)—i.e., logical parent pointer, double child pointers, and twin backward pointers.

SEQUENCE OF WRITING POINTERS   Whenever a record (or segment) is written and linked to another record by means of a pointer, there is a small but finite chance that the machine will fail before the operation is complete. If the new record is linked to only one existing record, it is generally better to write the new pointer *before* writing the record. If the record is written first, there is a small chance that the pointer to it may not be written because a machine failure intervenes. There may then be no means of locating the record.

The situation is different if the record is inserted into an already-existing pointer linkage. Suppose that record A points to record C. Record B is to be inserted into the linkage to form the sequence A   B   C. Here the last operation performed should be to change the pointer A   C to A   B. If this pointer is changed first and a machine failure occurs before B is written, C will be cut off with nothing pointing to it. On some installations records have been lost because pointers were written in the wrong sequence.

If B is written, as it should be, before the pointer in A is changed, B may be cut off due to a machine failure prior to writing the pointer to it. The source of B must therefore be retained until it is known that the linkage is complete. Even so a stray copy of B may be left in the storage without a pointer to it. This copy will be ignored when the next file maintenance run tidies up the physical data layout.

EMBEDDED VERSUS DIRECTORY POINTERS   The pointers in many types of files are embedded in the record, as in Fig. 22.2. To follow these pointers the storage-access mechanism must be moved from one record to another, and this may be a time-consuming operation.

There is another possible approach which sometimes has great advantages. The pointers could be stored separately from the records in a directory which describes the relationships between records. Where pointers form part of the records we will refer to them as *embedded* pointers. Where they are stored separately we will refer to them as *directory* pointers.

The advantage of directory pointers is that they can be followed more quickly than embedded pointers because the directory occupies far less space than the file of records. Furthermore, as new records are inserted or old ones deleted the modifications to the pointer linkages are made in the directory rather than in the file itself; this can be a neater, faster operation. The disadvantage of directory pointers may be that they do not fit naturally into the file addressing or index scheme that is used.

We will give a number of illustrations of directory pointers later in the book.

BOOK STRUCTURE

Chains or rings are one of the methods of representing associations between data. Chains are employed in the structures discussed in the four chapters following Chapter 23.

23 CHAINS AND RING STRUCTURES

Many data-base systems use chains to interconnect the records. A chain refers to a group of records scattered within the files and interconnected by a sequence of pointers. Record A has a pointer to record H, record H has a pointer to record Q, and so forth, as in Fig. 23.1. The software that is used to retrieve the chained records will make them appear to the application programmer as a contiguous logical file. The physical twin pointers of Fig. 22.2 constitute chains.

The primary disadvantage of chained records is that many *read* operations are needed in order to follow lengthy chains. Sometimes this does not matter because the records have to be read anyway. In most search operations, however, the chains have to be followed through records which would not otherwise be read. In some file organizations the chains can be contained within blocked physical records so that excessive reads do not occur. Often, however, they straggle from track to track and cylinder to cylinder, and much access time is consumed in following them. Chaining techniques are often more suited to the production of periodic reports than to interactive queries, because of the time penalty they incur.

The word *list* is also used to describe a chain and *list organization* to describe a chained file organization. Lists or chains are used for a variety of functions in data-base systems other than chaining the files. They may link together main-memory blocks, string items together to form a queue, link control blocks together in operating systems, and form push-down stacks of items in compilations. A list (or chain) is sometimes defined as *a technique which uses linkages between items to derive a logical organization of items from a physical organization.*

To employ a chain, an indication is needed of where it starts and where it ends. The start of the chain can be found by any of the addressing

Physical layout:

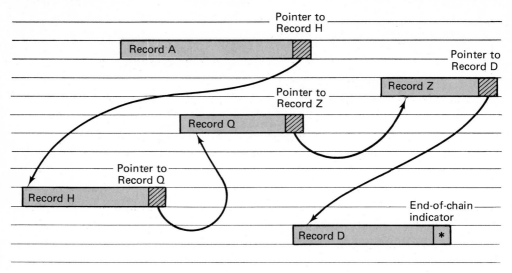

The software may make the chained records appear to the application programmer as a contiguous file:

Logical file:

Record A
H
Q
Z
D

Figure 23.1 Chained records.

methods that were discussed in Chapter 19. There may be one identifier for the entire chain. Commonly, index entries are used giving the starting addresses. Chains often have their starting address written in another record which is addressed separately.

The end of the chain may be indicated by a count of the number of records in the chain or by an end-of-chain indicator in place of the chain linkage in the last record of the chain. In the diagrams we will use an asterisk for the end-of-chain indicator.

VARIABLE-LENGTH INFORMATION

Figures 23.2 and 23.3 give two examples of chained files. The purpose of the first is to handle data which is highly variable in length—the text of employee resumés. Many files are organized in fixed-length blocks, and when the information exceeds the size of one block, another block is chained to it. This is the case with the overflow blocks shown in the diagram of an airline reservation data base in Fig. 34.8. Each record shown having an overflow block could, in fact, have any number of such blocks chained to it. In Fig. 23.2 the text can vary in length from one block to many. It would be extremely wasteful to organize it in fixed-length blocks without chaining. Furthermore, by separating the resumé text from the master file, the resumé details need not be read when other data in the master file, such as payroll data, are read.

In this case it may be possible to store the resumé records for one employee contiguously most of the time and so avoid a severe time penalty associated with following lengthy chains.

MASTER AND DETAIL RECORDS

Many files have a variable number of detail records associated with one master record, and these may be chained to it. In Fig. 23.3 the detail records are bank transactions, and they are chained to the customer record with which they are associated. When that customer's statement is printed the computer follows the chain, and each detail record becomes one line on the statement. The chain is strung through the detail records in order of the transaction's occurrence. When a new transaction is recorded it will be added to the chain.

SEQUENCED AND NONSEQUENCED CHAINS

The chains in Figs. 23.2 and 23.3 must be organized in a given sequence, the former because the records contain text which must not be shuffled and the latter because customer transactions must be printed on his bank statement chronologically. In many cases, however, there is no special sequence associated with the chained records. Figure 23.3 could have shown an invoice and its line items, rather than a bank statement and its transactions, and then the detail records could have been chained in any sequence.

When adding to a *sequenced* chain, a new item must be inserted into the requisite position. When adding an item to a nonsequenced chain, it can

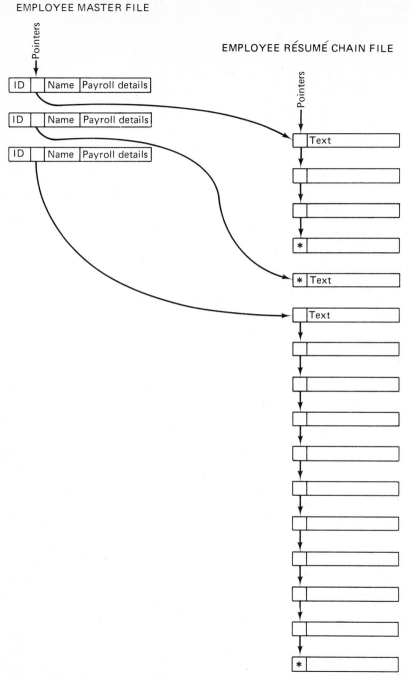

Figure 23.2 Text data, which is highly variable in length, stored in a chained file.

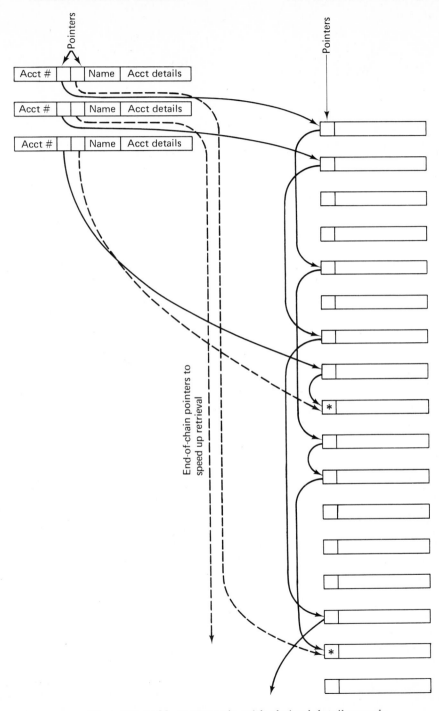

ACCOUNT MASTER RECORDS

TRANSACTION DETAIL RECORDS

Pointers

Pointers

Acct # | Name | Acct details

Acct # | Name | Acct details

Acct # | Name | Acct details

End-of-chain pointers to speed up retrieval

Figure 23.3 Master records, with chained detail records.

be inserted at the start of the chain, thereby avoiding the need to follow the chain when inserting it.

In Fig. 23.3, because new items are added at the beginning of the chain, the chain is in reverse chronological sequence. When a bank statement is printed or the account details are displayed on a terminal, the items will be read in chronological sequence, i.e., starting with the far end of the chain. It is a first-in-first-out (FIFO) chain. Such is the case with many chains. To speed up the retrieval process the address of the end of the chain is stored in the record at the head of the chain. This end-of-chain pointer is shown as a dotted line in Fig. 23.3. The *physical child (last)* pointers of Figs. 22.3 and 22.4 serve a similar function.

OPTIMIZATION

A nonsequenced chain can be organized so as to avoid, where possible, lengthy seeks, such as moving an access arm needlessly or skipping between pages in a paging mechanism. The file may be periodically reorganized and the chain linkages between newly added items reconnected to lessen the access time. No such optimization is possible on a sequenced chain.

Automatic optimization is possible on a nonvolatile chain. One form of this is referred to as *percolation* and has the objective of removing frequently referenced items close to the head of the chain. Each record may contain a percolation count, say 3 bits. The count is updated each time the record is used. When the record has been used, say, eight times it is moved up one position in the chain and its percolation count is reset to zero. To move it up, no data are moved, but the pointers linking the records are changed. Percolation will tend to cut down the time to access the most active records, and inactive records will languish at the far end of the chain.

ADDITIONS AND DELETIONS

When a new record is added to a sequenced chain, the item prior to the addition must have its address changed to that of the new item, and the address of the next link in the chain will be written in the new item. To find the item prior to the addition, the pointers will be followed from the start of the chain.

An item can be deleted from the chain with a similar process of relinking the pointers. A problem arises if the item to be deleted was found *without going to the head of the chain.* A different type of record may have pointed to the item which must now be deleted, or the item may have been addressed by some means other than following the chain. This often happens

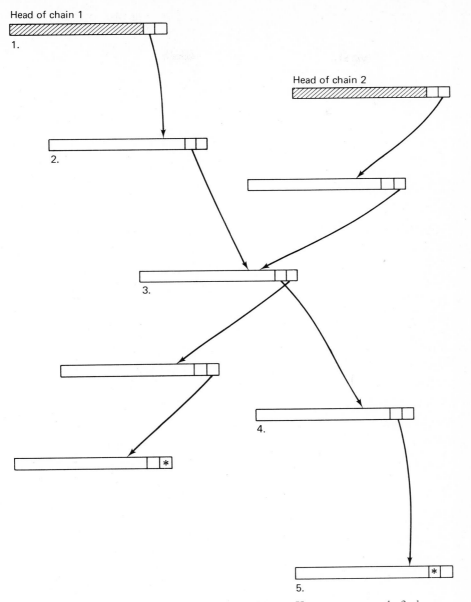

Figure 23.4 Intersecting chains. *Problem*: How can record 3 be deleted?

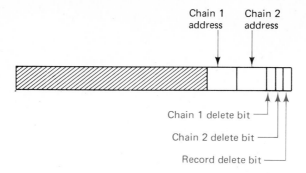

Figure 23.5   Delete bits in a record belonging to two chains.

with records having more than one key, which we will discuss in Chapter 26. When a simple chain such as that in Fig. 23.1 is entered in the middle there is no way of finding the prior link. The only way to delete the record from the chain is to set a bit in it saying that it is effectively deleted but to leave the record in the storage so that the string of pointers is not broken. Marking the record in this way has two disadvantages. First, storage space is taken up with deleted records, and, second, the chain is longer than it would otherwise be. A file in which records are deleted from chains will be periodically reorganized, the chains being rethreaded and the unwanted records removed.

INTERSECTING CHAINS
Figure 23.4 shows two chains of records which intersect. One record belongs to both chains. This record may be deleted, either from chain 1 or from chain 2, or it may be deleted from the file entirely. Such a record may therefore contain positions for 3 *delete bits*, as shown in Fig. 23.5. If records can belong to many chains, as is the case in examples we will discuss in Chapter 26, a delete bit for each chain is needed in the records.

The delete bits and their associated inefficiency can be avoided if it is possible to find the prior link in each chain so that the records can be relinked around the deleted record. This can be accomplished in two ways. First, the chains could be linked in both directions. Each record would contain a reverse pointer as well as a forward pointer, as shown in Fig. 23.6. Starting from record 3, in Fig. 23.6, all four neighbors of record 3 could be found and relinked. Two-way chains have double the storage overhead of one-way chains, and more operations are needed when items are added to them or deleted from them. Often data-base designers have felt that the

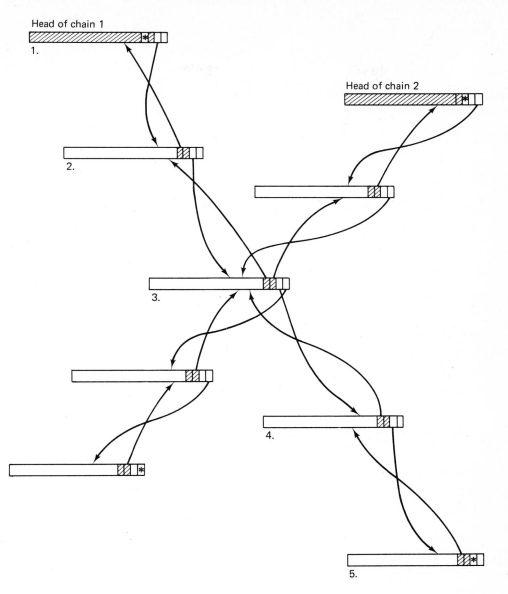

Figure 23.6 Chains with two-way pointers.

added overhead cannot be tolerated. A more important need for two-way chains, however, is to give recovery capability, as we will discuss shortly.

A second method would be to link the end of the chains back to the beginning. Record 5, for example, would point to record 1. When the end of

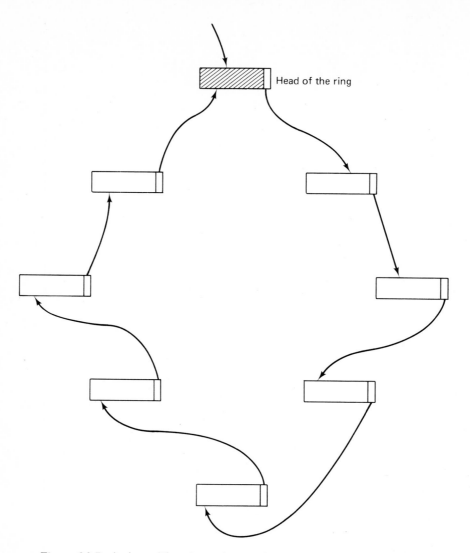

Figure 23.7 A ring with pointers in one direction only. *Problem*: What happens if a record is accidentally destroyed?

a chain is linked back to the beginning, the chain is referred to as a *ring*. To relink across the deleted record 3, the pointers would be followed around the entire ring until the record prior to record 3 were found and the chains could be relinked around record 3. This method uses little extra storage overhead but is slow because the entire ring must be followed.

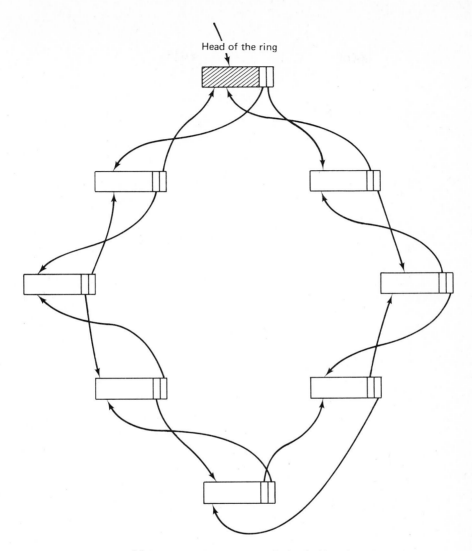

Figure 23.8   A ring with pointers in both directions.

RING
STRUCTURES

Rings have been used in many file organizations. They are used to eliminate redundancy, as we will illustrate in a later chapter. Figure 23.7 shows a simple ring with one-way pointers.

When a ring or a chain is entered at a point some distance from its head, it may be desirable to obtain the information at the head quickly, i.e., without stepping through all the intervening links. A direct linkage to the head of the ring or chain may be provided by means of a pointer in each record, as shown in Fig. 23.8.

Figure 23.9 shows an illustration of rings in which pointers to the head of the rings would be useful. Records of items which customers purchase are linked to the CUSTOMER record by a ring, and this ring is scanned when the computer produces periodic reports about what a customer has purchased. Records in an ITEM file are chained to the records of PURCHASES, and this ring is used for producing a periodic report of which customers have purchased each item. Whenever a new purchase occurs, it is linked into both a CUSTOMER ring and an ITEM ring. The file of PURCHASES does not contain the customer name and location, which is in the CUSTOMER record at the head of the purchases ring for that customer. Nor does it contain the item name or description, which is in the ITEM record at the head of the item ring. The report of what purchases a customer has made, however, must give the item names and descriptions, and so the head of each item ring must be read for each item printed on the report. Finding the head of the ring

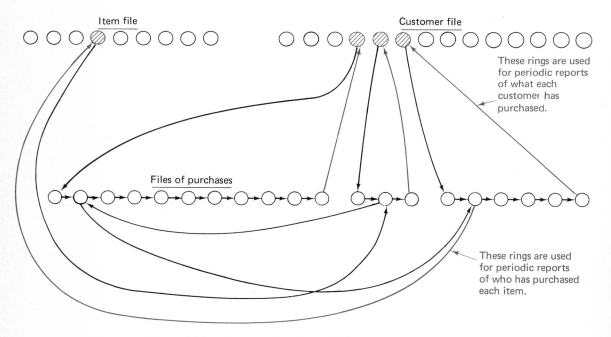

Figure 23.9 Intersecting rings. Pointers to the head of the ring (shaded) are needed, as in Fig. 23.10.

would be a lengthy operation without pointers to the head. Similarly, the report stating who has bought each item must give the customer names and locations, and so the head of the purchases ring must be read for every item in the item ring.

RECOVERY   A chain or ring can be *broken* by either a hardware or a programming fault. A disk track may become scratched. A program error may erase a record. A machine failure may occur while a pointer is being written with the result that the pointer is not written correctly. In practice, many systems have lost records because of damaged pointers. It is generally important that a system should be able to recover from damage to pointers without records being lost.

Where a pointer is the only means of accessing a record, the record is always vulnerable to pointer damage. Some of the bank account items in Fig. 23.3 will be inaccessible if one chain link is broken. A chain is as weak as its weakest link. When the pointers are embedded in data records there is generally no quick way of periodically dumping them for backup purposes.

The need for recovery is the strongest argument for using two-way rather than one-way lists. Figure 23.10 shows a ring with pointers in both directions. If any one record in the ring is destroyed, the other records are still accessible, and if any one pointer is damaged, it can be reconstructed.

The ring in Fig. 23.11 combines some of the benefits of those in Figs. 23.8 and 23.10 but still uses only two pointers. If record 1 or any even-numbered record is destroyed, all the others can still be reached. If an odd-numbered record is lost (except record 1), one other record also becomes inaccessible. This structure is referred to as a *coral ring*.

SEARCH   The main disadvantage of chains and rings is that
TIMES   they can take a long time to search. If there are N_c items in the chain and every item has an equal probability of being searched, the mean number of items that must be examined in order to find the required item is

$$\sum_{k=1}^{N_c} (k \times \text{Probability that the } k\text{th item examined is the one required})$$

$$= \sum_{k=1}^{N_c} k \; \frac{1}{N_c} = \frac{N_c + 1}{2} \tag{23.1}$$

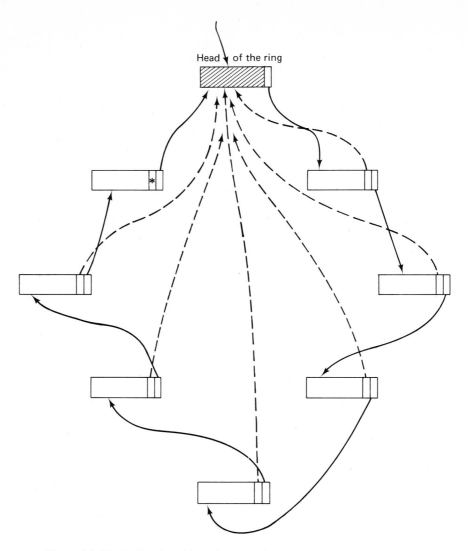

Figure 23.10 A ring in which the second pointer points to the head of the ring, so that a data path entering the ring part way around can be routed quickly to information at the head of the ring. *Problem*: Again, what happens if a record is accidentally destroyed?

SKIP-SEARCHED CHAINS

If the items are chained together *in sequence*, several techniques can be used for shortening the chain search time. The first enables the search to

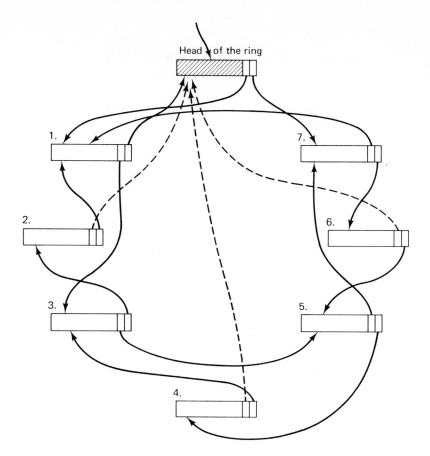

Head of the ring

1.
2.
3.
4.
5.
6.
7.

Figure 23.11 A *coral ring* combines the advantages of the two-way ring (Fig. 23.10) and those of the ring with pointers to its head (Fig. 23.8) with only two pointers per record.

skip along the chain (or ring), missing many of the items. The chain is divided into groups of items which are connected by reverse pointers in the first item of each group, as shown in Fig. 23.13. The search begins at the high end of the sequence of chained items and follows the reverse pointers until an item is found that is lower than the item sought or *is* the item itself.

Box 23.1   Optimum Skip Length in a Skip-Searched Chain

Let N_c be the number of items in a skip-searched chain and N_g be the number of items in a group that is skipped.

There are $\lceil N_c / N_g \rceil$ groups.

The mean number of groups that must be examined in order to find the required item is

$$\sum_{k=1}^{\left\lceil \frac{N_c}{N_g} \right\rceil} (k \times \text{Probability that the } k\text{th group examined contains the required item})$$

If the required record is equally likely to be in any group, then this mean number of groups examined is

$$= \sum_{k=1}^{\left\lceil \frac{N_c}{N_g} \right\rceil} k \, \frac{1}{\left\lceil \frac{N_c}{N_g} \right\rceil} = \frac{\left\lceil \frac{N_c}{N_g} \right\rceil + 1}{2}$$

Having found the right group in the chain, the search then examines the items in the group. The first item in the group has already been examined. The search must therefore examine between 0 and $N_g - 1$ other items. The mean number of items that must be examined is

$$\sum_{k=0}^{N_g-1} (k \times \text{Probability that the } k\text{th item examined is the one required})$$

If the required record is equally likely to be in any position in the group, then this mean number of items examined is

$$= \sum_{k=0}^{N_g-1} k \, \frac{1}{N_g} = \frac{N_g - 1}{2}$$

Box 23.1 *continued*

Let N_e be the number of items that must be examined in total in searching the chain.

The mean number of items that must be examined, $E(N_e)$, is the sum of the mean number of groups that are examined,

$$\frac{\left\lceil \dfrac{N_c}{N_g} \right\rceil + 1}{2}$$

and the mean number of items within a group that are examined, $(N_g - 1) / 2$, is

$$E(N_e) = \frac{\left\lceil \dfrac{N_c}{N_g} \right\rceil + 1}{2} + \frac{N_g - 1}{2} = \frac{1}{2}\left\lceil \frac{N_c}{N_g} \right\rceil + \frac{N_g}{2} \quad (23.2)$$

We can adjust N_g, the number of items in each group, to give the minimum value of $E(N_e)$:

$$\frac{dE(N_e)}{dN_g} \;\simeq\; -\,\frac{N_c}{2N_g{}^2} + \frac{1}{2}$$

$$= 0 \quad \text{when} \quad \frac{N_c}{2N_g{}^2} = \frac{1}{2} \quad\quad\quad (23.3)$$

$$N_g = \sqrt{N_c}$$

Thus, the optimum number of items in a chain group is $\sqrt{}$ (the number of items in the chain). The skip pointers point to the item $\sqrt{N_c}$ items away.

The number of items in the chain that must be inspected if there are $\lceil \sqrt{N_c} \rceil$ items in each group is [from Eq. (23.2)]

$$E(N_e) = \frac{1}{2}\left\lceil \frac{N_c}{\lceil \sqrt{N_c} \rceil} \right\rceil + \frac{\lceil \sqrt{N_c} \rceil}{2} \;\simeq\; \sqrt{N_c} \quad (23.4)$$

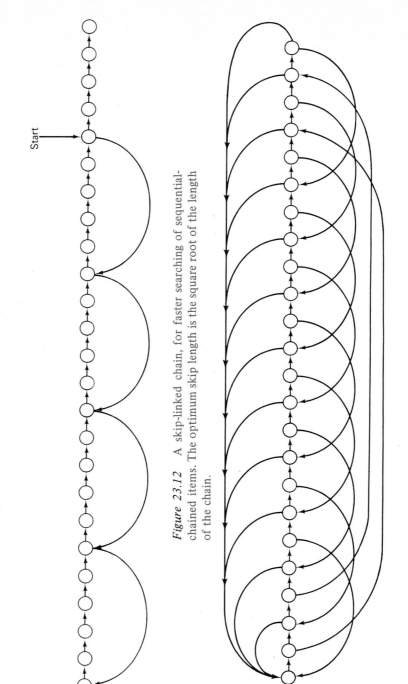

Figure 23.12 A skip-linked chain, for faster searching of sequential-chained items. The optimum skip length is the square root of the length of the chain.

Figure 23.13 A skip-linked coral ring.

If it is lower than the item sought, the forward pointers are followed to the item in question.

Where a chain is divided into groups of items for skip searching, the optimum size of a group is $\sqrt{N_c}$, where N_c is the number of items in the chain. (See Box 23.1.) The mean number of items that must be examined is then approximately $\sqrt{N_c}$.

Rings may similarly be organized with skip pointers. Figure 23.13 also shows a coral ring in which skip pointers alternate with pointers to the head of the ring.

MULTILIST CHAINS

A second approach to lowering the search time for a sequentially ordered chain is shown in Fig. 23.14. The chain is divided into segments, and an index gives the value of the first item in each segment and its starting address. This is sometimes known as a *multilist chain*.

If there are N_i index entries and the chain is chopped into equal segments, the mean number of items that must be examined when searching the chain is

$$E(N_e) = \frac{\left\lceil \dfrac{N_c}{N_i} \right\rceil + 1}{2} \qquad (23.5)$$

CELLULAR CHAINS

The total of the access times required when searching a chain is more important than the total of items inspected. The segments of multilist chain may be organized so that no piece extends beyond a certain hardware cell or boundary selected to minimize access times. For example, the segments may each be confined to a cylinder so that no seeks occur when following a chain. On a smaller scale, they may be confined to a track so that each segment is in core when it is searched.

PARALLEL CELLULAR CHAINS

Cellular chains may be organized so that different segments of them can be searched in parallel. The segments are spread out in modules on which simultaneous seeks and reads can occur. Figure 23.15 illustrates such a layout. This technique can be effective where the data sets are laid out with the sequence skipping from module to module, as

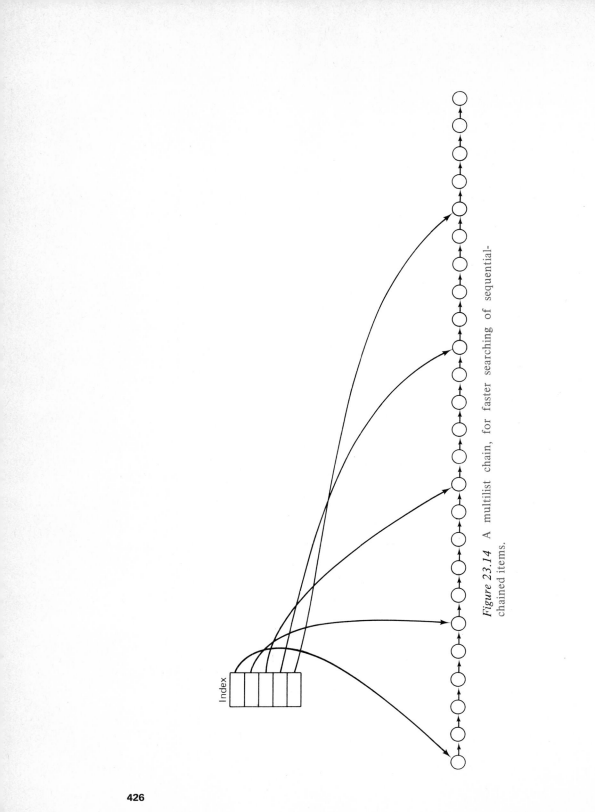

Figure 23.14 A multilist chain, for faster searching of sequential-chained items.

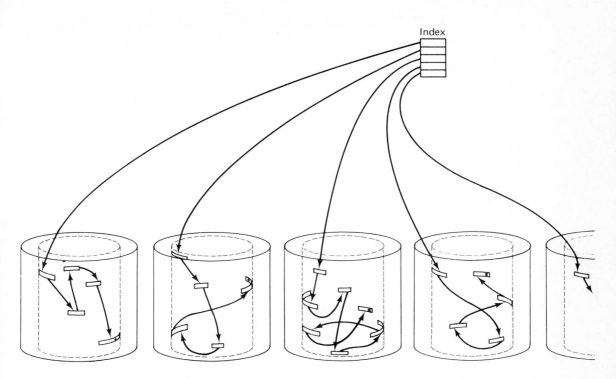

Figure 23.15 Parallel cellular chains. Separate chain segments can be searched simultaneously. This type of organization can be effective when the file is spread across several cells, as in the bottom half of Fig. 18.4, rather than the top half of Fig. 18.4.

in the lower half of Fig. 18.4, rather than the more common sequential-within-cylinder layout of the top half of Fig. 18.4.

We will discuss uses of these chain organizations later in the book.

SUMMARY   Box 23.2 summarizes the types of chains and rings.

Box 23.2 Summary of the Types of Chains and Rings

	Number of Pointers Per Record	Illus-trated in Fig.	
Simple one-way chain	1	23.2	
One-way chain with tail link	1	23.3	Pointer to the end of a sequenced chain enables new items to be added quickly.
One-way ring	1	23.7	The chain head can be found after locating a chain member.
Two-way ring	2	23.8	Recovery capability when the chain breaks.
Ring with head pointers	2	23.10	Quick access to the head of the ring.
Coral ring	2	23.11	Combines the advantages of two-way rings and rings with head pointers.
Skip-searched chain	2	23.12	Faster searching. N_c items per chain; $\sqrt{N_c}$ items per skip group.
Skip-searched coral ring	2	23.13	Combines the advantages of two-way rings, rings with head pointers, and skip searching.
Multilist chain	1	23.14	Fragmented chain with index permits faster searching.
Cellular chains	1		Chain fragmented into physical cells, or pages.
Parallel cellular chains	1	23.15	Chain fragmented into cells or pages which can be searched simultaneously.
Optimized chains	1		Most frequently referenced items percolate to head of chain.

BOOK STRUCTURE

Chapters 8 and 9 discussed tree and plex structures. Chapters 24 and 25 give methods of representing those structures physically.

Chapter 8   Tree Structures
Chapter 24   Physical Representation of Tree Structures

Chapter 9   Plex Structures
Chapter 25   Physical Representation of Plex Structures

24 PHYSICAL REPRESENTATIONS OF TREE STRUCTURES

Figure 9.11, showing tree structures, plex structures, and other schemas, says nothing about how they are laid out on the storage media or how their relationships are represented physically. There is a variety of different ways of representing them physically. In this chapter we will discuss the physical representation of tree structures, and in the following chapters we will examine more complex structures.

The relationships in trees can be represented by one or more of the following methods:

1. Physical positioning.

2. Pointers.

3. Chains or rings.

4. Directories.

5. Bit maps showing connections.

Often a combination of these methods is used, and there are several variations on each method.

A NOT-QUITE-FLAT FILE   We will begin with a simple example.

A flat file, in which each record has the same set of data items, can be represented physically in a simple sequential manner. Many file structures are, in reality, more complex. There may be multiple values of an attribute associated with one entity. Some attributes may in time become entities with their own family of attributes.

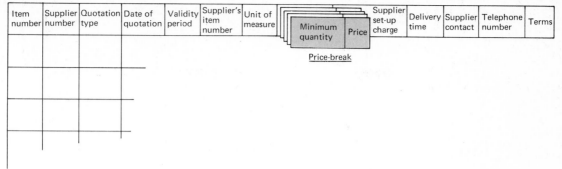

Figure 24.1 A not-quite-flat file.

Figure 24.1 shows a file which is not quite flat. It illustrates records used in the purchasing department of a factory to store the quotations which different suppliers have given for items to be purchased. The nonflatness arises from the fact that some suppliers quote different price breaks for different quantities, and hence the quotation records must store differing numbers of data-item pairs giving the price and minimum quantity that that price applies to. Some records have only one PRICE-BREAK; often, however, they have three or four. A few records have as many as 20 PRICE-BREAKS.

If variable-length records are used, the varying numbers of PRICE-BREAKS can be included in the QUOTATION record with no problem. Much of the software in common use, however, permits only fixed-length records, and then the designer must decide how many PRICE-BREAKS he will leave space for in the QUOTATION record.

He has three choices. First, he can include space in the QUOTATION record for 20 possible price quotations. This method wastes storage because most records have far fewer than 20 prices quoted.

Second, he can set up a separate record for the price breaks. The QUOTATION record would contain a pointer to the PRICE-BREAK records, as shown in Fig. 24.2. With this method an additional seek is always needed to the PRICE-BREAK record.

The third alternative is to leave space for *some* PRICE-BREAKS in the QUOTATION record and to provide an *overflow* record for the cases when this is not enough. The question then arises, How many PRICE-BREAKS should be stored in the QUOTATION record? Figure 24.3 plots two curves from a typical case, showing how the total storage needed and the mean additional access time incurred vary with the number of PRICE-BREAK data aggregates in the main quotation record. If no PRICE-BREAKS are included (Fig. 24.2), then an additional 56 seconds of access time is needed per 1000

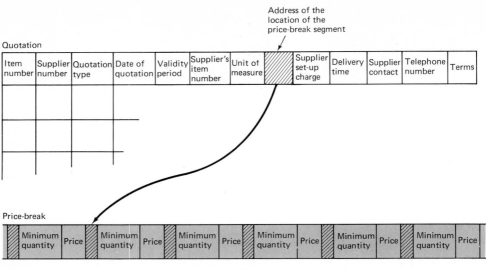

Figure 24.2

records to obtain the PRICE-BREAK record. At the other extreme, if 20 PRICE-BREAKS are included in the QUOTATION record, no additional access time is needed, but 200,000 numeric characters of storage are needed per 1000 records for the PRICE-BREAKS. Figure 24.3 suggests that a reasonable compromise would be to leave space for four PRICE-BREAKS in the QUOTATION record. This would be enough for most items, and for the few items with more than four an *overflow* access would occur and the remaining prices would be read from the PRICE-BREAK record.

MASTER-DETAIL FILES

Figures 24.2 and 24.4 are examples of simple two-level files. Many two-level files are employed in basic data processing, for example, a customer account record in a bank and the records of the transactions made by that customer. These are commonly referred to as master and detail records and are drawn in the form of a two-level tree. With any master-detail file, or, indeed, any pair of levels of a tree, the designer can choose to include some of the lower-level segments inside the higher-level segment. It is common that *all* lower-level segments are either stored separately or stored inside the higher-level segment. However, curves such as those in Fig. 24.3 usually apply, and the best solution may be a compromise like that in Fig. 24.4 rather than an *all-or-nothing* approach.

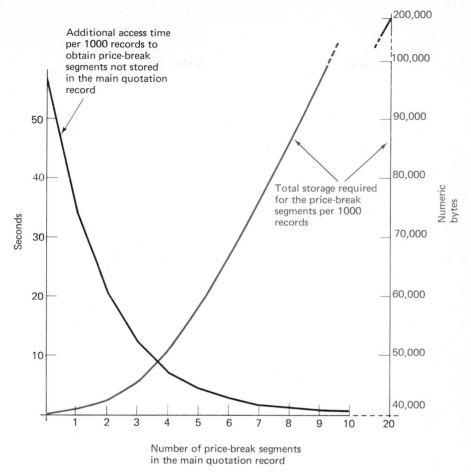

Figure 24.3

MULTILEVEL TREES

The quotation record in Fig. 24.4 could, in fact, be a subtree in a larger organization. A purchasing data base may contain many SUPPLIER records, and each SUPPLIER record may have several QUOTATION records, and each QUOTATION record may have several PRICE-BREAKS, thus giving a three-level tree as in Fig. 24.5.

Figure 24.6 shows a schema and an instance of a three-level tree. A second instance is also shown, after some insertions and deletions have occurred. The remaining figures in this chapter illustrate ways in which this tree can be represented physically.

434

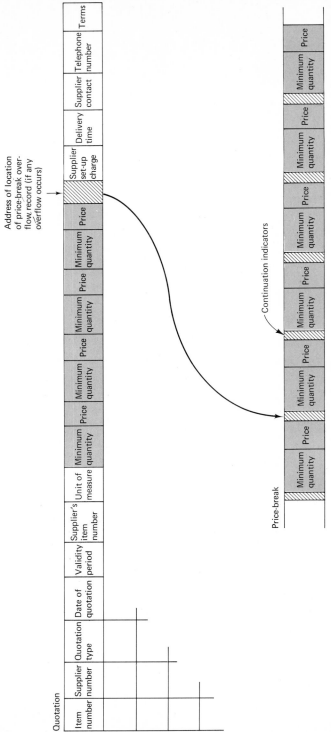

Figure 24.4

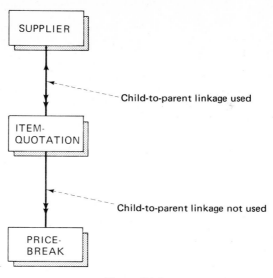

Figure 24.5

Method 1. A Physically Contiguous List

For the first two decades of computing most files were laid out serially on cards or tape, and tree structures were usually represented by contiguous physical positioning. Figure 24.7 shows this method of representing the tree of Fig. 24.6. The sequence of items in Fig. 24.7 is sometimes called a *left-list* layout; it is sometimes called a top-down-left-right sequence. It is the basis of the IBM Hierarchical Sequential Access Method (HSAM).

The rule determining the sequence is: *progress from the top of the tree down the left-hand side listing the nodes; when the bottom is reached, list that set of twin nodes from left to right; repeat the process omitting nodes already listed.*

The layout must indicate which level in the tree each record belongs to. This could be accomplished by a code in each record, for example, the record type could be determined from the key. Alternatively, some form of demarcation is used in the record sequence, as in the following representation:

$$A_1 \, (B_2 \, (C_5 \, C_{12} \, C_6) \, B_1 \, (C_{13} \, C_9) \, B_3 \, (C_{14} \, C_{11} \, C_7 \, C_{18}))$$

Sequences other than the left-list sequence can also be used to represent a tree.

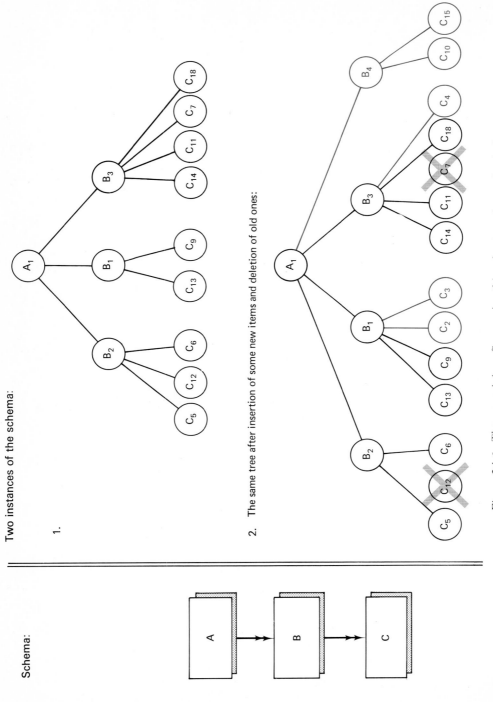

Schema:

Two instances of the schema:

1.

2. The same tree after insertion of some new items and deletion of old ones:

Figure 24.6 The remaining figures in this chapter show physical representations of this tree.

1. Original layout:

| A_1 | B_2 | C_5 | C_{12} | C_6 | B_1 | C_{13} | C_9 | B_3 | C_{14} | C_{11} | C_7 | C_{18} | |

2. Layout after the modifications have been merged into the file on a batch processing run:

| A_1 | B_2 | C_5 | C_6 | B_1 | C_{13} | C_9 | C_2 | C_3 | B_3 | C_{14} | C_{11} | C_{18} | C_4 | B_4 | C_{10} | C_{15} | |

Figure 24.7 The tree in Fig. 24.6 represented by means of physical contiguity: a top-down-left-right (left-list) layout, suitable only for batch processing.

A serial left-list layout does not permit the rapid answering of most questions relating to the lower levels of the tree because a scan of the list is needed. Its use is normally restricted to batch-processing applications or to on-line systems in which rapid query answering is not needed.

If the tree in question was the ITEM/QUOTATION/PRICE-BREAK tree, a left-list layout might be satisfactory if queries normally referred to ITEM records and required the QUOTATION and PRICE-BREAK information for the items.

If the tree were a DIVISION/DEPARTMENT/EMPLOYEE file, the technique would be poor for answering questions about a specified employee. It would be good for producing a printout of the form:

DIVISION: A

     DEPARTMENT: B_2

       EMPLOYEES: C_5

                           C_{12}

                           C_6

     DEPARTMENT: B_1

       EMPLOYEES: C_{13}

                           C_9

DEPARTMENT: B_3

.

.

.

ON-LINE INSERTIONS

Method 2. Left-List Layout with Overflow

As with any serial contiguous file, inserting and deleting items are relatively easy if done in a batch-processing fashion with a new file being written and the new items merged into it, as in Fig. 24.7. If direct-access updating in place is used, then insertions and deletions may be accommodated either with *overflow* techniques or with *distributed free space*—two maintenance methods used with the index sequential organization and illustrated in Figures 20.9 and 20.11.

Figure 24.8 shows a left-list layout with overflow. Fixed-length physical records are used, but the logical records within them may be of variable length. An index (not shown in the figure) may be used for locating the A, B, or C, records. In many applications no index is needed for the records on the lowest level; they may, for example, be transactions in a bank account, the schools an employee attended, the PRICE BREAKS in Fig. 24.4, or other items referred to *only* when the level above them is also read.

As new items are added to the file they may exceed the space available (in the first diagram in Fig. 24.8) and so are stored in overflow locations (second diagram in Fig. 24.8). Each physical record has a position for an overflow pointer. Periodically a maintenance operation will take place, and the file will be rewritten with the overflow items merged into the main records (third diagram in Fig. 24.8).

Method 3. Left-List Layout with Distributed Free Space

Figure 24.9 shows a left-list layout, again using fixed-length records, but now with distributed free space for accommodating insertions. When items are deleted, the remaining items are packed together within their block. When items are inserted, the free space within the block may be

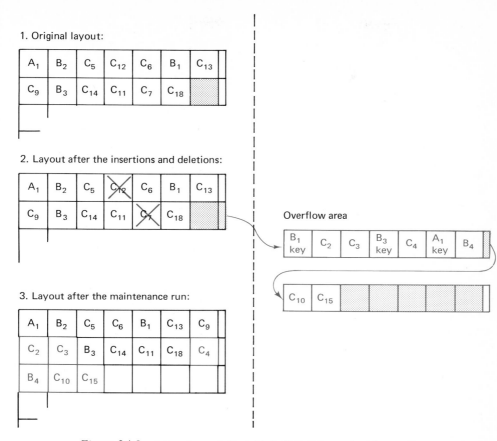

Figure 24.8   A top-down-left-right (left-list) layout with overflow.

sufficient for the insertion. If it is not, the block will have to be split as in Fig. 20.11.

SEQUENTIAL FILES   Any storage organization method which uses the physical sequence of records to represent a tree structure, as in above cases, cannot employ physical sequencing for other purposes. Often the physical sequence of records is determined by some other consideration, and the tree structure must then be represented by a different method. Files may, for example, be laid out sequentially, either because a sequential addressing method is used

1. Original layout:

A_1	B_2	C_5	C_{12}	C_6	
B_1	C_{13}	C_9			
B_3	C_{14}	C_{11}	C_7	C_{18}	

2. Layout after the insertions and deletions:

A_1	B_2	C_5	C_6		
B_1	C_{13}	C_9	C_2	C_3	
B_3	C_{14}	C_{11}	C_{18}	C_4	
B_4	C_{10}	C_{15}			

Figure 24.9   A left-list layout with distributed free space.

or because the majority of the processing is sequential. The following figures show sequential files with the tree structure represented by pointer linkages.

Method 4. Multiple Child Pointers

Figure 24.10 shows three types of pointers linking sequentially ordered records. The top diagram uses *child* pointers only. Any record other than those on the bottom level can have many children; therefore, variable-length lists of pointers are needed in the records. In some cases a record may need a very large number of such pointers. Pointer lists which are widely variable in length are clumsy to handle when insertions and deletions must be facilitated. For this reason variable-length pointer lists are often avoided.

Method 5. Child-and-Twin Pointers

Multiple child pointers can be clumsy to implement because of the large and variable number of pointers that may be needed in a record. For this reason many data-base systems use child-and-twin pointers, as in the bottom diagram in Fig. 24.10. In the organization illustrated, two pointers per

1. Multiple child pointers:

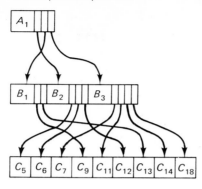

2. Parent pointers:

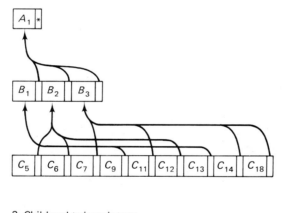

3. Child and twin pointers:

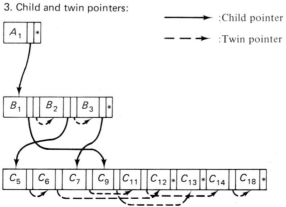

Figure 24.10 Sequential files with pointers; three types of pointers.

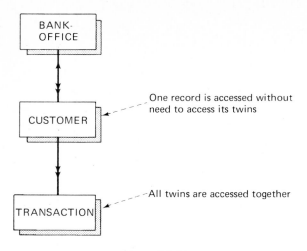

Figure 24.11

record are needed, and only one pointer for the lowest-level records. The problem with child-and-twin pointers is that long chains of pointers exist when there are many twins. To find record C_{18} in the illustration, five pointers must be followed. If a record had 100 children, the search for one at the end of the chain could be very time-consuming.

The lengths of the chains of twin pointers is not of concern on those applications in which when one child is read *all* of them are needed. If the tree is that in Fig. 24.11, for example, and when any TRANSACTION record is read, possibly for printing on a bank statement, *all* the twin TRANSACTION records are needed, then following a chain of twin pointers is not a serious disadvantage. On the other hand, the CUSTOMER records are read singly, and so some means of addressing them is needed other than scanning a twin chain that will link hundreds of customers.

In tree structures built with pointers, there is always a trade-off between the implementation difficulties of variable-length child pointer lists and the searching time associated with twin pointer chains.

PARENT POINTERS

The schema in Fig. 24.5 shows an arrow from the ITEM-QUOTATION record to its parent, SUP-PLIER. The ITEM-QUOTATION record may be accessed via the item number, and when a reference is made to it information from the associated SUPPLIER record is needed. In this case a parent pointer is needed to the CUSTOMER record. The center diagram of

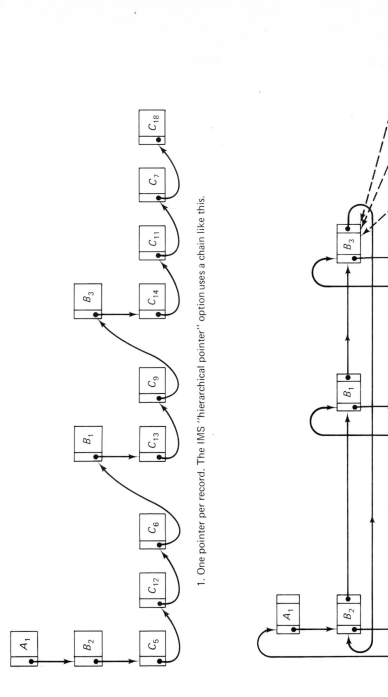

1. One pointer per record. The IMS "hierarchical pointer" option uses a chain like this.

2. Two pointers per record: a ring structure organization.

Figure 24.12   Chain and ring structures.

443

Fig. 24.10 shows parent pointers. As each record in a tree structure has only one parent, there is no difficulty with chains or multiple pointers.

Method 6. Ring Structures

Parent pointers are sometimes incorporated into ring structures for representing trees. The lower diagram in Fig. 24.12 shows a ring structure representation. The solid pointers show child-and-parent rings and twin rings. To provide two pointers per record uniformly the dotted pointers are added, giving parent pointers for all records on the lowest level. For the reasons discussed in Chapter 23 the rings could be made two-way rather than one-way, in which case there would be four pointers per record. The ring structure illustrated is similar to child-and-twin structure of Fig. 24.10 except that the rings are completed and the dotted parent pointers are added. The same search-time penalties are incurred.

The upper illustration in Fig. 24.12 shows a single-pointer chain. The space needed for pointers is less, but the search time is even longer. Such a representation is suitable for batch-processing applications or applications in which no parent has many children. IBM refers to this pointer configuration as *hierarchical pointers* in its IMS data-base management system. The user has the option of specifying hierarchical pointers or various configurations of child, twin, and parent pointers, such as those in Figs. 22.2 to 22.5.

INSERTIONS AND DELETIONS

When a tree structure is superimposed upon sequentially ordered files, a technique for handling insertions and deletions is necessary. As before they may be handled with overflow areas or with distributed free space. Figure 24.13 shows the use of overflow areas; Fig. 24.14 shows distributed free space.

DIRECTORIES

Method 7. Tree Directories

The pointers in the illustrations so far have all been *embedded* in the records. There is much to be said for removing the pointers from the records and placing them in a separate pointer *directory*.

A directory may be defined as a file which stores the relationships between records in other files.

Being small, a relevant section of the directory can usually be brought into main memory in one slice and searched at high speed. To follow chains of pointers in main memory is fast, whereas to follow chains embedded in

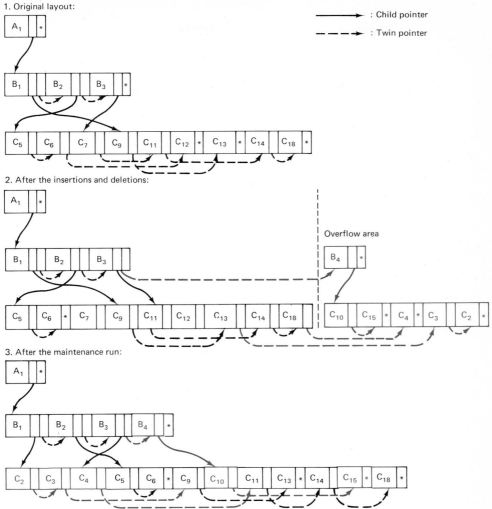

Figure 24.13 Sequential files with child and twin pointers and an overflow area.

records can be prohibitively slow. Making insertions and deletions in a directory can be much faster and easier than making them in data records.

There are many ways in which such directories can be organized, as we will discuss in Chapter 29. Figure 24.15 shows one way. Figure 24.15 does not show how the data records are laid out because they can be in any

1. Original layout:

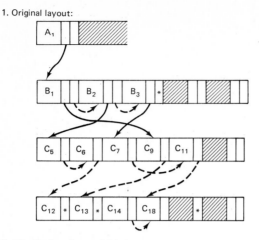

2. After the insertions and deletions:

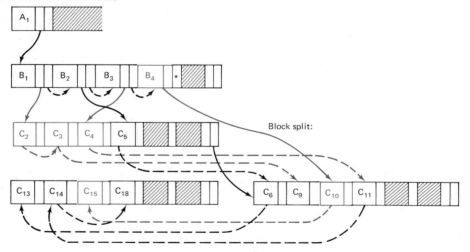

Block split:

Figure 24.14 Sequential files with child and twin pointers and distributed free space.

convenient layout and can utilize whatever addressing schema is most appropriate for them.

BIT MAP   **Method 8. Bit Maps**

Figure 24.16 shows a bit map which represents the relations in Fig. 24.6. Whether or not a bit map is a more compact way of

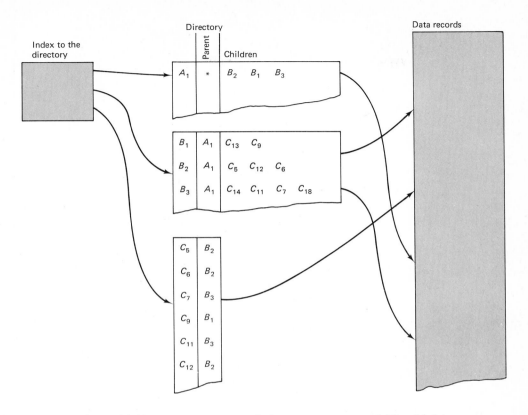

Figure 24.15 Representation of the tree structure of Fig. 24.6 in a directory.

	A_1	A ...	C_1	C_2	C_3	C_4	C_5	C_6	C_7	C_8	C_9	C_{10}	C_{11}	C_{12}	C_{13}	C_{14}	C_{15}	C_{16}	C_{17}	C_{18}	...
B_1	1		0	0	0	0	0	0	0	0	1	0	0	0	1	0	0	0	0	0	
B_2	1		0	0	0	0	1	1	0	0	0	0	0	1	0	0	0	0	0	0	
B_3	1		0	0	0	0	0	0	1	0	0	0	1	0	0	1	0	0	0	1	

Figure 24.16 The relationships in Fig. 24.6 represented by a bit map.

representing the relationships than a variable pointer list depends on the number of pointers used and the total number of possible pointer values. This trade-off was plotted in Fig. 18.9.

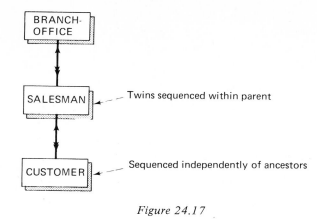

Figure 24.17

MIXED METHODS   It is often advantageous to mix more than one of
the above techniques in the representation of a
single tree, because different sections of the same tree have different
requirements. This is so when some of the record types *need* to be laid out
sequentially and others do not. In the tree in Fig. 24.17, for example, the
usage may require that the CUSTOMER records be sequenced independently
of their parents or grandparents, for example, sequenced in order of
customer number. SALESMAN records, on the other hand, may be
sequenced within the groups under each BRANCH-OFFICE. The BRANCH-
OFFICE → SALESMAN relationship could be represented by physical
contiguity, whereas the SALESMAN → CUSTOMER relationship could not.

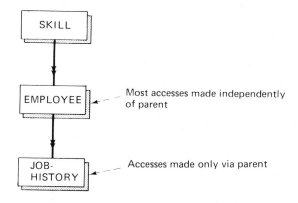

Figure 24.18

In Fig. 24.18 the lower level could be represented by physical contiguity. Access is made to the JOB-HISTORY records *only* via their EMPLOYEE parent. The upper level should not be represented by physical contiguity because most of the access to the EMPLOYEE records are independent of their parent in Fig. 24.18.

In Figs. 24.5 and 24.11 also the upper and lower heirarchical relationships may be differently represented because of their different characteristics. The methods of representation in all tree structures may be tailored to the characteristics of usage.

BOOK STRUCTURE

Chapter 24 discussed tree structures. Chapter 25 follows with an equivalent discussion of plex structures. Box 25.1 summarizes the techniques discussed in these two chapters.

Chapter 24	Physical Representation of Tree Structures
Chapter 25	Physical Representation of Plex Structures

25 PHYSICAL REPRESENTATIONS OF PLEX STRUCTURES

Many of the methods most commonly used for the physical representation of *tree* structures are not suitable for representation of *plex* structures. This is the reason much of the software which handles the tree structures in Fig. 9.11 will not operate with the *plex* structures in the same figure. To make matters more complicated, a technique which is appealing for one shape of plex structure is often unsatisfactory for another shape.

As with the tree relationships discussed in the previous chapter, plex structure relationships can be represented using a combination of the following techniques:

1. Physical contiguity.

2. Pointers.

3. Chains or rings.

4. Directories.

5. Bit maps.

Consider first the *simple plex structure* shown in Fig. 25.1, which could be described using two *sets* in the CODASYL DDL. Figures 25.2 to 25.5 show some methods of representing it. The methods shown in Figs. 25.8 to 25.10 could also be used.

PHYSICAL CONTIGUITY	Whereas tree structures can be represented by physical contiguity, without redundancy (for example, the left-list layout of Fig. 25.7), plex

Schema: An instance of the schema:

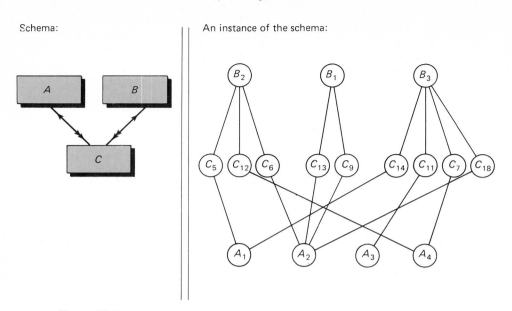

Figure 25.1 Figures 25.2, 25.4, and 25.5 show physical representations of this plex structure.

structures in general cannot. In some cases, however, it may be advantageous to represent one parent-child *set* of the structure by means of physical contiguity and use a different method for the other relationships. We can use physical contiguity to represent the A $\rightarrow$ C relationships in Fig. 25.1, or the B $\rightarrow$ C relationships, but not both unless we repeat the A or B records. In Fig. 25.2 the relationships between A and C are represented by physical contiguity and the relationships between B and C by pointers. As before, three types of pointers are shown: multiple-child pointers, parent pointers, and child-and-twin pointers. Multiple child pointers require variable-length pointer lists, whereas child-and-twin pointers incur lengthy chains.

The use of physical contiguity as in Fig. 25.2 might be acceptable if the C records are usually all required after the reading of an A record. For example, if A is a PURCHASE-ORDER record as in Fig. 25.3 and C is a LINE-ITEM on the order, the LINE-ITEMS will usually be required along with the PURCHASE-ORDER. When an INVENTORY-ITEM record is referred to, to see how much of an item is in stock, the program may also look up the LINE-ITEM records saying how much of the item is on order—hence the pointers from B to C. In such a case the organization at the top or bottom of Fig. 25.2 might be used.

1. Multiple child pointers

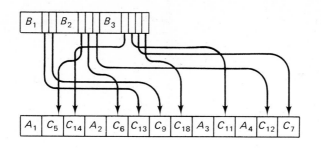

2. Parent pointers

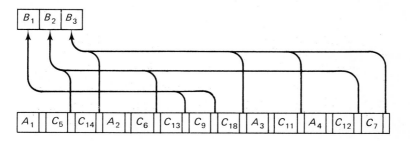

3. Child and twin pointers

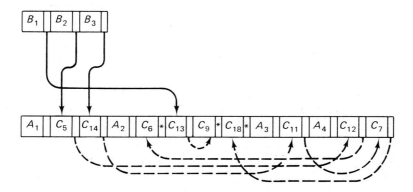

Figure 25.2 The relationship between A and C represented by physical layout of records, and the relationship between B and C represented by pointers.

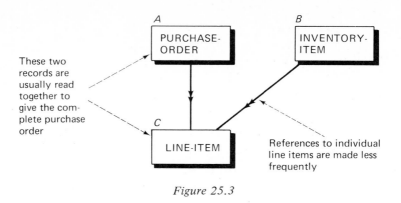

Figure 25.3

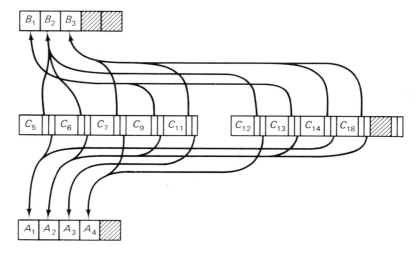

Figure 25.4   Sequential files with parent pointers (simple maps).

EMBEDDED POINTERS

Usually physical contiguity is not employed to represent plex structures. If pointers are used, they must represent the relationships both between A and C and between B and C. We might refer to the upper records in the schema of Fig. 25.1 as parents and the lower records as children. Figure 25.4 shows parent pointers and so represents only the simple mapping (the single arrows in Fig. 25.1). Figure 25.5 shows multiple child pointers and thus represents only the complex mapping (the double arrows in Fig. 25.1). To handle the variable numbers of pointers encountered, Fig. 25.5 shows a fixed number of pointers per record and an overflow pointer scheme.

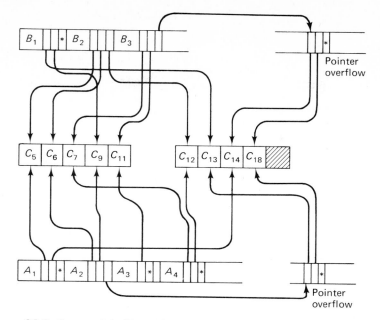

Figure 25.5 Sequential files with multiple child pointers (complex maps).

Figure 25.6 shows ring structures using child, twin, and parent pointers. As before, there are many possible variations on the configurations of pointers that are used.

Insertions and deletions must be handled, and so the structures illustrated must be further complicated with either an *overflow record* or a *distributed free-space* mechanism.

Some authorities have strongly advocated the use of ring structures. They formed the basis of the Honeywell IDS (Integrated Data Store) data-base management system, and they were recommended in the early CODASYL Data Base Task Group reports. A data base can have multiple rings as in Fig. 25.7, linking a variety of different types of record. They can represent a data map and its inverse with economical use of storage and are relatively easy to maintain.

Ring structures, like most other data structures, have cons as well as pros. They can give a poor response time when used with typical direct-access storage devices because of the time taken to follow all the pointers. Furthermore, the response times can be unpredictable and widely variable. Rings can give recovery problems. If a pointer is damaged or lost, the ring cannot be followed. Records may be lost unless two-way rings are used. Last, they cannot represent relationships with complex mapping in both directions.

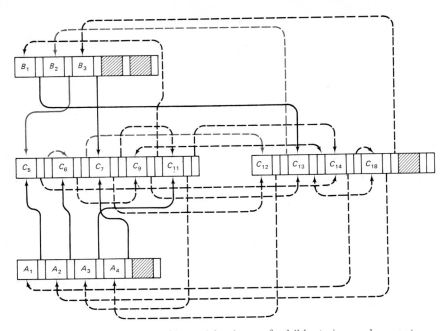

Figure 25.6   Sequential files with rings of child, twin, and parent pointers.

COMPLEX PLEX STRUCTURES   It is possible to employ physical contiguity, child-and-twin pointers, or ring structures for representing the above structures *because the child →
parent mapping is simple.* If any relationship is complex-complex, i.e., if any line connecting two blocks in a schema has double arrows going in both directions, then these three techniques are all unsuitable. Furthermore, *parent pointers*, which have required one or two pointers per record in the previous figures, now require variable-length pointer lists.

Using variable-length pointer lists a *complex plex structure* can be represented straightforwardly as in Fig. 25.8 (which uses the relationships previously illustrated in Fig. 13.5). In some applications the pointer lists will become very long, and for this reason many data-base management systems do not employ variable-length pointer lists like those in Fig. 25.8. Many such systems cannot represent complex plex structures. As discussed in Part I, they have to be converted to simpler structures.

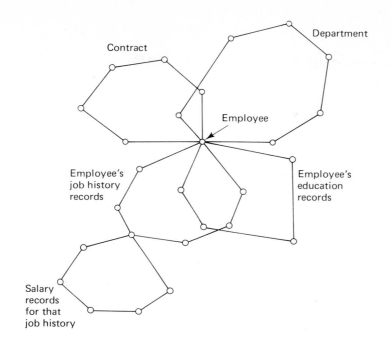

Figure 25.7 Rings related to an EMPLOYEE record.

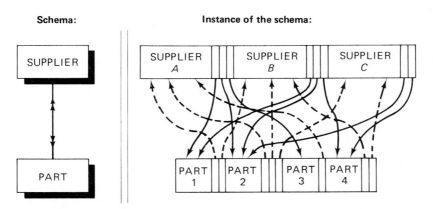

Figure 25.8 A complex plex structure can be represented by multiple pointer lists. However, physical contiguity, child-and-twin pointers, and ring structures are not suitable.

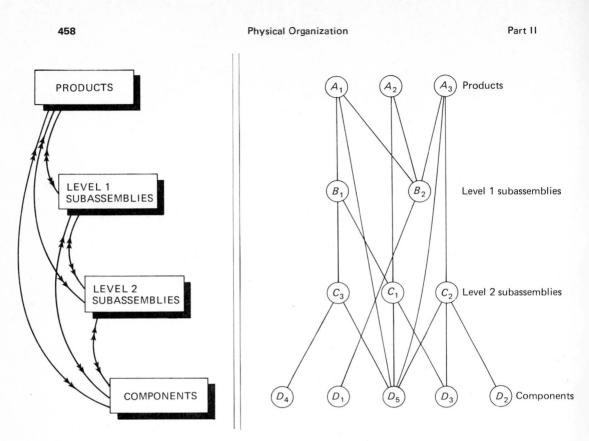

Figure 25.9   Figures 25.10 to 25.12 show physical representations of this plex structure.

The primary problem with embedded variable-length pointer lists is that of maintenance. To update the file the pointer lists must be capable of contraction and expansion, and this would normally warrant periodic reorganization of the records. However, reorganization is very difficult because when records are moved so many pointers have to be changed. This problem is partially overcome by using *symbolic pointers* which are not changed when records are moved but which rely upon the file's addressing mechanism to find the records. The use of symbolic pointers, however, is more time-consuming and usually requires more space than the use of direct pointers.

MULTILEVEL PLEX STRUCTURES

Many plex structures have multiple levels with relationships between nonadjacent levels, as in Fig. 25.9. In some cases it is not clear which record

Records	Pointers				
A_1	B_1	B_2	D_5		
A_2	B_2	C_1			
A_3	B_2	C_2	D_5		
B_1	A_1	C_1	C_3		
B_2	A_1	A_2	A_3	C_2	D_1
C_1	B_1	D_4	D_5		
C_2	A_3	B_2	D_2	D_3	D_5
C_3	B_1	D_4	D_5		
D_1	B_2				
D_2	C_2				
D_3	C_1	C_3			
D_4	C_3				
D_5	A_1	A_3	C_1	C_2	C_3

Figure 25.10 Variable-length pointer lists representing the plex structure of Fig. 25.9.

types should be called *parents* and which *children*. There is an amorphous interconnection of record types rather than any clear family structure.

One way to represent the structure is to use a variable-length list of pointers in each record, as in Fig. 25.10. The pointers may have to indicate what type of record they are pointing to. The variable-length pointer lists may be constructed using any software which permits variable-length records and handles insertions and deletions appropriately. For example, IBM's VSAM, illustrated in Fig. 20.9, could be used. The facilities would have to be added for relinking the pointers when records are inserted or deleted. Again, the maintenance of files with embedded variable-length pointer lists is cumbersome.

DIRECTORIES   As with tree structures there is much to be said for removing the pointers from the records and placing

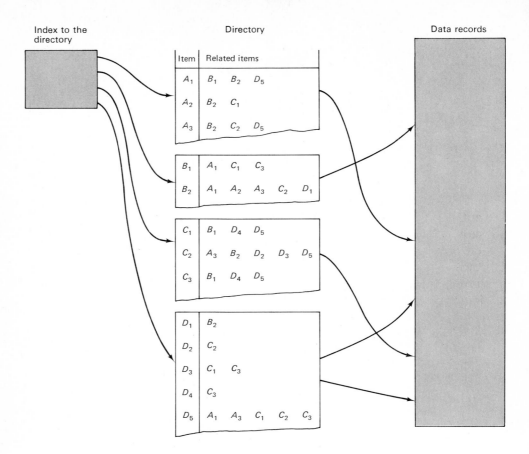

Figure 25.11   Representation of the plex structure of Fig. 25.9 in a
directory.

them in a separate directory, as in Fig. 25.11. The relevant section of the
directory can be searched more quickly than searching through embedded
pointers. It can be optimally and securely organized.

In general, the more complex the mapping, the stronger is the argument
for separating the relationships from the data and handling them in an
appropriately organized directory module. We will return to this point again
in Chapter 28.

BIT MAPS   As before, a variable-length pointer list may be
                                         more economically handled as a bit map. Figure
25.12 shows the relationships in Fig. 25.9 represented in the form of a
bit map.

	A_1	A_2	A_3	B_1	B_2	C_1	C_2	C_3
D_1	0	0	0	0	1	0	0	0
D_2	0	0	0	0	0	0	1	0
D_3	0	0	0	0	0	1	1	0
D_4	0	0	0	0	0	0	0	1
D_5	1	0	1	0	0	1	1	1

	A_1	A_2	A_3	B_1	B_2
C_1	0	1	0	1	0
C_2	0	0	0	0	1
C_3	0	0	0	1	0

	A_1	A_2	A_3
B_1	1	0	0
B_2	1	1	1

Figure 25.12 A bit map representation of the relationships in Fig. 25.9.

The use of directories or bit maps, rather than embedded pointers, can permit the data records to be laid out in such a way that they do not have to be moved when records are inserted or deleted. Ideally they should not have to be moved even when maintenance occurs. Instead, the entries in the directories or bit maps are changed. This speeds up the insertion and maintenance operations and avoids the risk of damaging data when periodically moving it.

SUMMARY   Box 25.1 summarizes the techniques for representing tree and plex structures.

Box 25.1 Summary of Techniques for Representing Tree and Plex Structures

	Illustrated in figs.:	Structures suitable for:			
		Tree	Simple Plex	Complex Plex	
Physical Contiguity on serial media	25.7	√			Batch processing only. Insertions and deletions accomplished by merging.
Physical Contiguity on Direct-access devices	25.8 25.9	√			Insertions and deletions accomplished by (1) overflows or (2) distributed free space. Useful when lower levels of a tree are accessed *only* via their parents. Not useful for records which should be organized sequentially.
Combination of physical contiguity and pointers	25.2	√	√		Useful when part of the structure yields to physical contiguity, e.g., one segtype accessed *only* via its parent.
Multiple child pointers	25.10 25.5	√	√		*Advantage*: No lengthy searches and hence useful for real-time inquiries. *Disadvantage*: Widely varying numbers of pointers per record; maintenance is difficult.
Fixed-position parent pointers	25.10	√			Simple but only useful for child-to-parent mapping.

Box 25.1 *continued*

	Illust-rated in figs.:	Structures suitable for:			
		Tree	Simplex Plex	Complex Plex	
Child-and-twin pointers	25.10 25.12 25.6	√	√		*Advantage*: Maintenance simpler than with multiple child pointers because there are no variable-length pointer lists. *Disadvantage*: Long time to search the pointer chain.
Ring Structures	25.12 25.6 25.7	√	√		*Advantage*: Maintenance simpler than with multiple child pointers because there are no variable-length pointer lists. *Disadvantage*: Long time to search the pointer chain.
Variable-length pointer lists	25.8 25.9	√	√	√	*Advantage*: No lengthy seeks and hence useful for real-time inquiries. *Disadvantage*: Widely varying numbers of pointers per record; maintenance is difficult.
Directory	25.15 25.11	√	√	√	*Advantages*: Fast-searching; suitable for paging structures; data records need not be moved during maintenance.
Bit maps	25.16 25.12	√	√	√	A form of directory. Whether or not a bit map is more compact than a variable pointer list depends on the number of pointers used and the total number of possible values.

BOOK STRUCTURE

Retrieval of data on the basis of multiple key values is much more complex than finding a record with a single key.

Chapter 26 gives the techniques for multiple-key retrieval. Chapter 27 and 28 illustrate these techniques. Chapter 29 discusses systems designed specially for multiple-key searching.

26 MULTIPLE-KEY RETRIEVAL

The file organizations discussed in the previous chapters were for records with a single key. Many applications require records with more than one key, and this makes the file organization more complex. In this chapter and Chapter 27 we will discuss multiple-key organizations.

Many *operations* files in the commercial world are organized with one key per record. The purchasing systems, accounting systems, airline reservation systems, and others used as examples in this book use single-key records. Multiple-key records are used in some operations systems but are more commonly found in *information* systems in which a variety of inquiries can be made about different aspects of the information.

PRIME KEY AND SECONDARY KEYS
On a file with many keys usually one key can be used to uniquely identify records. As we discussed earlier, this *unique identifier* is referred to as the *prime key*, and the other keys are referred to as *secondary keys.* A secondary key does not normally identify a record uniquely. There will often be many records with that same key value. A prime key might be PART-NUMBER. It identifies a part record uniquely because no two parts have the same part number. A secondary key might be PART-TYPE. There are many parts of the same type; nevertheless, PART-TYPE may be an important key with many inquiries based on it.

One way of finding a record by a secondary key is to use an index for that key. An index based on an attribute other than the prime key is referred to as a *secondary index.* In some information systems it is desirable to index many different attributes, and so many secondary indices are used.

EXAMPLE OF A
MULTIPLE-KEY
DATA BASE

A typical example of an information system with secondary indices is one for providing information about sales in a corporation. The users ask questions of the system such as the following:

Give me the top 10 customers in the Southern Region on net sales.
Give me this year's sales and on-order figures for customers in Branch Office 74.
List the on-order items for transportation industry customers in District 5.
Which customers in the Detroit area have ordered more than 500 of Item No. 721?
What have been the net sales to the cosmetics industry in July?
Which branch offices have net sales in excess of $100,000 for last month?

Customer name and location together form a prime key for addressing the customer records. Item number forms a prime key for addressing the item records. Secondary indices are needed for linking these two files and for indexing items such as region, net sales, number of items sold, number of items on order, and industry category.

When a batch-processing system is used there is often no need for secondary indices. The records will be scanned periodically, and a variety of listings will be produced. When the information system becomes on-line, large quantities of queries cannot be gathered together and sorted, as they would be in a batch system. A means must be provided for going directly from the query to those records which permit it to be answered.

The options available for the design of a multiple-key file permit the designer major trade-offs between increasing the quantity of secondary storage used, increasing the utilization of main memory, and increasing the time needed to locate the required records.

PHYSICAL
RECORD
POSITIONING

With most single-key addressing methods the *physical position* of the records on the files is usually determined by their key. Records on index sequential files are laid out in ascending key sequence. Records on directly accessed files are stored in a position determined by the key transformation algorithm. With multiple-key files, *only one key* can determine the physical positioning. If the records are in ascending sequence of key 1, for example, as in Fig. 26.1, then the other keys cannot be in sequence or in positions which are determinable by an algorithm.

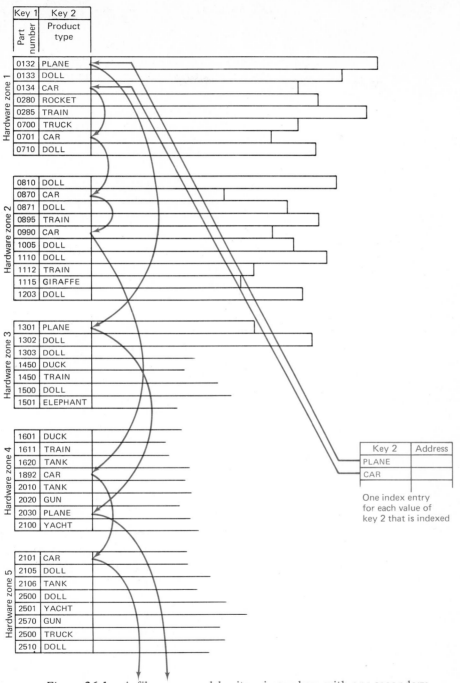

Key 1	Key 2
Part number	Product type

Hardware zone 1

0132	PLANE
0133	DOLL
0134	CAR
0280	ROCKET
0285	TRAIN
0700	TRUCK
0701	CAR
0710	DOLL

Hardware zone 2

0810	DOLL
0870	CAR
0871	DOLL
0895	TRAIN
0990	CAR
1005	DOLL
1110	DOLL
1112	TRAIN
1115	GIRAFFE
1203	DOLL

Hardware zone 3

1301	PLANE
1302	DOLL
1303	DOLL
1450	DUCK
1450	TRAIN
1500	DOLL
1501	ELEPHANT

Hardware zone 4

1601	DUCK
1611	TRAIN
1620	TANK
1892	CAR
2010	TANK
2020	GUN
2030	PLANE
2100	YACHT

Hardware zone 5

2101	CAR
2105	DOLL
2106	TANK
2500	DOLL
2501	YACHT
2570	GUN
2500	TRUCK
2510	DOLL

Key 2	Address
PLANE	
CAR	

One index entry
for each value of
key 2 that is indexed

Figure 26.1   A file sequenced by its primary key, with one secondary
key linked by chaining.

In most multiple-key files today the prime key determines the physical positioning of the records, just as it does with most single-key files. The secondary key addressing method must then be a technique which does not depend on the physical position of records. There are sometimes good reasons for making this independence of physical positioning apply to the prime key also. If the technique for finding the records is independent of where they are positioned, then the records can be left where they were first written and so not have to be reshuffled periodically to accommodate newcomers. Many of the difficulties that arise in maintaining a data base are a result of the periodic reorganizations of the records. Furthermore, files are becoming much larger as computer applications grow and storage costs drop. With very large files, periodic reshuffling of the records is time-consuming and costly.

CHAINED RECORDS   As we commented earlier, an index for a nonsequential file is usually much larger than that for a sequential file. If many different attributes are to be indexed, the total space occupied by the indices can become very large. On some information systems the secondary indices occupy substantially more space than the data.

An alternative to large indices is the use of chains of pointers embedded in the data records. Figure 26.1 illustrates a chained file. The example relates to a manufacturer of plastic toys. The prime key in this example is PART-NUMBER. The secondary key is PRODUCT-TYPE, and items of the same type are chained together. Such an organization would work efficiently for responding to certain categories of information requests. It would be good for the request "List the part numbers of all toy cars." For the request "What cars have part numbers between 1500 and 2000?" it would be less efficient. The computer would start at the record for part 1500 or the first one after that number and would then scan forward until the CAR chain is found. If only a small proportion of the part numbers are for cars, then many records which are not for cars might have to be examined before the CAR chain is found. The question would be answered more efficiently with a secondary index for cars. On the other hand, if a high proportion of the part numbers are for cars, say one-third, then the chain organization would be reasonably efficient, whereas a secondary index for cars would be very lengthy.

If the file is volatile, new links have to be added to the chain and old links removed. When a new CAR product is added to the file, the computer will scan backward from the location where the record is added until it reaches the closest link of the CAR chain. It will then change the pointer in this record to point to the new record, and the previous pointer will be written in the new record so that the chain is relinked. Similarly, when records are deleted the chain must be relinked, or else the deleted record must be marked and the relinking left for a periodic file reorganization. In Fig. 26.1, relinking the chain appears easy because the computer does not have to scan far to find the chain. In practice on some systems the chain links may be very far from one another, and a lengthy scan is needed.

The chain in Fig. 26.1 is shown as being a one-way chain. Often two-way rings are used instead, each item having a pointer to the previous link as well as to the next link. As we discussed in Chapter 23, two-way rings give protection against the accidental destruction of pointers and also facilitate the removal of records from the chain. With the one-way chain of Fig. 26.1, if a pointer is lost, it can be recovered only by a lengthy operation of scanning the secondary keys of the file.

MORE THAN ONE SECONDARY KEY   A chain such as that in Fig. 26.1 is satisfactory for certain systems which employ a *single* secondary key. Where the requests relate to more than one secondary key, lengthy chains can be inefficient.

Figure 26.2 shows the same file, using the same technique, but with two secondary keys. Key 3 is the *color* of the plastic toys. The organization in Fig. 26.2 may be satisfactory for requests concerning key 1 and either of the other keys but is less attractive for requests concerning key 2 and key 3.

Consider the request "List details of blue cars." Records concerning blue cars may be found either by searching the BLUE chain or by searching the CAR chain. In either case the entire chain has to be searched, and so the machine must seek and read many records which are not for blue cars.

COUNT   It will help if the machine can always follow the shortest chain. A *count* of the number of records in the chains should therefore be included in the index entries, as shown in Fig. 26.2. In practice the count of the chain links serves two purposes in data-base organization. First, it permits the shortest chains to be selected. In Fig. 26.2, the CAR chain would be searched, not the BLUE chain, when answering the above query. Second, it can give an indication of the reasonableness of a query. The terminal operators of an information system may unwittingly enter queries which could trigger extremely lengthy searches or result in an excess of items being printed in reply. The system

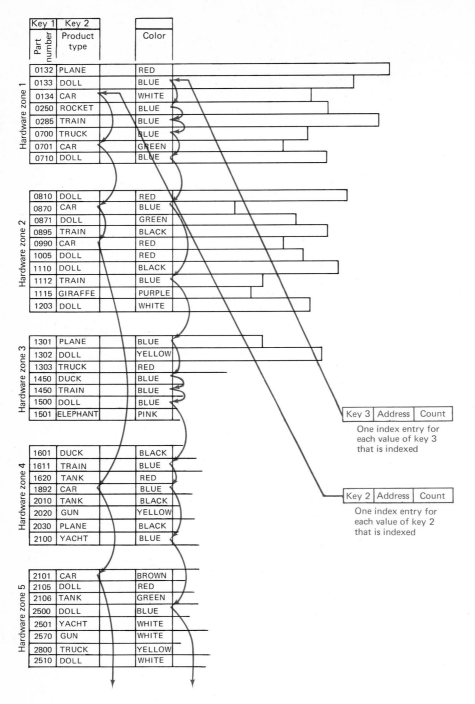

Figure 26.2 The same file as in Fig. 26.1 with two secondary keys and chains.

470

may use the count field to prevent such queries being handled on-line; they are better handled off-line. The operator will often be pleased to have been warned so that he can modify his query to encompass a smaller set of all items.

MULTILIST
ORGANIZATION

Some of the lengthy searches which are necessary with an organization such as that in Fig. 26.2 can be shortened if the chains are divided into smaller lengths. An index entry is then required giving the start of each piece of each chain. Figure 26.3 shows the same file as Fig. 26.1 with the lengths of the chains limited to three items.

The organization is sometimes referred to as a multilist organization ("list" referring to the "chain" of items). The length of the chains is a parameter which can be varied in a multilist file to give the best compromise between large indices and lengthy searches.

The inquiry "What cars have part numbers between 1500 and 2000?" can now be answered without the risk of having to search through many records from part 1500 onward before the CAR chain is found. The computer finds the address of the record for part 1500, and the CAR index gives the address of the chain which starts prior to that (the second dotted chain in Fig. 26.3). This chain is followed and it is quickly found that part 1892 (only) satisfies the requirements. The number of records read which do not satisfy the request can never be more than $L-1$, where L is the number of links in the chains.

Figure 26.4 plots the number of index entries and the mean number of record reads needed to locate one item, against chain length.

If there are L items per chain, the number of index entries per 1000 records is $\lceil 1000/L \rceil$.

The mean number of reads to locate one item is $L/2$.

It will be seen that the designer can exercise a trade-off between the number of index entries and the speed of locating an item.

HARDWARE-RELATED
CHAINS

The chain organizations discussed so far have not taken the hardware characteristics into consideration. The chains would therefore stretch heedlessly from one cylinder to another or from one module of a file to another. As with most other forms of file organization, the efficiency can be improved greatly by adapting the organization to specific hardware characteristics.

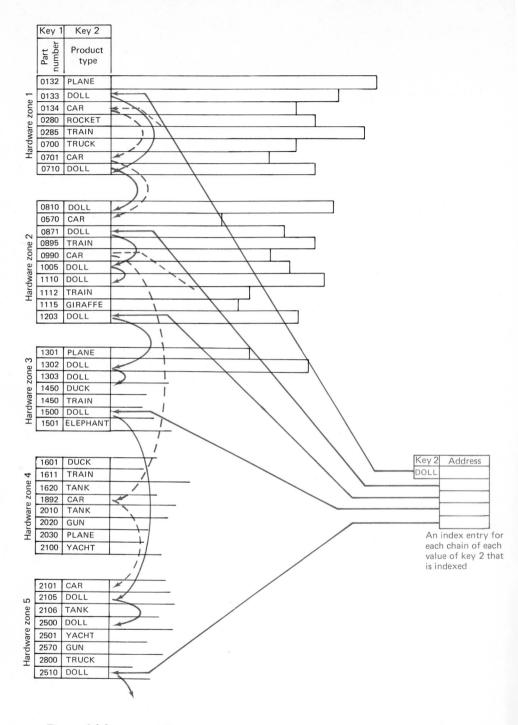

	Key 1	Key 2
	Part number	Product type

Hardware zone 1

0132	PLANE
0133	DOLL
0134	CAR
0280	ROCKET
0285	TRAIN
0700	TRUCK
0701	CAR
0710	DOLL

Hardware zone 2

0810	DOLL
0570	CAR
0871	DOLL
0895	TRAIN
0990	CAR
1005	DOLL
1110	DOLL
1112	TRAIN
1115	GIRAFFE
1203	DOLL

Hardware zone 3

1301	PLANE
1302	DOLL
1303	DOLL
1450	DUCK
1450	TRAIN
1500	DOLL
1501	ELEPHANT

Hardware zone 4

1601	DUCK
1611	TRAIN
1620	TANK
1892	CAR
2010	TANK
2020	GUN
2030	PLANE
2100	YACHT

Hardware zone 5

2101	CAR
2105	DOLL
2106	TANK
2500	DOLL
2501	YACHT
2570	GUN
2800	TRUCK
2510	DOLL

Key 2	Address
DOLL	

An index entry for each chain of each value of key 2 that is indexed

Figure 26.3 A multilist organization. The chains are cut into slices, and an index shows the start of each slice.

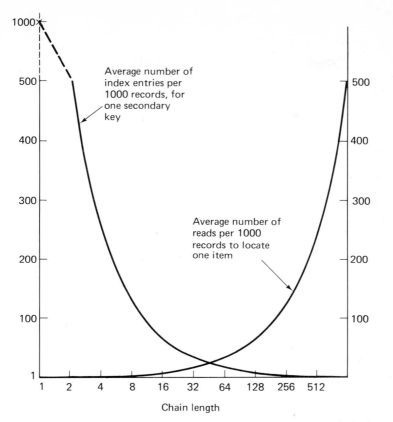

Figure 26.4   The effect of varying the number of items per chain in a multilist file. The designer can exercise a tradeoff between the number of index entries and the speed of locating a record from a secondary key.

CELLULAR CHAINS

In a chained data base the chains can be restricted in length so that they do not extend beyond certain hardware boundaries or cells. In this way lengthy seeks incurred when following the chains from one cell to another can be avoided. The records drawn in Figs. 26.1 to 26.3 are in five groups which are on different hardware zones or cells. These zones could be separate cylinders on a disk file, as in Fig. 26.6, separate cards on a magnetic card file, and so forth. Figure 26.5 shows the same toy manufacturer file, but now the chains are designed so that they each extend across one hardware zone and no further. These are sometimes called *cellular chains.* There is an index entry for each indexable key value—for each hardware

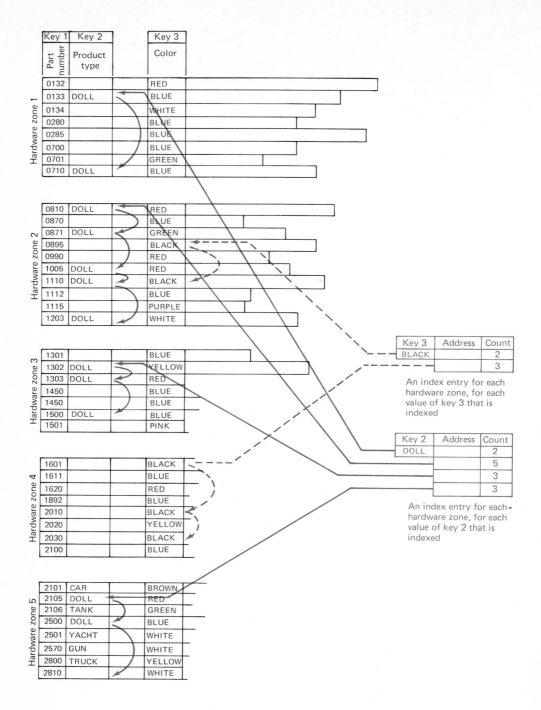

Figure 26.5 A cellular multilist organization. The same as fig. 26.3 except that no chain is permitted to extend beyond one hardware zone (to lessen search time).

474

Secondary index

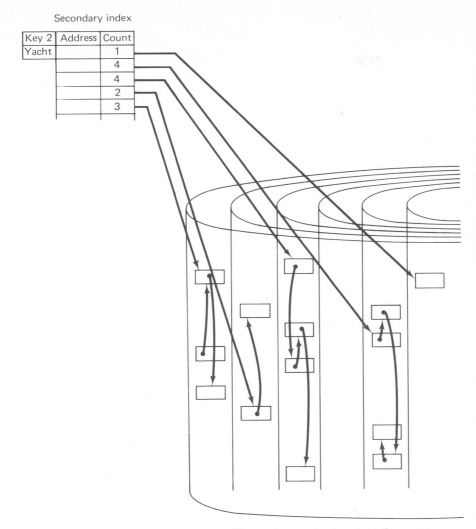

Key 2	Address	Count
Yacht		1
		4
		4
		2
		3

Figure 26.6   Cellular multilist. The chains are broken into fragments, each of which resides on one cell. The contents of a cell can be read without moving an access mechanism; hence the overall search time is shortened.

zone that contains that value. Hardware zone 4 does not contain any dolls, and so there is no entry for it in the doll table.

To answer a request such as "List all black dolls," the indices will first be examined to see which hardware zones contain both a "black" item and a "doll." Zone 4 does not contain a doll. Zones 1, 3, and 5 do not contain any black items. Therefore, of the five zones shown only zone 2 need be

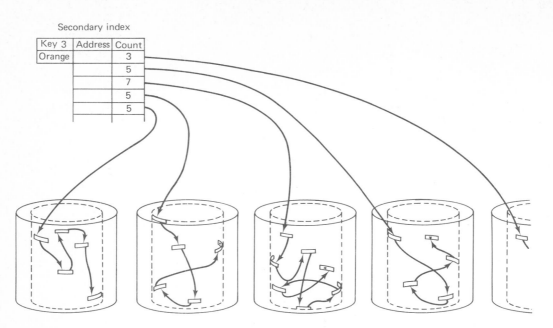

Figure 26.7 Parallel cellular multilist. The cells are organized so that they can be searched simultaneously, thus reducing the total search time.

examined. The count fields show that there are five dolls in zone 2 but only two black items. The two black item records will therefore be inspected to see which are black dolls.

To answer an inquiry such as "Which item numbers between 1500 and 2000 are cars?" the key 1 addressing mechanism will indicate that these item numbers extend over zones 3 and 4. Only zone 4 contains a car. The inquiry can therefore be answered without any chain searching.

PARALLEL CELLULAR CHAINS   The *cells* which contain the chains in Fig. 26.6 are cylinders of a disk module. If the module has only one access mechanism, only one chain can be searched at a time. Another way to lay out the data is to spread it across modules which can be read simultaneously. The layout may be designed to maximize the number of pieces of a chain that can be followed in parallel. Figure 26.7 shows a file spread across cylinders on separate disks and also the chains cut into pieces which can be read by access mechanisms on different disks at the same time. We will refer to a multilist organization in which the pieces of chain can be explored in parallel as a *parallel cellular multilist organization.*

476

When on-line systems use chained records it is sometimes necessary to design for a high level of parallel chain searching in order to meet the response-time requirements. Future systems designed to permit rapid searching of a large data base may require a substantial measure of parallel operation.

INVERTED
LIST

When multilist files with chains (lists) of controlled length are used, the length of chains can be varied from one link per chain to a length which can include every item. In the former extreme case the organization is referred to as an *inverted list.* There is an entry for *every* record in the index of *each* key, as shown in Fig. 26.8.

Only one access to the *data* is needed for each record that is part of the response to a query. Provided that the secondary indices can be examined rapidly, the inverted list organization gives the fastest response to real-time inquiries because no chains have to be followed. On the other hand, the indices can become enormous (have to be stored on secondary storage), and the organization of the indices themselves becomes a major file problem. The techniques used for storing and searching the indices are critical to the efficiency of inverted list files (or to multilist files with short chain lengths). We will discuss index organization in Chapters 29 and 30.

It should be noted that inverted list files are a special case of multilist files and in some cases have been implemented using multilist software.

INDIRECT
INDICES

The pointers that are shown in Figs. 26.1 to 26.8, whether they are embedded in records or are in an index, all give the address of the record pointed to. Secondary key pointers could, however, be *indirect* pointers; i.e., they give the primary key to the record pointed to rather than its address. This approach has the disadvantage that the pointers take longer to follow because the primary addressing mechanism has to be used to convert the primary key into an address. Following chains is a time-consuming occupation without this added burden. However, inverted lists such as that in Fig. 26.8 could use indirect pointers without too serious a time penalty. We will call an index with indirect pointers an *indirect index.*

There are two advantages to using an indirect index rather than one which gives record addresses. First, if records are moved physically, the secondary indices do not have to be updated. This is valuable if a file

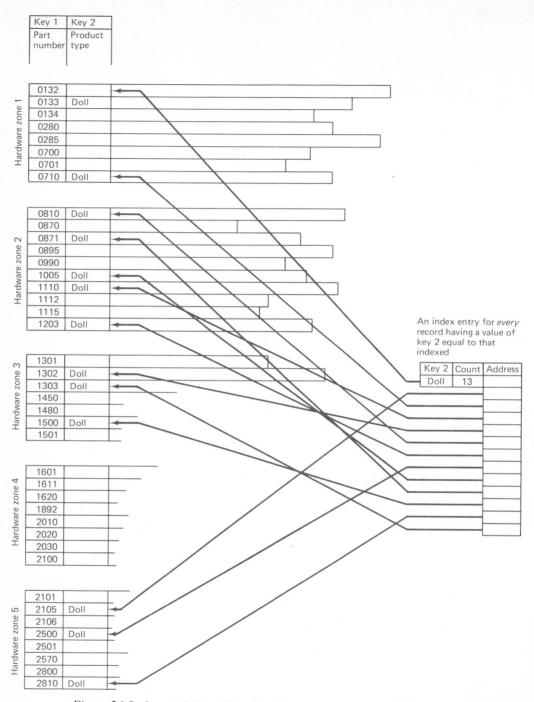

Figure 26.8 Inverted lists. *Every* attribute value of the secondary key is indexed so that there are no chains.

478

organization is used, such as that in Fig. 20.11, in which records sometimes have to be moved when new records are inserted. In general the use of indirect secondary indices substantially simplifies the work of maintaining the file, which is so burdensome with volatile files.

The second advantage is that many inquiries can be answered by using the index *without having to go to the data records.* Consider the request "List the part numbers of all dolls between 1000 and 1500." If the inverted list in Fig. 26.8 contained part numbers instead of addresses, the request could be answered by scanning the list. To facilitate the answering of queries involving multiple keys, a count of the items is included for each entry so that the smaller lists can be scheduled first.

CELLULAR INVERTED LISTS　　　The main disadvantage of inverted lists is the size of the indices. The index size can be reduced substantially on some files by storing not the address of each record but an indication of a hardware zone in which it resides. The zone will then have to be searched to find the required record. There is thus another trade-off between index size and the number of records that must be read. We will call this type of organization *cellular inverted lists.*

The cell or hardware zone may be a *track* of a disk or other device, in which case the read time is not substantially increased. It may be several tracks or a cylinder. To minimize index space the cell may be referred to in the index either with a binary number which can be converted into an address or with a single bit in a bit matrix like that in Fig. 26.9.

For a request like "List all black ducks" the bits for "black," 01010, and the bits for "duck," 00110, can be combined with an AND instruction to give 00010, revealing that only hardware zone 4 contains black duck records. Hardware zone 4 is then scanned to find them.

PARALLEL CELLULAR INVERTED LISTS　　　As with cellular chains, the cell positions can be selected so that cells can be searched in parallel in order to minimize the system response times. The multiple-key file, for example, may be spread across several disk packs, as shown in Fig. 26.10, perhaps occupying only a few cylinders on each, with differently organized data in the remaining cylinders. The cells which the indices refer to in Fig. 16.10 are cylinders, and several of them can be searched in parallel. If an inquiry asks for details of *blue elephants,* for example, the index in Fig. 26.10 reveals that cylinders 3 and 253 each

	Key 1	Key 2	Key 3
	Part number	Product type	Color

Hardware zone 1

Key 1	Key 2	Key 3
0132	Plane	Red
0133	Doll	Blue
0134	Car	White
0280	Rocket	Blue
0285	Train	Blue
0700	Truck	Blue
0701	Car	Green
0710	Doll	Blue

Hardware zone 2

Key 1	Key 2	Key 3
0810	Doll	Red
0870	Car	Blue
0871	Doll	Green
0895	Train	Black
0990	Car	Red
1005	Doll	Red
1110	Doll	Black
1112	Train	Blue
1115	Giraffe	Purple
1203	Doll	White

Hardware zone 3

Key 1	Key 2	Key 3
1301	Plane	Blue
1302	Doll	Yellow
1303	Truck	Red
1450	Duck	Blue
1480	Train	Blue
1500	Doll	Blue
1501	Elephant	Pink

Hardware zone 4

Key 1	Key 2	Key 3
1601	Duck	Black
1611	Train	Blue
1620	Tank	Red
1892	Car	Blue
2010	Tank	Black
2020	Gun	Yellow
2030	Plane	Red
2100	Yacht	Blue

Hardware zone 5

Key 1	Key 2	Key 3
2101	Car	Brown
2105	Doll	Red
2106	Tank	Green
2500	Gun	Blue
2501	Yacht	White
2570	Doll	White
2800	Truck	Yellow
2810	Doll	White

		Hardware zone				
		1	2	3	4	5
Key 2	Car	1	1	0	1	1
	Doll	1	1	1	0	1
	Duck	0	0	1	1	0
	Elephant	0	0	1	0	0
	⋮					
Key 3	Black	0	1	0	1	0
	Blue	1	1	1	1	1
	Brown	0	0	0	0	1
	Green	1	1	0	0	1
	⋮					

A 1 bit for each hardware zone containing a record with the key value in question

Figure 26.9 **Cellular** inverted lists.

480

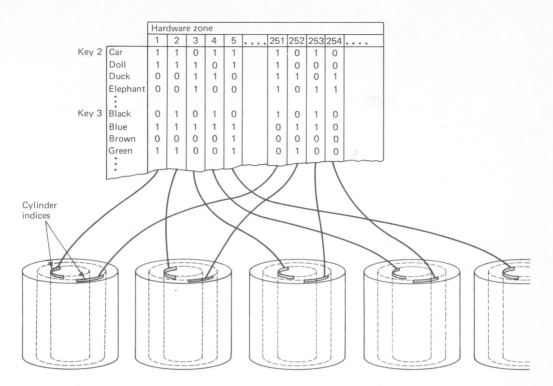

Hardware zone										
	1	2	3	4	5	. . . .	251	252	253	254	. . . .
Key 2 Car	1	1	0	1	1		1	0	1	0
Doll	1	1	1	0	1		1	0	0	0
Duck	0	0	1	1	0		1	1	0	1
Elephant	0	0	1	0	0		1	0	1	1
⋮										
Key 3 Black	0	1	0	1	0		1	0	1	0
Blue	1	1	1	1	1		0	1	1	0
Brown	0	0	0	0	1		0	0	0	0
Green	1	1	0	0	1		0	1	0	0
⋮										

Figure 26.10 Parallel cellular inverted lists. The main index is a bit index. A second-level index is used for searching each "cell" (i.e., cylinder).

contain *blue* items and *elephants.* The seek operations for locating the different cylinders to be searched can occur simultaneously. In Fig. 26.10 each cylinder has, itself, an index for speeding the search within the cylinder so that not every track has to be searched.

For many files a cylinder would be too large a *cell*, and smaller groups of tracks on the same cylinder would be used.

PARALLELISM IN SEARCH OPERATIONS

Any search operation in a data base can be speeded up if it can be divided into sections which are carried on simultaneously. In the parallel cellular organizations of Figs. 26.7 and 26.10, the seeks can be overlapped, but the read operations cannot be overlapped on conventional data-processing hardware unless the disks in question are attached to different computer channels.

It would be possible to overlap the disk read operations if each disk module had its own control unit with sufficient logic power to determine

481

whether a read satisfied the search criteria. We will refer to such a device as a *search controller.* The search controller would examine the keys of each record using a mask which would enable the controller to determine whether the record was a blue elephant, had a salary key greater than $3000, or satisfied whatever other search criteria were used. If no record on the track satisfied the search criteria, the controller would examine the next track. When a requisite record is found the main computer would be interrupted so that it can read the record from the controller.

There could be one search controller to a file unit of several disk spindles, one controller to each disk spindle or each access mechanism, or several controllers to a disk unit—possibly one to each read head. The number of controllers would affect the degree of parallelism that could be built into the search operation.

CHAINS IN   The chains we have discussed so far have all been
THE INDEX   constructed with pointers written in the data
                       records, i.e., *embedded* chains or *embedded*
pointers. A disadvantage of embedded chains is the file access time that is incurred in following them. Rather than embedding chains in the data, it may be better to put them in the indices where they can be followed without having to read the lengthy data records.

There are several ways in which relationships between records can be expressed in the indices. Figure 26.11 shows an organization with unbroken chains somewhat like Fig. 26.2 except that the chains are in the prime-key index instead of strung through the data file. They can be followed with far fewer track reads and seeks than the chains of Fig. 26.2.

As with the chains in the data records, chains in the index would probably be fragmented, in practice, into chains confined to related hardware zones. In fact, any of the organizations illustrated in Figs. 26.2 to 26.10 could be used *within the index itself.*

The structure of the index and the methods of compaction that are used in the index become very important for efficiency. These topics are discussed in the next few chapters.

Box 26.1 summarizes the techniques for multiple-key retrieval.

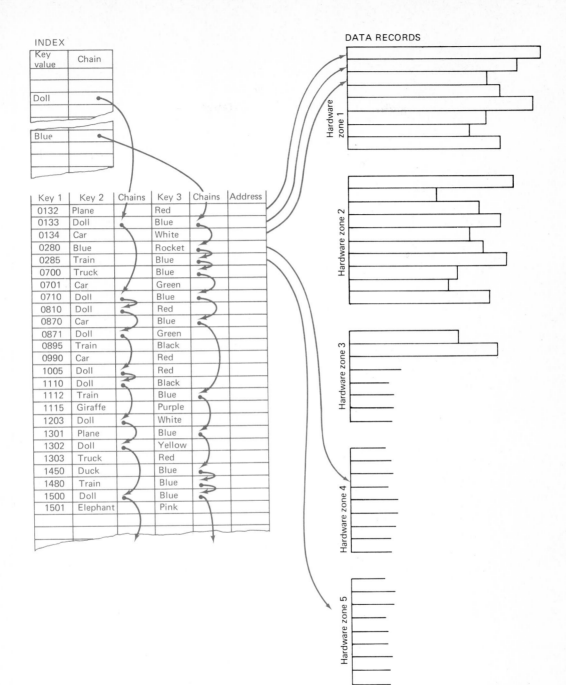

Figure 26.11 Index chains. The chains are in the index, not in the data records. The keys can be removed from the data records, and a file of key tuples can be organized in any of the ways illustrated in Figs. 26.1 to 26.10.

Box 26.1   Summary of Techniques for Multiple-Key Retrieval

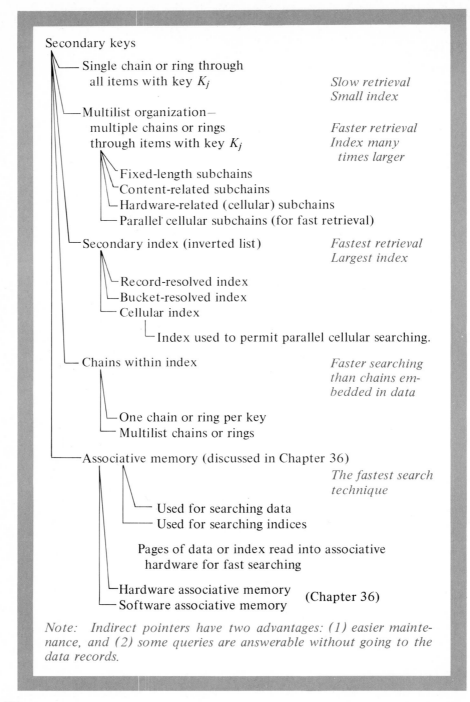

Secondary keys

    Single chain or ring through
    all items with key K_j *Slow retrieval*
                                     Small index

    Multilist organization—
    multiple chains or rings   *Faster retrieval*
    through items with key K_j *Index many*
                                  times larger

        Fixed-length subchains
        Content-related subchains
        Hardware-related (cellular) subchains
        Parallel cellular subchains (for fast retrieval)

    Secondary index (inverted list)   *Fastest retrieval*
                                  Largest index

        Record-resolved index
        Bucket-resolved index
        Cellular index

          Index used to permit parallel cellular searching.

    Chains within index   *Faster searching*
                                than chains em-
                                bedded in data

        One chain or ring per key
        Multilist chains or rings

    Associative memory (discussed in Chapter 36)

                                The fastest search
                                technique

           Used for searching data
           Used for searching indices

          Pages of data or index read into associative
            hardware for fast searching

        Hardware associative memory   (Chapter 36)
        Software associative memory

*Note: Indirect pointers have two advantages: (1) easier mainte-
nance, and (2) some queries are answerable without going to the
data records.*

BOOK STRUCTURE

Chapter 27 gives simple illustrations of the multiple-key retrieval techniques discussed in Chapter 26.

27 A COMPARISON OF MULTIPLE-KEY ORGANIZATIONS

To illustrate in a simple fashion the multiple-key organizations and indexing methods discussed in the previous two chapters, this chapter considers a data base of only 28 records, shown in Fig. 27.1, and shows 10 methods of organizing it. There are five indexable attributes in the records: A_0, man number (the unique identifier); A_1, his name; A_2, the department he works in; A_3, his skill code; and A_4, his salary. The remaining, and larger, part of the records consists of nonindexable details. The records in most cases are laid out in ascending sequence of the prime key, MAN NUMBER. They are shown occupying four hardware zones. The record addresses are written in the form X · Y, where X is the number of the hardware zone and Y is the number of the record within that zone.

Figures 27.2 to 27.11 are diagrams of organizations of these data. Many variations are possible on the organizations shown. When the reader inspects the diagrams he should extend them in his mind to a large file, perhaps occupying several disk modules, with more secondary keys and many more attribute values. He should consider how the organizations may differ in the response times incurred in responding to multiple-key queries. The reader should also consider the question of maintenance. Some of the organizations are difficult or time-consuming to maintain, whereas others are easier.

The attribute SALARY is a continuous range of numbers. To produce indices for this attribute it is *quantized* into discrete ranges. Ranges of $250 are used. Similarly, the attribute NAME is referred to by alphabetical ranges. In some of the illustrations the first letter of the surname is used as an index entry. (In practice it would be better to divide both the SALARY and the NAME data-items into ranges chosen not for equal key separation, as here, but so that each range relates roughly to an equal number of records—roughly equal chain lengths, for example.)

Keys:

A_0	A_1	A_2	A_3	A_4	Non-indexed details
Man number	Name	Depart-ment	Skill code	Salary	
07642	MARTJT	220	PL	1900	
07643	GREEJW	119	SE	2700	
07650	HALSPD	210	SE	2000	
07668	FEINPE	220	PL	1950	
07670	SCHAWE	119	AD	3100	
07671	MARSJJ	119	FI	1200	
07672	ALBEHA	210	SE	2100	
07700	LONDAJ	220	AD	3000	
07702	ANDEWF	119	FI	1000	
07710	MARTCH	220	PL	1750	
07715	FLINGA	119	AD	3000	
07716	MERLCH	220	FO	2200	
07760	JONEKB	119	PL	2200	
07761	REDFBB	119	SE	2650	
07780	BLANJE	220	FO	2100	
07805	ROPEES	220	PL	1900	
07806	KALNTD	119	MA	2300	
07815	EDWARB	220	PL	2040	
07850	DALLJE	119	FI	1050	
07883	JONETW	210	SE	2010	
07888	WEINSH	119	MA	2450	
07889	KLEINM	220	PL	1830	
07961	FREIHN	220	PL	1780	
07970	MANKCA	119	MA	2410	
07972	FIKETE	210	SE	2500	
08000	SCHEDR	210	FI	2100	
08001	FLANJE	119	PL	1920	
08100	JOOSWE	210	SE	3150	

Figure 27.1

It is assumed that fixed-length entries are used in the *name* index. The secondary key NAME is therefore truncated to the first four characters of the surname followed by the first two initials. The remainder of a person's name is stored in the nonindexable details portion of the record. Two people will occasionally have the same NAME key, in which case both their records will have to be examined to find the required name.

Assume that a file consists of 100,000 records of 500 bytes each. The records have one primary key of 10 bytes in total.

A₁ Index		
Name	Address of start of chain	Count
A	1.0	2
B	2.0	1
D	2.4	1
E	2.3	1
F	0.3	5
G	0.1	1
H	0.2	1
J	1.6	3
K	2.2	2
L	1.1	1
M	0.0	5
R	1.7	2
S	0.4	2
W	3.1	1

A₂ Index		
Department	Address of start of chain	Count
119	0.1	12
210	0.2	6
220	0.0	10

A₃ Index		
Skill code	Address of start of chain	Count
AD	0.4	3
FI	0.5	4
FO	1.5	2
MA	2.2	3
PL	0.0	9
SE	0.1	7

A₄ Index		
Salary	Address of start of chain	Count
1000	0.5	3
1750	0.0	7
2000	0.2	8
2250	2.2	3
2500	0.1	3
3000	0.4	4

Figure 27.2 A simple chained file. The index gives the address of the start of each chain and a count of the number of items in the chain. The data records contain a chain address for each of the four secondary keys. An asterisk indicates the end of a chain. To answer the query "List the names of all employees with a Skill Code PL in Department 119" either the Skill Code PL chain or the Department 119 chain could be followed. The Skill Code PL chain would be used because the count fields in the indices indicate that it is shorter.

Address	A_0 Man number	A_1 Name	Chain address	A_2 Department	Chain address	A_3 Skill code	Chain address	A_4 Salary	Chain address	Non-indexed details
C_0	07642	MARTJT	0.5	220	0.3	PL	0.3	1900	0.3	
$C_0 + L$	07643	GREEJW	*	119	0.4	SE	0.2	2700	1.7	
$C_0 + 2L$	07650	HALS PD	*	210	1.0	SE	1.0	2000	1.0	
$C_0 + 3L$	07668	FEINPE	1.4	220	1.1	PL	1.3	1950	1.3	
$C_0 + 4L$	07670	SCHAWE	3.6	119	0.5	AD	1.1	3100	1.1	
$C_0 + 5L$	07671	MARSJJ	1.3	119	1.2	FI	1.2	1200	1.2	
C_1	07672	ALBEHA	1.2	210	3.0	SE	1.7	2100	1.5	
$C_1 + L$	07700	LONDAJ	*	220	1.3	AD	1.4	3000	1.4	
$C_1 + 2L$	07702	ANDEWF	*	119	1.4	FI	2.4	1000	2.4	
$C_1 + 3L$	07710	MARTCH	1.5	220	1.5	PL	1.6	1750	2.1	
$C_1 + 4L$	07715	FLINGA	3.3	119	1.6	AD	*	3000	3.8	
$C_1 + 5L$	07716	MERLCH	3.4	220	2.0	FO	2.0	2200	1.6	
$C_1 + 6L$	07740	JONE KB	3.0	119	1.7	PL	2.1	2200	2.0	
$C_1 + 7L$	07761	REDFBD	2.1	119	2.2	SE	3.0	2650	3.5	
C_2	07780	BLANJE	*	220	2.1	FO	*	2100	2.3	
$C_2 + L$	07805	ROPEES	*	220	2.3	PL	2.3	1900	3.2	
$C_2 + 2L$	07806	KALNTD	3.2	119	2.4	MA	3.1	2300	3.1	
$C_2 + 3L$	07515	EDWARS	*	220	3.2	PL	3.2	2040	3.0	
$C_2 + 4L$	07850	DALLJE	*	119	3.1	FI	3.6	1050	*	
C_3	07883	JONETW	3.8	210	3.5	SE	3.5	2010	3.6	
$C_3 + L$	07888	WEINSH	*	119	3.4	MA	3.4	2450	3.4	
$C_3 + 2L$	07889	KLEINM	*	220	3.3	PL	3.3	1830	3.3	
$C_3 + 3L$	07961	FREIHN	3.5	220	*	PL	3.7	1780	3.7	
$C_3 + 4L$	07970	MANKCA	*	119	3.7	MA	*	2410	*	
$C_3 + 5L$	07972	FIKETE	3.7	210	3.6	SE	3.8	2500	*	
$C_3 + 6L$	08000	SCHEDR	*	210	3.8	FI	*	2100	*	
$C_3 + 7L$	08001	FLANJE	*	119	*	PL	*	1920	*	
$C_3 + 8L$	08100	JOOSWE	*	210	*	SE	*	3150	*	

Figure 27.2 (continued)

A₁ Index				A₂ Index				A₃ Index				A₄ Index		
Name	Address of start of chain	Count		Department	Address of start of chain	Count		Skill code	Address of start of chain	Count		Salary	Address of start of chain	Count
A	1.0	2		119	0.1	4		AD	0.4	3		1000	0.5	3
B	2.0	1			1.4	4		FI	0.5	4		1750	0.0	4
D	2.4	1			2.4	4		FO	1.5	2			3.2	3
E	2.3	1		210	1.2	4		MA	2.2	3		2000	0.2	4
F	0.3	4			3.6	2		PL	0.0	4			2.0	4
	3.7	1		220	0.0	4			2.1	4		2250	2.2	3
G	0.1	1			1.5	4			3.7	1		2500	0.1	3
H	0.2	1			3.2	2		SE	0.1	4		3000	0.4	4
J	1.6	3							3.0	3				
K	2.2	2												
L	1.1	1												
M	0.0	4												
	3.4	1												
R	1.7	2												
S	0.4	2												
W	3.1	1												

Address	A₀ Man number	A₁ Name	Chain address	A₂ Department	Chain address	A₃ Skill code	Chain address	A₄ Salary	Chain address	Non-indexed details
C₀	07642	MARTJT	0.5	220	0.3	PL	0.3	1900	0.3	
C₀ + L	07643	GREEJW	*	119	0.4	SE	0.2	2700	1.7	
C₀ + 2L	07650	HALSPD	*	210	1.0	SE	1.0	2000	1.0	
C₀ + 3L	07668	FEINPE	1.4	220	1.1	PL	1.3	1950	1.3	
C₀ + 4L	07670	SCHAWE	3.6	119	0.5	AD	1.1	3100	1.1	
C₀ + 5L	07671	MARSJJ	1.3	119	1.2	FI	1.2	1200	1.2	
C₁	07672	ALBEHA	1.2	210	3.0	SE	1.7	2100	1.5	
C₁ + L	07700	LONDWJ	*	220	1.3	AD	1.4	3000	1.4	
C₁ + 2L	07702	ANDEWF	*	119	*	FI	2.4	1000	2.4	
C₁ + 3L	07710	MARTCH	1.5	220	*	PL	1.6	1750	2.1	
C₁ + 4L	07715	FLINGA	3.3	119	1.6	AD	*	3000	3.8	
C₁ + 5L	07716	MERLCH	*	220	2.0	FO	2.0	2200	1.6	
C₁ + 6L	07740	JONEKB	3.0	119	1.7	PL	*	2200	*	
C₁ + 7L	07761	REDFBB	2.1	119	2.2	SE	*	2650	3.5	
C₂	07780	BLANJE	*	220	2.1	FO	*	2100	2.3	
C₂ + L	07805	ROPEES	*	220	2.3	PL	2.3	1900	*	
C₂ + 2L	07806	KALNTD	3.2	119	*	MA	3.1	2300	3.1	
C₂ + 3L	07815	EDWARB	*	220	*	PL	3.2	2040	3.0	
C₂ + 4L	07850	DALLJE	*	119	3.1	FI	3.6	1050	*	
C₃	07883	JONETW	3.8	210	3.5	SE	3.5	2010	3.6	
C₃ + L	07888	WEINSH	*	119	3.4	MA	3.4	2450	3.4	
C₃ + 2L	07889	KLEINMA	*	220	3.3	PL	3.3	1830	3.3	
C₃ + 3L	07961	FREIHN	3.5	220	*	PL	*	1780	3.7	
C₃ + 4L	07970	MANKCA	*	119	3.7	MA	*	2410	*	
C₃ + 5L	07972	FIKETE	*	210	*	SE	3.8	2500	*	
C₃ + 6L	08000	SCHEDR	*	210	3.8	FI	*	2100	*	
C₃ + 7L	08001	FLANJE	*	119	*	PL	*	1920	*	
C₃ + 8L	08100	JOOSWE	*	210	*	SE	*	3150	*	

Figure 27.3 A multilist organization with controlled list length. This organization is similar to that in Fig. 27.2 except that no chain can be more than four items in length. Each entry in the index therefore has a variable number of chain addresses associated with it. The time to find a record from a secondary key is in many cases shorter than with the organization Fig. 27.2.

Name	Address of start of chain	Count
F	0.3	1
G	0.1	1
H	0.2	1
M	0.0	2
S	0.4	1
A	1.0	2
F	1.4	1
J	1.6	1
L	1.2	1
M	1.3	2
R	1.7	1
B	2.0	1
D	2.4	1
E	2.3	1
K	2.2	1
R	2.1	1
F	3.3	3
J	3.0	2
K	3.2	1
M	3.4	1
S	3.6	1
W	3.1	1

A_1 Index

Department	Address of start of chain	Count
119	0.1	3
	1.2	4
	2.2	2
	3.1	3
210	0.2	1
	1.0	1
	3.0	4
220	0.0	2
	1.1	3
	2.0	3
	3.2	2

A_2 Index

Skill	Address of start of chain	Count
AD	0.4	1
	1.1	2
FI	0.5	1
	1.2	1
	2.4	1
FO	1.5	1
	2.0	1
MA	2.2	1
	3.1	2
PL	0.0	2
	1.3	2
	2.1	2
	3.2	3
SE	0.1	2
	1.0	2
	3.0	3

A_3 Index

Salary	Address of start of chain	Count
1000	0.5	1
	1.2	1
	2.4	1
1750	0.0	2
	1.3	1
	2.1	1
	3.2	3
2000	0.2	1
	1.0	3
	2.0	2
	3.0	2
2250	2.2	1
	3.1	2
2500	0.1	1
	1.7	1
	3.5	1
3000	0.4	1
	1.1	2
	3.8	1

A_4 Index

	Address	A_0 Man number	A_1 Name	Chain address	A_2 Depart-ment	Chain address	A_3 Skill code	Chain address	A_4 Salary	Chain address	Non-indexed details
Cell 0	C_0	07642	MARTJT	0.5	220	0.3	PL	0.3	1900	0.3	
	$C_0 + L$	07643	GREEJW	*	119	0.4	SE	0.2	2700	*	
	$C_0 + 2L$	07650	HALSPD	*	210	*	SE	*	2000	*	
	$C_0 + 3L$	07668	FEINPE	,*	220	*	PL	*	1950	*	
	$C_0 + 4L$	07670	SCHAWE	*	119	0.5	AD	*	3100	*	
	$C_0 + 5L$	07671	MARSJJ	*	119	*	FI	*	1200	*	
Cell 1	C_1	07672	ALBEHA	1.2	210	1.7	SE	1.7	2100	1.5	
	$C_1 + L$	07700	LONDAJ	*	220	1.3	AD	1.4	3000	1.4	
	$C_1 + 2L$	07702	ANDEWF	*	119	1.4	FI	*	1000	*	
	$C_1 + 3L$	07710	MARTCH	1.5	220	1.5	PL	1.6	1750	*	
	$C_1 + 4L$	07715	FLINGA	*	119	1.6	AD	*	3000	*	
	$C_1 + 5L$	07716	MERLCH	*	220	*	FO	*	2200	1.6	
	$C_1 + 6L$	07740	JONEKB	*	119	1.7	PL	*	2200	*	
	$C_1 + 7L$	07761	REDFBB	*	119	*	SE	*	2650	*	
Cell 2	C_1	07780	BLANJE	*	220	2.1	FO	*	2100	2.3	
	$C_2 + L$	07805	ROPEES	*	220	2.3	PL	2.3	1900	*	
	$C_2 + 2L$	07806	KALNTD	*	119	2.4	MA	*	2300	*	
	$C_2 + 3L$	07815	EDWARB	*	220	*	PL	*	2040	*	
	$C_2 + 4L$	07850	DALLJE	*	119	*	FI	*	1050	*	
Cell 3	C_3	07883	JONETW	3.8	210	3.5	SE	3.5	2010	3.6	
	$C_3 + L$	07888	WEINSH	*	119	3.4	MA	3.4	2450	3.4	
	$C_3 + 2L$	07889	KLEINM	*	220	3.3	PL	3.3	1830	3.3	
	$C_3 + 3L$	07961	FREIHN	3.5	220	*	PL	3.7	1780	3.7	
	$C_3 + 4L$	07970	MANECA	*	119	3.7	MA	*	2410	*	
	$C_3 + 5L$	07972	FIKETE	3.7	210	3.6	SE	3.8	2500	*	
	$C_3 + 6L$	08000	SCHEDA	*	210	3.8	FI	*	2100	*	
	$C_3 + 7L$	08001	FLANJE	*	119	*	PL	*	1920	*	
	$C_3 + 8L$	08100	JOOSWE	*	210	*	SE	*	3150	*	

Figure 27.4 A multilist organization with cellular chains. This organization is similar to that in Fig. 27.3 except that the chain lengths are determined by hardware boundaries. (See Fig. 26.6.) No seek need be required when following a chain. If records in different cells can be read simultaneously, parallel searching of the chains is possible. To answer the query "List the names of all employees with a Skill Code MA who are in Department 210" an inspection of the Skill Code MA and Department 210 index entries shows that Cells 0, 1 and 2 do not contain such a combination. Only Cell 3 need be searched.

	A1 Index		A2 Index		A3 Index		A4 Index	
	Name	Address	Department	Address	Skill code	Address	Salary	Address
	ALBEHA	1.0	119	0.1	AD	0.4	1000	1.2
	ANDRWF	1.2		0.4		1.1	1050	2.4
	BLANJE	2.0		0.5		1.4	1200	0.5
	DALLJE	2.4		1.2	FI	0.5	1750	1.3
	EDWARB	2.3		1.4		1.2	1780	3.3
	FEINPE	0.3		1.6		2.4	1830	3.2
	FIKETE	3.5		1.7		3.6	1900	0.0
	FLANJE	3.7		2.2	FO	1.5		2.1
	FLINGA	1.4		2.4		2.0	1920	3.7
	FREIHN	3.3		3.1	MA	2.2	1950	0.3
	GREEJW	0.1		3.4		3.1	2000	3.0
	HALSPD	0.2		3.7		3.4	2010	3.0
	JONEKB	1.6	210	0.2	PL	0.0	2040	2.3
	JONETW	3.0		1.0		0.3	2100	1.0
	JOOSWE	3.8		3.0		1.3		2.0
	KALNTD	2.2		3.5		1.6		3.6
	KLEINM	3.2		3.6		2.1	2200	1.5
	LONDAJ	1.1		3.8		2.3		1.6
	MANKCA	3.4	220	0.0		3.2	2300	2.2
	MARSJJ	0.5		0.3		3.3	2410	3.4
	MARTCH	1.3		1.1		3.7	2450	3.1
	MARTJT	0.0		1.3	SE	0.1	2500	3.5
	MERLCH	1.5		1.5		0.2	2650	1.7
	REDFBB	1.7		2.0		1.0	2700	0.1
	ROPEES	2.1		2.1		1.7	3000	1.1
	SCHAWE	0.4		2.3		3.0		1.4
	SCHEDR	3.6		3.2		3.5	3100	0.4
	WEINSH	3.1		3.3		3.8	3150	3.8

Figure 27.5 An inverted list organization. The index contains an entry or set of entries for *each* key value. There are no chains in the data records, but the indices are substantially larger.

The complete name key is included in the name index rather than merely the initial letter that was in the indices of the previous examples. Similarly, the salary index contains the actual salaries rather than the salary ranges that were in the previous examples. The inclusion of the actual key rather than key ranges does not increase the number of entries in the inverted list, although it does increase the index size. It increases both the resolving power of the index and the number of inquiries that can be answered without going to the data records.

Address	A_0 Man number	A_1 Name	A_2 Department	A_3 Skill code	A_4 Salary	Non-indexed details
C_0	07642	MARTJT	220	PL	1900	
$C_0 + L$	07643	GREEJW	119	SE	2700	
$C_0 + 2L$	07650	HALSPD	210	SE	2000	
$C_0 + 3L$	07668	FEINPE	220	PL	1950	
$C_0 + 4L$	07670	SCHAWE	119	AD	3100	
$C_0 + 5L$	07671	MARSJJ	119	FI	1200	
C_1	07672	ALBEHA	210	SE	2100	
$C_1 + L$	07700	LONDAJ	220	AD	3000	
$C_1 + 2L$	07702	ANDEWF	119	FI	1000	
$C_1 + 3L$	07710	MARTCH	220	PL	1750	
$C_1 + 4L$	07715	FLINGA	119	AD	3000	
$C_1 + 5L$	07716	MERLCH	220	FO	2200	
$C_1 + 6L$	07760	JONEKB	119	PL	2200	
$C_1 + 7L$	07761	REDFBB	119	SE	2650	
C_2	07780	BLANJE	220	FO	2100	
$C_2 + L$	07805	ROPEES	220	PL	1900	
$C_2 + 2L$	07806	KALNTD	119	MA	2300	
$C_2 + 3L$	07815	EDWARB	220	PL	2040	
$C_2 + 4L$	07850	DALLJE	119	FI	1050	
C_3	07883	JONETW	210	SE	2010	
$C_3 + L$	07888	WEINSH	119	MA	2450	
$C_3 + 2L$	07889	KLEINM	220	PL	1830	
$C_3 + 3L$	07961	FREIHN	220	PL	1780	
$C_3 + 4L$	07970	MANKCA	119	MA	2410	
$C_3 + 5L$	07972	FIKETE	210	SE	2500	
$C_3 + 6L$	08000	SCHEDR	210	FI	2100	
$C_3 + 7L$	08001	FLANJE	119	PL	1920	
$C_3 + 8L$	08100	JOOSWE	210	SE	3150	

A1 index

	Name	Address
1	ALBEY. HA	1.0
2	ANDREWS. WF	1.2
3	BLANAGAN. JE	2.0
4	DALL. JED	2.4
5	EDWARDS. RB	2.3
6	FEINBURG. PE	0.3
7	FIKE. TE	3.5
8	FLANNEL. JE	3.7
9	FLINT. GA	1.4
10	FREIMAN. HN	3.3
11	GREENWOOD. JW	0.1
12	HALSEY. PD	0.2
13	JONES. KB	1.6
14	JONES. TW	3.0
15	JOOST. WE	3.8
16	KALNER. TD	2.2
17	KLEINROCK. NM	3.2
18	LONDON. AJC	1.1
19	MANKOVITZ.CA	3.4
20	MARSHAL. JJ	0.5
21	MARTIN. CHA	1.3
22	MARTIN. JT	0.0
23	MERLIN. CH	1.5
24	REDFERN. BB	1.7
25	ROPELY. ES	2.1
26	SCHARTZ. WE	0.4
27	SCHEAFER. DR	3.6
28	WEINBURG. SH	3.1

A_2 index

Department	No.
119	11
	26
	20
	2
	9
	13
	24
	16
	4
	28
	19
	8
210	12
	1
	14
	7
	27
	15
220	22
	6
	18
	21
	23
	3
	25
	5
	17
	10

A_3 index

Skill code	No.
AD	26
	18
	9
FI	20
	2
	4
	27
FO	23
	3
MA	16
	28
	19
PL	20
	6
	21
	13
	25
	5
	17
	10
	8
SE	11
	12
	1
	24
	14
	7
	15

A_4 index

Salary	No.
1000	2
1050	4
1200	20
1750	21
1780	10
1830	17
1900	22
	25
1920	8
1950	6
2000	12
2010	14
2040	5
2100	1
	3
	27
2200	23
	13
2300	16
2410	19
2450	28
2500	7
2650	24
2700	11
3000	18
	9
3100	26
3150	15

Address	A_0 Man number	A_1 Name	A_2 Department	A_3 Skill code	A_4 Salary	Non-indexed details
C_0	07642	MARTJT	220	PL	1900	
$C_0 + L$	07643	GREEJW	119	SE	2700	
$C_0 + 2L$	07650	HALSPD	210	SE	2000	
$C_0 + 3L$	07668	FEINPE	220	PL	1950	
$C_0 + 4L$	07670	SCHAWE	119	AD	3100	
$C_0 + 5L$	07671	MARSJJ	119	FI	1200	
C_1	07672	ALBEHA	210	SE	2100	
$C_1 + L$	07700	LONDAJ	220	AD	3000	
$C_1 + 2L$	07702	ANDEWF	119	FI	1000	
$C_1 + 3L$	07710	MARTCH	220	PL	1750	
$C_1 + 4L$	07715	FLINGA	119	AD	3000	
$C_1 + 5L$	07716	MARLCH	220	FO	2200	
$C_1 + 6L$	07760	JONEKB	119	PL	2200	
$C_1 + 7L$	07761	REDFBB	119	SE	2650	
C_2	07780	BLANJE	220	FO	2100	
$C_2 + L$	07805	ROPEES	220	PL	1900	
$C_2 + 2L$	07806	KALNDD	119	MA	2300	
$C_2 + 3L$	07815	EDWARB	220	PL	2040	
$C_2 + 4L$	07850	DALLJE	119	FI	1050	
C_3	07883	JONETW	210	SE	2010	
$C_3 + L$	07888	WEINSH	119	MA	2450	
$C_3 + 2L$	07889	KLEINM	220	PL	1830	
$C_3 + 3L$	07961	FREIHN	220	PL	1780	
$C_3 + 4L$	07970	MANKCA	110	MA	2410	
$C_3 + 5L$	07972	FIKETE	210	SE	2500	
$C_3 + 6L$	08000	SCHEDR	210	FI	2100	
$C_3 + 7L$	08001	FLANJE	119	PL	1920	
$C_3 + 8L$	08100	JOOSWE	210	SE	3150	

Figure 27.6 Inverted lists with indirect addressing. This organization is similar to that in Fig. 27.5 except that the A_2, A_3, and A_4 indices do not contain machine addresses, but an index serial number based upon the sequence of entries in the A_1 index. This has two advantages over the organization in Fig. 27.5. First, when the data files are reorganized and the physical addresses of the records are changed, the A_2, A_3, and A_4 indices need not be rewritten. Only the A_1 index must be changed.

Second, more questions can be answered using the indices *without going to the data files*. To enhance this property, the full name rather than a truncated key is included in the A_1 index. If the question is asked "What are the names of employees in Department 119 who earn $3,000 or more?" an inspection of the Department and Salary indices shows that employees with index numbers 9 and 26 are the ones required. The A_1 index gives their names: FLINT, G. A. and SCHWARTZ, W. E. The primary key A_0 could have been used instead of the index serial number, but the latter is shorter.

If the inquiry had asked for the records of the employees, the addresses of these records would have taken longer to find than with the index organization of Fig. 27.5.

Name	Bucket		Depart-ment	Bucket		Skill code	Bucket		Salary	Bucket
A	2		119	0		AD	1		1000	1
B	5			1			2			2
D	6			2			3			6
E	6			3		FI	1			0
F	1			4			2		1750	0
	3			5			6			1
	8			6			9			3
	9			7			3			5
G	0			9		FO	5			7
H	0		210	0			5			8
J	4			2		MA	7			9
	7			7			8		2000	0
	9			8			0			2
K	5			9		PL	1			3
	7		220	0			3			4
L	2			1			4			5
M	0			2			5			6
	1			3			6			7
	3			5			7			9
	8			6			8		2250	5
R	4			7			9			7
	5			8			0			8
S	1					SE	2		2500	0
	9						4			4
W	7						7			8
							8		3000	1
							9			2
										3
										9

	A₀	A₁	A₂	A₃	A₄	Non-indexed details
	Man number	Name	Depart-ment	Skill code	Salary	
Bucket 0	07642	MARTJT	220	PL	1900	
	07643	GREEJW	119	SE	2700	
	07650	HALSPD	210	SE	2000	
Bucket 1	07668	FEINPE	220	PL	1950	
	07670	SCHAWE	119	AD	3100	
	07671	MARSJJ	119	FI	1200	
Bucket 2	07672	ALBEHA	210	SE	2100	
	07700	LONDAJ	220	AD	3000	
	07702	ANDEWF	119	FI	1000	
Bucket 3	07710	MARTCH	220	PL	1750	
	07715	FLINGA	119	AD	3000	
	07716	MERLCH	220	FO	2200	
Bucket 4	07760	JONEKB	119	PL	2200	
	07761	REDFBB	119	SE	2650	
Bucket 5	07780	BLANJE	220	FO	2100	
	07805	ROPEES	220	PL	1900	
	07806	KALNTD	119	MA	2300	
Bucket 6	07815	EDWARB	220	PL	2040	
	07850	DALLJE	119	FI	1050	
Bucket 7	07883	JONETW	210	SE	2010	
	07888	WEINSH	119	MA	2450	
	07889	KLEINM	220	PL	1830	
Bucket 8	07961	FREIHN	220	PL	1780	
	07970	MANKCA	119	MA	2410	
	07972	FIKETE	210	SE	2500	
Bucket 9	08000	SCHEDR	210	FI	2100	
	08001	FLANJE	119	PL	1920	
	08100	JOOSWE	210	SE	3150	

Figure 27.7 A bucket-resolved inverted list organization. In an attempt to reduce the bulky indices of Fig. 27.5, bucket-resolved inverted lists may be used. In this illustration the bucket size is 3. Unfortunately, in this case only a few of the buckets contain more than one identical attribute value, so the savings is small. The saving would have been greater if larger buckets had been used. The bucket size could be made equal to the cell size—*cellular inverted lists*.

If the question is asked "What employees in Department 200, with a Skill Code FI, earn more than $2,250?" an inspection of the indices for Department, Skill Code, and Salary shows that Buckets 1 and 2 must be inspected.

Name	Bucket
A	7
B	2
D	7
E	0
F	3
	5
	6
	8
	5
G	5
H	1
J	4
	8
	9
K	3
	4
	6
L	0
M	1
	2
	7
	3
R	5
S	6
	8
W	4

Department	Bucket
119	2
	4
	5
	6
	8
210	1
	5
	8
	9
220	0
	3
	6
	7

Skill code	Bucket
AD	6
FI	2
	8
	7
FO	4
MA	1
	3
	7
	8
SE	1
	5
	9

Salary	Bucket
1000	2
1750	0
	3
	8
2000	1
	7
	8
2250	4
2500	5
3000	6
	9

	A_0 Man number	A_1 Name	A_2 Department	A_3 Skill code	A_4 Salary	Non-indexed details
Bucket 0	07642	MARTJT	220	PL	1900	
	07668	FEINPE	220	PL	1950	
	07710	MARTCH	220	PL	1750	
Bucket 1	07650	HALSPD	210	SE	2000	
	07672	ALBEHA	210	SE	2100	
	07970	MANKCA	210	SE	2010	
Bucket 2	07671	MARSJJ	119	FI	1200	
	07702	ANDEWF	119	FI	1000	
	07850	DALLJE	119	FI	1050	
Bucket 3	07805	ROPEES	220	PL	1900	
	07888	KLEINM	220	PL	1830	
	07961	FREIHN	220	PL	1780	
Bucket 4	07806	KALNTD	119	MA	2300	
	07883	JONETW	119	MA	2410	
	07888	WEINSH	119	MA	2450	
Bucket 5	07643	GREEJW	119	SE	2700	
	07761	REDFBB	119	SE	2650	
	07972	FIKETE	210	SE	2500	
Bucket 6	07670	SCHAWE	119	AD	3100	
	07715	FLINGA	119	AD	3000	
	07700	LONDAJ	220	AD	3000	
Bucket 7	07716	MERLCH	220	FO	2200	
	07780	BLANJE	220	FO	2100	
	07815	EDWARB	220	PL	2040	
Bucket 8	07760	JONEKB	119	PL	2200	
	08001	FLANJE	119	PL	1920	
	08000	SCHEDR	210	FI	2100	
Bucket 9	08100	JOOSWE	210	SE	3150	

Figure 27.8 A bucket-resolved inverted-list organization with the file sequenced so as to minimize the inverted-list lengths. The technique illustrated in Fig. 27.7 is improved by sorting the data records in such a way as to place records with similar sets of the A_2, A_3, and A_4 attributes in the same buckets. This sorting substantially reduces the sizes, and hence the search times, of the A_2, A_3, and A_4 indices. However, file maintenance is *much* more complicated, and because the records are no longer in sequence by prime key A_0, the primary index cannot be bucket-resolved. Because of the increased complexity of maintenance, sorting the files to reduce the size of secondary indices is a technique that is desirable only when the files are not updated on-line. The technique is used in library science application, for example. It is sometimes referred to as *automatic classification*.

	Bucket									
Attribute value	0	1	2	3	4	5	6	7	8	9
Name										
A	0	0	1	0	0	0	0	0	0	0
B	0	0	0	0	0	1	0	0	0	0
D	0	0	0	0	0	0	1	0	0	0
E	0	0	0	0	0	1	0	0	0	0
F	0	1	0	1	0	0	0	0	1	1
G	1	0	0	0	0	0	0	0	0	0
H	1	0	0	0	0	0	0	0	0	0
J	0	0	0	0	1	0	0	1	0	1
K	0	0	0	0	0	1	0	1	0	0
L	0	0	1	0	0	0	0	0	0	0
M	1	1	0	1	0	0	0	0	1	0
R	0	0	0	0	1	1	0	0	0	1
S	0	1	0	0	0	0	0	0	0	1
W	0	0	0	0	0	0	0	1	0	0
Department 119	1	1	1	1	1	1	1	1	0	1
210	1	0	1	0	0	0	0	1	1	1
220	1	1	1	1	0	1	1	1	1	0
Skill code AD	0	1	1	1	0	0	0	0	0	0
FI	0	1	1	0	0	0	1	0	0	1
FO	0	0	0	1	0	1	0	0	0	0
MA	0	0	0	0	0	1	0	1	1	0
PL	1	1	0	1	1	1	1	1	1	1
SE	1	0	1	0	1	0	0	1	1	1
Salary 1000	0	1	1	0	0	0	1	0	0	0
1750	1	1	0	1	0	1	0	1	1	1
2000	1	0	1	1	1	1	1	1	0	1
2250	0	0	0	0	0	1	0	1	1	0
2500	1	0	0	0	1	0	0	0	1	0
3000	0	1	1	1	0	0	0	0	0	1

Figure *27.9* A bucket-resolved inverted-list organization represented by bit strings. This organization is similar to that in Fig. 27.7 except that bit strings are used to indicate the contents of the buckets. In this illustration the use of bit strings results in more compact indices than those in Fig. 27.7. This is not always the case. Whether or not bit strings represent the most economical form of index depends upon the total number of buckets and the fractions of them which contain each secondary key (as illustrated by Fig. 18.9). If a bit string index is used, the technique used in Fig. 27.8 of sorting the data records into related sets gives no storage saving but does lessen the number of buckets that must be examined in answering a given query.

To answer the request "Find the records for employees in Department 210 with a Skill Code FI and a salary in the range of $1,750 to $2,000" an OR operation will be done on the bit strings for Salary $1,750, Department 210 and Skill Code FI. Only bucket 9 contains a 1 bit in each of these three rows of the matrix. The records in bucket 9 will therefore be inspected.

	A_0	A_1	A_2	A_3	A_4	Non-indexed details
	Man number	Name	Department	Skill code	Salary	
Bucket 0	07642	MARTJT	220	PL	1900	
	07643	GREEJW	119	SE	2700	
	07650	HALSPD	210	SE	2000	
Bucket 1	07668	FEINPE	220	PL	1950	
	07670	SCHAWE	119	AD	3100	
	07671	MARSJJ	119	FI	1200	
Bucket 2	07672	ALBEHA	210	SE	2100	
	07700	LONDAJ	220	AD	3000	
	07702	ANDEWF	119	FI	1000	
Bucket 3	07710	MARTCH	220	PL	1750	
	07715	FLINGA	119	AD	3000	
	07716	MERLCH	220	FO	2200	
Bucket 4	07760	JONEKB	119	PL	2200	
	07761	REDFBB	119	SE	2650	
Bucket 5	07780	BLANJE	220	FO	2100	
	07805	ROPEES	220	PL	1900	
	07806	KALNTD	119	MA	2300	
Bucket 6	07815	EDWARB	220	PL	2040	
	07850	DALLJE	119	FI	1050	
Bucket 7	07883	JONETW	210	SE	2010	
	07888	WEINSH	119	MA	2450	
	07889	KLEINM	220	PL	1830	
Bucket 8	07961	FREIHN	220	PL	1780	
	07970	MANKCA	119	MA	2410	
	07972	FIKETE	210	SE	2500	
Bucket 9	08000	SCHEDR	210	FI	2100	
	08001	FLANJE	119	PL	1920	
	08100	JOOSWE	210	SE	3150	

No.	Name	Department	Chain	Skill code	Chain	Salary	Chain	Address
1	ALBEHA	210	0	SE	0	2100	0	1.0
2	ANDREWF	119	0	FI	0	1000	0	1.2
3	BLANJE	220	0	FO	2	2100	0	2.0
4	DALLJE	119	0	FI	1	1050	1	2.4
5	EDWARB	220	0	PL	0	2040	1	2.3
6	FEINPE	220	0	PL	0	1950	0	0.3
7	FIKETE	210	1	SE	1	2500	1	3.5
8	FLANJE	119	0	PL	0	1920	1	3.7
9	FLINGA	119	1	AD	1	3000	1	1.4
10	FREIHN	220	1	PL	1	1780	1	3.3
11	GREEJW	119	1	SE	1	2700	2	0.1
12	HALSPD	210	1	SE	1	2000	1	0.2
13	JONEKB	119	1	PL	1	2200	1	1.6
14	JONETW	210	1	SE	1	2010	1	3.8
15	JOOSWE	210	2	SE	2	3150	1	3.8
16	KALNTD	119	1	MA	1	2300	1	2.2
17	KLEINM	220	1	PL	2	1830	2	3.2
18	LONDAJ	119	2	AD	2	3000	1	1.1
19	MANKCA	119	1	MA	2	2410	2	3.4
20	MARSJJ	119	2	FI	2	1200	*	0.5
21	MARTCH	220	2	PL	2	1750	2	1.3
22	MARTJT	220	2	PL	2	1900	2	0.0
23	MERLCH	220	2	FO	*	2200	2	.15
24	REDFBB	119	2	SE	*	2650	*	1.7
25	ROPEES	220	*	PL	*	1900	*	2.1
26	SCHAWE	119	2	AD	*	3100	*	0.4
27	SCHEDR	210	*	FI	*	2100	*	3.6
28	WEINSH	119	*	MA	*	2450	*	3.1

(Index record 0: rows 1–10; Index record 1: rows 11–20; Index record 2: rows 21–28)

Department	Index record in which chain starts
119	0
210	0
220	0

Skill code	Index record in which chain starts
AD	0
FI	0
FO	0
MA	1
PL	0
SE	0

Salary	Index record in which chain starts
1000	0
1750	0
2000	0
2250	1
2500	0
3000	0

Figure 27.10 An organization with secondary keys removed from the data into a chained index. In this organization the secondary key fields are removed from the data records and stored in the index. The total storage requirement is similar to that in Fig. 27.2, but the organization permits more queries to be answered without going to the data records. The chains are in the index where they can be followed much more quickly than if they were in the bulky data records. Maintenance activities are carried out in the index rather than in the data file.

The center portion of this figure can be regarded as a multiple-key data file itself, with pointers to a separate single-key data file. Its prime key is NAME and it is sequentially organized by that key. It is organized with chains, but it could equally well have been organized with any other multiple-key technique.

A disadvantage of the structure shown here is that if the pointers are accidentally damaged, it may not be possible to reassociate a data record and its secondary keys. For this reason the secondary keys may be stored in the data record also.

Address	A_0 Man number	Non-indexed details
C_0	07642	
$C_0 + L$	07643	
$C_0 + 2L$	07650	
$C_0 + 3L$	07668	
$C_0 + 4L$	07670	
$C_0 + 5L$	07671	
C_1	07672	
$C_1 + L$	07700	
$C_1 + 2L$	07702	
$C_1 + 3L$	07710	
$C_1 + 4L$	07715	
$C_1 + 5L$	07716	
$C_1 + 6L$	07740	
$C_1 + 7L$	07761	
C_2	07780	
$C_2 + L$	07805	
$C_2 + 2L$	07806	
$C_2 + 3L$	07815	
$C_2 + 4L$	07850	
C_3	07883	
$C_3 + L$	07888	
$C_3 + 2L$	07889	
$C_3 + 3L$	07961	
$C_3 + 4L$	07970	
$C_3 + 5L$	07972	
$C_3 + 6L$	08000	
$C_3 + 7L$	08001	
$C_3 + 8L$	08100	

Index to the index record file

Attribute value	Index record 0	1	2	3	4
119	1	1	1	1	1
210	1	1	1	0	1
220	1	1	1	1	1
AD	0	1	1	1	1
FI	1	0	0	1	1
FO	1	0	0	1	0
MA	0	0	1	1	1
PL	1	1	1	1	1
SE	1	1	1	1	0
1000	1	0	0	1	0
1750	1	1	1	1	1
2000	1	1	1	1	1
2250	0	0	1	1	1
2500	0	1	0	1	1
3000	0	1	1	0	1

Name	Index record
FE	0
H	1
L	2
RE	3
W	4

Index record file

	A_1 Name	A_2 Dept-ment	A_3 Skill code	A_4 Salary	A_0 Man number
Index record 0	ALBEHA	210	SE	2100	07672
	ANDEWF	119	FI	1000	07702
	BLANJE	220	FO	2100	07780
	DALLJE	119	FI	1050	07850
	EDWARB	220	PL	2040	07815
	FEINPE	220	PL	1950	07668
Index record 1	FIKETE	210	SE	2500	07972
	FLANJE	119	PL	1920	08001
	FLINGA	119	AD	3000	07715
	FREIHN	220	PL	1780	07961
	GREEJW	119	SE	2700	07643
	HALSPD	210	SE	2000	07650
Index record 2	JONEKB	119	PL	2200	07760
	JONETW	210	SE	2010	07883
	JOOSWE	210	SE	3150	08100
	KALNTD	119	MA	2300	07806
	KLEINM	220	PL	1830	07889
	LONDAJ	220	AD	3000	07700
Index record 3	MANKCA	119	MA	2410	07970
	MARSJJ	119	FI	1200	07671
	MARTCH	220	PL	1150	07710
	MARTJT	220	PL	1900	07642
	MERLCH	220	FO	2200	07716
	REDFBB	119	SE	2650	07761
Index record 4	ROPEES	220	PL	1900	07805
	SCHAWE	119	AD	3100	07670
	SCHEDR	210	FI	2100	08000
	WEINSH	119	MA	2450	07888

Address	A_0 Man number	Non-indexed details
C_0	07642	
$C_0 + L$	07643	
$C_0 + 2L$	07650	
$C_0 + 3L$	07668	
$C_0 + 4L$	07670	
$C_0 + 5L$	07671	
C_1	07672	
$C_1 + L$	07700	
$C_1 + 2L$	07702	
$C_1 + 3L$	07710	
$C_1 + 4L$	07715	
$C_1 + 5L$	07716	
$C_1 + 6L$	07740	
$C_1 + 7L$	07761	
C_2	07780	
$C_2 + L$	07805	
$C_2 + 2L$	07806	
$C_2 + 3L$	07815	
$C_2 + 4L$	07850	
C_3	07883	
$C_3 + L$	07888	
$C_3 + 2L$	07889	
$C_3 + 3L$	07961	
$C_3 + 4L$	07970	
$C_3 + 5L$	07972	
$C_3 + 6L$	08000	
$C_3 + 7L$	08001	
$C_3 + 8L$	08100	

Figure 27.11 Secondary keys removed from the data into an index file organized with cellular inverted lists. This organization is similar to the one in Fig. 27.10 except that instead of chains being used in the index file, cellular inverted lists in the form of a bit matrix are used. The "cells" now refer to index records which contain tuples of the keys which are employed.

The file in the center portion of the figure does not give the addresses of the main data records, as in Fig. 27.10. Instead it gives their primary keys, and the data records can then be found with any other addressing method. With such a method the main data records can remain untouched while maintenance activities take place in the relatively small index file. The index file may be sorted on faster and more expensive direct-access devices than the main data file.

The index record file could be sorted, just as the data record file was sorted in Fig. 27.8, to place tuples with similar groups of A_2, A_3, and A_4 keys in the same index record. This sort would lower the numbers of index records that must be read when answering queries relating to secondary keys. It would, however, necessitate a longer separate name index, and would complicate maintenance of the index record file.

The reader should consider the following five questions and with them reexamine the 10 organizations:

1. Which organizations of those shown would be most suitable for a fast-response real-time inquiry system for this file using disk storage?

2. Assume that 2 million bytes of solid-state memory with an access time of about 1 microsecond are available to buffer data-base operations. Directories can be paged from disks or other devices into this main memory. With this hardware, which organizations would be suitable for a fast-response system?

3. For each of the 10 organizations, consider how records might be added and deleted. Which organizations would tend to facilitate maintenance, and which would be bad for maintenance?

4. For each of the organizations, consider the effect of a pointer becoming damaged. What would have to be done to repair the pointer? How could the organization best be protected from the effects of pointer destruction?

5. Taking maintenance, pointer damage, and fast-response requirements into consideration, which organization would you prefer for a moderately volatile file?

BOOK STRUCTURE

The structures discussed in Chapters 24 to 28 can be represented by separating the data themselves from the structure representation. This is discussed in Chapter 28.

28 SEPARATING DATA AND RELATIONSHIPS

Most of the data bases installed today use physical structures in which the relationships between data are stored along with the data themselves. Pointers between records have been stored in the records. The combining of data items into data aggregates or records has been accomplished by making them physically contiguous. The relationships between data have been inherent in most traditional data structures.

An approach, which is becoming more important as data-base complexity grows, is to store the relationships between the data separately from the data, as shown in Fig. 28.1. The separation can be done at the segment level, i.e., relationships between segments are stored separately from those segments, or it can be done at the data-item level and relationships between data-item values can be stored separately from those values.

The major objectives of storing the relationships separately from the data are first to make possible faster data retrieval and second to provide more complete data independence.

In addition storage may be saved. Pointers in relationship files are generally shorter than pointers between data records, and if substantial *distributed free space* is used to accommodate insertions, the unoccupied space is in the relationship file, where it is much smaller than the equivalent space in the data records.

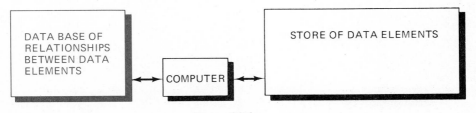

Figure 28.1

Relationships

No.	Name→Department	Name→Skill	Name→Salary	Name→Man number
1	2	6	13	7
2	1	2	1	9
3	3	3	13	15
4	1	2	2	19
5	3	5	12	18
6	3	5	9	4
7	2	6	18	25
8	1	5	8	27
9	1	1	21	11
10	3	5	5	23
11	1	6	20	2
12	2	6	10	3
13	1	5	14	13
14	2	6	11	20
15	2	6	23	28
16	1	4	15	17
17	3	5	6	22
18	3	1	21	8
19	1	4	16	24
20	1	2	3	6
21	3	5	4	10
22	3	5	7	1
23	3	3	14	12
24	1	6	19	14
25	3	5	7	16
26	1	1	22	5
27	2	2	13	26
28	1	4	17	21

Man number	Name
1	22
2	11
3	12
4	6
5	26
6	20
7	1
8	18
9	2
10	21
11	9
12	23
13	13
14	24
15	3
16	25
17	16
18	5
19	4
20	14
21	28
22	17
23	10
24	19
25	7
26	27
27	8
28	15

Department	Name
1	2
	4
	8
	9
	11
	13
	16
	19
	20
	24
	26
	28
2	1
	7
	12
	14
	15
	27
3	2
	5
	6
	10
	17
	18
	21
	22
	23
	25

Skill	Name
1	9
	18
	26
2	2
	4
	20
	27
3	3
	23
4	16
	19
	28
5	5
	6
	8
	10
	13
	17
	21
	22
	25
6	1
	7
	11
	12
	14
	15
	24

Salary	Name
1	2
2	4
3	20
4	21
5	10
6	17
7	22
	25
8	8
9	6
10	12
11	14
12	5
13	1
	3
	27
14	13
	23
15	16
16	19
17	28
18	7
19	24
20	11
21	9
	18
22	26
23	15

No.	Name
1	Albey. H A
2	Andrews. W F
3	Blanagan. J E
4	Dall. J E D
5	Edwards. R B
6	Feinburg. P E
7	Fike. T E
8	Flannel. J E
9	Flint. G A
10	Freiburg. H N
11	Greenwood. J W
12	Halsey. P D
13	Jones. K B
14	Jones. T W
15	Joost. W E
16	Kalner. T D
17	Kleinrock. NM
18	London. A J C
19	Mankowitz. C A
20	Marshal. J J
21	Martin. C H A
22	Martin. J T
23	Merlin. C H I
24	Redfern. B B
25	Ropely. E S
26	Schartz. W E
27	Scheaffer. D R
28	Weinburg. S H

No.	Department
1	119
2	210
3	220

No.	Skill
1	Administrator
2	Fitter
3	Foreman
4	Mason
5	Plumber
6	Secretary

No.	Salary
1	1000
2	1050
3	1200
4	1750
5	1780
6	1830
7	1900
8	1920
9	1950
10	2000
11	2010
12	2040
13	2100
14	2200
15	2300
16	2410
17	2450
18	2500
19	2650
20	2700
21	3000
22	3100
23	3150

No.	Man number	Non-indexed details
1	07642	
2	07643	
3	07650	
4	07668	
5	07670	
6	07671	
7	07672	
8	07700	
9	07702	
10	07710	
11	07715	
12	07716	
13	07760	
14	07761	
15	07780	
16	07805	
17	07806	
18	07815	
19	07850	
20	07883	
21	07888	
22	07889	
23	07961	
24	07970	
25	07972	
26	08000	
27	08001	
28	08100	

Figure 28.2 The file used in Chapter 27, with the data and the relationships between data stored separately.

SEPARATE STORAGE   Several of the illustrations in the book have shown
OF DATA-ITEM VALUES   relationships between records stored separately
from the records. They are separate in the inverted
list structures of Figs. 26.8 and 26.9 and Figs. 27.5 to 27.9.

Figure 28.2 takes the separation process a stage further, using the same
data as in the previous chapter. Each data-item *value* is stored only once and
is given a serial number, as shown on the right-hand side of Fig. 28.2. The
relationships are stored separately in terms of the serial numbers, as shown
on the left-hand side of Fig. 28.2. There are four inverted lists of binary
relations for the four secondary keys and a noninverted file of relations
sequenced by the prime key, MAN-NUMBER.

Storing the values separately saves storage space with those data-item
types for which multiple data items have the same value. In the illustration
there are only six SKILL values. The file contains many *secretaries*, but the
value SECRETARY is stored only once. In the relationship lists a SKILL
value in Fig. 28.2 could be referred to with 3 bits.

On the other hand, there is no duplication of names and initials, so
storing the NAME values separately gives no savings. On the contrary, it
takes extra space because the NAME values must each be given a serial
number. (With a large file of names there may be some saving if front-end
compression is used, as in Fig. 29.3).

Storing the values separately does, however, make the relationship lists
occupy as little storage as possible and thus can enhance the speed of
searching operations. A larger fraction of the list to be searched can be
contained on one *page* or can be made available for searching in main
memory.

RELATIONAL   The term *relational data base* is used to describe a
DATA BASE   data base composed of the two-dimensional "relations" discussed in Chapter 13—in other words, a
data base of normalized files. The redundancy between *key* data items that
can be seen in Figs. 13.2 and 13.3 is not replicated physically if the data-
item values are separate from the relations as in Fig. 28.2.

Even when the data-item values are not stored separately there is no
need to repeat data-item values such as EMPLOYEE- # in Fig. 13.2. A
pointer to the EMPLOYEE relation will suffice. In some prototype
implementations of relational data bases, such pointers are not *embedded*
with the data but are stored separately. Regardless of how the other data
items are stored the *key* data-item values may be stored separately, and files
of pointers to these values represent the key domains.

There is much to be said for storing the data in normalized (relational) files with no pointers in these files and storing the indices and domain dictionary in separate physical storage.

TREE AND PLEX STRUCTURES

When tree and plex structures are not normalized, the relationships between the records or data aggregates may still be stored separately from the data in a *directory*, as in Figs. 24.15, 24.16, 25.11, and 25.12. The advantages of separate tree and plex directories are

1. A lower level in the structure can be found without intermediate seeks between data records.
2. The pointers are generally smaller.
3. *Distributed free space* occupies less storage.

LARGE RECORDS AND LONG ACCESS TIME

The longer the seek time in *data* storage units and the longer the record read time, the greater is the case against having to follow pointers embedded in the data.

In some uses of data storage the records will be very long, and in some storage hardware the seek time will be very long. As storage units of 10^{11} or 10^{12} bits come into more widespread use both seek time and record size will tend to increase. Information retrieval systems will store text where they now store abstracts. Documents will be stored in digitized facsimile form so that key punching or manual data entry is not necessary and so that signatures, diagrams, and corporate logos can be stored. Storage of information in digitized facsimile form requires an order of magnitude more bits than when the information is in alphanumeric form, but as storage costs drop it will become economical because it bypasses manual input procedures.

In such cases it will be highly desirable that directories to the files be separate from the data storage and that seeks in the slow-access file be kept to minimum.

BINARY RELATIONS

Some designers of prototype data-base systems have advocated that all relations be stored in a binary form [1]. The inverted relations in Fig.

28.2 are binary, and the noninverted relations on the left of Fig. 28.2 are not. The noninverted relations could be replaced by four binary lists.

We showed in Chapter 13 how any data-base schema, no matter how complex, can be replaced by a set of two-dimensional files or relations. This laudable simplification is obtained at the expense of increased redundancy, at least in the *logical* data description. The decomposition of the data can be taken further by splitting it into binary relations. Redundancy in pointers, if not in data, is further increased, but the relations can be highly compact and can be searched rapidly.

Figure 28.3 shows the bill-of-materials file of Fig. 9.13 represented by data records and separate binary relations. The data records give the details of each product, subassembly, and part. The relations show first what items the product and subassemblies are composed of and, second, how many.

If any engineering change is now made to the products in Fig. 28.3, the change can be represented by additional data items and relationships without disturbing any existing items. Such a change is shown in Fig. 28.4. Item A has been redesigned and is replaced in new products by item A1, which contains 2 of item C, 9 of item H3, and 1 of item H4.

Any logical data base, no matter how complex, can be represented physically by named binary relations. The value of binary relations, however, is of value primarily in *interactive* query systems.

The advantages of using *binary* relation lists are

1. Each relation list is as compact as possible, and hence as much of it as possible can be brought into main memory at one time for searching. Searching the binary lists can be relatively fast.

2. The data base has a uniform structure. Only mechanisms for manipulating binary lists are needed.

3. The structure provides the maximum flexibility and the maximum data independence. New data-item types can be added without any change in what is already there. A data-item type can be included simply in any *logical* record, and hence the programmers have maximum freedom to change their use of logical records.

The disadvantages of going binary are

1. More storage is needed, although this disadvantage is partially offset by the applicability of data compression techniques to the lists. The relationship lists in Fig. 28.4, for example, yield effectively to compaction techniques (Chapter 32).

2. Several lists have to be searched to construct a logical record with several data items. Suppose that the record [MAN-NUMBER, NAME, DEPARTMENT, SKILL, SALARY] is needed. This can be derived more quickly from the organization in Fig. 28.2 than from an organization with binary relations.

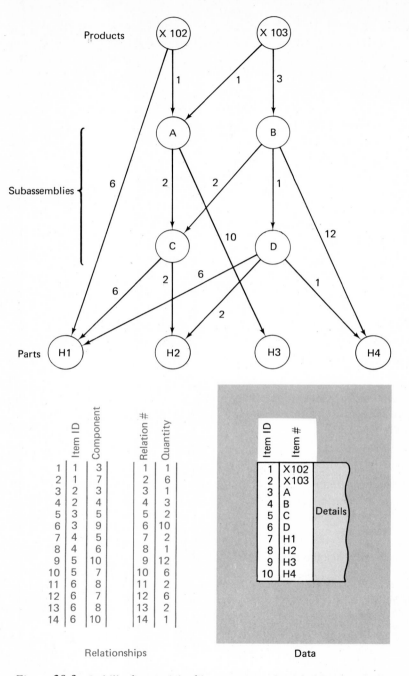

Figure 28.3 A bill-of-materials file represented with binary relation-ships and a separate data file.

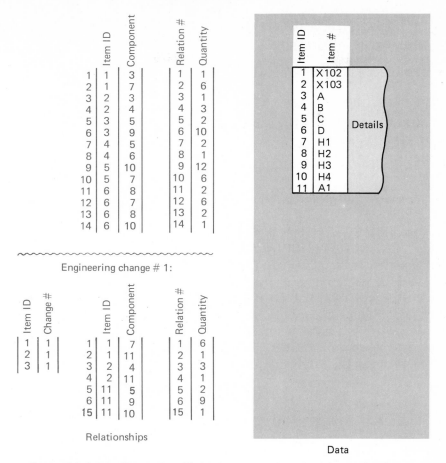

Figure 28.4 The file in Fig. 28.3 after an engineering change has been made.

Most systems to date using binary relations have been experimental in nature, and many owe their derivation to the ideas of Feldman and Rovner [1] implemented in ALGOL on the TX-2 at M.I.T. Lincoln Laboratories. Feldman and Rovner designed and implemented a language called LEAP which can handle binary relations.

A binary relation has the form $R(X, Y)$, where X and Y are two data items and R is the name of the relation between them. A meaningful segment of information is thus regarded as having three components, R, X, and Y. The grouping of the three components has been referred to as a *triad* [2,3]. The reader might think of the three components as two bubbles and the link between them on a bubble chart such as those in Chapters 6 and 15.

Consider the following relation from Fig. 13.2:

```
DEPARTMENT (DEPT-#, DEPT-NAME, REPORTS-TO,
MANAGER, BUDGET)
```

This relation can be split into the following four binary relations:

1. DEPT-NAME (DEPT #, NAME)
2. DEPT-REPORTS-TO (DEPT-#, EMPLOYEE-#)
3. DEPT-MANAGER (DEPT-#, EMPLOYEE-#)
4. DEPT-BUDGET (DEPT-#, BUDGET)

An instance of this group of binary relations can be represented by a list of triads.

    The splitting into triads is not quite so simple with the relation SALES (ITEM #, BRANCH-OFFICE- #, MONTH, QUANTITY). QUANTITY has no meaning unless it is related to ITEM-#, BRANCH-OFFICE, *and* MONTH. This could be achieved as in the bubble charts of Chapter 15 by making a concatenated key of ITEM-# + BRANCH-OFFICE-# + MONTH and treating it as one data item—one bubble.

    Alternatively a triad itself could be regarded as a data item and each instant of it given an identification number. The representation of the above relations then has the following schema:

```
TRIAD #:    SALES (ITEM-#, TRIAD-#)

TRIAD #:    SALES-BO (BRANCH-OFFICE-#, TRIAD-#)

TRIAD #:    SALES-MONTH (MONTH, QUANTITY)
```

An instance of this schema is as follows:

```
      103:    SALES (7182,902)

      902:    SALES-BO (7, 670)

      670:    SALES-MONTH (9, 2001)
```

The triad name would be replaced by a number:

```
      103:    1 (7182, 902)

      902:    2 (7, 670)

      607:    3 (9, 2001)
```

The triad names may be stored separately as follows:

```
1001:   4   (1,  SALES)

1002:   4   (2,  SALES-BO)

1003:   4   (3,  SALES-MONTH)

1004:   4   (4,  TRIAD-NAME)
```

To avoid having to read three triads, another method of representation would be to have different triad types for each branch office and month, as follows:

```
101:              SALES-IN-BRANCH-OFFICE-1-FOR-MONTH-1
                  (7182,  65)
    .                 .
    .                 .
    .                 .
193:              SALES-IN-BRANCH-OFFICE-7-FOR-MONTH-9
                  (7182,  200)
    .                 .
    .                 .
    .                 .
```

Again, the triad names would be replaced by numbers to provide a brief relation identifier:

```
101:              1       (7182,  65)
    .
    .
    .
193:              93      (7182,  200)
```

**TRIAD
QUERIES**
A triad thus consists of three data items *A*, *B*, and *C* and a triad identification number. Any of the three data items could be a relation identifier, and the other two are a pair of values related at one instant in that relation. Any data base, no matter how complex, could be represented as a collection of triads.

The data-base operations will be of the following forms:

A?? Find all *B* and *C* values of triads with a stated *A* value.

Test for the existence of triads with a stated *A* value.

AB? Find *C* values of triads with a stated *A* and *B* pair of values.

ABC Test for the existence of triads with stated *A*, *B*, and *C* values.

Create a triad.

Delete a triad.

Physical representation of triads will take somewhat more storage than physical representation of relations in third normal form. However, it provides an extremely flexible structure for the data base which must relate data items in multiple different ways and give fast responses to widely differing queries.

Triad representation can form an effective basis for the use of associative storage, as we will discuss in Chapter 36.

**BINARY AND
NONBINARY QUERIES**
On some interactive systems which are unrelated to their batch predecessors many of the queries concern binary relations or combinations of binary relations. For example, "Is a seat available on Flight 2?", "What commercial paper is giving the maximum interest rate?", or "Which salesman sold the most last month?" With such queries a binary relation could be searched to find a specific value or a maximum. A binary relation structure would be efficient.

On the other hand, other systems process queries which normally require the groups of data items stored together in records. A system may, for example, be designed to display purchase orders or utility bills or give all the facts about a certain customer. These queries would be more efficiently answered with appropriate *tuples* or groupings of related data items.

Some information systems (as opposed to operational systems) also handle queries which relate to groupings of data items. For example, "List all unemployed actresses between 18 and 21 with movie experience and talents for singing and sky-diving." If the data required to answer this query were stored in a binary fashion, the query would have to be processed as a combination of binary queries; i.e., find a person whose

$$
\begin{aligned}
\text{PROFESSION} &= \text{ACTRESS} \\
\text{JOB-STATUS} &= \text{UNEMPLOYED} \\
\text{AGE} &= \text{18 to 21} \\
\text{EXPERIENCE} &= \text{MOVIE-ACTING} \\
\text{SKILL} &= \text{SINGING} \\
\text{SKILL} &= \text{SKY-DIVING}
\end{aligned}
$$

Each of these (with the exception of SKILL = SKY-DIVING perhaps) would produce a lengthy list of names which would have to be merged. The search would probably be faster if the data about an individual were all stored together and a secondary index or multilist structure were used for searching. The attribute value producing the shortest list of related entities could be employed (SKILL = SKY-DIVING) and the records of sky-divers examined to see whether they were unemployed singing movie actresses of the requisite age.

While the use of binary relations can provide great flexibility, the maximum data independence, and fast-search capability for some queries, it is nevertheless likely that most data-base structures will benefit from the use of well-selected n-ary relations as well as binary relations.

REFERENCES

1. J. A. Feldman and P. D. Rovner, "An ALGOL-Based Associative Language," *Comm. ACM 12*, No. 8, Aug. 1969, 439–449.

2. A. J. Symonds, "Auxilary-Storage Associative Data Structure for PL/1," *IBM Systems J. 7*, Nos. 3 and 4, 1968, 229–245.

3. A. J. Symonds, "Use of Relational Programming to Manipulate a Structure in a Software Associative Memory," presented at 1969 ACM/SIAM/EEE Conference on Mathematical and Computer Aids to Design, Oct. 1969.

BOOK STRUCTURE

Chapter 29 discusses systems specially designed for multiple-key searches of data.

29 INDEX ORGANIZATION

We have mentioned in passing a variety of structures for primary indices, secondary indices, and directories giving relationships between records. In this chapter we will summarize the categories of index and directory and in Chapter 30 will review the techniques for searching them.

Most of the data-base organizations we have been discussing require large indices. Some require many indices because multiple keys in each record are indexed. On some systems, indeed, the total space occupied by the indices is larger than the space occupied by the data. It is important that the indices be organized as efficiently as possible. The designer will wish to minimize the space that they occupy and minimize the time needed to search them. As with the data files, they must be designed so that insertions and deletions can be handled and so that index maintenance is not excessively time-consuming.

TABLE LOOK-UP OPERATION
An index is a table on which we must perform a table look-up operation. The main problem is that it is often a very large table and we are concerned with the time taken to search it.

As with any table, the field we use for searching it is called the *argument*, and the field that we obtain from the table is called the *function*. An argument can have one or more functions associated with it. The reader might think of the index as being like a telephone directory. In a telephone directory the argument is the name of the person to be called, and the function is that person's telephone number.

FUNCTIONS   The output, or function, of a data-base index can take one of several forms:

1. Record Address

The most common form of index ultimately provides the machine address of the record that is sought. Several levels of index are often needed before the record address is found. The machine may have to examine a cylinder index and track index, for example, and then at a third level of index the record address is found (as in Fig. 20.7).

2. Relative Record Address

In some cases the index provides a relative address rather than an actual address. When this is done blocks of records can be moved without having to change all the index entries. This will become extremely important as *paging* in storage hierarchies becomes more common.

3. Symbolic Record Address

Where the index provides the locations of specific records it is in effect a table of *pointers*, and like all pointers these can be machine addresses, relative addresses, or symbolic addresses. *Secondary* indices and relationship directories sometimes use symbolic pointers in order to separate the secondary index structure from the physical record layout. Secondary index sets are sometimes very large, and it would be very time-consuming to rewrite them every time the file is reorganized. They may therefore provide the prime key of the record that is sought, and this will be used by whatever file-addressing method is employed to find the record (possibly a primary index). This use of symbolic addresses increases the time taken to find a record but greatly facilitates index *maintenance*. The latter may be an overriding consideration.

4. Bucket Location

Some indices do not point to a record but to a location which contains a number of records, as in Fig. 26.10. The location is sometimes referred to as a *bucket*. It may be a track, a VSAM *control interval*, or an area selected to be of suitable size for the indexing technique in question. When the bucket is accessed the records in it must be inspected to find the one required.

The term *resolution* is used to describe the number of records in the bucket an index refers to. An index which points to individual records is referred to as a *record-resolved* index. An index which points to buckets is referred to as a *bucket-resolved* index. A bucket-resolved index is usually much smaller than a record-resolved index and can be searched more quickly. A bucket-resolved index can be used only if records with the property that is indexed *can* be grouped together in buckets. A bucket-resolved primary index can be used when the data records are stored sequentially by prime key, for example, but not when they are stored in a random sequence.

As with record-resolved indices, the pointers provided by bucket-resolved indices can be machine addresses, relative addresses, or possibly symbolic pointers. A symbolic pointer for a bucket may be the prime key of the first record in the bucket.

5. Chain Address

Where chaining is used, as, for example, in Fig. 26.2, a secondary index may give the address of the head of the chain. It may also give a count of the number of items in the chain.

6. Attribute Values

Some secondary indices do not give addresses but, instead, give attribute values. This enables many questions involving secondary keys to be answered without going to the data records. An attribute value provided by a secondary index may, after additional indexing operations, be converted to a data record address. The index in some cases consists of tuples of keys, one of the keys being the prime key with which the data records can be found if needed in a further addressing operation. Figure 27.11 illustrates this technique.

In some systems the distinction between index records and data records becomes blurred. The index records contain data which may not be repeated in the data records.

7. Multiple Outputs

Each entry in a prime index provides a single pointer. Each entry in a secondary index or relationship directory may provide many pointers. They may point to records, buckets, or chain fragments. They may be machine addresses, relative addresses, symbolic addresses, or attribute values. Each entry in a relationship directory may provide multiple pointers to children or other relatives, as in Fig. 15.10.

A FINITE SET OF FUNCTIONS

Where an index entry can assume one of a finite set of values, it is often possible to save storage space by giving each of the entry values a binary number. The binary number is then stored in the index instead of the entry value. If there are N possible entry values, then the binary number has $\lceil \log_2 N \rceil$ bits, and this is often much smaller than the number of bits needed to store the value itself. A penalty of storing the entries in the form of binary numbers is that a further table inspection is needed to obtain the entry value. If N is small enough, the entry value table may be in main memory, or at least accessible by a paging operation.

MULTIFUNCTION INDICES

In some indices each argument can have many functions from a finite set of functions. It is desirable to minimize the number of bits needed to store these functions. As with all such data there are two possible ways to store them (indicated in Chapter 18). They may be stored as a string of values, possibly values reduced to binary numbers, or they may be stored as a bit matrix like that shown in Fig. 15.12. The second method will be preferable when $K \lceil \log_2 N \rceil > N$, where N is the number of possible function values and K is the mean number of function entries associated with one index argument. Figure 18.9 indicated the break-even points between these two methods.

ARGUMENT

The argument of a primary index or relationship directory is usually the prime key of a record. The argument of a secondary index is usually a secondary key.

In some cases a *combination* of attribute values form the argument. A unique record identifier may be a combination of values such as PASSEN-GER-NAME + FLIGHT-NUMBER + DATE. Fields which are *hierarchically* related may be used as the input, for example, DEPARTMENT-NUMBER and EMPLOYEE-NAME. A secondary index also may use a combination of attribute values as its input, for example JOB-CODE combinations or a combination of ITEM-TYPE and SIZE. When an index employs a combination of values as its argument the index is sometimes referred to as a *composite index*.

An index which has as its argument *all possible* values of a given key is referred to as a *dense index*. The secondary index is often dense, i.e., contains all possible values of the secondary key. A primary index need not be dense if the records are laid out in sequence of their prime keys; the index may point to a track or area of the file which must be scanned. In this case the index is referred to as a *sparse index*; all attribute values can be found by means of the index but are not physically present in the index.

In some secondary indices not all attribute values are indexed. Only certain *specific* ones can be found via the index. Such an index is sometimes referred to as a *marked index.*

Many indexed attributes have discrete values. Some, however, have a continuous spread of values. In the latter case the spread of values may be split for indexing purposes into divisions like the divisions on a ruler. This is called *quantizing* and reduces the number of index entries that are required.

The index argument may refer to a specific value; argument $= x$ or argument $\neq x$, or it may refer to a range of values, for example, argument $< x$, argument $\leqslant x$, argument $> x$, or argument $> x_1$ *and* $< x_2$. An index of this type is called a *range index.*

WHAT ATTRIBUTES SHOULD BE INDEXED?

When a multiple-key file is designed for answering a wide variety of spontaneous queries about the data it contains, the designer must ask, For which of the attributes should an index be established? It may be desirable to avoid indices which are too large. The designer may prefer to index an attribute with a small set of values so that its inverted list has a small number of entries. Unfortunately, attributes with a small set of values are generally not very selective. In a library, for example, the attribute value *fiction* might refer to half the books on the shelves and so an index on this value alone is of little help in the indexing process. Conversely, an attribute which would produce a small number of items per query is likely to have a large number of indexable values.

One way out of this dilemma is to *combine* attributes in the indexing, as indeed they would be combined in the search criteria. An index is sometimes established on two or more combined attribute values.

Figure 29.1 illustrates some of the useful index types.

KEY COMPRESSION

Because of the size of indices, especially secondary indices, techniques for compressing the index entries are important. Some indices can be com-

Keys:	A_0	A_1	A_2	A_3
L_0	P	1	8	M
L_1	Q	2	11	F
L_2	R	3	16	M
L_3	S	4	15	M
L_4	T	1	30	M
L_5	U	2	17	F
L_6	V	4	9	F
L_7	W	4	5	F
L_8	X	2	21	M
L_9	Y	4	14	F
L_{10}	Z	1	12	M

Record locations: (left labels for the table above)

The following are some of the types of index that may be used with this file:

1. A bucket-resolved prime-key index

(like ISAM or VSAM)

A_0	Bucket address
R	L_0
U	L_3
X	L_6
Z	L_9

This index is sparse

2. Key A_1 relative-address pointer-list index

A_1	Relative address
1	0, 4, 10
2	1, 5, 8
3	2
4	3, 6, 7, 9

This index is dense

3. Key A_1 symbolic pointer-list index

A_1	A_0
1	P, T, Z
2	Q, U, X
3	R
4	S, V, W, Y

4. Key A_1 bit-stream index

A_1	Relative address										
	0	1	2	3	4	5	6	7	8	9	10
1	1	0	0	0	1	0	0	0	0	0	1
2	0	1	0	0	0	1	0	0	1	0	0
3	0	0	1	0	0	0	0	0	0	0	0
4	0	0	0	1	0	0	1	1	0	1	0

5. Key A_2 bucket-resolved quantized bit-stream index

A_2	Relative bucket address			
	0	3	6	9
5	0	0	1	0
10	1	0	1	0
15	1	1	0	1
20	1	1	0	0
25	0	0	1	0
30	0	1	0	0

6. Key A_2 range index (Is $A_2 \leqslant x$?)

x	Address										
	L_0	L_1	L_2	L_3	L_4	L_5	L_6	L_7	L_8	L_9	L_{10}
5	0	0	0	0	0	0	0	1	0	0	0
10	1	0	0	0	0	0	1	1	0	0	0
15	1	1	0	1	0	0	1	1	0	1	1
20	1	1	1	1	0	1	1	1	0	1	1
25	1	1	1	1	0	1	1	1	1	1	1
30	1	1	1	1	1	1	1	1	1	1	1

7. Keys A_1 and A_3 composite index

A_1	A_3	Relative address
1	F	0, 4, 10
1	M	—
2	F	1, 5
2	M	8
3	F	
3	M	2
4	F	6, 7, 9
4	M	3

Figure 29.1

pressed by binary encoding. Some can be compressed by removing inessential parts of the keys.

Figure 29.2 shows a multiple-level index with the rear part of the keys truncated. The index entry for each bucket of data records contains as its argument the highest key in that bucket. All that is really necessary to locate a record are enough high-order characters to distinguish it from the next highest key in the next bucket. The data bucket which is at the bottom right-hand corner of the Fig. 29.2, contains as its highest key LIU JOE. This key value therefore appears in the index, and enough characters must be used to distinguish it from the next key, LIU KATE. The LIU JOE key in the lowest level of index is there truncated to LIU J.

Figure 29.3 shows the same index with the front end of the keys truncated also. LIU J follows LIU HI. The first four letters are the same, and so LIU J is shortened to 4J, the digit 4 meaning that the first four characters of the previous key are repeated. This technique is effective because the characters which did not yield to rear-end compression in Fig. 29.2 tend to yield to front-end compression in Fig. 29.3. For example, the string of LOCKWOOD'S in the lowest level of the index

LOCKWOOD

LOCKWOOD AR

LOCKWOOD ART

LOCKWOOD B

LOCKWOOD D

LOCKWOOD ED

LOCKWOOD F

LOCKWOOD M

LOCKWOOD MI

LOCKWOOD P

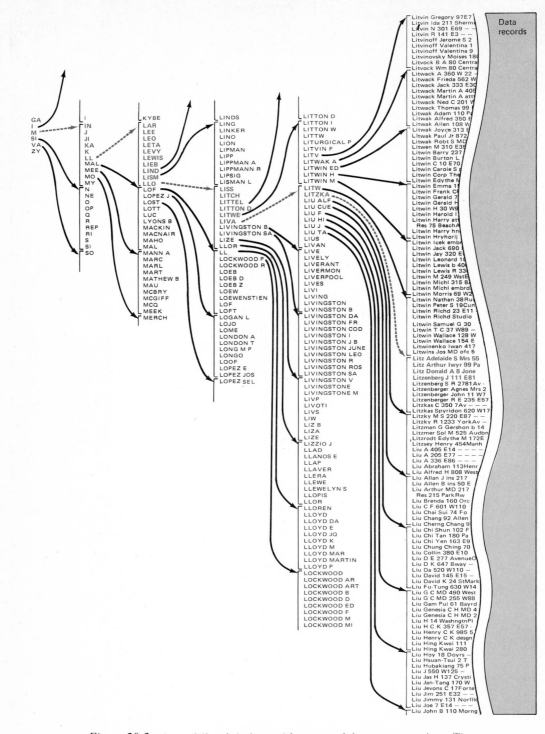

Figure 29.2 A multilevel index with rear-end key compression. The shaded path shows the items inspected when searching for the index entry LITZENBERG J.

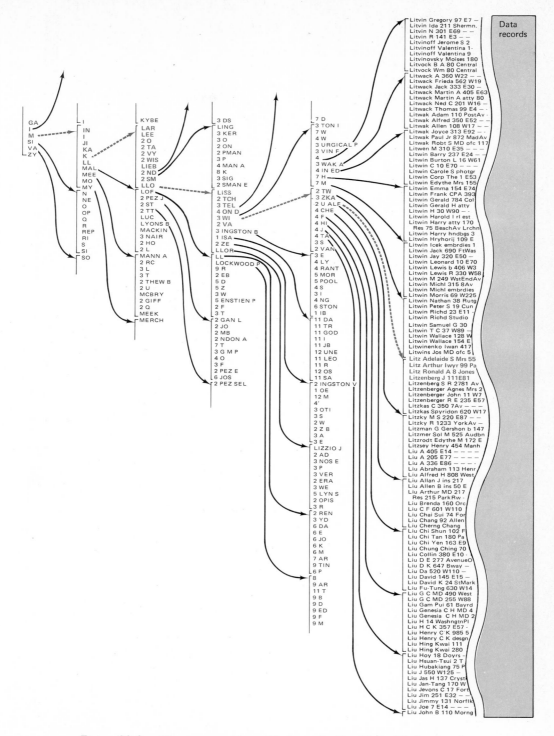

Figure 29.3   The same portion of index as in Fig. 29.2 with front-end key compression as well as rear-end key compression. The red path shows the items inspected when searching for the index entry LITZENBERG J.

become

LOCKWOOD

9AR

11T

9B

9D

9ED

9F

9M

10I

9P

To find the data record for LITZENBERG J the path shown red is followed. The top (leftmost) segment of the index is scanned from the top down until an entry higher in alphabetical sequence than LITZENBERG J is found. This is the entry M. The block the entry M points to is scanned from the top down until an entry higher than LITZENBERG J is found. This is LL. The next block yields LLO on a top-down search. When the next block is scanned, the entries

LISS

2TCH

3TEL

4ON D

3WI

2VA

are converted to

LISS

LITCH

LITTEL

LITTON D

LITWI

LIVA

The LIVA entry points to a block which begins 2TW, which is converted to LITW. The next entry in this block is 3ZKA, which is converted to LITZKA. LITZKA is higher than LITZENBERG J, and so the LITZKA pointer is followed, and the bucket it points to contains the required record.

PARSING   Still further compression can be obtained with a technique called *parsing*. With parsing, the highest level of index contains a portion of the key. The next level of index contains the following character or characters but *does not repeat those which were in the higher index*. Figure 29.4 illustrates parsing. The top three levels of index contain one-letter entries—the first three letters of the keys, respectively. The fourth level of index does not repeat these three letters.

The fact that the top three levels of index in Fig. 29.4 have one-character entries makes them easier to construct than those with variable-length entries in Figs. 29.2 and 29.3. No facility is needed for indicating where the entries begin and end. The fourth level of index in Fig. 29.4 could have been made fixed-length also if the data record buckets that it points to had been made of variable capacity. The disadvantage of the technique in Fig. 29.4 is that some of the index blocks will contain substantially more entries than the 10-entry blocks of Fig. 29.3. The blocks in the first three levels of index can, however, be binary-searched, whereas they could not in Fig. 29.3. The fourth level would also be binary-searchable if fixed-length entries were used. It may pay to add an extra level of index also containing one-letter entries between the third and fourth levels of Fig. 29.4.

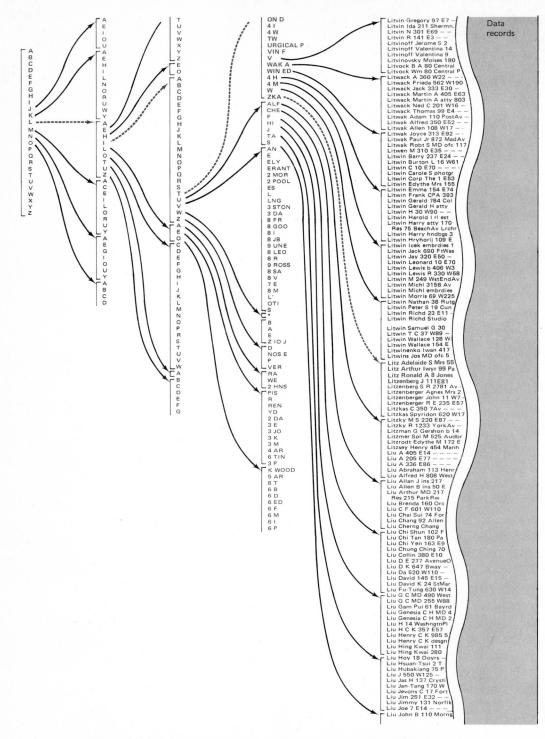

Figure 29.4 The same portion of the index as in Fig. 29.3, but now using a *parsing* technique to achieve further index compression.

Box 29.1 Summary of Index Categories

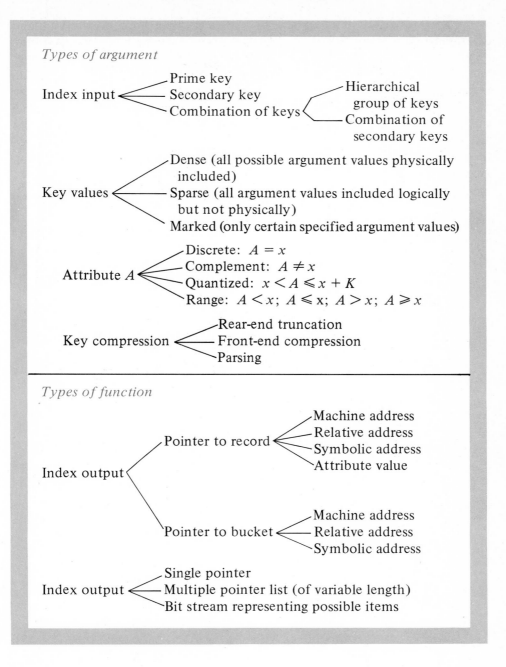

Types of argument

Index input
- Prime key
- Secondary key
- Combination of keys
  - Hierarchical group of keys
  - Combination of secondary keys

Key values
- Dense (all possible argument values physically included)
- Sparse (all argument values included logically but not physically)
- Marked (only certain specified argument values)

Attribute A
- Discrete: $A = x$
- Complement: $A \neq x$
- Quantized: $x < A \leqslant x + K$
- Range: $A < x$; $A \leqslant x$; $A > x$; $A \geqslant x$

Key compression
- Rear-end truncation
- Front-end compression
- Parsing

Types of function

Index output
- Pointer to record
  - Machine address
  - Relative address
  - Symbolic address
  - Attribute value
- Pointer to bucket
  - Machine address
  - Relative address
  - Symbolic address

Index output
- Single pointer
- Multiple pointer list (of variable length)
- Bit stream representing possible items

In any index it is necessary to have a mechanism for insertions and deletions (we will discuss this in Chapter 30). A further advantage of the index in Fig. 29.4 is that the file can be highly volatile with many names being added and deleted, and yet there can be very little change to the top three levels of index. The reader can observe this property by taking new names from a telephone directory and adding them to the portion of the file shown. If no index entries are ever deleted from the top three levels, these levels do not increase in size very much from that shown in Fig. 29.4, and they eventually become completely nonvolatile. The insertion and deletion mechanisms concentrate on the fourth level of index.

SUMMARY   Box 29.1 summarizes the categories of index types.

BOOK STRUCTURE

Chapters 30 and 31 discuss indices and means of searching them. Such indices are needed to implement the techniques of Chapters 20, 26, 27 and 29.

30 INDEX-SEARCHING TECHNIQUES

A data-base index is itself a data file, and we have to tackle the problem of organizing it much as we would any other data file. The difference is that it is a simple data file, and we have more control over it. There is far more scope for compaction and optimization techniques than with the main data files. As with the main data files it must be organized so that additions and deletions can be handled and so that maintenance is not excessively time-consuming.

A major problem with the main data files is the addressing problem—how to find out where a record is located. We may use an index to solve that problem, but then we have the same problem on a smaller scale with the index itself. *How do we find a specified item in the index with suitable speed?*

The computer may have to read many items in the index before it finds the one that is needed, just as you read many entries in a telephone directory before you find the number you are searching for. We will refer to the reading of one item as a *probe* and will estimate how many probes will occur, on average, when searching an index. The mean number of probes needed for different index techniques is shown in Fig. 30.6. The calculations that produced those curves assume that all items have an equal probability of being searched for.

Let N_I be the number of entries in the index and N_P be the number of probes when searching it.

One indication of the efficiency of the index-searching method is the ratio of the mean number of probes needed to the number of entries in the index, $E(N_P)/N_I$. This is by no means a complete measure of the search efficiency, however, because different probes require different amounts of time, and this difference in time will depend on the hardware that is employed. Some probes need a new seek, some need a track reading without a seek, and some merely require a further reference to data already in main memory.

To locate an item in the index, any of the addressing techniques used in Chapter 19 can be employed. The following pages review these techniques.

INDEX-SEARCHING TECHNIQUES

Technique 1: Scanning the Index

The arguments in the index can be examined sequentially until the required argument is found. There are usually far too many items for this to be a good technique for the index as a whole. Assuming that all items have an equal probability of being searched for, the mean number of probes is $E(N_P) = (N_I + 1)/2$.

Technique 2: A Block Search

Rather than scan an entire index, the index may be subdivided into blocks and block-searched in a fashion similar to the file block search that was illustrated in Fig. 19.1. The search may start at the block with the lowest arguments. The higher argument in each block is examined. If it is too low, the search passes on to the next block.

The size of block which gives the minimum number of probes is a block holding $\sqrt{N_I}$ items, where a total of N_I items are to be searched. (The calculation of optimum block size given in Chapter 19, Box 19.1, applies.)

Suppose that each block contains $\lceil \sqrt{N_I} \rceil$ items. The number of blocks is then $\lceil N_I / \lceil \sqrt{N_I} \rceil \rceil$.

Assuming again that all items are equally likely to be searched for, the mean number of probes needed to find the requisite block is $\lceil N_I / \lceil \sqrt{N_I} \rceil \rceil / 2$.

When the requisite block has been identified by inspecting the highest item in it, the other items will be scanned and the mean number of probes required for this scan is $(\lceil \sqrt{N_I} \rceil + 1) / 2 - 1$.

The mean number of probes in total is then

$$E(N_P) = \frac{\lceil N_I / \lceil \sqrt{N_I} \rceil \rceil + 1}{2} + \frac{\lceil \sqrt{N_I} \rceil + 1}{2} - 1$$

$$= \frac{\lceil N_I / \lceil \sqrt{N_I} \rceil \rceil + \lceil \sqrt{N_I} \rceil}{2} \qquad (30.1)$$

$$\simeq \sqrt{N_I}$$

A block search is rarely applied to an entire index, but it is an important technique for searching a portion of an index. A portion of an index may occupy one track of a file unit, for example; it is read into core and block-searched.

Technique 3: A Binary Search

Figure 19.2 illustrated a binary search of a data file. An index can be binary-searched in a similar fashion. The mean number of probes approximates to $\log_2 N_I - 1$ when N_I is large. (See Appendix A.) This is a substantially smaller number of probes than that for a serial scan or block search. The larger the index, the greater is the saving of probes that results from a binary search.

If all probes took an equal time, a binary search would be more efficient than a block search or searching a tree-structured index. Unfortunately, many of the indices that need searching cannot be held entirely in main memory; they are held on electromechanical files. The entries probed in a binary search are some distance apart, and where a mechanical *seek* is needed between one probe and the next, binary searching is a poor technique because it results in the access mechanism being moved repeatedly backward and forward.

We can find a better method than binary searching for an index on electromechanical files. However, a final or interim stage of many search techniques is to search a block of entries sufficiently small to be contained in main memory, and for this a binary search may be the best. Figure 30.1 compares the mean number of probes needed with a serial scan, a block search, and a binary search.

The binary searching of sequenced items has two other disadvantages besides the darting backward and forward that can incur a high penalty in seek time. Most index compaction techniques cannot be used when a binary search is employed. They delete part of the key that is needed for binary searching, as can be seen in Fig. 29.3. Compaction is valuable in the storage of most indices. The designer of the index techniques is faced with a choice between compaction and the binary searching of index blocks in main memory. In most cases the choice has been in favor of compaction.

The other disadvantage is the difficulty of deleting and inserting items. When new items are added this must be done in such a way that the entire block is still in sequence. In other words, the items in the block must be moved whenever new items are added. This operation can be avoided if a binary tree search is used.

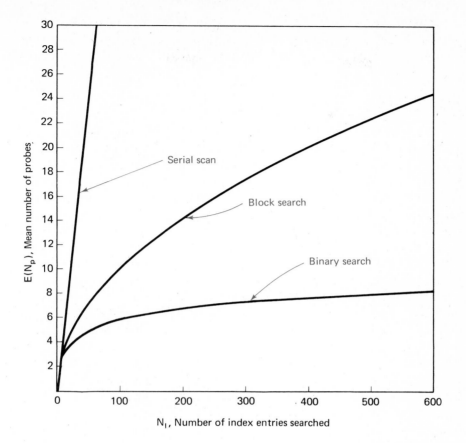

Figure 30.1 The number of probes needed to locate an item in a single-level index or table, using a serial scan, a block search, and a binary search. The calculation, as with the other curves in this chapter, assumes that any two index entries are equally likely to be searched for.

Technique 4: A Binary Tree Search

If the items to be searched are arranged in the form of a binary tree linked with pointers, it is possible to add new items without always having to shuffle the existing ones. Figure 30.2 illustrates this. It shows a block which can hold 16 items, and each item can have two short pointers to another location in the block. In the first illustration the block contains 12 items. The first item is not the first in sequence, A, but that item at which a binary

1. Initially the block contains these twelve entries:

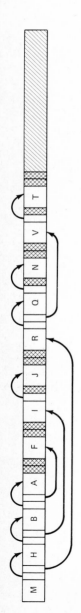

2. Entry K is added:

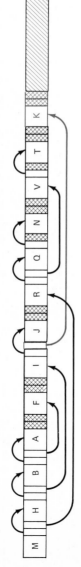

3. Entry L is added, and N is removed:

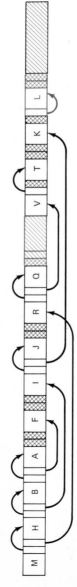

4. Entry D, then G, are added, and M is deleted:

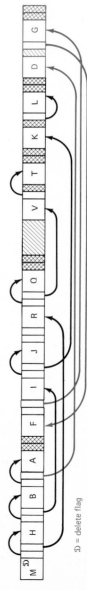

ⅅ = delete flag

5. The block is now full. If another entry is added the block will be reorganized.
If yet another entry is added without one being deleted the block must be split.

Figure 30.2 A block of index entries organized in the form of a binary tree. Characteristics: fast searching, easy addition of new items, and space taken up with pointers.

search would begin, *M*. The second two items are those which would be probed second with a binary search and so forth. Instead of having to calculate which item to probe next, the decision is made by inspecting one of two pointers appended to each item, one for the next item to probe lower in sequence and the other for the next item to probe higher in sequence. The pointers are followed until the required item is located. The mean number of probes is the same as with a conventional binary search.

The items are laid out in a sequence sometimes referred to as a *preorder traversal* of the binary tree. This traversal requires three steps:

1. Store the root of the tree.
2. Traverse the root's left subtree in preorder traversal sequence.
3. Traverse the root's right subtree in preorder traversal sequence.

There is a variety of sequences in which the binary tree can be laid out. The advantage of this one is that pointers to items lower in the sequence point to the *next* item. *H* is next to *M*, *B* is next to *H*, and so forth. Consequently, these pointers can be represented with 1 bit. The higher-in-sequence pointers can point to any position, and in the 16-entry block of Fig. 30.2 they would require 4 bits.

The second illustration in Fig. 30.2 shows a new item, *K*, being added. It is added at the end and luckily fits into an empty slot in the binary tree.

The third illustration shows item *L* being added and *N* removed. *L* cannot fit into an empty slot in the tree, and so a new level in the tree is created for it (right-hand diagram). It is again added at the end of the other items with no need to change the other items except to add a pointer from *K* to *L*.

The fourth illustration shows two more items added, *D* and then *G*. A further level is added to the tree. Item *M* is deleted but cannot be removed because its pointers are still needed to find the other items. Instead, it is flagged to indicate deletion. If item *D* were added below item *F* in the tree, a lower-in-sequence pointer would be needed which would span part of the block and hence be longer than 1 bit. To retain the use of 1-bit lower-in-sequence pointers, item *D* is switched in its tree position with item *F*.

The block is now full. If other items are added, the block will be reorganized and possibly split. Block splitting may be accommodated by *overflow pointers* or *distributed free space*, as before.

One-bit pointers can be used only if the items are of fixed length. If the items are of fixed length, compaction like that in Fig. 29.3 cannot be used within the block. With variable-length items, some measure of front-end compaction can be employed because an entry need not repeat the front characters which are identical to those of the entry which pointed to it.

If many items are added to and deleted from a binary tree, the time taken to search it increases. If this volatility continues indefinitely and in a random fashion, the mean number of probes needed to search the tree will be $1.386 \log_2 N$ where N is the number of items in the tree.

Whenever the tree is reorganized the search time will drop to that given in Appendix A (Fig. A.1), which approximates to $\log_2 N - 1$ probes when N is large.

The disadvantage of binary tree searching is the extra space needed for pointers in each entry and also the absence of a lower degree of compaction. Where index space is a primary consideration a block search is usually preferable, using parsing as used in Fig. 29.4. Binary tree searching is also disadvantageous when the items are commonly required in key sequence.

Technique 5:   A Balanced Tree Index with a Serial Scan of the Nodes

Most indices are constructed with more than one level, in the form of a tree. Figure 30.3 shows a tree index of three levels. It is a balanced tree (Fig. 8.3), and it is full; i.e., all the nodes and entries are in use. The highest-level node is searched first and points to the next-level node. This level node is searched and points to the lowest-level node.

The search of each node can be made by any of the four previous techniques—a scan, a block search, a binary search or a binary tree search.

A tree index like that in Fig. 30.3 occupies more space than a single-level index because the highest (or lowest) key of each node is repeated at the next highest node. It can be searched with fewer probes than most nontree indices—or, more important, with fewer seeks. It is desirable to select the optimum number of levels and the optimum number of entries per node.

Let there be N_B index entries per node and L levels. The lowest level of the index, level 1, will require $\lceil N_I / N_B \rceil$ nodes. Level 2 of the index will contain one entry for each node in level 1 and hence will require $\lceil \lceil N_I / N_B \rceil / N_B \rceil = \lceil N_I / N_B^2 \rceil$ nodes. Level 3 will require $\lceil \lceil N_I / N_B^2 \rceil / N_B \rceil = \lceil N_I / N_B^3 \rceil$ nodes. In general, level j will require $\lceil N_I / N_B^j \rceil$ nodes.

The top level of the index, level L, will contain only one node. Therefore,

$$\left\lceil \frac{N_I}{N_B{}^L} \right\rceil = 1$$

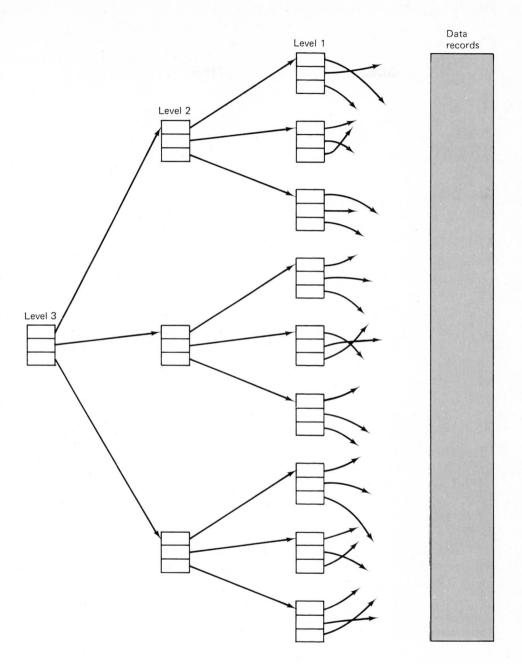

Figure 30.3 A full balanced tree index. The nodes may be scanned, block-searched, or binary-searched.

For the number of levels L

$$L = \lceil \log_{N_B} N_I \rceil$$

$$= \left\lceil \frac{\log_2 N_I}{\log_2 N_B} \right\rceil \tag{30.2}$$

The total number of index entries will be

$$N_B \sum_{j=1}^{L} \left\lceil \frac{N_I}{N_B^{\,j}} \right\rceil = \sum_{j=1}^{\lceil \log_{N_B} N_I \rceil} \left\lceil \frac{N_I}{N_B^{\,(j-1)}} \right\rceil \tag{30.3}$$

To serially scan each node requires an average of $(N_B + 1) / 2$ probes. The mean number of probes in searching the entire index is therefore

$$E(N_P) = L \, \frac{N_B + 1}{2}$$

$$= \left\lceil \frac{\log_2 N_I}{\log_2 N_B} \right\rceil \frac{N_B + 1}{2} \tag{30.4}$$

This equation can be used to calculate the index node size which results in the minimum number of probes. Figure 30.4 shows the result of this calculation.

From equation (30.4),

$$\frac{E(N_P)}{\log_2 N_I} \simeq \frac{N_B + 1}{2 \log_2 N_B}$$

The ratio $E(N_P) / \log_2 N_I$ has been plotted against N_B in Fig. 30.4. It will be seen that to minimize $E(N_P) / \log_2 N_I$ the number of entries per block should be small.

Technique 6: A Balanced Tree Index with a Block-Search of the Nodes

It is better to block-search the nodes of an index than to scan them. The node is divided into blocks of $\lceil \sqrt{N_B} \rceil$ items, and as with technique 2 the mean number of probes per node is

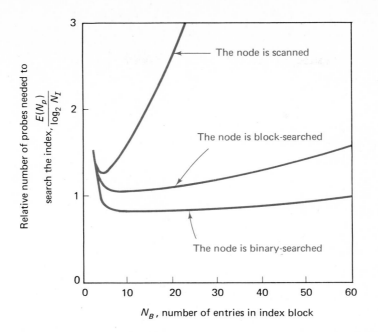

Figure 30.4 An indication of the effect of index block size on the number of probes needed to search the three types of tree index. Small blocks are preferable.

$$\frac{\left\lceil \dfrac{N_B}{\lceil \sqrt{N_B} \rceil} \right\rceil + \lceil \sqrt{N_B} \rceil}{2}$$

The mean number of probes for searching the entire index is therefore

$$E(N_P) = \frac{L}{2}\left(\left\lceil \frac{N_B}{\lceil \sqrt{N_B} \rceil} \right\rceil + \lceil \sqrt{N_B} \rceil \right)$$

As in Eq. (30.2),

$$L = \left\lceil \frac{\log_2 N_I}{\log_2 N_B} \right\rceil$$

Therefore,

$$E(N_P) = \frac{1}{2}\left\lceil \frac{\log_2 N_I}{\log_2 N_B} \right\rceil \left(\left\lceil \frac{N_B}{\lceil \sqrt{N_B} \rceil} \right\rceil + \lceil \sqrt{N_B} \rceil \right) \tag{30.5}$$

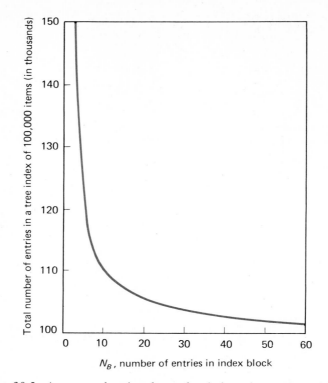

Figure 30.5 A curve showing how the index size varies with the number of entries per index block. Compare with Fig. 30.4.

This equation, as before, can be used to calculate the index block size which results in the minimum number of probes. Figure 30.4 shows the result of this calculation also. Again a fairly small block size is desirable.

On the other hand, the smaller the block size, the greater the total number of index entries. Figure 30.5 plots Eq. (30.3) for an index to 100,000 items. Comparing Fig. 30.5 with the curve for a block search in Fig. 30.4, it might be concluded that a block size of 20 to 30 items gives a reasonable compromise between saving index space and minimizing the number of probes. This is much smaller than the number of index entries that can be stored on a typical disk track. A disk track or other hardware subdivision should therefore contain more than one block of a tree index.

In reality the number of entries per block may be tailored to fit the hardware that is used. One higher-level block may, for example, point to all the index blocks that are stored on a track. An index on each cylinder is often used to point to each track on a cylinder. A *hardware-independent* storage organization, on the other hand, such as that shown in Fig. 20.4, may use the values suggested by the above equations.

Technique 7: A Balanced Tree Index with a Binary Search of the Nodes

One of the objections to a binary search is that time-consuming seeks may be required in the early stages of the search if the index is on an electromechanical file. Most of the seeks can be avoided if a tree index is used as in Fig. 30.3 and the nodes of the tree are binary-searched in main memory.

Suppose, again, that the tree has L levels, and that the nodes contain N_B items. As before,

$$L = \left\lceil \frac{\log_2 N_I}{\log_2 N_B} \right\rceil \tag{30.2}$$

The number of probes needed to binary-search a block is given in Appendix A [Eq. (A.1)] as

$$\sum_{j=1}^{\lfloor \log_2 N_I \rfloor} j \frac{2^{(j-1)}}{N_I} + \left(\lfloor \log_2 N_I \rfloor + 1 \right) \left(1 - \sum_{j=1}^{\lfloor \log_2 N_I \rfloor} \frac{2^{(j-1)}}{N_I} \right)$$

(We need to be more accurate than the approximation $\log_2 N_B - 1$.)

The mean number of probes needed to search the index is therefore

$$E(N_P) = \left\lceil \frac{\log_2 N_I}{\log_2 N_B} \right\rceil \left\{ \sum_{j=1}^{\lfloor \log_2 N_I \rfloor} j \frac{2^{(j-1)}}{N_I} + \right.$$

$$\left. \left(\lfloor \log_2 N_I \rfloor + 1 \right) \left(1 - \sum_{j=1}^{\lfloor \log_2 N_I \rfloor} \frac{2^{(j-1)}}{N_I} \right) \right\} \tag{30.6}$$

The lower curve in Fig. 30.4 shows the effect of varying the block size on a tree index with binary searching. When binary searching is used, the block size is less sensitive.

If time is the overriding consideration, a binary search of an index tailored into blocks so as to avoid seeks where possible is the best of the table look-up techniques. However, as we commented before, a simple

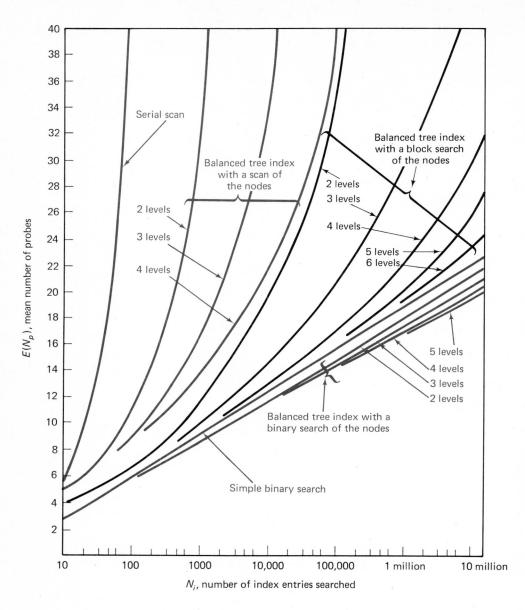

Figure 30.6

binary search cannot be used with index entry compaction, and compaction can have a major effect on saving index space (Fig. 29.3). Furthermore, the insertion of new items into a block that will be binary-searched (without a binary tree) is a clumsy operation, as many of the existing items have to be moved. For these reasons a multilevel block search rather than a multilevel binary search is used in much file software. IBM's VSAM, for example, uses the tree index illustrated in Fig. 20.3 with key compaction, and the nodes are block-searched.

As shown in Fig. 30.6 the number of probes needed for a binary search is not too much lower than the number needed for a block-searched tree index. Figure 30.6 shows the numbers of probes for the three types of tree indices with different numbers of levels in the tree.

Technique 8: Sequence Set Operations

The bottom level of a tree index, level 1 in Fig. 30.3, is referred to as the *sequence set.* The entries (arguments) in the sequence set are normally in collating sequence. Index operations may be carried out either by going from the root of the tree down the branches to the sequence set or by operating at the sequence set level alone. The position for starting a search of the sequence set might be found by any of the techniques in this chapter. The sequence set is often used directly in sequential file operations.

A computer run may read every record in a file sequentially, for example, a run producing electricity bills. The records may not be stored physically in collating sequence, and so the run proceeds by reading the sequence set index sequentially to locate the records.

A *skip sequential* run requires records to be read in collating sequence but with many of them skipped. Often a skip sequential run requires only a very small percentage of the records. Where there is no index, for example, with a file in collating sequence, the computer must read all the records, ignoring the unwanted ones. Such a procedure wastes time, and so a sequence set index can be advantageous even when records themselves on a direct-access device are in sequence. The sequence set index is scanned rather than the entire file.

If the sequence set nodes are not all physically contiguous, then the set must have *horizontal* chains between the nodes, as shown by the dotted arrows in Fig. 30.7. The chains may be one-way as in Fig. 30.7 or may be two-way to permit forward or backward scanning of the sequence set.

The sequence set of the index can, itself, be organized as an indexed sequential file, and any of the techniques in Chapter 20 are applicable to it. Its organization must include a convenient method of handling additions and

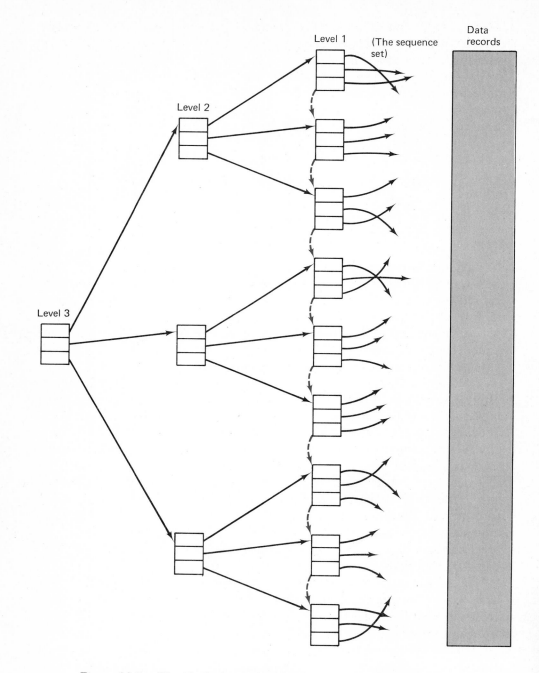

Figure 30.7   The blocks in the lowest level of the index, the sequence
set, are chained together for sequence set operations.

deletions. They could be handled using *distributed free space,* as in Fig. 20.10. The reader might regard the entries in Fig. 20.10 as index entries rather than data records.

Technique 9: Look-aside Buffers

The file activity on many systems is such that the file references are highly clustered. That is, when reference is made to a record with a given key it is likely that a recent previous reference was to a record with the same key or a key close in value. In some cases skip sequential activity causes this property. In other cases one group of records is much more frequently referenced than the rest. An area of high activity may move from one part of the file to another. For example, on an airline system the records associated with a flight close to takeoff are frequently referenced. In a stockbroker system a certain group of hot stocks may elicit most of the current inquiries, but next week different stocks will be fashionable.

Whatever the cause of the clustering, it is a property that might be taken advantage of in the organization of the storage. Where paging is used, the page replacement algorithm can retain the most frequently referenced items in the main memory or faster-access storage. When indexing is used, *look-aside buffers* have been employed to retain in main memory a given number of recently used index references. If a tree index is used as in Fig. 30.3, a look-aside buffer may be employed for some, or all, levels of the tree. When the computer has to find a record it glances first at the look-aside buffers to see whether an index entry is there for the item in question.

Consider the portion of a tree index shown in Fig. 30.8. Look-aside buffers for the three levels of index shown are in main memory. A request comes in for record 721. The level 1 look-aside buffer is inspected, and there is an entry in it which points to appropriate sequence set block. A request comes for record 801. The computer finds no entry for it in the level 1 buffer, and so it goes on to inspect the level 2 buffer. This does contain an entry which points to the requisite block in level 2 of the index.

There are many variations possible in the organization of look-aside buffers. In particular there are many possible algorithms for deciding which entries will be stored in the buffers. The buffers could store the *most recently used* index entries. They could store those entries which were *most frequently used* in the last hour—or other specified period. They could store an *unchanging* group of frequently used index entries. Which look-aside algorithm is the most efficient will vary from one system to another depending upon the patterns of file usage.

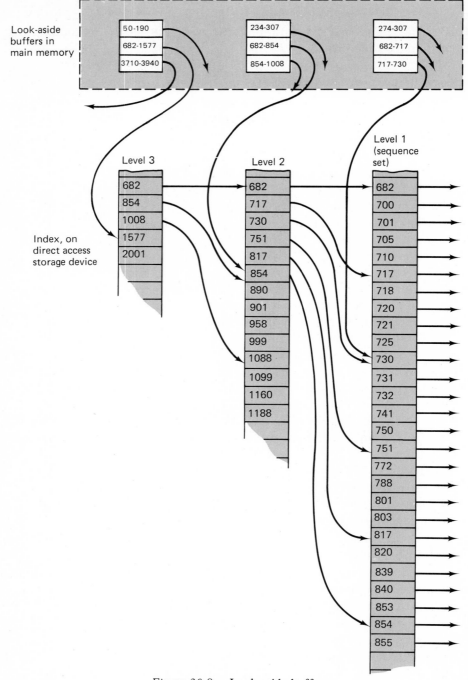

Figure 30.8   Look-aside buffers.

Technique 10: Unbalanced Trees

We have so far shown balanced trees with an equal number of entries per block. Trees need not have an equal number of entries per block (Fig. 29.4) nor need they be balanced. One of the disadvantages cited for balanced tree indices is that every index level must be read for each record that is accessed. The frequently read records or records for which fast access is important do not have preferential treatment.

Preferential treatment can be given in an unbalanced tree index. Figure 30.9 illustrates an unbalanced tree. A small number of records can be found using only the top level of the tree. A larger number can be found with two levels of the tree. The majority need an inspection of all the levels. The most popular items in the file in Fig. 30.9 are BETTY and JUNE. These are indexed at the top level of the tree. The next most popular are CHLOE, KRISTEN, YVONNE, and MOLLY, and these are indexed at the next-to-top level. And so forth.

The frequency of reference may change. If the data base is to be adjusted because BETTY and JUNE fall from popularity, this change can be made *in the index* without moving the data records. In Fig. 30.10, CHLOE and SCARLETT have become the most frequently used, so their index entries are now placed at the top of the tree. The other index entries are also shuffled.

A disadvantage of an unbalanced tree is that it needs more levels than a balanced tree. The records which require four index levels in Fig. 30.9 would require only three if a balanced tree as in Fig. 30.3 were used with the same number of entries per node.

Even a large file is unlikely to have more than five or six levels of index, so not too much time can be saved by unbalancing the tree unless the shorter access paths (i.e., to CHLOE and SCARLETT in Fig. 30.10) can avoid a movement of a physical access mechanism that would otherwise be necessary.

Technique 11: Calculated Guess Addressing

An index search may be shortened if an estimate can be made of the approximate position of the entry in the index. If the estimate is accurate enough to narrow down the search to 1% of the index, the saving in number of probes can be substantial, as can be seen by imagining N to be divided by 100 in Fig. 30.1 or 30.6.

The ability to make such an estimate is highly dependent on the nature of the application. Table 30.1 relates to finding names which are indexed in

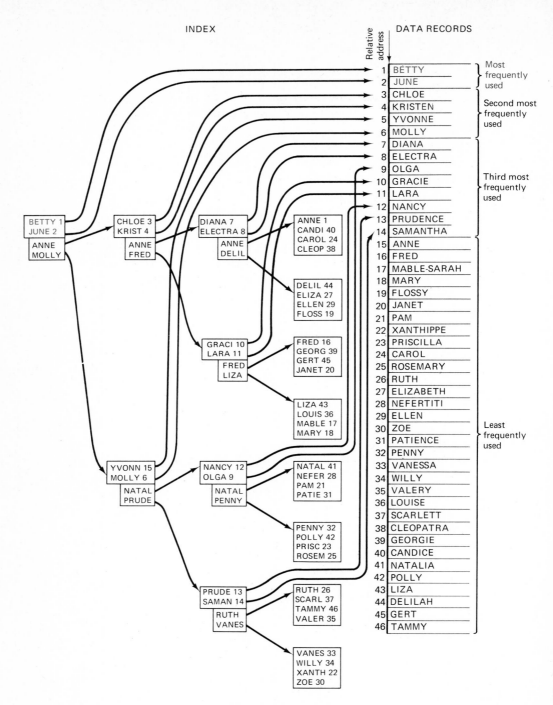

Figure 30.9   An unbalanced tree index.

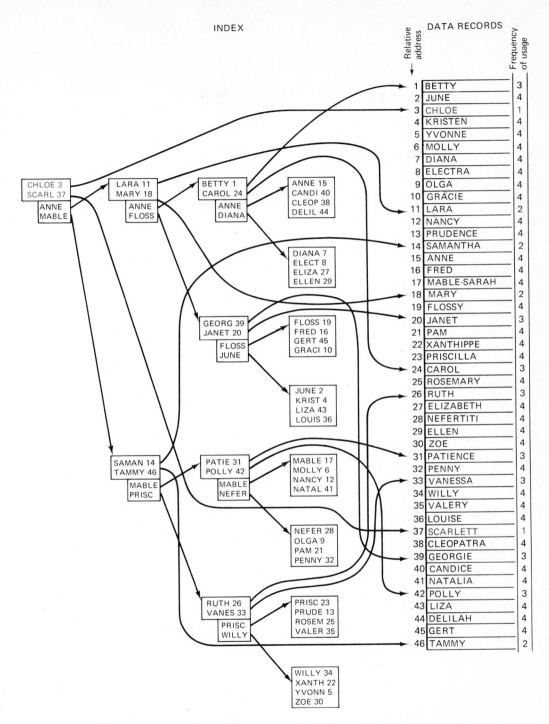

INDEX

DATA RECORDS

Figure 30.10 The unbalanced tree of Fig. 30.9 when the frequency of use changes.

Table 30.1. A table for Calculated Guess Addressing.

	First Letter	Second Letter
A	0	0
B	0.0500	0.0781
C	0.1285	0.0909
D	0.2005	0.1202
E	0.2425	0.1613
F	0.2661	0.2918
G	0.3108	0.3206
H	0.3688	0.3345
I	0.4220	0.3930
J	0.4333	0.4607
K	0.4554	0.4630
L	0.4968	0.4672
M	0.5495	0.5032
N	0.6323	0.5294
O	0.6608	0.6022
P	0.6753	0.6843
Q	0.7220	0.7058
R	0.7237	0.7072
S	0.7952	0.7736
T	0.8833	0.8382
U	0.9167	0.9284
V	0.9269	0.9561
W	0.9403	0.9661
X	0.9871	0.9810
Y	0.9871	0.9840
Z	0.9925	0.9991

alphabetical order. The second column relates to the first letter of the surname and indicates after what fraction of the index that letter begins. The third column relates in a similar fashion to the second letter of the surname. Items beginning with K begin approximately 0.4554 of the way through the index. Items beginning with KE begin approximately $0.4554 + 0.1613 \times (0.4968 - 0.4554)$ of the way through the index. Knowing the number of the entries in the index, the address of the required index entry can be estimated. The search begins at that point in the index. (The figures in Table 30.1 relate to names in New York and would be somewhat different for names elsewhere).

Technique 12: Algorithm Indexing

In Chapter 19 we discussed various algorithms used as a means of file addressing. Any such schemes could be used to locate an index block rather than the data themselves. They can give a faster means of locating the required record than a tree index because they provide a single-seek access to an index block which is equivalent to the bottom level of the tree (Fig. 30.11). On the other hand, they are not as fast as direct addressing without an index.

What are the possible advantages of using this combination of algorithm and index? First, the combination makes possible a large variety of algorithms not sufficiently precise to find the record but which could locate an indexable group of records. Second, the method overcomes a major disadvantage of direct addressing, namely that there is no independence between the physical positioning of a record on the files and its logical key. The physical positioning cannot be changed independently of the addressing algorithm.

An example of algorithm indexing which illustrates both advantages is the location of passenger name records on an airline reservation system. These records contain details of the passenger booking and are several hundred characters in length. *Fast* access is needed to them because of the tight response time requirements. The file is both *large* (a million passenger name records are stored by the large airlines) and *highly volatile* (many thousand new records are added each day). Because of the high volatility, it is undesirable to store the records sequentially. Too many out-of-sequence additions would have to be chained to the records. Because of the fast response-time requirements, it is desirable that most accesses should require no more than two seeks, and the first of these seeks should be short if possible. In other words, an addressing scheme faster than a tree index is desirable.

The passenger names fall into natural groups—those passengers who are booked on the same flight. An algorithm can be devised based on the flight number and date with which a simple calculation and main memory table reference can produce a unique file address—the address of a *passenger name index* record for that flight. The passenger name index record is in a fixed location on a part of the storage that is rapidly accessible. It contains an index, or set of pointers. to the passenger name records for that flight, which, because of their volatility, can be scattered anywhere within a large "pool" of fixed-length record locations.

The index in this example is in segments among the data records. This is sometimes referred to as an *embedded* index. The variable pointer lists discussed in Chapters 24 and 25, for the representation of tree and plex structures, for example, that in Fig. 25.8, are in a sense embedded indices.

Technique 13: Hash Indexing

A particularly important type of algorithm is hashing, discussed in Chapter 21. Hashing is usually used to locate a record directly. It could,

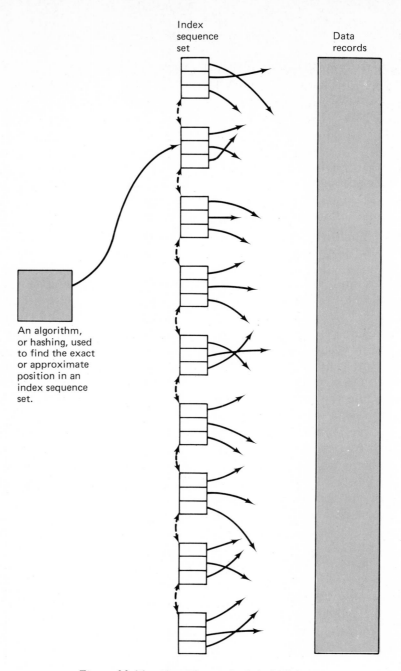

An algorithm, or hashing, used to find the exact or approximate position in an index sequence set.

Figure 30.11 Algorithm or hash indexing.

however, be used to locate an index block, thereby avoiding the need for higher levels of indexing (Fig. 30.11). The combination of hashing and indexing can be better than indexing alone in that fewer index probes or access arm movements are needed.

The main advantage of pure hash addressing, namely that records can be found with one seek, is lost. However, hash indexing may be preferable to pure hash addressing because it allows the records to be stored in an order determined by other considerations. The records could be stored sequentially by prime key, for example, or stored with their parents in a tree structure. The most frequently referenced records can be placed on rapidly accessible parts of the storage devices. On some systems it may be valuable to be able to change the record layout without changing the hashing algorithm. Furthermore, the empty spaces in the buckets, which are characteristic of hashing techniques, are spaces in the index, not spaces in the data storage location. Hash indexing is thus less wasteful of space than pure hash addressing of records. Furthermore, the overflows that are inevitable with hashing can be handled in the index rather than in the data records, where they incur time-consuming seeks. The bucket sizes can be large enough to give a low proportion of overflows (See Fig. 21.4.)

HOW ARE THE INDEX BLOCKS LAID OUT?

Where a tree index is used, there are various possible sequences in which the blocks can be laid out. In some software packages the levels of the tree have corresponded to sections of hardware such as a disk track. However, it is clear from Fig. 30.4 that the optimum block size is quite small, and hence two or possibly three compacted index levels could fit onto one disk track. The index may spread over many contiguous tracks or reside in a large solid-state module, in which case four, five, or six levels might be contiguously stored.

Consider the three-level tree index in Fig. 30.12. The subscript 1 indicates a pointer to level 1, and the subscript 2 indicates a pointer to level 2. Figure 30.12 shows three common ways of laying out such an index sequentially. Other ways are also possible.

The first method lays out the three levels each without a break. This method has the advantage that all the sequence set items are contiguous and hence facilitates sequential operations.

The second method is similar to the method of laying out tree structures sequentially, discussed in Chapter 24 (Fig. 24.7). Such a layout is advantageous with data in certain applications because the records are

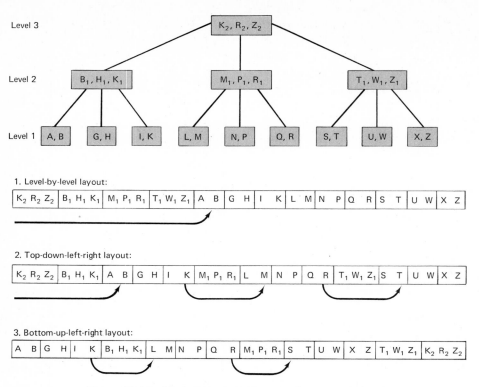

Figure 30.12 Three sequential layouts for a tree index.

needed in a top-down-left-right sequence. The sequence set items may be chained together to facilitate sequential processing.

The third method stores the parent node *after* their children. If an entry is changed, all the necessary modifications can be made scanning in a left-right direction. First the level 1 entry is changed, then the level 2 entry if necessary, then the level 3, and so forth if higher levels exist. Left-right operations like this are convenient on serial storage devices which do not permit a backward scan, like some magnetic tape units.

INSERTIONS AND DELETIONS

Perhaps more important than the layout sequence is the method of inserting and deleting entries. As before, either *distributed free space* or *overflows* are applicable, and often both are used together, overflows coming into operation when the free space in an area runs out.

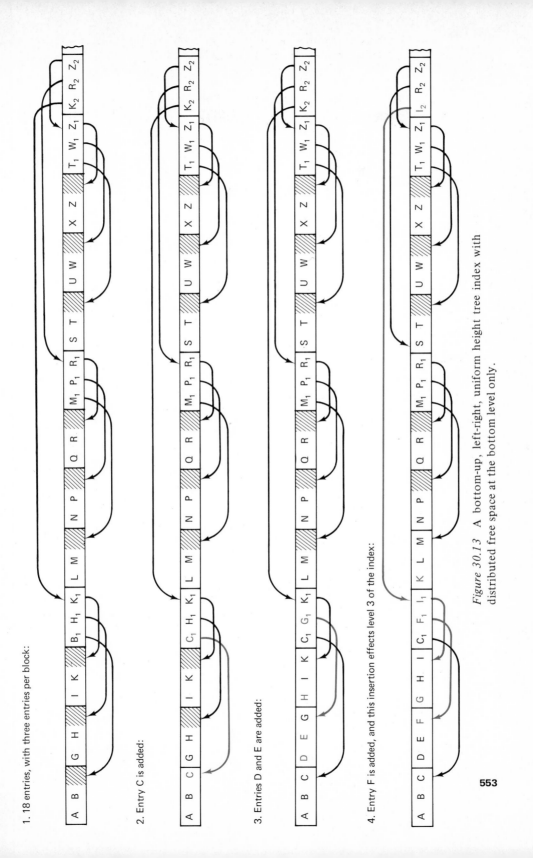

1. 18 entries, with three entries per block:

2. Entry C is added:

3. Entries D and E are added:

4. Entry F is added, and this insertion effects level 3 of the index:

Figure 30.13 A bottom-up, left-right, uniform height tree index with distributed free space at the bottom level only.

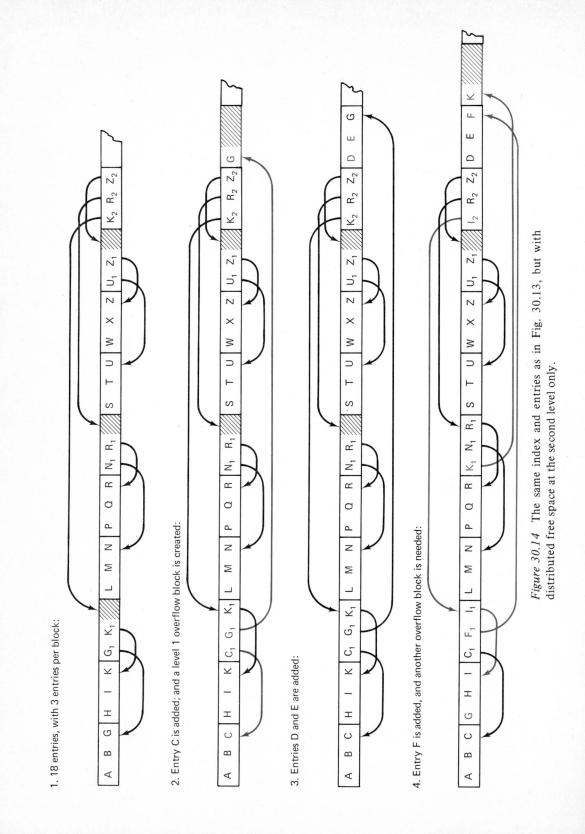

1. 18 entries, with 3 entries per block:

2. Entry C is added; and a level 1 overflow block is created:

3. Entries D and E are added:

4. Entry F is added, and another overflow block is needed:

Figure 30.14 The same index and entries as in Fig. 30.13, but with distributed free space at the second level only.

If distributed free space and overflows are used in conjunction, at what level in the index should the free space be distributed? Figure 30.13 shows the index of Fig. 30.12 with free space distributed at level 1. Figure 30.14 shows the same but with the free space at level 2. The shaded parts of the diagrams are the free space. The diagrams show four new entries being added, and, to make life difficult, the entries are highly clustered.

In Fig. 30.13, because the free space is at the lowest level, a shuffling of entries at the lowest level accommodates the new arrivals. Only when the fourth item in the cluster is added does level 3 of the index have to be modified.

In Fig. 30.14 the total storage space utilized is less because the free space is at level 2. However, lengthy jumps are needed when following the sequence set. If these jumps do not extend beyond a cell boundary, i.e., do not incur a seek, then they are of little concern, and the layout in Fig. 30.14 is better than that in Fig. 30.13. The free space could be pushed to higher index levels or could be eliminated entirely in favor of overflows. This decision should depend on where seeks are incurred and on the trade-off between saving space and saving time.

SUMMARY   Box 30.1 summarizes index-searching techniques.

Box 30.1   Index-Searching Techniques

Technique	Illustrated in Fig.	Comment
Serial scan		Poor. Use only for small blocks.
Block search	19.1	Suitable for a small index or a portion of a large index.
Binary search	19.2	*Advantage*: Fast for an index in main memory. *Disadvantages*: Very poor if it involves mechanical seeks to and fro. Entry compaction not possible. Insertions and deletions difficult.

Box 30.1 *continued*

Technique	Illustrated in Fig.	Comment
Binary-tree search	30.2	*Advantages*: Fast insertions and deletions handled efficiently. *Disadvantages*: Space taken up with pointers. Entry compaction not possible.
Balanced tree index	30.3	Nodes searched by Serial scan, poor Block search, better Binary search, no compaction Fast. Economical, Can be tailored to hardware. Techniques are needed to handle insertions and deletions.
Unbalanced tree index	30.9	*Advantage*: Frequently used records found more quickly. *Disadvantages*: Infrequently used records found more slowly. Complex maintenance.
Algorithm index	30.11	Faster than a pure index. May destroy data independence.
Hash index	30.11	Faster than a pure index. Better space utilization than pure hashing.
Other techniques		
Look-aside buffers	30.8	Can take advantage of clustered file reference patterns to speed to addressing.
Sequence set chain	30.7	Can speed up sequential or skip sequential operations.

BOOK STRUCTURE

Chapter 31 discusses means of searching indices such as those discussed in Chapter 30.

31 INVERTED FILE SYSTEMS

In this and the following two chapters we will describe the application of the techniques we have discussed to three categories of data bases which have somewhat more stringent requirements than the average. In this chapter we will discuss inverted file systems. In the next chapter we will discuss files of high volatility, and in Chapter 35 we will discuss systems with tight response-time requirements.

Inverted file systems are ones in which records are normally addressed on the basis of attribute values or combinations of attribute values. In the notation of Fig. 5.5, they answer queries of the form

$$A(?) \quad \genfrac{}{}{0pt}{}{=}{\genfrac{}{}{0pt}{}{\neq}{\genfrac{}{}{0pt}{}{<}{>}}} \quad V_1 \quad \text{and} \quad \genfrac{}{}{0pt}{}{=}{\genfrac{}{}{0pt}{}{\neq}{\genfrac{}{}{0pt}{}{<}{>}}} \quad V_2 \ldots$$

In this chapter we are concerned primarily with *interactive* inverted file systems in which the responses are returned to users at terminals. A user can successively refine his queries until he obtains the information he needs from the data base. Such systems need multiple secondary indices, and usually the total space taken up by the indices is greater than that taken up by the data.

To achieve conversational response times, especially in a time-shared environment, it is essential to be able to search the files without following chains or rings embedded in data on electromechanical storage.

SECONDARY INDICES VERSUS INVERTED FILES

We may distinguish three varieties of systems that use inverted indices, as summarized in Box 31.1. The first may be called a *secondary index system*. The records or segments are organized sequentially

Box 31.1   Inverted Index Systems

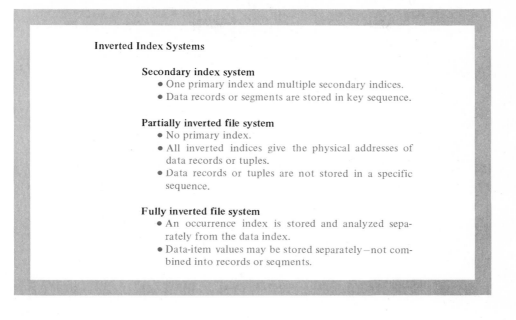

Inverted Index Systems

Secondary index system
- One primary index and multiple secondary indices.
- Data records or segments are stored in key sequence.

Partially inverted file system
- No primary index.
- All inverted indices give the physical addresses of data records or tuples.
- Data records or tuples are not stored in a specific sequence.

Fully inverted file system
- An occurrence index is stored and analyzed separately from the data index.
- Data-item values may be stored separately—not combined into records or seqments.

by some primary key and are usually designed for specific types of usage. One primary index and multiple secondary indices are used as discussed in earlier chapters.

The next is sometimes called a *partially inverted file system*. In this the records or segments can be in any sequence, and hence there is no primary index—only secondary indices. There is no concern with inserting new records into the middle of the files; they can be stored anywhere, but the indices must be appropriately updated. The indices give the physical address of the records directly, not merely a reference to the primary key.

The third category is referred to as a *fully inverted file system*. In this a file of data values may be kept, and the values forming a particular record or tuple may not necessarily be stored contiguously. There is an *occurrence index* which is examined to find occurrences of a particular data value, and a separate *data index* to find the data associated with those occurrences.

This chapter discusses fully inverted file systems. Fig. 31.1 shows four essential components of such systems. A dictionary is employed to point to the occurrence index. The lists of occurrences in this index are examined and compared, and then the required data values are found via a data index. Figs. 31.2 and 31.4 give more details of typical inverted file structures.

Inverted file storage structure:

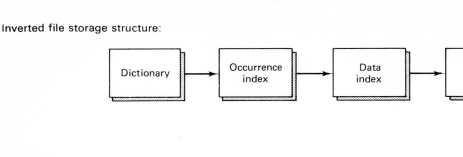

Inverted file dialogue structure:

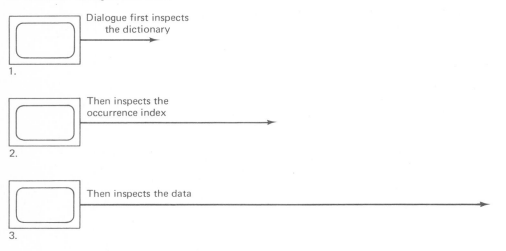

Figure 31.1 Typical inverted file storage and dialogue structure.

The dialogue for searching an inverted file system may proceed in three stages. First the dictionary is inspected, then the occurrence index. The occurrence index may be searched multiple times before proceeding to the data index to locate the required data.

A fully inverted file system may be the best for interactive searching of a data base, but it can be slow or cumbersome for conventional data processing such as payroll or invoicing operations, where a predefined group of data items is always accessed together.

DOCUMENT-SEARCHING SYSTEMS   An important category of inverted file system is the document-searching or text-retrieval system. Many of these systems are now in successful operation, and they will probably become very common as storage costs drop and the information explosion grows.

There is a great difference in usability between an information retrieval system with which a user can carry out a fast search of the documents and one which is off-line or too slow for effective interactive searching. Many off-line information retrieval systems inundate their users with long listings of abstracts which are often dumped in waste bins without reading. A fast interactive system can be employed by a user when he needs to find information on a particular subject. His search will progress rapidly through the files, rejecting many references as it goes. It will need the speed of a visual display terminal and an inverted file system.

Figure 31.2 shows a typical file structure of an interactive document-searching system. It is the file structure of the IBM STAIRS system [1,2].

On the right-hand side of Fig. 31.2 is the *document file*, which stores the documents. The documents are numbered by the system. They are subdivided into paragraphs and sentences. The sentences are numbered. The paragraphs are given codes to indicate the type of paragraph, such as "Title," "Author," "Abstract," "Text," or general categorization.

On the left-hand side of Fig. 31.2 is a *word dictionary*. It gives the names of English-language (or other) words which are in the documents. The dictionary can be large and needs a higher-level index. A character-pair matrix is used. For each pair of characters the matrix stores a pointer to the dictionary block containing words beginning with these characters. The characters can be letters, digits, or a special character. The second character can also be a blank. There are thus $37 \times 38 = 1406$ entries in the matrix. The dictionary contains variable-length groups or entries, each entry in the group being for a word beginning with the same two characters. (The first two characters are not repeated in the dictionary entries but they have been left in in Fig. 31.2 for ease of reading. Some words in the dictionary may have identical meanings, and these are linked by "synonym" pointers (dotted lines in Fig. 31.2).

Each entry in the dictionary points to an *occurrence list* giving every occurrence in the document file of the word in question. The occurrence list is headed by fields giving the number of documents containing the word and the total number of occurrences of the word in the entire document file. These numbers are given to the user who is carrying out a search. If they are too large, he may not employ the word in question but will attempt to find a more suitable word or words as the basis of his search.

The system gives all documents a unique number which is as compact as possible. It is unrelated to any external number by which the user may

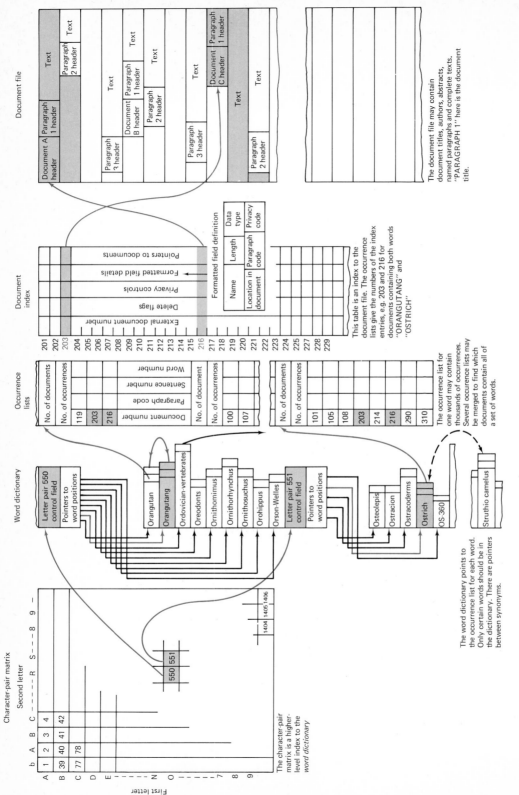

Figure 31.2 An inverted file structure for document retrieval. The marked path shows the answering of the query: "Give me the titles of documents with both the words ORANGUTANG and OSTRICH in the text."

refer to the document. The occurrence list contains this document number for each occurrence. A search criterion may be *search for all documents containing both of two specified words*, for example, all documents containing the words *computer* and *chess*. The program then obtains from the occurrence list file the numbers of all documents containing the word *computer* and all documents containing the word *chess*. These lists are merged to produce a list of the numbers of documents containing both words.

There are many other possible search criteria. The criteria often specify that two or more words must be adjacent, for example, *nuclear* and *particle* or *data*, *base*, *management*, and *system*. For this reason the positions of words in the sentences are recorded in the occurrence list.

The user may attempt to narrow down the search by specifying that more than one sentence contains the key word or words. If the documents are long—say 30-page reports—then many irrelevant documents could be included in the occurrence list, and so the user may specify that the key words must appear in well-separated sentences.

Particularly important is the *paragraph type*. The user may specify that the key word appear in the title, the abstract, the introduction, or in specially designated paragraphs or that the key word be an author's name, place of origination, or date of publication. Whatever the search criteria, a list of numbers of documents which satisfy them is produced without going further into the files than the occurrence list.

The user is shown how many documents are in the list which results from his search criteria. He may then change his criteria or instruct the machine to display the document titles, authors, abstracts, or text, one screenful at a time.

The internal document numbers form a key to the *document index*, and the document index points to the location in the storage of the document itself. The occurrence list *could* have pointed to the document directly, but such a pointer would contain more bytes than the brief internal document number. Lists containing many thousands, occasionally hundreds of thousands, of document references are merged as part of the searching process, so the document references must be as short as possible. For this reason the document index is kept separately.

The document index, in addition to giving the storage address of the document, gives the external document number, delete flags to indicate whether all or part of the document has been removed from the files, and controls relating to privacy, which can prevent certain users or certain terminals from having access to classified documents.

FORMATTED   The documents may contain processable data items
FIELDS   in certain specified locations. These are referred to
                   as *formatted fields.* A data set contains the
definitions of the formatted fields, stating their names, locations, lengths,
type of data, privacy level, and the type code of the paragraph from which
their contents derive. Specified formatted fields may be stored in the
document index. These may be inspected in the search operation before the
decision is made to retrieve the documents in question.

SUCCESSION   The search thus begins with the *dictionary* and
OF SEARCH   may proceed no further until the operator modifies
LEVELS   his search criteria. It continues into the *occurrence
                   list* and again may not proceed further without
refinement of the search criteria. It may continue into the *document index*,
possibly searching the *formatted fields.* Finally, the documents themselves
are inspected. This succession of search levels (indicated in Fig. 31.1) makes
it possible to give the terminal users conversational response times.
    A key to success in designing inverted file operations is to structure this
succession of search levels in an appropriate fashion, confining the search
where possible to sections of the storage which do not require large numbers
of time-consuming seeks.

DICTIONARY   It is very important to contol which words are
CONTROL   employed in the dictionary. Users of such a system
                   often want to put too many words in the dictio-
nary and to employ words which are too common. If a word is too common,
its occurrence list will be very long, and the search operations which merge
occurrence lists will be excessively time-consuming. The system can become
flooded by the use of inappropriate dictionary entries.
    On some STAIRS installations, occurrence lists with nearly a million
entries for one word have been encountered before the word was pruned
from the dictionary.

GENERAL-PURPOSE   Many inverted file systems do not search docu-
INVERTED-FILE   ments but search data which have been assembled
SYSTEMS   for purposes of providing an information system.
                   These systems have much in common with the

document-searching systems we have described but introduce some additional complications.

One complication is that there may be relationships between the records or segments that are searched. Any of the relationships shown in Fig. 9.11 might exist, but some inverted file systems restrict themselves to tree (hierarchical) data structures.

Whereas document retrieval systems are searched primarily on the basis of words in documents, general-purpose systems employ a wide variety of different data-item types and so require a dictionary of data-item types.

TDMS
The first major inverted file data management system for interactive use was TDMS, the Time-shared Data Management System produced by the Systems Development Corporation [3] (later repackaged under the name CDMS). A TDMS system could answer most multiple-key queries from its terminal users with a response time of a few seconds. Today the main use of TDMS is in military systems, but the file structures which TDMS used remain typical of commercial fully-inverted file systems. (Most inverted file systems in current commercial use are *partially* inverted.)

Figure 31.3 shows a schema of a tree structure, and Fig. 31.4 illustrates the TDMS files for representing it. The entries shown in Fig. 31.4 relate to the blocks which are shaded in Fig. 31.3.

The data stored are in the two right-hand columns. They would all be stored in the *data-item table* if no data items were longer than 4 bytes. TDMS, however, stores all data-item values longer than 4 bytes in a separate

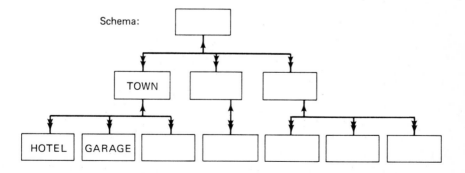

Figure 31.3 The TDMS and CDMS files for this tree structure are shown in Fig. 31.4. The labelled entries in Fig. 31.4 correspond to labelled records in this figure.

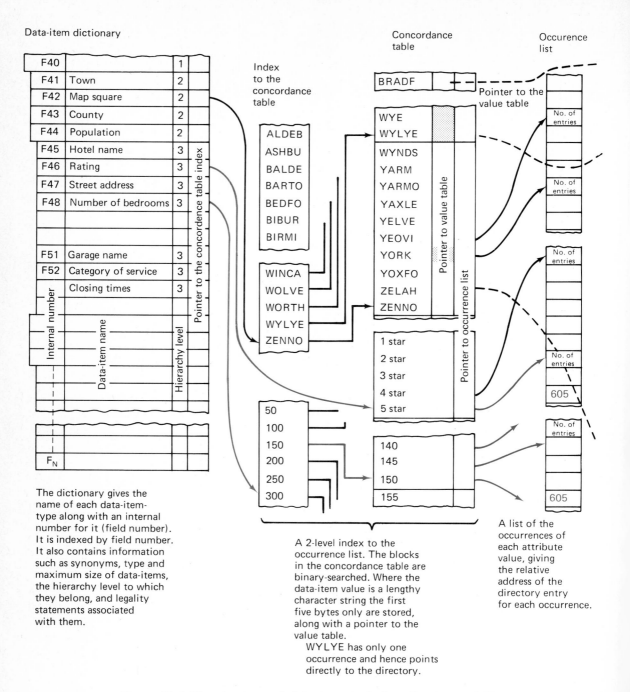

The dictionary gives the name of each data-item-type along with an internal number for it (field number). It is indexed by field number. It also contains information such as synonyms, type and maximum size of data-items, the hierarchy level to which they belong, and legality statements associated with them.

A 2-level index to the occurrence list. The blocks in the concordance table are binary-searched. Where the data-item value is a lengthy character string the first five bytes only are stored, along with a pointer to the value table.

WYLYE has only one occurrence and hence points directly to the directory.

A list of the occurrences of each attribute value, giving the relative address of the directory entry for each occurrence.

Figure 31.4 The structure of data in a typical on-line inverted file system, the System Development Corporation TDMS (Time-shared Data Management System) and CDMS. The marked path shows the

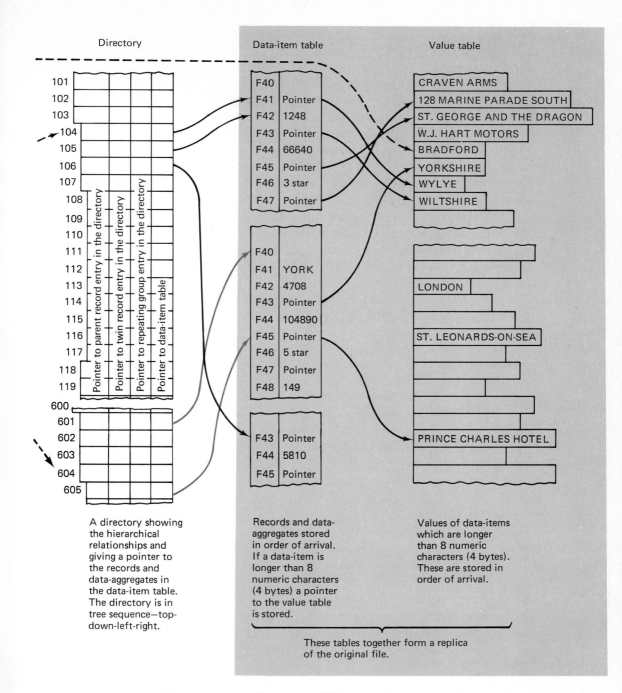

Directory	Data-item table	Value table

Directory

101
102
103
104 →
105
106
107
108
109
110
111
112
113
114
115
116
117
118
119

Pointer to parent record entry in the directory
Pointer to twin record entry in the directory
Pointer to repeating group entry in the directory
Pointer to data-item table

600
601
602
603
604
605

Data-item table

F40	
F41	Pointer
F42	1248
F43	Pointer
F44	66640
F45	Pointer
F46	3 star
F47	Pointer

F40	
F41	YORK
F42	4708
F43	Pointer
F44	104890
F45	Pointer
F46	5 star
F47	Pointer
F48	149

F43	Pointer
F44	5810
F45	Pointer

Value table

CRAVEN ARMS
128 MARINE PARADE SOUTH
ST. GEORGE AND THE DRAGON
W.J. HART MOTORS
BRADFORD
YORKSHIRE
WYLYE
WILTSHIRE

LONDON

ST. LEONARDS-ON-SEA

PRINCE CHARLES HOTEL

A directory showing the hierarchical relationships and giving a pointer to the records and data-aggregates in the data-item table. The directory is in tree sequence—top-down-left-right.

Records and data-aggregates stored in order of arrival. If a data-item is longer than 8 numeric characters (4 bytes) a pointer to the value table is stored.

Values of data-items which are longer than 8 numeric characters (4 bytes). These are stored in order of arrival.

These tables together form a replica of the original file.

steps taken to answer the query: "What are the names and towns of hotels with a five-star rating and more than 140 bedrooms?" The Prince Charles Hotel in York is one such hotel.

table of values. The reasoning behind this strategy is that in most data the same data-item value occurs many times. If the value is lengthy, space can be saved by storing it only once and pointing to it. As we commented earlier, this strategy sometimes pays off and sometimes does not. The value LONDON, for example, in the file of Fig. 31.4 would be pointed to many times, and its existence in a separate table would save storage space. The value 128 MARINE PARADE SOUTH, on the other hand, probably occurs only once, and so space and time are wasted by storing it separately from the record occurrence of which it is a part.

The entries in both the data-item table and the value table are stored in the sequence in which they arrive. New entries are simply added to the end of the file without displacing any previous entries. On-line insertions thus cause no problem as far as the *data* storage is concerned. However, the updating of the *index* tables is complex.

The leftmost table in Fig. 31.4 is a *data-item dictionary*, which defines the data-item type. It gives the name of each data-item type, along with its level in the tree structure, and an internal number for it (field number). It is indexed by field number. It also contains information not shown in Fig. 31.4 such as synonyms (data items which have more than one name), type and maximum size of data items, and legality statements associated with them. Other such data dictionaries sometimes contain details of privacy controls.

The TDMS *data-item dictionary* contains for each data-item type a pointer to the *concordance table*, which lists the stored values of that data item. In some cases the value list in the concordance table is quantized. For example, not every possible value of NUMBER-OF-BEDROOMS is stored; every fifth possible value is stored in sequence. With a lengthy data item the entire value is not stored but rather only five characters followed by a pointer to the complete value in the *value table.* For example, the town Yarmouth is stored as YARMO. Two different values may have the same first five characters, and if so, a duplication indicator is stored.

There may be many entries in the concordance table for one data-item type—so many, in fact, that a binary search of them would necessitate moving an access arm backward and forward. There is therefore a higher-level index to the concordance table, as shown. This makes it possible to read into main memory blocks of the concordance table sufficiently small to be binary-searched. The optimum block size can be chosen as discussed in Chapter 30.

The *concordance table* gives a pointer to the *occurrence list*, which lists all the occurrences of each data-item value. The concordance table is, in effect, an index to the occurrence list and is analogous to the *word dictionary* in Fig. 31.2. However, if a data-item value occurs only once, it does not appear in the occurrence list. Instead, the concordance table points to the next table in Fig. 31.4, the *directory*.

The *occurrence list* contains a pointer to the *directory* for each occurrence. The directory uses parent and twin pointers and repeating group pointers, along with its sequential positioning to indicate the tree structure relationships, and points to the data-item table. The entries in the directory are in top-down-left-right tree sequence (as in Fig. 24.7).

The tables on the left of the data-item table thus combine to form an elaborately structured set of inverted indices and directory to the data items.

EXAMPLE OF
TDMS USE

The marked path in Fig. 31.4 shows the steps taken to answer the query "What are the names and towns of hotels with a 5-star rating and more than 140 rooms?" The query would be expressed in the TDMS terminal language with a statement such as PRINT HOTEL NAME AND TOWN WHERE RATING EQ 5 STAR AND NUMBER OF BEDROOMS GR 140.

Answering the query begins with the *data-item dictionary*. HOTEL-NAME, TOWN, RATING, and NUMBER-OF-BEDROOMS are found in the dictionary. The inquirer might have used names other than these, for example, BEDROOM CAPACITY, and the dictionary contains all the allowable synonyms for the data-item names. The dictionary indicates that HOTEL-NAME, RATING, and NUMBER-OF-BEDROOMS are in the same record type and that TOWN is in its parent in the tree structure.

The dictionary points to the index to the *concordance table*. The concordance table entries corresponding to RATING value of 5 STAR, and a NUMBER-OF-BEDROOMS greater than 140 are found. There are many occurrences of 5 STAR hotels and hotels with more than 140 bedrooms. The concordance table points to the *occurrence lists* for each of these.

At the head of each occurrence list is a statement of the number of occurrences in that list. If the list is excessively long, the operator will be informed and asked whether he wants the search to proceed. As with document-searching systems a key to successful operation is to avoid inclusion in inverted structure of data items which occur too often and hence would have excessively long occurrence lists.

The computer merges the occurrence list looking for identical entries. Entry number 605 appears in both the lists in this case (and perhaps other entries not shown). 605 is an internal number of an entry in the *directory*. This entry points to a HOTEL-NAME item in the *data-item table,* which in turn points to the value PRINCE CHARLES HOTEL in the *value table.* The

605 entry in the directory also points to the parent record of this entry, which itself points to the data-item table. In this way the TOWN entry in the data-item table is found, revealing that the PRINCE CHARLES HOTEL is in YORK. Any of the data items associated with the PRINCE CHARLES HOTEL or YORK could have been found from the directory and data-item table.

MAINTENANCE OF
INVERTED FILE
SYSTEMS

With all inverted file systems, the occurrence lists which have to be merged are sometimes very long. It is therefore necessary to design the occurrence lists to occupy as little space as possible. That is why the occurrence lists are separate from the other tables in Fig. 31.3 and contain compacted binary pointers to the directory.

When the values of data items change new entries must be inserted into the occurrence lists and old entries deleted. Thus, for an active file, the occurrence lists are *volatile* even when the file itself is not.

For a volatile file the maintenance of the concordance table and directory, as well as the occurrence lists, is complex. Inserting one new record may require an upheaval in all three tables. Because these tables can be very long, lengthy sorting operations are required to maintain them along with the restringing of very large numbers of pointers.

Today's inverted file systems can give fast responses to terminal users and provide a powerful file-searching capability, but a price is paid in the updating of records and, worse, in the insertion of new records with their associated index entries.

If the inverted structure is updated in real time, much distributed free space or overflow space must be left for insertions to the tables. Because of the expensive and complex nature of the maintenance operations, most inverted file systems do not attempt to carry up-to-the-minute data. Instead, they are updated off-line and, if possible, not too frequently. The *information system* data base built with an inverted file structure is separate from any *operations system* data base using the same data. As in Fig. 16.2 the information system may be updated periodically with data collected for this purpose by the operations system.

The inverted file structure, while excellent for certain types of *information* systems, is far from ideal for most *operational* systems. The structures in Figs. 31.2 and 31.4 are poor for batch processing and even for answering simple queries like "What is the NUMBER OF BEDROOMS in the PRINCE CHARLES HOTEL in YORK?"

The periodic updates require the time-consuming process of reconstructing, sorting, and restringing the tables. This operation will be delayed as long as the data users' requirements permit. A simple technique is used in STAIRS systems to postpone the evil day when the tables are reconstructed. Periodically, perhaps once a week, a new batch of documents is added to the system. A *separate* inverted file is created of the new documents, with tables *separate* from those that already exist. This new data base is then chained to the existing one so that users' requests will cause both of them to be searched. The users do not know that they are searching disjoint data bases. Up to 16 such data bases can be chained together, and then the day of reckoning arrives—all the files must be merged and a joint set of tables constructed for them.

INVERTED FILES WITH COMPLEX STRUCTURES

Historically, both fully inverted and partially inverted file systems have had difficulty handling complex data structures. If the complexities of plex structures are added to complexities of the structures in Figs. 31.2 or 31.4, it becomes apparent that techniques of greater conceptual clarity are needed.

When data must be searched in multiple ways, the relative simplicity and flexibility *relational* data base techniques become attractive. The inversion processes can then be restricted to flat files, and fast means of searching flat files can be devised.

One day we will have data-base structures that are good for *both* operations systems and the spontaneous queries and interactive searching of information systems. To achieve this will probably require hardware better than today's, and it seems likely that in many such systems relational structures will be used.

REFERENCES

1. "STAIRS, Storage and Information Retrieval System," *General Information Manual No. GH 12.5107* IBM World Trade Corp., Stuttgart, Germany, 1973.

2. "STAIRS," *Program Reference Manual SH.12-5407*, IBM World Trade Corp., Stuttgart, Germany, 1973.

3. Robert E. Bleier and Alfred H. Vorhaus, "File Organization in the SDC Time-Shared Data Management System (TDMS)," IFIP Congress, Edinburgh, Aug. 1968.

32 DATA COMPACTION

A variety of techniques is available for compressing data in order to reduce the space it occupies. In many instances *data compaction* can achieve dramatic savings. Most files can be cut to half their size, and some existing commercial files can be cut by as much as 80 or even 90%. Data compaction techniques are not new, and in view of the savings they can give it is surprising that they have not been used more frequently.

Compaction techniques may be used when storing any data but are perhaps of most value with large archival files that are infrequently read. We have already discussed the use of compaction to reduce the size of indices (Figs. 29.2, 29.3, and 29.4). Compaction may also be used when transmitting data and can often double or triple the effective speed of a communication line.

Compaction methods fall into two categories: first, those which are dependent on the structure of the records or the content of the data and hence must be specially written for a given application, and, second, those which can be applied to many applications and hence can be built into general-purpose software, hardware, or microcode. Packages for reducing file size are available from a number of software firms.

The work for reducing the size of a file may begin with methods which are dependent on the content of the data and then continue by using application-independent coding methods. We will review the content-dependent methods first.

1. Elimination of Redundant Data Items

An important method of reducing data-base storage size is to eliminate the redundancy that exists due to the multiple storage of identical data items

Julian Date

4 packed decimal digits
counting days sequentially
from May 24, 1967 = 0000

Binary Date

Year	Month	Day
7 bits	4 bits	5 bits

Figure 32.1   Two ways of representing dates with 16 bits.

in separate files. This is one of the major objectives of data-base management systems, and it uses the techniques discussed in earlier chapters.

2. Conversion from Human Notation to Compact Notation

When fields are stored in the form in which humans prefer to read them they often contain more characters than are necessary. Dates, for example, we may write as 12 NOV 1976, or, in our most compact written form 11.12.76, and so dates are often stored as 6 bytes in computer files. In the machine, however, the month needs no more than 4 bits, the day can be encoded in 5 bits, and the year usually needs no more than 7 bits—a total of 16 bits, or two 8-bit bytes (Fig. 32.1). Conversion from the 2-byte form to human-readable form needs only a few lines of code.

Another common way of representing dates is in the Julian form proposed by Joseph Scalizer in 1582 for astronomical uses. Scalizer represented dates as the number of elapsed days since Jan. 1, 4713 B.C. Using this scheme, Jan. 1, 1979 is 2,443,874. Often, only the four low-order digits are used. May 23, 1968 is then 0000, and dates are counted from that day, requiring 16 bits in packed decimal notation. Many other items such as part numbers and street addresses can often be compressed similarly.

3. Supression of Repeated Characters

Numeric fields in some files contain a high proportion of leading or trailing zeros. More than two zeros can be encoded into two (packed decimal) characters—one character to indicate repetition and the next to say how much repetition. Some files contain repetitive blanks or other characters, and these can be dealt with in a similar manner.

One character suppression scheme uses a unique group of characters to indicate that the character following that character is repeated. Where the conventional 8-bit EBCDIC character encoding is employed the majority of bit combinations are usually not used to represent data characters (see Fig. 32.2). Any character with a zero in the second position is not normally

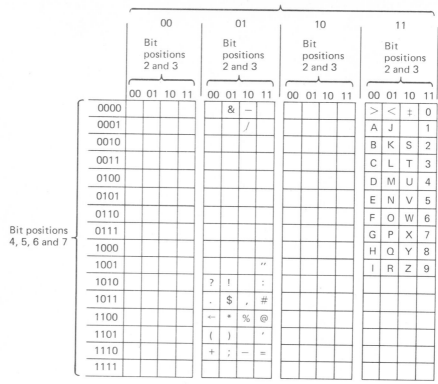

Figure 32.2   Most of the bit combinations in the conventional 8-bit EBCDIC code (which most computers employ) are not used for data characters. In an EBCDIC-encoded record any byte with a zero as its second bit (bit position 1) may be used for special control purposes, such as eliminating repeated characters or blanks.

employed as a data character. Such a character could therefore be employed to indicate repetition of other characters.

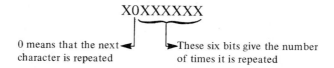

There are certain types of files which benefit greatly from suppression of repeated characters, and others on which the effect is slight.

4. Avoidance of Empty Space in the Files

In some files the records *and* data items are highly variable in length. A data item giving a person's address, for example, or giving *comments* is variable. The organization of a file for variable-length items is usually more complex than for fixed-length items.

A related question concerns records which contain a varying set of data items rather than a fixed set—or another way of wording the same problem, records containing a set of data items of which some may be missing. This is a severe problem with some files; at any one time the majority of the data' items which the records must make provision for have no value. A data compression scheme may be devised such that the data items with no value occupy no space. Figure 32.3 shows a record format for such a scheme. A bit map precedes the data items to indicate whether they are present or not.

5. Substitution for Commonly Used Data Items

Where only a limited set of attribute values exist, there is no need to spell the item out in full. Instead a code can be used. With some data items, such as "type of license," a code would normally be used. Others, such as "name," are often spelled out in full.

Most of the names that are used in name data items belong to a relatively small set. The first names of persons, for example, could be encoded into one 8-bit byte. The 256 names which this makes possible could include almost all the first names that are used. The first bit may have the

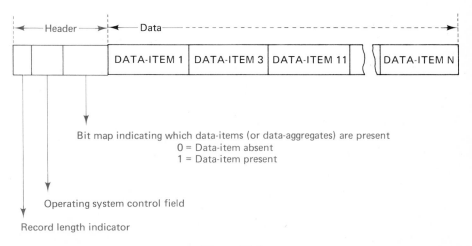

Figure 32.3

additional function of encoding sex, giving 128 female names and 128 male names. However, there would always be the occasional person seeking baptismal distinction whose first name would defy the encoding scheme. What could we do about this? There are several possibilities. We could use 2 bytes instead of 1. We could pass a law saying that people's first names must be taken from a set of 256. We could use one 8-bit combination as an exception byte which indicates that the following bytes spell out the name in full. The latter course seems the best.

Surnames do not yield so well to code substitution, especially in the United States, where the names of so many national origins are mixed together. Nevertheless, even in the United States 128 entries could include about 80% of all surnames and 256 entries more than 90%. We will represent more than 90% of the names by 1 byte and spell the remainder out in full. Two bytes (65,536 combinations) would encompass almost all surnames, but the substitution table would be excessively large, and an extra seek would be needed to access it.

Where substitution tables are used it is desirable to achieve a reasonable compromise between increase in processing time and data compaction. Substituting 2 bytes for 65,536 possibilities would usually be unreasonable. An 8-bit substitution table might require 5000 or so bytes of core, and this may be regarded as too expensive. A 6-bit substitution table might be better, and the code byte could then also give "marital status" or other required information.

6. Substitution for English Text

English words and text are often stored in computer files. Where English constitutes a substantial portion of the file, words or phrases may be substituted with code characters. Suppose that a file stores 8-bit bytes. Each byte may contain combinations of bits that represent the 200 or so most commonly used words. Suppose, also, that 32 of the 256 possible combinations indicate that this character alone does not give the word in question but that the next character is also needed. This gives $32 \times 256 = 8192$ additional words that may be encoded. Another combination of bits in the first character indicates that the word is spelled out in EBCDIC code. The machine receiving this string of data converts it into verbal English with a table look-up operation.

The vocabulary required for many specific applications is small, and it may be necessary to store no more than, say, 256 words. Alternatively, such a scheme may generate not words but messages or phrases.

Original	Compression Step 1:	Step 2:	Approach 3:
WESTCOTT D.L.	WESTCOTT DL	WESTCOTT DL	WESCDL
WEST JOHN C.	3T JOHN C	3T40C	3TJC
WEST JOHN J. JR.	9 J JR	9 J‡	4JJ
WEST PHILLIP	5PHILLIP	561	4P
WESTBROOK C.	4BROOK C	4BROOK C	4C
WESTCOTT C. RAYMOND	4COTT C RAYMOND	4COTT C65	5R
WESTERMAN C.R. MRS.	4ERMAN C R MRS	4ERMAN CR*	6
WESTERN THOMAS C.	6N THOMAS C	6N80C	4TC
WESTERN T.P. MRS.	8T P MRS	8T P*	5P
WESTERN UNION INC.	8UNION INC	8UNION @	4U@
WINGATE WILLIAM	WINGATE WILLIAM	WINGATE 89	1INGW
WINSTON ROBERT	3STON ROBERT	3STON69	3SW
WINTRAIL ETHEL E. MRS.	3TRAL ETHEL E. MRS.	3TRAL12E*	3TEE

1. Front compression	2. Name and word substitution	3. First four letters of surname and two initials

Figure 32.4

7. Compression of Sorted Data

Where a set of data items has been sorted the leading characters tend to repeat each other. The names listed on the left-hand side of Fig. 32.4 are taken from the telephone directory of a small town. These data-item elements can be shortened by substituting a digit for the repeated characters and then shortened further if common first names are replaced by code. Let us suppose that the 100 most common first names are replaced by digits. (An encoded byte is more likely to be used in practice, but we can illustrate digital encoding more easily on a printed book page.) The substitutions relating to Fig. 32.4 are as follows:

$$12 = \text{Ethel}$$
$$40 = \text{John}$$
$$61 = \text{Philip}$$
$$65 = \text{Raymond}$$
$$69 = \text{Robert}$$
$$80 = \text{Thomas}$$
$$89 = \text{William}$$

Common descriptive words on the listing can be replaced by special characters, as follows:

$$* = \text{Mrs.}$$
$$\ddagger = \text{Jr.}$$
$$@ = \text{Inc.}$$

If the list is being used as an index or directory, then further compression is possible because not all the details of each entry are needed to make that entry unique. We may, for example, store only the first two initials and the first four letters of the surname for each entry (approach 3 of Fig. 32.4).

Occasionally this technique will produce duplicates. Westcott, C. Raymond, and Westerman C. R. Mrs., for example, both condense to WESTCR, and any such duplicates other than the first appear as a 6 in the above coding. Where a 6 appears it is necessary to go to an overflow table which stores the original in a unique form. The use of overflow tables in this way can make powerful compression schemes practical.

Such schemes are particularly valuable with the directories or tables that are an essential part of many file organization methods. The tables used are often ordered in ascending sequence with little change between one item and the next. The following, for example, is a directory of engineering changes that have been added to a bill-of-materials file:

Part No.	Engineering Change No.
73012	1380 A
73013	1380 A
79292	1781 A
79293	1781 A
79294	1781 B
79295	1781 B
79296	1781 B
79811	1046 A
79812	1046 A

The items may be preceded by a group of bits which indicate the type of compression, for example,

00: Identical to the previous item
01: Next sequential value

> 1000: Identical to previous item except for last character
> 1001: Identical to previous item except for last two characters
> 1010: Identical to previous item except for last three characters
> 1011: Identical to previous item except for last four characters
> 11 (*n* bits): No relation to previous item; length indicated by the *n* bits

CHARACTER ENCODING

The effectiveness of all the above techniques is highly dependent on the nature of the data that they are used upon. Some of them are entirely application-dependent and could not be included in a general-purpose compaction algorithm. Some, like the technique for suppressing repeated characters, *could* be in a general-purpose algorithm.

One generally applicable way to compress data for storage or transmission is to use the most efficient form of character encoding. The conventional EBCDIC code which most files use (Fig. 32.2) does not give tight encoding for most data. Nor does the U.S. ASCII code, which is widely insisted upon for data transmission.

Numeric characters are often stored in a 4-bit form (packed decimal) on files which store 8-bit bytes, but numeric information is more economically stored in a binary form. Alphabetical data and most punctuation could be transmitted as 5-bit characters. In fact, there is much to be said for using the old 5-bit Baudot code for compact data transmission.[†] It uses "letters shift" and "figures shift" characters to switch the meaning of the big combinations between letters and figures (plus special characters), somewhat like the shift key on a typewriter. It is interesting to reflect that a 5-bit code with three shifts could carry all the data that most users would be likely to want to transmit. A minor modification of the Baudot code could achieve this, as shown in Fig. 32.5. The character 00010 has been given the meaning "transparency shift." When this character is transmitted, the characters following it have the meanings shown in the rightmost column, until a "letters shift" or "figures shift" character is sent. Some of these are control characters. A variety of control characters is used on modern terminals. The remainder are 4-bit binary characters, bits 1, 2, 3, and 5 being used, with the fourth (always a 0) being ignored. Any 8-bit binary character can thus be sent in two of the 4-bit characters, and so programs could be transmitted in this code.

A somewhat tidier 5-bit, three-shift code could be devised if the Baudot code were ignored. The Baudot code is, however, the most commonly used telegraph code outside North America. The character 00010 is "carriage

---

[†] See the author's *Teleprocessing Network Organization*, Prentice-Hall, Inc., Englewood Cliffs, N.J., Chapter 2. 1970.

Code	Letters shift — CCITT standard international telegraph alphabet No. 2	Figures shift	Transparency shift — Control characters or four-bit binary combinations (T)
11000	A	—	T
10011	B	?	Control
01110	C	:	Control
10010	D	Who are you?	Control
10000	E	3	T
10110	F	Note 1	Control
01011	G	Note 1	Control
00101	H	Note 1	T
01100	I	8	T
11010	J	Bell	Control
11110	K	(	Control
01001	L	)	T
00111	M	.	Control
00110	N	,	Control
00011	O	9	Control
01101	P	0	T
11100	Q	1	T
01010	R	4	Control
10100	S	,	T
00001	T	5	T
11100	U	7	T
01111	V	=	Control
11001	W	2	T
10111	X	/	Control
10101	Y	6	T
10001	Z	+	T
00000	Blank		T
00100	Space		T
01000	Line feed		T
11111	Letters shift		
11011	Figures shift		
00010	Transparency shift		

Note 1: Not allocated internationally by CCITT, available to each country for internal use

Figure 32.5 The Baudot code encodes alphanumeric formation with five bits per character. A third shift added to the Baudot code would permit it to encode characters not in its basic character set in binary form.

return" in the Baudot code and "transparency shift" in Fig. 32.5. To communicate with a Baudot code machine, a machine using the code in Fig. 32.5 need inhibit only its "transparency shift" feature and substitute "carriage return."

If a large number of machines using a 5-bit, three-shift code came into use, the translation circuitry could be on one LSI chip and would not be expensive. The throughput with alphanumeric data on a given data channel would be almost 40% higher than with the 8-bit codes in use.

VARIABLE-LENGTH
CHARACTER ENCODING

Character-encoding schemes in normal use have a fixed number of bits per character. Tighter packing of data can be achieved with a code which employs a variable number of bits per character. With such a code the most commonly occurring characters would be short, and the infrequently occurring characters would be long. The shortest character—the most frequently occurring one—would be only one bit.

To provide a simple illustration, suppose that it were necessary to encode only four characters **A**, **B**, **C** and **D**. To encode these in a conventional fixed-length manner would require two bits per character. Suppose the **A** is a frequently occurring character and that **C** and **D** are infrequently occurring. The relative popularity of the characters is as follows:

$$\text{A:} \quad 60\%$$

$$\text{B:} \quad 25\%$$

$$\text{C:} \quad 10\%$$

$$\text{D:} \quad 5\%$$

Because **A** occurs most frequently it will be coded with one bit, a 0 bit. To recognize the start of a character, every other character must begin with a 1 bit. **B** is the second most frequently occurring character, so **B** will be encoded with two bits: 10. To avoid confusion with **B**, no other character may now begin with 10. **C** and **D** must therefore be encoded with three bits, 110 and 111, respectively,

We thus have

Character	Code	Length (bits)	Probability of Occurrence	Probability × length
A	0	1	0.60	0.6
B	10	2	0.25	0.5
C	110	3	0.10	0.3
D	111	3	0.05	0.15

Weighted mean length $= 1.55$

Character	Frequency of occurrence (%)
0	55.5
1	6.7
2	4.5
8	3.5
3	3.3
A	3.2
5	3.0
6	2.7
4	2.7
9	2.2
7	1.9
F	1.5
B	1.2
Blank	1.1
D	1.0
E	0.9
Z	0.7
P	0.6
N	0.5
U	0.4
C	0.4
H	0.4
R	0.3
M	0.3
L	0.3
S	0.25
I	0.20
T	0.15
K	0.15
Y	0.13
X	0.12
G	0.10
J	0.10
O	0.06
Q	0.03
V	0.03
W	0.03
.	0.01
—	
,	
&	
/	
+	
<	below
)	0.001
(	
%	
=	
#	
?	
'	
@	

Figure 32.6 Where the distribution of characters is highly skewed, as here, variable-length character coding can be used to good effect, as in Figs. 32.7 and 32.8.

Character	Frequency of occurrence (%)	Code	Number of bits
0	55.5	0	1
1	6.7	100	3
2	4.5	101	3
8	3.5	11000	5
3	3.3	11001	5
A	3.2	11010	5
5	3.0	11011	5
6	2.7	111000	6
4	2.7	111001	6
9	2.2	111010	6
7	1.9	111011	6
F	1.5	1111000	7
B	1.2	1111001	7
Blank	1.1	1111010	7
D	1.0	1111011	7
E	0.9	11111000	8
Z	0.7	11111001	8
P	0.6	11111010	8
N	0.5	11111011	8
u	0.4	111111000	9
C	0.4	111111001	9
H	0.4	111111010	9
R	0.3	111111011	9
M	0.3	1111111000	10
L	0.3	1111111001	10
S	0.25	1111111010	10
I	0.20	1111111000	10
T	0.15	11111111000	11
K	0.15	11111111001	11
Y	0.13	11111111010	11
X	0.12	11111111011	11
G	0.10	111111111000	12
J	0.10	111111111001	12
O	0.06	111111111010	12
Q	0.03	111111111011	12
V	0.03	1111111111000	13
W	0.03	1111111111001	13
.	0.01	1111111111010	13
—	↑	1111111111011	13
,		11111111111000	14
&		11111111111001	14
/		11111111111010	14
+		11111111111011	14
<		111111111111000	15
)	below	111111111111001	15
(	0.001	111111111111010	15
%		111111111111011	15
=		1111111111111000	16
#		1111111111111001	16
?		1111111111111010	16
'		1111111111111011	16
@	↓	11111111111111000	17
		11111111111111001	17

Average character length =
0.555 × 1 + 0.112 × 3
+ 0.130 × 5 + 0.095 × 6
+ 0.048 × 7 + 0.027 × 8
+ 0.015 × 9 + 0.0105 × 10
+ 0.0055 × 11 + 0.0029 × 12
+ 0.0007 × 13
= 3.01 bits per character

Figure 32.7

Character	Frequency of occurrence (%)	Code	Number of bits
O	55.5	0	1
1	6.7	1000	4
2	4.5	1100	4
8	3.5	10010	5
3	3.3	10100	5
A	3.2	10101	5
5	3.0	10110	5
6	2.7	11100	5
4	2.7	11101	5
9	2.2	11110	5
7	1.9	100110	6
F	1.5	101110	6
B	1.2	111110	6
Blank	1.1	110110	6
D	1.0	110100	6
E	0.9	110101	6
Z	0.7	1011110	7
P	0.6	1111110	7
N	0.5	1101110	7
u	0.4	10011110	8
C	0.4	10011100	8
H	0.4	10011101	8
R	0.3	10111110	8
M	0.3	11111110	8
L	0.3	11111111	8
S	0.25	11011110	8
I	0.20	100111110	9
T	0.15	110111110	9
K	0.15	110111111	9
Y	0.13	1001111110	10
X	0.12	1001111111	10
G	0.10	1011111100	10
J	0.10	1011111101	10
O	0.06	10111111100	11
Q	0.03	10111111101	11
V	0.03	10111111110	11
W	0.03	101111111110	12
.	0.01	1011111111110000	16
—	↑	1011111111110001	16
?		1011111111110010	16
&		1011111111110011	16
/		1011111111110100	16
+		1011111111110101	16
<	below	1011111111110110	16
)	0.001	1011111111110111	16
(		1011111111111000	16
%		1011111111111001	16
=		1011111111111010	16
#		1011111111111011	16
?		1011111111111100	16
'		1011111111111101	16
@	↓	1011111111111110	16
		1011111111111111	16

Average character length. =
0.555 x 1 + 0.112 x 4
+ 0.206 x 5 + 0.76 x 6
+ 0.018 x 7 + 0.24 x 8
+ 0.005 x 9 + 0.0045 x 10
+ 0.0017 x 11 + 0.0003 x 12
+ 0.0001 x 16

= 2.91 bits per character

Figure 32.8

The mean length of all characters is now 1.55 bits, which is better than the two bits of fixed-length encoding.

This type of coding was originally proposed by D. A. Huffman [1] and is called a Huffman code.

Note that such a scheme pays off only with the skewed character distribution. If all characters were used equally often, the mean number of bits per character would be $1 \times 0.25 + 2 \times 0.25 + 3 \times 0.25 + 3 \times 0.25 = 2.25$—worse than with fixed-length characters.

The more skewed the character distribution, the more effective is Huffman and other variable-length encoding. In English text the letters of the alphabet occur with varying frequency, and Huffman encoding gives a mean of about 4.12 bits per character [2]. Most commercial data files have a distribution of characters which is more skewed than this. On one commercial file the relative frequency of occurrence of characters was measured and found to be that shown in Fig. 32.6. Such a distribution is typical and can be encoded with a mean of about 3 bits per character.

A variety of variable-length codes can be used. Figure 32.7 shows one of them. The rule for determining the number of bits per character in Fig. 32.7 is as follows.

If the first bit is 0, the character has one bit.

If the first 2 bits are 10, the character has three bits.

Otherwise character length is the number of leading 1s + 3.

The result indicated in Fig. 32.7 is a mean of 3.01 bits per character.

Figure 32.8 shows a Huffman code which is slightly more efficient and gives a mean of 2.91 bits per character, but it is somewhat more complex to decode.

Figure 32.7 and 32.8 give a low mean number of bits per character because one single character is far more common than any other. In some files two or more characters may share this distinction. If two characters are far more popular than any others, they may both be coded with 2 bits. The encoding in order of decreasing popularity may begin as follows:

0 0

0 1

1 0 0

1 0 1

1 1 0 0

1 1 0 1

1 1 1 0 0 0

There are many possible variations on this idea. If variable-length encoding is used, it is desirable that the method best suited to the data in question be employed.

IMPLEMENTATION   A compaction algorithm designed for use on multiple systems could be implemented in one of three ways—software, microprogramming, or special hardware.

Software packages have been written by different organizations which combine variable-length character encoding and suppression of repeated characters—two operations that can be conveniently built into the same algorithm. They are fairly expensive in machine time. Typically on an IBM 370 Model 155, about 30 microseconds is needed per character encoded or decoded. This may be acceptable on a file which is read or written only very infrequently, but it would not be generally acceptable for real-time file-updating operations. It may be worthwhile when data are transmitted over long and expensive transmission lines or when a very large number of copies of a given set of data have to be distributed. Although this high processing time is needed, the total time the processor is tied up may be *reduced* on some input/output-bound jobs.

When microprogramming is used the time per character drops to about 1 or 2 microseconds on the 370 Model 155. If it were built into hardware logic, perhaps part of the file control unit, the time would be a small fraction of a microsecond.

Most compaction methods result in variable-length records and data items. They should be used with those types of file organization methods which support variable-length items.

HOW EFFECTIVE ARE   On most commercial files the use of a code
COMPACTION TECHNIQUES?   such as the Huffman code, carefully selected to
                           fit the file's character distribution, will halve
the file size, or better. Suppression of repeated characters also halves the file size in many cases. The elimination of unused data elements has a major effect on some files. The other techniques are highly dependent on the application.

Three typical files for a manufacturing application gave the following figures for possible size reductions:

Original File Size (Bytes)	Reduction Using Suppression of Repeated Characters (%)	Reduction Using Huffman Code (%)
300,000	54	82
3 million	34	46
19 million	64	83

The reduction would have been greater if repeated characters had been suppressed first and then the Huffman code used. These figures are typical. A few files give more dramatic savings.

A study of the use of the Huffman code for compacting programs gave savings in the range of 35 to 45% for object code and 55 to 75% for source code.

SIMULATION It is desirable to know in advance how effective compaction will be on existing files. This can be found out using simulation. The files in question, or portions of them, should be processed against the proposed algorithms, and statistics should be gathered. The effect of different techniques and different variable-length character codes may be tested.

REFERENCES

1. D. A. Huffman, "A Method for the Construction of Minimum-Redundancy Codes," *Proc. I.R.E. 40*, Sept. 1952, 1098.

2. E. N. Gilbert and E. F. Moore, "Variable-Length Binary Encodings," *Bell System Tech. J.*, July 1959, 933.

33 VIRTUAL MEMORY AND STORAGE HIERARCHIES

The reason for virtual memory techniques in today's computer systems is to make the computer's main memory appear larger than it really is. This illusion is achieved by dividing the memory contents into pages and storing pages on a backing store. When a program refers to a page which is not in main memory, the operation of the program is temporarily suspended, and the missing page is read in as quickly as possible. When a program modifies the data on a page, the page is moved out to the backing store. The operating system attempts to meet the needs of the programs by judiciously moving the pages in and out of main memory. It takes storage blocks away from one program and gives them to another rather like kiting checks.

The same conjuring trick can also be applied to direct-access storage devices. If a drum is used, for example, a slower, larger, and cheaper storage device can back up the drum, creating what might be described as a *virtual drum.* The objective is to make the drum seem larger than it really is, or, in different words, to make the large slow storage appear to have an access time comparable to that of the drum. The IBM 3850 Mass Storage System uses a large random-access cartridge storage to back up 3330 disk units, and has a storage control computer which makes the entire complex appear like a large array of *virtual* disk units. The software in a 370 behaves as though it were using only 3330 disks.

Ever since direct-access devices were first used there have been proposals that computer storage should consist of a hierarchy of devices of increasing capacity. The devices lower in Fig. 33.1 are larger in capacity and store data at a lower cost per bit, but have longer access times than the higher devices. We will refer the lower devices in Fig. 33.1 as being "lower in the storage hierarchy."

When the computer program requests data, the request goes to the

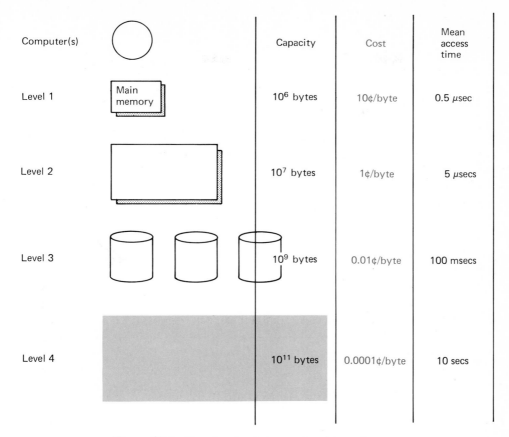

Computer(s)		Capacity	Cost	Mean access time
Level 1	Main memory	10^6 bytes	10¢/byte	0.5 μsec
Level 2		10^7 bytes	1¢/byte	5 μsecs
Level 3		10^9 bytes	0.01¢/byte	100 msecs
Level 4		10^{11} bytes	0.0001¢/byte	10 secs

Figure 33.1   Four levels of storage in a hierarchy.

highest storage device in the hierarchy—computer main memory, or a high-speed cache which is faster than main memory. If the data request is not in this level 1 storage, the request goes to level 2. If it is not in level 2, the request goes to level 3, and so forth. In the worst case the data will have to be brought in from the lowest level.

Figure 33.1 shows four levels of storage. In practice there could be from two to five levels. It is doubtful whether it will ever be economically necessary to use more than four or possibly five levels. Today's virtual systems use two and sometimes three levels. Whether four- or five-level systems are used will depend on the relative speeds, capacities, and costs of available storage devices. Whatever the number of levels, the techniques for paging data between levels in storage hierarchies will be an increasingly important aspect of storage technology. They will have a very important effect on physical data-base organization.

Box 33.1 Typical Cost Per Bit, Size, and Access Time
of Today's Storage Technologies (order-of-
magnitude figures). Cost includes the
transport mechanism cost.

How can these devices be fitted together to form a unified storage system?

Type of Storage	Cost per Bit ($)	Size of Storage (bits)	Access Time (seconds)
Register	10	10^3	10^{-8}
High-speed cache	1	10^4	10^{-7}
Main memory	10^{-1}	$10^6, 10^7$	5×10^{-7}
Large core storage	10^{-2}	$10^7, 10^8$	5×10^{-6}
			◄────── Access-time gap
Drum and fixed-head disk	10^{-3}	$10^7, 10^8$	10^{-2}
Movable-head disk	10^{-4}	$10^8, 10^9, 10^{10}$	10^{-1}
Magnetic strip	10^{-5}	$10^9, 10^{10}$	1
Mass (library) cartridge	10^{-6}	$10^{11}, 10^{12}$	10

Box 33.1 shows some order-of-magnitude figures for cost per bit, size, and access time of today's on-line storage devices. It is because these figures range over such large scales that storage hierarchy systems are needed.

The figures will change somewhat in the future as cost per bit drops but will probably continue to range over equally large or larger scales as new technologies come into the scene. There is a marked break in the access-time scale between solid-state devices and electromechanical devices (arrow in Box 33.1). This gap gives rise to the need for today's virtual memory. It will become economical to build much larger solid-state storages, but at the same time much larger storages with mechanical movement will be available, so during the next 10 years a gap will remain in the access-time scale of three orders of magnitude or thereabouts.

The reader might think of the four levels in Fig. 33.1 as being

1. Computer main memory.

2. Large core storage—larger and cheaper than main memory but substantially slower.

3. Drums or disks.

4. An on-line *archival* or *library* device such as the Ampex Terabit Memory [1,2] (terabit

means 10^{12} bits) or the Precision Instruments Unicon Store which is attached to the ARPA computer network and which also stores 10^{12} bits [3,4,5,6], or the IBM 3850 Mass Storage System [13].

TRILLON-BIT MEMORIES

The last of those four levels has a seek time of up to 15 seconds and a cost per bit that is one or two orders of magnitude lower than disk storage. Such devices are sometimes referred to as *trillon-bit* memories and sometimes as *mass stores* [7]. They will be an increasingly important component of data-base technology, doubtless dropping in both cost per bit and seek time.

Trillon-bit memories in their various future forms can be employed in two ways. First, they can be used in a relatively simple fashion as a replacement for a tape library, without a hierarchical storage arrangement employing drums or disks. To be equivalent to a system with many tape units, many data paths to the reading mechanisms are needed. Second, they can form the lowest component of a hierarchical store, as in Fig. 33.1. In this case they can be used either for serial access or for random access and need not necessarily have many data paths. A block of data, possibly consisting of many pages, will be transferred to the next highest level of storage (e.g., disk storage) when needed.

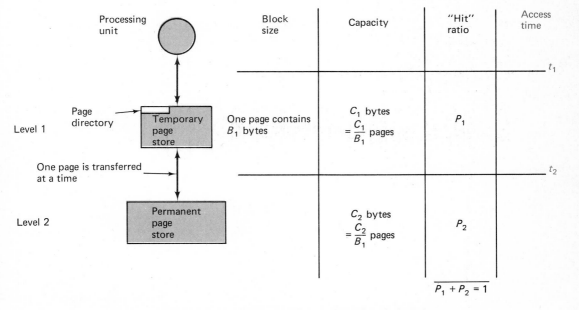

Figure 33.2   A two-level hieararchy: conventional virtual memory.

PAGING   We will briefly describe a paging system such as
                                today's virtual systems and then extend the con-
cept to multilevel hierarchies.

Figure 33.2 shows a two-level memory. It consists of a backing store of
capacity C_2 bytes in which data are kept permanently and a main memory
of C_1 bytes in which some of the data reside temporarily. The data are
organized in fixed-length pages of B_1 bytes. Level 1, the main memory,
holds C_1/B_1 pages. Level 2 holds C_2/B_1 pages. Both of these are an integral
number of pages.

When a program makes a reference to data the probability of its being
found in level 1 is P_1. This is referred to as the *hit ratio* for level 1. The
probability of it being accessed from level 2 is P_2.

$$P_1 + P_2 = 1.$$

The time to access level 1 is t_1, and the time to access level 2 is t_2.
These are the total access times including any queuing delays.

Using $E(x)$ to indicate the mean value (expected value) of x, the mean
access time, $E(t_a)$, of the two-level memory is

$$E(t_a) = P_1 E(t_1) + P_2 E(t_2)$$

$E(t_2)$ may be more than 1000 times greater than $E(t_1)$, so the
performance of the system is highly sensitive to P_1.

P_1 is dependent on four factors:

1. C_1, the storage capacity of level 1.

2. B_1, the page size.

3. The stream of data references.

4. The replacement algorithm, i.e., the decision about which page will be overwritten in
   level 1 storage when a new page is brought in.

THE REFERENCE   The processing unit or units which use the store
STREAM   generate a series of references to the data stored.
                                These may be represented as a series of page
addresses: Z_1, Z_2, Z_3, $\ldots$, Z_L. Different reference patterns will greatly
change P_1.

Suppose that the following string of letters represents a reference
stream:

A B Z T B G H A L K L B Z A X K L K L K L A B T A

A P K L K L A B B G H X Z K L

Each letter represents the identification of a page which is referenced.

Suppose that level 1 storage receives this reference stream but can hold only three pages (for the sake of a simple illustration). The contents of the storage as the reference stream is processed will change as shown in Fig. 33.3. The asterisks mark the time when a page has to be read in from a lower, slower level of storage. After the third reference the memory is full. When the fourth page is brought in one of the first three must be overwritten. The decision is made, in this illustration, always to overwrite that page which was least recently referred to.

If the storage in the above illustration could hold four pages instead of three, there would be fewer times when pages had to be read from the lower level of storage (although the improvement is minor in this case). The contents of the storage would be as shown in Fig. 33.4.

REPLACEMENT ALGORITHMS The decision to always throw out the *least recently used* item in level 1 storage when space is needed is referred as a *replacement algorithm.* A variety of different replacement algorithms could have been used, including

1. *Random replacement.* This is harmful because it frequently removes useful pages.

2. *First-in-first-out* (FIFO). Simple to implement but not necessarily efficient because the item that was the first to be read in may be a popular item which should not be removed.

3. *Least recently used item replacement* (LRU). Generally fairly efficient but more complex to implement because a record must be kept of when each item was last used.

4. *Least frequently used item replacement* (LFU). Often but not always more efficient than least-recently-used replacement but equally complex to implement.

5. *ATLAS loop detection method.* A page-turning technique originally implemented on the Ferranti ATLAS computer, which attempted to minimize program page transfers by detecting looping in programs. It is inappropriate for data paging.

6. *Working set control.* A working set is the set of pages referenced by a program during the previous t seconds, where t is a variable parameter. The storage may be used by many programs at the same time. The working set replacement algorithm decrees that only pages which are not part of current working sets maybe replaced. If necessary,

Figure 33.3 — A reference stream being processed against a store which can hold three items, using *least-recently-used* replacement.

Time	1	2	3	4	5	6	7	8	9	10	11	12	13	14	15	16	17	18	19	20	21	22	23	24	25	26	27	28	29	30	31	32	33	34	35	36	37	38	39	40
Reference stream:	A	B	Z	T	B	G	H	A	L	K	L	B	Z	A	X	K	L	K	L	K	L	A	B	T	A	A	P	K	L	K	L	A	B	B	G	H	X	Z	K	L
Storage contents:	A	B	Z	T	B	G	H	A	L	K	L	B	Z	A	X	K	L	K	L	K	L	A	B	T	A	A	P	K	L	K	L	A	B	B	G	H	X	Z	K	L
		A	B	Z	T	B	G	H	A	L	K	L	B	Z	A	X	K	L	K	L	K	L	A	B	T	T	A	P	K	L	K	L	A	A	B	G	H	X	Z	K
			A	B	Z	T	B	G	H	A	A	K	L	B	Z	A	X	X	X	X	X	K	L	A	B	B	T	A	P	P	P	K	L	L	A	B	G	H	X	Z
(reads)	*	*	*	*		*	*	*	*	*		*	*	*	*	*	*					*	*	*			*	*	*			*	*		*	*	*	*	*	*

(Asterisks indicate that a read from a lower, slower, level of storage is necessary.)

Time:

Reference stream:

Storage contents:

Time	Reference	Storage (1)	Storage (2)	Storage (3)	Storage (4)	Read needed
1	A	A				*
2	B	B	A			*
3	Z	Z	B	A		*
4	T	T	Z	B	A	*
5	B	B	T	Z	A	
6	G	G	B	T	Z	*
7	H	H	G	B	T	*
8	A	A	H	G	B	*
9	L	L	A	H	G	*
10	K	K	L	A	H	*
11	L	L	K	A	H	
12	B	B	L	K	A	*
13	Z	Z	B	L	K	*
14	A	A	Z	B	L	*
15	X	X	A	Z	B	*
16	K	K	X	A	Z	*
17	L	L	K	X	A	*
18	K	K	L	X	A	
19	L	L	K	X	A	
20	A	A	L	K	X	
21	B	B	A	L	K	*
22	T	T	B	A	L	*
23	A	A	T	B	L	
24	A	A	T	B	L	
25	P	P	A	T	B	*
26	K	K	P	A	T	*
27	L	L	K	P	A	*
28	K	K	L	P	A	
29	L	L	K	P	A	
30	A	A	L	K	P	
31	B	B	A	L	K	*
32	B	B	A	L	K	
33	G	G	B	A	L	*
34	H	H	G	B	A	*
35	X	X	H	G	B	*
36	Z	Z	X	H	G	*
37	K	K	Z	X	H	*
38	L	L	K	Z	X	*

(Asterisks indicate that a read from a lower, level of storage is necessary.)

Figure 33.4 The same reference stream as in Fig. 33.3 processed against a store which can hold four items. The storage contents in Fig. 33.3 are a subset of the storage contents here, at all times.

595

execution of a program can be suspended in order to achieve working set control. This replacement algorithm, advocated by Denning [8,9], is intended to minimize *thrashing*—wasteful flip-flopping of a program's pages in and out of main memory. It is primarily relevant to paging between levels 1 and 2 rather than lower storage levels.

STAGING   When multiple levels of storage are used with blocks of pages being passed upward from the lower levels when data are requested, the process is referred to as *staging*. Two-level systems are often concerned with the passing of blocks of *program* between main memory and a backing store. With staging hierarchies it is usually blocks of *data* that are passed. The reference pattern when blocks of data records are passed is likely to be different from that with programs. Program block references relate to the flow of control within a program, whereas record references relate to the physical structure of data bases. Data staging, while simple in principle, has some complex ramifications.

A FOUR-LEVEL   To use words which may help the reader to
SYSTEM   visualize pictorially what is happening, we will refer to the blocks of pages which reside in level 2 as *folders* and the blocks of folders which reside in level 3 as *drawers*. A four-level hierarchy is shown in Fig. 33.5. The lowest level is a permanent store of drawers. The reader may think of an analogy with a hypothetical machine which could store a large number of filing cabinet drawers. Each drawer contains a fixed number of folders, and each folder contains a fixed number of pages. All the data reside permanently in level 4 of the storage, in drawers. Any piece of data may also exist, temporarily duplicated, in any of the other levels.

When a computer program requests data, the logical address or identification number of that data is determined. The logical address does not identify where the data are stored, at least in levels 1, 2, or 3, but does identify its *page number*, *folder number*, and *drawer number.* Level 3 has a directory saying which drawers it contains at any one instant and where they are located. Similarly, level 2 has a directory saying which folders it contains, and level 1 has a directory saying which pages it contains.

When a program requests data, the level 1 directory is inspected to see if the pages containing that data are in level 1. If not, the level 2 directory is inspected to see if the folder containing the required page is in level 2. If so, the page is transferred to level 1 for processing. If the page is not found yet, the level 3 directory is inspected to see whether the drawer containing it is in

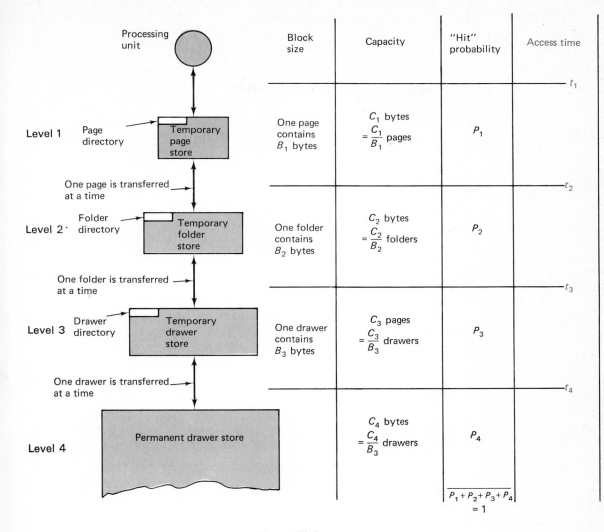

Figure 33.5

level 3. In the worst case the drawer will have to be retrieved from level 4, the folder transferred to level 2, and the page transferred to level 1.

Only complete drawers are passed from level 4 to level 3. Only complete folders are passed from level 3 to level 2. Pages are passed from level 2 to main memory as with two-level virtual memory.

When a block of data is *staged* in this way to a higher level it usually has to overwrite a block currently stored at that level, and so a replacement algorithm is needed for every storage level except the lowest, where the data reside permanently.

When the processor updates the data in a page this page must be transferred to the permanent storage. The page is inserted into its folder in level 2, and the folder is inserted into its drawer in levels 3 and 4.

A page which is being updated may be held at level 1 until the updating is completed or until the page is displaced by the movement of new pages into level 1. If the displaced page contains updated data, it must be moved to its folder in level 2. If not, it can be simply overwritten. Similarly, when a folder is displaced in level 2 or a drawer is displaced in level 3, it must first be moved to its parent location if and only if it contains new data.

A folder is generally held in level 2 as long as its constituent pages are active in level 1, and a drawer is held in level 3 as long as *its* constituents are active in a lower level.

UNEVEN DATA USAGE

The access time of the overall storage subsystem will depend on the level in the hierarchy of the page being accessed, just as it does with today's virtual memory. The objective of the data organization and the replacement algorithms will be to maximize the probability of a page being high in the hierarchy when it is needed.

If successive references to the same page tend to be clustered in time, the *least-recently-used* or *least-frequently-used* replacement algorithms will tend to minimize the mean access time. If a program's data references tend to be close in address space, the page-folder-drawer structure will tend to minimize access time. In many systems data references tend to be clustered in time or clustered in address space. A page once read may be referred to multiple times, perhaps a search operation. A file once opened has multiple records processed. During any brief period of operation most of the references are to a small proportion of the data. The majority of the data is infrequently referenced. It is these tendencies to uneven data usage that make data staging workable. If the data references were randomly distributed among all the data in level 4, staging would be of no value.

MEAN ACCESS TIME

As shown in Fig. 33.5, P_i is the probability that an item will be accessed from level i. For a four-level system $P_1 + P_2 + P_3 + P_4 = 1$.

t_i is the total access time to an item in level i.

The mean access time, $E(t_a)$, is then

$$E(t_a) = P_1 \cdot E(t_1) + P_2 \cdot E(t_2) + P_3 \cdot E(t_3) + P_4 \cdot E(t_4)$$

or in general for an L-level system:

$$E(t_a) = \sum_{i=1}^{L} P_i \cdot E(t_i)$$

To quote the mean access time alone, or even the mean and standard deviation, can be grossly misleading because some of the accesses will be many thousands of times longer than others. We recommend that only a distribution of access times, or the P_i and $E(t_i)$ values, be quoted.

It is desirable to make P_i for the higher level of storage as large as possible. In a four-level system, P_4 should be as small as possible because $E(t_4)$ is likely to be large enough to seriously degrade response times.

DESIGN
OPTIONS

P_i is referred to as the *hit ratio* at level *i*. What strategies will make the hit ratios at higher levels as high as possible, especially at the higher storage levels?

1. The larger the storage capacities of levels 1, 2, and 3, the higher will be the hit ratios. However, the purpose of using a storage hierarchy is to lower the overall storage cost, so it is self-defeating to make the expensive levels of storage too large. Nevertheless, we will show that too small a capacity at any of the three levels will result in *gross* system inefficiency.

2. The replacement algorithm will have an effect on P_i. Different levels may have different replacement algorithms.

3. It is desirable to select the optimum page size, folder size, and drawer size. If these sizes are too small, the directory will be lengthy and will be time-consuming to search. If the sizes are too large, the transfer time will be higher, and the number of transfers will be increased for some types of processing.

4. The number of levels in the hierarchy could be changed. For example, level 2 might be eliminated and the pages stored directly in drawers, without folders. The number of levels which form the most economical mix will depend on the available storage devices—their cost, size, and speed. Detailed analyses show that it is desirable to avoid too big a gap in access times between one level and another.

5. The scheduling of jobs in the computer may have a major effect on the reference stream. On some interactive systems little can be done to improve the reference stream, but batch-processing appropriate job scheduling may be a key to efficient use of a storage hierarchy.

ANTICIPATORY AND   The system we have described moves the blocks of
DEMAND STAGING   data only *on demand*. This is referred to as *demand
                                staging*. No block is fetched from lower levels of
storage unless it has been requested.

An alternative is to move many blocks of data upward in the hierarchy
when a program begins to execute or when a file is opened, in *anticipation*
that these blocks will be needed. This is referred to as *anticipatory* staging.
Anticipatory staging can decrease the average access time but may worsen
the utilization of the higher, expensive levels of storage.

Any form of staging is to be contrasted with *static* allocation of
hierarchical storage. Most storage hierarchies have been allocated in a static
fashion to date. There is likely to be swing to dynamic allocation for much
the same reasons as the swing to virtual memory—more efficient utilization
of resources and an attempt to disguise the long access times of mass
storages.

THE SUCCESS   A ratio called the *success function* is used in
FUNCTION   evaluating storage hierarchies. The success function
                                for level i depends on the capacity of that level, C_i,
and will be written $F_i(C)$. It represents the fraction of references that could
be found in level i if level i were the highest level of storage.

The success function is calculated by taking the computer reference
stream and running it against the level i storage. A set of values of $F_i(C)$ is
calculated for a given reference stream, a given replacement algorithm, and a
given block size in level i. At level 1, the success function equals the hit ratio.
At lower levels it is greater than the hit ratio because some hits are always
found at level 1:

$$F_1(C) = P_1$$
$$F_i(C) > P_i \quad \text{where } i > 1$$

We will calculate the success function first for level 1 and then for
higher levels.

STACK REPLACEMENT   Referring back to the three- and four-item storage
ALGORITHMS   of Figs. 33.3 and 33.4, the reader should note that
                                at each instant in time the set of four items in

storage in Fig. 33.4 *includes* the three items in storage in Fig. 33.3. In fact, if the storage could hold N items, the N items stored would include the $N - 1$ items that would be stored if the storage capacity were $N - 1$. This *inclusion property* is a property of the least-recently-used replacement algorithm used in Figs. 33.3 and 33.4. The least-frequently-used replacement algorithm and most other important replacement algorithms have the same property. Such algorithms are referred to as *stack* replacement algorithms, and for them there is a particularly neat method of obtaining the success function $F_i(C)$. The method is called *stack processing*. It was first used by Mattson et al. [10].

If S(D) is the set of blocks in the storage at a given point in the processing of a given reference stream with a given stack replacement algorithm and D is the capacity of the storage in blocks, then S(D) ⩽ S(D + 1) if at least D + 1 blocks have been referenced.

Figure 33.6 takes advantage of this property to show which pages would be in the storage for *any* storage capacity. The first two rows of the storage contents box show what pages would be in the storage at each time if the capacity of the storage were two pages. The first three rows correspond to Fig. 33.3. The first N rows show what pages would be in the storage if its capacity were N pages.

The columns in the box are sequenced by decreasing desirability of the pages. The page lowest in each column is the one most elegible for replacement. Because Fig. 33.6 employs the least-recently-used replacement algorithm, the lowest page in each column is the least recently used page, and the column is sequenced by previous time of use. The columns are referred to as *stacks*, sometimes as *probability stacks.*

When a new page is referred to, it appears at the top of the stack. Its position in the previous stack is referred to as the *stack distance.* At time 5, for example, B appears in the reference stream. At time 4, B was in position 3 of the stack. The stack distance in this case is 3. If B had not existed in the previous stack, the stack distance would have been written as *infinity.* If the storage capacity is equal to or greater than the stack distance, then no access is needed to a lower level of storage. The asterisks in Fig. 33.4 (storage capacity = 4) thus correspond to stack distances in Fig. 33.6, which are greater than 4 and hence necessitate an access to a lower-level store.

From any reference stream a set of stack distances can be produced as in Fig. 33.6. The stack distances can then be examined statistically.

The following table relates to Fig. 33.6:

Time: 1 2 3 4 5 6 7 8 9 10 11 12 13 14 15 16 17 18 19 20 21 22 23 24 25 26 27 28 29 30 31 32 33 34 35 36 37 38 39 40

Reference stream: A B Z T B G H A L K L B Z A X K L K L A B T A A P K L A B B G H X Z K L

Level 1 stacks:

Pages
1
2
3
4
5
6
7
8
9
10

Stack distance (pages): ∞ 3 ∞ ∞ 3 ∞ ∞ 6 ∞ ∞ 2 6 8 2 ∞ 6 2 2 2 4 6 2 ∞ 1 8 6 2 4 6 1 ∞ 8 6 1 10 10 9 10 8 8

An access to level 2 storage is needed if the storage capacity
of level 1 is less than these figures

Figure 33.6 **Level-1 probability stacks for the above reference stream,
with *least-recently-used* replacement.** The position of item B in the
stacks is red.

602

Stack Distance (D)	Frequency of Occurrence of D	Frequency of Occurrence of Distance $\leqslant D$	Probability that Stack Distance $\leqslant D$
1	2	2	0.050
2	7	9	0.225
3	2	11	0.275
4	2	13	0.325
5	1	14	0.350
6	8	22	0.550
7	0	22	0.550
8	3	25	0.625
9	2	27	0.675
10	3	30	0.750
∞	10	40	1.000

The probability that the stack distance $\leqslant D$ is equivalent to the probability that a referenced page will be found in the storage if the storage capacity is D pages—in other words, this probability equals the success function $F_1(C)$.

Figure 33.7 plots $F_1(C)$ against D and C for the reference stream in question. In reality a much longer reference stream should be examined by means of a program. The stream of 40 references is not long enough to reach

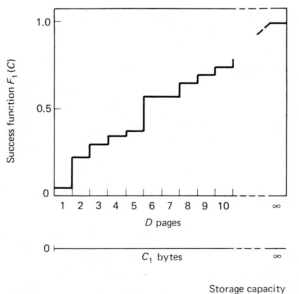

Figure 33.7 The success function plotted from the stack distances in Fig. 33.6.

Time:
1 2 3 4 5 6 7 8 9 10 11 12 13 14 15 16 17 18 19 20 21 22 23 24 25 26 27 28 29 30 31 32 33 34 35 36 37 38 39 40

Reference stream:
A B Z T B G H A L K L B Z A X K L K L A B T A A P K L K L A B B G H X Z K L

Level 1 stacks:

Stack																																							
1	A	B	Z	T	B	G	H	A	L	K	L	K	K	X	K	L	L	L	B	A	L	T	A	P	K	K	K	L	L	B	B	G	H	X	N	K	A	K	K	L
2		A	B	Z	T	B	G	B	B	B	B	B	B	B	B	B	B	K	A	L	A	L	L	A	A	A	A	A	A	A	A	A	A	A	A	A	L	A	A	K
3			A	B	Z	T	B	G	G	L	L	A	A	B	B	A	A	A	K	K	K	K	K	L	L	L	L	K	B	L	L	L	L	L	L	L	B	L	L	A
4				A	A	Z	T	H	H	G	G	L	L	A	A	K	K	B	X	B	B	B	B	K	K	K	K	B	K	K	K	K	K	B	B	B	K	B	B	B
5						A	Z	T	G	H	H	H	H	L	L	X	X	X	N	N	N	N	N	B	B	B	P	P	P	P	P	P	T	K	K	K	T	K	Z	Z
6							A	Z	T	T	T	G	G	H	H	H	H	H	X	X	X	X	X	N	T	T	T	T	T	T	T	T	P	T	T	G	X	X	X	X
7								A	Z	Z	N	T	T	G	G	G	G	G	H	H	H	H	H	X	X	X	X	X	X	X	X	X	X	P	P	T	Z	H	H	H
8									A	N	Z	N	N	T	T	T	T	T	G	G	G	G	G	H	H	H	H	N	N	N	N	N	N	N	Z	P	H	G	G	G
9										A	A	Z	Z	N	N	N	N	N	T	T	T	T	T	G	G	G	G	H	H	H	H	H	H	X	X	P	G	T	T	T
10												A	A	Z	Z	Z	Z	Z	Z	Z	Z	Z	Z	T	Z	Z	Z	G	G	G	G	G	G	G	H	X	P	P	P	P

Stack distance (pages):
8 8 3 8 6 8 8 8 4 4 2 2 4 8 8 8 5 4 2 2 3 4 3 9 3 1 8 3 5 3 2 3 4 1 10 10 10 9 5 3

Figure 33.8 The same as Fig. 33.6, except that *least-frequently-used* replacement is employed. Item B remains higher in the stacks than in Fig. 33.6. It would be in the storage when needed more frequently than in Fig. 33.6 if the storage capacity is 4 or 5 items.

Pages

604

a steady-state condition. Much of it is filling up stacks which start empty. If a long reference stream were analyzed, the curve in Fig. 33.7 would be much smoother.

COMPARISON OF
REPLACEMENT
ALGORITHMS

Using the method shown, different replacement algorithms can be compared. If an algorithm has the property of *inclusion*, which makes it a stack replacement algorithm, then a set of stack distances can be analyzed. If it does not have this property, then a separate analysis of the reference stream must be done for each storage size.

FIFO, for example, is *not* a stack replacement algorithm.

Figure 33.8 shows a stack analysis using the same reference stream but with a least-frequently-used replacement algorithm. A count is maintained of the number of times each page is used and when space is needed the page with the lowest count is thrown out. If there is more than one page with the same lowest count, the least recently used of these is replaced.

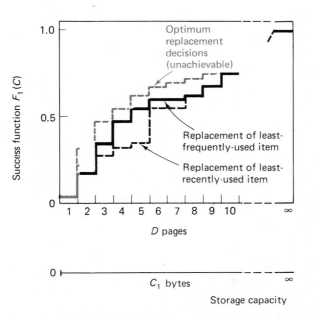

Figure 33.9 A comparison of replacement algorithms using the reference stream of the previous figures. If long steady-state reference streams were analyzed, these would be smooth curves.

Figure 33.9 compares the values of $F_1(C)$ for the least-frequently-used replacement algorithm with those for the least-recently-used. It will be seen that for storage capacities 3 through 7 the least-frequently-used algorithm is the better of the two. This is not true for all reference streams. Which algorithm performs best depends on the clustering in the reference stream.

AN OPTIMAL
REPLACEMENT
ALGORITHM

Figure 33.9 also shows the success function that would have been achieved if each replacement decision had been the best possible decision. How can we tell what would have been the optimal replacement decision? To do this it is necessary to look ahead at the future references. For each replacement, the page to be thrown out is that which is referenced furthest in the future in the reference stream.

For demand paging (or staging) this *optimum* replacement algorithm cannot be achieved in practice. The computer is not clairvoyant and cannot predict the future. It is, however, valuable as a yardstick with which other replacement algorithms can be compared.

The optimal algorithm is a *stack* replacement algorithm. Figure 33.10 illustrates it, and it is from the stack distances in Fig. 33.10 that the optimum is plotted in Fig. 33.9. It will be seen that in this example the least frequently used replacement algorithm is fairly closed to the optimum.

MULTILEVEL
ANALYSES

The success function will be calculated in a similar fashion for the other storage levels. To provide an easily illustrated example we will assume that the staging blocks of level 2 (folders) each contain two pages. Figure 33.11 shows the stacks for level 2, using the same reference stream as before. The replacement algorithm replaces the least frequently used folders. The stacks are of folders rather than pages as in the previous diagrams. The stack distance is measured in folders.

Figure 33.12 plots the level 1 and level 2 success functions calculated from Figs. 33.8 and 33.11.

The stream of requests that go from level 1 to level 2 will vary with the capacity of level 1. P_2, the probability of a *hit* in level 2, is dependent on the size of level 1. If level 1 is large, there will be more hits in level 1 and hence fewer in level 2. In Fig. 33.13, level 1 has been fixed at a capacity of five pages and level 2 at a capacity of six folders.

Although the level 2 hit probability is dependent on level 1, the level 2 priority stacks are entirely *independent* of level 1. The replacement

Time:

Time	Reference stream	Stack distance (pages)
1	A	∞
2	B	∞
3	Z	∞
4	T	∞
5	B	2
6	G	∞
7	H	∞
8	A	3
9	L	8
10	K	8
11	L	2
12	B	4
13	Z	5
14	A	3
15	X	8
16	K	4
17	L	2
18	K	2
19	L	2
20	A	2
21	B	4
22	T	6
23	A	2
24	A	1
25	P	8
26	K	3
27	L	4
28	K	2
29	L	2
30	A	3
31	B	6
32	B	1
33	G	7
34	H	8
35	X	5
36	Z	9
37	K	2
38	L	3
39	K	
40	L	

Level 1 stacks: (rows 1–10)

Figure 33.10 The optimum replacement algorithm—unachievable in practice for demand paging, but a useful yardstick to measure what is achievable.

Time:

1 2 3 4 5 6 7 8 9 10 11 12 13 14 15 16 17 18 19 20 21 22 23 24 25 26 27 28 29 30 31 32 33 34 35 36 37 38 39 40

Reference stream:

A B Z T B G H A L K L B Z A X K L K L A B T A A P K L K L A B B G H X Z K L

Level 2 Stacks

Blocks																																						
1	A B	A B	A Y N	A S T	A G H	G H	A G B	A K L	K L	K L	K L	K A B	Y N	A Y B	A W X	K L	K L	K L	K L	W K L	A O B P	A O P	K L	K L	K L	K L	A B	A B	A A B	G H	G H	G W X	A B	A B	W G X H	O P	O P	K L	K L
2		A B	A B	S T	A B	A B	S T	A B	A B	A B	A B	K L	A B	K L	K L	A B	A B	A B	A B	A B	K L	K L	A B	A B	A B	A B	K L	K L	K L	K L	K L	A B	K L	K L	K L	A B	A B	A B	A B
3			Y N	Y N	S T	S T	S T	S G H	G H	G H	G H	G H	K L	K L	Y N	Y Z N	Y N	Y N	Y N	K Y L N	S K T L	S T	S T	S T	S T	A K B L	S T	S T	S T	S T	S T	K L	S T	S T	A B	G H	G H	Y N	Y N
4				Y N	Y N	Y N	Y N	S T	S T	S T	Y N	G H	G H	Y G H	Y N	G G H	G H	G H	G H	G W X	Y Y N	Y N	Y N	Y N	S K T L	S T	Y N	Y N	Y N	Y N	Y N	Y N	Y N	Y N	S T	S T	W X	W X	W X
5						Y N	Y N	Y N	Y N	Y N	Y N	S T	S S T	S T	S T	W W X	W X	W X	W X	S S T	G W H X	G H	G H	G H	G H	Y N	G H	G H	G H	G H	G H	G H	G H	O P	Y N	Y N	S T	S T	S T
6							Y N	Y N	Y N	Y N	Y N					S T	S T	S T	S T		S T	S T	W X	W X	G H	G H	O P	O P	O P	O P	O P	W W X	O P	O P	O P	W X	Y N	Y N	O P
7																									W X	W X	W X	W X	W X	W X	W X		W X	W X	W X	S T	O P	O P	O P

Stack distance (blocks):

8 1 8 8 8 2 1 8 2 1 2 5 1 2 8 3 1 1 1 1 2 1 6 1 3 1 1 1 3 2 1 1 5 1 7 1 6 2 1

Figure 33.11 Probability stacks for level 2 using the same reference stream, *least-frequently-used* replacement, and a block size of two pages.

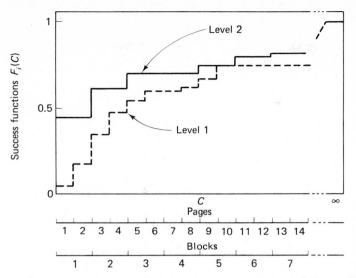

Figure 33.12 Success functions for storage levels 1 and 2 drawn from the stack diagrams, Figs. 33.8 and 33.11 *Least-frequently-used* replacement algorithms are used for both.

algorithm used by level 2 in Fig. 33.11 is based on the original reference stream, not on anything that happens in level 1.

A similar argument can apply to all levels in the hierarchy. The priority stacks for level i are independent of what takes place at level j, where $j < i$. The success function $F_i(C)$ is therefore also independent of level j.

SELECTING THE STORAGE CAPACITY	A data-base designer using a staging hierarchy must select the storage capacities to give an appropriate set of hit ratios, P_i, and hence an appropriate set of response times.

From a reference stream he can compute the success functions $F_i(C)$ for each level. He can then estimate the values of P_i by subtracting values of success functions for adjacent levels, as illustrated in Fig. 33.14. This technique can be used when the following two properties apply:

Property 1: The replacement algorithm at level i is independent of the storage capacity of level j, where $i > j$, for all values of i and j.

Property 2: The presence of a data block in storage level i implies the presence of its parent block in level $i + 1$, for all levels except the lowest.

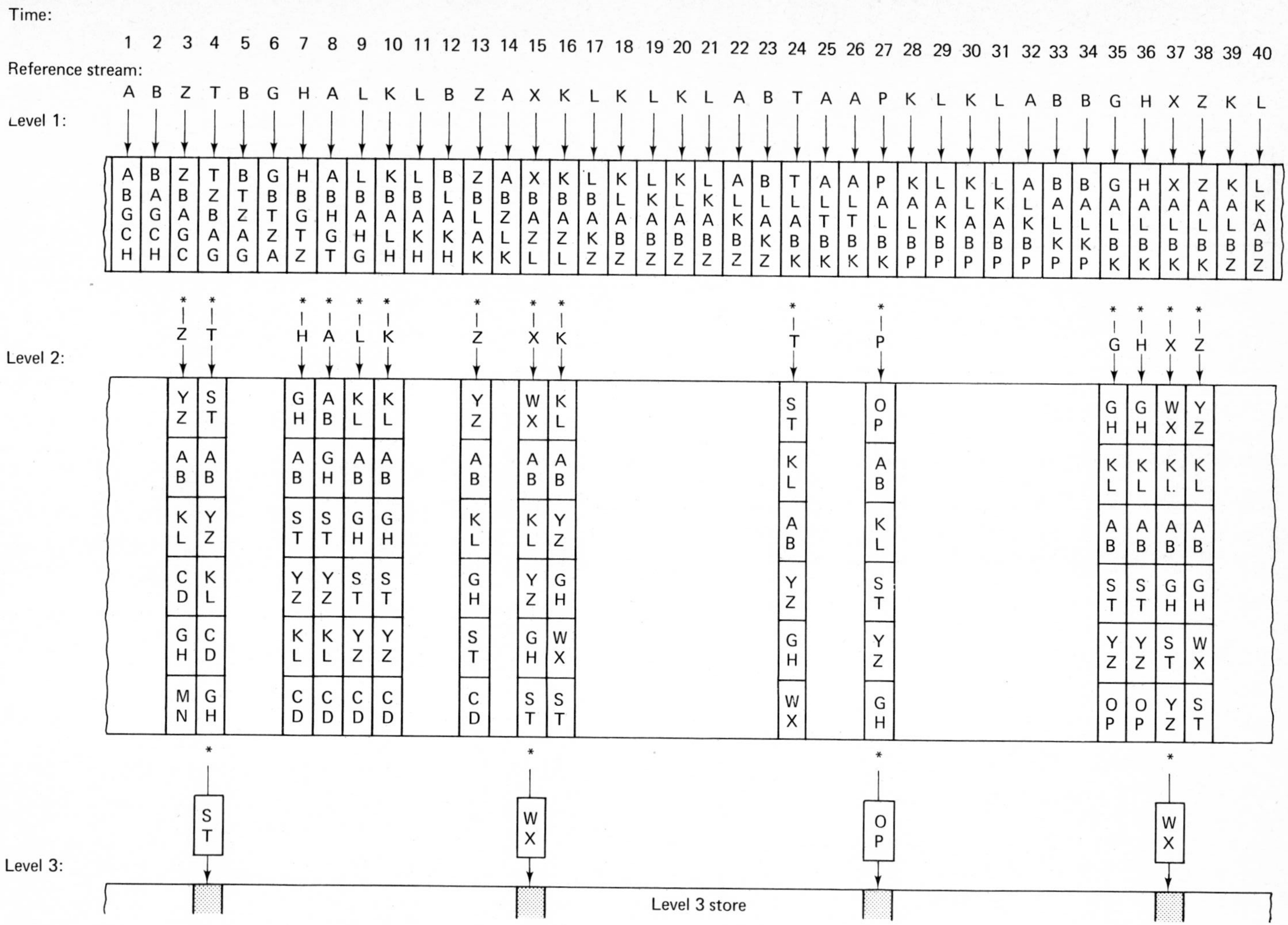

Figure 33.13 The contents of levels 1 and 2 when processing the reference stream in Figs. 33.8 and 33.11 with least-frequently-used replacement. The level 1 capacity is set at five pages, the level 2 capacity is set at twelve pages.

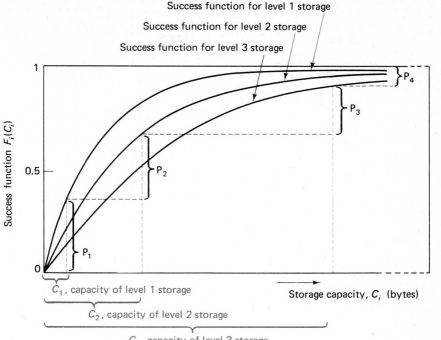

Figure 33.14 For important classes of replacement algorithms the hit ratios, $P_1, \ldots, P_L$, are related to the success functions as shown. This provides a simple method of selecting the storage capacities to obtain acceptable performance.

It was proved by Slutz and Traiger [11,12] that in a staging hierarchy of L levels having capacities C_i, which obeys the above two properties, hit ratios P_i are determined by

$$P_i = F_i(C_i) - F_{i-1}(C_{i-1}), \qquad i = i \ldots L$$

where $F_0(C) = 0$ and $F_L(C) = 1$.

Given the curves of Fig. 33.14, the designer can slide the values of C_1, C_2, and C_3 until he finds an acceptable set of P_i values and storage costs.

DEPENDENCE ON THE REFERENCE STREAM   The P_i values are highly dependent on the *sequence* of data references in the reference stream. A reference stream in which successive references are

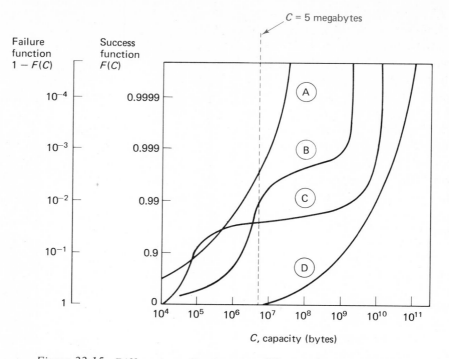

Figure 33.15 Different applications or different data bases result in different reference streams, and the same staging techniques yield widely varying success functions.

highly clustered within pages can have a mean access time close to t_1. A stream in which successive references are randomly scattered across the entire storage will have a mean reference time close to t_4 —a million times greater perhaps. It therefore does not make much sense to quote P_i values or a distribution of storage subsystem access times as though they are a characteristic *of the hardware.* The subsystem access times are very highly dependent on the application or mix of applications that are being processed simultaneously.

The success functions may be plotted for different applications or different data bases, assuming a given block size and replacement algorithm. It is often desirable to plot this for a very wide range of values of C, and hence logarithmic scales are used, as in Fig. 33.15.

Example 1

A solid state memory comes onto the market with a capacity of 5 megabytes. The success function of four existing systems are shown in Fig.

33.15 using a block size and a replacement algorithm that would give good performance with the memory. Should it be used?

With system B it would have a major effect on system performance because of the kink in the success function curve. 99% of the requests could be handled by the solid-state memory, thus taking much of the load of the lower-level disk storage. This would permit much higher system throughput and better response times. The memory would also be effective with system A. With system D it would give negligible improvement. With system C the success function is little different from that with disks of 10^8 or even 10^9 bytes, which give a much lower cost per byte. If the disks are given adequate throughput and response time, the intermediate solid-state memory may give little benefit to the system but substantially increases its cost.

Example 2

An order entry system has terminals in hundreds of sales offices·which are used to enter data into and make inquiries on a data base which occupies a large number of disk modules. A mass storage comes onto the market capable of holding the entire data base. Its mean access time is 5 seconds. Should it be used?

This interactive system generates 20 requests per second to the data base. The mean access time of the mass store is 5 seconds. Because of queuing it is assumed that the access mechanism should not have more than 75% utilization. The device can then handle $1/5 \times 0.75 = 0.15$ requests per second:

$$\frac{\text{Maximum mass store access rate}}{\text{System reference rate}} = \frac{0.15}{20} = 0.0075$$

The capacity of the storage level above the mass storage must therefore be such that the value of its success function is $\leqslant 1 - 0.0075 (= 0.9925)$.

The reference stream of the existing system is captured and analyzed with a block size suitable for the transfers from the mass store. Curve 1 in Fig. 33.16 shows the result. Unfortuantely most of the curve lies below the horizontal dotted line at $F(C) = 0.9925$. The storage level *below* the mass store would need a capacity of about 8 billion bytes. The entire data base occupies only 20 billion bytes. Eight billion bytes would require at least five of the large disk storage units which are employed today. The design team concludes that it would not be economical to use a mass store if it must be backed up by so much disk storage.

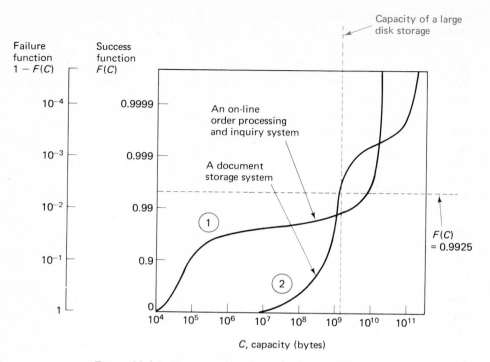

Figure 33.16   Examples: Should a mass store be used?

Example 3

A system is being designed to store bulky documents (possibly documents stored in digitized facsimile form). Documents which are currently of interest are referred to much more frequently than most. The majority of the documents are requested only rarely. The number of requests is not high enough to make the throughput critical, as in the previous example, but a fast response time is needed to some of the documents.

A typical stream of document requests is analyzed and results in curve 2 of Fig. 33.16. The shape of the curve suggests that the mass store should be backed up with a disk storage unit which is available, having the capacity of the vertical dotted line.

THRASHING   One of the most troublesome problems that afflicts some of today's two-level virtual systems is *thrash-*

ing. Thrashing means that needed pages are repeatedly displaced from main memory and have to be brought in again. The term denotes severe performance degradation caused by too much paging. On some systems which have behaved well earlier, an increase in load can cause a relatively sudden onset of thrashing, which can reduce a powerful computer to stammering efficiency.

Thrashing can also occur in storage hierarchies, but the causes are generally somewhat different because the storage references are to blocks of data rather than pages of program. It conjures up visions of slapstick comedy to imagine a large storage hierarchy thrashing, bringing in quantities of folders and drawers, rejecting them without using their data, and rushing to bring in more.

The cause of thrashing in programs has been investigated in detail by many authorities. The primary causes are that a main storage is too small, that an access time to the level 2 storage is too large, and that scheduling techniques allow too many programs to begin work that cannot continue without excessive paging [8]. Systems designers sometimes insist on simulating large virtual memories with real memories that are too small. This is dangerous when the difference in speed between the main memory and backing store is very large. The great difference in access time makes system efficiency very sensitive to changes in missing-page probability. A system thus susceptible to thrashing has the disease brought on by paging algorithms which fail to control a rise in missing-page probability.

In data bases, certain physical structures are prone to excessive paging or staging if a hierarchy storage is used. Chains or rings, for example, which straggle from page to page or block to block will be very wasteful of the staging capability. Binary searches which jump from page to page are to be avoided. Indices should be divided into tree structures in which each block is confined to a page. In general the more the clustering of data accesses into pages or blocks the better. To facilitate clustering, the data and relationships should be separated as discussed in Chapter 28. The uneven distribution of data-base references must be exploited. It is essential to avoid accessing the lowest-level storage with accesses which are scattered randomly throughout the storage.

Tailoring the data base to the storage hierarchy and its block sizes will make major changes to the reference streams that are used. It is thus not really adequate to take the reference stream of an existing nonhierarchy system and use it for designing a hierarchy system. There is an intimate trade-off between data structures and storage structures which needs to be explored.

As storage hierarchies come into use and become better understood they will change much of the conventional wisdom about physical data-base structures.

REFERENCES

1. S. Damron, J. Lucas, J. Miller, E. Salbu, and M. Wildmann, "A Random Access Terabit Magnetic Memory," *Proc. AFIPS FJCC 33*, Part 2, 1968, 1381–1387.

2. Richard B. Gentile and Joseph R. Lucas, "The TABLON Mass Storage Network," *Proc. AFIPS SJCC 38*, 1971, 345–356.

3. C. H. Becker, "Unicon Mass Memory System," *Proc. AFIPS FJCC 29*, 1966, 711–716.

4. K. McFarland and M. Hashiguchi, "Laser Recording for High-Density Permanent Digital Store," *Proc. AFIPS FJCC 23*, Part 2, 1968, 1369–1380.

5. S. Parnas and C. J. Peters, "Laser Recorders Pick Up Where Magnetic Machines Leave Off," *Electronics*, Feb. 16, 1970, 101.

6. Harold L. Pickering, "Planned Application of a Massive Memory Device," in *Proceedings of the IEEE 5th Annual International Computer Society Conference Digest, 1971*, pp. 151–152.

7. George B. Houston, "Trillion Bit Memories," *Datamation*, Oct. 1973, 52–58.

8. Peter J. Denning, "Thrashing: Its Causes and Prevention," in *Proceedings of the Fall Joint Computer Conference, 1968*, p. 915.

9. Peter J. Denning, "The Working Set Model for Program Behavior," *Comm. ACM 11*, No. 5, May 1968.

10. R. L. Mattson, J. Gecsei, D. R. Slutz, and I. L. Traiger, "Evaluation Techniques for Storage Hierarchies," *IBM System J. 9*, No. 2, 1970.

11. D. R. Slutz and I. L. Traiger, "Determination of Hit Ratios for a Class of Staging Hierarchies," *IBM Research Report No. RJ1044*, IBM, Yorktown Heights, N.Y., May 1972.

12. I. L. Traiger and D. R. Slutz, "One-Pass Techniques for the Evaluation of Memory Hierarchies," *IBM Research Report No. RJ892*, IBM, Yorktown Heights, N.Y., July 1971.

13. "Introduction to the IBM 3850 Mass Storage System (MSS)" IBM Manual No. GA32-0028, IBM, Harrison, N.Y., 1974.

BOOK STRUCTURE

Chapters 34 and 35 discuss two special requirements: highly volatile systems, and systems requiring fast response times.

34 VOLATILE FILES

A volatile file is one into which new records are inserted, and possibly old ones deleted, at a high rate. Some of the techniques we have discussed facilitate the handling of a high rate of insertions and deletions. Other techniques are generally unsatisfactory. The techniques which are suitable are more limited if volatility is combined with a requirement for fast response time.

Some files are fairly static; that is, new records are not added very often, nor are records removed. The customers of a bank do not change very rapidly. The customers of an airline, on the other hand, do, and this file needs to be organized to cater to the change. Some files, such as a store of messages to be sent in a message-switching system, change constantly minute by minute.

A slowly changing file on a direct-access device can be reorganized periodically when the system is off the air so that the gaps left by deleted records do not cause a waste of space. A rapidly changing file must be organized so that the space left by deleted records can be filled by new ones as the need arises, in real time.

In the latter case, the organization of the file may become steadily more inefficient. In other words, it takes longer to gain access to a record than need be because the records are not in the best locations. It should therefore be cleaned up periodically. This may be done when the system is not on the air, or it may be done, using multiprogramming, during the system's idler periods of operation. When there are few real-time transactions arriving, the computer may work through the files' indices moving records to fill up gaps.

If a file is volatile, storage organizations which involve cumbersome maintenance operations should be avoided. It is desirable to select

Box 34.1　Volatile File Techniques　(Compare with Box 35.1)

Techniques Which Tend To Be Poor for Volatile Files	Techniques Which Tend To Be Better
• Embedded pointers	• Relational data base
• Relationships mixed up with data • Relationships represented by physical contiguity • Intersecting chains or rings	• All relationships in a separate directory
• Machine-address pointers	• Symbolic pointers
• Real-time insertions and deletions	• Insertions and deletions deferred to off-line operation • *Information system* data base separate from *operations system* data base (Fig. 16.2)
• Files ordered in key sequence	• Files ordered randomly or in sequence of record origination
• Files ordered hierarchically	• Circular files • Dynamic block allocation
• Moving data records to accommodate insertions	• Insertions accommodated by index or pointer modification, without moving data records

techniques with which to allow many new records to be added to a file without having to shuffle the records already there.

Box 34.1 lists techniques of physical data organization according to whether they are likely to be better or worse for volatile files.

**REAL-TIME
INSERTIONS
AND DELETIONS**
On some systems it is possible to defer the insertion of new records into the files until the end of the day. Similarly, old records need not be deleted in real time but simply flagged to indicate that they are not available. If new records can be retained until later rather than inserted into the files in real time, then they are generally easier and less disruptive to handle.

On many *information* systems (as opposed to *operations* systems) most of the complexities in data structures arise from the secondary keys and searching requirements. When records are inserted the prime keys may be dealt with without much trouble, but the secondary keys require chains to be relinked or large secondary indices to be reshuffled. While it is more difficult to handle insertions and deletions in the secondary key files, these changes may be less urgent. It often does not matter if a management information system gives information which is 24 hours out of date.

**VERY HIGH
VOLATILITY**
Some files are so volatile that the volatility dominates the entire design. The mechanisms must be designed so that new records can be added at a rapid rate without degrading the response time. The space for the new records must be assigned in advance. Old records must be systematically removed from the files with appropriate modifications to chains or indices. It is usually better to remove the deleted records in a planned periodic operation which makes the space available for new records rather than to remove them in real time when the deletion occurs.

**POLICE
EMERGENCY
SYSTEM**
An example of a system in which the main file is highly volatile is one for enabling the police to react efficiently to incidents that are taking place in a city. When a person dials the police emergency number in the city, his call is routed immediately to an operator of a computer terminal. The operator enters details of the situation into the computer, and the computer provides a group of radio vehicle dispatchers

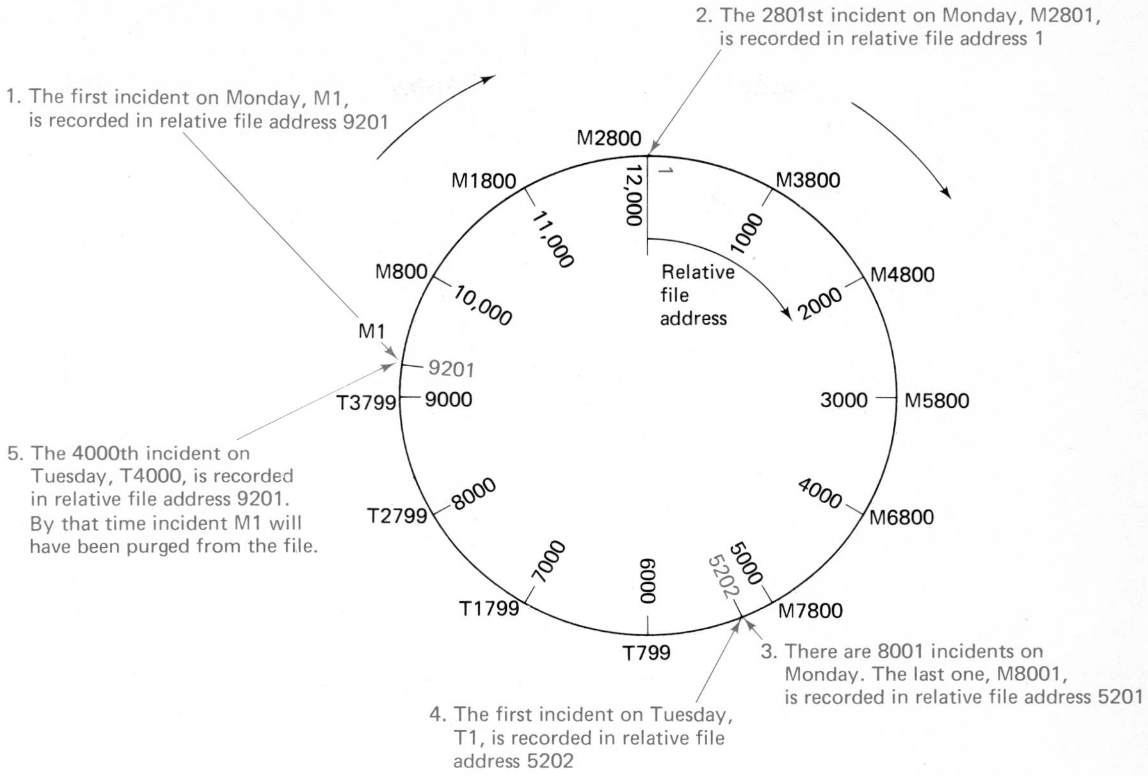

Figure 34.1 The concept of a circular file. The circle represents 12,000 blocks of contiguous storage.

with details of all such situations. The dispatchers send police cars or ambulances to the scene of the incident if they are needed.

The computer must maintain a file of all incidents taking place in the city. In New York City this file can hold details of up to 12,000 incidents per day. Both the input operator and the radio dispatchers must interrogate the file in a variety of different ways. New incidents may happen at a fast and furious rate, and the information first received about an incident is often wrong. The file is as volatile as the streets of New York.

CIRCULAR FILES

In some of the police emergency systems the incidents are stored in a circular file, as shown in Fig. 34.1; 12,000 blocks of contiguous storage are employed in this illustration. Each block can hold the record for one incident. A relative file address is used for the storage, extending from 1 to 12,000. The incident records are stored sequentially in the storage in the order in which they are created. When relative file address 12,000 is filled, the next record is stored in relative file address 1. The storing of incident records thus circulates continuously through the 12,000 storage blocks. Each incident record stored will overwrite the one 12,000 incidents ago, and by that time this record must have been purged from the file.

With the police systems the details of an incident must be available on-line up to 24 hours after it was first reported. An incident is "closed" after the police who were assigned to deal with it have been taken off the assignment and the incident has been given a final disposition code. There are thus two logical on-line incident files—one of active incidents and one of closed incidents. The two logical files are handled by the same physical circular file structure.

Suppose that the first incident of the day is written in relative file address A_1. When referring to the xth incident of the day, its relative file address A_x will be computed as follows:

$$\text{IF } x \leqslant 12001 - A_1 \quad \text{THEN } A_x = x + A_1 - 1$$

$$\text{IF } x > 12001 - A_1 \quad \text{THEN } A_x = x + A_1 - 12001$$

In Fig. 34.1, the first incident on Monday is referred to by an incident number M1. There are 8001 incidents on Monday, and the last of these, number M8001, is written in relative file address 5201. The first incident on Tuesday, number T1, is then written in relative file address 5202. The 4000th incident on Tuesday overwrites incident M1. When reference to a specified incident record is communicated within the machines, program to program, the relative file address is used. When reference to the incident involves communication with people, the incident number, e.g., T1, is used.

Incident records are normally dumped from the file onto tape from 24 to 25 hours after they occur. The dumping of a few hundred contiguous records thus takes place every hour. The tapes are then available for batch processing if needed. The records could be dumped onto a separate nonvolatile *information system* data base, which could be utilized by detectives.

It is regarded as highly improbable that there will be more than 12,000 incidents in one day. If the city is in more turmoil than normal and the incidents pass the 12,000 count, then the last incidents for that day will begin to overwrite the first. The system will detect the high volume long

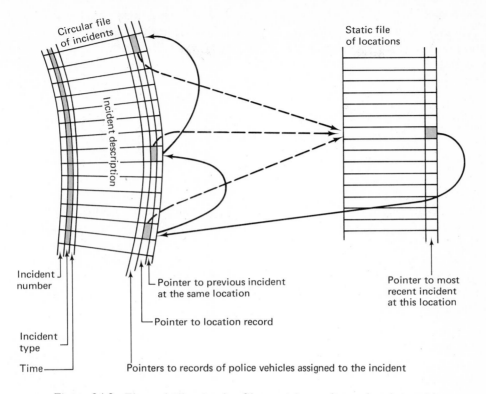

Circular file of incidents

Incident description

Static file of locations

Incident number

Incident type

Time

Pointer to previous incident at the same location

Pointer to location record

Pointers to records of police vehicles assigned to the incident

Pointer to most recent incident at this location

Figure 34.2 The volatile circular file contains codes and pointers to static files which permit a variety of inquiries to be processed.

before the overwriting takes place and will ensure that incidents are logged onto tape before they are destroyed. If the city repeatedly approaches a number of incidents near to 12,000, the size of the circular file will have to be increased.

This volatile file is accessed in a variety of different ways. It may be accessed by INCIDENT-NUMBER, which is, in effect, its prime key. It may be accessed by pointers from the records of the status of police vehicles which have been assigned to the incident. A member of the public may telephone and say "Why has nothing been done about the incident I reported half an hour ago?" The operator receiving the call does not know the number of the incident in question, so he enters its location—for example, street intersection. A record exists for every such location in the city, and this record contains a pointer to the *most recent* incident which occurred at that location (Fig. 34.2). Each INCIDENT record is chained to the previous INCIDENT which occurred at the same location. The computer can follow this chain looking for an incident of a given type or types or an incident reported at a stated time. The INCIDENT records contain pointers to the records of police vehicles (primary and second vehicles) assigned to the incident.

Note that although the file is highly volatile, there is no problem with linking and unlinking chains.

OVERFLOW   The major part of the incident record is a verbal description of incident and comments about it. The incident records are of fixed length, and sometimes the description extends far beyond the allotted record size. An overflow pointer is therefore used to a block or chain of blocks in which the verbiage can continue. This file of overflow blocks is as volatile as its parent file. It could therefore be constructed as another circular file, as in Fig. 34.3. In reality, however, it is often more economical to use a technique of assigning blocks at random from a pool of available blocks. This technique is called *dynamic block allocation.*

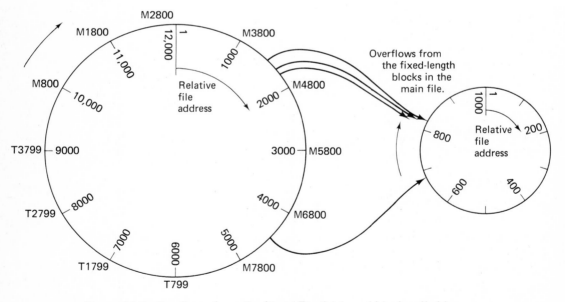

Figure 34.3 Overflows from the file in Fig. 34.1 could be handled by a second circular file, as here. In reality, it is usually more economical to use dynamically allocated storage blocks as in Fig. 34.6.

DYNAMIC
BLOCK
ALLOCATION

Using dynamic block allocation, a pool of fixed-length blocks is set up with a mechanism for allocating an unused block to any file which needs the space. Many different files may share the pool of blocks. A file may be stored in a chain of blocks, as in Fig. 34.4. This file, unlike a circular file, can be expanded or contracted to meet changing requirements. On the other hand, the blocks are not contiguous as with a circular file, and so a seek may be needed in going from one record to the next. A circular file can thus give faster response time. A chain of blocks can be organized as a first-in-first-out chain, as in Fig. 34.4, or as a *push-down stack* in which blocks are removed from the end of chain that new blocks are attached to, i.e., first-in-last-out.

The control mechanism must keep track of all the blocks which are not in use at any one time. The easiest way to do this is to chain together all the unused blocks, as in Fig. 34.5. This chain is referred to as an *uncommitted storage list.*

Records which are an overflow from another file because the other file did not have large enough blocks, as with the police INCIDENT record overflows, would not be stored in one chain. Instead, there would be pointers from the original file, as shown in Fig. 34.6. A large number of extra blocks could be added to a record if it needed the space. When the parent record is deleted, the overflow blocks will be chained back to the uncommitted storage list.

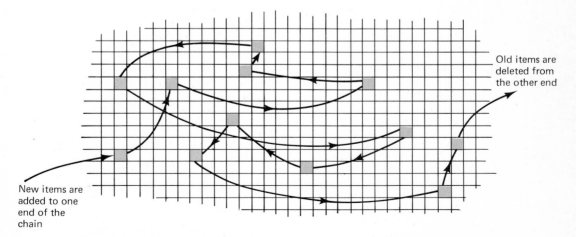

Figure 34.4 A volatile file may be constructed by chaining together blocks from a pool of blocks, as here.

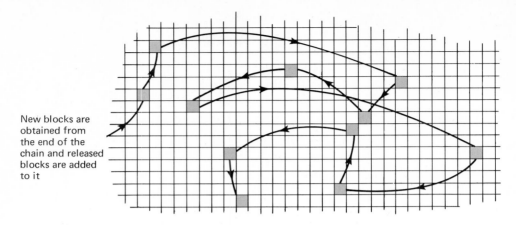

New blocks are
obtained from
the end of the
chain and released
blocks are added
to it

Figure 34.5 Uncommitted storage list. The blocks in the pool which
are not in use are also chained together.

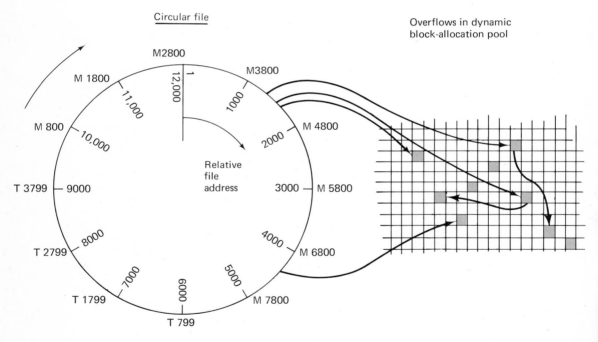

Circular file

Overflows in dynamic
block-allocation pool

M2800

M 1800   M3800

M 800   M 4800

Relative
file
address

T 3799   9000   3000 — M 5800

T 2799   M 6800

T 1799   M 7800

T 799

Figure 34.6 Overflows from a circular file handled by dynamic block
allocation.

The circular file itself could be constructed from blocks in the pool, but
in order to eliminate needless seeks they may be contiguous blocks chained
together in a ring. With this mechanism the size of the circular file can be
expanded when necessary.

FILES WHICH VARY GREATLY IN LENGTH   The designers of the police INCIDENT file had one advantage. Although it was highly volatile, they could make an assumption about its length and use a fixed number of records. Some files are both volatile and vary greatly in length. For these it is usually uneconomical to use a fixed-length circular file like that in Fig. 34.1.

In an airline the passenger booking records constitute a volatile file. Thousands of new bookings are made each day, hundreds of cancelations occur, and thousands of old bookings are purged from the files. The record giving details of a passenger and his booking must be linked to the flight record. The flight record may have no passengers yet, or it may have any number up to 400 (for certain 747s). We thus have a two-level structure, but the file which constitutes the lower level is both volatile and widely varying in length. In practice the higher-level record type is referred to as a PNI (passenger name index) record, and the lower-level record type is referred to as a PNR (passenger name record). The PNR contains full details about the passenger and his booking, and the PNI contains some brief information about the flight followed by a set of pointers to the PNRs of passengers on that flight. Figure 34.7 shows the schema for this and has the added complications of wait lists for a flight and "other airlines" (passengers may book journeys which include legs on other airlines).

A typical airline reservation system handles its volatile and variable-length files by using two dynamically allocated block pools, one with larger

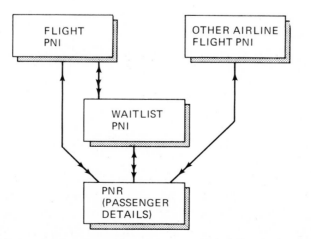

Figure 34.7 Schema for airline booking records.

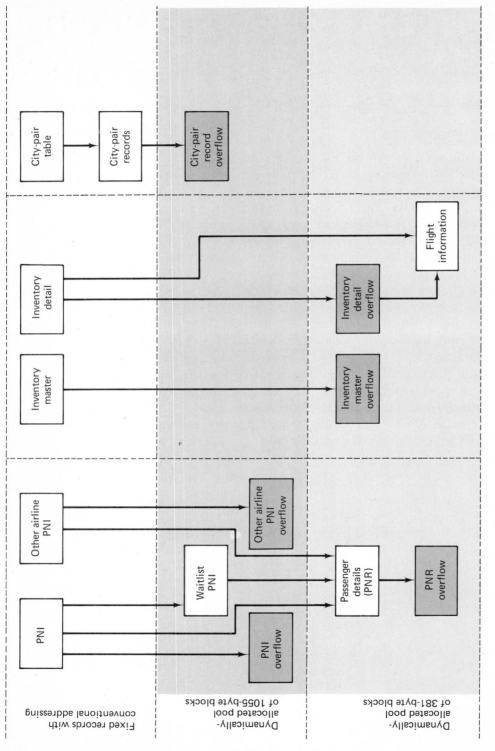

Figure 34.8 The volatile records in an airline reservation system are stored in two pools of dynamically allocated blocks, one of shorter and one of longer blocks. Once stored, no record need be moved.

and one with smaller blocks. The left-hand side of Fig. 34.8 shows the PNR and PNI records with their overflows. The remainder of the figure shows the other major records which share the block pools. The flights which require few blocks will tend to balance the flights which require many blocks, and that is the reason for dynamic block allocation. Once stored in a block, the records will never have to be moved until they are purged from the storage.

BOOK STRUCTURE

Chapters 34 and 35 discuss two special requirements: highly volatile systems, and systems requiring fast response times.

Chapter 34   Volatile Files
Chapter 35   Fast-Response Systems

35 FAST-RESPONSE SYSTEMS

A design requirement of many real-time systems is that they should give suitably fast responses to messages originating at terminals. How fast the responses should be depends on the nature of the messages and the application. I have discussed this subject elsewhere [1]. Many *dialogue* systems need a response in about 2 seconds—not much longer than the response time required in human conversations. The contracts for some systems have stated that 90% of the messages will have a response time of 3 seconds or less, where response time is defined as *the interval between the last action the terminal operator takes on input and the first character of the response being printed or displayed.* If a real-time system has this 90-percentile response time of 3 seconds, its mean response time will normally be less than 2 seconds [2].

The requirement for fast responses constrains the design of both the teleprocessing subsystem and the data-base subsystem. If the teleprocessing subsystem introduces delays (perhaps of a second or so), then the data-base subsystem must react appropriately faster. Sometimes the response requires the accessing of two or more files or the accessing of many records. In this case the access times must be low. The need for fast access is still greater on systems which handle a high transaction volume in which several, or many, responses must be generated each second.

Of the techniques we have discussed for physical storage organization, some are inherently fast and others inherently slow. High-volume, short-response time systems must use the fast ones. Fast retrieval techniques can generally be found when all accesses are to single records via their *prime* keys. It is often much more difficult to find a fast retrieval method when files have to be searched or accessed with multiple keys. A general-purpose high-speed "search engine" has yet to be built, although the associative memory techniques discussed in the following chapter are promising.

In general the methods for giving fast responses include combinations of the following:

1. Storing frequently referenced data on fast devices.

2. Positioning data so that lengthy seeks are avoided where possible.

3. Selection of addressing and search schemes which require few seeks, preferably only one per retrieval.

4. The use of multiple operations in parallel.

Box 35.1 categorizes techniques described in earlier chapters according to whether they tend to be good or bad for achieving fast responses. If Box 35.1 is compared with Box 34.1, it will be seen that some of the techniques which tend to be good for fast response are also good for volatile files. This fact may be helpful, as some fast-response systems are indeed volatile.

EMBEDDED CHAINS

The first block of items in Box 35.1 relates to embedded chains. As we have discussed before, there is no hope of achieving fast responses if lengthy chains have to be followed from record to record with seeks between the reading of the records. Rather than use embedded pointers it is better to store the relationships separately from the data where they can be accessed rapidly. For fast multiple-key searches, inverted list files rather than chained files are used. Inverted list structures take more storage, and, as is often the case, there is a trade-off between retrieval speed and storage utilization.

ADDRESSING TECHNIQUES

As indicated earlier, the trade-off between storage and time exists also in the techniques available for addressing single records. Indices can be designed to minimize storage space or to minimize index-searching time. Algorithm addressing can avoid index searching entirely but is likely to waste storage space. Binary searches of indices are fast but prohibit most forms of entry compaction.

SERIAL VERSUS PARALLEL OPERATIONS

Where a lengthy search is necessary, the more it can be broken into fragments which proceed simultaneously, the faster the results will be

Box 35.1 (Compare with Box 34.1)

Techniques Which Tend To Be Poor for Fast-Response Systems	Techniques which Tend To Be Faster
Embedded chains and ring structures	Relations in a unit separate from the data Inverted list structures
Indices designed for space optimization (or low storage cost)	Indices in main memory Algorithm or hash addressing
Scanning large cells	Binary searches in main memory
Single-server queues for channel or access mechanism	Layout of files to permit multiple simultaneous operations
Serial organization	Parallel organization
Machine-independent organizations	Organization tailored to hardware
Application-independent organizations	Organization tailored to application
Insistence on similar tuning for all responses	Man-machine dialogue tailored to storage organization to minimize the effects of time-consuming actions

obtained. On systems in which a queue builds up, the more servers serve the queue simultaneously, the shorter the queuing time will be. Queues build up for the file channel and also for the file-access mechanism. The latter is usually the more serious because the access time is substantially longer than the channel time. It is therefore desirable on some fast-response systems to have multiple channels and, more important, multiple access mechanisms operating in parallel. To achieve this on a disk unit the files are sometimes laid out spanning the disks as in Figs. 18.3 and 18.5, with the most frequently used files clustered together on the central cylinders as in Fig. 18.6.

Box 35.1 *continued*

Techniques Which Tend To Be Poor for Fast-Response Systems	Techniques which Tend To Be Faster
Real-time updating	Lengthy updates deferred until later
Real-time insertions and deletions	Insertions deferred to off-line operation
Poor techniques for storing insertions (especially clustered insertions)	Informational data base separate from operational data base
	Redundant · storage of certain items, designed to minimize response times
	Adaptive organizations
	Use of peripheral machines in handling dialogue
	Hardware designed to facilitate parallel searching

MACHINE AND APPLICATION INDEPENDENCE   It is generally desirable to construct data-base software which is *application-independent.* In other words, it can be used on a wide variety of different applications. Software producers also strive for techniques which are *machine-independent*, i.e., can be run on different computers and with different file hardware. The more machines and applications a given software package can be used with, the greater the return on the cost of writing it.

Nevertheless, much of the software which is successful in achieving fast response times has its physical storage mechanisms tailored to specific file units (for example, takes advantage of specific track lengths or puts an index at the head of each cylinder). Further, some of the applications which are most demanding in their response-time requirements use physical storage techniques which are specifically tailored to the applications. This is especially true when short response-time requirements are combined with a high transaction volume.

It is usually easier to achieve fast response times when the accessing techniques are tailored to the hardware and to the application. There may thus be a trade-off between generality and speed of response at a given cost.

DIALOGUE
CONSIDERATIONS

The reason for fast response times is usually to provide a psychologically attractive man-machine dialogue. In dialogues, however, it is not necessarily the case that *every* terminal action needs a fast retrieval from the data base. At certain points in the dialogue an operator may have completed a set of entries and is mentally prepared to relax for a moment while the machine acts upon what it has been told. Such a strategic moment in the dialogue is referred to by some phychologists as a *closure* [3,4]. The closure points can be useful in designing the programming in that exceptionally lengthy retrieval operations can be saved for these moments.

In an airline reservation dialogue, for example, a sequence of fast (average < 2 seconds) responses is needed as the terminal operator establishes what seats are available and what flight connections the traveler will make and as details of the passenger are entered. The operator then presses an END TRANSACTION key and relaxes. This is a moment of closure. At this point a 5-second response would be acceptable. The closure concept could have been put to use in the data-base design because it is when the closure occurs that the time-consuming updates of the files and the insertion of the new passenger record are performed.

System designers often make the mistake of demanding a blanket response-time requirement (90% of the responses in less than 3 seconds) rather than tailoring the response times to the dialogue structure.

Again, a given reasonable file design may not be able to provide a fast response to certain retrieval operations. An operation may need a search which takes many seconds or a lengthy *paging* access to a backup store. In such cases the dialogue should be designed to disguise the delay, saying *something* to the operator and perhaps eliciting his response while the retrieval is taking place. The operator must not suddenly be left in prolonged suspense in the middle of an otherwise fast dialogue. If the designer can "keep him talking" while the search goes on, he has gained time which might allow more economical but slower searching techniques.

NON-REAL-TIME
UPDATES

It usually takes longer to update a record than to read it. The updated copy has to be written back on the files and checked, and sometimes chains or secondary indices have to be modified. On some systems, however, it is not necessary to update all of the records in real time. Certain files can be updated later, or at least new records can be saved until later before insertion. The access mechanisms and channels are then less utilized, and it is easier to achieve fast responses on the remaining real-time operations.

Figure 16.2 illustrated the separating of an operations system and information system using the same data. This separation facilitated the handling of volatile files. It can also facilitate the provision of fast responses. The operational system files may be updated in real time, and information system files may not because it does not matter if the information searched for is 24 hours out of date. In practice many information systems use this approach and may obtain their data input, off-line, from more than one operational system.

REDUNDANT
DATA

Separating the information and operations data introduces a form of redundancy into the storage. Much of the data is kept twice. One of the objectives of data-base organization is to minimize redundancy. Nevertheless, to achieve fast responses many systems duplicate certain critical portions of the data and place a portion of it, often highly condensed, where it can be accessed quickly.

Airline reservation systems, for example, have a high throughput of transactions as well as stringent requirements for fast response times. To meet the response-time requirements the data base contains a carefully planned measure of redundancy in the data elements, the data paths, and the data structures. It is designed so that the most frequently occurring data accesses can be handled with one seek and less frequently occurring accesses can be handled with two seeks. As few accesses as possible need more than two seeks.

By far the most common transactions are the *availability requests*, which ask whether seats are available on certain flights. Inventory records are maintained for all flights, giving details of the seats sold and the numbers of seats on the plane. These records could provide an answer to the seat availability requests. Most airline systems, however, provide another record which gives the answer in a much more compact form. Only 4 bits are required to indicate whether seats are available for a given class of a given flight. The first 3 bits indicate the number of seats available from 0 to 7 (bit pattern 111 indicates 7 or more seats available), and the fourth bit indicates whether there is any restriction on selling the seats (the seats may be for a single leg, e.g., London to Rome, on a long multileg flight, e.g., London to Australia, and selling them may be prohibited unless the passenger books a long multileg journey; this restriction is designed to maximize the profitability of the operation).

The 4-bit groups for many flights, legs, and classes may be stored compactly in one record. In many airlines, the availability status of an entire day's flights is contained in a single record. These AVAILABILITY records are then stored in a location selected for fast access. The AVAILABILITY record is entirely redundant, but it takes up only a small fraction of the storage and substantially improves performance.

ADAPTIVE ORGANIZATIONS

Another way to reduce the mean response time is to employ an *adaptive* organization which uses some automatic method of moving the most frequently referenced items into locations in which they can be referenced most quickly. In Chapter 23 we mentioned *percolation* for moving frequently referenced items to the head of a chain. This is an adaptive organization but is usually not fast enough for real-time systems. A multilist organization (Fig. 26.3) can be made adaptive by using variable-length lists (chains). Short lists can be used for frequently used keys and long lists for infrequently used keys. In other words, there is a higher degree of inversion for the frequently referenced items. Such an organization may be modified automatically at maintenance time on the basis of key-usage statistics, which are continuously recorded.

A better technique than either of these, given appropriate hardware, is the use of the staging mechanisms discussed in Chapter 33. An algorithm is used which attempts to keep those items most likely to be referenced in the fastest level of storage.

A systems analyst today often does not have available to him adaptive multilist software or storage hierarchies with suitable staging control. To make his system adaptive he must construct some means of reorganizing the data periodically.

One stockbroker system, for example, uses tape and disk units. Data which are stored about stocks are sufficiently bulky that they have to be on

Box 35.2 Use of a Double Record Type to Improve
Mean Access Time

A selected number of days into the future on an airline reservation system are called the *current period*. Separate PASSENGER NAME INDEX (PNI) and seat INVENTORY records are maintained for the current period, which can be accessed quickly. Also the seat availability information in the INVENTORY records if stored in a highly abbreviated form in the AVAILABILITY records, which are referred to very frequently and are hence quickly accessible.

For the *current period* a DETAIL INVENTORY record is maintained. It gives full details of the seats sold for each class, leg, and segment of the flight (*segment* refers to a combination of a boarding and leaving point, thus, a three-leg flight involving London-Rome-Athens-Tehran will have six segments, London-Rome, London-Athens, Rome-Tehran, etc., and the DETAIL INVENTORY will keep a count for each).

For the noncurrent period a GROSS INVENTORY record is kept with a single combined total of all seats sold on a flight for any segment or class. One such record contains the gross inventory for a flight for 61 days, and six records keep it for the whole year. When a flight moves into the current period a DETAIL INVENTORY record must be created from the passenger booking records. Figure 35.1 shows the separation of gross and detail records.

DETAIL INVENTORY records are also created for flights outside the current period which are heavily loaded. DETAIL INVENTORY records will be automatically created for flights that have more than N seats booked, say 20. N, like the number of days in the current period, is a system parameter which can be adjusted to achieve the best compromise between speedy operation and conservation of storage.

A similar strategy is used with the storage of passenger names. Two different structures are used, a DETAIL PASSENGER NAME INDEX for the current period and a GROSS PASSENGER NAME INDEX for the noncurrent period. As with the inventory records a DETAIL record will be created in advance for peak days such as Christmas. The gross index contains an indication of those days for which a detail index has been redundantly created.

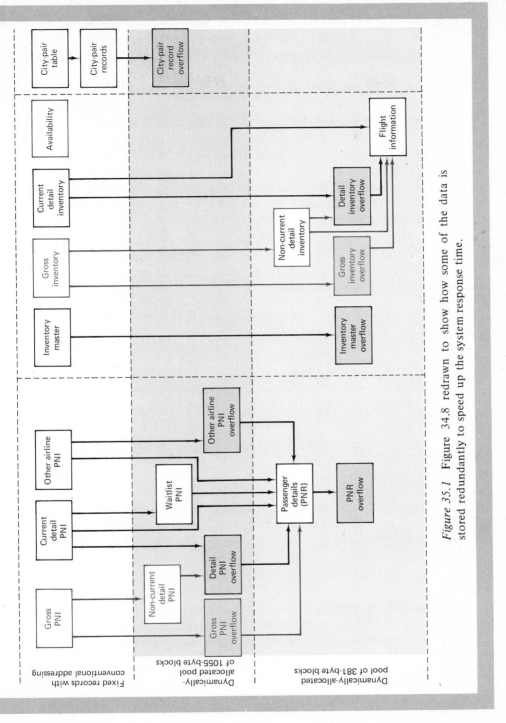

Figure 35.1 Figure 34.8 redrawn to show how some of the data is stored redundantly to speed up the system response time.

tape. On any given day, however, a relatively small number of stocks are highly active. Data for this active group are stored on disk where they can be accessed quickly. The members of the active group change as new stocks become "hot." Consequently, a periodic batch run transfers the newly hot stocks from tape to disk.

Sometimes the systems analyst can predict ahead of time that certain records will be more active than others but that the active group will change. For example, in an airline data base most of the activity relates to flights that take off in the next few days. A large quantity of bookings may exist for flights months ahead, but these will be rarely read. Because of this, two types of inventory records are used which are entirely different in structure: DETAIL records, which relate to a selected number of days into the future called the current period, and GROSS records, which relate to the time beyond that period. The records contain similar information, but the DETAIL records are more quickly accessible at the expense of taking up more store. Box 35.2 illustrates these.

FUTURE HARDWARE   There are several ways in which hardware can be designed in the future to facilitate fast-response file operations.

First, disk or other electromechanical devices can be designed with more logic in their control units to permit *parallel* searching. With today's disks, if a track is being searched for a record with a given key, it is not necessary for the entire contents of the track to be read into main memory. A controlling device can be used to recognize the requisite key and read only the record with that key.

It would be possible to build a "search engine" which looks for specified secondary keys as well as primary keys and which searches more than one track at a time. The upper part of Fig. 35.2 shows a disk unit with a *module search controller* on each module. The lower part extends the idea, showing a *head search controller* on each track, all searching in parallel for records with certain specified key characteristics. The module search controller may have the capability to advance the access mechanism as the search progresses. A similar arrangement could be employed on any future electromechanical storage unit. Prior to the advent of *large-scale-integration* circuitry and microcomputers, search controllers on each read head were too expensive to be practical. As the cost of mass-produced logic circuitry drops, so parallel search controllers become more attractive.

An entirely different approach to fast file operations is to build a very large solid-state buffer—let us say between 10 million and 1 billion bytes. In

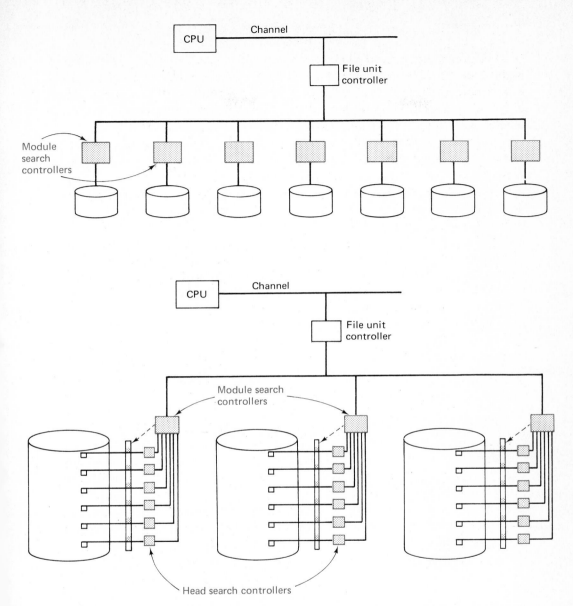

Figure 35.2 Microprocessors in the file control hardware could speed up data retrieval by facilitating parallel operations. This technique could be employed on any form of electromechanical storage and become economical as the cost of large-scale integration circuitry drops.

this buffer search operations can proceed with an access time of a microsecond or so. The buffer may contain a relational data base, indices, and directories, so that a search takes place in the buffer and the records located are then read from a larger, more permanent backup storage. The indices and directories may not reside permanently in the solid-state storage. This would probably be undesirable if only because most solid-state devices, unlike magnetic storage, lose their data when power fails. Instead, a *paging* mechanism would read them into the buffer when needed, as described in Chapter 33. Segments of files would also be paged into the buffer on demand. The algorithms for controlling the *demand paging* will be critical to the goal of achieving fast response times.

Again, prior to the advent of large-scale integration, such a large data buffer would have been far too expensive to be practical. Now it is economically feasible.

Given the capability to build large solid-state storage devices, a technique which has existed for 20 years in laboratories begins to appear viable—associative memory. An associative memory is one in which records are addressable *by their contents* rather than by their physical addresses. In the next chapter we will discuss associative memory.

The mechanisms of data-base storage can be changed dramatically with the use of large solid-state buffers, demand paging, parallel searching both in the buffers and in electromechanical devices, and associative memory.

REFERENCES

1. James Martin, *Design of Man-Computer Dialogues*, Prentice-Hall, Inc., Englewood Cliffs, N.J., 1973, Chapter 18.

2. James Martin, *Systems Analysis for Data Transmission*, Prentice-Hall, Inc., Englewood Cliffs, N.J., 1972, Chapter 31.

3. Robert B. Miller, "Response Time in Man-Computer Conversational Transactions," in *AFIPS Conference Proceedings (Fall Joint Computer Conference 1968)*, Thompson Book Company, Washington, D.C., 1968.

4. James Martin, *Design of Man-Computer Dialogues, op. cit.*, Chapter 18.

BOOK STRUCTURE

The last chapter discusses a type of hardware not yet in common use which could give greater assistance to searching data, multiple-key retrieval and secondary indices.

Chapter 36   Associative Memory

36 ASSOCIATIVE MEMORY

An idea can be powerful when its time has come. Associative memory is an old idea whose time does not seem to have come yet—but it may come soon. When it does it will change much in physical storage structures.

Small associative memories have been in existence since the early 1960s. In associative memory the storage locations are addressed by data content rather than by a hardware address. Figure 36.1 shows the difference between a conventional memory array and an associative memory array.

Both arrays in the diagram contain a set of words of M bits. In the conventional array an address of N bits is used to read out one of the words. In the associative array a search argument of M bits is employed as input, and the output consists of a bit for each of the words, indicating whether it is identical to the search argument or not. A 1 bit indicates a match and a 0 bit a mismatch. Associative arrays usually have facilities for masking the search argument so that only selected bits in the words are compared.

The output of an associative array may be employed to read data from a conventional storage array. In Fig. 36.2, 2^N lines could go from the associative array to the storage array. Often, however, this is far too many lines, and so the output of the associative array is encoded and taken to the conventional storage on a smaller number of lines. N lines connect the associative and conventional arrays in Fig. 36.2. One set of N bits may be transmitted for each match that occurs in the associative array, giving the address of the word in question and causing the cell with that address in the conventional storage to be read.

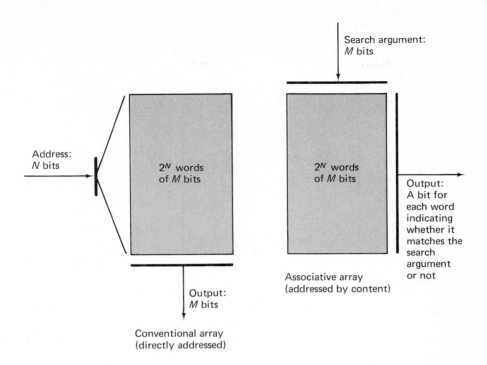

Figure 36.1 Comparison of a conventional memory array and an associative memory array.

<table>
<tr><td>**THE RESPONSE STORAGE**</td><td>The store which contains the output of the associative array in Fig. 36.1 is called the *response store*. In Fig. 36.1, the response store has at least 1</td></tr>
</table>

THE RESPONSE
STORAGE

The store which contains the output of the associative array in Fig. 36.1 is called the *response store*. In Fig. 36.1, the response store has at least 1 bit for each storage location in the array.

In another design of associative storage the response is *the contents* of the storage location satisfying the search criterion. In this case the device must have the ability to output the contents of successive locations when more than one satisfy the search criterion.

MORE COMPLEX
OPERATIONS

Associative memory hardware thus carries out a series of compare operations in a parallel-by-word, serial-by-bit fashion on a selected group of bits in each storage location.

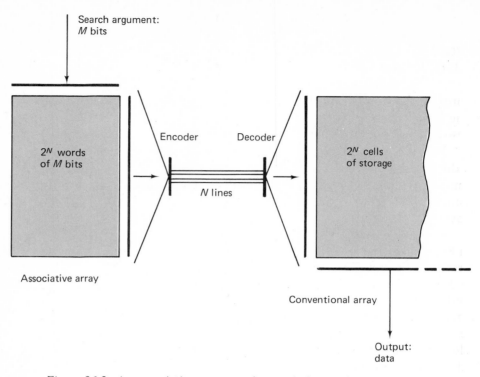

Figure 36.2 An associative array used as an index to data stored in a conventional memory.

In addition to carrying out *compare* operations it may also execute other operations in parallel upon the selected bits. It may be able to test for equality, inequality, greater than, greater than or equal to, less than, less than or equal to, between limits, maximum, minimum, next higher, or next lower. All these operations are of value when searching data. More complex logic may be used which can carry out Boolean operations within the words. However, such operations could be carried out less expensively by multiple searches of the same data with different search criteria.

There have been proposals that associative memories carry out arithmetic or logical operations in parallel on the stored data as well as merely executing search fuctions. They could, for example, add a constant to a specific field in every storage location or increment the field if it contains a certain value. The greater the variety of operations, the greater the cost, and as cost is the main objection to associative memory we will confine our attention to search functions.

PHYSICAL CONSTRUCTION　Small associative arrays on single LSI (large-scale-integration) chips are purchasable from semiconductor manufacturers. As LSI technology improves, the number of bits stored per chip will increase. However, to be of value in data-base construction much larger associative memories are needed. These can be built from multiple chips.

The cost of producing an LSI chip drops dramatically as the quantity produced rises. When associative storage becomes a widely accepted technology the cost of LSI associative arrays may become low because of the economics of mass production of memories containing many identical arrays.

Associative designs have also used magnetic disks on which many tracks can be scanned in parallel. Figure 36.3 shows a system built by the Goodyear Aerospace Corporation [1] that is used for military applications. The disk at the left of the diagram has 72 tracks of which 64 are used to store data. There is one head per track, and the 64 tracks are read in parallel into 64 storage locations of an associative array like that in Fig. 36.1. Each sector of the disk holds 256 bits per track, and each word of the associative array holds 256 bits. It takes 100 microseconds to read 64 sectors into the array and 100 microseconds to search the array. Therefore, as the disk rotates,

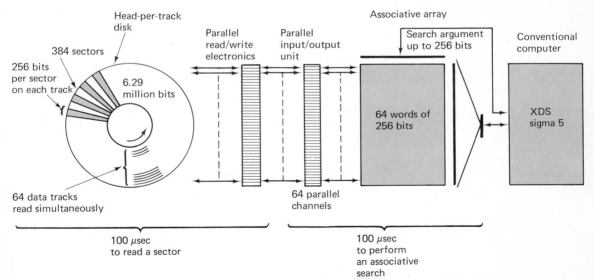

Figure 36.3 An associative memory system using a head-per-track disk implemented by the Goodyear Aerospace Corporation [1].

alternate sectors are read and searched. The entire disk may be searched in this manner in two disk rotations. There are 384 sectors on the disk, and the disk takes approximately 38.4 milliseconds to rotate. The contents of the disk—about 6.29 million bits—may thus be searched associatively in about 76.8 milliseconds.

The associative array is attached to a conventional computer, an XDS SIGMA 5, which controls the searches, giving appropriate search arguments and instructions to the array.

The associative array has a capacity of 256 words, and only 64 of these are used. If four disk surfaces were employed for four times the reading facilities, four times as much data could be searched associatively.

THE BEST OF
TWO WORLDS

In view of the small size of associative arrays, the way in which storage may be organized is to store data conventionally in *pages* but to read the pages into an associative memory for searching. This, in effect, is what is done in Fig. 36.3. Any conventionally organized storage could be used instead of the disk in Fig. 36.3 provided that its read rate is high enough to fill the associative memory sufficiently fast for effective searching.

Richard Moulder [1], discussing the system in Fig. 36.3, claims "An associative processor working in conjunction with a sequential processor affords the best configuration. With this marriage comes the best of two computer worlds, each performing what it is best capable of doing. Associative processing brings to data base management designers and users the ability to query and update data bases, in a fast and efficient manner with a minimum amount of software." No additional storage is needed for inverted files, and updates can be made straightforwardly without the problems of inverted files, described in Chapter 31.

ASSOCIATIVE PAGE
ORGANIZATION

If data are to be divided into pages which will be associatively searched, how should the data be organized?

An associative processor searches flat files—every "word" in the associative array must contain the same set of data-item types. The data should therefore be in a relational (normalized) form, as described in Chapters 13 and 14. Some of the normalized *relations* may contain more bits per tuple than the number of bits per word in the associative array. Such oversize relations must be divided physically into domain groups that fit into the associative array. In Chapter 28 we discussed separating data and relationships. If associative storage is used in data-base management systems, it seems likely that it should be applied to a relatively small file of relationships, not to the larger file of data. It is possible, for example, to imagine an "index box" built associatively for searching primary or secondary indices. If such a device were to become a mass-produced unit, it could have a major effect on the design of interactive information systems.

BINARY
RELATIONS

Because of the limited size of associative arrays, it is desirable to load them with only those data which are actively involved in the search. If third normal form tuples are loaded into the array, some of the data items in the tuples may not be involved in the search when responding to a particular query. For this reason *binary* relations may be preferable to third normal form or *n*-ary relations (although the *logical* data description may still be in third normal form as discussed in Chapter 14).

As we discussed in Chapter 28, any data-base schema, no matter how complex, can be represented by binary relations. Furthermore, complex queries can be answered by dealing with the data-item types in the query one pair at a time. The binary relations will be loaded into the associative memory for searching. The word length of the associative memory need not be long in this case. The 256 bit words used in the Goodyear associative array would be adequate for most binary relations but insufficient for most third normal form relations.

SOFTWARE ASSOCIATIVE
MEMORIES

Associative memory hardware large enough for data-base use has not been available for most systems. However, file storage with properties similar to associative memories can be built from conventional storage hardware by using software techniques. Such file organizations are sometimes referred to as *software associative memories.*

Software associative memory is slow, clumsy, and often error-prone compared with its hardware equivalent, but at the time of writing it is cheaper. If a manufacturer provides only conventional storage, associativity has to be provided by appropriate data structures such as hashing and rings.

CONTENT
ADDRESSABILITY

The term *content addressable* is used to describe associative storage. The primary property of content addressable memory is

*Property 1:   The address of a segment of data is a function of its
              information content.*

With software associative memory the term is sometimes used to imply
a second property:

Property 2:   Segments similar in content are stored close in address space.

The second property may imply that items similar in content, for
example, having the same secondary key, are on the same *page* so that they
can be searched for rapidly when that page is brought into main memory.
This technique will minimize access time when retrieving related pieces of
information.

There have been several implementations of software-associative memories [2—7]. One has been built at the IBM Cambridge Scientific Center
[8,9] and used for a variety of applications with complex data structures
requiring fast responses. The physical data structure employed provides both
properties of content addressability. It is called RAM (relational access
method).

The system employs binary relations, and these are in the form of
triads,· as discussed in Chapter 28. A triad consists of three elements, *A*, *B*,
and *C*, two of which are data items on a bubble chart and the third of which
is the identification of the link associating them. They can be in any
sequence, but in the following description *A* or *B* will usually be the association name.

To ensure that triads similar in content are close in address space
(property 2 of content addressability), the Cambridge group required an
addressing method which would place similar triads on the same *page*. The
page could then be searched at high speed in main memory. The technique
used is illustrated in Fig. 36.4.

Triads with the same value of *A* are stored on the same page, with
overflow to a page close in address space if necessary. A page-addressing
algorithm is employed to convert the value of *A* to the page on which *A* is
stored. Hashing on the combined values of *A* and *B* is used to convert their
values to the location within the page where the value of *B* associated with *A*
is stored.

All the values of *B* associated with a given *A* value are chained together
into a *B* ring, as shown in Fig. 36.4. The head of the *B* ring is the location
where that *A* value is stored. All the values of *C* associated with a given *AB*
pair are chained together into a *C* ring. The head of the *C* ring is the location
where that related *B* value is stored. If the *AB* pair has only one associated *C*

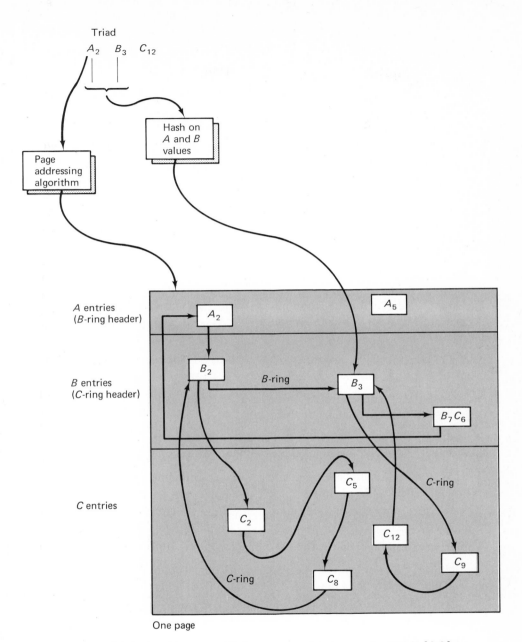

Figure 36.4   A software associate memory structure, using triads [8 9].

value, there is no C ring. The C value is stored along with the related B value, as with C_6 and B_7 in Fig. 36.4.

The hashing technique allows AB pairs to be found most of the time with one page read. The rings on the page can then be searched fast in main memory, thus providing an effective simulation of associative storage. Synonyms are dealt with by using a separate *conflict ring*, not shown in Fig. 36.4.

As large-scale-integration circuits improve in the years ahead the cost of associative arrays will drop. On the other hand, the cost of conventional solid-state storage will drop also, and it may still remain more economical to build software associative memory than hardware. As technology changes there should be continual reassessment of the merits and role of associative storage.

REFERENCES

1. Richard Moulder, "An Implementation of a Data Management System on an Associative Processor," in *Proceedings of the National Computer Conference*, New York, 1973.

2. J. A. Feldman and P. D. Rovner, "An ALGOL-Based Associative Language," *Comm. ACM 12*, No. 8, Aug. 1969, 439-449.

3. W. L. Ash, "A Compiler for an Associative Object Machine," *CONCOMP Technical Report 17*, University of Michigan, Ann Arbor, May 1969.

4. W. Ash and E. Sibley, "TRAMP: A Relational Memory with an Associative Base," *CONCOMP Technical Report 5*, University of Michigan, Ann Arbor, June 1967.

5. A. J. Symonds, "Auxiliary-Storage Associative Data Structure for PL/I," *IBM Systems J. 7*, Nos. 3 and 4, 1968, 229-245.

6. A. J. Symonds, "Use of Relational Programming To Manipulate a Structure in a Software Associative Memory," presented at 1969 ACM/SIAM/EEE Conference on Mathematical and Computer Aids to Design, Oct. 1969.

7. Jack Miuker, "An Overview of Associative and Content-Addressable Memory Systems and a KWIC Index to the Literature' 1956-1970," *Computing Rev.*, Oct. 1971.

8. M. F. C. Crick, R. A. Lorie, E. J. Mosher and A. J. Symonds, "A Data-Base System for Interactive Applications," *Report G 320-2058*, Cambridge Scientific Center, IBM Corporation, July 1970.

9. M. F. C. Crick and A. J. Symonds, "A Software Associative Memory for Complex Data Structures," *Report G 320-2060*, Cambridge Scientific Center, IBM Corporation, Aug. 1970.

THE MEAN NUMBER OF PROBES IN A BINARY SEARCH

Parts of this book discussed a binary search of files or indices (Fig. 23.2) and referred to the mean number of reads or probes necessary in executing a binary search. This mean number of probes is calculated here. The calculation assumes that any of the items are equally likely to be searched for.

Let N_I be the number of items that are to be searched, and let N_p be the number of reads or probes necessary.

The maximum possible number of probes are shown in the following table:

N_I	Maximum Possible Number of Probes
1	1
2–3	2
4–7	3
8–15	4
.	.
.	.
.	.

In general the maximum possible number of probes is $\lfloor \log_2 N_I \rfloor + 1.$*

Let P_j be the probability of finding the item on the jth probe. The mean number of probes is then

*$\lfloor x \rfloor$ is the next integer below x.

$$E(N_p) = \sum_{j=1}^{\lfloor \log_2 N_I \rfloor + 1} j P_j \qquad (A.1)$$

First Probe

There is only one possible candidate for inspection by the first probe. The probability of the first probe finding the required item is therefore $P_1 = 1/N_I$.

Second Probe

There are two possible candidates for inspection by the second probe. The probability that the second probe will locate the required item is therefore $P_2 = 2/N_I$.

jth Probe Where $j \leqslant \lfloor \log_2 N_I \rfloor$

There are $2^{(j-1)}$ possible candidates for inspection by the jth probe if $j \leqslant \lfloor \log_2 N_I \rfloor$. The probability that the jth probe will locate the required item is therefore $P_j = 2^{(j-1)}/N_I$.

Last Probe

If there is a final probe after the $\lfloor \log_2 N_I \rfloor$th probe, there may be less than $2^{(j-1)}$ items remaining to be inspected. The probability that this $(\lfloor \log_2 N_I \rfloor + 1)$th probe will locate the required item is $(1 - $ the sum of the probabilities that no previous item located it). That is,

$$P_j \ (\text{where } j = \lfloor \log_2 N_I \rfloor + 1) = 1 - \sum_{j=1}^{\lfloor \log_2 N_I \rfloor} \frac{2^{(j-1)}}{N_I}$$

Substituting these probabilities into Eq. (A.1),

$$E(N_p) = \sum_{j=1}^{\lfloor \log_2 N_I \rfloor} j \frac{2^{(j-1)}}{N_I} + \left(\lfloor \log_2 N_I \rfloor + 1 \right) \left(1 - \sum_{j=1}^{\lfloor \log_2 N_I \rfloor} \frac{2^{(j-1)}}{N_I} \right) \qquad (A.2)$$

$E(N_P)$ is plotted in Fig. A.1. It will be observed that the mean number of probes approximates $\log_2 N_I - 1$ when N_I is large.

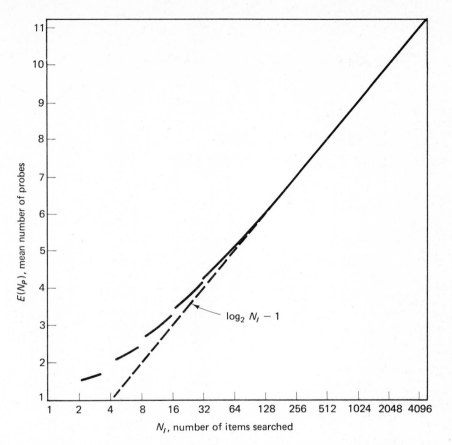

Figure A.1 The mean number of probes in a binary search. When a large number, N_I, of items are searched, the mean number of probes approximates $\log_2 N_I - 1$.

B SAMPLE LOGICAL DATA DESCRIPTIONS†

Different data-base languages have different methods of describing data. The following pages give samples of typical data descriptions using the

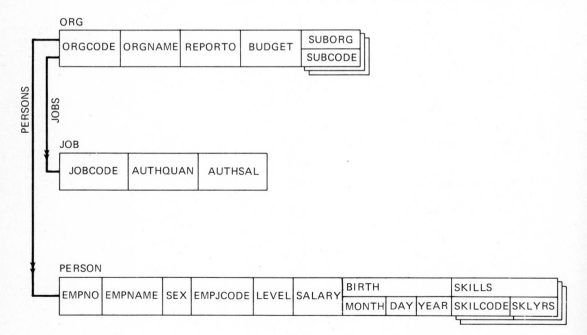

Figure B.1

†Reproduced from the *CODASYL Systems Committee Technical Report, May 1971.*

schema in Fig. B.1. For various reasons the data structures coded in the different systems are not exactly the same.

1. COBOL

```
DATA DIVISION

FILE SECTION

FED SDCDATA

01        ORG
  02        ORGCODE ; PICTURE IS 9999
  02        ORGNAME ; PICTURE IS A(25)
  02        REPORTO ; PICTURE IS 9999
  02        BUDGET ; PICTURE IS Z(8); USAGE IS COMPUTATIONAL-1
  02        JOB ; OCCURS 1 TO 50 TIMES ASCENDING KEY IS JOBCODE
    03        JOBCODE ; PICTURE IS 9999
    03        AUTHQUAN ; PICTURE IS 99; USAGE IS COMPUTATIONAL
    03        AUTHSAL ; PIC ZZZZZZ ; USAGE-COMP-1
  02        SUBORG ; OCCURS 0 TO 20 TIMES ASCENDING KEY IS SUBCODE
    03        SUBCODE ; PIC 9999
  02        PERSON ; OCCURS 1 TO 999 TIMES ASCENDING KEYS ARE
              EMPJCODE, EMPNO
    03      EMPNO ; PIC Z9999
    03      EMPNAME ; PIC A(20)
    03      SEX ; PIC A
    03      EMPJCODE ; PIC 9999
    03      LEVEL ; PIC AAAA
    03      SALARY ; PIC ZZZZZ ; USAGE COMP-1
    03      BIRTH
      04      MONTH ; PIC 99
      04      DAY ; PIC 99
      04      YEAR ; PIC 99
    03      SKILLS ; OCCURS 1 TO 9 TIMES ASCENDING KEY IS SKILCODE
      04      SKILCODE ; PIC 9999
      04      SKLYRS ; PIC 99
```

2. The Proposed CODASYL Data Description Language (Chapter 11)

```
SCHEMA NAME IS ORGDATA

AREA NAME IS ORGPART

RECORD NAME IS ORG

PRIVACY LOCK IS SESAME

  01        ORGCODE   PICTURE IS "9(4)"
  01        ORGNAME   TYPE IS CHARACTER 25
  01        REPORTO   PICTURE IS "9999"
  01        BUDGET TYPE DECIMAL FLOAT ; IS ACTUAL RESULT OF SALSUM
              ON MEMBERS OF PERSONS
  01        NOSUBORG   TYPE BINARY
```

```
01      SUBORG OCCURS NOSUBORG TIMES
   02      SUBCODE PICTURE "9999"
RECORD NAME IS JOB
01      JOBCODE   PICTURE "9999"
01      AUTHQUAN  PICTURE "99"
01      AUTHSAL   TYPE FLOAT
RECORD NAME IS PERSON
01      EMPNO   PICTURE "9(5)"
01      EMPNAME   TYPE CHARACTER 20
01      SEX   PICTURE "A"
01      EMPJCODE   PICTURE "9999"
01      LEVEL   PICTURE "X(4)"
01      SALARY   PICTURE "9(5)V99" ; PRIVACY LOCK FOR GET IS
          PROCEDURE AUTHENT
01      BIRTH
   02      MONTH   PICTURE "99"
   02      DAY   PICTURE "99"
   02      YEAR   PICTURE "99"
01      NOSKILLS   TYPE BINARY
01      SKILLS OCCURS NOSKILLS TIMES
   02      SKILCODE   PICTURE "9999"
   02      SKLYRS   PICTURE "99"
SET NAME IS JOBS; ORDER IS SORTED
  OWNER IS ORG
  MEMBER IS JOB OPTIONAL AUTOMATIC; ASCENDING KEY IS
  JOBCODE DUPLICATES NOT ALLOWED
SET NAME IS PERSONS; ORDER IS SORTED
    OWNER IS ORG
    MEMBER IS PERSON OPTIONAL AUTOMATIC ; ASCENDING KEY IS
      EMPJCODE,EMPNO DUPLICATES NOT ALLOWED
```

3. Informatics Mark IV File Management System

The data are described by filling in this form:

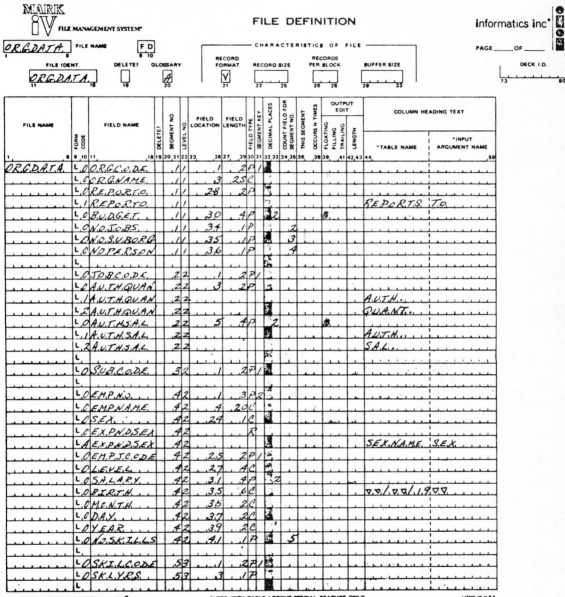

MARK IV FILE MANAGEMENT SYSTEM®   FILE DEFINITION   Informatics inc®

FILE NAME: ORGDATA   FD

FILE IDENT. ORGDATA   DELETE?   GLOSSARY: A   RECORD FORMAT: V   RECORD SIZE   RECORDS PER BLOCK   BUFFER SIZE   PAGE____OF____   DECK I.D.

CHARACTERISTICS OF FILE

FILE NAME	FORM CODE	FIELD NAME	DELETE?	LEVEL NO	SEGMENT NO	FIELD LOCATION	FIELD LENGTH	FIELD TYPE	SEGMENT KEY	DECIMAL PLACES	COUNT FIELD FOR SEGMENT NO.	THIS SEGMENT	OCCURS N TIMES	OUTPUT EDIT FLOATING	FILLING	TRAILING	LENGTH	*TABLE NAME	*INPUT ARGUMENT NAME
ORGDATA	L	O ORGCODE		1	1	1	2	P	/										
	L	C ORGNAME		1	1	3	25	C											
	L	O REPORTO		1	1	28	2	P											
	L	I REPORTO		1	1													REPORTS TO	
	L	O BUDGET		1	1	30	4	P		2		B							
	L	O NOJOBS		1	1	34	1	P			2								
	L	O NOSUBORG		1	1	35	1	P			3								
	L	O NOPERSON		1	1	36	1	P			4								
	L																		
	L	O JOBCODE		2	2	1	2	P	/										
	L	O AUTHQUAN		2	2	3	2	P											
	L	I AUTHQUAN		2	2													AUTH.	
	L	2 AUTHQUAN		2	2													QUANT.	
	L	O AUTHSAL		2	2	5	4	P		2		B							
	L	I AUTHSAL		2	2													AUTH.	
	L	2 AUTHSAL		2	2													SAL.	
	L																		
	L	O SUBCODE		3	2	1	2	P	/										
	L																		
	L	O EMPNO		4	2	1	3	P	X										
	L	C EMPNAME		4	2	4	20	C											
	L	O SEX		4	2	24	1	C											
	L	O EXPNDSEX		4	2			R											
	L	A EXPNDSEX		4	2													SEXNAME	SEX
	L	O EMPJCODE		4	2	25	2	P	/										
	L	O LEVEL		4	2	27	4	C											
	L	O SALARY		4	2	31	4	P		2									
	L	O BIRTH		4	2	35	6	C							▽▽/▽▽/19▽▽				
	L	O MONTH		4	2	35	2	C											
	L	O DAY		4	2	37	2	C											
	L	O YEAR		4	2	39	2	C											
	L	O NOSKILLS		4	2	41	1	P			5								
	L																		
	L	O SKILCODE		5	3	1	2	P	/										
	L	O SKLYRS		5	3	3	1	P												
	L																		

MK IV FDSC COPYRIGHT 1969 INFORMATICS INC. ®   *USED WITH TABLE LOOKUP SPECIAL FEATURE ONLY.   LITHO IN USA

4. IDS—Honeywell Information Systems' Integrated Data Store

```
DATA DIVISION
IDS SECTION
MD ORGDATA

    01      ORG                 TYPE IS 100 ; AUTHORITY 2192

        02      ORGCODE ; PIC 9999
        02      ORGNAME ; PIC A(25)
        02      REPORTO ; PIC 9999
        02      BUDGET ; PIC Z(8)
        02      SUBORG OCCURS 0 TO 20 TIMES ASCENDING KEY IS SUBCODE
            03      SUBCODE ; PIC 9999

        98      CALC CHAIN DETAIL RANDOMIZE ON ORGCODE
        98      JOBS CHAIN MASTER CHAIN-ORDER IS SORTED
        98      PERSONS CHAIN MASTER CHAIN-ORDER IS SORTED

    01      JOB             TYPE IS 101

        02      JOBCODE ; PIC 9999
        02      AUTHQUAN ; PIC 99
        02      AUTHSAL ; PIC Z(6)

        98      JOBS CHAIN DETAIL
                SELECT CURRENT MASTER
                ASCENDING KEY IS JOBCODE
                DUPLICATES NOT ALLOWED

    01      PERSON          TYPE IS 102

        02      EMPNO ; PIC Z9999
        02      EMPNAME ; PIC A(20)
        02      SEX ; PIC A
        02      EMPJCODE ; PIC 9999
        02      LEVEL ; PIC AAAA
        02      SALARY ; PIC ZZZZZ
        02      BIRTH
            03    MONTH ; PIC 99
            03    DAY ; PIC 99
            03    YEAR ; PIC 99
        02      SKILLS OCCURS 1 TO 9 TIMES
            03    SKILCODE ; PIC 9999
            03    SKLYRS ; PIC 99

        98      PERSONS CHAIN DETAIL
                SELECT CURRENT MASTER
                ASCENDING KEY IS EMPJCODE,EMPNO
                DUPLICATES NOT ALLOWED
```

5. IBM Data Language/I (used in IMS) (Chapter 12)

```
DBD      NAME = ORGDATA

SEGM     NAME = ORG, BYTES = 38, START = 1
FIELD    NAME = (ORGCODE SEQ, U), BYTES = 2, TYPE = P
FIELD    NAME = ORGNAME, BYTES = 25, START = 3, TYPE = C
FIELD    NAME = REPORTO, BYTES = 2, START = 28, TYPE = P
FIELD    NAME = BUDGET, BYTES = 4, START = 30, TYPE = P

SEGM     NAME = JOB, BYTES = 8, FREQ = 31, PARENT = ORG
FIELD    NAME = (JOBCODE, SEQ, U), BYTES = 2, TYPE = P

SEGM     NAME = SUBORG, BYTES = 2, PARENT = ORG
FIELD    NAME = (SUBCODE, SEQ, U), BYTES = 2, TYPE = P

SEGM     NAME = PERSON, BYTES = 40, PARENT = ORG
FIELD    NAME = (EMPJCODE, SEQ, M), BYTES = 2, TYPE = P
FIELD    NAME = (EMPNO, SEQ, U), BYTES = 3, TYPE = P

SEGM     NAME = SKILLS, BYTES = 3, PARENT = PERSON
FIELD    NAME = (SKILCODE, SEQ, U), BYTES = 2, TYPE = P

DBDGEN

FINISH

END
```

6. GIS—IBM Generalized Information System, a System for File Searching

```
DDT
FILE:NAME = ORGDATA

FLD:NAME = ORGCODE, UNITS = PACD, LENGTH = 2
    EDIT:TYPSPC = RNGE, ERRORD = E, CONVA = PACD, LGTHA = 2,
    EEDVAL = 2000, 2999
FLD:NAME = ORGNAME, UNITS = EBCD, JUST = L, LENGTH = 25
FLD:NAME = REPORTO, UNITS = PACD, LENGTH = 2, HEADER = REPORTS TO,
    EDIT:TYPSPC = RNGE, ERRORD = E, CONVA = PACD, LGTHA = 2,
    EEDVAL = 2000, 2999
FLD:NAME = BUDGET, UNITS = PACD, LENGTH = 4
FLD:NAME = NOJOBS, UNITS = PACD, LENGTH = 1
FLD:NAME = NOSUBORG, UNITS = PACD, LENGTH = 1
FLD:NAME = NOPERSON, UNITS = PACD, LENGTH = 1
SEGM:NAME = ORG, LEVEL = 0, UNIND = Y,
     SORT = ORGCODE, A

FLD:NAME = JOBCODE, UNITS = PACD, LENGTH = 2
FLD:NAME = AUTHQUAN, UNITS = PACD, LENGTH = 2,
    HEADER = AUTH. QUANT.
FLD:NAME = AUTHSAL, UNITS = FLPT, LENGTH = 4, HEADER = AUTH. SAL.
SEGM:NAME = JOB, LEVEL = 1, OPTION = CNT, OPFFNM = NOJOBS,
    UNIND = Y, SORT = JOBCODE, A
```

```
FLD:NAME = SUBCODE, UNITS = PACD, LENGTH = 2
SEGM:NAME = SUBORG, LEVEL = 1, OPTION = CNT, OPTFNM = NOSUBORG,
   UNIND = Y, SORT = SUBCODE, A

FLD:NAME = EMPNO, UNITS = PACD, LENGTH = 3
FLD:NAME = EMPNAME, UNITS = EBCD, JUST = L, LENGTH = 20
FLD:NAME = SEX, UNITS = EBCD, JUST = L, LENGTH = 1
   EDIT:TYPSPC = LKUP, ERRORD = E, CONVA = EBCD, LENGTH = 1,
   EEDVAL = M, F
FLD:NAME = EMPJCODE, UNITS = PACD, LENGTH = 2
FLD:NAME = LEVEL, UNITS = EBCD, JUST = L, LENGTH = 4,
   EDIT:TYPSPC = PICT, ERRORD = E, LGTHA = 4, EEDVAL = ZZZZ
FLD:NAME = SALARY, UNITS = FLPT, LENGTH = 4, QSEC = 102, USEC = 57
FLD:NAME = BIRTH, UNITS = EBCD, JUST = L, LENGTH = 6
   RDFN MONTH, 2, DAY, 2, YEAR, 2
FLD:NAME = SKILL1, UNITS = PACD, LENGTH = 2
FLD:NAME = SKLYRS1, UNITS = PACD, LENGTH = 1
FLD:NAME = SKILL2, UNITS = PACD, LENGTH = 2
FLD:NAME = SKLYRS2, UNITS = PACD, LENGTH = 1
SEGM:NAME = PERSON LEVEL = 1, OPTION = CNT,
   OPTFNM = NOPERSON, SORT = EMPJCODE, A, EMPNO, A
END
```

7. TDMS and CDMS—The System Development Corporation's Time-Shared Data Management System

```
DATA BASE NAME IS:  ORGDATA
TERMINATOR IS:  END

1   ORGCODE (NUMBER) VALUES ARE 2000 . . . 2999
2   ORGNAME (NAME)
3   REPORTO (NUMBER) VALUES ARE 2000 . . . 2999
4   BUDGET (NUMBER)
5   JOB (RG)
      6    JOBCODE (NUMBER IN 5) FORMAT IS 9999
      7    AUTHOUAN (NUMBER IN 5)
      8    AUTHSAL (NUMBER IN 5)
9   SUBORG (RG)
     10    SUBCODE (NAME IN 9) VALUES ARE 2000 . . . 2999
11  PERSON (RG)
     12    EMPNO (NUMBER IN 11) FORMAT IS 09999
     13    EMPNAME (NAME IN 11)
     14    SEX (NAME IN 11) VALUES ARE M, F
     15    EMPJCODE (NAME IN 11) FORMAT IS 9999
     16    LEVEL (NAME IN 11) FORMAT IS LLLL
     17    SALARY (NUMBER IN 11)
     18    BIRTH (NAME IN 11) FORMAT IS 99 / 99 / 99
           181   YEAR (1...2 IN 18)
           182   MONTH (4...5 IN 18)
           183   DAY (R1...2 IN 18)
     19    SKILLS (RG IN 11)
           20 SKILL (NAME IN 19) FORMAT IS 9999
           21 SKLYRS (NUMBER IN 19)
END
```

8. UL/1—RCA User Language/1

```
ESTABLISH    ORGDATA

IDENTIFICATION

#1   N    ORGCODE
#2   A    ORGNAME
#3   N    REPORTO          REPORTS TO
#4   N    BUDGET
#5   N    JOBCODE          JOB CODE
#6   N    AUTHQUAN         AUTH.QUANT.
#7   N    AUTHSAL          AUTH.SAL.
#8   N    SUBCODE          SUBORG. CODE
#9   N    EMPNO
#10  A    EMPNAME          EMPLOYEE NAME
#11  C    SEX
#12  N    EMPJCODE         EMPL. JOB CODE
#13  A    LEVEL
#14  N    SALARY
#15  A    MONTH
#16  A    DAY
#17  A    YEAR
#18  N    SKILL
#19  N    SKLYRS

STRUCTURE

     JOBS (EMPJCODE AUTHQUAN AUTHSAL) REPEATS
     SUBCODE REPEATS
     PERSONS (NUMBER EMPNAME  SEX EMPJCODE LEVEL SALARY
         MONTH DAY YEAR SKILL SKLYRS) REPEATS
     BIRTH (MONTH DAY YEAR)
     SKILLGR (SKILL SKLYRS)
     SKILLGR REPEATS UNDER PERSONS

CODES
     SEX M MALE F FEMALE
```

CLASS QUESTIONS

Chapter 2

1. What is the difference between logical and physical data description?

2. What words describe the logical components of a data base?

3. What words have the same meaning as (*i*) *data item* and (*ii*) *data aggregate*?

4. Define "data item."

5. What words describe the physical subdivisions of data?

6. What is the difference in meaning between "virtual" and "transparent"?

Chapter 3

1. The term "data base" has sometimes been used to mean "management information system." In fact, these terms are entirely separate in meaning. What is the difference?

2. How small could a data base be?

3. What is meant by "data independence"? Make a list of data independence capabilities.

4. Can a data base be of value in a system which uses only batch processing with no terminals? Under what circumstances would such a system be better off using the traditional concept of data files?

5. List what you think the functions of a data administrator should be. What do you think is likely to be the most difficult part of a data administrator's job in a large corporation?

6. When this book is rewritten in some years time there might be a Stage 5 in Fig. 3.1. List what you think the Stage 5 attributes might be.

Chapter 4

1. If the ultimate ideal in data-base software could be written, what should it do? Make a list of functions.

2. "The data base designer has to steer a delicate course through compromises." Why?

3. What are the most important data-base objectives for the following:

    i.   A dedicated airline reservation system?

    ii. A batch-processing system for purchasing and inventory control?

    iii. A crime data base to give police detectives information which would enable them to do their job better?

Chapter 5

1. What are the three realms of data? What words are used to describe data in each realm?

2. What is the difference between a primary and secondary key?

3. Draw an example of an inverted list relating to a crime information system for use by police detectives.

4. List the six types of query relating to entities, attributes, and attribute values. Give an example of each from a crime information system.

Chapter 6

1. What is the difference between a "data-item type," an "instance of a data item," and a "data-item value"?

2. Why should a schema be independent of physical data organization? Can it be entirely independent?

3. Why should a subschema be independent of a schema? How complete does this independence need to be?

4. Fig. 6.2 shows two subschemas derived from the schema in Fig. 6.1. Draw a third subschema derived from the same schema.

5. What is the difference between simple and complex mapping?

6. Draw a schema for a simple data base intended to show what movies are playing in a group of towns. The schema should include the following data-items: TOWN, STATE, THEATER NAME, MOVIE NAME, ACTOR, DIRECTOR, SEAT PRICE, TIME OF SHOWING, ADDRESS OF THEATER, MOVIE RATING, REVIEW OF MOVIE.

Chapter 7

1. List the events that take place when a COBOL program updates a record, using a data-base management system.

2. One programmer should be able to change his data structure without effecting the work of other programmers who may use the same data. How does the data-base management system make this possible?

3. What types of languages may be employed in a data-base system? Give examples of each.

4. What facilities should a data-base system have for privacy and security protection? Where in the software should they reside?

5. In computers of the future the data-base management system and the operating system could be merged. What would be the advantages and disadvantages of merging them?

Chapter 8

Questions relating to this chapter are at the end of Chapter 9.

Chapter 9

1. Think of an example of data which could be represented by a four-level tree.

2. Think of examples of data which could be represented by (*i*) a simple plex structure, (*ii*) a complex plex structure, (*iii*) a cycle, (*iv*) a loop.

3. Decompose the structures in Fig. 9.1 into equivalent tree structures.

4. Think of examples of data in which there can be multiple types of relationships between the same two segments of data. How might these be represented in a schema?

5. Devise a method for *physical* representation of a tree structure which would not work with a plex structure.

6. Devise a method for *physical* representation of a simple plex structure which would not work with a complex plex structure.

Chapter 10

1. Why are three types of data description needed?

2. Should the subschema description method be independent of the host programming language?

3. In what ways may the subschema description differ from the schema description?

4. It is extremely important in implementing corporate data bases to select a logical data description language which is sure to be in use many years in the future. Why? Which of today's languages do you think are safe bets for this criterion?

5. Why is it important that a logical data description language should be independent of physical data structuring? Give examples of types of data descriptions which would violate this requirement.

Chapter 11

1. What are the characteristics of a CODASYL set?

2. Draw the set structures required to represent the schemas in Figs. 8.9, 6.8, and 9.4.

3. Describe a schema in the CODASYL Data Description Language for representing information of the type in Fig. 8.6. What is the simplest schema that could be employed?

4. Draw a DDL schema for representing information of the type in Fig. 9.13.

5. Loops are not permitted in the CODASYL language. Can you think of an example of data with which this would be a disadvantage? Is it serious?

6. Why is an area defined? What are the characteristics of an area?

Chapter 12

1. What is the difference between a physical child and a logical child in DL/I? Draw a data structure that contains both.

2. Give an illustration of the use of logical twin pointers.

3. Draw a DL.I structure to represent the schemas in Fig. 11.1, 9.4, and 9.6.

4. Draw a DL.I structure for representing information of the type in Fig. 9.2. What is the simplest structure that can be employed?

5. Draw a DL.I structure for representing information of the type in Fig. 9.13.

6. What is intersection data? Give an example of its use.

7. How does DL/I represent the three views of data which are necessary?

Chapter 13

1. What is a relation? What is a tuple? What is a domain? Define the properties of a relation.

2. Give normalized versions of the schemas in Figs. 6.1, 11.1, 9.5, and 9.6.

3. Draw a normalized structure for representing information of the type in Fig. 9.2. What is the simplest structure that can be employed?

4. Write normalized relations for a simple data base intended to show what movies are playing in a group of towns. The relations should include at least the following data-items: TOWN, STATE, THEATER NAME, MOVIE NAME, ACTOR, DIRECTOR, SEAT PRICE, TIME OF SHOW-ING, ADDRESS OF THEATER, MOVIE RATING, REVIEW OF MOVIE.

5. Devise an economical physical structure for the normalized data from the previous question.

6. To what extent does normalization introduce redundancy into data? Why is this not in conflict with the data base objective of minimizing redundancy?

7. Give an illustration of *projection* and *join* operations on a relation of your choice.

Chapter 14

1. Represent the file shown in Fig. 5.1 in third normal form.

2. Consider the relations shown in first normal form in Fig. 13.2. What additional normalization step would you apply?

3. Define the terms "functionally dependent" and "fully functionally dependent."

4. Draw functional dependency diagrams, such as that in Fig. 14.1, of the following relations. Decide for each of them whether you think further normalization is necessary.

    i.   INV   (INVOICE #, CUSTOMER #, CUSTOMER-NAME, CUS-TOMER ADDRESS, DATE, $ TOTAL)

    ii. STU   (STUDENT #, STUDENT-NAME, COURSE #, COURSE-TITLE, GRADE)

    iii. PO   (PART #, PURCHASE-ORDER #, PART-NAME, QUAN-ITITY-ORDERED, DELIVERY-DATE)

    iv. DENT   (DENTIST #, PATIENT #, DATE-OF-VISIT, TIME-OF-VISIT, DURATION-OF-VISIT, TYPE-OF-WORK-PERFORMED, COMPLETION-CODE, CHARGE)

5. Devise a set of relations in third normal form to represent the information in Fig. 10.3.

6. Give an example of how a relation not in third normal form can change due to application development in such a way that file restructuring and hence program rewriting is necessary.

7. List the advantages that would result from employing normalization in a data base management system.

Chapter 15

1. In terms of the nodes and links on bubble charts, define:

    i.   a primary key

    ii.   an attribute

    iii.   a secondary key

    iv.   a root key

    v.   an intersecting attribute.

2. The following are three views of data. Combine them into an integrated data-base structure.

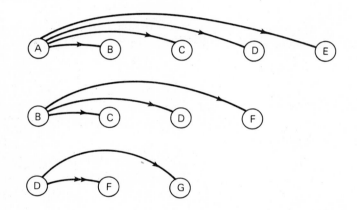

3. Construct a canonical schema containing the following data items, intended to show what movies are showing in group of towns for the next month:

    DATE, TOWN, STATE, THEATER NAME, MOVIE NAME, ACTOR, DIRECTOR, SEAT PRICE, TIME OF SHOWING, ADDRESS OF THEATER, TELEPHONE NUMBER, MOVIE RATING, MOVIE REVIEW.

4. Write down the data-items types which your librarian would use if she employed a computer to assist in managing the library. Arrange these data items into a canonical schema.

5. A delivery firm has a small data base. The systems analysts perceive applications of the data which they think require the following data structures:

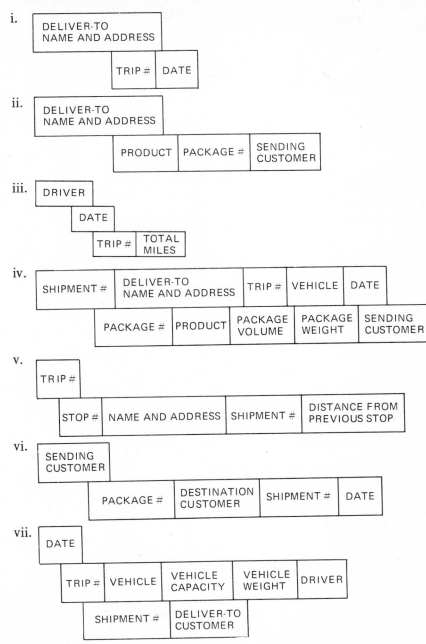

Design a canonical schema for this set of user views. Is the data likely to be used in other ways and if so will your design be appropriate? Have you designed a stable structure that represents the inherent properties of the data?

6. Convert your design from Question 5 into CODASYL, DL/I, and relational, schemas. What performance considerations should effect this design?

7. Design a canonical schema for a bill-of-materials data base.

8. What data-items do you think should be kept in a data base for a nation-wide car rental corporation relating to its cars, customers and reservations? Arrange these into a canonical schema.

9. A wine merchant has an on-line minicomputer with a data base. He wants it to accomplish the following activities:

   i.   Permit inquiries about vintages

   ii.   Permit inquiries about specific wine types

   iii.   Produce a customer mailing list

   iv.   Maintain an inventory of bottles in stock

   v.   Maintain an accounts receivable file

   vi.   Maintain an accounts payable file

   vii.   Maintain details of suppliers

   viii. Assist in ordering supplies

   ix.   Maintain a file of supplier invoices

   x.   Maintain a file of customer orders

   xi.   Send bills to customers

   xii.   Send notices to customers of overdue payment

   xiii. Keep records of deliveries

Design a canonical schema for his data base. Draw versions of this schema which are (a) CODASYL, (b) DL/I, (c) Relational.

Chapter 16

1. What is the difference between static and dynamic data independence?

2. At what times can binding take place?

3. To what extent do the following systems differ in their requirements for data independence:

   i. A dedicated airline reservation system?

   ii. A batch-processing system for purchasing and inventory control?

   iii. A crime data base to give police detective information which would enable them to do their job better?

Chapter 17

1. If perfect software existed, what should be the differences between the objectives of logical and physical data organization?

2. List those properties of data which should effect the choices of physical organization.

Chapter 18

1. What possible purposes can the physical sequencing of data records serve?

2. How might parallel cellular organizations of data be used?

3. What differences may exist between the physical and logical representations of relationships between segments?

4. A system employs a security scheme which permits up to 1000 authorized users to use a data base. The system makes three security checks:

   i. The user must type in a unique 5-character security code allocated to him and changed each month.

   ii. The user can employ only certain terminals. The system has 200 terminals, and any one user is permitted to use up to eight of them.

   iii. The system contains 400 data record categories. An average user is permitted to read 30% of the record categories but is permitted to modify not more than two categories.

To prevent the user taking non-permitted actions, an authorization table is employed; for each user it gives the terminals he is authorized to use, the data record categories he is authorized to read and to modify, and his security number. The information in the table is summarized as follows:

User	Security Code (Five digits)	Terminals this user may employ (Up to ten)	Data Records Categories this user may (a) read and (b) modify
1	S_1		
2	S_2		
3	S_3		
.	.		
.	.		
.	.		
1000	S_{1000}		

The data record category authorizations fall into patterns. That is, several users may have the same set of record category authorizations. Users with identical sets of record category authorizations may be grouped, and there are 50 such groups.

Devise a means of encoding the data in the authorization table in the minimum number of bits. (It is suggested that you refer to Figure 18.9.)

Chapter 19

1. What is the optimum number of records per block in a block-searched file?

2. What are the disadvantages of an indexed *non-sequential* organization compared with an indexed *sequential organization*? Why, then, are indexed non-sequential files used?

3. Application-oriented algorithms for key conversion are used to good effect on some systems. What are their disadvantages?

4. List the steps that occur when a file is loaded using hashing. What are the advantages of hashing over an index sequential organization?

5. Which type of addressing would be a good choice and which a bad choice for:

    i.   A batch processing billing operation?

    ii.   A consumer credit enquiry system?

    iii. An extremely volatile file?

Chapter 20

1. One of the differences between ISAM and VSAM is that VSAM is "hardware independent." What does this mean? How has it been accomplished?

2. What techniques can be used to shorten the overall access times of index sequential organizations?

3. Refer to Box 22.1. What are the advantages and disadvantages of the methods of handling insertions which are listed?

4. If a file has many highly clustered insertions, what would be a good way of handling them?

Chapter 21

1. Why is "randomizing" not a good name for the hashing technique?

2. If a record with the key "PEGGY" were added to the file in Fig. 23.3, where would it go? If a record with the key "ALICE" were added, what overflow chains would exist from the bucket it is allocated to?

3. A storage unit has a capacity of 10,000 records. A file of 9000 records is to be stored in it using hashing. Space for 1000 records (of the 10,000) is designated the overflow area, and a bucket capacity of 20 is selected. Is this likely to be adequate? Would it have been better to use a smaller overflow area, leaving more space in the prime area?

4. Under what conditions is it efficient to store the overflows in the prime area? What could be the advantages of doing so in preference to using a separate overflow area?

5. Contrast the advantages and disadvantages of hashing and indexing for file organization in

    i.   A batch-processing billing system.

ii.   An interactive system with requirements for fast response to complex queries.

iii. A system with highly volatile files.

Chapter 22

Class questions are at the end of the following chapter.

Chapter 23

1. What three types of pointers are in common use? When might each be used?

2. What is the difference between embedded pointers and directory pointers? What are the advantages of the latter?

3. Why is a pointer sometimes used from the head of a chain to its farthest end?

4. How may records be deleted when they are members of chains which intersect?

5. Give an example of effective use of (*i*) a coral ring, (*ii*) a ring with pointers to the head of the ring.

6. List the techniques which can be used to speed up the searching of chained files.

Chapter 24

1. What tradeoffs exist in the methods of representing a repeating group?

2. Represent the tree in Fig. 8.5 as a physically contiguous list. Devise a method of handling additions or deletions with such an organization.

3. What are the advantages and disadvantages of the three types of pointer organizations shown in Fig. 24.10?

4. What is a directory? What are its advantages in handling tree structures?

5. Consider the files in Figs. 24.5, 24.11, 24.17, and 24.18. Which techniques would be good, and which poor, for each of these?

6. Summarize the methods of handling insertions and deletions in tree structures.

7. Devise an efficient method of organizing the data in Fig. 13.2 first as a tree, and second in normalized form. What methods are possible for phvsical representation of normalized files?

Chapter 25

1. Which techniques can handle a tree structure but not a plex structure? Which techniques can handle a simple plex structure but not a complex plex structure?

2. What are the advantages of using directories to represent plex structures? When is a bit map representation advantageous?

3. Which techniques of representing plex structures would be good with highly volatile files?

4. Devise an efficient method of organizing the data in Fig. 13.5, first as a plex structure, and second in normalized form.

Chapter 26

1. Why should a count of items be given in a chained file?

2. List the techniques which can speed up the search of a chained file.

3. When should indirect pointers be used in preference to direct pointers?

4. What parameters can be varied in a multilist file?

5. Which of the multiple-key retrieval techniques are to be preferred and which are disadvantageous

    i.   If the file is frequently updated?

    ii. If the file is highly volatile (many new records inserted and old ones deleted)?

    iii. If conversational response times are needed?

    iv. If storage space saving is of primary importance?

See also questions at the end of Chapter 28.

Chapter 27

Assume that a file consists of one hundred thousand records of 500 bytes each. The records have one primary key of ten bytes in total.

1. Which organizations of those shown would be most suitable for a fast-response real-time inquiry system for this file using disk storage?

2. Assume that two million bytes of solid-state memory with an access time of about 1 microsecond are available to buffer data-base operations. Directories can be paged from disks or other devices into this main memory. With this hardware, which organizations would be suitable for fast-response systems?

3. For each of the ten organizations, consider how records might be added and deleted. Which organizations would tend to facilitate maintenance, and which would be bad for maintenance?

4. For each of the organizations, consider the effect of a pointer becoming damaged. What would have to be done to repair the pointer? How could the organization best be protected from the effects of pointer destruction?

5. Taking maintenance, pointer damage, and fast-response requirements into consideration, which organization would you prefer for a moderately volatile file?

Chapter 28

1. Give three advantages of storing relationships between data separately from the data.

2. Under what circumstances is it advantageous to store data-item *values* separately as in Fig. 29.2, rather than in records or segments? Under what circumstances is it disadvantageous?

3. Draw a file structure for the data in Figs. 6.8 and 10.3 in which the data segments are stored separately from the relationships between segments.

4. What effect does the separation of data and relationships between data have on the handling of insertions and deletions?

5. Some designers of prototype data-base systems have used *binary* relations. What are the advantages and disadvantages of using binary relations? In what types of data base might they be preferable?

6. What is a triad? Give an illustration of data for which a triad organization can be used effectively.

Chapter 29

1. What is the difference between a sparse and a dense index? Give an illustration of the use of a sparse index.

2. What does the term index "resolution" refer to? Give an example of a situation in which it would be advantageous to use a bucket-resolved index with relative pointers.

3. Under what circumstances can front-end compression *not* be used?

4. What are likely differences in structure between a primary index and a secondary index?

Chapter 30

1. What is the mean number of probes needed in a block search? What is the mean number of probes needed in a binary search?

2. If a binary search is the fast way to search an index block in main memory, why is it often not used?

3. When is a binary tree search technique better than a binary search? Organize the items in Fig. 22.2 into a binary tree and draw the insertions shown in that figure.

4. Demonstrate that small blocks are desirable in tree indices.

5. Select a large direct-access storage device with which you are familiar and demonstrate how a tree index may be tailored to the hardware. How much waste occurs if the block sizes are not tailored to the hardware but instead assume the values shown in this chapter which minimize the mean number of probes?

6. When should the sequence set of an index be linked with pointers?

7. Could look-aside buffers be useful with the index of an airline reservation system?

8. In what circumstances would an unbalanced tree index be of use? What are the snags of unbalanced tree indices?

9. Is a hash index likely to be better than

    i.   Pure hashing?

    ii. A tree index without hashing?

10. What indexing techniques are appropriate for a highly volatile file?

Chapter 31

1. What steps can be taken to improve the performance of inverted file systems?

2. What maintenance problems are encountered on inverted file systems?

3. How may large hierarchical storages using staging (previous chapter) effect the design of inverted file systems?

Chapter 32

1. Consider the index at the back of this book. Assuming that the reader had the patience of a computer, what compaction techniques could be applied to it?

2. What compaction techniques can be implemented in hardware in an application-independent fashion?

3. When information is to be stored in facsimile form, documents are scanned a line at a time and converted into a bit stream. When the document is black at a scanning point a 1 bit results; when it is white a 0 bit results. To obtain good resolution, 125 scanning points per inch are used, and a typical document may thus be represented by about 1.3 million bits. Devise a compaction algorithm which could be applied to such a bit stream. What compaction ratio do you think could be achieved with a typical document page?

4. If files are stored in the form of binary relations, or triads, as discussed in Chapter 29, what compaction techniques can be applied?

5. What is Huffman encoding? When is it most effective?

Chapter 33

1. What are the advantages and disadvantages of using staging in a storage hierarchy?

2. Under what circumstances will staging be effective? Do such conditions apply (or can they be made to apply) to the majority of large-storage applications?

3. What design options does the designer of a staging system have?

4. What are the differences between static and dynamic staging, and between demand and anticipatory staging? Which do you think will be the most commonly used five years in the future?

5. What is a stack replacement algorithm?

6. Verify, by examining a suitable example, that *first-in-first-out* is not a stack replacement algorithm.

7. Why can we draw curves for an "optimal" replacement algorithm? Verify by examining an example that an optimal replacement algorithm is a stack replacement algorithm.

8. What application characteristics could cause the shapes of the curves in Fig. 32.15?

9. When staging hierarchies are used, some types of data organization will be very poor; others will be efficient. Make a list of each.

Chapter 34

1. Re-examine Boxes 20.2, 21.2, 22.1, 23.1, 26.1, 27.1, and 30.1, and consider which of the techniques listed would be good, and which bad, for highly volatile files?

Chapter 35

1. Re-examine Boxes 20.2, 21.2, 22.1, 23.1, 26.1, 27.1, and 30.1, and consider which of the techniques listed would be good, and which bad, for systems which must give fast responses.

2. What techniques are appropriate for fast-response systems with highly volatile files?

3. What trade-offs can be excercised in the design of man-terminal dialogues and terminal network design to make the dialogues phychologically effective but still have them conform to the realities of data-base accessing?

4. What techniques will be appropriate and what inappropriate in fast-response systems using large storage hierarchies with staging (Chapter 32)?

GLOSSARY

ACCESS. The operation of seeking, reading, or writing data on a storage unit.

ACCESS MECHANISM. A mechanism for moving one or more reading and writing heads to the position at which certain data are to be read or written. Alternatively the data medium may be moved to the read/write station.

ACCESS METHOD. A technique for moving data between a computer and its peripheral devices, e.g. serial access, random access, remote access, virtual sequential access method (VSAM), hierarchical indexed sequential access method (HISAM).

ACCESS TIME. The time that elapses between an instruction being given to access some data and that data becoming available for use.

ACTIVITY RATIO. The fraction of records in a file or data set, which have activity (are updated or inspected) in a given period or during a given run.

ADDRESS. An identification (number, name, label) for a location in which data is stored.

ADDRESSING. The means of assigning data to storage locations, and subsequently retrieving them, on the basis of the key of the data.

ALGORITHM. A computational procedure.

ALTERNATE TRACK. A track which is automatically substituted for a damaged track on a disk or other storage device.

ANTICIPATORY STAGING. Blocks of data are moved from one storage device to another device with a shorter access time, in anticipation of their being needed by the computer programs. This is to be contrasted with demand staging in which the blocks of data are moved *when* programs request them, not *before*.

AREA (CODASYL). A named sub-division of the addressable storage space in the data base which may contain occurrences of records and sets or parts of sets of various types. Areas may be opened by a run-unit with *usage modes* which permit, or do not permit, concurrent run-units to open the same area. An area may be declared in the schema to be a *temporary area*. The effect of this is to provide a different occurrence of the temporary area to each run-unit opening it and at the termination of the run-unit, the storage space involved becomes available for re-use.

ASSEMBLE. To convert a routine coded in non-machine language into actual machine language instructions.

To perform some or all of the following functions: (1) translation of symbolic operation codes into machine codes; (2) allocation of storage, to the extent at least of assigning storage locations to successive instructions; (3) computation of absolute or relocatable addresses from symbolic addresses; (4) insertion of library routines; (5) generation of sequences of symbolic instructions by the insertion of specific parameters into macro instructions.

ASSOCIATIVE STORAGE (MEMORY). Storage which is addressed by content rather than by location, thus providing a fast way to search for data having certain contents. (Conventional storage had addresses related to the physical location of the data.)

ATTRIBUTE. A field containing information about an entity.

AVAILABILITY. A measure of the capability of a system to be used for performing its intended function, as a result of the system's being in an operating state.

BINARY SEARCH. A method of searching a sequenced table or file. The procedure involves selecting the upper or lower half based upon an examination of its midpoint value. The selected portion is then similarly halved, and so on until the required item is found.

BLOCKING. The combining of two or more records so that they are jointly read or written by one machine instruction.

BUCKET. An area of storage which may contain more than one record and which is referred to as a whole by some addressing technique.

BUFFER. An area of storage which holds data temporarily while it is being received, transmitted, read or written. It is often used to compensate for differences in speed or timing of devices. Buffers are used in terminals, peripheral devices, storage units and in the CPU.

CANONICAL SCHEMA. A model of data which represents the inherent structure of that data and hence is independent of individual applications of the data and also of the software or hardware mechanisms which are employed in representing and using the data.

CATALOG. A directory of all files available to the computer.

CELL. Contiguous storage locations referred to as a group in an addressing or file searching scheme. The cell may be such that it does not cross mechanical boundaries in the storage unit; for example it could be a track or cylinder.

CELLULAR CHAINS. Chains which are not permitted to cross cell boundaries.

CELLULAR MULTILIST. A form of multilist organization (q. v.) in which the chains cannot extend across cell boundaries.

CELLULAR SPLITTING. A technique for handling records added to a file. The records are organized into cells and a cell is split into two cells when it becomes full.

CHAIN. An organization in which records or other items of data are strung together by means of pointers.

CHANNEL. A subsystem for input to and output from the computer. Data from storage units, for example, flows into the computer via a channel.

CHECKPOINT/RESTART. A means of restarting a program at some point other than the beginning, used after a failure or interruption has occurred. Checkpoints may be used at intervals throughout an application program; at these points records are written giving enough information about the status of the program to permit its being restarted at that point.

CIRCULAR FILE. An organization for a file of high volatility, in which new records being added replace the oldest records.

CODASYL. Conference of Data Description Languages. The organization that specified the programming language COBOL. It has now specified a set of manufacturer-independent, application-independent languages designed to form the basis of data-base management.

COMPACTION. A technique for reducing the number of bits in data without destroying any information content.

COMPILER. A computer program which in addition to performing the functions of an assembler has the following characteristics: (1) it makes use of information on the overall logical structure of the program to improve the efficiency of the resulting machine program; (2) its language does not parallel the actual form of the machine language, but is rather oriented toward convenient problem or procedure statement; (3) it usually generates more than one machine instruction for each symbolic instruction.

CONCATENATE. To link together. A *concatenated data set* is a collection of logically connected data sets. A *concatenated key* is composed of more than one field.

CONCEPTUAL MODEL. Conceptual schema (q.v.).

CONCEPTUAL SCHEMA. The overall logical structure of a data base. Schema (q.v.).

CORE STORAGE. A high-speed random-access memory consisting of many ferromagnetic toroids (cores) strung on wires in matrix arrays. The term is now used loosely to mean the main memory of a computer even though that computer may employ a more advanced memory technology than magnetic cores.

CYLINDER. A concept of storage: that area of storage which can be read without the movement of an access mechanism. The term originated with disk files, in which a cylinder consisted of one track on each disk surface such that each of these tracks could have a read/write head positioned over it simultaneously.

DASD. Direct-Access Storage Device.

DATA ADMINISTRATOR. An individual with an overview of an organization's data.

DATA AGGREGATE (CODASYL definition). A named collection of data-items within a record. There are two types: vectors and repeating groups. A vector is a one-dimensional, ordered collection of data-items, all of which have identical characteristics. A repeating group is a collection of data that occurs an arbitrary number of times within a record occurrence. The collection may consist of data-items, vectors, and repeating groups.

DATA BANK. A collection of data relating to a given set of subjects.

DATA BASE.
(1) A collecton of interrelated data stored together with controlled redundancy to serve one or more applications; the data are stored so that they are independent of programs which use the data; a common and controlled approach is used in adding new data and in modifying and retrieving existing data within a data base. A system is said to contain a collection of data bases if they are disjoint in structure.
(2) CODASYL definition: A DATA BASE consists of all the record occurrences, set occurrences and areas which are controlled by a specific schema. If an installation has multiple data bases, there must be a separate schema for each data base. Furthermore, the content of different data bases is assumed to be disjoint.

DATA-BASE ADMINISTRATOR. An individual with an overview of one or more data bases, who controls the design and use of these data bases.

DATA-BASE MANAGEMENT SYSTEM. The collection of software required for using a data base.

DATA DESCRIPTION LANGUAGE. A language for describing data (in some software for describing the logical, not the physical, data; in other software for both).

DATA DICTIONARY. A catalogue of all data types giving their names and structures.

DATA DIVISION *(COBOL)*. That division of a COBOL program which consists of entries used to define the nature and characteristics of the data to be processed by the object program.

DATA ELEMENT. Synonymous with DATA ITEM (q.v.) or FIELD.

DATA INDEPENDENCE. The property of being able to change the overall logical or physical structure of the data without changing the application program's view of the data.

DATA INDEPENDENCE, LOGICAL. The property of being able to change the overall logical structure of the data base (schema) without changing the application program's view of the data.

DATA INDEPENDENCE, PHYSICAL. The property of being able to change the physical structure of the data without changing the logical structure.

DATA ITEM. The smallest unit of data that has meaning in describing information; the smallest unit of named data. Synonymous with DATA ELEMENT or FIELD.

DATA MANAGEMENT. A general term that collectively describes those functions of the system that provide creation of and access to stored data, enforce data storage conventions, and regulate the use of input/output devices.

DATA MANIPULATION LANGUAGE. The language which the programmer uses to cause data to be transferred between his program and the data base.

    The data manipulation language is not a complete language by itself. It relies on a host programming language to provide a framework for it and to provide the procedural capabilities required to manipulate data.

DATA SET. A named collection of logically related data items, arranged in a prescribed manner, and described by control information to which the programming system has access.

DBDC. Data base/data communications.

DEMAND STAGING. Blocks of data are moved from one storage device to another device with a shorter access time, when programs request them and they are not already in the faster-access storage. Contrast with ANTICIPATORY STAGING (q.v.).

DEVICE/MEDIA CONTROL LANGUAGE. A language for specifying the physical layout and organization of data.

DIALOGUE. A generic word for a preplanned man-machine interaction; it encompasses formal programming languages, languages for interrogating data bases, and innumerable non-formal conversational interchanges, many of which are designed for one specific application.

DICTIONARY. See DATA DICTIONARY.

DIRECT ACCESS. Retrieval or storage of data by a reference to its location on a volume, rather than relative to the previously retrieved or stored data.

DIRECT-ACCESS STORAGE DEVICE (DASD). A data storage unit on which data can be accessed directly at random without having to progress through a serial file such as tape. A disk unit is a direct-access storage device.

DIRECTORY. A table giving the relationships between items of data. Sometimes a table (index) giving the addresses of data.

DISTRIBUTED FREE SPACE. Space left empty at intervals in a data layout to permit the possible insertion of new data.

DL/I. IBM's Data Language/I, for describing logical and physical data structures.

DOMAIN. The collection of data items (fields) of the same type, in a relation (flat file).

DYNAMIC STORAGE ALLOCATION. The allocation of storage space to a procedure based on the instantaneous or actual demand for storage space by that procedure, rather than allocating storage space to a procedure based on its anticipated or predicted demand.

EMBEDDED POINTERS. Pointers in the data records rather than in a directory.

ENTITY. Something about which data is recorded.

ENTITY IDENTIFIER. A key which uniquely identifies an entity or data concerning that entity.

EXTENT. A contiguous area of data storage.

EXTERNAL SCHEMA. A user's or programmer's view of the data. Subschema (q.v.).

FIELD. See DATA ITEM.

FILE. A set of similarly constructed records.

FLAT FILE. A 2-dimensional array of data items.

FUNCTIONAL DEPENDENCE. Attribute B of a relation R is functionally dependent on attribute A or R if, at every instant in time, each value of A has no more than one value of B associated with it in relation R. (Equivalent to saying that A identifies B).

   An attribute or collection of attributes, B, of a relation, R, is said to be *fully functionally dependent* on another collection of attributes, A, of R, if B is functionally dependent on the whole of A but not on any subset of A.

HASH TOTAL. A meaningless total of the values of a certain field in a file, maintained for control purposes to ensure that no items are lost or changed invalidly.

HASHING. A direct addressing technique in which the key is converted to a pseudorandom number from which the required address is derived.

HEADER RECORD OR HEADER TABLE. A record containing common, constant, or identifying, information for a group of records which follows.

HEURISTIC. Pertaining to trial-and-error methods of obtaining solutions to problems.

HIERARCHICAL FILE. A file in which some records are subordinate to others in a tree structure.

HIERARCHICAL STORAGE. Storage units linked together to form a storage subsystem, in which some are fast but small and others are large but slow. Blocks of data are moved from the large slow levels to the small fast levels when required.

HIT RATE. A measure of the number of records in a file which are expected to be accessed in a given run. Usually expressed as a percentage:

$$\frac{Number\ of\ input\ transactions\ \times\ 100\%}{Number\ of\ records\ in\ the\ file}$$

HOME ADDRESS. (1) A storage location (e.g., a home bucket) into which a data record is logically assigned; as opposed to overflow address. (2) A field that contains the physical address of a track, recorded at the beginning of a track.

HUFFMAN CODE. A code for data compaction in which frequently used characters are encoded with a smaller number of bits than infrequently used characters.

INDEPENDENCE, DATA. See DATA INDEPENDENCE.

INDEPENDENCE, DEVICE. Data organization which is independent of the device on which the data is stored.

INDEX. A table used to determine the location of a record.

INDEX CHAINS. Chains within an index.

INDEX POINT. A hardware reference mark on a disk or drum; used for timing purposes.

INDEX, SECONDARY. See SECONDARY INDEX.

INDEXED-SEQUENTIAL STORAGE. A file structure in which records are stored in ascending sequence by key. Indices showing the highest key on a cylinder/track/ bucket, etc., are used for the selected retrieval of records.

INDICATIVE DATA. Data that identifies or describes; e.g., in a stock file, the product number, description, pack size. Normally, indicative data does not change on a regular, frequent basis during processing (as in, for example, an account balance).

INDIRECT ADDRESSING. Any method of specifying or locating a storage location whereby the key (of itself or through calculation) does not represent an address. For example, locating an address through indices.

INFORMATION SYSTEM. Contrasted with OPERATING SYSTEM, to mean a system in which the data stored will be used in spontaneous ways which are not fully predictable in advance for obtaining information.

INTERNAL SCHEMA. The physical structure of the data.

INTERPRETIVE ROUTINE. A routine which decodes instructions written as pseudo-codes and immediately executes those instructions, as contrasted with a compiler which decodes the pseudo-codes and produces a machine-language routine to be executed at a later time.

INTERSECTION DATA. Data which is associated with the conjunction of two segments (or other data groupings) but which has no meaning if associated with only one of the two segments.

INVERTED FILE. A file structure which permits fast spontaneous searching for previous unspecified information. Independent lists or indices are maintained in records keys which are accessible according to the values of specific fields.

INVERTED LIST. A list organized by a secondary key (q.v.) not a primary key.

ISAM. Index sequential access method (IBM).

KEY. A data item used to identify or locate a record (or other data grouping).

KEY COMPRESSION. A technique for reducing the number of bits in keys; used in making indices occupy less space.

KEY, PRIMARY. A key which uniquely identifies a record (or other data grouping).

KEY, SECONDARY. A key which does not uniquely identify a record, i.e., more than one record can have the same key value. A key which contains the value of an attribute (data item) other than the unique identifier.

LABEL. A set of symbols used to identify or describe an item, record, message, or file. Occasionally it may be the same as the address in storage.

LATENCY. The time taken for a storage location to reach the read/write heads on a rotating surface. For general timing purposes, average latency is used; this is the time taken by one half-revolution of the surface.

LFU. Least frequently used. A replacement algorithm in which when new data has to replace existing data in an area of storage, the least frequently used items are replaced.

LIBRARY.
   (1) The room in which volumes (tapes and diskpacks) are stored.
   (2) An organized collection of programs, source statements, or object modules,

maintained on a direct-access device accessible by the operating system.

LIST. An ordered set of data items. A chain.

LOGICAL. An adjective describing the form of data organization, hardware, or system that is perceived by an application program, programmer, or user; it may be different to the real (physical) form.

LOGICAL DATA BASE. A data base as perceived by its users; it may be structured differently from the physical data-base structure. In IBM's Data Language/I, a logical data base is a tree-structured collection of segments derived from one or more physical data bases by means of pointer linkages.

LOGICAL DATA-BASE DESCRIPTION. A schema. A description of the overall data-base structure as perceived for the users, which is employed by the data-base management software.

LOGICAL FILE. A file as perceived by an application program; it may be in a completely different form from that in which it is stored on the storage units.

LRU. Least recently used. A replacement algorithm in which when new data has to replace existing data in an area of storage, the least recently used items are replaced.

LVIEW. A user's view of data. Subschema (q.v.).

MACHINE-INDEPENDENT. An adjective used to indicate that a procedure or a program is conceived, organized, or oriented without specific reference to the system. Use of this adjective usually implies that the procedure or program is oriented or organized in terms of the logical nature of the problem or processing, rather than in terms of the characteristics of the machine used in handling it.

MACROINSTRUCTION. One line of source program code which generates a program routine rather than one program instruction.

MAINTENANCE OF A FILE. Periodic re-organization of a file to better accommodate items that have been added or deleted.

MANAGEMENT, DATA BASE. See DATA BASE MANAGEMENT SYSTEM.

MAPPING. A definition of the way records are associated with one another.

MIGRATION. Frequently used items of data are moved to areas of storage where they are more rapidly accessible; infrequently used items are moved to areas which are less rapidly accessible and possibly less expensive.

MODEL. The logical structure of the data. Schema (q.v.)

MODULE. The section of storage hardware which holds one volume, such as one spindle of disks.

MULTILIST ORGANIZATION. A chained file organization in which the chains are divided into fragments in each fragment indexed, to permit faster searching.

MULTIPLE-KEY RETRIEVAL. Retrieval which requires searches of data based on the values of several key fields (some or all of which are secondary keys).

NETWORK STRUCTURE. See PLEX STRUCTURE.

NORMAL FORM, FIRST. Data in flat file form.

NORMAL FORM, SECOND. A relation R is in second normal form if it is in first normal form and every nonprime attribute of R is fully functionally dependent (q.v.) on each candidate key of R (E. F. Codd's definition).

NORMAL FORM, THIRD. A relation R is in third normal form if it is in second normal form and every nonprime attribute of R is nontransitively dependent on each candidate key of R (E. F. Codd's definition).

NORMALIZATION. The decomposition of more complex data structures into flat files (relations). This forms the basis of relational data bases.

ON-LINE. An on-line system is one in which the input data enter the computer directly from their point of origin and/or output data are transmitted directly to where they are used. The intermediate stages such as punching data, writing tape, loading disks, or off-line printing are avoided.

ON-LINE STORAGE. Storage devices, and especially the storage media which they contain, under the direct control of a computing system, not off-line or in a volume library.

OPERATING SYSTEM. Software which enables a computer to supervise its own operations, automatically calling in programs, routines, language, and data, as needed for continuous throughput of different types of jobs.

OVERFLOW. The condition when a record (or segment) cannot be stored in its *home address*; i.e., the storage location logically assigned to it on loading. It may be stored in a special OVERFLOW LOCATION, or in the home address of other records.

PAGE FAULT. A program interruption that occurs when a page which is referred to is not in main memory and has to be read in.

PAGING. In virtual storage systems, the technique of making memory appear larger than it is by transferring blocks (pages) of data or programs into that memory from external storage when they are needed.

PARALLEL DATA ORGANIZATIONS. Organizations which permit multiple access arms to search, read, or write, data simultaneously.

PHYSICAL. An adjective, contrasted with LOGICAL (q.v.), which refers to the form in which data or systems exist in reality. Data is often converted by software from the form in which it is *physically* stored to a form in which a user or programmer perceives it.

PHYSICAL DATA BASE. A data base in the form in which it is stored on the storage media, including pointers or other means of interconnecting it. Multiple logical data bases may be derived from one or more physical data bases.

PHYSICAL RECORD. A collection of bits that are physically recorded on the storage medium and which are read or written by one machine input/output instruction.

PLEX STRUCTURE. A relationship between records (or other groupings) in which a child record can have more than one parent record. Also called NETWORK STRUCTURE.

POINTER. The address of a record (or other data groupings) contained in another record so that a program may access the former record when it has retrieved the latter record. The address can be absolute, relative, or symbolic, and hence the pointer is referred to as absolute, relative, or symbolic.

PRIMARY KEY. See KEY, PRIMARY.

PROGRESSIVE OVERFLOW. A method of handling overflow in a randomly stored file which does not require the use of pointers. An overflow record is stored in the first available space and is retrieved by a forward serial search from the home address.

PURGE DATE. The date on or after which a storage area is available to be overwritten. Used in conjunction with a file label, it is a means of protecting file data until an agreed release date is reached.

RANDOM ACCESS. To obtain data directly from any storage location regardless of its position with respect to the previously referenced information. Also called DIRECT ACCESS.

RANDOM ACCESS STORAGE. A storage technique in which the time required to obtain information is independent of the location of the information most recently obtained. This strict definition must be qualified by the observation that we usually mean relatively random. Thus, magnetic drums are relatively non-random access when compared to magnetic cores for main memory, but relatively random access when compared to magnetic tapes for file storage.

RANDOMIZING. An old word for HASHING (q.v.).

REAL TIME.
(1) Pertaining to actual time during which a physical process transpires.
(2) Pertaining to the performance of a computation during the actual time that the related physical process transpires in order that results of the computation can be used in guiding the physical process.
(3) Pertaining to an application in which response to input is fast enough to effect subsequent input, as when conducting the dialogues that take place at terminals on interactive systems.

RECORD.

(1) A group of related fields of information treated as a unit by an application program.

(2) CODASYL definition: A named collection of zero, one or more data-items or data-aggregates. There may be an arbitrary number of occurrences in the data base of each record type specified in the schema for that data base. For example, there would be one occurrence of the record type PAYROLL-RECORD for each employee. This distinction between the actual occurrences of a record and the type of the record is an important one.

(3) IBM's DL/I terminology: A logical data-base record consists of a named hierarchy (tree) of related segments. There may be one or more segment types, each of which may have a different length and format.

RELATION. A flat file. A two-dimensional array of data elements. A file in normalized form.

RELATIONAL ALGEBRA. A language providing a set of operators for manipulating relations.

RELATIONAL CALCULUS. A language in which the user states the results he requires from manipulating a relational data base.

RELATIONAL DATA BASE. A data base made up of relations (as defined above). Its data-base management system has the capability to recombine the data elements to form different relations thus giving great flexibility in the usage of data.

RING STRUCTURE. Data organized with chains such that the end of the chain points to its beginning, thus forming a ring.

ROOT. The base node of a tree structure. Data in the tree may be accessed starting at its root.

SCHEMA.

(1) A map of the overall logical structure of a data base.

(2) CODASYL definition: A SCHEMA consists of DDL (Data Description Language) entries and is a complete description of all of the area, set occurrences, record occurrences and associated data-items and data-aggregates as they exist in the data base.

SCHEMA LANGUAGE. Logical data-base description language.

SEARCH. To examine a series of items for any that have a desired property or properties.

SECONDARY INDEX. An index composed of secondary keys rather than primary keys.

SECONDARY KEY. See KEY, SECONDARY.

SECONDARY STORAGE. Storage facilities forming not an integral part of the computer but directly linked to and controlled by the computer, e.g., disks, magnetic tapes, etc.

SECTOR. The smallest address portion of storage on some disk and drum storage units.

SEEK. To position the access mechanism of a direct-access storage device at a specified location.

SEEK TIME. The time taken to execute a SEEK operation.

SEGMENT. A named fixed-format quantum of data containing one or more fields. A segment is the basic quantum of data which is passed to and from the application programs when IBM Data Language/I is used.

SENSITIVITY. A programmer may view only certain of the data in a logical data base. His program is said to be *sensitized* to that data.

SEQUENCE SET INDEX. The lowest level in a tree-structured index. The entries in this level are in sequence. Searches and other operations may be carried out in the sequence set index; those are called SEQUENCE SET OPERATIONS.

SEQUENTIAL PROCESSING. Accessing records in ascending sequence by key; the next record accessed will have the next higher key, irrespective of its physical position in the file.

SERIAL-ACCESS STORAGE. Storage in which records must be read serially one after the other, e.g. tape.

SERIAL PROCESSING. Accessing records in their physical sequence. The next record accessed will be the record in the next physical-position/location in the field.

SET (CODASYL definition). A SET is a named collection of record types. As such, it establishes the characteristics of an arbitrary number of occurrences of the named set. Each set type specified in the schema must have one record type declared as its OWNER and one or more record types declared as its MEMBER records. Each occurrence of a set must contain one occurrence of its owner record and may contain an arbitrary number of occurrences of each of its member record types.

SET, SINGULAR. A CODASYL set without owner records; the owner is declared to be "SYSTEM." A singular set is used to provide simple nonhierarchical files such as a file of customer records.

SKIP-SEARCHED CHAIN. A chain having pointers which permit it to be searched by skipping, not examining every link in the chain.

SORT. Arrange a file in sequence by a specified key.

STAGING. Blocks of data are moved from one storage device to another with a shorter access time, either before or at the time they are needed.

STORAGE HIERARCHY. Storage units linked together to form a storage subsystem, in which some are fast but small and others are large but slow. Blocks of data are moved (STAGED) from the large slow levels to the small fast levels as required.

SUBMODEL. A user's or programmer's view of the data. Subschema (q.v.).

SUBSCHEMA. A map of a programmer's view of the data he uses. It is derived from the global logical view of the data—the schema, and external schema. Also called LVIEW.

TABLE. A collection of data suitable for quick reference, each item being uniquely identified either by a label or by its relative position.

TERABIT STORAGE. Storage which can hold 10^{12} bits of data.

THIRD NORMAL FORM. A record, segment, or tuple, which is normalized (i.e. contains no repeating groups) and in which every nonprime data item is nontransitively dependent and fully dependent on each candidate key.

In other words: the *entire* primary key or candidate key is needed to identify each other data item in the tuple and no data item is identified by a data item which is not in the primary key or candidate key.

TRACK. The circular recording surface transcribed by a read/write head on a drum, disk, or other rotating mechanism.

TRANSACTION. An input record applied to an established file. The input record describes some "event" that will either cause a new file record to be generated, an existing record to be changed, or an existing record to be deleted.

TRANSFER RATE. A measure of the speed with which data is moved between a direct-access device and the central processor. Usually expressed as thousands of characters per second or thousands of bytes per second).

TRANSPARENT DATA. Complexities in the data structure are hidden from the programmers or users (made transparent to them) by the software.

TREE INDEX. An index in the form of a tree structure.

TREE STRUCTURE. A hierarchy of groups of data such that
1. the highest level in the hierarchy has only one group, called a *root*;
2. all groups except the root are related to one and only one group on a higher level than themselves.
A simple master/detail file is a two-level tree. Also called a HIERARCHICAL structure.

TUPLE. A group of related fields. *N* related fields are called an *N*-tuple.

VIRTUAL. Conceptual or appearing to be, rather than actually being. An adjective which implies that data, structures, or hardware, appear to the application programmer or user to be different to what they are in reality, the conversion being performed by software.

VIRTUAL MEMORY. Memory which can appear to the programs to be larger than it really is because blocks of data or program are rapidly moved to or from secondary storage when needed.

VOLATILE FILE. A file with a high rate of additions and deletions.

VOLATILE STORAGE. Storage which loses its contents when the power supply is cut off. Solid-state (LSI) storage is volatile; magnetic storage is not.

VOLUME. Demountable tapes, disks, and cartridges are referred to as *volumes*. The word also refers to a nondemountable disk or other storage medium. It has been defined as "that portion of a single unit of storage medium which is accessible to a single read/write mechanism"; however, some devices exist in which a volume is accessible with two or more read/write mechanisms.

VOLUME TABLE OF CONTENTS (VTOC). A table associated with a volume which describes each file or data set on the volume.

VSAM. Virtual sequential access method, an IBM volume independent indexed sequential access method.

VTOC. See Volume Table of Contents.

WORKING STORAGE. A portion of storage, usually computer main memory, reserved for the temporary results of operations.

WRITE. To record information on a storage device.

INDEX

THE JAMES MARTIN BOOKS ON COMPUTER

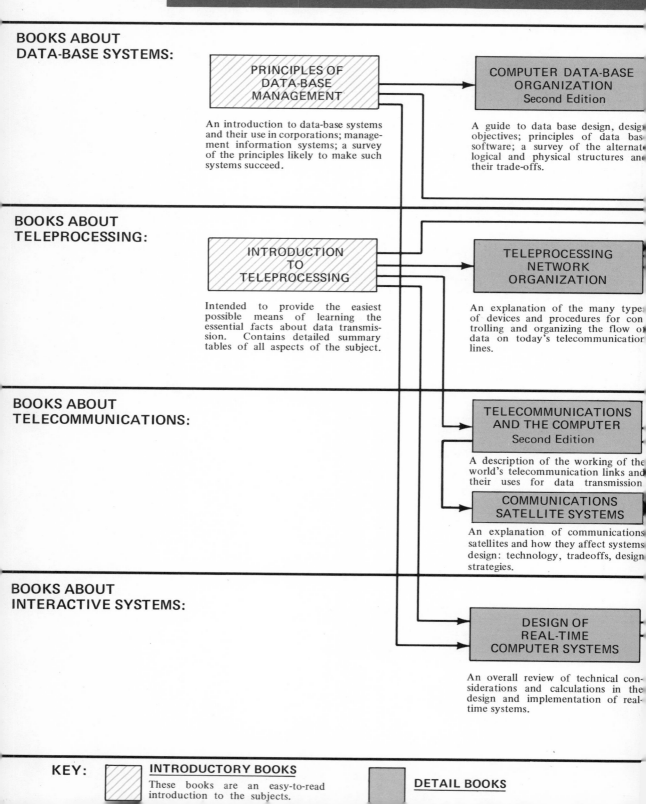

BOOKS ABOUT DATA-BASE SYSTEMS:

PRINCIPLES OF DATA-BASE MANAGEMENT

An introduction to data-base systems and their use in corporations; management information systems; a survey of the principles likely to make such systems succeed.

COMPUTER DATA-BASE ORGANIZATION
Second Edition

A guide to data base design, design objectives; principles of data base software; a survey of the alternate logical and physical structures and their trade-offs.

BOOKS ABOUT TELEPROCESSING:

INTRODUCTION TO TELEPROCESSING

Intended to provide the easiest possible means of learning the essential facts about data transmission. Contains detailed summary tables of all aspects of the subject.

TELEPROCESSING NETWORK ORGANIZATION

An explanation of the many types of devices and procedures for controlling and organizing the flow of data on today's telecommunication lines.

BOOKS ABOUT TELECOMMUNICATIONS:

TELECOMMUNICATIONS AND THE COMPUTER
Second Edition

A description of the working of the world's telecommunication links and their uses for data transmission.

COMMUNICATIONS SATELLITE SYSTEMS

An explanation of communications satellites and how they affect systems design: technology, tradeoffs, design strategies.

BOOKS ABOUT INTERACTIVE SYSTEMS:

DESIGN OF REAL-TIME COMPUTER SYSTEMS

An overall review of technical considerations and calculations in the design and implementation of real-time systems.

KEY:

INTRODUCTORY BOOKS
These books are an easy-to-read introduction to the subjects.

DETAIL BOOKS